Introduction to Physical Anthropology

Arctic Ocean

NORWAY

SWEDEN FINLAND

RUSSIA

ARCTIC CIRCLE

60N

Sungir

80N

Neander Valley
Spy • Heidelberg (Mauer)
Mladeč, Předmostí, Dolní Věstonice
Krapina • Oase
Arago • Dmanisi
Ceprano • Petralona
Tighenif

KAZAKHSTAN

MONGOLIA

Jinniushan

Zhoukoudian
Ordos
Lantian
CHINA
Hexian
Dali

NORTH KOREA
SOUTH KOREA

JAPAN

40N

Teshik Tash

TURKEY

Amud
Skhul/Tabun
Jebel Qafzeh
Shanidar

IRAN
IRAQ

AFGHANISTAN

PAKISTAN

Liujiang
Maba

TAIWAN

Pacific
Ocean

TROPIC OF CANCER

20N

Toros-Menalla

NIGER

CHAD

NIGERIA

SUDAN
Hadar
Bodo •
ETHIOPIA
Omo
East and West Turkana
Tugen Hills • Kanapoi
Olduvai/Laetoli

Middle Awash (Aramis, Bouri, Herto, Dikika)

INDIA

MYANMAR
(BURMA)

THAILAND
CAMBODIA
VIETNAM

LAOS

SRI LANKA

MALDIVES

PHILIPPINES

MALAYSIA
Borneo
SINGAPORE

BRUNEI

NORTHERN
MARIANA
ISLANDS
(U.S.)

REPUBLIC OF THE
MARSHALL ISLANDS

FEDERATED STATES
OF MICRONESIA

EQUATOR

0

SEYCHELLES

INDONESIA
Sangiran
Ngandong
Trinil
Flores

PAPUA
NEW GUINEA

SOLOMON
ISLANDS

TUVALU

COMOROS IS.

Indian Ocean

MADAGASCAR
MAURITIUS

VANUATU

NEW
CALEDONIA
(Fr.)

FIJI

20S

TROPIC OF CAPRICORN

Kabwe

AUSTRALIA

Taung
Florisbad
Border Cave
SOUTH
AFRICA
Klasies River Mouth

Sterkfontein/Swartkrans/Drimolen

Lake Mungo

Kow Swamp

NEW
ZEALAND

40S

1. SLOVENIA
2. CROATIA
3. BOSNIA AND HERZEGOVINA
4. ALBANIA
5. MACEDONIA
6. SERBIA AND MONTENEGRO

60S

ANTARCTIC CIRCLE

ANTARCTICA

80S

Introduction to Physical Anthropology

ELEVENTH EDITION

Robert Jurmain

Professor Emeritus, San Jose State University

Lynn Kilgore

University of Colorado, Boulder

Wenda Trevathan

New Mexico State University

with Russell L. Ciochon

University of Iowa

THOMSON

WADSWORTH

Australia • Brazil • Canada • Mexico • Singapore • Spain
United Kingdom • United States

THOMSON
━━━━━━★━━━━━━ ™
WADSWORTH

Introduction to Physical Anthropology, **Eleventh Edition**
Robert Jurmain, Lynn Kilgore, Wenda Trevathan, with Russell L. Ciochon

Senior Acquisitions Editor: *Lin Marshall*
Senior Development Editor: *Sherry Symington*
Editorial Assistant: *Jessica Jang*
Technology Project Manager: *David Lionetti*
Executive Marketing Manager: *Caroline Concilla*
Marketing Assistant: *Mary Anne Payumo*
Senior Marketing Communications Manager: *Shemika Britt*
Project Manager, Editorial Production: *Marti Paul*
Creative Director: *Rob Hugel*
Executive Art Director: *Maria Epes*
Print Buyer: *Judy Inouye*

Permissions Editor: *Roberta Broyer*
Production Service: *Hespenheide Design*
Compositor: *Hespenheide Design*
Text Designer: *Yvo Riezebos*
Photo Researcher: *Hespenheide Design*
Copy Editors: *Christianne Thillen and Bridget Neumayr*
Illustrator: *Alexander Productions, Joanne Bales, Robert Greisen,
    Randy Miyake, Paragon 3, Sue Sellars, Cyndie Wooley*
Cover Designer: *Yvo Riezebos*
Cover Image: *Photomosaic® by Robert Silvers*
Text and Cover Printer: *Courier Corporation/Kendallville*

Library of Congress Control Number: 2007920765

Student Edition:
ISBN-13: 978-0-495-18779-0
ISBN-10: 0-495-18779-8

Thomson Higher Education
10 Davis Drive
Belmont, CA 94002-3098
USA

For more information about our products, contact us at:
Thomson Learning Academic Resource Center
1-800-423-0563

For permission to use material from this text or product, submit a request online at **http://www.thomsonrights.com.**
Any additional questions about permissions can be submitted by e-mail to **thomsonrights@thomson.com.**

BRIEF CONTENTS

CONTENTS

Biophoto Associates / Photo Researchers, Inc

PRIMATES
Chapter 6
Survey of the Living Primates

Chapter 7
Primate Behavior

CONTENTS

Manoj Shah/The Image Bank

Chapter 8
Primate Models for Human Behavioral Evolution

Chapter 9
Overview of the Fossil Primates

© Russell Ciochon, University of Iowa

HOMINID EVOLUTION

Chapter 10
Paleoanthropology: Reconstructing Early Hominid Behavior and Ecology

Chapter 11
Hominid Origins in Africa

National Museums of Kenya

Chapter 12
The Earliest Dispersal of the Genus *Homo*: *Homo Erectus* and Contemporaries

CONTENTS

© Russell Ciochon, University of Iowa

© Randall White, New York University

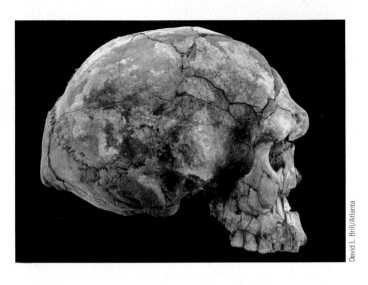

David L. Brill/Atlanta

CONTEMPORARY HUMAN EVOLUTION

Chapter 15
Modern Human Biology: Patterns of Variation

Chapter 16
Modern Human Biology: Patterns of Adaptation

Chapter 17
Legacies of Human Evolutionary History

LIST OF FEATURES

Craig King, Armed Forces DNA Identification Laboratory

© Russell Ciochon, University of Iowa

HOMINID EVOLUTION

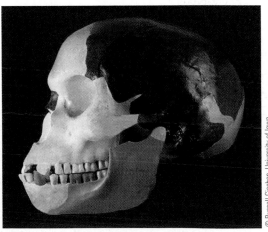

© Russell Ciochon, University of Iowa

CONTEMPORARY HUMAN EVOLUTION

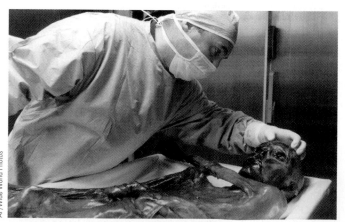

AP/Wide World Photos

PREFACE

Welcome to *Introduction to Physical Anthropology,* Eleventh Edition. Eleven editions may seem like a lot of revisions of our book—and it is. Both students and instructors may wonder why so many revisions are required and why new editions appear with regularity.

Consider, however, how fast things change in our culture. How often do any of us have to upgrade our computers, both for new software and hardware? How many of you still listen to cassette players?

Science too changes rapidly, and you may be surprised to learn it can change even more rapidly than many aspects of popular culture, like those we mentioned above. In some areas of scientific research what we knew just last year is now obsolete. So, out go the Walkman®, the old laptop, and last year's textbook.

This physical anthropology textbook is about human biology, most especially from an evolutionary perspective. Since all our main topics are *biological,* many are particularly prone to rapid scientific modification. Everyone is at least partly familiar with the rapid advances in DNA research, now often called "genomics." New techniques have fueled a massive revolution in all the biological sciences, including physical anthropology. Knowledge is exploding so fast that researchers race to stay up-to-date. Sometimes, what was adequate knowledge last month is now incomplete. While professional journals churn out exciting results, in some cases weekly, textbooks obviously can't keep up with that sort of pace.

Since the last edition of *Introduction to Physical Anthropology* came out, much has changed in our field. For example, at that time the entire pattern of chimpanzee DNA (that is, the chimpanzee genome) was not yet published. Moreover, many of you saw or heard, in the fall of 2004, the announcement in the popular press of the discovery of what have been called "the hobbits," found on an island in Indonesia. This fascinating discovery of 3-foot-tall, small-brained humans living as recently as 13,000 years ago is the most startling human evolutionary discovery in many decades. Yet, it was not discussed at all in our last edition.

We should also reemphasize some key points related to what this text is about and what we authors are trying to accomplish. As we've said, our approach is grounded in an evolutionary understanding of human beings. In many public schools evolutionary theory is no longer taught, and in others it is handled superficially or, we're sad to say, incorrectly. Moreover, you're all probably aware of wide popular debate regarding evolutionary biology and how it should be taught in public schools. We'll address these issues (in Chapter 2), but from the outset you should recognize how humans fit within the evolutionary development of life on earth. This is the main focus of our book.

What's more, medical and other applications taken directly from the biological sciences will increasingly impact all of us in coming years. Many of you who are taking a course in physical/biological anthropology are doing so to fulfill a general education life science requirement. As educated and engaged citizens in a 21st-century democracy, it's crucial that you be well informed. The authors (all teachers) have taught introductory physical anthropology as a general education course. Consequently, for all of us another major goal of this text is to provide students with essential tools for understanding scientific information; in this way, you'll be better prepared to deal with the rapidly changing world you'll face in the years ahead.

Because genetic mechanisms lie at the heart of understanding evolution, we'll address basic aspects of life, cells, DNA, and the ways species change in the early chapters (2–5) of this text. We'll next turn (in Chapters 6–8) to an exploration of our evolutionary cousins, the non-human primates and how they relate to us both physically and behaviorally. In Chapter 9, we'll discuss the evolutionary history of early primates in order to better understand the many ways in which primates have adapted to their environments.

More details of our specific human evolutionary history over the past five million years are covered over the next five chapters. We'll begin with our small-brained ancestors in Africa and follow the development of their descendants through time and over their expanding ranges into Asia and Europe—and much later into Australia and the Americas.

In the last section of this book (Chapters 15–17), we'll conclude our coverage of human evolution with a discussion of modern human biology and trace the ongoing evolution of our species. Our major topics will include the nature of human variation (including the meaning of "race") and patterns of adaptation in recent human populations.

What's New in the Eleventh Edition

For those familiar with earlier editions, the most obvious change you'll note, even from a glance at the cover, is that we have a new coauthor (Russell Ciochon from the University of Iowa). Moreover, we have a new chapter ("Overview of the Fossil Primates"). This new chapter provides an interpretation and concise summary of the evolution of our early primate ancestors from the most primitive prosimians through the emergence of monkeys, apes, and humans. We will trace the roots of our primate cousins, beginning around 65 million years ago, and follow the evolution of their descendants. You'll be able to see how many species have come and gone and discover what can be learned from fossils about the ancestry of the living primates—including us.

As mentioned, we have also updated materials throughout and expanded certain sections to reflect contemporary research. Updates include those discussed above relating to molecular biology and new fossil finds from Indonesia. Other significant new fossil and molecular research is also represented, including the discovery of the earliest modern human fossils from Ethiopia and the first DNA sequencing of early modern humans found in Europe (involving fossils from France, Belgium, Italy, and Russia). Finally, we have updated our coverage of the evolution of human disease, including expanded materials on both AIDS and SARS.

Prior users will also notice many changes to the figures, including new versions of all maps, and the addition of dozens of new photos. As in earlier editions, all of these photos are carefully selected to enhance the material discussed directly in the text. These changes greatly enhance the visual appeal as well as the teaching effectiveness of the presentation.

Since a central goal of our text is to stimulate critical thinking, the **Critical Thinking Questions** at the end of each chapter have been thoroughly revised to emphasize a more critical and intellectually creative approach to incorporating *and* applying knowledge. These components, as well as other new ones and those retained from earlier editions are listed below.

FEATURES

New Frontiers in Research boxes are major between-chapter features highlighting some of the newest and most innovative research in physical anthropology. Four areas of research are covered, including:

- Molecular Applications in Forensic Anthropology (following Chapter 4)
- Molecular Applications in Primatology (following Chapter 8)
- Ancient DNA (following Chapter 12)
- Molecular Applications in Modern Human Biology (following Chapter 16)

Issues are major features found between many chapters. They focus on intriguing topics that have produced debates among the general public as well as among professional anthropologists. Each is written in informal style and challenges readers to think critically about the scientific and moral questions raised.

Boxed highlights titled **A Closer Look** are high-interest features found throughout the book. They expand on the topic under discussion in the chapter by providing a more in-depth perspective.

IN-CHAPTER LEARNING AIDS

- **Chapter outlines** at the beginning of each chapter list all major topics covered.
- **Key Questions** appear at the beginning of each chapter and highlight the central topic of that chapter.
- A **running glossary** in the margins provides definitions of terms immediately adjacent to the text when the term is first introduced. A **full glossary** is provided in the back of the book.
- **At a Glance** boxes are features found throughout the book that briefly summarize complex or controversial material in a visually simple fashion.
- **Figures**, including numerous photographs, line drawings, and maps, most in full color, are carefully selected to clarify text materials and are placed to directly support discussion in the text.
- **Critical Thinking Questions** at the end of each chapter have been completely revised to reinforce key concepts and to encourage students to think critically about what they have read.
- **Full bibliographic citations** throughout the entire book provide sources from which the materials are drawn. This type of documentation guides students to published source materials and illustrates for students the proper use of references. All cited sources are listed in the comprehensive bibliography at the back of the book.
- A **"Click!"** guide at the beginning of each chapter directs students to the appropriate media covering materials pertinent to that chapter. One or more of the three supplemental multimedia products will be listed: *Virtual Laboratories for Physical Anthropology, Fourth Edition; Basic Genetics for Anthropology CD-ROM: Principles and Applications;* and *Hominid Fossils CD-ROM: An Interactive Atlas.*

 Click!   An example of the Click! icon in the margins.

ACKNOWLEDGMENTS

Over the years many friends and colleagues have assisted us with our books. For this edition we are especially grateful to the reviewers who so carefully commented on the manuscript and made such helpful suggestions:

Diane E. Barbolla (Mesa College); Doug Broadfield (Florida Atlantic University); Mary Glenn (Humboldt State University); Barbara J. King (College of William and Mary); Andrew Kramer (University of Tennessee); Catherine M. Leonard, (Pennsylvania State University); Ann Magennis (Colorado State University); Erik Ozolins (Mt. San Jacinto College); Karen R. Rosenberg (University of Delaware); and Mary K. Sandford (University of North Carolina, Greensboro).

We also wish to thank the following at Wadsworth Publishing: Lin Marshall, Anthropology Editor; Jessica Jang, Editorial Assistant; Sherry Symington, Development Editor; David Lionetti, Technology Project Manager, Caroline Concilla, Executive Marketing Manager; Catherine Morris, Project Editor; Eve Howard, VP and Editor in Chief; Sean Wakely, President, Thomson Higher Education, Humanities and Behavioral and Social Sciences; and Susan Badger, President and CEO of Thomson Higher Education. Moreover, for their unflagging expertise and patience we are grateful to our copy editor, Chris Thillen, together with our production service at Hespenheide Design, especially Christine Rocha, production coordinator, and Bridget Neumayr, proofreader/editor.

To the many friends and colleagues who have generously provided photographs we are greatly appreciative: Zeresenay Alemsegel, David Begun, Brenda Benefit, Jonathan Bloch, C.K. Brain, Günter Bräuer, Michel Brunet, Peter Brown, Chip Clark, Desmond Clark, Ron Clarke, Raymond Dart, Henri de Lumley, Louis de Bonis, Jean deRousseau, Denis Etler, John Fleagle, Diane France, Robert Franciscus, David Frayer, Kathleen Galvin, Philip Gingerich, Gregg Gunnell, David Haring, John Hodgkiss, Almut Hoffman, Ellen Ingmanson, Fred Jacobs, Peter Jones, John Kappelman, Richard Kay, William Kimbel, Leslie Knapp, Arlene Kruse, Richard Leakey, Carol Lofton, David Lordkipanidze, Giorgio Manzi, Margaret Maples, Monte McCrossin, Lorna Moore, Stephen Nash, Gerald Newlands, Xijum Ni, John Oates, Bonnie Pedersen, Lorna Pierce, David Pilbeam, William Pratt, Judith Regensteiner, Sastrohamijoyo Sartono, Jeffrey Schwartz, Eugenie Scott, Rose Sevick, Elwyn Simons, Meredith Small, Fred Smith, Thierry Smith, Judy Suchey, Masanaru Takai, Heather Thew, Li Tianyuan, Phillip Tobias, Erik Trinkaus, Alan Walker, Carol Ward, Dietrich Wegner, James Westgate, Randy White, Milford Wolpoff, and Xinzhi Wu.

To the many students who have pledged their time and expertise, we would like to thank: Lindsay Eaves-Johnson, Scott Maddux, Hannah Marsh, and Nathan Holton for their help editing and researching the manuscript; James Rogers, Nathan Totten, Joshua Gruber, Natalie Anne Petersen, Emma Rainey, Kirk Scott, and Audrey Cropp for their help with computer graphics; Anaid Hernandez for her sketches; Lindsay Eaves-Johnson, Anna Waterman, and Kara Bantz for their meticulous work on the index and bibliography; as well as Cerisa Reynolds and Kiran Patel for their organizational skills. Special mention goes to Lindsay Eaves-Johnson and James Rogers for their valued assistance in facilitating coordination of the text and art within the context of the Ciochon Lab. These students have worked to ensure that the text is as accessible as possible for their peers. Also at the University of Iowa, Linda Maxson, Dean of the College of Liberal Arts and Sciences provided invaluable support. Others who have assisted in forming our concepts and putting them into written form include John Fleagle, Gregg Gunnell, and Philip Rightmire. Jessica White provided a detailed comparative evaluation of the text.

Robert Jurmain
Lynn Kilgore
Wenda Trevathan
Russell Ciochon

SUPPLEMENTS

Introduction to Physical Anthropology comes with an outstanding supplements program to help instructors create an effective learning environment so students can master the latest discoveries and interpretations in the field of physical anthropology.

SUPPLEMENTS FOR INSTRUCTORS

Instructor's Manual and Test Bank This comprehensive manual offers chapter outlines, learning objectives, key terms and concepts, lecture suggestions and enrichment topics as well as 40–60 test questions per chapter.

ExamView® Computerized Testing Create, deliver, and customize tests and study guides (both print and online) in minutes with this easy-to-use assessment and tutorial system. ExamView offers both a Quick Test Wizard and an Online Test Wizard that guide you step-by-step through the process of creating tests, while the unique "WYSIWYG" capability allows you to see the test you are creating on the screen exactly as it will print or display online. You can build tests of up to 250 questions, using up to 12 question types. Using ExamView's complete word processing capabilities, you can enter an unlimited number of new questions or edit existing questions.

Multimedia Manager for Anthropology: A Microsoft® PowerPoint® Link Tool This new CD-ROM contains digital media and Microsoft PowerPoint presentations for all of Wadsworth's © 2008 introductory anthropology texts, placing images, lectures, and video clips at your fingertips. This CD-ROM includes preassembled Microsoft PowerPoint presentations using charts, graphs, maps, line art, and images with a NEW zoom feature from all Wadsworth © 2008 anthropology texts. You can add your own lecture notes and images to create a customized lecture presentation. Also, an Earthwatch Institute Research Expedition feature offers even more images.

JoinIn™ on Turning Point® The Anthropology discipline at Thomson Wadsworth is pleased to offer **JoinIn**™ (clicker) content for Audience Response Systems tailored to this text. Use the program by posing your own questions and display students' answers instantly within the Microsoft PowerPoint slides of your existing lecture. Or, utilize any or all of the following content that will be included with your Anthropology **JoinIn** product:

- Opinion polls on issues important to each chapter in the text (5 questions per chapter). **JoinIn** gives students complete anonymity and facilitates student participation.
- Conceptual quiz questions for each chapter. Give students a quick quiz during or after the chapter lecture to determine if they have understood the material.

- Plus, pre-assembled PowerPoint lecture slides for each chapter of the book are included with the above material integrated into the slides. All of the work integrating clicker questions into the chapter lecture slides has been done for you!

The program can be used to simply take roll, or it can assess your students' progress and opinions with in-class questions. Enhance how your students interact with you, your lecture, and each other. For college and university adopters only. *Contact your local Thomson representative to learn more.*

Wadsworth Anthropology Video Library Qualified adopters may select full-length videos from an extensive library of offerings drawn from such excellent educational video sources as *Films for the Humanities and Sciences.*

ABC Anthropology Video Series This exclusive video series was created jointly by Wadsworth and ABC for the anthropology course. Each video contains approximately 60 minutes of footage originally broadcast on ABC within the past several years. The videos are broken into short two- to seven-minute segments, perfect for classroom use as lecture launchers. An annotated table of contents accompanies each video, providing descriptions of the segments and suggestions for their possible use within the course.

Thomson Learning Connects Get trained, get connected, and get the support you need for seamless integration of technology resources into your course with **Thomson Learning Connects [TLC]**. This unparalleled technology service and training program provides robust online resources, peer-to-peer instruction, personalized training, and a customizable program you can count on. Visit www.thomsonedu.com/tlc to sign up for online seminars, first days of class services, technical support, or personalized, face-to-face training. Our online or onsite trainings are frequently led by one of our Lead Teachers, faculty members who are experts in using Thomson Learning technology and can provide best practices and teaching tips.

ONLINE RESOURCES FOR INSTRUCTORS AND STUDENTS

Anthropology Resource Center This online center offers a wealth of information and useful tools for both instructors and students in all four fields of anthropology. For students, it includes interactive maps, learning modules, video exercises, breaking news in anthropology, and more. For instructors, the Resource

Center is a gateway to time-saving teaching tools, such as image banks, sample syllabi, and more. Access to the website is available free when bundled with the text or for purchase at a nominal fee. To purchase online, students are directed to http://thomsonedu.com where they can create an account through 1Pass™.

Book Premium Companion Website Access to this text-specific website is available free when bundled with the text or for purchase at a nominal fee. This site includes learning modules on key concepts in physical anthropology, animations, interactive exercises, map exercises, video exercises with critical thinking questions, tutorial quizzes with feedback, and essay questions, all of which can be e-mailed to professors.

NOW ONLINE!

Virtual Laboratories for Physical Anthropology, Version 4.0
by John Kappelman

Virtual Laboratories provides students with an interactive learning environment to complete lab assignments at school, home, or in the library. Each laboratory is a self-contained instructional module that combines a wide range of digital images, 3-D animation, video, and sound, to help students master the many techniques and concepts taught in the normal laboratory class. Students actively participate in the physical anthropology labs and develop critical thinking and problem-solving skills by taking measurements and plotting data, assessing primates in the wild, evaluating data, and much more. When you order *Virtual Laboratories* on the web-based ThomsonNOW platform, a powerful course management component allows you to reorder the labs, move content within the labs, utilize pre- and post-lab tests for each lab, and track how much time students spend on each lab. *Virtual Laboratories* includes weblinks, outstanding fossil images, exercises, a notebook feature, and a post-lab self-quiz. (Also available on CD with a portion of the features and functionality of the online version.)

Thomson InSite™ for Writing and Research-With Turnitin™ Originality Checker InSite features a full suite of writing, peer review, online grading, and e-portfolio applications. It is an all-in-one tool that helps instructors manage the flow of papers electronically and allows students to submit papers and peer reviews online. Also included in the suite is Turnitin, an originality check that offers a simple solution for instructors who want a strong deterrent against plagiarism, as well as encouragement for students to employ proper research techniques. Access is available for packaging with each copy of this book. For more information, visit http://insite.thomsom.com.

InfoTrac® College Edition Ignite discussions or augment lectures with the latest developments in physical anthropology. InfoTrac College Edition (available as a free option with newly purchased texts) gives instructors and students 4 months free access to an easy-to-use online database of reliable, full-length articles (not abstracts) from hundreds of top academic journals and popular sources. Among the journals which are available 24-hours a day, seven days a week, are *American Anthropologist*, *Current Anthropology*, *Journal of Contemporary Ethnography*, *Canadian Review of Sociology and Anthropology*, and thousands more. To get started with InfoTrac, students are directed to http://thomsonedu.com where they can create an account through 1Pass.

SUPPLEMENTS FOR STUDENTS

Thomson Audio Study Products *Thomson Audio Study Products* provide audio reinforcement of key concepts students can listen to from their personal computer or MP3 player. Created specifically for *Introduction to Physical Anthropology*, 11e, *Thomson Audio Study Products* provide approximately ten minutes of up-beat audio content, giving students a quick and convenient way to master key concepts, test their knowledge with quiz questions, and listen to a brief overview on the major themes of each chapter. Students may purchase access to *Thomson Audio Study Products* for this text online at www.ichapters.com.

Study Guide This useful guide enables students to fully comprehend and appreciate what the text has to offer. Each chapter of the study guide features learning objectives, chapter outlines, key terms, concept applications, and practice tests consisting of 30–40 multiple-choice questions and 5–10 true/false questions with answers and page references, in addition to several short-answer and essay questions.

Telecourse Study Guide A NEW enhanced Telecourse, *Physical Anthropology: The Evolving Human*, available in the fall of 2007 provides online and print companion study guide options that include quizzing, study aids, interactive exercises, video, and more.

Lab Manual and Workbook for Physical Anthropology, Sixth Edition *by Diane L. France* Now in full color, France's **Lab Manual** balances the study of human osteology, forensic anthropology, anthropometry, primates, human evolution, and genetics with a new chapter on growth and development, more material on disease, and new information on the anomalies of the human skeleton caused by disease and mechanical stress. This edition's art program has been greatly enhanced with color images that include scales and orientation information, as well as reprinted images for chapter exercises where needed. With hands-on lab assignments that help students apply physical anthropology perspectives and techniques to real situations, the **Lab Manual** provides a wealth of solid information and photographs that help make the concepts of physical anthropology easier to understand. *Contact your Thomson sales representative to package with the text.*

Modules in Physical Anthropology
Evolution of the Brain *by Daniel D. White* The human species is the only species that has ever created a symphony, written a poem, developed a mathematical equation, or studied its own origins. The biological structure that has enabled humans to perform these feats of intelligence is the human brain. This module explores the basics of neuroanatomy, brain development, lateralization, sexual dimorphism, and the fossil evidence for hominid brain evolution.

Human Environment Interactions *by Cathy Galvin* This module begins with a brief discussion of the history and core concepts of the field of human ecology, before looking in-depth at how the environment influences cultural practices (environmental determinism) and how aspects of culture, in turn, affect the environment. Human Behavioral Ecology is presented within the context of natural selection and how ecological factors influence the development of cultural and behavioral traits and how people subsist in different environments. The module concludes with a discussion of resilience and global change as a result of human-environment interactions.

Molecular Anthropology Module *by Leslie Knapp* This module explores how molecular genetic methods are used to understand the organization and expression of genetic information in humans and nonhuman primates. Students will learn about the common laboratory methods used to study variation and evolution in molecular anthropology. Examples are drawn from up-to-date research on human evolutionary origins and comparative primate genomics to demonstrate that scientific research is an ongoing process with theories frequently being questioned and reevaluated.

Forensic Anthropology Module *by Diane France* This module introduces students to the essentials of forensic anthropology as it is practiced in the United States and Canada. It explores the field's myths and realities of the search for human remains in crime scenes, the expectations from a forensic anthropology expert in the courtroom, some of the challenges of mass fatality incident responses, and the issues a student should consider if pursuing a career in forensic anthropology.

Basic Genetics in Anthropology CD-ROM: Principles and Applications *by Robert Jurmain, Lynn Kilgore and Wenda Trevathan* Available *free* bundled with the text, this CD-ROM helps students to review and more easily comprehend biological inheritance (genes, DNA sequencing, etc.) and its application to modern human populations at the molecular level (human variation and adaptation to disease, diet, growth, and development). Interactive animations and simulations bring these important concepts to life.

Hominid Fossils: An Interactive Atlas CD-ROM *by James Ahern* This CD-based interactive atlas explores more than 75 key fossils that are important for a clear understanding of human evolution. The QuickTime® Virtual Reality (QTVR) format enables each fossil to be rotated 360 degrees. Compelling and highly visual *Tutorials* help students learn fossil and species identification, while a compare/contrast feature aids in student mastery of key fossils. "Hot Spot" labeling, an audio glossary, and a dynamic quizzing section, geared to users with varying levels of prior knowledge, further enhance student learning. An online instructor resource site is also available.

CHAPTER 1

Introduction to Physical Anthropology

Robert Jurmain

Courtesy Bonnie Pedersen/Arlene Kruse

Lynn Kilgore

Lynn Kilgore

KEY QUESTIONS

What do physical anthropologists do?

Why is physical anthropology a scientific discipline, and what is its importance to the general public?

Introduction

Click!

Go to the following media for interactives and exercises on topics covered in this chapter:

- Online Virtual Laboratories for Physical Anthropology, Fourth Edition
- Basic Genetics for Anthropology CD-ROM: Principles and Applications
- Hominid Fossils CD-ROM: An Interactive Atlas

One day, perhaps during the rainy season some 3.7 million years ago, two or three animals walked across a grassland savanna in what is now northern Tanzania in East Africa. These individuals were early members of the taxonomic family **Hominidae**, the family that also includes us, modern *Homo sapiens*. Fortunately for us, a record of their passage on that long-forgotten day remains in the form of fossilized footprints, preserved in hardened volcanic deposits.

As chance would have it, shortly after heels and toes were pressed into the dampened soil, a nearby volcano erupted. The ensuing ashfall blanketed everything on the ground surface. In time, the ash layer hardened into a deposit that remarkably preserved the tracks of numerous animals including the early **hominids** (Fig. 1-1).

These now famous prints indicate that two hominids, one smaller than the other and perhaps walking side by side, left parallel sets of tracks. But because the larger individual's prints are obscured, possibly by those of a third, it's unclear how many actually made that journey so long ago. But, what is clear is that the prints were made by an animal that habitually walked **bipedally** (on two feet), and that fact tells us that those ancient travelers were hominids.

Besides the footprints, scientists working at this site (called Laetoli) and at other locations have discovered many fossilized parts of skeletons of an animal we call *Australopithecus afarensis*. After analyzing these remains, we know that these hominids were anatomically similar to ourselves, although their brains were only about one-third the size of ours. But, even though they may have used stones and sticks as simple tools, there's no evidence to

FIGURE 1-1
Early hominid footprints at Laetoli, Tanzania. The tracks to the left were made by one individual, while those to the right appear to have been formed by two individuals, the second stepping in the tracks of the first.

Hominidae The taxonomic family to which humans belong; also includes other, now extinct, bipedal relatives.

hominids Colloquial term for members of the family Hominidae, which includes all bipedal hominoids back to the divergence from African great apes.

bipedally On two feet. Walking habitually on two legs.

Courtesy, Peter Jones

suggest that they actually made stone tools. In fact, these early hominids were very much at the mercy of nature's whims. They certainly couldn't outrun most predators, and since their canine teeth were fairly small, they were pretty much defenseless.

We've asked hundreds of questions about the Laetoli hominids, but we'll never be able to answer them all. Those individuals walked down a path into what became their future, and their immediate journey has long since ended. So, it remains for us to learn as much as we can about them and their **species**; and as we continue to do so, their greater journey continues.

On July 20, 1969, a television audience numbering in the hundreds of millions watched as two human beings stepped out of a spacecraft onto the surface of the moon. To anyone born after that date, this event is taken more or less for granted. But the significance of that first moonwalk can't be overstated, because it represents humankind's presumed mastery over the natural forces that govern our presence on earth. For the first time ever, people had actually walked upon the surface of a celestial body that has never given birth to biological life.

As the astronauts gathered geological specimens and frolicked in near weightlessness, they left traces of their fleeting presence in the form of footprints in the lunar dust (Fig. 1-2). On the surface of the moon, where no rain falls and no wind blows, the footprints remain undisturbed to this day. They survive as mute testimony to a brief visit by a medium-sized, big-brained creature who presumed to challenge the very forces that created it.

You may be wondering why anyone would care about early hominid footprints and how they can possibly be relevant to your life. And even though you know that there was a moon landing in the late 1960s, you may not have spent much time actually thinking about it. You may also wonder why a physical anthropology textbook would begin by discussing two such seemingly unrelated events as hominids walking across a savanna and a moonwalk. The fact is, these two events aren't unrelated at all.

Physical, or biological, anthropology is a scientific discipline concerned with the biological and behavioral characteristics of human beings; our closest relatives, the nonhuman **primates** (apes, monkeys, and prosimians); and their ancestors. This kind of research helps us explain what it means to be human. This is an ambitious goal, and it probably isn't fully attainable. But it's certainly worth pursuing. We're the only species to ponder our own existence and wonder how we fit into the spectrum of life on earth. Most people view humanity as separate from the rest of the animal kingdom. But at the same time, some are curious about the similarities we share with other species. Maybe, as a child, you looked at your dog and tried to figure out how his front legs might correspond to your arms. Perhaps, during a visit to zoo, you noticed the similarities between a chimpanzee's hands or facial expressions and your own. Maybe you wondered if they also shared your thoughts and feelings. If you've ever had thoughts and questions like these, then you've indeed been curious about humankind's place in nature.

We humans, who can barely comprehend a century, can't begin to grasp the enormity of nearly 4 million years. But we still want to know more about those creatures who walked across the savanna that day. We want to know how an insignificant but clever bipedal primate such as *Australopithecus afarensis*, or perhaps a close relative, gave rise to a species that would eventually walk on the surface of a moon some 230,000 miles from earth.

How did *Homo sapiens*, a result of the same evolutionary forces that produced all other life on this planet, gain the power to control the flow of rivers and alter the very climate in which we live? As tropical animals, how were we able to leave the tropics and eventually occupy most of the earth's land surfaces? How did we adjust to different environmental conditions as we dispersed? How could our species, which numbered fewer than 1 billion until the mid-nineteenth century, come to number more than 6 billion worldwide today and, as we now do, add another billion people every 11 years?

These are some of the many questions that physical anthropologists attempt to answer, and these questions are largely the focus of the study of human **evolution**, variation, and **adaptation**. These issues, and many others, are the topics covered directly or indirectly in this textbook— because physical anthropology is, in part, human biology seen from an evolutionary perspective.

As biological organisms, humans are subjected to the same evolutionary forces as all other species are. On hearing the term *evolution*, most people think of the appearance of new species. Certainly, new species formation is one important consequence of evolution;

FIGURE **1-2**
Human footprints left on the lunar surface during the *Apollo* mission.

species A group of organisms that can interbreed to produce fertile offspring. Members of one species are reproductively isolated from members of all other species (i.e., they cannot mate with them to produce fertile offspring).

primates Members of the order of mammals *Primates* (pronounced "pry-may´-tees"), which includes prosimians, monkeys, apes, and humans.

evolution A change in the genetic structure of a population. The term is also frequently used to refer to the appearance of a new species.

adaptation An anatomical, physiological, or behavioral response of organisms or populations to the environment. Adaptations result from evolutionary change (specifically, as a result of natural selection).

FIGURE 1-3

(a) An early stone tool from East Africa. This artifact represents one of the oldest types of stone tools found anywhere. (b) Assortment of just a few of the thousands of implements available today in a modern hardware store.

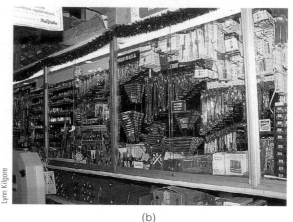

(a)   (b)

culture   Behavioral aspects of human adaptation, including technology, traditions, language, religion, marriage patterns, and social roles. Culture is a set of *learned* behaviors transmitted from one generation to the next by nonbiological (i.e., nongenetic) means.

worldview   General cultural orientation or perspective shared by members of a society.

behavior   Anything organisms do that involves action in response to internal or external stimuli. The response of an individual, group, or species to its environment. Such responses may or may not be deliberate and they aren't necessarily the results of conscious decision making, as in one-celled organisms, insects, and many other species.

biocultural evolution   The mutual, interactive evolution of human biology and culture; the concept that biology makes culture possible and that developing culture further influences the direction of biological evolution; a basic concept in understanding the unique components of human evolution.

but it isn't the only one, because evolution is an ongoing biological process with more than one outcome. Simply stated, evolution is a change in the genetic makeup of a population from one generation to the next, and it can be defined and studied at two levels. Sometimes genetic changes over time in populations do result in the appearance of a new species or *speciation*, especially when those populations are isolated from one another. Change at this level is called *macroevolution*. At the other level, there are genetic alterations *within* populations; and while this type of change may not lead to speciation, it often causes populations of a species to differ from one another regarding the frequency of certain traits. Evolution at this level is referred to as *microevolution*. Evolution as it occurs at both these levels will be addressed in this book.

But physical anthropologists don't just study physiological and biological systems. When these topics are considered within the broader context of human evolution, another factor must be considered, and that factor is **culture**. Culture is an extremely important concept, not only as it relates to modern human beings but also because of its critical role in human evolution. Quite simply, and in a very broad sense, culture can be said to be the strategy by which humans adapt to the natural environment. In fact, culture is the environment in which we live. Culture includes technologies ranging from stone tools to computers; subsistence patterns, from hunting and gathering to global agribusiness; housing types, from thatched huts to skyscrapers; and clothing, from animal skins to high-tech synthetic fibers (Fig. 1-3). Technology, religion, values, social organization, language, kinship, marriage rules, gender roles, inheritance of property, and so on are all aspects of culture. And each culture shapes people's perceptions of the external environment, or **worldview**, in particular ways that distinguish that culture from all others.

One very basic point about culture is that it's passed from one generation to the next independently of biological factors (that is, genes). In other words, culture is *learned*, and the process of learning one's culture begins, quite literally, at birth. As we just discussed, humans are products of the culture they're raised in, and since most of human **behavior** is learned, it follows that most behaviors, perceptions, and reactions are shaped by culture.

At the same time, however, it's important to emphasize that even though culture isn't genetically determined, the human *predisposition to assimilate culture and function within it is profoundly influenced by biological factors*. Most nonhuman animals, including birds and especially primates, rely to varying degrees on learned behavior. This is especially true of the great apes which exhibit numerous aspects of culture.

We can't overemphasize that the predisposition for culture is perhaps the most critical component of human evolutionary history, and it was inherited from early hominid or prehominid ancestors. In fact, the common ancestor we share with chimpanzees may have had this predisposition. But during the course of human evolution, the role of culture became increasingly important. Over time, culture came to influence biology; and in turn, aspects of biology influenced cultural practices. For this reason, humans are said to be the result of interactions between biology and culture or **biocultural evolution**. In this respect, humans are unique among biological organisms.

In humans, biocultural interactions have resulted in many anatomical, biological, and behavioral changes: the shape of the pelvis and hip, increased brain size, reorganization of neurological structures, decreased tooth size, and the development of language, to list a few. Today, biocultural interactions are still crucial, for example, as humans are increasingly exposed to environmental pollutants, some of which cause diseases (for example, respiratory problems and various forms of cancer). Human activities have also altered the patterns of infectious diseases such as tuberculosis, malaria, and now avian flu. And HIV, the virus that causes AIDS, provides a dramatic example. Rapid culture change (particularly in Africa) and changing social and sexual mores may have influenced evolutionary rates of HIV. Certainly these cultural changes, as well as air travel and other factors, influenced the spread of HIV throughout populations in both the developed and developing worlds. So, it's clear that we humans have influenced the development and spread of infectious disease; but what isn't so clear, at least to most people, is that the changes in infectious disease patterns also are affecting human biology and behavior.

What Is Anthropology?

Human biologists also study many biological aspects of humankind, including adaptation and evolution. However, particularly in the United States, when this kind of research also considers the role of evolution and cultural factors, it's placed within the discipline of **anthropology**

In the United States, anthropology comprises three main subfields: cultural, or social, anthropology; archaeology; and physical, or biological, anthropology. Additionally, some universities include linguistic anthropology as a fourth area. Each of these subdisciplines, in turn, is divided into several specialized areas of interest. Following is a brief discussion of the main subdisciplines of anthropology.

Cultural Anthropology

Cultural anthropology is the study of all aspects of human behavior. The beginnings of cultural anthropology are found in the nineteenth century, when Europeans became increasingly aware of what they termed "primitive" societies in Africa, Asia, and the New World.

The interest in traditional societies led numerous early anthropologists to study and record lifeways that unfortunately are now all but extinct. These studies produced many descriptive **ethnographies** that emphasized various phenomena, such as religion, ritual, myth, use of symbols, subsistence strategies, technology, gender roles, child-rearing practices, and so on. Ethnographic accounts, in turn, formed the basis for comparative studies of numerous cultures. Such *cross-cultural* studies, called *ethnologies*, broadened the context within which cultural anthropologists studied human behavior.

The focus of cultural anthropology shifted over the course of the twentieth century. For example, ethnographic techniques have been applied to the study of diverse subcultures and their interactions with one another in contemporary metropolitan areas (urban anthropology). Another relevant area for cultural anthropologists today is the resettlement of refugees in many parts of the world.

Medical anthropology is the subfield of cultural anthropology that explores the relationship between various cultural attributes and health and disease. One area of interest is how different groups view disease processes and how these views affect treatment or the willingness to accept treatment. When a medical anthropologist focuses on the social dimensions of disease, physicians and physical anthropologists may also collaborate. In fact, many medical anthropologists have received much of their training in physical anthropology.

Many cultural anthropology subfields (for example, medical anthropology) have practical applications and are pursued by anthropologists working outside the university setting. This approach is called *applied anthropology*. While most applied anthropologists regard themselves as cultural anthropologists, the term is also sometimes used to describe

anthropology The field of inquiry that studies human culture and evolutionary aspects of human biology; includes cultural anthropology, archaeology, linguistics, and physical, or biological, anthropology.

ethnographies Detailed descriptive studies of human societies. In cultural anthropology, an ethnography is traditionally the study of a non-Western society.

the work of archaeologists and physical anthropologists. Indeed, the various fields of anthropology, as practiced in the United States, overlap considerably—which after all was the rationale for combining them under the umbrella of anthropology in the first place.

Archaeology

Archaeology is the study of earlier cultures and lifeways by anthropologists who specialize in the scientific recovery, analysis, and interpretation of the material remains of past societies. Archaeologists are concerned with culture but, instead of interviewing living people, they obtain information from artifacts and structures left behind by earlier societies. Obviously, no one has ever excavated such aspects of culture as religious belief, spoken language, or a political system. But archaeologists assume that the surviving evidence of human occupation reflects some of those important but less-tangible features of the culture that created them.

Unlike in the past, sites aren't excavated simply because they exist, or for the artifacts they may contain; rather, they're excavated to gain information about human behavior. For example, patterns of behavior are reflected in the dispersal of human settlements across a landscape and in the distribution of cultural remains within them. Archaeological research questions may focus on specific localities or peoples and attempt to identify, for example, various aspects of social organization, subsistence techniques, or factors that led to the collapse of a civilization. Alternatively, inquiry may reflect an interest in broader issues relating to human culture in general, such as the development of agriculture or the rise of cities.

Archaeological techniques are used to identify and excavate not only remains of human cities and settlements but also sites that contain remains of extinct species, including everything from dinosaurs to early hominids. Together, prehistoric archaeology and physical anthropology form the core of a joint science called *paleoanthropology*, described later in this book.

Linguistic Anthropology

Linguistic anthropology is the study of human speech and language, including the origins of language in general as well as specific languages. By examining similarities between contemporary languages, linguists have been able to trace historical ties between languages and groups of languages, thus facilitating the identification of language families and perhaps past relationships between human populations.

Because the spontaneous acquisition and use of language is a uniquely human characteristic, it's an important topic for linguistic anthropologists, who, along with specialists in other fields, study the process of language acquisition in infants. Since insights into the process may well have implications for the development of language skills in human evolution, as well as in growing children, it's also an important subject to physical anthropologists.

Physical Anthropology

As we've already said, *physical anthropology* is the study of human biology within the framework of evolution and with an emphasis on the interaction between biology and culture. This subdiscipline is also referred to as *biological anthropology*, and you'll find the terms used interchangeably. *Physical anthropology* is the original term, and it reflects the initial interests anthropologists had in describing human physical variation. The American Association of Physical Anthropologists, its journal, as well as many college courses and numerous publications, retain this term. The designation *biological anthropology* reflects the shift in emphasis to more biologically oriented topics, such as genetics, evolutionary biology, nutrition, physiological adaptation, and growth and development. This shift occurred

FIGURE **1-4**
Paleoanthropologists excavating at the Drimolen site, South Africa.

largely because of advances in the field of genetics since the late 1950s. Although we've continued to use the traditional term in the title of this textbook, you'll find that all the major topics pertain to biological issues.

The origins of physical anthropology can be found in two principal areas of interest among nineteenth-century European and American scholars. First, many scientists (at the time called *natural historians*) were becoming increasingly curious about the origins of modern species. In other words, they were beginning to doubt the literal interpretation of the biblical account of creation, and scientific explanations emphasizing natural, rather than supernatural, phenomena were becoming more popular.

The sparks of interest in biological change over time were fueled into flames by the publication of Charles Darwin's *On the Origin of Species* in 1859. Today, **paleoanthropology**, or the study of human evolution, particularly as evidenced in the fossil record, is a major subfield of physical anthropology (Fig. 1-4). Thousands of specimens of human ancestors (mostly fragmentary) are now kept in research collections. Taken together, these fossils span at least 4 million years of human prehistory; and although incomplete, they provide us with significantly more knowledge than was available just 15 years ago. It's the ultimate goal of paleoanthropological research to identify the various early hominid species, establish a chronological sequence of relationships among them, and gain insights into their adaptation and behavior. Only then will we have a clear picture of how and when humankind came into being.

Primate paleontology can really be viewed as a subfield of paleoanthropology because it's the study of the primate fossil record that extends back to the beginning of primate evolution some 60 million years ago (mya). Virtually every year, fossil-bearing beds in North America, Africa, Asia, and Europe yield important new discoveries. By studying fossil primates and comparing them with anatomically similar living species, primate paleontologists are learning a great deal about factors such as diet or locomotion in earlier forms. They can also make certain assumptions about behavior in some extinct primates and try to clarify what we know about evolutionary relationships between extinct and modern species, including ourselves.

The other major area of interest that directly affected early anthropological studies was *human variation*, especially observable physical variation, most obvious in skin color. Enormous effort was aimed at describing and explaining the biological differences between various human populations. Although some attempts were misguided and even racist, they gave birth to literally thousands of body measurements that are sometimes still used to compare people. Physical anthropologists also use many of the techniques of **anthropometry** to study skeletal remains from archaeological sites (Fig. 1-5).

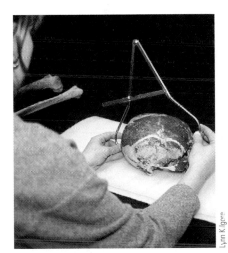

FIGURE **1-5**
Anthropology student using spreading calipers to measure cranial length.

paleanthropology   The interdisciplinary approach to the study of earlier hominids—their chronology, physical structure, archaeological remains, habitats, and so on.

primate paleontology   The study of fossil primates, especially those that lived before the appearance of hominids.

anthropometry   Measurement of human body parts. When osteologists measure skeletal elements, the term *osteometry* is often used.

FIGURE 1-6
This researcher is using a treadmill test to assess a subject's heart rate, blood pressure, and oxygen consumption.

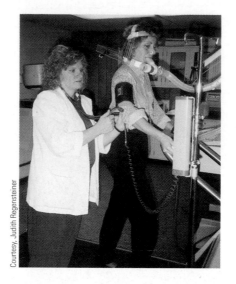

Courtesy, Judith Regensteiner

Anthropologists today are concerned with human variation because of its possible *adaptive significance*, and because they want to identify the genetic and other related evolutionary factors that have acted to produce variation. In other words, many traits that typify certain populations are seen as having evolved as biological adaptations, or adjustments, to local environmental conditions, including infectious disease. Other characteristics may be the results of geographical isolation or the descent of populations from small founding groups. Examining biological variation between populations of any species provides valuable information as to the mechanisms of genetic change in groups over time, which is really what the evolutionary process is all about.

Modern population studies also examine other important aspects of human variation, including how various groups respond physiologically to different kinds of environmentally induced stress (Fig. 1-6). Such stresses may include high altitude, cold, or heat. Many biological anthropologists conduct nutritional studies, investigating the relationships between various dietary components, cultural practices, physiology, and certain aspects of health and disease (Fig. 1-7). Investigations of human fertility, growth, and development also are closely related to the topic of nutrition. These fields of inquiry, which are fundamental to studies of adaptation in modern human populations, can provide insights into hominid evolution too.

It would be impossible to study evolutionary processes without knowledge of how traits are inherited. For this reason and others, **genetics** is a crucial field for physical anthropologists. Modern physical anthropology wouldn't exist as an evolutionary science if it weren't for advances in the understanding of genetic mechanisms.

In this exciting time of rapid advances in genetic research, *molecular anthropologists* use cutting-edge technologies to investigate evolutionary relationships between human populations as well as between humans and nonhuman primates. To do this, they examine similarities and differences in **DNA** sequences between individuals, populations, and species. What's more, by extracting DNA from certain fossils, these researchers have contributed to

FIGURE 1-7
Dr. Kathleen Galvin measures upper arm circumference in a young Maasai boy in Tanzania. Data derived from various body measurements, including height and weight, were used in a health and nutrition study of groups of Maasai cattle herders.

genetics The study of gene structure and action and the patterns of inheritance of traits from parent to offspring. Genetic mechanisms are the foundation for evolutionary change.

DNA (deoxyribonucleic acid) The double-stranded molecule that contains the genetic code. DNA is a main component of chromosomes.

Courtesy, Judith Regensteiner

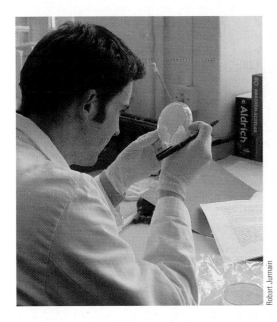

Robert Jurmain

Courtesy, Bonnie Pedersen/Arlene Kruse

FIGURE 1-8
Cloning and sequencing methods are frequently used to identify genes in humans and nonhuman primates. This graduate student identifies a genetically modified bacterial clone.

FIGURE 1-9
Yahaya Alamasi, a member of the senior field staff at Gombe National Park, Tanzania. Alamasi is recording behaviors in free-ranging chimpanzees.

our understanding of relationships between extinct and living species. As genetic technologies continue to be developed, molecular anthropologists will play a key role in explaining human evolution, adaptation, and our biological relationships with other species (Fig. 1-8).

Primatology, the study of nonhuman primates, has become increasingly important since the late 1950s (Fig. 1-9). Behavioral studies, especially those conducted on groups in natural environments, have implications for many scientific disciplines. Because nonhuman primates are our closest living relatives, identifying the underlying factors related to social behavior, communication, infant care, reproductive behavior, and so on helps us to develop a better understanding of the natural forces that have shaped so many aspects of modern human behavior.

Moreover, nonhuman primates are important to study in their own right. This is particularly true today because the majority of primate species are threatened or seriously endangered. Only through study will scientists be able to recommend policies that can better ensure the survival of many nonhuman primates and thousands of other species as well.

Osteology, the study of the skeleton, is central to physical anthropology. In fact, it's so important that when many people think of biological anthropology, the first thing that comes to mind is bones (although they often ask about dinosaurs). The emphasis on osteology is due partly to the fact that a thorough knowledge of skeletal structure and function is critical to the interpretation of fossil material.

Bone biology and physiology are of major importance to many other aspects of physical anthropology besides paleontology. Many osteologists specialize in studies that emphasize various measurements of skeletal elements. This type of research is essential, for example, to identifying stature and growth patterns in archaeological populations.

One subdiscipline of osteology, called **paleopathology**, is the study of disease and trauma in archaeologically derived skeletal populations. Paleopathology is a prominent subfield that investigates the prevalence of trauma, certain infectious diseases (including syphilis and tuberculosis), nutritional deficiencies, and numerous other conditions that may leave evidence in bone (Fig. 1-10). This research tells us a great deal about the lives of individuals and populations

primatology   The study of the biology and behavior of nonhuman primates (prosimians, monkeys, and apes).

osteology   The study of skeletal material. Human osteology focuses on the interpretation of the skeletal remains from archaeological sites, skeletal anatomy, bone physiology, and growth and development. Some of the same techniques are used in paleoanthropology to study early hominids.

paleopathology   The branch of osteology that studies the evidence of disease and injury in human skeletal (or, occasionally, mummified) remains from archaeological sites.

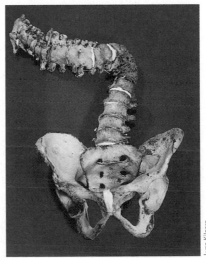

Lynn Kilgore

FIGURE 1-10
Severe congenital scoliosis in an adult male from Nubia. The curves are due to several developmental defects that affect individual vertebrae. (This is not the most common form of scoliosis.)

FIGURE 1-11

(a) Physical anthropologists Lorna Pierce (left) and Judy Suchey (center) working as forensic consultants. The dog has just located a concealed human cranium during a training session. (b) Forensic anthropologists at the location on Staten Island where all materials from the World Trade Center were taken for investigation after September 11, 2001. The scientists are wearing HAZMAT (hazardous materials) suits for protection.

Courtesy, Lorna Pierce/Judy Suchey

(a)

Provided by D. France

(b)

from the past. Paleopathology also yields information regarding the history of certain disease processes, and for this reason it's of interest to scientists in biomedical fields.

Forensic anthropology is directly related to osteology and paleopathology, and many people have become interested in it because of forensic shows on television. Technically, this approach is the application of anthropological (usually osteological and sometimes archaeological) techniques to legal issues (Fig. 1-11). Forensic anthropologists help identify skeletal remains in mass disasters or other situations where a human body has been found. Forensic anthropologists have been involved in numerous cases having important legal, historical, and human consequences. They were instrumental in identifying the skeletons of most of the Russian imperial family, executed in 1918; and many participated in the overwhelming task of trying to identify the remains of victims of the September 11, 2001, terrorist attacks in the United States (Fig.1-11b).

forensic anthropology An applied anthropological approach dealing with legal matters. Forensic anthropologists work with coroners and others in identifying and analyzing human remains.

FIGURE **1-12**
Dr. Linda Levitch teaching a human anatomy class at the University of North Carolina School of Medicine.

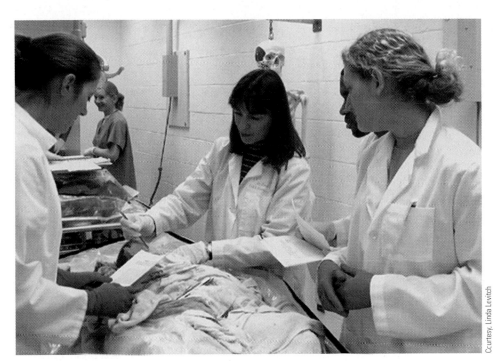

Courtesy, Linda Levitch

Anatomy is yet another important area of interest for physical anthropologists. In living organisms, bones and teeth are intimately linked to the soft tissues that surround and act on them. Consequently, a thorough knowledge of soft tissue anatomy is essential to the understanding of biomechanical relationships involved in movement. Such relationships are important in accurately assessing the structure and function of limbs and other components of fossilized remains. For these reasons and others, many physical anthropologists specialize in anatomical studies. In fact, several physical anthropologists hold professorships in anatomy departments at universities and medical schools (Fig. 1-12).

Applied approaches in biological anthropology are numerous. And while *applied anthropology* is aimed at the practical application of anthropological theories and methods outside the academic setting, applied and academic anthropology aren't mutually exclusive approaches. In fact, applied anthropology relies on the research and theories of academic anthropologists and at the same time has much to contribute to theory and techniques. Within biological anthropology, forensic anthropologists are a good example of the applied approach. But the practical application of the techniques of physical anthropology isn't new. During World War II, for example, physical anthropologists were extensively involved in designing gun turrets and airplane cockpits. Since then, many physical anthropologists have pursued careers in genetic and biomedical research, public health, evolutionary medicine, medical anthropology, and conservation of nonhuman primates, and many hold positions in museums and zoos. In fact, a background in physical anthropology is excellent preparation for almost any career in the medical and biological fields.

From this brief overview, you can see that physical anthropology is the subdiscipline of anthropology that focuses on many varied aspects of the biological and behavioral nature of human beings. Humans are a product of the same forces that produced all life on earth. As such, we're just one contemporary component of a vast biological **continuum** at one point in time; and in this regard, we aren't particularly unique. Stating that humans are part of a continuum doesn't imply that we're at the peak of development on that continuum. Depending on the criteria used, humans can be seen to exist at one end of the spectrum or the other, or somewhere in between, but we don't necessarily occupy a position of inherent superiority over other species.

However, human beings are truly unique in one dimension, and that is intellect. After all, humans are the only species, born of earth, to stir the lunar dust. We're the only species to develop language and complex culture as a means of buffering nature's challenges; and by so doing, we have gained the power to shape the planet's very destiny.

continuum A set of relationships in which all components fall along a single integrated spectrum. All life reflects a single biological continuum.

Physical Anthropology and the Scientific Method

Science is a process of explaining natural phenomena by means of observation, developing explanations or **hypotheses**, and then devising a research design or series of experiments to test those hypotheses. By this we mean that there's an **empirical** approach to gaining information. Because biological anthropologists are engaged in scientific pursuits, they adhere to the principles of the **scientific method**, whereby they identify a research problem and then gather information to solve it.

Once a question has been asked, the first step usually is to explore the existing literature (books and journals) to determine what other people have done to resolve the issue. Based on this preliminary research and other observations, one or even several tentative explanations (hypotheses) are then proposed. The next step is to develop a research design or methodology aimed at testing the hypothesis. These methods involve collecting information or **data** that can then be studied and analyzed. Data can be analyzed in many ways, most of them involving various statistical tests. During the data collection and analysis phase, it's critical for scientists to use a rigorously controlled approach so they can precisely describe their techniques and results. This precision is critical because it enables others to repeat the experiments and allows scientists to make comparisons between their study and the work of others.

For example, when scientists collect data on tooth size in hominid fossils, they must specify which teeth are being measured, how they're measured, and the results of the measurements (expressed numerically, or **quantitatively**). Then, by analyzing the data, the investigators try to draw conclusions about the meaning and significance of their measurements. This body of information then becomes the basis of future studies, perhaps by other researchers, who can compare their own results with those already obtained.

Hypothesis testing is the very core of the scientific method and, although it may seem contradictory at first, it's based on the potential to *falsify* the hypothesis. Falsification doesn't mean that the entire hypothesis is untrue, but it does indicate there may be exceptions to it. Or the hypothesis may need to be refined and subjected to further testing.

Eventually, if a hypothesis stands up to repeated testing, it may become part of a **theory**, or perhaps a theory itself. There's a popular misconception that a theory is mere conjecture, or a "hunch." But in science, theories are proposed explanations of relationships between natural phenomena. Theories usually concern a broader or more universal view than hypotheses, which have a narrower focus and deal with more specific relationships between phenomena. But, like hypotheses, theories aren't facts. *They're tested explanations of facts.* For example, it's a fact that when you drop an object, it falls to the ground. The explanation for this fact is the theory of gravity. But, like hypotheses, theories can be altered over time with further experimentation and by using newly developed technologies in testing.

There's one more important fact about hypotheses and theories: *Any proposition that's stated as absolute and/or doesn't allow the possibility of falsification is not a scientific hypothesis, and it should never be considered as such.* We've emphasized that a crucial aspect of scientific statements is that there must be way to evaluate their validity. Statements such as "Heaven exists" may well be true (that is, they describe some actual state), but there's no rational, empirical means (based on experience or experiment) of testing them. Therefore, acceptance of such a view is based on faith rather than on scientific verification. The purpose of scientific research isn't to establish absolute truths; rather, it's to generate ever more accurate and consistent explanations of phenomena in our universe, based on observation and testing. At its very heart, scientific methodology is an exercise in rational thought and critical thinking (see Issue, pp. 16–17).

Scientific testing of hypotheses may take several years (or longer) and may involve researchers who weren't involved with the original work. What's more, new methods may permit different kinds of testing that weren't previously possible, and this is a strength of scientific research. For example, since the 1970s primatologists have reported that male nonhuman primates (as well as males of many other species) sometimes kill infants. One hypothesis has been that since the males were usually new to a group, they were killing infants fathered by other males. Many scientists have objected to this hypothesis, and

science A body of knowledge gained through observation and experimentation; from the Latin *scientia*, meaning "knowledge."

hypotheses (*sing.*, hypothesis) A provisional explanation of a phenomenon. Hypotheses require verification or falsification through testing.

empirical Relying on experiment or observation; from the Latin *empiricus*, meaning "experienced."

scientific method An approach to research whereby a problem is identified, a hypothesis (or provisional explanation) is stated, and that hypothesis is tested by collecting and analyzing data.

data (sing., datum) Facts from which conclusions can be drawn; scientific information.

quantitatively Pertaining to measurements of quantity and including such properties as size, number, and capacity. When data are quantified, they're expressed numerically and can be tested statistically.

theory A broad statement of scientific relationships or underlying principles that has been substantially verified through the testing of hypotheses.

scientific testing The precise repetition of an experiment or expansion of observed data to provide verification; the procedure by which hypotheses and theories are verified, modified, or discarded.

they've proposed several alternatives. For one thing, there was no way to know for certain that the males weren't killing their own offspring; but if they were, this would argue against the hypothesis. However, in a fairly recent study, scientists collected DNA samples from dead infants and the males who killed them and showed that most of the time, the males weren't related to their victims. This result doesn't prove that the original hypothesis is accurate. But it does strengthen it. This study is described in more detail in Chapter 7, but we mention it here to emphasize that science is an ongoing process that builds on previous work and benefits from newly developed techniques (that is, DNA testing) in ways that constantly expand our knowledge.

Using the scientific method allows for the development and testing of hypotheses, and it allows scientists to try to eliminate various types of *bias*. It's important to realize that bias occurs in all studies. Sources of bias include how the investigator was trained and by whom; what particular questions the researcher is asking; what specific skills and talents he or she possesses; what earlier results (if any) have been established in this realm of study and by whom (for example, the researcher, close colleagues, or those with rival approaches or even rival personalities); and what sources of data are available (such as in accessible countries or museums) and thus what samples can be collected.

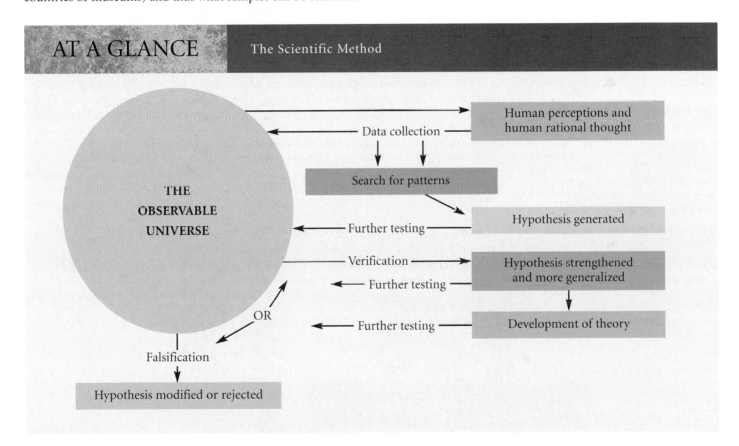

AT A GLANCE   The Scientific Method

The Anthropological Perspective

Perhaps the most important benefit you'll receive from this textbook, and this course, is a wider appreciation of the human experience. To understand human beings and how our species came to be, we must broaden our viewpoint, both through time and space. All branches of anthropology fundamentally seek to do this in what we call the *anthropological perspective*.

Physical anthropologists, for example, are interested in how humans differ from—and are similar to—other animals, especially nonhuman primates. For example, we've defined *hominids* as bipedal primates, but what are the major anatomical components of bipedal locomotion, and how do they differ from, say, those in a quadrupedal ape? To answer these questions, we would need to study the anatomical structures involved in human locomotion (muscles, hips, legs, and feet) and compare them to the same structures in various nonhuman primates.

Through a perspective that is broad in space and time, we can begin to grasp the diversity of the human experience within the context of biological and behavioral continuity with other species. In this way, we may better understand the limits and potentials of humankind. And by extending our knowledge to include cultures other than our own we may hope to avoid the **ethnocentric** pitfalls inherent in a more limited view of humanity.

In addition to broadening perspectives over space (that is, encompassing many cultures and ecological circumstances as well as nonhuman species), an anthropological perspective also extends our horizons *through time*. For example, in Chapter 17 we'll discuss human nutrition. The vast majority of the foods people eat today (coming from domesticated plants and animals) were unavailable until 10,000 years ago. Human physiological mechanisms for chewing and digesting foods nevertheless were already well established long before that date. These adaptive complexes go back millions of years. Besides the obviously different diets prior to the development of agriculture (approximately 10,000 years ago), earlier hominids might well have differed from humans today in average body size, **metabolism**, and activity patterns. How, then, does the basic evolutionary "equipment" (that is, physiology) inherited from our hominid forebears accommodate our modern diets? Clearly, the way to understand such processes is not just by looking at contemporary human responses, but by placing them in the perspective of evolutionary development through time.

We hope that after reading the following pages, you'll have an increased understanding not only of the similarities we share with other biological organisms but also of the processes that have shaped the traits that make us unique. We live in what may well be our planet's most crucial period in the past 65 million years. We are members of the one species that, through the very agency of culture, has wrought such devastating changes in ecological systems that we must now alter our technologies or face potentially unspeakable consequences. In such a time, it's vital that we attempt to gain the best possible understanding of what it means to be human. We believe that the study of physical anthropology is one endeavor that aids in this attempt, and that is indeed the goal of this text.

ethnocentric   Viewing other cultures from the inherently biased perspective of one's own culture. Ethnocentrism often results in other cultures being seen as inferior to one's own.

metabolism   The chemical processes within cells that break down nutrients and release energy for the body to use. (When nutrients are broken down into their component parts, such as amino acids, energy is released and made available for the cell to use.)

VISUAL SUMMARY

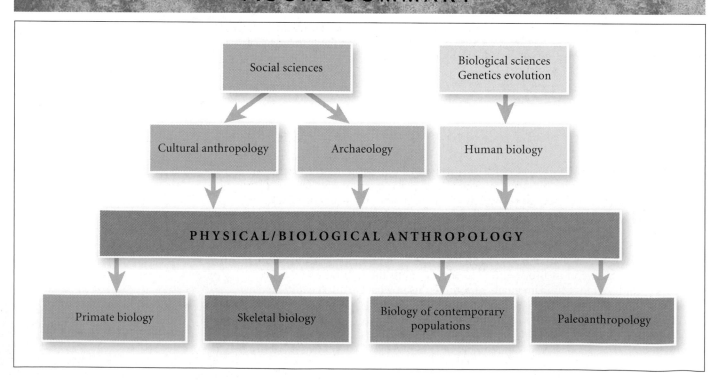

Summary: Putting It All Together

In this chapter, we've introduced you to the field of physical, or biological, anthropology, placing it within the overall context of anthropological studies. As a major academic discipline within the social sciences, anthropology also includes cultural anthropology, archaeology, and linguistic anthropology as major subfields.

Physical anthropology is the study of many aspects of human biology, including genetics, genetic variation, adaptations to environmental factors, nutrition, and anatomy. These topics are discussed within an evolutionary framework because all human characteristics are either directly or indirectly the results of biological evolution, which in turn is driven by genetic change. Hence, biological anthropologists also study our closest relatives, the nonhuman primates, primate evolution, and the genetic and fossil evidence for human evolution.

Because biological anthropology is a scientific discipline, we also discussed the role of the scientific method in research. We presented the importance of objectivity, observation, data collection, and analysis; and we described the formation and testing of hypotheses to explain natural phenomena. We also emphasized that this approach is an empirical one that doesn't rely on supernatural explanations.

Because evolution is the core of physical anthropology, in the next chapter we present a brief historical overview of changes in Western scientific thought that led to the discovery of the basic principles of biological evolution. As you're probably aware, evolution is a highly controversial subject in the United States. However, it's not particularly controversial in other countries. In the next chapter we'll address some of the reasons for this controversy and explain the evidence for evolution as the single thread uniting all the biological sciences.

Critical Thinking Questions

1. Given that you've only just been introduced to the field of physical anthropology, why do you think subjects such as anatomy, genetics, nonhuman primate behavior, and human evolution are integrated into a discussion of what it means to be human?

2. Is it important to you, personally, to know about human evolution? Why or why not?

3. Do you see a connection between hominid footprints that are almost 4 million years old and human footprints left on the moon in 1969? If so, do you think this relationship is important? What does the fact that there are human footprints on the moon say about human adaptation? (You may wish to refer to both biological and cultural adaptation.)

Anthropology Resource Center Online

Go to the Anthropology Resource Center at **http://anthropology.wadsworth.com** for a wealth of online resources, including a companion Premium Online Study Center for your text that provides study aids such as self-quizzes for each chapter and a practice final exam, as well as links to anthropology websites and information on the latest theories and discoveries in the field. Also check out InfoTrac College Edition®, your online library that offers full-length articles from thousands of scholarly and popular publications. Just click on the InfoTrac button at the companion website and use the passcode that came with your book.

Evaluation in Science: Lessons in Critical Thinking

At the end of various chapters throughout this book, you'll find a brief discussion of a contemporary topic. Some of these subjects aren't usually covered in anthropology textbooks. However, we think it's important to address such issues because scientists shouldn't simply dismiss those views or ideas they're skeptical of. Similarly, you should be reluctant to *accept* a view based solely on its personal appeal. Accepting or rejecting an idea based on personal feelings is as good a definition of "bias" as one could devise. Science is an approach—indeed, a *tool*—used to eliminate (or at least minimize) bias.

Scientific evaluation is, in fact, a part of a broader framework of intellectual rigor called *critical thinking.* The development of critical thinking skills should be an important and lasting benefit of a college education. These skills are valuable in everyday life because they enable people to evaluate, compare, analyze, critique, and synthesize information so they won't accept everything they hear and read at face value.

The advertising industry provides an excellent illustration of the need for critical thinking. Cosmetics companies tell us, among other things, that collagen creams will reduce wrinkles because collagen is a principal protein component of connective tissue, including skin. It's true that collagen is a major protein constituent of skin tissue. Moreover, collagen fibers do break down over time, and this damage is one factor that contributes to the development of wrinkles. But, the most beneficial properties of the creams are probably the UV filters and moisturizers they contain, although they won't eliminate wrinkles. What's more, the collagen isn't absorbed into skin cells, and even if it were, it still wouldn't be incorporated in a way that would replenish what's been destroyed. But most people don't know what collagen is, and they don't take the time to find out. When they hear it's an important component of skin tissue and that, as such, it can help reduce wrinkles, the argument sounds reasonable; so, they buy the cream, which won't reduce wrinkles and is usually expensive.

Critical thinking is probably most important in the area of politics. Politicians routinely make claims, frequently in 30-second sound bites that use catchphrases and misleading statistics. (Remember, their speechwriters are well informed, skillful at manipulating language, and they know they're targeting a generally uninformed public.)

In many situations, an informed public should call government leaders to task. As one example, global climate change has become a political issue, especially in the United States. The vast majority of scientists worldwide now agree that global warming is happening, and that it's caused largely by human activity. And many governments, especially in Europe, are beginning to formulate policies aimed at slowing the warming trend. However, many politicians in the United States and a few other countries continue to say that we still don't have enough scientific data to justify spending billions of dollars on preventive measures that may not even work. Given the stakes involved, if the concerns expressed by so many scientists today are real, an informed populace should take it upon itself to investigate these issues and ask why some governments are concerned but others aren't.

When politicians say, "Scientists aren't in complete agreement on the issue of global warming," what they imply—and what most people hear—is that scientists aren't in agreement that climate is changing. Certainly some climate scientists still aren't convinced, but most of them are. If you understand the nature of science and the scientific method, then you realize that actually much of the disagreement among scientists isn't whether warming is happening, but rather how fast it's happening, how warm it will get, and how disastrous the consequences will be.

People are also ambivalent toward, and intimidated by, science. In general, people accept scientific results when they support their personal views and reject them when they don't. They're also ambivalent because science changes so rapidly. A study in 2004, before the presidential election, revealed that one-third of Americans had never even heard of stem cells, even though stem cell research was a major political issue and had been prominent in the news. One reason is that most respondents in the survey were old enough not to have learned about stem cells in school and, once out of school, most people avoid scientific issues. Moreover, primary and secondary science and math education in the United States has suffered a deplorable decline in recent years and now ranks behind that in all European countries; and over half of high school graduates don't complete a college degree. Fortunately, most colleges and universities require at least one year of science for a degree—in fact, that requirement may be why you're taking this course.

Education is crucial to the development of critical thinking and, in order to make important decisions and understand the many profound issues that we must confront, people need to have critical thinking skills. Among other things, critical thinkers are able to assess the evidence supporting their own beliefs (in a sense, to step outside themselves) and to identify the weaknesses in their own positions. They recognize that knowledge is not merely a collection of facts, but an ongoing process of examining information to expand our understanding of the world. Critical thinking people look beyond the often superficial (and even ill-informed) statements made by political leaders and advertising and ask questions like these: "What is the evidence for that?" "Who made that statement?" "What research supports that claim?" "Was the research published in a peer-reviewed journal, or quoted out of context in a biased publication?" They also may take the time to research issues before making up their mind about them.

Throughout this book, you'll be presented with the results of numerous studies using numerical data. For example, it might be stated that Neandertal males were bigger than females, or that the gene for cystic fibrosis is more common in European populations than in other groups. First and always, be cautious of generalizations. What is the specific nature of the argument? What data support it? Can these data be quantified? If so, how is this information presented? (*Note:* Always carefully read the tables in textbooks or articles.)

Regardless of the discipline you ultimately study, at some point in your college career you should take a course in statistics. Many universities now make statistics a general education requirement (sometimes under the category "quantitative reasoning"). Statistics often seems like a dry subject, and many students are intimidated by the math it requires. Nevertheless, perhaps more than any other skill you'll acquire in your college years, quantitative critical reasoning is a tool you'll be able to use every day of your life.

A responsibility of an educated society is to be both informed and vigilant. The knowledge we possess and attempt to build on is neither good nor bad; however, the ways that knowledge may be used can have highly charged moral and ethical implications. Thus, a goal of the chapter-closing issues is to stimulate your interest and give you a basis for reaching your own conclusions. Here are some useful questions to ask in making critical evaluations about these issues or any other controversial scientific topic:

1. What data are presented?

2. What conclusions are presented, and how are they organized (as tentative hypotheses or as more dogmatic assertions)?

3. Are these views simply the authors' opinions, or are they supported by a larger body of research?

4. What are the research findings? Are they adequately documented?

5. Is the information consistent with information that you already possess? If not, can the inconsistencies be explained?

6. Are the conclusions (hypotheses) testable? How might one go about testing the various hypotheses that are presented?

7. If presentation of new research findings is at odds with previous hypotheses (or theories), must these hypotheses now be modified (or completely rejected)?

8. How do your own personal views bias you in interpreting the results?

9. Once you've identified your own biases, are you able to set them aside in order to evaluate the information objectively?

10. Can you discuss both the pros and cons of a scientific topic in an evenhanded manner?

SOURCES

Gregory, J.M., P. Huybrecths, and S.C.B. Raper. 2004. "Threatened Loss of the Greenland Ice-sheet," Brief Communications, *Nature*, 428:616.

Gross, Liza. 2006. "Scientific Illiteracy and the Partisan Takeover of Biology." *PloS Biology*, 4(5): 206. DOI: 10,1371/journal.pbio. 0040167.

CHAPTER 2

The Development of Evolutionary Theory

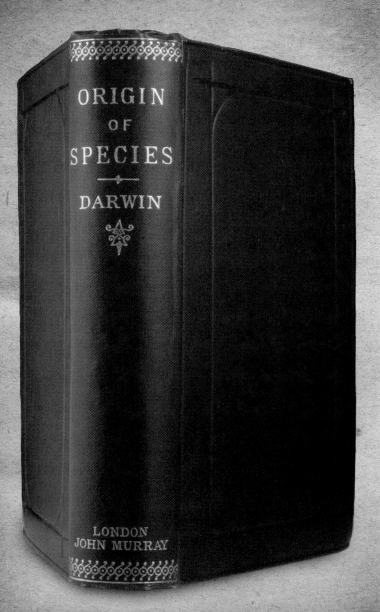

© Russell L. Ciochon, University of Iowa

OUTLINE

KEY QUESTIONS

What are the basic premises of natural selection?

What were the technological and philosophical changes that led people to accept notions of evolutionary change?

Introduction

Has anyone ever asked you, "If humans evolved from monkeys, then why do we still have monkeys?" Or maybe you've heard this one: "If evolution happens, then why don't we ever see new species?" These are the kinds of questions asked by people who have no understanding of evolutionary processes and who usually don't even believe those processes exist. That anyone today, given the overwhelming evidence for biological evolution, would ask such questions is a reflection of the poor quality of primary and secondary biological education.

Evolution is one of the most fundamental of biological processes, and it's one of the most misunderstood. This is partly because, in the United States, the topic is commonly avoided in primary and secondary schools, so students frequently aren't exposed to it. And at colleges and universities, evolution is covered only in classes that directly relate to it. Indeed, if you're not an anthropology or biology major and you're taking a class in biological anthropology mainly to fill a science requirement, you'll probably never study evolution again.

By the end of this course, you'll know the answers to the above questions. Briefly, no one who studies evolution would ever say that humans evolved from monkeys, because they didn't. They didn't evolve from chimpanzees, either. The earliest human ancestors evolved from a species that lived some 5 to 8 million years ago (mya). That ancestral species was the *last common ancestor* we share with chimpanzees. In turn, the lineage that led to the apes and humans separated from a monkey-like ancestor some 20 mya, and monkeys are still around because as lineages diverged from a common ancestor, each group went its separate way. Over time, some of these groups became extinct while others evolved into the species we see today. So, each living species is the current product of processes that go back millions of years. Because evolution takes time, and lots of it, we rarely witness the appearance of new species except in microorganisms. But we do see *microevolutionary* changes (briefly referred to in Chapter 1) in many species.

The subject of evolution is controversial especially in the United States, because some religious views hold that evolutionary statements run counter to biblical teachings. In fact, as you're probably aware, there is strong opposition to the teaching of evolution in public schools.

People who deny that evolution happens say, "evolution is only a theory," implying that evolution is mere supposition. You'll remember from Chapter 1 that we pointed out why scientific theories aren't just suppositions or guesses, although that's how the word *theory* is commonly used in everyday conversation. Actually, as you learned, when dealing with scientific issues, referring to a concept as "theory" supports it. As we discussed in Chapter 1, theories have been tested and subjected to verification through accumulated evidence—and they haven't been disproved, sometimes even after decades of experimentation. It's true; evolution *is* a theory, one that's being supported by a mounting body of genetic evidence that, quite literally, expands daily. It's a theory that explains how biological change occurs in species over time, and it's stood the test of time. Today evolutionary theory stands as the most fundamental unifying force in biological science.

Because physical anthropology is concerned with all aspects of how humans came to be and how we adapt physiologically to the external environment, the details of the evolutionary process are crucial to the field. And, given the central importance of evolution to biological anthropology, it's beneficial to know how the mechanics of the process came to be discovered. Also, if we want to understand and make critical assessments of the controversy still surrounding the issue today, we need to explore the social and political events that influenced the discovery of evolutionary principles.

Click!

Go to the following media for interactives and exercises on topics covered in this chapter:

- Basic Genetics for Anthropology CD-ROM: Principles and Applications
- Online Virtual Laboratories for Physical Anthropology, Fourth Edition

A Brief History of Evolutionary Thought

The discovery of evolutionary principles first took place in Western Europe and was made possible by advances in scientific thinking that date back to the sixteenth century. Having said this, we must recognize that Western science borrowed many of its ideas from other cultures, especially the Arabs, Indians, and Chinese. In fact, intellectuals in these cultures and in ancient Greece had developed notions of biological evolution (Teresi, 2002), but they never formulated them into a cohesive theory.

Charles Darwin was the first person to explain the basic mechanics of the evolutionary process. But while he was developing his theory of **natural selection**, a Scottish naturalist named Alfred Russel Wallace independently reached the same conclusion. That natural selection, the single most important force of evolutionary change, should be proposed at more or less the same time by two British men in the mid-nineteenth century may seem like a strange coincidence. But, if Darwin and Wallace hadn't made their simultaneous discoveries, someone else soon would have, and that someone would probably have been British or French. That's because the groundwork had already been laid in Britain and France, and many scientists there were prepared to accept explanations of biological change that would have been unacceptable even 25 years before.

Like other human endeavors, scientific knowledge is usually gained through a series of small steps rather than giant leaps. And just as technological change is based on past achievements, scientific knowledge builds on previously developed theories. For this reason, it's informative to examine the development of ideas that led Darwin and Wallace to independently develop the theory of evolution by natural selection.

Throughout the Middle Ages, one predominant feature of the European worldview was that all aspects of nature, including all forms of life and their relationships to one another, never changed. This view was partly shaped by a feudal society that was itself a hierarchical, rigid class system that hadn't changed much for centuries. But the most important influence was an extremely powerful religious system, wherein the teachings of Christianity were taken literally. Consequently, it was generally accepted that all life on earth had been created by God exactly as it existed in the present, and the belief that life-forms couldn't and didn't change came to be known as **fixity of species**. To question the assumptions of fixity, especially publicly, was seen as a challenge to God's perfection and could be considered heresy, a crime punishable by a nasty and potentially fiery death.

The plan of the entire universe was viewed as God's design. In what's called the "argument from design," anatomical structures were engineered to meet the purpose for which they were required. Limbs, internal organs, and eyes fit the functions they performed; and they, along with the rest of nature, were a deliberate plan of the Grand Designer. Also, pretty much everybody believed that the Grand Designer had completed his works fairly recently. An Irish archbishop named James Ussher (1581–1656) analyzed the "begat" chapter of Genesis and determined that the earth was created in 4004 B.C. While Ussher wasn't the first person to suggest a recent origin of the earth, he was the first to propose a precise date for it.

The prevailing notion of the earth's brief existence, together with fixity of species, was a huge obstacle to the development of evolutionary theory. Evolution takes time; and the idea of immense geological time, which today we take for granted, simply didn't exist. In fact, until the concepts of fixity and time were fundamentally altered, it was impossible to conceive of evolution by means of natural selection.

THE SCIENTIFIC REVOLUTION

So, what transformed centuries-old beliefs in a rigid, static universe to a view of worlds in continuous motion? How did the earth's brief history become an immense expanse of incomprehensible time? How did the scientific method as we know it today develop? These are important questions, but it would be equally appropriate to ask why it took so long for Europe to break from the constraints of traditional belief systems when Arab and Indian scholars had developed concepts of (for example) planetary motion centuries earlier.

For Europeans, the discovery of the New World and circumnavigation of the globe in the fifteenth century overturned some very basic ideas about the planet. For one thing, the earth could no longer be thought of as flat. Also, as Europeans began to explore the New

natural selection The most critical mechanism of evolutionary change, first articulated by Charles Darwin; refers to genetic change or changes in the frequencies of certain traits in populations due to differential reproductive success between individuals.

fixity of species The notion that species, once created, can never change; an idea diametrically opposed to theories of biological evolution.

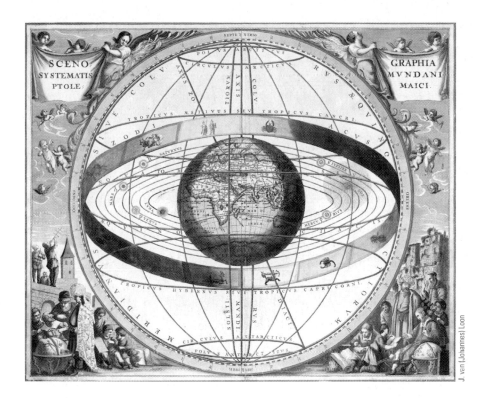

J. van (Johannes) Loon

FIGURE 2-1
This beautifully illustrated seventeenth-century map shows the earth at the center of the solar system. Around it are 7 concentric circles depicting the orbits of the moon, sun, and the 5 planets that were known at the time. (Note also the signs of the zodiac.)

World, their awareness of biological diversity was greatly expanded as they became aware of plants and animals previously unknown to them.

There were other attacks on traditional beliefs. In 1514, a Polish mathematician named Copernicus challenged a notion proposed more than 1,500 years earlier by the fourth-century B.C. Greek philosopher, Aristotle. Aristotle had taught that the sun and planets existed in a series of concentric spheres that revolved around the earth (Fig. 2-1). This system of planetary spheres was, in turn, surrounded by the stars; and this meant that the earth was the center of the universe. In fact, in India, scholars had figured out that the earth orbited the sun long before Copernicus did; but Copernicus is generally credited with removing the earth as the center of all things by proposing a sun-centered solar system.

Copernicus' theory was openly discussed in intellectual circles, but it didn't attract much attention from the Catholic Church. Nevertheless, it did contradict a major premise of Church doctrine, which, at that time, wholeheartedly embraced the teachings of Aristotle. By the 1300s, the Church had accepted this view as dogma because it reinforced the notion that the earth, and the humans on it, was the central focus of God's creation and must therefore have a central position in the universe.

However, in the early 1600s, an Italian mathematician named Galileo Galilei restated Copernicus' views in print, and he used logic and mathematics to support his claim. (In fact, Galileo is credited with having introduced the empirical approach to Western science.) To his misfortune, Galileo eventually was confronted by the Catholic Church regarding his publications and spent the last nine years of his life under house arrest. Nevertheless, in intellectual circles, the solar system had changed from being earth-centered to sun-centered, and from being fixed to being in motion.

Throughout the sixteenth and seventeenth centuries, European scholars developed methods and theories that revolutionized scientific thought. The seventeenth century, in particular, saw the discovery of the principles of physics, motion, and gravity. Other achievements included discovery of the true function of the heart and circulatory system as well as development of numerous scientific instruments including the telescope (perfected by Galileo), barometer, and microscope. These advances permitted investigations of natural phenomena and opened up entire new worlds for discoveries that had never before been imagined. But even with these advances, the idea that living forms could change over time simply didn't occur to people.

PRECURSORS TO THE THEORY OF EVOLUTION

Before early naturalists could begin to understand the many forms of organic life, it was necessary to list and describe them. And as research progressed, scholars were increasingly impressed with the amount of biological diversity they saw.

The concept of species, as we think of it today, wasn't proposed until the seventeenth century when John Ray, a minister educated at Cambridge University, developed the concept. Importantly, he recognized that groups of plants and animals could be differentiated from other groups by their ability to mate with one another and produce offspring. He placed such groups of **reproductively isolated** organisms into a single category, which he called the species (*pl.*, species). Thus, by the late 1600s, the biological criterion of reproduction was used to define species, much as it is today (Young, 1992).

Ray also recognized that species frequently shared similarities with other species, and he grouped these together in a second level of classification he called the genus (*pl.*, genera). He was the first to use the labels *genus* and *species* in this way, and they're the terms we still use today.

Carolus Linnaeus (1707–1778) was a Swedish naturalist who developed a method of classifying plants and animals. In his famous work, *Systema Naturae* (Systems of Nature), first published in 1735, he standardized Ray's use of genus and species terminology and established the system of **binomial nomenclature**. He also added two more categories: class and order. Linnaeus' four-level system became the basis for **taxonomy**, the system of classification we continue to use.

Linnaeus also put humans in his classification of animals, placing them in the genus *Homo* and species *sapiens*. Including humans in this scheme was controversial because it defied contemporary thought that humans, made in God's image, should be considered unique and separate from the rest of the animal kingdom.

For all his progressive tendencies, Linnaeus still believed in fixity of species—although in later years, faced with mounting evidence to the contrary, he came to question it. Indeed, fixity was being challenged on many fronts, especially in France, where voices were being raised in favor of a universe based on change and, more to the point, in favor of a biological relationship between similar species based on descent from a common ancestor.

A French naturalist, Georges-Louis Leclerc de Buffon (1707–1788), recognized the dynamic relationship between the external environment and living forms. In his *Natural History*, first published in 1749, he stressed the importance of change in the universe and in the changing nature of species. Buffon believed that when groups of organisms migrated to new areas, they gradually became altered as a result of adapting to a different environment. Although Buffon rejected the idea that one species could give rise to another, his recognition of the external environment as an agent of change in species was extremely important.

Today, Erasmus Darwin (1731–1802) is best known as Charles Darwin's grandfather. But, he was also a physician, inventor, naturalist, philosopher, and leading member of an important intellectual community in Lichfield, England. During his lifetime, Erasmus Darwin was also a famous poet and, in his most famous work, expressed his views that life had originated in the seas and that all species had descended from a common ancestor. Thus he introduced many of the ideas that his grandson would propose 56 years later. These concepts include vast expanses of time for life to evolve, competition for resources, and the importance of the environment in evolutionary processes. From letters and other sources, we know that Charles Darwin read his grandfather's writings; but we don't know how much Erasmus influenced his grandson's theories.

One important point is that neither Buffon nor Erasmus Darwin attempted to *explain* the evolutionary process. The first person to attempt to do this was a French naturalist named Jean-Baptiste Lamarck (1744–1829). Lamarck (Fig. 2-2) suggested a dynamic relationship between species and the environment such that if the external environment changed, an animal's activity patterns would also change to accommodate the new circumstances. This would result in the increased or decreased use of certain body parts; and consequently, those body parts would be modified. According to Lamarck, these physical changes would occur in response to bodily "needs," so that if a particular part of the body felt a certain need, "fluids and forces" would be directed to that point and the structure would be modified. Since the alteration would make the animal better suited to its habitat, the new trait would be passed on to offspring.

reproductively isolated   pertaining to groups of organisms that, mainly because of genetic differences, are prevented from mating and producing offspring with members of other groups.

binomial nomenclature   (*binomial*, meaning "two names") In taxonomy, the convention established by Carolus Linnaeus whereby genus and species names are used to refer to species. For example, *Homo sapiens* refers to human beings.

taxonomy   The branch of science concerned with the rules of classifying organisms on the basis of evolutionary relationships.

Lamarck's theory is known as the *inheritance of acquired characteristics*, or the *use-disuse* theory, and it's often described by giving the giraffe as a hypothetical example. Having stripped all the leaves from the lower branches of a tree (environmental change), the giraffe tries to reach leaves on upper branches. As "vital forces" move to tissues of the neck, it becomes slightly longer, and the giraffe can reach higher. The longer neck is then transmitted to offspring, with the eventual result that all giraffes have longer necks than their predecessors had (Fig. 2-3). So, according to this theory, *a trait acquired by an animal during its lifetime can be passed on to offspring.* Today we know that this explanation is incorrect, because only those traits that are influenced by genetic information contained within sex cells (eggs and sperm) can be inherited (see Chapter 3).

Because Lamarck's explanation of species change isn't genetically correct, it's frequently made fun of and dismissed. But, in point of fact, Lamarck deserves a lot of credit because he emphasized the importance of interactions between organisms and the external environment in the evolutionary process. What's more, he was one of the first to acknowledge the need for a distinct branch of science that dealt solely with living things (that is, separate from geology). For this new science, Lamarck coined the term *biology*, and a central feature of this new discipline was the idea of species change.

Lamarck's most vehement opponent was a French vertebrate paleontologist named Georges Cuvier (1769–1832). Cuvier (Fig. 2-4) introduced the concept of extinction to explain the disappearance of animals represented by fossils. Although he was a brilliant anatomist, Cuvier never grasped the dynamic concept of nature, and he insisted on the

FIGURE 2-2
Lamarck believed that species change was influenced by environmental change. He is best known for his theory of the inheritance of acquired characteristics.

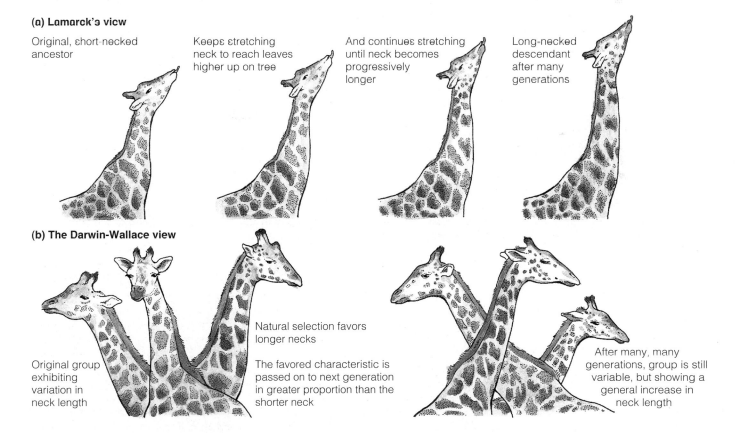

(a) Lamarck's view

Original, short-necked ancestor

Keeps stretching neck to reach leaves higher up on tree

And continues stretching until neck becomes progressively longer

Long-necked descendant after many generations

(b) The Darwin-Wallace view

Original group exhibiting variation in neck length

Natural selection favors longer necks

The favored characteristic is passed on to next generation in greater proportion than the shorter neck

After many, many generations, group is still variable, but showing a general increase in neck length

FIGURE 2-3
Contrasting ideas about the mechanism of evolution. (a) Lamarck's theory holds that acquired characteristics can be passed to subsequent generations. Short-necked giraffes stretched their necks to reach higher into trees for food, and, according to Lamarck, this acquired trait was passed on to offspring, who were born with longer necks. (b) The Darwin-Wallace theory of natural selection states that among giraffes there is variation in neck length. If having a longer neck provides an advantage for feeding, the trait will be passed on to a greater number of offspring, leading to an overall increase in the length of giraffe necks over many generations.

FIGURE 2-4
Cuvier explained the fossil record as the result of a succession of catastrophes followed by new creation events.

FIGURE 2-5
Thomas Malthus' *Essay on the Principle of Population* led both Darwin and Wallace to the principle of natural selection.

catastrophism The view that the earth's geological landscape is the result of violent cataclysmic events. Cuvier promoted this view, especially in opposition to Lamarck.

uniformitarianism The theory that the earth's features are the result of long-term processes that continue to operate in the present as they did in the past. Elaborated on by Lyell, this theory opposed catastrophism and contributed strongly to the concept of immense geological time.

fixity of species. Just as the abundance of fossils in geological strata was becoming increasingly apparent, it also became more important to explain what they were. But, rather than assuming that similarities between fossil forms and living species indicated evolutionary relationships, Cuvier proposed a variation of a doctrine known as **catastrophism**.

Catastrophism was the belief that the earth's geological features are the results of sudden, worldwide cataclysmic events. Cuvier's version of catastrophism suggested that a series of regional disasters had destroyed most or all of the local plant and animal life. These areas were then restocked with new, similar forms that migrated in from unaffected regions. Since he needed to be consistent with emerging fossil evidence, which indicated that organisms had become more complex over time, Cuvier proposed that after each disaster, the incoming migrants had a more modern appearance because they were the results of more recent creation events. (The last of these creations was the Noah flood, described in Genesis.) In this way, Cuvier's explanation of increased complexity over time avoided any notion of evolution while still being able to account for the evidence for change that was preserved in the fossil record.

In 1798, an English economist named Thomas Malthus (1766–1834) wrote *An Essay on the Principle of Population* (Fig. 2-5). This important essay inspired both Charles Darwin and Alfred Russel Wallace in their separate discoveries of natural selection. Considering the enormous influence that Malthus had on these two men, it's noteworthy that he wasn't interested in species change at all. Instead, he was arguing for limits to human population growth because, as he pointed out, in nature the tendency for populations to increase is constantly being held in check by the availability of resources. That is, population size increases exponentially while food supplies remain relatively stable. Even though humans can reduce constraints on population size by producing food, Malthus argued that the lack of resources would always be a constant source of "misery" for humankind if our numbers continued to increase. What both Darwin and Wallace recognized from this observation was that, given limited resources, all organisms are constantly competing for food and other necessities. In time, as you'll see in the following few pages, both Darwin and Wallace used these concepts to develop their theories of species change.

Charles Lyell (1797–1875) is considered the founder of modern geology (Fig. 2-6). He was a lawyer, a geologist, and for many years, Charles Darwin's friend and mentor. Before meeting Darwin in 1836, Lyell had earned acceptance in Europe's most prestigious scientific circles, thanks to his highly praised *Principles of Geology,* first published during the years 1830–1833.

In this immensely important work, Lyell argued that the geological processes observed in the present are the same as those that occurred in the past. This theory, called geological **uniformitarianism**, didn't originate entirely with Lyell, having been proposed by James Hutton in the late 1700s. Even so, it was Lyell who demonstrated that forces such as wind, water erosion, local flooding, frost, decomposition of vegetable matter, volcanoes, earthquakes, and glacial movements had all contributed in the past to produce the geological landscape that we see today. What's more, these processes were ongoing, indicating that geological change was still happening and that the forces driving such change were consistent, or *uniform*, over time. In other words, various aspects of the earth's surface (for example, climate, plants, animals, and land surfaces) are variable through time, but the *underlying processes* that influence them are constant.

Additionally, Lyell emphasized the obvious: namely, that for such slow-acting forces to produce momentous change, the earth must be far older than anyone had previously suspected. By providing an immense time scale and thereby altering perceptions of earth's history from a few thousand to many millions of years, Lyell changed the framework within which sci-

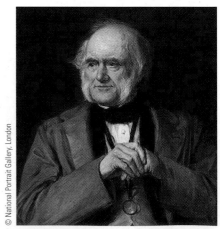

FIGURE 2-6
Portrait of Charles Lyell.

entists viewed the geological past. So the concept of "deep time" (Gould, 1987) remains one of Lyell's most significant contributions to the discovery of evolutionary principles. The immensity of geological time permitted the necessary time depth for the inherently slow process of evolutionary change.

As you can see, the roots of evolutionary theory are deeply imbedded in the late eighteenth and early nineteenth centuries. During that time, many less-famous people, whom we haven't discussed, also contributed to this intellectual movement. One of these lesser-known figures is someone we think deserves mention; her name is Mary Anning (1799–1847), and she lived in the town of Lyme Regis on the south coast of England (Fig. 2-7).

Anning's father died when she was 11 years old, leaving his family destitute. But fortunately, he had taught Mary to recognize marine fossils embedded in the cliffs near the town, and she began to collect and sell these fossils to support her family. She was able to do this because of a growing public interest in collecting fossils, many of which were believed to be the remains of creatures killed in the Noah flood.

After Anning's discovery of the first *complete* fossil of *Ichthyosaurus*, a large fishlike marine reptile, and the first *Pleiosaurus* fossil (another ocean-dwelling reptile), some of the most famous scientists in England repeatedly visited her home. Over the years, Anning supplied researchers and museums with hundreds of fossils. In fact, many of her discoveries became the foundation of some of the best-known collections in the world. Often excavating in perilous conditions, she became known as one of the world's leading "fossilists" and, by sharing her extensive knowledge of fossil species with many of the leading scientists of the day, she contributed to the understanding of the evolution of marine life over 200 million years ago. But because she was a woman, and of lowly social position, she wasn't acknowledged in the numerous scientific publications she facilitated. In recent years, however, she has achieved the recognition she deserves; her portrait hangs prominently in the British Museum (Natural History) in London, near one of her famous *Pleiosaurus* fossils.

The Natural History Museum, London

FIGURE 2-7
Portrait of Mary Anning.

The Discovery of Natural Selection

Having already been introduced to Erasmus Darwin, you shouldn't be surprised that his grandson Charles grew up in an educated family with ties to intellectual circles. Charles Darwin (1809–1882) was one of six children of Dr. Robert and Susanna Darwin (Fig. 2-8). Being the grandson not only of Erasmus Darwin but also of the wealthy Josiah Wedgwood (of Wedgwood china fame), Charles grew up enjoying the comfortable lifestyle of the landed gentry in rural England.

As a boy, Darwin had a keen interest in nature and spent his days fishing and collecting shells, birds' eggs, and rocks. However, this interest in natural history didn't dispel the generally held view of family and friends that he was in no way remarkable. In fact, his performance at school was no more than ordinary. (Perhaps this can be a source of inspiration to us all!)

After the death of his mother when he was eight years old, Darwin was raised by his father and older sisters. Because he showed little interest in anything except hunting, shooting, and perhaps science, his father sent him to Edinburgh University to study medicine. It was there that Darwin first became acquainted with the evolutionary theories of Lamarck and others.

During that time (the 1820s), notions of evolution were becoming feared in England and elsewhere. Anything identifiable with postrevolutionary France was viewed with suspicion by the established order in England, and Lamarck, partly because he was French, was especially vilified by British scientists.

It was also a time of growing political unrest in Britain. The Reform Movement, seeking to undo many inequalities of the traditional class system, was under way and, like most social movements, it had a radical faction. Because many of the radicals were atheists and socialists who also supported Lamarck's ideas, many people came to associate evolution with atheism and political subversion. The growing fear of evolutionary ideas led many to believe that, if these ideas were generally accepted, "the Church would crash, the moral fabric of society would be torn apart, and civilized man would return to savagery" (Desmond and Moore,

© Bettmann/CORBIS

FIGURE 2-8
Charles Darwin, photographed 5 years before the publication of *Origin of Species*.

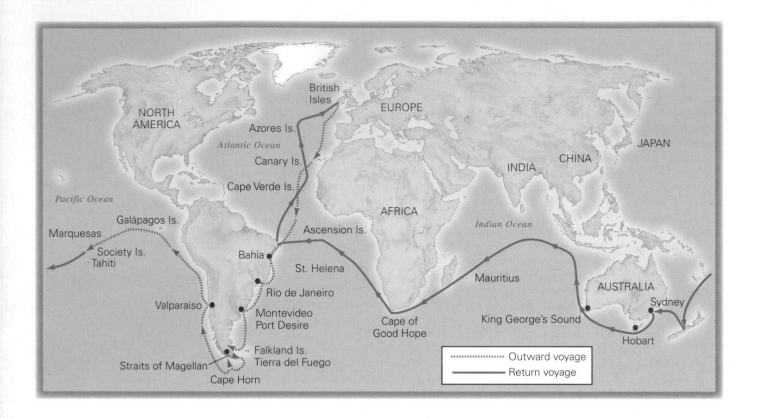

FIGURE 2-9
The route of HMS *Beagle*.

1991, p. 34). It's unfortunate that some of the most outspoken early proponents of **transmutation** were so vehemently anti-Christian, because their rhetoric helped establish the entrenched suspicion and misunderstanding of evolutionary theory that persists today.

While at Edinburgh, Darwin studied with professors who were outspoken supporters of Lamarck. So, even though he hated medicine and left Edinburgh after two years, his experience there was a formative period in his intellectual development.

Darwin was fairly indifferent to religion, but he next went to Christ's College, Cambridge, to study theology. It was during his Cambridge years that he cultivated his interests in natural science, immersing himself in botany and geology. It's no wonder that following his graduation in 1831, he was invited to join a scientific expedition that would circle the globe. And so it was that Darwin set sail aboard HMS *Beagle* on December 17, 1831. The famous voyage of the *Beagle* would take almost 5 years and would forever change not only the course of Darwin's life but also the history of biological science (Fig. 2-9).

Darwin went aboard the *Beagle* believing in fixity of species. But during the voyage, he privately began to have doubts. For example, he came across fossils of ancient giant animals that, except for size, looked very much like species that still lived in the same vicinity, and he began to wonder if the fossils represented ancestors of those living forms.

During the famous stopover at the Galápagos Islands off the coast of Ecuador (see Fig. 2-9), Darwin noticed that the vegetation and animals (especially birds) shared many similarities with those on the mainland of South America. But they weren't identical to them. What's more, the birds of one island were somewhat different from those on another. Darwin collected 13 varieties of Galápagos finches, and it was clear that they represented a closely affiliated group; but some of their physical traits were different, particularly the shape and size of their beaks (Fig. 2-10). Darwin also collected finches from the mainland, and these appeared to represent only one group, or species.

transmutation The change of one species to another. The term *evolution* did not assume its current meaning until the late nineteenth century.

The insight that Darwin gained from the finches is legendary. He recognized that the various Galápagos finches had all descended from a common, mainland ancestor and had been modified over time in response to different island habitats and dietary preferences. But actually, it wasn't until *after* he returned to England that he recognized the significance of the variation in beak structure. In fact, during the voyage, he had paid little attention to the finches. It was only later that he considered the factors that could lead to the modification of one species into many (Gould, 1985; Desmond and Moore, 1991).

Darwin arrived back in England in October of 1836 and was immediately accepted into the most prestigious scientific circles. He married his cousin, Emma Wedgwood, and moved to the village of Down, near London, where he spent the rest of his life writing on topics ranging from fossils to orchids. But the question of species change was his overriding passion.

At Down, Darwin began to develop his views on what he called *natural selection.* This concept was borrowed from animal breeders, who choose or "select" as breeding stock those animals having certain traits they want to emphasize in offspring. Animals with undesirable traits are "selected against," or prevented from breeding. A dramatic example of the effects of selective breeding can be seen in the various domestic dog breeds shown in Fig. 2-11. Darwin applied his knowledge of domesticated species to naturally occurring ones—recognizing that in undomesticated organisms, the selective agent was nature, not humans.

By the late 1830s, Darwin had realized that biological variation within a species (that is, differences among individuals) was crucial. What's more, he recognized that sexual reproduction increased variation, although he didn't know why. Then, in 1838, he read Malthus' essay; and there he found the answer to the question of how new species came to be. He accepted from Malthus the idea that populations increase at a faster rate than resources do, and he recognized that in nonhuman animals, population size is continuously limited by the amount of food available. He also accepted Lyell's observation that in nature there is a constant "struggle for existence." The idea that in each generation more offspring are born than will survive to adulthood, coupled with the notions of competition for resources and biological diversity, was all Darwin needed to develop his theory of natural selection. He wrote: "It at once struck me that under these circumstances favourable variations would tend to be preserved, and unfavourable ones to be destroyed. The result of this would be the formation of a new species" (F. Darwin, 1950, pp. 53–54). Basically, this quotation summarizes the entire theory of natural selection.

By 1844 Darwin had written a short summary of his views on natural selection, but he didn't think he had enough data to support his hypothesis, so he continued his research without publishing. He also had other reasons for not publishing what he knew would be, to say the least, a highly controversial work. He was deeply troubled that his wife, Emma, saw his ideas as running counter to her strong religious convictions (Keynes, 2002). Also, as a member of the established order, he knew that many of his friends and associates were concerned with threats to the status quo, and evolutionary theory was viewed as a very serious threat.

(a) Ground finch
Main food: seeds
Beak: heavy

(b) Tree finch
Main food: leaves, buds, blossoms, fruits
Beak: thick, short

(c) Tree finch (called woodpecker finch)
Main food: insects
Beak: stout, straight

(d) Ground finch (known as warbler finch)
Main food: insects
Beak: slender

FIGURE 2-10
Beak variation in Darwin's Galápagos finches.

Wolf: John Giustina/Getty Images   Dogs surrounding wolf: Lynn Kilgore and Lin Marshall

FIGURE 2-11
All domestic dog breeds share a common ancestor, the wolf. The extreme variation exhibited by dog breeds today has been achieved in a relatively short time through artificial selection. In this situation, humans allow only certain dogs to breed in order to emphasize specific characteristics. (We should note that not all traits desired by human breeders are advantageous to the dogs themselves.)

FIGURE 2-12
Alfred Russel Wallace independently discovered the key to the evolutionary process.

IN DARWIN'S SHADOW

Unlike Darwin, Alfred Russel Wallace (1823–1913) was born into a family of modest means (Fig. 2-12). He went to work at the age of 14, and with little formal education, he moved from one job to the next. He became interested in collecting plants and animals, and in 1848 he joined an expedition to the Amazon, where he acquired firsthand knowledge of many natural phenomena.

In 1855, Wallace published an article suggesting that species were descended from other species and that the appearance of new species was influenced by environmental factors (Trinkaus and Shipman, 1992). This article caused Lyell and others to urge Darwin to publish, but still he hesitated.

Then, in 1858, Wallace sent Darwin another paper, "On the Tendency of Varieties to Depart Indefinitely from the Original Type." In this paper, Wallace described evolution as a process driven by competition and natural selection. When he received Wallace's paper, Darwin was afraid that Wallace might get credit for a theory (natural selection) that he himself had developed. He quickly wrote a paper presenting his ideas, and both men's papers were read before the Linnean Society of London. Neither author was present. Wallace was out of the country, and Darwin was mourning the recent death of his young son.

The papers received little notice at the time. But in December 1859, when Darwin completed and published his greatest work, *On the Origin of Species,** the storm broke; and it still hasn't abated. Although public opinion was negative, there was much scholarly praise for the book, and scientific opinion gradually came to Darwin's support. The riddle of species was now explained: Species were mutable (changeable), not fixed; and they evolved from other species through the mechanism of natural selection.

Natural Selection

Early in his research, Darwin had realized that natural selection was the key to evolution. With the help of Malthus' ideas, he saw *how* selection in nature could be explained. In the struggle for existence, those *individuals* with favorable variations would survive and reproduce, but those with unfavorable variations wouldn't. For Darwin, the explanation of evolution was simple. These are the basic processes, as he understood them:

1. All species are capable of producing offspring at a faster rate than food supplies increase.

2. There is biological variation within all species.

3. Because in each generation more offspring are produced than can survive, and owing to limited resources, there is competition among individuals. (*Note:* This statement doesn't mean that there is constant fierce fighting.)

4. Individuals who possess favorable variations or traits (for example, speed, resistance to disease, protective coloration) have an advantage over those who don't have them. In other words, they have greater **fitness** because favorable traits increase the likelihood of survival and reproduction.

5. The environmental context determines whether or not a trait is beneficial. What is favorable in one setting may be a liability in another. Consequently, the traits that become most advantageous are the results of a natural process.

6. Traits are inherited and passed on to the next generation. Because individuals who possess favorable traits contribute more offspring to the next generation than others do, over time, those favorable traits become more common in the population; less favorable ones aren't passed on as frequently, and they become less common. Individuals who produce more offspring in comparison to others are said to have greater **reproductive success** or fitness.

fitness   Pertaining to natural selection, a measure of *relative* reproductive success of individuals. Fitness can be measured by an individual's genetic contribution to the next generation compared to that of other individuals. The terms *genetic fitness, reproductive fitness*, and *differential reproductive success* are also used.

reproductive success   The number of offspring an individual produces and rears to reproductive age; an individual's genetic contribution to the next generation.

---

*The full title is *On the Origin of Species by Means of Natural Selection, or the Preservation of Favoured Races in the Struggle for Life*.

7. Over long periods of geological time, successful variations accumulate in a population, so that later generations may be distinct from ancestral ones. Thus, in time, a new species may appear.

8. Geographical isolation also contributes to the formation of new species. As populations of a species become geographically isolated from one another, for whatever reasons (for example, distance, natural barriers like rivers, etc.), they begin to adapt to different environments. Over time, as populations continue to respond to different **selective pressures** (that is, different ecological circumstances), they may become distinct species. The 13 species of Galápagos finches are presumably all descended from a common ancestor on the South American mainland, and they exemplify the role of geographical isolation.

Before Darwin, individual members of species weren't considered important, so they weren't studied. But as we've seen, Darwin recognized the uniqueness of individuals and realized that variation among them could explain how selection occurred. Favorable variations were selected, or chosen, for survival by nature; unfavorable ones were weeded out. *Natural selection operates on individuals*, either favorably or unfavorably, but *it's the population that evolves*. It's important to emphasize that the unit of natural selection is the individual; the unit of evolution is the population. This is because individuals don't change genetically, but over time, populations do.

Natural Selection in Action

The most frequently cited example of natural selection relates to changes in the coloration of a species of moth. In recent years, the moth story has come under some criticism; but the premise remains valid, so we use it to illustrate how natural selection works.

Before the nineteenth century, the most common variety of the peppered moth in England was a mottled gray color. During the day, as the moths rested on lichen-covered tree trunks, their coloration provided camouflage (Fig. 2-13). There was also a dark gray variety of the same species, but since the dark moths weren't as well camouflaged, they were more frequently eaten by birds and so they were less common. (In this example, the birds are the *selective agent*, and they apply *selective pressures* on the moths.) Yet, by the end of the nineteenth century, the darker form had almost completely replaced the common gray one.

What brought about this rapid change? The traditionally cited answer is air pollution. Coal dust, ubiquitous in industrial areas of Britain during the industrial revolution, killed the lichen and turned the trees dark gray. With this environmental change, the lighter moths became more conspicuous, and birds began to prey on them more frequently. Consequently, lighter moths contributed fewer genes to the next generation than darker moths did, and the proportion of darker moths increased.

In the 1950s a series of experiments, conducted under somewhat artificial conditions, seemed to confirm that the color shift was due to the absence of lichen (Kettelwell, 1956). But some aspects of the study were questionable. For instance, the same shift in coloration had occurred in North America, where lichen wasn't generally present on trees. Besides, there is evidence that birds can see ultraviolet (UV) light and, in the UV spectrum, moths and lichen wouldn't look like each other. For these reasons, a resemblance to lichen may not have played a significant part in protecting the moths (Weiss, 2003). Yet, the color shift occurred in both regions during periods of increased air pollution. As clean air acts in both Britain and the United States have reduced the amount of air pollution (at least from coal), the predominant color of the peppered moth is once again the light mottled gray. Even though the explanation for the observed changes in moth color is probably more complex than originally believed and may involve factors in addition to bird predation, this phenomenon is still a very good example of microevolution in a contemporary population.

The medium ground finch of the Galápagos Islands gives us another example of natural selection. In 1977, drought killed many of the plants that produced the smaller, softer seeds favored by these birds. This forced a population of finches on one of the islands to feed on larger, harder seeds. Even before 1977, some birds had smaller, less robust beaks than others (that is, there was variation); and during the drought, because they were less able to

(a)

Michael Tweed e/Photo Researchers

(b)

FIGURE 2-13

Variation in the peppered moth. (a) The dark form is more visible on the light, lichen-covered tree. (b) On trees darkened by pollution, the lighter form is more visible.

Breck P. Kent/Animals Animals

selective pressures Forces in the environment that influence reproductive success in individuals.

process the larger seeds, more smaller-beaked birds died than did larger-beaked birds. So, although overall population size declined, average beak thickness in the survivors and their offspring increased, simply because thicker-beaked individuals were surviving in greater numbers and producing more offspring. In other words, they had greater reproductive success. But during heavy rains in 1982–1983, smaller seeds became more plentiful again and the pattern in beak size reversed itself, demonstrating again how reproductive success is related to environmental conditions (Grant, 1975, 1986; Ridley, 1993).

The best illustration of natural selection, however—and certainly one with potentially grave consequences for humans—is the recent increase in resistant strains of disease-causing microorganisms. When antibiotics were first introduced in the 1940s, they were seen as the end of bacterial disease. But that optimistic view didn't take into account that bacteria, like other organisms, possess genetic variability. Consequently, while an antibiotic will kill most bacteria in an infected person, any bacterium with an inherited resistance to that particular therapy will survive. In turn, the survivors reproduce and pass their drug resistance to future generations so that eventually, the population is mostly made up of bacteria that don't respond to treatment. What's more, because bacteria produce new generations every few hours, antibiotic-resistant strains are continuously appearing. As a result, many types of infection no longer respond to treatment. For example, tuberculosis was once thought to be well controlled, but there's been a resurgence of TB in recent years because some strains of the bacterium that causes it are resistant to most of the antibiotics used to treat TB.

These three examples (moths, finches, and bacteria) provide the following insights into the fundamentals of evolutionary change produced by natural selection:

1. *A trait must be inherited if natural selection is to act on it.* A characteristic that isn't hereditary (such as a temporary change in hair color produced by the hairdresser) won't be passed on to offspring. In finches, for example, beak size is a hereditary trait.

2. *Natural selection can't occur without population variation in inherited characteristics.* If, for example, all the peppered moths had initially been gray (you'll recall that some dark forms were always present) and the trees had become darker, the survival and reproduction of all moths could have been so low that the population might have become extinct. *Selection can work only with variation that already exists.*

3. *Fitness is a relative measure that changes as the environment changes.* Fitness is simply *differential reproductive success.* In the initial stage, the lighter moths were more fit because they produced more offspring. But as the environment changed, the dark gray moths became more fit, and a further change reversed the pattern. Likewise, the majority of Galápagos finches will have larger or smaller beaks, depending on exter-

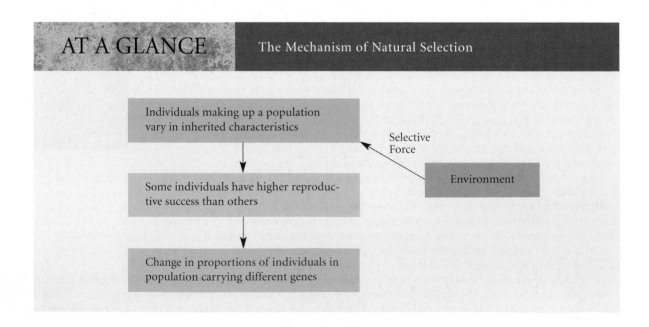

nal conditions. So it should be obvious that statements regarding the "most fit" don't mean anything without reference to specific environments.

4. *Natural selection can act only on traits that affect reproduction.* If a characteristic isn't expressed until later in life, after organisms have reproduced, then natural selection can't influence it. This is because the trait's inherited components have already been passed on to offspring. Many forms of cancer and cardiovascular disease are influenced by hereditary factors, but because these diseases usually affect people after they've had children, natural selection can't act against them. By the same token, if a condition usually kills or compromises the individual before he or she reproduces, natural selection can act against it because the trait won't be passed on.

So far, our examples have shown how different death rates influence natural selection (for example, moths or finches that die early leave fewer offspring). But mortality isn't the complete picture. Another important aspect of natural selection is **fertility**, because an animal that gives birth to more young passes its genes on at a faster rate than one that bears fewer offspring. But fertility isn't the entire story either, because the crucial element is the number of young raised successfully to the point where they themselves reproduce. We call this *differential net reproductive success*. The way this mechanism works can be demonstrated through another example.

In swifts (small birds that resemble swallows), data show that producing more offspring doesn't necessarily guarantee that more young will be successfully raised. The number of eggs hatched in a breeding season is a measure of fertility. The number of birds that mature and are eventually able to leave the nest is a measure of net reproductive success, or successfully raised offspring. The following table shows the correlation between the number of eggs hatched (fertility) and the number of young that leave the nest (reproductive success), averaged over four breeding seasons (Lack, 1966):

Number of eggs hatched (fertility)	2 eggs	3 eggs	4 eggs
Average number of young raised (reproductive success)	1.92	2.54	1.76
Sample size (number of nests)	72	20	16

As you can see, the most efficient number of eggs is three, because that number yields the highest reproductive success. Raising two offspring is less beneficial to the parents since the end result isn't as successful as with three eggs. Trying to raise more than three is actually detrimental, since the parents may not be able to provide enough nourishment for any of the offspring. Offspring that die before reaching reproductive age are, in evolutionary terms, equivalent to never being born. Actually, death of an offspring can be a minus to the parents, because before it dies, it drains parental resources. It may even inhibit their ability to raise other offspring, thus reducing their reproductive success even further. Selection favors those genetic traits that yield the maximum net reproductive success. If the number of eggs laid is a genetic trait in birds (and it seems to be), natural selection in swifts should act to favor the laying of three eggs as opposed to two or four.

Constraints on Nineteenth-Century Evolutionary Theory

Darwin argued for the concept of evolution in general and the role of natural selection in particular. But he didn't entirely comprehend the exact mechanisms of evolutionary change.

As we have seen, natural selection acts on *variation* within species, though neither Darwin nor anyone else in the nineteenth century understood the actual source of this variation. Also, no one understood how parents pass traits to offspring. Almost without exception, nineteenth-century scholars believed that inheritance was a *blending* process in which parental characteristics were mixed together to produce intermediate expressions in offspring. Given this notion, we can see why the true nature of genes was unimaginable; and with no alternative explanations, Darwin accepted it. As it turns out, a contemporary of Darwin's had actually worked out the rules of heredity. However, the work of this

fertility The ability to conceive and produce healthy offspring.

Augustinian monk named Gregor Mendel (whom you'll meet in Chapter 4) wasn't recognized until the beginning of the twentieth century.

The first three decades of the twentieth century saw the merger of natural selection theory and Mendel's discoveries. This was a crucial development because until then, scientists thought these concepts were unrelated. Then, in 1953, the structure of DNA was discovered. This landmark achievement has been followed by even more amazing advances in the field of genetics, including the sequencing of the human **genome**. We may finally be on the threshold of revealing the remaining secrets of the evolutionary process. If only Darwin could know!

Opposition to Evolution Today

Almost 150 years after the publication of *Origin of Species*, the debate over evolution is far from over, most especially in the United States, and it's primarily based in religious opposition. For the majority of biological scientists today, evolution is indisputable. The genetic evidence for it is solid and accumulating daily. What's more, most Christians don't believe that biblical depictions should be taken literally. But at the same time, some surveys show that about half of all Americans don't believe that evolution occurs. There are a number of reasons for this.

The mechanisms of evolution are complex and don't lend themselves to simple explanations. Understanding them requires some familiarity with genetics and biology, a familiarity that most people don't have. What's more, many people who haven't been exposed to scientific training want definitive, clear-cut answers to complex questions. But as you learned in Chapter 1, science doesn't always provide definitive answers to questions; it doesn't establish absolute truths; and it doesn't *prove* facts. Another thing to consider is that regardless of their culture, most people are raised in belief systems that don't emphasize **biological continuity** between species or offer scientific explanations for natural phenomena.

The relationship between science and religion has never been easy (remember Galileo), even though both systems serve, in their own ways, to explain natural phenomena. Scientific explanations are based in data analysis, hypothesis testing, and interpretation. Religion, meanwhile, is a system of faith-based beliefs that, like science, often attempts to explain natural phenomena. One difference between science and religion is that religious beliefs and explanations aren't amenable to scientific testing. Religion and science concern different aspects of the human experience, and they aren't inherently mutually exclusive approaches. That is, belief in God doesn't exclude the possibility of biological evolution; and acknowledgement of evolutionary processes doesn't preclude the existence of God. What's more, evolutionary theories aren't considered anathema by all religions or even by most forms of Christianity.

Some years ago, the Vatican hosted an international conference on human evolution; and in 1996, Pope John Paul II issued a statement that "fresh knowledge leads to recognition of the theory of evolution as more than just a hypothesis." Today, the official position of the Catholic Church is that evolutionary processes do occur, but that the human soul is of divine creation and not subject to evolutionary processes. Likewise, mainstream Protestants don't generally see a conflict. Unfortunately, those who believe in an absolutely literal interpretation of the Bible (called *fundamentalists*) accept no compromise.

A BRIEF HISTORY OF RELIGIOUS-BASED OPPOSITION TO EVOLUTION IN THE UNITED STATES

Reacting to rapid cultural change after World War I, conservative Christians in the United States sought a revival of what they considered to be "traditional values." In their view, one way to do this was to prevent any mention of Darwinism in public schools. One result of this effort was a law passed in 1925 that banned the teaching of any theory (particularly evolution) that doesn't support the biblical version of the creation of humankind. To test the validity of the law, the American Civil Liberties Union persuaded a high school teacher named John Scopes to submit to being arrested and tried for teaching evolution. The subsequent trial, called the Scopes Monkey Trial, was a 1920s equivalent of current celebrity trials. In the end, Scopes was convicted and fined $100, though the conviction was later over-

genome The entire genetic makeup of an individual or species.

biological continuity Refers to a biological continuum. When expressions of a phenomenon continuously grade into one another so that there are no discrete categories, they exist on a continuum. Color is one such phenomenon, and life-forms are another.

turned. Although most states didn't actually forbid the teaching of evolution, Arkansas, Tennessee, and a few others continued to prohibit any mention of it until 1968, when the U.S. Supreme Court struck down the ban against teaching evolution in public schools (One coauthor of this textbook remembers when her junior high school science teacher was fired for mentioning evolution in Little Rock, Arkansas.)

As coverage of evolution in textbooks increased by the mid-1960s, **Christian fundamentalists** renewed their campaign to eliminate evolution from public school curricula or to introduce antievolutionary material into public school classes. Out of this effort, the *creation science* movement was born.

Proponents of creation science are called "creationists" because they explain the existence of the universe as the result of a sudden creation event, directed by an omnipotent, supernatural being, occurring over the course of six 24-hour days as described in the book of Genesis. The premise of creation science is that the biblical account of the earth's origins and the Noah flood can be supported by scientific evidence.

Creationists have insisted that what they used to call "creation science" and now call "intelligent design" (ID) is as much a scientific endeavor as is evolution, and that there's scientific evidence to support creationist views. They've argued that in the interest of fairness, a balanced view should be offered: If evolution is taught as science, then creationism should also be taught as science. Sounds fair, doesn't it? But "creation science" or ID isn't science at all, for the simple reason that creationists insist that their view is absolute and infallible. Therefore, creationism isn't a hypothesis that can be tested, nor is it amenable to falsification. And, because hypothesis testing is the basis of all science, creationism, by its very nature, cannot be considered science.

Since the 1970s, creationists have become increasingly active in local school boards and state legislatures, promoting laws that mandate the teaching of creationism in public schools. In 1981, the Arkansas state legislature passed one such law that was subsequently overturned in 1982. In his ruling against the state, the judge justifiably stated "a theory that is by its own terms dogmatic, absolutist and never subject to revision is not a scientific theory." And, he added, "Since creation is not science, the conclusion is inescapable that the only real effect of [this law] is the advancement of religion." In 1987, the U.S. Supreme Court struck down a similar law in Louisiana.

In Dover, Pennsylvania, ID proponents suffered a setback in 2004 when voters ousted all eight of the nine-member Dover Area School Board who were up for reelection. This school board, composed entirely of ID supporters, had established a policy requiring high school teachers to discuss ID as an alternative to evolution. Then, in late 2005, U.S. District Judge John Jones struck down the policy because it violated the First Amendment to the Constitution (see the following discussion).* In his written opinion, Judge Jones stated, "ID is not science and cannot be adjudged a valid, accepted scientific theory. . . . [It] is grounded in theology, not science. . . . It has no place in a science curriculum." He further wrote, "ID's negative attacks on evolution have been refuted by the scientific community. . . . It has not generated peer-reviewed publications, nor has it been the subject of testing and research." ID takes a natural phenomenon and, instead of accepting or seeking a natural explanation, argues that the explanation is supernatural" (Mervis, 2006).

State and federal courts consistently overrule these and other similar laws because they violate the "establishment clause" of the First Amendment of the U.S. Constitution, which states that "Congress shall make no law respecting an establishment of religion, or prohibiting the free exercise thereof." This statement guarantees the separation of church and state, and it means that the government can neither promote nor inhibit the practice of any religion. Therefore, the use of public institutions (including schools) paid for by taxpayers' dollars to promote any particular religion is unconstitutional. Of course this doesn't mean that individuals can't have private religious discussions or pray in public places, but they can't have organized religious events.

The establishment clause was initially proposed to ensure that the government could neither promote nor restrict any particular religious view, as it did in England at the time the U.S. Constitution was written. But this hasn't stopped creationists, who encourage teachers to claim "academic freedom" to teach creationism.

---

* For the full text of this ruling, go to www.pamd.uscourts.gov/kitzmiller/kitzmiller_342.pdf

Christian fundamentalists
Adherents to a movement in American Protestantism that began in the early twentieth century; this group holds that the teachings of the Bible are infallible and are to be taken literally.

By the mid-1980s, and especially after the 1987 Supreme Court ruling, creationists dropped the terms *creationism* and *creation science* in favor of the less religious-sounding term *intelligent design theory*, which harkens back to the argument from design (see p. 20). The term *intelligent design* is based on the notion that most biological functions and anatomical traits (one favorite example is the eye) are too complex to be explained by a theory that doesn't include the presence of a creator or designer. To avoid objections based on the guarantee of separation of church and state, proponents of ID claim that they don't emphasize any particular religion. But this argument doesn't address the essential point that teaching *any* religious views, in a way that promotes them in publicly funded schools, is a violation of the U.S. Constitution.

But, even after numerous defeats in state, district, and federal courts, the attacks on evolution continue. In the first 6 weeks of 2006 alone, 12 antievolution bills were introduced in 9 states. That's more than in any year in the history of the United States (Gross, 2006). Clearly, antievolution sentiment also remains extremely strong among many politicians, particularly those with support from Christian fundamentalists. The president of the United States (as of this writing) has publicly supported teaching intelligent design in public schools; and in 1999, one very powerful ex-U.S. congressman went so far as to state that the teaching of evolution a factor behind violence in America today! Now, that's a stretch!

VISUAL SUMMARY

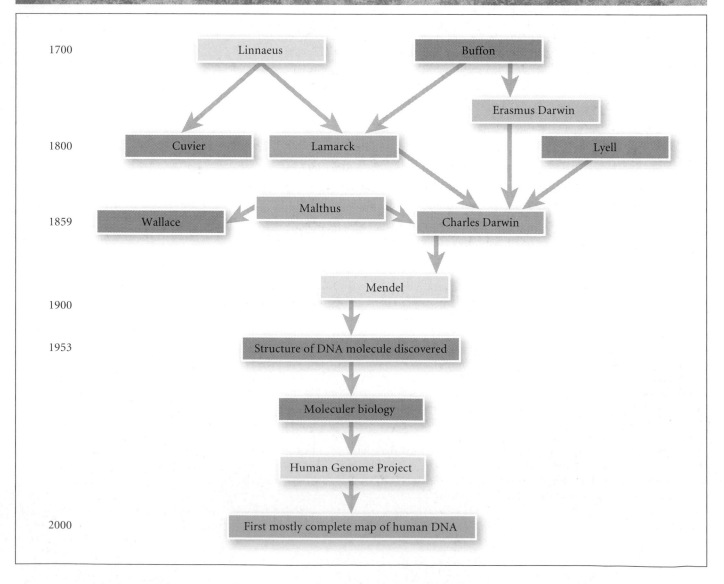

Summary: Putting It All Together

Our current understanding of evolutionary processes is directly traceable to developments in intellectual thought in Western Europe, with significant influences from the East, over the past 400 years. Many people contributed to this shift in perspective, and we've named only a few. Linnaeus placed humans in the same taxonomic scheme as all other animals. With remarkable insight, Lamarck and Buffon both recognized that species could change in response to environmental circumstances; Lamarck also attempted to explain *how* the changes occurred. He proposed the idea of the *inheritance of acquired characteristics*, which was later discredited. Lyell, in his theory of geological uniformitarianism, provided the necessary expanse of time for evolution to occur, and Malthus discussed how population size is kept in check by the availability of resources.

Darwin and Wallace, influenced by their predecessors, independently recognized that because of competition for resources, individuals with favorable characteristics would tend to survive and pass those traits on to offspring. Those lacking beneficial traits would produce fewer offspring, if they survived to reproductive age at all. That is, they would have lower reproductive success and reduced fitness. Thus, over time, advantageous characteristics accumulate in a population (because they have been selected for) while disadvantageous ones are eliminated (selected against). This, in a nutshell, is the theory of evolution by means of natural selection.

Despite mounting evidence in support of evolutionary theory for almost 150 years, there is still very strong public sentiment against it, most especially in the United States. The opposition has been fueled mostly by fundamentalist Christian groups attempting to either ban the teaching of evolution in public schools or introduce religious-based views into public school curricula in the name of "fair and balanced treatment." These attempts have repeatedly been struck down in state and federal courts because they violate the First Amendment to the U.S. Constitution.

Critical Thinking Questions

1. After having read this chapter, how would you respond to the question, "If humans evolved from monkeys, why do we still have monkeys?"

2. Given what you've read about the scientific method in Chapter 1, how would you explain the differences between science and religion as methods of explaining natural phenomena? Do you personally see a conflict between evolutionary and religious explanations of how species came to be?

3. Can you think of other examples of artificial and natural selection than the ones discussed in this chapter? For your examples, what traits have been selected for? In the case of natural selection, what was the selective agent?

CHAPTER 3

The Biological Basis of Life

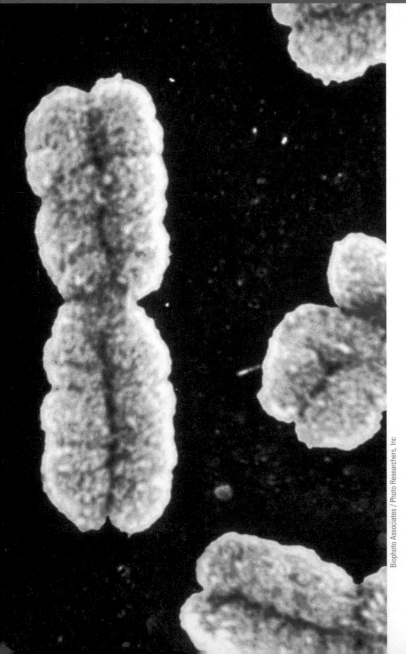

Biophoto Associates / Photo Researchers, Inc

KEY QUESTIONS

What is the molecular basis for life? Does it vary from species to species? How do human beings fit into a biological continuum?

Introduction

Envision yourself after a rotten day, watching the news on TV. The first story, following an endless string of commercials, is about genetically modified foods, a newly cloned species, or the controversy over stem cell research. What do you do? Change the channel? Leave the room? Go to sleep? Or do you follow the story? And if you do follow it, do you understand it? Do you think it's important or relevant to you personally? The fact is, you live in an age when genetic discoveries and genetically based technologies are advancing daily, and they're going to profoundly affect your life.

At some point, you or someone you love will probably need lifesaving medical treatment, perhaps for cancer, and this treatment will be based on genetic research. Like it or not, you already eat genetically modified foods. You may take advantage of developing reproductive technologies, and sadly, you may soon see the development of biological weapons based on genetically altered bacteria and viruses. But fortunately, you'll also probably live to see many of the secrets of evolution revealed through genetic research. So even if you've been uninterested in (or intimidated by) genetic issues, you should be aware that they affect your life every day.

As you already know, this book is about human evolution and adaptation, both of which are intimately linked to life processes that involve cells, the duplication and decoding of genetic information, and the transmission of this information between generations. So, to present human evolution and adaptation in the broad sense, we need to examine how life is organized at the cellular and molecular levels. This, in turn, requires a discussion of the fundamental principles of genetics.

Genetics is the study of how genes work and how traits are transmitted from one generation to the next. Because physical anthropologists are concerned with human evolution, adaptation, and variation, they must thoroughly understand the factors lying at the very root of these phenomena. In fact, although many physical anthropologists don't actually specialize in genetics, it's genetics that ultimately links the various subdisciplines of biological anthropology.

The Cell

To discuss genetic and evolutionary principles, it's necessary to understand basic cell functions. Cells are the fundamental units of life in all living organisms. In some forms, such as bacteria, a single cell constitutes the entire organism. However, more complex *multicellular* forms, such as plants, insects, birds, and mammals, are composed of billions of cells. As a matter of fact, an adult human is made up of perhaps as many as 1,000 billion (1,000,000,000,000) cells, all functioning in complex ways that ultimately promote the survival of the individual.

Life on earth can be traced back at least 3.7 billion years, in the form of single-celled organisms, represented today by bacteria (Fig. 3-1) and blue-green algae. Structurally more complex cells appeared approximately 1.2 billion years ago, and these are referred to as *eukaryotic* cells. Because eukaryotic cells are found in all multicellular organisms, they're the focus of this discussion. Despite the numerous differences between various life-forms and the cells that constitute them, it's important to understand that the cells of all living organisms share many similarities as a result of their common evolutionary past.

In general, a eukaryotic cell is a three-dimensional structure composed of *carbohydrates, lipids (fats), nucleic acids,* and *proteins.* It also contains several kinds of substructures called **organelles**, one of which is the **nucleus** (*pl.,* nuclei), a discrete unit surrounded by a thin

 Click!

Go to the following media for interactives and exercises on topics covered in this chapter:

- Basic Genetics for Anthropology CD-ROM: Principles and Applications

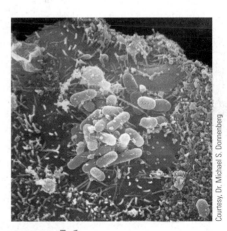

Courtesy, Dr. Michael S. Donnenberg

FIGURE 3-1
Each one of these oval-shaped structures is a single-celled bacterium.

organelles Structures contained within cells. There are many organelle types, each performing specific functions.

nucleus A structure (organelle) found in all eukaryotic cells. The nucleus contains chromosomes (nuclear DNA).

molecules   Structures made up of two or more atoms. Molecules can combine with other molecules to form more complex structures.

deoxyribonucleic acid (DNA)   The double-stranded molecule that contains the genetic code. DNA is a main component of chromosomes.

ribonucleic acid (RNA)   A single-stranded molecule, similar in structure to DNA. Three forms of RNA are essential to protein synthesis. They are messenger RNA (mRNA), transfer RNA (tRNA), and ribosomal RNA (rRNA).

cytoplasm   The portion of the cell contained within the cell membrane, excluding the nucleus. The cytoplasm consists of a semifluid material and contains numerous structures involved with cell function.

proteins   Three-dimensional molecules that serve a wide variety of functions through their ability to bind to other molecules.

protein synthesis   The assembly of chains of amino acids into functional protein molecules. The process is directed by DNA.

mitochondria   (*sing.*, mitochondrion) Structures contained within the cytoplasm of eukaryotic cells that convert energy, derived from nutrients, into a form that's used by the cell.

ribosomes   Structures composed of a form of RNA called ribosomal RNA (rRNA) and protein. Ribosomes are found in the cell's cytoplasm and are essential to the manufacture of proteins.

mitochondrial DNA (mtDNA)   DNA found in the mitochondria; mtDNA is inherited only from the mother.

somatic cells   Basically, all the cells in the body except those involved with reproduction.

gametes   Reproductive cells (eggs and sperm in animals) developed from precursor cells in ovaries and testes

zygote   A cell formed by the union of an egg cell and a sperm cell. It contains the full complement of chromosomes (in humans, 46) and has the potential of developing into an entire organism.

nucleotides   Basic units of the DNA molecule, composed of a sugar, a phosphate, and one of four DNA bases.

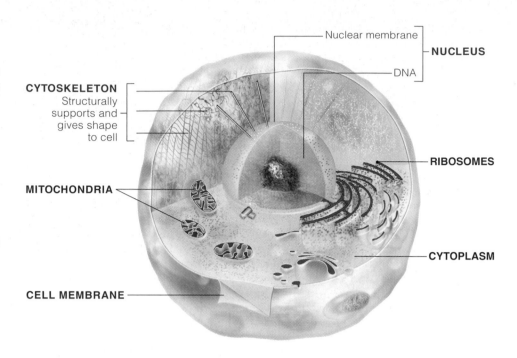

FIGURE 3-2

Structure of a generalized eukaryotic cell, illustrating the cell's three-dimensional nature. Various organelles are shown, but for simplicity only those we discuss are labeled.

membrane called the *nuclear membrane* (Fig. 3-2). Inside the nucleus are two types of **molecules** containing the genetic information that controls the cell's functions. These two critically important molecules are **deoxyribonucleic acid (DNA)** and **ribonucleic acid (RNA)**. (In single-celled organisms, genetic information isn't contained within a walled nucleus.) The nucleus is surrounded by a gel-like substance called the **cytoplasm**, which contains numerous other types of organelles involved in various activities, such as breaking down nutrients and converting them to other substances, storing and releasing energy, eliminating waste, and manufacturing **proteins** through a process called **protein synthesis**.

Two of these organelles, **mitochondria** (*sing.*, mitochondria) and **ribosomes**, require further mention. Mitochondria (see Fig. 3-2) are responsible for producing energy within the cell, and they can be loosely thought of as the cell's engines. Mitochondria are oval structures enclosed within a folded membrane, and they contain their own distinct DNA, called **mitochondrial DNA (mtDNA)**, which directs mitochondrial activities. Mitochondrial DNA has the same molecular structure and function as nuclear DNA (that is, DNA found in the nucleus), but it's organized somewhat differently. In recent years, mtDNA has attracted much attention, because it has numerous forensic applications and because it's significant for studies of certain evolutionary processes. For these reasons, we'll discuss mitochondrial inheritance in more detail in Chapters 4 and 14. Ribosomes are roughly spherical in shape and are the most common type of cytoplasmic organelle. They're made up partly of RNA and are essential to protein synthesis (see p. 43).

There are basically two types of cells: **somatic cells** and **gametes**. Somatic cells are the cellular components of body tissues, such as muscle, bone, skin, nerve, heart, and brain. Gametes, or sex cells, are specifically involved in reproduction and aren't important as structural components of the body. There are two types of gametes: egg cells, produced in female ovaries, and sperm cells, which develop in male testes. The sole function of a sex cell is to unite with a gamete from another individual to form a **zygote**, which has the potential of developing into a new individual. In this way, gametes transmit genetic information from parent to offspring.

DNA Structure

Because it directs all cellular functions, DNA is the very basis of life. So, if we want to understand these functions and how characteristics are inherited, we need to know something about the structure and function of DNA.

The exact physical and chemical properties of DNA were unknown until 1953 when, at the University of Cambridge in England, an American researcher named James Watson and three British scientists, Francis Crick, Maurice Wilkins, and Rosalind Franklin, developed a structural and functional model (Fig. 3-3) of DNA (Watson and Crick, 1953a, 1953b). It's impossible to overstate the importance of this achievement because it completely revolutionized the fields of biology and medicine and forever altered our understanding of biological and evolutionary mechanisms (see "A Closer Look," below).

The DNA molecule is composed of two chains of even smaller molecules called **nucleotides**. A nucleotide, in turn, is made up of three components: a sugar molecule (deoxyribose), a phosphate unit, and one of four nitrogenous bases (Fig. 3-4). In DNA, nucleotides are stacked onto one another to form a chain that is bonded along its bases to another nucleotide chain. Together the two chains twist to form a spiral, or helical, shape. The DNA molecule, then, is double-stranded and is described as forming a *double helix* that resembles a twisted ladder. If we follow the twisted ladder analogy, the sugars and phosphates represent the two sides, while the bases and the bonds that join them form the rungs (Fig. 3-5).

A. Barrington Brown / Photo Researchers, Inc.

FIGURE **3-3**

James Watson (left) and Francis Crick in 1953 with their model of the structure of the DNA molecule.

A CLOSER LOOK Rosalind Franklin: The Fourth (but Invisible) Member of the Double Helix Team

The Novartis Foundation

FIGURE 1
Rosalind Franklin

In 1962, three men—James Watson, Francis Crick, and Maurice Wilkins—won the Nobel Prize for medicine and physiology. They earned this most prestigious of scientific honors for their discovery of the structure of the DNA molecule, on which they had published in 1953. But due credit was not given to a fourth, equally deserving person—Rosalind Franklin, who had died of ovarian cancer in 1958. Even if she had been acknowledged in 1962, she still wouldn't have been a Nobel recipient because the Nobel Prize isn't awarded posthumously.

Franklin, a physical chemist, arrived at the University of Cambridge in 1951. She was invited there to study the structure of DNA using a technique called X-ray diffraction, which she'd been working with in Paris. (X-ray diffraction is a process that reveals the positions of atoms in crystalline structures.) What Franklin didn't know was that a colleague in her lab, Maurice Wilkins, was working on the same project. And he, not having been informed of her position, thought she'd been hired as his assistant. This was hardly a good way to begin a working relationship; and as you might expect, there were some tense moments.

Franklin soon produced some excellent X-ray diffraction images of wet DNA fibers, provided by Wilkins. The images clearly showed that the structure was helical, and she worked out that there were two strands. Wilkins innocently (but without Franklin's knowledge) showed the images to Watson and Crick, who were working in another laboratory, also at Cambridge. Within two weeks, Watson and Crick had developed their now famous model of a double-stranded helix.

Desperately unhappy at Cambridge, Franklin took a position at King's College, London, in 1953. In April of that year, she and a student published an article in the journal *Nature* that dealt indirectly with the helical structure of DNA. In the same issue were the Watson and Crick article and another by Wilkins and two colleagues.

During her life, Franklin did gain recognition for her work in carbons, coals, and viruses, topics on which she published many articles; and she was happy with the reputation she achieved. After her death, Watson made many rather nasty comments about Rosalind Franklin, several in print. Nevertheless, it appears they remained on friendly terms until she died at age 37. She also remained friendly with Crick, but she never knew that their revolutionary discovery was made possible in part by her photographic images.

replicate   To duplicate. The DNA molecule is able to make copies of itself.

enzymes   Specialized proteins that initiate and direct chemical reactions in the body.

complementary   In genetics, referring to the fact that DNA bases form base pairs in a precise manner. For example, adenine can bond only to thymine. These two bases are said to be *complementary* because one requires the other to form a complete DNA base pair.

hemoglobin   A protein molecule that occurs in red blood cells and binds to oxygen molecules.

FIGURE **3-4**

Part of a DNA molecule. The illustration shows the two DNA strands with the sugar and phosphate backbone (red and yellow) and the bases (blue) extending toward the center.

P = Phosphate

S = Sugar

BASES

A = Adenine

G = Guanine

T = Thymine

C = Cytosine

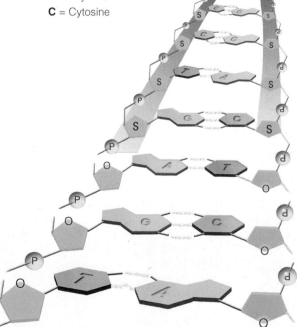

The four bases are the key to how DNA works. These bases are *adenine, guanine, thymine,* and *cytosine,* and they're usually referred to by their initial letters—A, G, T, and C. In forming the double helix, one type of base can pair or bond with only one other type. In other words, base pairs can form *only* between adenine and thymine and between guanine and cytosine (see Figs. 3-4 and 3-5). This specificity is essential to the DNA molecule's ability to **replicate**, or make an exact copy of itself.

DNA Replication

So that organisms can develop and grow, and injured tissues can be repaired, cells have to multiply; and cell multiplication is made possible by cell division. In the simpler type of cell division, cells multiply by dividing in a way that ensures that each new cell receives a full set of genetic material. This process is important, because a cell can't function properly without the appropriate amount of DNA; and for it to happen, the DNA must first replicate.

Before a cell divides, **enzymes** break the bonds between bases throughout the DNA molecule, leaving the two previously joined strands of nucleotides with their bases exposed (see Fig. 3-5). These exposed bases then attract unattached DNA nucleotides, which are present in the cell nucleus. Since each base can pair with only one other, the attraction between bases occurs in a **complementary** way. What this means is that the two previously joined parental nucleotide chains serve as models or templates for forming new strands of nucleotides. As each new strand is formed, its bases are joined to the bases of an original strand. When the process is complete, there are two double-stranded DNA molecules exactly like the original one. And each newly formed molecule consists of one original nucleotide chain joined to a newly formed chain (see Fig. 3-5).

Protein Synthesis

One of the most important activities of DNA is to direct the manufacture of proteins (protein synthesis) within the cell. Proteins are complex, three-dimensional molecules that function through their ability to bind to other molecules (Fig. 3-6). For example, the protein **hemoglobin**, found in red blood cells, is able to bind to oxygen, which it carries to cells throughout the body.

Proteins function in countless ways. Some are structural components of tissues. Collagen, which we mentioned in Chapter 1, is the most common protein in the body and is a major component of all connective tissues. Enzymes are also proteins, and they initiate and enhance chemical reactions. For instance, a digestive enzyme called *lactase* breaks down *lactose,* or milk sugar, into two simpler sugars. Another class of proteins includes

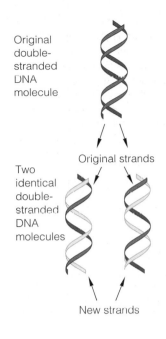

Original double-stranded DNA molecule

Original strands

Two identical double-stranded DNA molecules

New strands

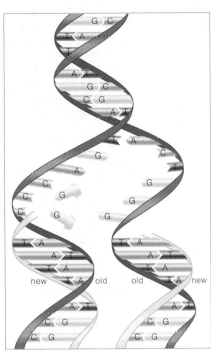

DNA double helix

Replication under way

Unattached nucleotides are attracted to their complementary nucleotides and thereby form a new strand

new   old   old   new

Replication complete

FIGURE 3-5
DNA replication. During DNA replication, the two strands of the DNA molecule (blue) are separated, and each strand serves as a template for the formation of a new strand (yellow). When replication is complete, there are two DNA molecules. Each molecule consists of one new and one original DNA strand.

many types of **hormones**. Hormones are produced by specialized cells and then released into the bloodstream to circulate to other areas of the body, where they produce specific effects in tissues and organs. Insulin, for example, is a hormone produced by cells in the pancreas, and it causes cells in the liver and certain types of muscle tissue to absorb energy-producing glucose (sugar) from the blood. (Enzymes and hormones are discussed in more detail in Chapter 17.) Lastly, many kinds of proteins can enter a cell's nucleus and attach directly to the DNA. These proteins are called **regulatory proteins** or molecules because, when they bind to the DNA, they can regulate DNA activity. From this brief description, you can see that proteins make us what we are. Thus protein synthesis has to occur accurately, because if it doesn't, physiological development and cellular activities can be disrupted or even prevented.

Alpha chain   Alpha chain

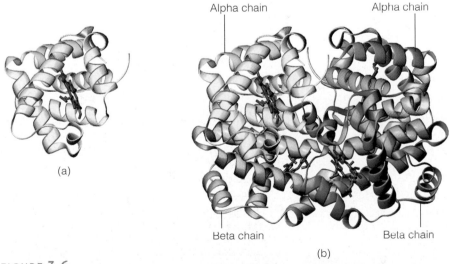

(a)

Beta chain   Beta chain

(b)

hormones Substances (usually proteins) that are produced by specialized cells; hormones travel to other parts of the body, where they influence chemical reactions and regulate various cellular functions.

regulatory proteins Proteins that can bind to DNA and modify the action of genes. Many are active only during certain stages of development.

FIGURE 3-6
Diagrammatic representation of a hemoglobin molecule. Hemoglobin molecules are composed of 4 chains of amino acids (2 "alpha" chains and 2 "beta" chains). They're discussed in more detail on p. 48.

Proteins are made up of chains of smaller molecules called **amino acids**. In all, there are 20 amino acids, 8 of which must be obtained from foods (see Chapter 17). The remaining 12 amino acids are produced in cells. These 20 amino acids are combined in different amounts and sequences to produce at least 90,000 different proteins. What makes proteins different from one another is the number and sequence of their amino acids. And, for a protein to function accurately, its amino acids must be arranged in the proper sequence.

In part, DNA is a recipe for making a protein, since it's the sequence of DNA bases that ultimately determines the order of amino acids in a protein molecule. In the DNA instructions, a *triplet,* or group of three bases, specifies a particular amino acid. For example, if a triplet consists of the base sequence cytosine, guanine, and adenine (CGA), it specifies the amino acid *alanine.* If the next triplet in the chain consists of the sequence guanine, thymine, and cytosine (GTC), it refers to another amino acid—*glutamine.* So a DNA recipe might look like this:

AGA CGA ACA ACC TAC TTT TTC CTT AAG GTC (without the spaces)

Protein synthesis actually takes place outside the cell nucleus in the cytoplasm at one of the types of organelles we mentioned earlier, the *ribosomes.* But, the DNA molecule can't leave the cell's nucleus. So the first step in protein synthesis is to copy the DNA message into a form of RNA called **messenger RNA (mRNA),** which can pass through the nuclear membrane into the cytoplasm. RNA is similar to DNA, but it's different in some important ways:

1. It's single-stranded. (This is true for the forms we discuss here, but it's not true for all.)

2. It contains a different type of sugar.

3. It contains the base uracil as a substitute for the DNA base thymine. (Uracil binds to adenine, just as thymine does.)

amino acids   Small molecules that are the components of proteins.

messenger RNA (mRNA)   A form of RNA that's assembled on a sequence of DNA bases. It carries the DNA code to the ribosome during protein synthesis.

TABLE 3-1	The Genetic Code		
Amino Acid Symbol	**Amino Acid**	**DNA Triplet**	**mRNA Codon**
Ala	Alanine	CGA, CGG, CGT, CGC	GCU, GCC, GCA, GCG
Arg	Arginine	GCA, GCG, GCT, GCC, TCT, TCC	CGU, CGC, CGA, CGG, AGA, AGG
Asn	Asparagine	TTA, TTG	AAU, AAC
Asp	Aspartic acid	CTA, CTG	GAU, GAC
Cys	Cysteine	ACA, ACG	UGU, UGC
Gln	Glutamine	GTT, GTC	CAA, CAG
Glu	Glutamic acid	CTT, CTC	GAA, GAG
Gly	Glycine	CCA, CCG, CCT, CCC	GGU, GGC, GGA, GGG
His	Histidine	GTA, GTG	CAU, CAC
Ile	Isoleucine	TAA, TAG, TAT	AUU, AUC, AUA
Leu	Leucine	AAT, AAC, GAA, GAG, GAT, GAC	UUA, UUG, CUU, CUC, CUA, CUG
Lys	Lysine	TTT, TTC	AAA, AAG
Met	Methionine	TAC	AUG
Phe	Phenylalanine	AAA, AAG	UUU, UUC
Pro	Proline	GGA, GGG, GGT, GGC	CCU, CCC, CCA, CCG
Ser	Serine	AGA, AGG, AGT, AGC, TCA, TCG	UCU, UCC, UCA, UCG, AGU, AGC
Thr	Threonine	TGA, TGG, TGT, TGC	ACU, ACC, ACA, ACG
Trp	Tryptophan	ACC	UGG
Tyr	Tyrosine	ATA, ATG	UAU, UAC
Val	Valine	CAA, CAG, CAT, CAC	GUU, GUC, GUA, GUG
Terminating triplets		ATT, ATC, ACT	UAA, UAG, UGA

A CLOSER LOOK   Characteristics of the DNA Code

1. **The code is universal.** In other words, the same basic messages apply to all life-forms on the planet, from bacteria to oak trees to humans. The same triplet code, specifying each amino acid, thus applies to all life on earth. This commonality is the basis for the methods used in recombinant DNA technology.

2. **The code is triplet.** Each amino acid is specified by a sequence of three bases in the mRNA (the codon), which in turn is coded for by three bases in the DNA.

3. **The code is continuous—without pauses.** There are no pauses separating one codon from another. Thus, if a base should be deleted, the entire frame would be moved, drastically altering the message downstream for successive codons. Such a gross alteration is termed a *frame-shift mutation*. Note that although the code lacks "commas," it does contain "periods"; that is, three specific codons act to stop translation.

4. **The code is redundant.** While there are 20 amino acids, there are 4 DNA bases and 64 possible triplets or mRNA codons. Even considering the three "stop" messages, that still leaves 61 codons specifying the 20 amino acids. Thus, many amino acids are specified by more than one codon (see Table 3-1). For example, leucine and serine are each coded for by six different codons. In fact, only two amino acids (methionine and tryptophan) are coded for by a single codon. Redundancy is useful. For one thing, it serves as a safety net by helping to reduce the likelihood of severe consequences if there is a change, or *mutation*, in a DNA base. For example, four different DNA triplets—CGA, CGG, CGT, and CGC—code for the amino acid alanine. If, in the codon CGA, A mutates to G, the resulting triplet, CGG, will still specify alanine; thus, there will be no functional change.

The mRNA molecule forms on the DNA template in much the same way that new DNA molecules are assembled. As in DNA replication, the two DNA strands separate, but only partially, and one of these strands attracts free-floating RNA nucleotides (also produced in the cell), which are joined together on the DNA template. The formation of mRNA is called *transcription* because, in fact, the DNA code is being copied or transcribed (Fig. 3-7). Transcription continues until a section of DNA called a terminator region (composed of one of three DNA triplets) is reached and the process stops (see Table 3-1). At this point, the mRNA strand, comprising anywhere from 5,000 to perhaps as many as 200,000 nucleotides, peels away from the DNA model, and a portion of it travels through the nuclear membrane to the ribosome. Meanwhile, the bonds between the DNA bases are reestablished, and the DNA molecule is once more intact.

As the mRNA strand arrives at the ribosome, its message is translated in groups of three mRNA bases called "codons". (This stage of the process is called *translation* because at this point, the genetic instructions are actually being decoded and implemented.) Therefore, mRNA codons specify one amino acid just as DNA triplets do (see Table 3-1).

Another form of RNA, **transfer RNA (tRNA)**, is also essential to the assembly of a protein. Each tRNA molecule can bind to one specific amino acid and, during protein synthesis, a tRNA molecule takes the amino acid that matches the codon that is being translated to the ribosome (Fig. 3-8). The ribosome then joins that amino acid to another one in the order dictated by the sequence of mRNA codons. In this way, amino acids are linked together to form a structure that eventually functions as a protein or part of a protein.

transfer RNA (tRNA) The type of RNA that binds to specific amino acids and transports them to the ribosome during protein synthesis.

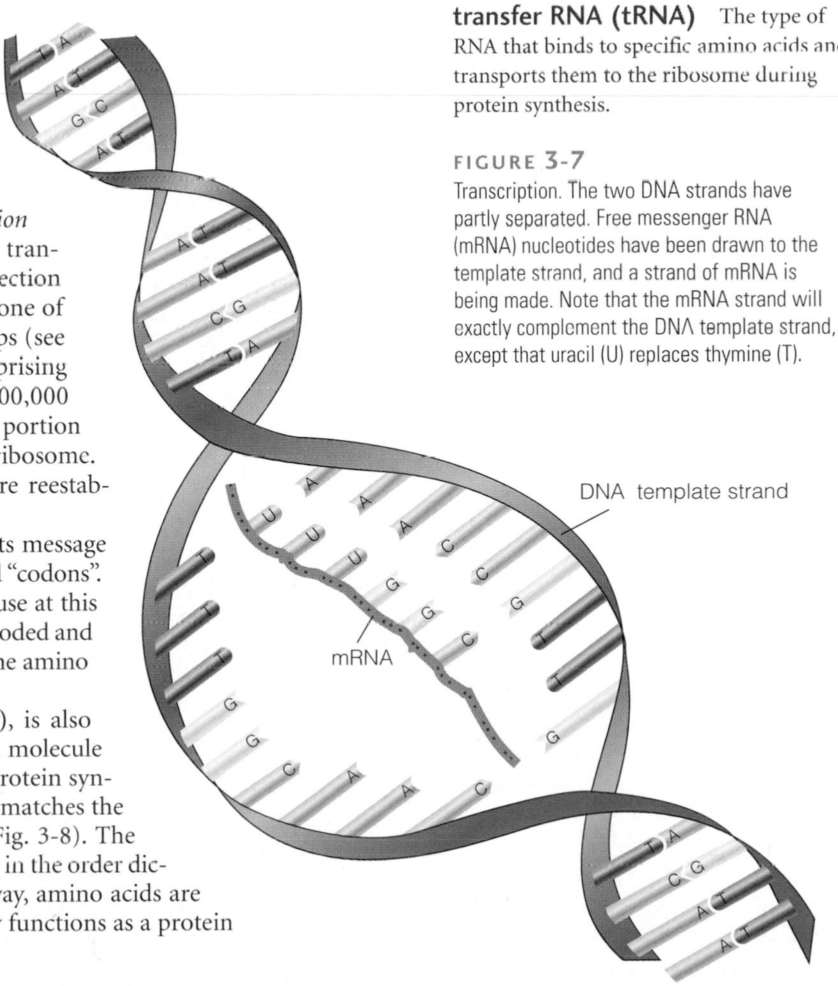

FIGURE 3-7
Transcription. The two DNA strands have partly separated. Free messenger RNA (mRNA) nucleotides have been drawn to the template strand, and a strand of mRNA is being made. Note that the mRNA strand will exactly complement the DNA template strand, except that uracil (U) replaces thymine (T).

DNA template strand

mRNA

FIGURE 3-8
Assembly of an amino acid chain in protein synthesis.

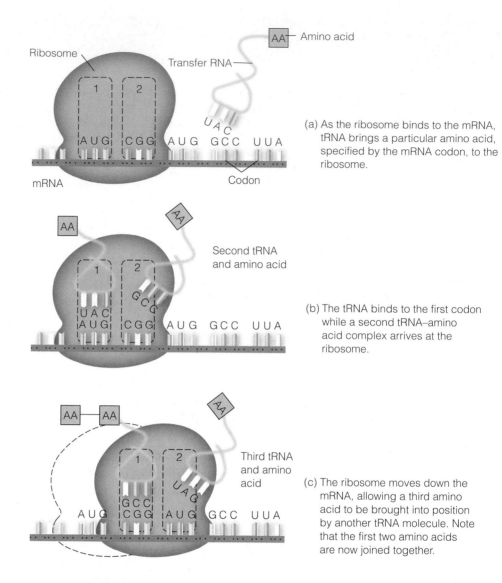

(a) As the ribosome binds to the mRNA, tRNA brings a particular amino acid, specified by the mRNA codon, to the ribosome.

(b) The tRNA binds to the first codon while a second tRNA–amino acid complex arrives at the ribosome.

(c) The ribosome moves down the mRNA, allowing a third amino acid to be brought into position by another tRNA molecule. Note that the first two amino acids are now joined together.

What Is a Gene?

A **gene** is the entire sequence of DNA bases responsible for synthesizing a protein or, in some cases, part of a protein. That is to say, a gene is a segment of DNA that specifies the sequence of amino acids in a particular protein. Even more precisely, a gene codes for the production of a **polypeptide chain**. Those proteins composed of only a single polypeptide chain are produced through the action of a single gene. However, some proteins (such as collagen and hemoglobin) are composed of two or more polypeptide chains, each resulting from the action of a different gene. So, while some proteins result from the action of only one gene, others are produced by two or more. A gene may be composed of only a few hundred bases, or it may comprise thousands. If the sequence of bases is altered by **mutation** (a change in the DNA), then the manufacture of proteins may not happen, and the cell (or indeed the organism) may not function properly, if it functions at all.

The preceding definition of a gene is a functional one, and it's technically correct. But over the years, the definition of a gene has changed to keep up with genetic research. (Incidentally, this situation is a good example of what we said in Chapter 1—scientific hypotheses and theories can, and do, change over time with the gathering of new data.) For example, the notion of *one gene–one protein*, which was a core concept of biology for a few decades, has been

gene A sequence of DNA bases that specifies the order of amino acids in an entire protein, a portion of a protein, or any functional product. A gene may be made up of hundreds or thousands of DNA bases organized into coding and noncoding segments.

polypeptide chain A sequence of amino acids that may act alone or in combination with others as a functional protein.

mutation A change in DNA. *Mutation* refers to changes in DNA bases (specifically called point mutations) as well as to changes in chromosome number and/or structure.

A CLOSER LOOK   Genetic Junk and Jumping Genes

In all fields of inquiry, important discoveries always raise new questions that eventually lead to further revelations. Probably, there's no statement that could be more aptly applied to the field of genetics. For example, in 1977, geneticists recognized that during protein synthesis (see p. 40), the initially formed mRNA molecule contained many more nucleotides than were represented in the subsequently produced proteins. This finding led to the discovery of *introns* (discussed later in this box), portions of genes that don't code for, or specify, proteins. What happens is that once the mRNA molecule peels away from the DNA template, but before it leaves the cell's nucleus, enzymes snip out the introns. The original mRNA molecule is sometimes called *pre-mRNA*, but once the introns have been deleted, the remainder is mature mRNA (Fig. 1). It's the mature mRNA that leaves the nucleus carrying its code for protein production.

In the 1980s, geneticists learned that only about 2 percent of the roughly 3 billion DNA bases in the human genome is contained within *exons*, the segments that actually provide the code for protein synthesis. This means that while an estimated 28 percent of human DNA is composed of genes (including introns and exons), only 5 percent of the DNA within these genes is actually composed of coding sequences (Baltimore, 2001). And we also know that a human gene can specify the production of as many as three different proteins by using different combinations of the exons interspersed within it (Pennisi, 2001). So the notion that one gene specifies only one protein has fallen by the wayside.

With only 2 percent of the human genome directing protein synthesis, humans have more noncoding DNA than any other species so far studied (Vogel, 2001). Invertebrates and some vertebrates have only small amounts of noncoding sequences, and yet they're fully functional organisms. So just what does all this noncoding DNA (originally called "junk DNA") do in humans? Scientists are beginning to answer that question.

It appears that repeated segments near the ends of chromosomes contain genes that may be involved in many of the activities of the telomeres, crucial structures at the very ends of chromosomes. Among other things, telomeres (composed of the same repeated sequence of apparently noncoding DNA) influence cellular aging and the regulation of cell cycles (Reithman et al., 2001).

Almost half of all human DNA consists of noncoding segments that are repeated over and over and over. Depending on their length, these segments are referred to as *tandem repeats, satellites,* or *microsatellites.* Microsatellites have an extremely high mutation rate and can gain or lose repeated segments and then return to their former length. But this tendency to mutate means that the number of repeats in a given microsatellite varies between individuals. And this tremendous variation has been the basis for DNA fingerprinting, a technique commonly used to provide evidence in criminal cases (see p. 58). Actually, anthropologists are now using microsatellite variation for all

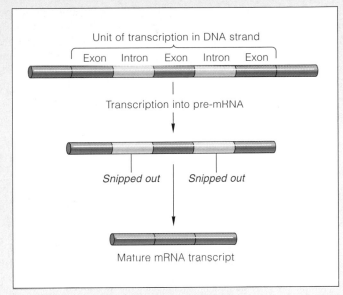

FIGURE 1

Diagram of a DNA sequence being transcribed. The introns are deleted from the pre-mRNA before it leaves the cell nucleus. The remaining mature mRNA contains only exons.

kinds of research, from tracing movements of peoples to paternity testing in chimpanzees (see p. 173).

Some of the variations in microsatellite composition are associated with neurological disorders, so we can't help wondering why humans have them. One possible answer is that some noncoding regions may switch functioning genes on and off. Or they may modulate the activities of genes in other ways. Also, by losing or adding material, they can alter the sequences of bases in genes, thus becoming a source of mutation in functional genes. What's more, these mutations and the enormous abundance of noncoding sequences combine to provide a source of variation for natural selection to act on.

Lastly, there are transposable elements (TEs), the so-called *jumping genes.* These are DNA sequences that can change position within the genome. They mainly code for proteins that enable them to move about, and because they can land right in the middle of coding sequences, they can change the function of genes. So TEs are also a cause of mutations since they change the DNA sequence. Frequently, these alterations are harmful; TEs have been associated with numerous disease conditions, including a form of breast cancer (Deragon and Capy, 2000). But if the changes are neutral or even beneficial, then TEs are generating variations that may prove to be advantageous in certain environmental conditions, that is, as more fuel for natural selection.

refuted, partly in recognition of the fact that DNA also codes for RNA and DNA nucleotides (see "A Closer Look," previous page). One new and more inclusive definition simply states that a gene is "a complete chromosomal segment responsible for making a functional product" (Snyder and Gerstein, 2003).

In recent years, geneticists have also learned that only some parts of a gene, called **exons**, are actually transcribed into mRNA and thus code for specific amino acids. But most of the nucleotide sequences in a gene aren't expressed during protein synthesis. In fact, some sequences, called **introns**, are initially transcribed but subsequently clipped out (see "A Closer Look," previous page). This means that introns aren't represented in the newly formed mature mRNA segment, so they aren't translated into amino acid sequences. But, they're still a part of the DNA molecule, and it's the combination of introns and exons, interspersed along a strand of DNA, that comprises the unit we call a gene.

Regulatory Genes

Some genes act solely to control the expression of other genes. Basically, these *regulatory genes* make products that switch other DNA segments on or off. Thus, functions are critical for individual organisms, and they play an important role in evolution.

One example of regulatory genes concerns DNA deactivation during embryonic development. All somatic cells contain the same genetic information; but in any given cell, only a fraction of the DNA contained within exons is actually involved in protein synthesis. For example, like the cells of the stomach lining, bone cells have DNA that codes for the production of digestive enzymes. But fortunately for us all, bone cells don't produce digestive enzymes. Instead, they manufacture collagen, the major organic component of bone. This is because cells become specialized during embryonic development to perform only certain functions, and most of their DNA is permanently deactivated by regulatory genes. In other words, they become specific types of cells, such as bone cells.

Homeobox or *Hox* genes are extremely important regulatory genes. *Hox* genes direct early segmentation of embryonic tissues, including those that give rise to the spine and thoracic muscles. They also interact with other genes to determine the identity and characteristics of developing body segments and structures, but not their actual development. For example, homeobox genes determine where, in a developing embryo, limb buds will appear. They also establish the number and overall pattern of the different types of vertebrae, the bones that make up the spine (Fig. 3-9).

exons Segments of genes that are transcribed and are involved in protein synthesis. (The prefix *ex–* denotes that these segments are expressed.)

introns Segments of genes that are initially transcribed and then deleted; therefore, they aren't expressed, that is, they aren't involved in protein synthesis.

homeobox genes An evolutionarily ancient family of regulatory genes that directs the development of the overall body plan and the segmentation of body tissues.

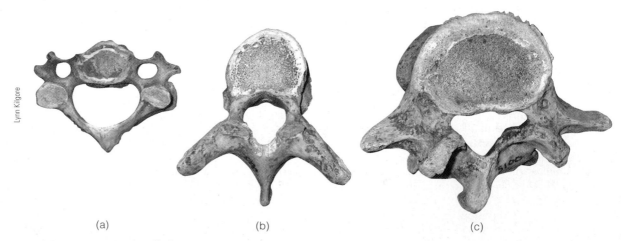

(a)   (b)   (c)

Lynn Kilgore

FIGURE 3-9

The differences in these three vertebrae, from different regions of the spine, are caused by the action of *Hox* genes during embryonic development. The cervical (neck) vertebrae (a) have characteristics that differentiate them from thoracic (b) vertebrae (attached to the ribs), and also from the lumbar vertebrae (c) of the lower back. *Hox* genes determine the overall pattern not only of each type of vertebra but also of each individual vertebra.

Homeobox genes are highly conserved, meaning they've been maintained pretty much throughout evolutionary history. They're present in all insects and vertebrates and don't vary greatly from species to species. Counterparts of human homeobox genes are present in fruit flies, for example, where they perform similar functions. This type of conservation means that not only are these genes vitally important, but they evolved from genes that were present in some of the earliest forms of life. Also, alterations in the behavior of homeobox genes are probably responsible for various physical differences between closely related species. For example, some of the anatomical differences between humans and chimpanzees are almost certainly the results of evolutionary changes in homeobox and other regulatory genes in both lineages. For these reasons, homeobox genes are now a critical area of research in evolutionary and developmental biology.

There's one final point to be made about genes and DNA: The genetic code is universal and, at least on earth, DNA is the genetic material in all forms of life. The DNA of all organisms, from bacteria to oak trees to human beings, is composed of the same molecules using the same kinds of instructions. Consequently, the DNA triplet CGA, for example, specifies the amino acid alanine, regardless of species. These similarities imply biological relationships among, and an ultimate common ancestry for, all forms of life. What makes oak trees distinct from humans isn't differences in the DNA material itself, but differences in how that material is arranged.

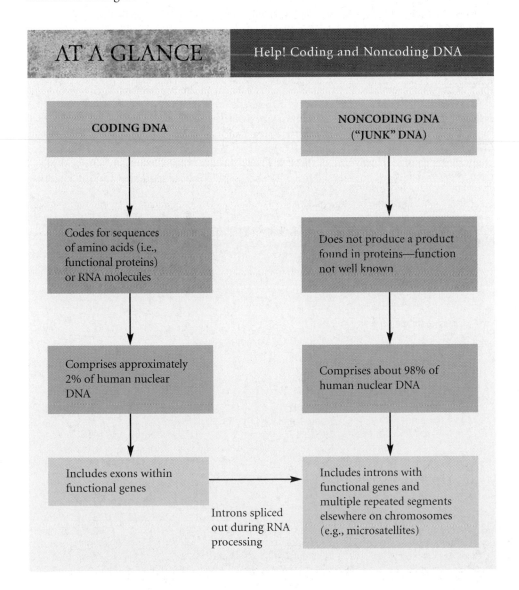

AT A GLANCE

Help! Coding and Noncoding DNA

CODING DNA

Codes for sequences of amino acids (i.e., functional proteins) or RNA molecules

Comprises approximately 2% of human nuclear DNA

Includes exons within functional genes

Introns spliced out during RNA processing

NONCODING DNA ("JUNK" DNA)

Does not produce a product found in proteins—function not well known

Comprises about 98% of human nuclear DNA

Includes introns with functional genes and multiple repeated segments elsewhere on chromosomes (e.g., microsatellites)

(a)

(b)

FIGURE **3-10**

(a) Scanning electron micrograph of a normal, fully oxygenated red blood cell. (b) Scanning electron micrograph of a collapsed, sickle-shaped red blood cell that contains HB^S.

FIGURE **3-11**

Diagram showing the cascade of symptoms that can occur in people with sickle-cell anemia.

Mutation: When Genes Change

The best way to understand how genetic material functions is to see what happens when it changes, or mutates. Normal adult hemoglobin is made up of four polypeptide chains (two *alpha* chains and two *beta* chains) that are the direct products of gene action. Each beta chain is in turn composed of 146 amino acids. There are several hemoglobin disorders with genetic origins, and perhaps the best known of these is **sickle-cell anemia**, which results from a defect in the beta chain. People with sickle-cell anemia inherit, from *both* parents, a mutated form of the gene that directs the formation of the beta chain. This mutation is caused by the substitution of one amino acid (*valine*) for the amino acid that's normally present (*glutamic acid*). This single amino acid substitution on the beta chain results in the production of a less-efficient form of hemoglobin called hemoglobin S (Hb^S) instead of the normal form, which is called hemoglobin A (Hb^A). In situations where the availability of oxygen is reduced, such as at high altitude, or when oxygen requirements are increased through exercise, red blood cells with Hb^S collapse and become sickle-shaped (Fig. 3-10). What follows is a cascade of events, all of which result in severe anemia and its consequences (Fig. 3-11). Briefly, these consequences include impaired circulation from blocked capillaries, red blood cell destruction, oxygen deprivation to vital organs (including the brain), and, without treatment, death.

People who inherit the altered form of the gene from only one parent don't have sickle-cell anemia, but they do have what's called *sickle-cell trait*. But, because only about 40 percent of their hemoglobin is abnormal, they're much less severely affected and usually have a normal life span.

The cause of all the serious problems associated with sickle-cell anemia is a change in the *Hb* gene. Remember that the beta chains of normal hemoglobin and the sickle-cell variety each have 146 amino acids, and 145 of the amino acids in both forms are identical. What's more, to emphasize the importance of a seemingly minor alteration, consider that triplets of DNA bases are required to specify amino acids. Therefore, it takes 438 bases (146 × 3) to produce the chain of 146 amino acids forming the adult hemoglobin beta chain. But a change in only one of these 438 bases produces the life-threatening complications seen in sickle-cell anemia. Figure 3-12 shows a DNA base sequence and the resulting

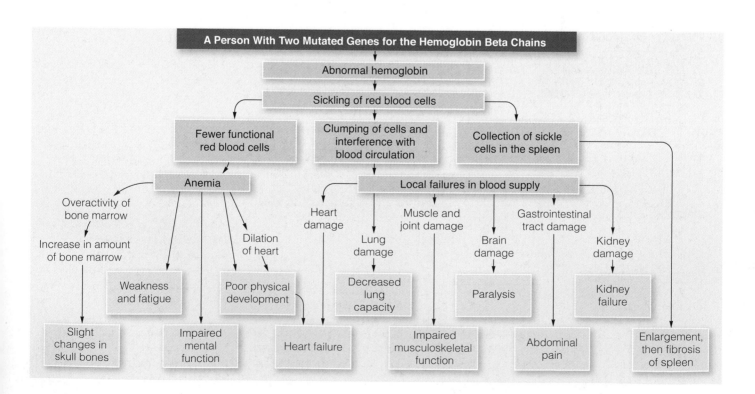

A Person With Two Mutated Genes for the Hemoglobin Beta Chains

Abnormal hemoglobin

Sickling of red blood cells

Fewer functional red blood cells   Clumping of cells and interference with blood circulation   Collection of sickle cells in the spleen

Anemia   Local failures in blood supply

Overactivity of bone marrow

Increase in amount of bone marrow   Dilation of heart   Heart damage   Muscle and joint damage   Gastrointestinal tract damage

Lung damage   Brain damage   Kidney damage

Weakness and fatigue   Poor physical development   Decreased lung capacity   Paralysis   Kidney failure

Slight changes in skull bones   Impaired mental function   Heart failure   Impaired musculoskeletal function   Abdominal pain   Enlargement, then fibrosis of spleen

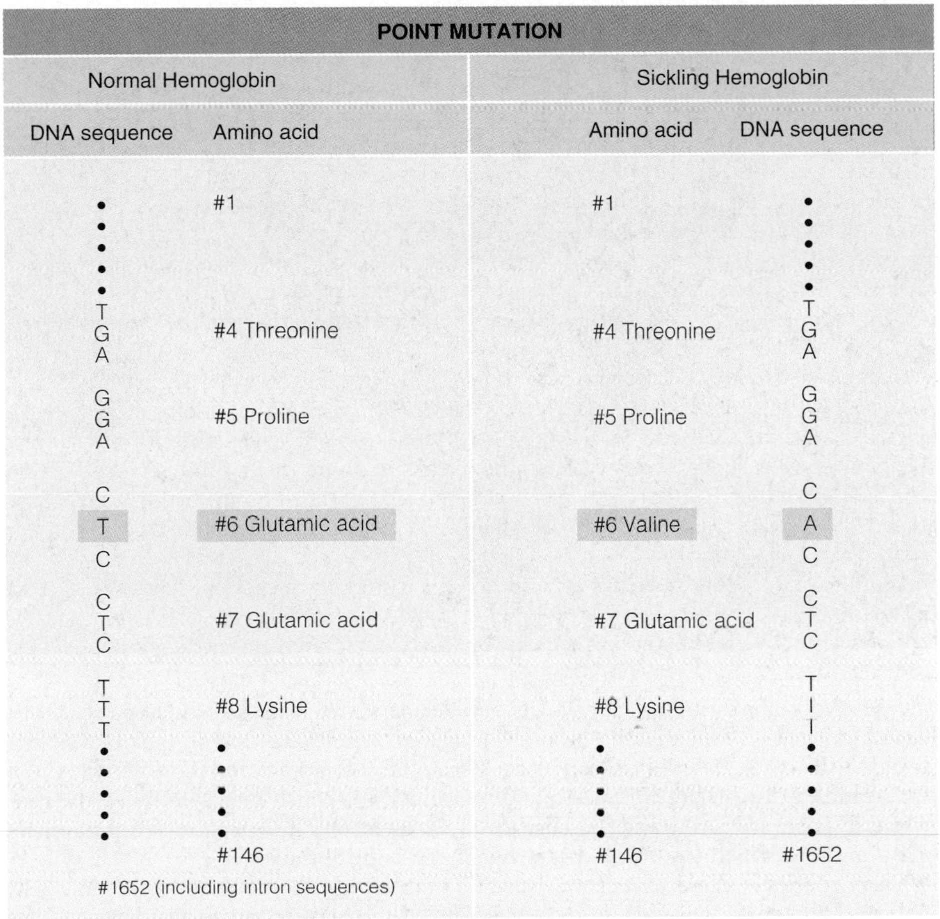

POINT MUTATION				
Normal Hemoglobin			Sickling Hemoglobin	
DNA sequence	Amino acid		Amino acid	DNA sequence
• • • • • T G A	#1 #4 Threonine		#1 #4 Threonine	• • • • • T G A
G G A	#5 Proline		#5 Proline	G G A
C T C	#6 Glutamic acid		#6 Valine	C A C
C T C	#7 Glutamic acid		#7 Glutamic acid	C T C
T T T • • • • •	#8 Lysine #146		#8 Lysine #146	T T T • • • • • #1652
#1652 (including intron sequences)				

FIGURE 3-12
Substitution of one base at position 6 produces sickling hemoglobin.

amino acid products for both normal and sickling hemoglobin. As you can see, a single base substitution (from CTC to CAC) can result in an altered amino acid sequence, from:

... proline—*glutamic acid*—glutamic acid ...

to

... proline—*valine*—glutamic acid ...

This kind of change in the genetic code is referred to as a **point mutation**, and in evolution, it's a common and important source of new genetic variation in populations. Point mutations, like the one that causes sickle-cell anemia, probably occur fairly frequently. But, for a new mutation to become significant in an evolutionary sense, it must be passed on to offspring and eventually become more common in a population. Once point mutations occur, their fate in populations will depend on the other evolutionary forces, especially natural selection. In fact, sickle-cell anemia is the best-demonstrated example of natural selection acting on human beings, a point that we'll consider in more detail in Chapter 4.

Chromosomes

Throughout much of a cell's life, its DNA (all six feet of it!) is involved in directing cellular functions and exists as an uncoiled, granular substance called **chromatin**. However, at various times in the life of most types of cells, normal functions are interrupted and the cell divides. Cell division produces new cells, and it's during this process that the chromatin becomes tightly coiled and is visible under a microscope as a set of discrete structures called **chromosomes** (Fig. 3-13).

sickle-cell anemia A severe inherited hemoglobin disorder in which red blood cells collapse when deprived of oxygen. It results from inheriting two copies of a mutant allele. This allele is caused by a single base substitution in the DNA.

point mutation A chemical change in a single base of a DNA sequence.

chromatin The loose, diffuse form of DNA seen when a cell isn't dividing. When it condenses, chromatin forms into chromosomes.

chromosomes Discrete structures composed of DNA and protein found only in the nuclei of cells. Chromosomes are visible under magnification only during certain phases of cell division.

FIGURE 3-13
Scanning electron micrograph of human chromosomes during cell division. Note that these chromosomes are composed of two strands, or two DNA molecules.

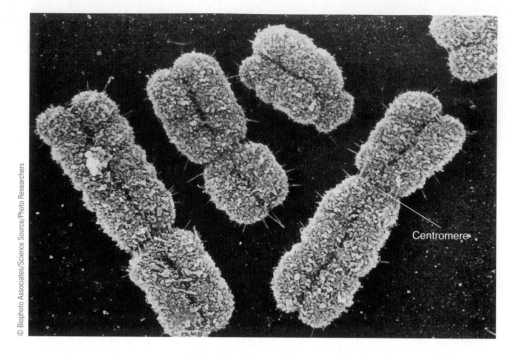

Centromere

A chromosome is composed of a DNA molecule and associated proteins (Fig. 3-14). During normal cell function, if chromosome s were visible, they would look like single-stranded structures. During the early stages of cell division, however, they're made up of two strands, or two DNA molecules, joined together at a constricted area called the **centromere**. There are two strands because the DNA molecules have *replicated* during interphase, and one strand of a chromosome is an exact copy of the other.

Every species is characterized by a specific number of chromosomes in somatic cells (Table 3-2). Humans, have 46 chromosomes, while chimpanzees and gorillas have 48. This difference doesn't mean that humans have less DNA than chimpanzees and gorillas do. It just means that the DNA is packaged differently.

There are two basic types of chromosomes: **autosomes** and **sex chromosomes**. Autosomes carry genetic information that governs all physical characteristics except primary sex determination. The two sex chromosomes are the X and Y chromosomes; in mammals, the Y chromosome is directly involved in determining maleness. Although the X chromosome is called a "sex chromosome," it actually functions more like an autosome because it's not involved in primary sex determination, and it influences several other traits.

Among mammals, all genetically normal females have two X chromosomes (XX), and they're female only because they don't have a Y chromosome. (In other words, female is the default setting.) All genetically normal males have one X and one Y chromosome (XY). In other classes of animals, such as birds or insects, primary sex determination is governed by various other chromosomal mechanisms.

Chromosomes occur in pairs, so all normal human somatic cells have 22 pairs of autosomes and one pair of sex chromosomes. Abnormal numbers of autosomes, with few exceptions, are fatal—usually soon after conception. Although abnormal numbers of sex chromosomes aren't usually fatal, they may result in sterility and frequently have other consequences as well (see p. 57 for further discussion). So, to function normally, it's essential for a human cell to possess both members of each chromosomal pair, or a total of 46 chromosomes.

Offspring inherit one member of each chromosomal pair from the father (paternal) and one member from the mother (maternal). Members of chromosomal pairs are alike in size and position of the centromere, and they carry genetic information governing the same *traits*. This doesn't mean that partner chromosomes are genetically identical; it just means they influence the same traits. For example, on both copies of a person's ninth chromosomes, there's a **locus**, or gene position, that determines which of the four ABO blood types (A, B, AB, or O) he or she will have. However, these two ninth chromosomes might not have

centromere   The constricted portion of a chromosome. After replication, the two strands of a double-stranded chromosome are joined at the centromere.

autosomes   All chromosomes except the sex chromosomes.

sex chromosomes   In mammals, the X and Y chromosomes.

locus   (*pl.,* loci) (lo´-kus, lo-sigh´) The position on a chromosome where a given gene occurs. The term is sometimes used interchangeably with *gene.*

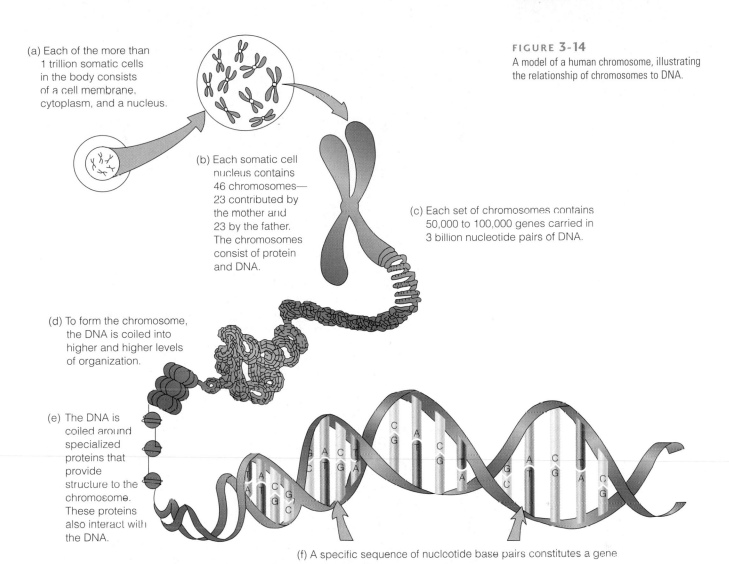

(a) Each of the more than 1 trillion somatic cells in the body consists of a cell membrane, cytoplasm, and a nucleus.

(b) Each somatic cell nucleus contains 46 chromosomes—23 contributed by the mother and 23 by the father. The chromosomes consist of protein and DNA.

(c) Each set of chromosomes contains 50,000 to 100,000 genes carried in 3 billion nucleotide pairs of DNA.

(d) To form the chromosome, the DNA is coiled into higher and higher levels of organization.

(e) The DNA is coiled around specialized proteins that provide structure to the chromosome. These proteins also interact with the DNA.

(f) A specific sequence of nucleotide base pairs constitutes a gene

FIGURE 3-14
A model of a human chromosome, illustrating the relationship of chromosomes to DNA.

TABLE 3-2	Standard Chromosomal Complement in Various Organisms	
Amino Acid	Chromosome Number in Somatic Cells	Chromosome Number in Gametes
Human (*Homo sapiens*)	46	23
Chimpanzee (*Pan troglodytes*)	48	24
Gorilla (*Gorilla gorilla*)	48	24
Dog (*Canis familiaris*)	78	39
Chicken (*Gallus domesticus*)	78	39
Frog (*Rana pipiens*)	26	13
Housefly (*Musca domestica*)	12	6
Onion (*Allium cepa*)	16	8
Corn (*Zea mays*)	20	10
Tobacco (*Nicotiana tabacum*)	48	24

Source: Cummings, 2000, p. 16.

identical DNA segments at the ABO locus. In other words, at numerous genetic loci, there may be more than one possible form of a gene, and these different forms are called **alleles**. Alleles are alternate forms of a gene that can direct the cell to produce slightly different forms of the same product and, ultimately, different expressions of traits—as in the hemoglobin S (Hb^S) example.

At the ABO locus, there are three possible alleles: *A, B,* and *O.* However, since individuals have only two ninth chromosomes, only two alleles are present in any one person. And, the variation in alleles at the ABO locus is what accounts for the variation among humans in ABO blood type.

Karyotyping Chromosomes

One method frequently used to examine chromosomes in an individual is to produce a **karyotype**. (An example of a human karyotype is shown in Fig. 3-15.) Chromosomes used in karyotypes are obtained from dividing cells. (You'll remember that chromosomes are visible as discrete entities only during cell division.) For example, white blood cells, because they're easily obtained, can be cultured, chemically treated, and microscopically examined to identify the ones that are dividing. These cells are then photographed through a microscope to produce *photomicrographs* of intact, double-stranded chromosomes. Partner chromosomes are then matched up, and the entire set is arranged in descending order by size so that the largest (number 1) appears first.

Karyotyping has numerous practical applications. Physicians and genetic counselors routinely use karyotypes to help diagnose chromosomal disorders in patients, or in prenatal testing to identify chromosomal abnormalities in developing fetuses. Karyotype analysis has also revealed many chromosomal similarities shared by different species, including humans and nonhuman primates. The similarities in overall karyotype, as well as the biochemical and DNA similarities indicated by banding patterns (discussed in Chapter 6), point to close *genetic* relationships, especially between humans and the African great apes (chimpanzees and gorillas). But, since scientists can now compare the genomes of species directly, karyotyping probably won't continue being used for this purpose.

FIGURE 3-15

A karyotype of a male, with the chromosomes arranged by size and position of the centromere, as well as by the banding patterns.

alleles Alternate forms of a gene. Alleles occur at the same locus on paired chromosomes and thus govern the same trait. But because they're different, their action may result in different expressions of that trait. The term is sometimes used synonymously with *gene*.

karyotype The chromosomal complement of an individual, or what is typical for a species. Usually displayed in a photomicrograph, the chromosomes are arranged in pairs and according to centromere size and position.

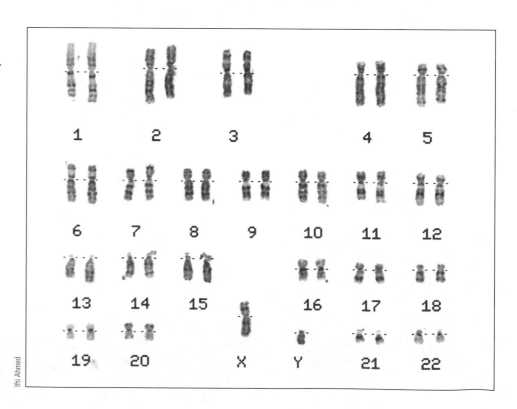

Ifti Ahmed

Cell Division

As we mentioned earlier, normal cellular function is periodically interrupted so the cell can divide. Cell division in somatic cells is called **mitosis**, and it's the way these cells reproduce. Mitosis occurs during growth and development; it also repairs injured tissues and replaces older cells with newer ones. But, while mitosis produces new cells, **meiosis** may lead to the development of new individuals, since it produces reproductive cells, or gametes.

MITOSIS

In the early stages of mitosis, a human somatic cell has 46 double-stranded chromosomes and, as the cell begins to divide, these chromosomes line up in random order along the center of the cell (Fig. 3-16). As the cell wall starts to constrict at the center, the chromosomes split apart at the centromere, so that the two strands are separated. Once the two strands

mitosis Simple cell division; the process by which somatic cells divide to produce two identical daughter cells.

meiosis Cell division in specialized cells in ovaries and testes. Meiosis involves two divisions and results in four daughter cells, each containing only half the original number of chromosomes. These cells can develop into gametes.

FIGURE **3-16**
Mitosis.

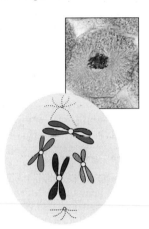
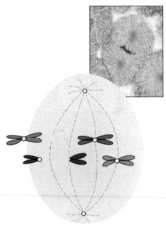

(a) The cell is involved in metabolic activities. DNA replication occurs, but chromosomes are not visible.

(b) The nuclear membrane disappears, and double-stranded chromosomes are visible.

(c) The chromosomes align themselves at the center of the cell.

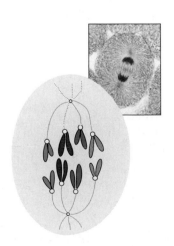

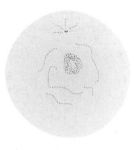

(d) The chromosomes split at the centromere, and the strands separate and move to opposite ends of the dividing cell.

(e) The cell membrane pinches in as the cell continues to divide. The chromosomes begin to uncoil (not shown here).

(f) After mitosis is complete, there are two identical daughter cells. The nuclear membrane is present, and chromosomes are no longer visible.

are apart, they pull away from each other and move to opposite ends of the dividing cell. Each strand is now a distinct chromosome, *composed of one DNA molecule*. Following the separation of chromosome strands, the cell membrane pinches in and becomes sealed, so that two new cells are formed, each with a full complement of DNA, or 46 chromosomes.

Mitosis is referred to as "simple cell division" because a somatic cell divides one time to produce two daughter cells that are genetically identical to each other and to the original cell. In mitosis, the original cell possesses 46 chromosomes, and each new daughter cell inherits an exact copy of all 46. This precision is made possible by the ability of the DNA molecule to replicate, so DNA replication is what ensures that the quantity and quality of the genetic material remain constant from one generation of cells to the next.

We should mention that not all somatic cells undergo mitosis. Red blood cells are produced continuously by specialized cells in bone marrow, but they can't divide since they have no nucleus and no nuclear DNA. Once the brain and nervous system are fully developed, brain and nerve cells (neurons) don't divide, although there's currently some debate over this issue. Liver cells also don't divide after growth has stopped, unless this vital organ is damaged through injury or disease. With these three exceptions (red blood cells, mature neurons, and liver cells), somatic cells are regularly duplicated through the process of mitosis.

MEIOSIS

In some ways, meiosis is similar to mitosis, but it's a more complicated process. In meiosis there are two divisions instead of one. Also, meiosis produces four daughter cells, not two, and each of the four cells contains only half the original number of chromosomes.

During meiosis, specialized cells in male testes and female ovaries divide and eventually develop into sperm and egg cells. Initially, these cells contain the full complement of chromosomes (46 in humans), but after the first division (called "reduction division") the number of chromosomes in the two resulting daughter cells is 23, or half the original amount (see Fig. 3-17). This reduction of chromosome number is a critical feature of meiosis because the resulting gamete, with its 23 chromosomes, may eventually unite with another gamete that also has 23 chromosomes. The product of this union is a *zygote*, or fertilized egg, in which the original number of chromosomes (46) has been restored. In other words, a zygote inherits the exact amount of DNA it needs (half from each parent) to develop and function normally. But, if it weren't for *reduction division* in meiosis, it wouldn't be possible to maintain the correct number of chromosomes from one generation to the next.

During the first meiotic division, partner chromosomes come together to form pairs of double-stranded chromosomes. Then, the *pairs* of chromosomes line up along the cell's center (see Fig. 3-17). Pairing of partner chromosomes is essential, because while they're together, members of pairs exchange genetic information in a process called **recombination**. Pairing is also important because it ensures that each new daughter cell receives only one member of each pair.

As the cell begins to divide, the chromosomes themselves remain intact (that is, double-stranded), but *members of pairs* separate and migrate to opposite ends of the cell. After the first division, there are two new daughter cells, but they aren't identical to each other or to the parental cell. They're different because each cell contains only one member of each chromosome pair and thus only 23 chromosomes, each of which still has two strands (see Figs. 3-17 and 3-18). Also, because of recombination, each chromosome is somewhat different from its predecessor because it now contains some alleles it may not have had before.

The second meiotic division happens pretty much the same way as in mitosis. In the two newly formed cells, the 23 double-stranded chromosomes line up at the cell's center and, as in mitosis, the strands of each chromosome separate and move apart. Once this second division is completed, there are four daughter cells, each with 23 single-stranded chromosomes, or 23 DNA molecules (see Figs. 3-17 and 3-18).

THE EVOLUTIONARY SIGNIFICANCE OF MEIOSIS

Meiosis occurs in all sexually reproducing organisms, and it's an extremely important evolutionary innovation because it increases genetic variation in populations. Members of sexually reproducing species aren't genetically identical **clones** of other individuals, because

recombination (also sometimes called crossing over) The exchange of genetic material between homologous chromosomes during meiosis.

clones Organisms that are genetically identical to another organism. The term may also be used in referring to genetically identical DNA segments, molecules, and cells.

random assortment The chance distribution of chromosomes to daughter cells during meiosis; along with recombination, the source of variation resulting from meiosis.

they result from the genetic contributions of two parents. In human matings a staggering number of genetic combinations can result in the possible offspring of two parents. From just the **random assortment** of chromosome pairs lining up along the center of the cell during the first division of meiosis, each parent can produce 8 million genetically different gametes. And, given the joint probability accounting for both parents, the total number of possible genetic combinations for any human mating is about 70 trillion! Each individual thus represents a unique combination of genes that, in all likelihood, has never occurred before and will never occur again. This genetic uniqueness is solely due to

FIGURE **3-17**
Meiosis.

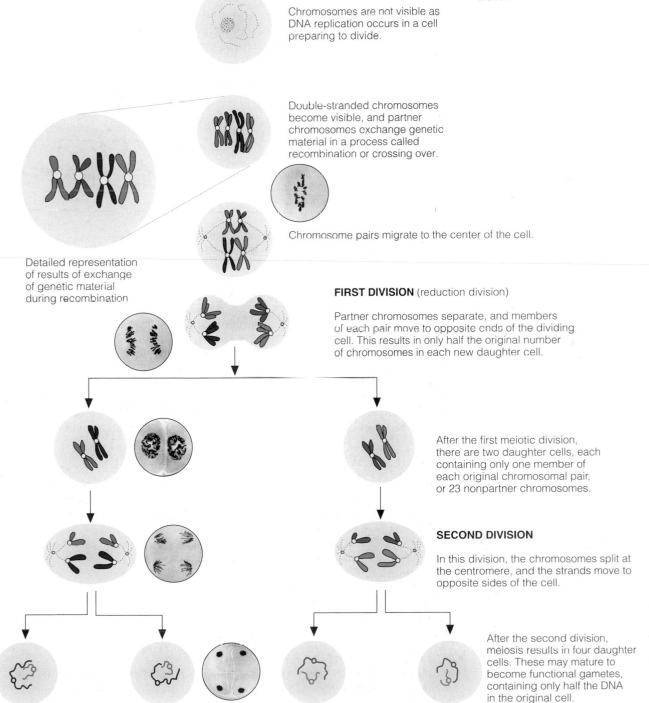

Chromosomes are not visible as DNA replication occurs in a cell preparing to divide.

Double-stranded chromosomes become visible, and partner chromosomes exchange genetic material in a process called recombination or crossing over.

Chromosome pairs migrate to the center of the cell.

Detailed representation of results of exchange of genetic material during recombination.

FIRST DIVISION (reduction division)

Partner chromosomes separate, and members of each pair move to opposite ends of the dividing cell. This results in only half the original number of chromosomes in each new daughter cell.

After the first meiotic division, there are two daughter cells, each containing only one member of each original chromosomal pair, or 23 nonpartner chromosomes.

SECOND DIVISION

In this division, the chromosomes split at the centromere, and the strands move to opposite sides of the cell.

After the second division, meiosis results in four daughter cells. These may mature to become functional gametes, containing only half the DNA in the original cell.

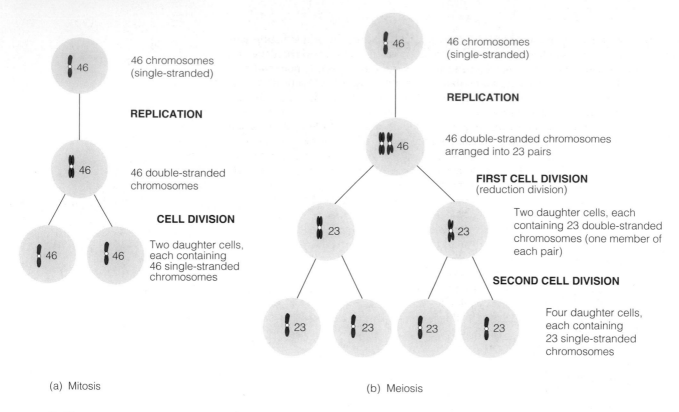

(a) Mitosis

(b) Meiosis

FIGURE 3-18

Mitosis and meiosis compared. In mitosis, one division produces two daughter cells, each of which contains 46 chromosomes. Meiosis is characterized by two divisions. After the first, there are two cells, each containing only 23 chromosomes (one member of each original chromosome pair). Each daughter cell divides again, so that the final result is four cells, each with only half the original number of chromosomes.

random assortment of chromosomes and recombination during meiosis, and it insures that in every generation, parental genetic contributions are reshuffled in an almost infinite number of combinations.

As you can see, genetic diversity is considerably enhanced by meiosis, and diversity is essential if species are to adapt to changing selective pressures. As we mentioned in Chapter 2, natural selection acts on genetic variation in populations; so if all individuals were genetically identical, natural selection would have nothing to act on and evolution couldn't occur. In all species, *mutation* is the only source of *new* genetic variation because it produces new alleles. But, sexually reproducing species have an additional advantage because recombination produces new *arrangements* of genetic information, which potentially provide additional material for selection to act on.

It's been argued that its influence on variation is the principal adaptive advantage of sexual reproduction. Thus, sexual reproduction and meiosis are of major evolutionary importance because they contribute to the role of natural selection in populations.

PROBLEMS WITH MEIOSIS

For meiosis to ensure an opportunity for normal fetal development, the process needs to be exact. If chromosomes or chromosome strands don't separate during either of the two divisions, serious problems can develop. This failure to separate is called **nondisjunction**. The result of nondisjunction is that one of the daughter cells receives two copies of the affected chromosome, while the other daughter cell receives none. If such an affected gamete unites with a normal gamete containing 23 chromosomes, the resulting zygote will have either 45 or 47 chromosomes. Having only one member of a chromosome pair is referred to as *monosomy*. The term *trisomy* refers to the presence of three copies of a particular chromosome.

You can appreciate the potential effects of an abnormal number of chromosomes if you remember that the zygote reproduces itself through mitosis. Consequently, every cell in the developing body will also have the abnormal chromosome number. Most abnormal numbers of autosomes are lethal, and the embryo is usually spontaneously aborted, frequently before the pregnancy is even recognized.

Trisomy 21, formerly called "Down syndrome," is caused by the presence of three copies of chromosome 21, and it's the only example of an abnormal number of autosomes that's

nondisjunction   The failure of partner chromosomes or chromosome strands to separate during cell division.

compatible with life beyond the first few years after birth. Trisomy 21 occurs in approximately 1 out of every 1,000 live births and is associated with various developmental and health problems. These problems include congenital heart defects (seen in about 40 percent of affected newborns), increased susceptibility to respiratory infections, and leukemia. However, the most widely recognized effect is mental impairment, which is variably expressed and ranges from mild to severe.

Trisomy 21 is partly associated with advanced maternal age. For example, the risk of a 20-year-old woman giving birth to an affected infant is just 0.05 percent (5 in 10,000). However, 3 percent of babies born to mothers 45 and older are affected (a 60-fold increase). Actually, most affected infants are born to women under the age of 35; but this statistic exists because the majority of babies are born to women in this age category. The increased prevalence of trisomy 21 with maternal age is thought to be related to the fact that meiosis actually begins in females during their own fetal development and then stops, only to be resumed and completed at ovulation. This means that a woman's gametes are as old as she is, and age-related changes in the chromosomes themselves appear to increase the risk of nondisjunction at least for some chromosomes.

Nondisjunction also occurs in sex chromosomes, producing individuals who, for example, are XXY (47 chromosomes), XO (45 chromosomes), XXX (47 chromosomes), or XYY (47 chromosomes). While these conditions don't result in death, some are associated with impaired mental function and/or sterility (Table 3-3). What's more, still greater numbers of X chromosomes, such as XXXX or XXXY, result in marked mental deficiency, and some nondisjunctions of sex chromosomes are lethal. It's possible to survive without a Y chromosome (roughly half of all humans do), but it's impossible to live without an X chromosome. Indeed, the evidence suggests that embryos possessing only a Y chromosome are spontaneously aborted before the woman is aware she is pregnant.

Clearly, the importance of accuracy during meiosis can't be overstated. If normal development is to occur, the correct number of both autosomes and sex chromosomes must be present.

TABLE 3-3	Examples of Nondisjunction in Sex Chromosomes		
Chromosomal Complement	Condition	Estimated Incidence	Manifestations
XXX	Trisomy X	1 per 1,000 female births	Affected women are usually clinically normal, but there is a slight increase in sterility and mental impairment compared to the general population. In cases with more than three X chromosomes, mental retardation can be severe.
XYY	XYY syndrome	1 per 1,000 male births	Affected males are fertile and tend to be taller than average.
XO	Turner syndrome	1 per 10,000 female births	Affected females are short-statured, have broad chests and webbed necks, and are sterile. There is usually no mental impairment, but concepts relating to spatial relationships, including mathematics, can pose difficulties. Between 95 and 99 percent of affected fetuses die before birth.
XXY	Klinefelter syndrome	1 per 1,000 male births	Symptoms are noticeable by puberty: reduced testicular development, reduced facial and body hair, some breast development in about half of all cases, and reduced fertility or sterility. Some individuals exhibit lowered intelligence. Additional X chromosomes (XXXY) are associated with mental impairment.

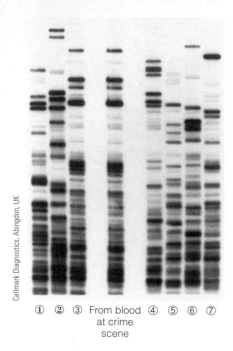

Cellmark Diagnostics, Abingdon, UK

① ② ③ From blood ④ ⑤ ⑥ ⑦
at crime
scene

FIGURE 3-19

Eight DNA fingerprints, one of which is from a blood sample left at an actual crime scene. The other seven are from suspects. By comparing the banding patterns, it is easy to identify the guilty party.

polymerase chain reaction (PCR)
A method of producing thousands of copies of a DNA segment using the enzyme DNA polymerase.

recombinant DNA technology
A process in which genes from the cell of one species are transferred to somatic cells or gametes of another species.

New Frontiers

Since the discovery of DNA structure and function in the 1950s, the field of genetics has revolutionized biological science and reshaped our understanding of inheritance, genetic disease, and evolutionary processes. For example, a technique developed in 1986, called **polymerase chain reaction** (PCR), enables scientists to make copies of small samples of DNA for subsequent analysis. This is a hugely important innovation because in the past, DNA samples such as those from crime scenes or from fossils were too small to be studied. But PCR has made it possible to examine nucleotide sequences in, for example, Neandertal fossils and Egyptian mummies. By using the techniques of PCR, scientists separate the two strands of a DNA sample. Then an enzyme synthesizes complementary strands on the exposed bases, as in DNA replication. Because this process can be repeated many times, it's possible to produce over a million copies of the original DNA material! As you can imagine, PCR has limitless potential for many disciplines, including forensic science, medicine, and evolutionary biology.

Another application of PCR allows scientists to identify *DNA fingerprints,* so called because they appear as patterns of repeated DNA sequences that are unique to each individual. For example, one person might have a segment of six bases such as ATTCTA repeated 3 times; another person might have the same sequence repeated 10 times.

DNA fingerprints are produced by forcing the DNA through an electrically charged gel. This process breaks up the DNA into fragments, which in turn separate into bands that vary in thickness. Each person has a unique banding pattern, and it's these patterns that comprise the DNA fingerprint (Fig. 3-19).

DNA fingerprinting is perhaps the most powerful tool available for human identification. Scientists have used it to identify scores of unidentified remains, including those belonging to members of the Russian royal family murdered in 1918 and victims of the September 11, 2001, terrorist attacks. The technique has also been used to exonerate innocent people wrongly convicted and imprisoned for crimes—in some cases decades after they were imprisoned.

Over the last two decades, using the techniques of **recombinant DNA technology**, scientists have been able to transfer genes from the cells of one species into those of another. The most common method has been to insert human genes that direct the production of various proteins into bacterial cells. The altered bacteria can then produce human gene products such as insulin. Until the early 1980s, diabetic patients relied on insulin derived from nonhuman animals. This insulin wasn't plentiful, however, and some patients developed allergies to it. But since 1982, abundant supplies of human insulin, produced by bacteria, have been available; and bacteria-derived insulin doesn't cause allergic reactions.

In recent years, genetic manipulation has become increasingly controversial owing to questions related to product safety, environmental concerns, and animal welfare. For example, the insertion of bacterial DNA into certain crops has made them toxic to leaf-eating insects, thus reducing the need for pesticide use. And cattle and pigs are commonly treated with antibiotics and genetically engineered growth hormone to increase growth rates. (The faster an animal grows, the less time and expense are involved before it's ready for slaughter.) There's no current evidence that humans are susceptible to the insect-repelling bacterial DNA or affected by consuming meat and dairy products from animals treated with growth hormone. But there are concerns over the unknown effects of long-term exposure. In fact, tremendous opposition to genetically modified foods has resulted in greatly increased demand for organically grown produce and hormone-free meats.

No matter how contentious these new techniques may be, nothing has generated as much controversy as cloning. The controversy escalated in 1997 with the birth of Dolly, a clone of a female sheep (Wilmut et al., 1997). Actually, cloning isn't as new as you might think. Anyone who has ever taken a cutting from a plant and rooted it to grow a new one has produced a clone. In the 1960s, an African toad became the first animal to be cloned. Since then, cloning has become almost commonplace; the list of cloned mammals includes mice, rats, rabbits, cats, sheep, cattle, a horse, a mule, and recently a dog (Woods et al., 2003).

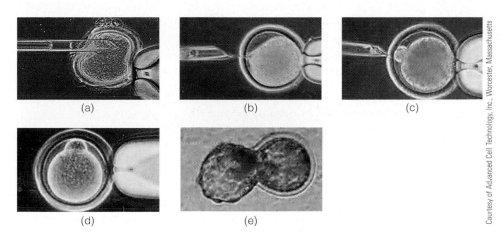

Courtesy of Advanced Cell Technology, Inc., Worcester, Massachusetts

FIGURE 3-20
A series of photomicrographs showing a nuclear transfer process. (a) The nucleus of an egg cell (from a donor) is drawn into a hollow needle. (b) The enucleated egg with only the cytoplasm remaining. (c) The nucleus of a skin cell from the individual being cloned is injected into the enucleated egg. (d) Electric shock causes the nucleus of the skin cell to fuse with the egg's cytoplasm. (e) The egg begins to divide, and a few days later the cloned embryo will be transferred into the uterus of a host animal.

Cloning is accomplished by a technique called nuclear transfer (Fig. 3-20). This process involves several stages. First, egg cells are taken from an animal and the nucleus is removed. Then, the nucleus (containing DNA) is taken from tissue cells of another animal (the animal being cloned). This nucleus is then inserted into the egg cell, and the fused egg is placed in the uterus of a host mother. If all goes well, the mother eventually gives birth to an infant that's genetically identical to the animal that provided the tissue cells containing the DNA.

The harangue among politicians and others about the ethics of human cloning, whether for reproductive purposes or not, may be in vain, at least for now (see Issue, p. 62–63). Apparently, it's going to be harder to clone a human than scientists originally thought because so far, all attempts to clone nonhuman primates have failed (Simerly et al., 2003).

How successful cloning will be hasn't yet been determined. Dolly, who had developed health problems, was euthanized in February 2003 at the age of 6 years (Giles and Knight, 2003). Long-term studies have yet to show whether cloned animals live out their normal life span, but some evidence in mice suggests that they don't. Also, only about 3 percent of cell nuclei inserted into donor eggs result in a live birth (Giles and Knight, 2003).

As exciting as these innovations are, probably the single most important advance in genetics has been the progress made by the **Human Genome Project**. The goal of this international effort, begun in 1990, was to sequence the entire human **genome**, which consists of some 3 billion bases comprising approximately 30,000 genes. In 2003, the project was completed; now, all human chromosomes have been provisionally mapped. The next step is to sort out which DNA segments operate as functional genes and which don't. It will also be several years before scientists identify the functions of many of the proteins produced by these genes. It's one thing to know a gene's chemical makeup but quite another to know what it does. Still, the magnitude and importance of the achievement can't be overstated; it will ultimately transform biomedical and pharmaceutical research, changing forever the way many human diseases are diagnosed and treated.

While scientists were sequencing human genes, the genomes of other organisms were also being studied. As of September 2000, the genomes of over 600 species (mostly microorganisms) had been either partially or completely identified. In December 2002, the mouse genome had been completely sequenced (Waterston et al., 2002). Then, in December 2003, a rough draft of the chimpanzee genome was announced. Already scientists have begun to compare human and chimpanzee DNA for evidence as to how our lineage became distinct from that of chimpanzees (Clark, A.G. et al., 2003). This research has enormous implications not only for biomedical research but also for studies of evolutionary relationships among species. We already know that humans share many genes with other organisms, but just how many and which ones will partly be clarified by upcoming projects aimed at sequencing nonhuman primate genomes. Eventually, comparative genome analysis should provide a thorough assessment of genetic similarities and differences, and thus the evolutionary relationships, between humans and other primates. In fact, it wouldn't be exaggerating to say that this is the most exciting time in the history of evolutionary biology since Darwin published *On the Origin of Species*.

Human Genome Project An international effort aimed at sequencing and mapping the entire human genome, completed in 2003.

genome The entire genetic makeup of an individual or species. In humans, it's estimated that each individual possesses approximately 3 billion DNA nucleotides.

VISUAL SUMMARY

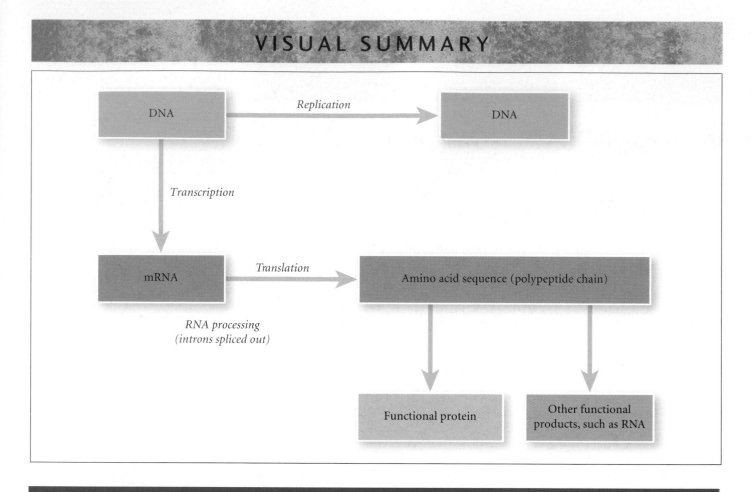

Summary: Putting It All Together

The topics covered in this chapter relate almost entirely to discoveries made after Darwin and Wallace described the fundamentals of natural selection. But all the issues presented here are basic to an understanding of biological evolution, adaptation, and human variation.

We've shown that cells are the fundamental units of life and that there are basically two types of cells. Somatic cells make up body tissues, while gametes (eggs and sperm) are reproductive cells that transmit genetic information from parent to offspring.

Genetic information is contained in the DNA molecule, found in the nuclei of cells. The DNA molecule is capable of replication, or making copies of itself. Replication makes it possible for daughter cells to receive a full complement of DNA (contained in chromosomes).

DNA also controls protein synthesis by directing the cell to arrange amino acids in the proper sequence for each particular type of protein. Also involved in the process of protein synthesis is another, similar molecule called RNA.

There are many genes that regulate the function of other genes. Homeobox genes are expressed only in embryonic development, and they direct the development of the body plan. Other regulatory genes turn genes on and off. In some cases, this results in the production of different forms of a protein, such as hemoglobin, during different stages of life.

Many segments of DNA don't code for protein production, and much of their function is unknown. We do know that genes contain noncoding segments called introns are initially transcribed into mRNA but are then deleted before the mRNA leaves the cell nucleus.

Cells multiply by dividing, and during cell division, DNA is visible under a microscope in the form of chromosomes. In humans there are 46 chromosomes (23 pairs). If the full complement isn't precisely distributed to succeeding generations of cells, there may be serious consequences.

Somatic cells divide during growth or tissue repair or to replace old, worn-out cells. Somatic cell division is called mitosis. A cell divides one time to produce two daughter cells, each possessing a full and identical set of chromosomes. Sex cells are produced when specialized cells in the ovaries and testes divide during meiosis. Unlike mitosis, meiosis is characterized by two divisions that produce four nonidentical daughter cells, each containing only half the amount of DNA (23 chromosomes) that's carried by the original cell.

Critical Thinking Questions

1. We only briefly touched on the topic of recombinant DNA technologies. From what we said and from things you've heard elsewhere, what is your view on this important topic? Are you generally in favor of most of the goals of recombinant DNA research? What are your objections?

2. Before reading this chapter, were you aware that the DNA in your body is structurally the same as in all other organisms? Do you see this fact as having potential to clarify some of the many questions we still have regarding biological evolution? Why?

Stem Cell Research: Promise and Controversy

Stem cells are undifferentiated, or unspecialized, cells that can divide and replicate indefinitely. Depending on their origins (and given the right circumstances), they can give rise to many, if not all, of the specialized cells that make up an organism.

Adult stem cells are found in specialized tissues, such as bone marrow, skin, and the gastrointestinal tract. They're able to replicate themselves throughout the life of the organism and can also give rise to all the specialized types of cells *that make up the tissue in which they're found*. For example, stem cells in bone marrow give rise to all the cells that comprise blood, including oxygen-transporting red cells and all the white cells involved in the immune response. In short, adult stem cells replace certain types of cells that have lived out their life span or have been lost through disease or trauma.

For years, one type of adult stem cell, hematopoietic (blood-producing) stem cells (HSCs), has been transplanted into patients with immune disorders and various forms of cancer, especially leukemias. In these procedures, called bone marrow transplants, bone marrow cells are extracted from a donor and then transplanted into a recipient. Nowadays, bone marrow transplants are be ing replaced by injections of HSCs extracted directly from the donor's circulating blood. Stem cell transfer, as this procedure is called, is dangerous, particularly in the treatment of cancer, because the chemotherapy or radiation required before the stem cell transfer virtually destroys not only the patient's cancerous blood-producing cells but also the immune system; thus, there's a risk of death due to infection or graft-versus-host immune reactions. But success rates are increasing, and in many cases, the stem cells give rise to healthy white and red blood cells in a patient whose cancer has been eradicated or at least put into remission.

By the late 1980s, researchers recognized that HSCs are also present in the approximately 3 ounces of blood contained in umbilical cords. Since 1988, HSCs derived from cord blood have been used to treat thousands of children with various forms of leukemia. Human embryonic stem cells (ESCs) are, as the name implies, derived from embryos consisting of 200 to 250 cells. Most of these embryos are the unused products of *in vitro* fertilization of eggs at fertility clinics and are donated by patients. At this developmental stage, an embryo consists of two portions: one that becomes the placenta and one, an inner cell mass consisting of about 40 cells, that develops into the fetus. The cells that make up the inner cell mass are the undifferentiated ESCs that can potentially give rise to the more than 200 types of cells found in mammals. It's this potential that makes ESCs so attractive to researchers, because it isn't yet known if adult stem cells have this same capacity.

When ESCs are exposed to certain chemicals, they give rise to specialized cells that replace damaged ones. For example,

ESCs transplanted into mouse brains have given rise to neurons that produce an enzyme necessary for the synthesis of dopamine, the neurochemical lacking in patients with Parkinson's disease.

Such findings have led researchers to consider the possibility that in the future, embryonic stem cells can be implanted into patients with Alzheimer disease or those with brain and spinal cord injuries to replace damaged or destroyed neurons. It is also hoped that nonfunctioning pancreatic cells in diabetic patients can be replaced with stem cells that will produce healthy, insulin-producing cells. Or perhaps it will be possible to replace damaged cardiac muscle cells in patients with heart disease—and even skin cells in burn victims.

But there are many ethical objections to the use of embryonic stem cells and many technical problems to overcome. Abortion opponents raise the strongest objections; they believe that any fertilized egg, with the potential to develop into a human being if implanted into a woman's uterus, shouldn't be destroyed. It's this objection that has led, in the United States, to a presidential executive order that limits federal funding for embryonic stem cell research to the approximately 60 cell lines already established by the summer of 2001. There's also a funding ban on all projects that create cloned embryos solely for research, but privately funded research remains unaffected.

The scientific community has become increasingly concerned over the federal government's efforts to limit or ban all stem cell research involving the use of human embryos. For one thing, in reality only about 20 cell lines are available for study (Check, 2004). And the scientific community has argued that, in the course of fertility treatments, it's necessary to create more embryos than will actually be used, so that fertility clinics destroy thousands of surplus embryos every year. It's these surplus embryos that have been used in past research, and scientists argue that it's better to use them for the benefits they may provide than to destroy them.

Since 2001, controversy over stem cell research had continued with well-known celebrities, such as the late Christopher Reeves (Superman), lobbying for a reinstatement of federal funding. (Reeves was paralyzed from the neck down after he suffered a broken neck in a horse-riding accident.) But in 2006, when the U.S. Congress passed a bill that would have reinstated public funding for stem cell research, George W. Bush vetoed it.

Funding limitations similar to those in the United States exist in some other countries, including Germany and Italy. But in Britain, public funds are available for embryonic stem cell studies, even those that involve nonreproductive cloning and the creation of embryos for research purposes.

Besides funding constraints, there are other concerns the scientific community must address. First, the potential of stem cells to produce malignant (that is, constantly replicating) cell lines isn't known; but there are increasing fears that stem cells are involved in the development of some cancers. Second, there's the problem of tissue rejection in patients receiving stem cell transplants that are recognized as foreign by their own immune systems.

Scientists are also exploring alternatives to using embryos left over from *in vitro* procedures. One alternative that's been looked at is using embryos that have "died" after they were produced for *in vitro* fertilization. Although there's been some success with this technique, serious questions arise over fears that some underlying genetic defects may have caused these embryos to stop dividing.

This discussion illustrates the conflicts between technology, ethical standards, and the legal system. The questions raised by developing technologies challenge traditionally held views about fundamental aspects of life. In the past, people with hereditary disorders frequently died. They still do. But now there are treatments, however costly, for some conditions. How we view these new discoveries and how we come to terms with the ethical and legal issues surrounding our new technologies will increasingly become social, religious, and ultimately political concerns. Solutions won't come easily, and they certainly won't please everyone.

SOURCES

Check, E. 2004. "Bush Pressured as Nancy Reagan Pleads for Stem-Cell Research." *Nature,* 429:116.

Kline, Ronald M. 2001. "Whose Blood Is It, Anyway?" *Scientific American* 284(4): 42–49.

Pearson H. and A. Abbott. "Stem Cells Derived from 'Dead' Human Embryos."*Nature* 433, 2005:376–377.

Stem Cells: Scientific Progress and Future Research Directions. Report from the National Institutes of Health to Secretary of Health and Human Services, Tommy G. Thompson, February 2001. Internet version obtained from the NIH website: www.nih.gov/news/stemcell/scireport/htm.

CHAPTER 4

Heredity and Evolution

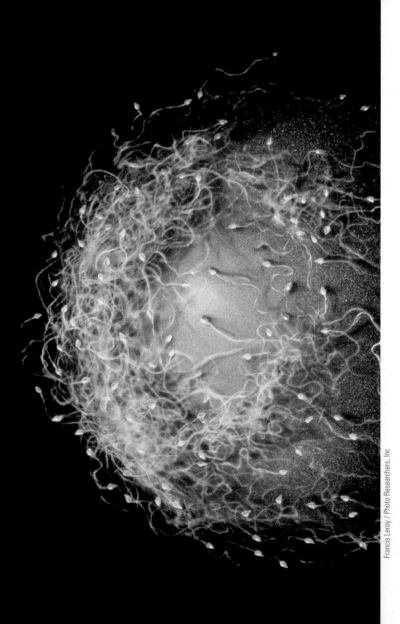

Francis Leroy / Photo Researchers, Inc

KEY QUESTIONS

Why is it important to know the basic mechanisms of inheritance to understand the processes of evolution?

How do the patterns of human inheritance compare with those of other organisms?

Introduction

Have you ever had a cat with five, six, or even seven toes? Even if you haven't you may have seen one, because this condition is fairly common in cats. Maybe you've known someone with an extra finger or toe, because it's not unheard of. Anne Boleyn, mother of England's Queen Elizabeth 1, and the first of Henry VIII's wives to lose her head, apparently had at least part of an extra little finger. (Of course, this had nothing to do with her early demise; that's another story altogether.)

Having extra fingers or toes is called polydactyly, and it's likely that one of Anne Boleyn's parents was also polydactylous. It's also likely that any polydactylous cat has a parent with extra toes. But how can we know this? Actually, it's fairly simple. We know this because polydactyly is a Mendelian characteristic, meaning that its pattern of inheritance is one of those discovered almost 150 years ago by a monk named Gregor Mendel (Fig. 4-1).

For at least 10,000 years, beginning with the domestication of plants and animals, people have tried to explain how offspring inherit characteristics from their parents. Even though their explanations were wrong, farmers have known for millennia that they could enhance the frequency and expression of desirable attributes through **selective breeding**. But they didn't know why.

Since the ancient Greek philosophers considered the problem of inheritance, until well into the nineteenth century, one common belief was that the traits seen in offspring resulted from the *blending* of parental traits. Blending supposedly happened because of certain particles that existed in every part of the body. These particles contained miniature versions of the body part (limbs, organs, and so on) they came from, and they traveled through the blood to the reproductive organs and ultimately blended with particles of another individual during reproduction. There were variations on this theme; and numerous scholars, including Charles Darwin, adhered to some aspects of the theory.

The Genetic Principles Discovered by Mendel

It wasn't until Gregor Mendel (1822–1884) addressed the question of heredity that it began to be resolved (see Fig. 4-1). Mendel was living in an abbey in what is now the Czech Republic. By the time he began his research, he had already studied botany, physics, and mathematics at the University of Vienna, and he had conducted various experiments in the monastery gardens. These experiments led him to explore the ways that physical traits, such as color or height, could be expressed in plant **hybrids**.

Mendel worked with garden peas, concentrating on seven different traits, each of which could be expressed in two different ways (Fig. 4-2). It's important here to realize that the principles Mendel discovered apply not just to peas, but to all biological organisms, including humans. You may think it's strange that we discuss the pea experiments in a biological anthropology book, but we do it because they provide a simple example of the basic rules of inheritance.

 Click!

Go to the following media for interactives and exercises on topics covered in this chapter:

- Basic Genetics for Anthropology CD-ROM: Principles and Applications

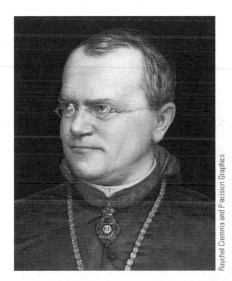

FIGURE 4-1
Portrait of Gregor Mendel

selective breeding A practice whereby animal and plant breeders choose which animals will be allowed to mate based on traits (such as coat color, body size, shape of face) they hope to produce in offspring. Animals that don't have the desirable traits aren't allowed to breed.

hybrids Offspring of individuals that differ with regard to certain traits or certain aspects of genetic makeup; heterozygotes.

FIGURE 4-2
The traits Mendel studied in peas.

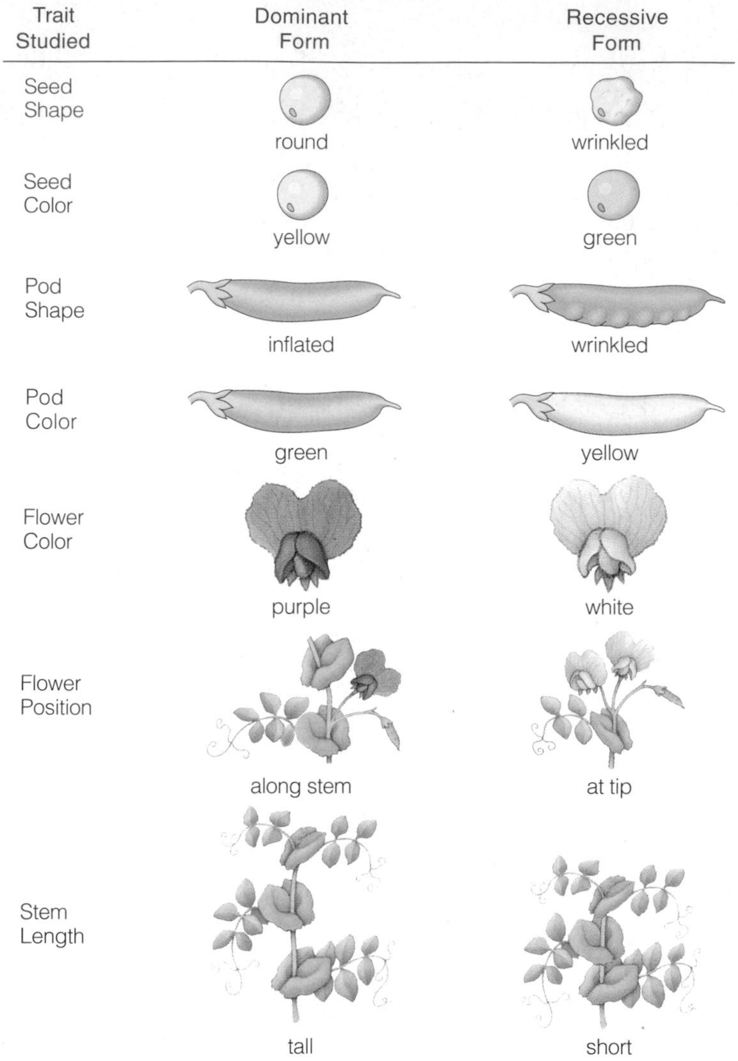

Trait Studied	Dominant Form	Recessive Form
Seed Shape	round	wrinkled
Seed Color	yellow	green
Pod Shape	inflated	wrinkled
Pod Color	green	yellow
Flower Color	purple	white
Flower Position	along stem	at tip
Stem Length	tall	short

SEGREGATION

Mendel began by crossing parent (P) plants that produced only tall plants with other plants that produced only short ones (Fig. 4-3). But, instead of being intermediate in height, as blending theories would have predicted, the hybrid offspring, called the F_1 generation, were all tall.

Next, Mendel allowed the F_1 plants to self-fertilize to produce a second generation (the F_2 generation). But this time, only about ¾ of the offspring were tall, and the remaining ¼ were short. One expression of the trait had completely disappeared in the F_1 generation and then reappeared in the F_2 generation. What's more, the expression that was present in all the F_1 plants was more common in the F_2 plants, occurring in a ratio of approximately 3:1 (three tall plants for every short one).

These results suggested that different expressions of traits were controlled by discrete units, or what Mendel called "particles" (we would call them genes), occurring in pairs and that offspring inherited one unit from each parent. Mendel realized that the members of a pair of units somehow separated into different sex cells and were again united with another member during fertilization of the egg. This is Mendel's *first principle of inheritance,* known as the **principle of segregation**.

Today we know that meiosis explains Mendel's principle of segregation: during meiosis, paired chromosomes and the genes they carry separate from each other and end up in different gametes. But in the zygote, the original number of chromosomes is restored, and both members of each chromosome pair are present in the offspring.

principle of segregation Genes (alleles) occur in pairs because chromosomes occur in pairs. During gamete formation, the members of each pair of alleles separate so that each gamete contains one member of each pair. During fertilization, the full number of chromosomes is restored, and members of gene or allele pairs are reunited.

recessive Describes a trait that isn't expressed in heterozygotes; also refers to the allele that governs the trait. For a recessive allele to be expressed, an individual must have two copies of it (i.e., the person must be homozygous).

DOMINANCE AND RECESSIVENESS

Mendel also realized that the expression that was absent in the F₁ plants hadn't actually disappeared at all. It was still present, but somehow it was masked and couldn't be expressed. Mendel described the trait that seemed to be lost as **recessive**, and he called the expressed trait **dominant**. Thus he formulated the important principles of *dominance* and *recessiveness*, and today, they're still extremely important concepts in the field of genetics.

As it turns out, height in pea plants is controlled by two different alleles at one genetic locus. The allele that determines that a plant will be tall is dominant to the allele for short. (It's worth mentioning that height isn't controlled this way in all plants.) In Mendel's experiments, all the parent (P) plants had two copies of the same allele, either dominant or recessive, depending on whether they were tall or short. When two copies of the same allele are present, the individual is said to be **homozygous**. So, all the tall P plants were homozygous for the dominant allele, and all the short P plants were homozygous for the recessive allele. (This homozygosity explains why tall plants crossed with tall plants produced only tall offspring, and short plants crossed with short plants produced only short offspring. Because they were homozygous, they had no genetic variation at this locus and could pass on only one form of the gene.) But all the F₁ plants (hybrids) had inherited a different allele from each parent plant, so they weren't homozygous. Instead, they all had two *different* alleles at specific loci, and plants (or individuals) that have two different alleles at a locus are **heterozygous**. (Since heterozygotes have two forms of a gene at a particular locus, they can pass on two variants of that gene.)

Figure 4-3 illustrates the crosses that Mendel initially performed. Uppercase letters refer to dominant alleles (or dominant traits), and lowercase letters refer to recessive alleles (or recessive traits). Therefore,

T = the allele for tallness
t = the allele for shortness

The same symbols are combined to describe an individual's actual genetic makeup, or **genotype**. The term *genotype* can be used to refer to an organism's entire genetic makeup or to the alleles at a specific genetic locus. Thus, the genotypes of the plants in Mendel's experiments were

TT = homozygous tall plants
Tt = heterozygous tall plants
tt = homozygous short plants

Figure 4-4 is a *Punnett square* that represents the different ways alleles can be combined when the F₁ plants are self-fertilized to produce an F₂ generation. It shows all the *genotypes* that are possible in the F₂ generation; it also demonstrates that approximately ¼ of the F₂ plants are homozygous dominant (TT), ¼ are heterozygous (Tt), and the remaining ¼ are homozygous recessive (tt).

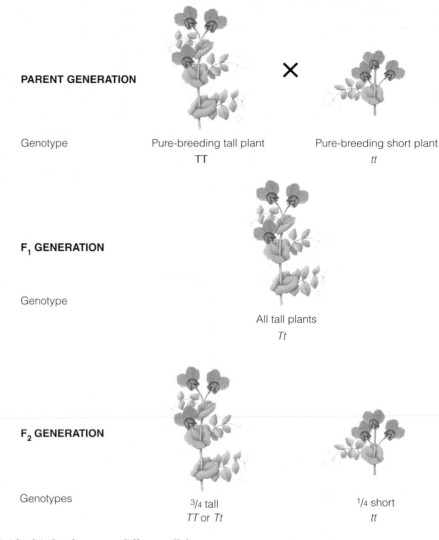

PARENT GENERATION

Genotype

Pure-breeding tall plant
TT

×

Pure-breeding short plant
tt

F₁ GENERATION

Genotype

All tall plants
Tt

F₂ GENERATION

Genotypes

3/4 tall
TT or Tt

1/4 short
tt

FIGURE **4-3**
Results of crosses when only one trait at a time is considered.

dominant   Describes a trait governed by an allele that's expressed in the presence of another allele (i.e., in heterozygotes). Dominant alleles prevent the expression of recessive alleles in heterozygotes. (This is the definition of *complete* dominance.)

homozygous   Having the same allele at the same locus on both members of a pair of chromosomes.

heterozygous   Having different alleles at the same locus on members of a pair of chromosomes.

genotype   The genetic makeup of an individual. Genotype can refer to an organism's entire genetic makeup or to the alleles at a particular locus.

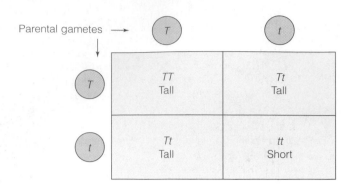

Parental gametes →

	T	*t*
T	*TT* Tall	*Tt* Tall
t	*Tt* Tall	*tt* Short

FIGURE **4-4**

Punnett square representing possible genotypes and their proportions in the F$_2$ generation. The circles across the top and at the left of the Punnett square represent the gametes of the F$_1$ parents. The four squares illustrate that ¼ of the F$_2$ plants can be expected to be homozygous tall (*TT*); another half can also be expected to be tall but will be heterozygous (*Tt*); and the remaining ¼ can be expected to be short because they are homozygous for the recessive "short" allele (*tt*). Thus, ¾ can be expected to be tall and ¼ to be short."

phenotype   The observable or detectable physical characteristics of an organism; the detectable expressions of genotypes, frequently influenced by environmental factors.

phenotypic ratio   The proportion of one phenotype to other phenotypes in a group of organisms. For example, Mendel observed that there were approximately three tall plants for every short plant in the F$_2$ generation. This is expressed as a phenotypic ratio of 3:1.

Mendelian traits   Characteristics that are influenced by alleles at only one genetic locus. Examples include many blood types, such as ABO. Many genetic disorders such as sickle-cell anemia and Tay-Sachs disease are also Mendelian traits.

principle of independent assortment   The distribution of one pair of alleles into gametes does not influence the distribution of another pair. The genes controlling different traits are inherited independently of one another.

assort   To sort out or separate.

The Punnett square also illustrates proportions of the different **phenotypes** (physical manifestations of genes) that can be expected in the F$_2$ plants. By examining the Punnett square, you can see that ¼ of the F$_2$ plants are tall because they have the *TT* genotype. An additional half of the plants, which are heterozygous (*Tt*), will also be tall because *T* is dominant to *t* and will therefore be expressed in the phenotype. The remaining ¼ are homozygous recessive (*tt*), and they'll be short because no dominant allele is present. It's important to understand that, in general, the *only* way a recessive allele can be expressed is if it occurs with another recessive allele—that is, if the individual is homozygous recessive at the particular locus in question.

In conclusion, ¾ of the F$_2$ generation will express the dominant phenotype, and ¼ will show the recessive phenotype. This relationship is expressed as a **phenotypic ratio** of 3:1 and typifies all **Mendelian traits** (characteristics governed by only one genetic locus) when only two alleles are involved, and one of them is completely dominant to the other.

INDEPENDENT ASSORTMENT

Mendel also showed that traits aren't necessarily inherited together by demonstrating that plant height (stem length) and seed color are independent of each other (Fig. 4-5). That is, he observed that any tall pea plant had a 50-50 chance of producing either yellow or green seeds (peas). This relationship is called the **principle of independent assortment**, which states that the "units" (genes) that control plant height and seed color **assort** independently of one another during gamete formation. Today we know this happens because the genes that control plant height and seed color are located on different, non-partner chromosomes; and, because of random assortment (see p. 54), those non-partner chromosomes don't necessarily end up together in the same newly forming cells.

Mendel made this discovery by making crosses between plants that differed in the expression of two traits (such as height and seed color). But if he had used just *any* two traits, his results would have been very different because genes that are located on the *same* chromosome aren't independent of each other and, unless they're separated during recombination, they stay together during meiosis. So, the traits they influence don't conform to Mendel's expectations of independent assortment. Even though Mendel didn't know about chromosomes, he was certainly aware that, while all traits weren't independent of one another, many were; and since independence was what he wanted to emphasize, he reported only on those characteristics that did in fact illustrate independent assortment.

In 1866, Mendel's results were published; but the methodology and statistical nature of the research were beyond the thinking of the time, and their significance was overlooked and unappreciated. By the end of the nineteenth century, however, several investigators had made important contributions to the understanding of chromosomes and cell division. These discoveries paved the way for the acceptance of Mendel's work by 1900, when three different groups of scientists, conducting similar breeding experiments, came across his paper. Regrettably, Mendel had died 16 years earlier and never saw his work vindicated.

Mendelian Inheritance in Humans

Mendelian traits, also called *discrete traits* or *traits of simple inheritance*, are characteristics controlled by alleles at only one genetic locus (or, in some cases, two or more very closely linked loci). The most comprehensive listing of Mendelian traits in humans is V. A. McKusick's (1998) *Mendelian Inheritance in Man*, first published in 1965 and now in its twelfth edition. This volume, as well as its continuously updated Internet version, *Online Mendelian Inheritance in Man* (www.ncbi.nlm.nih.gov/omim/), currently lists over 17,000 human characteristics that are inherited according to Mendelian principles.

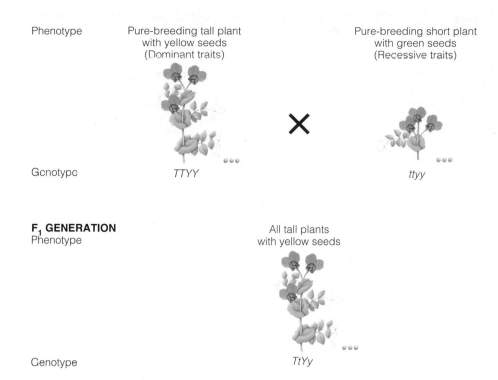

Phenotype

Pure-breeding tall plant
with yellow seeds
(Dominant traits)

X

Pure-breeding short plant
with green seeds
(Recessive traits)

Genotype   *TTYY*   *ttyy*

FIGURE **4-5**

Results of crosses when two traits are considered simultaneously. Stem length and seed color are independent of each other. Also shown are the genotypes associated with each phenotype. Notice that the ratio of tall plants to short plants is ¾ to ¼, or 3:1, the same as in Figure 4-3. The phenotypic ratios in the F₂ generation are 9:3:3:1.

F₁ GENERATION
Phenotype

All tall plants
with yellow seeds

Genotype   *TtYy*

F₂ GENERATION
Phenotype

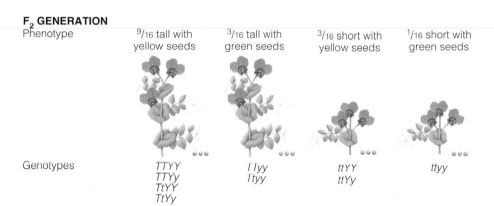

| ⁹/₁₆ tall with yellow seeds | ³/₁₆ tall with green seeds | ³/₁₆ short with yellow seeds | ¹/₁₆ short with green seeds |

Genotypes

TTYY	*Ttyy*	*ttYY*	*ttyy*
TTYy	*Ttyy*	*ttYy*	
TtYY			
TtYy			

Although some Mendelian characteristics have readily visible phenotypic expressions (for example, polydactyly), most don't. Most Mendelian traits are biochemical in nature, and many genetic disorders result from harmful alleles inherited in Mendelian fashion. So, if it seems like textbooks overly emphasize genetic disease when they discuss Mendelian traits, it's because many of the known Mendelian characteristics are the results of harmful alleles.

Some genetic disorders are inherited as dominant traits (see Table 4-1). This means that if a person inherits only one copy of a harmful, dominant allele, the condition it causes will be present, regardless of the existence of a different, recessive allele on the partner chromosome.

Recessive conditions are commonly associated with the lack of a substance, usually an enzyme (see Table 4-1). For a person actually to have a recessive disorder, he or she must have *two* copies of the recessive allele that causes it. Heterozygotes who have only one copy of a harmful recessive allele are unaffected, but they're frequently called *carriers* because they can pass the allele to their children. (Remember, half their gametes will carry the recessive allele.) If their mate is also a carrier, it's possible for them to have a child who will be homozygous for the allele, and that child will be affected. In fact, in a mating between two carriers, the risk of having an affected child is 25 percent (look back to Fig. 4-4).

TABLE 4-1   Some Mendelian Traits in Humans

Dominant Traits		Recessive Traits	
Condition	**Manifestations**	**Condition**	**Manifestations**
Achondroplasia	Dwarfism due to growth defects involving the long bones of the arms and legs; trunk and head size usually normal.	Cystic fibrosis	Among the most common genetic (Mendelian) disorders among European Americans; abnormal secretions of the exocrine glands, with pronounced involvement of the pancreas; most patients develop obstructive lung disease. Until the recent development of new treatments, only about half of all patients survived to early adulthood.
Brachydactyly	Shortened fingers and toes.		
Familial hyper-cholesterolemia	Elevated cholesterol levels and cholesterol plaque deposition; a leading cause of heart disease, with death frequently occurring by middle age.		
Neurofibromatosis	Symptoms range from the appearance of abnormal skin pigmentation to large tumors resulting in gross deformities; can, in extreme cases, lead to paralysis, blindness, and death.	Tay-Sachs disease	Most common among Ashkenazi Jews; degeneration of the nervous system beginning at about 6 months of age; lethal by age 2 or 3 years.
		Phenylketonuria (PKU)	Inability to metabolize the amino acid phenylalanine; results in mental retardation if left untreated during childhood; treatment involves strict dietary management and some supplementation.
Marfan syndrome	The eyes and cardiovascular and skeletal systems are affected; symptoms include greater than average height, long arms and legs, eye problems, and enlargement of the aorta; death due to rupture of the aorta is common. (Abraham Lincoln may have had Marfan syndrome.)	Albinism	Inability to produce normal amounts of the pigment melanin; results in very fair, untannable skin, light blond hair, and light eyes; may also be associated with vision problems. (There is more than one form of albinism.)
Huntington disease	Progressive degeneration of the nervous system accompanied by dementia and seizures; age of onset variable but commonly between 30 and 40 years.	Sickle-cell anemia	Abnormal form of hemoglobin (Hb_S) that results in collapsed red blood cells, blockage of capillaries, reduced blood flow to organs, and, without treatment, death.
Camptodactyly	Malformation of the hands whereby the fingers, usually the little finger, is permanently contracted.	Thalassemia	A group of disorders characterized by reduced or absent alpha or beta chains in the hemoglobin molecule; results in severe anemia and, in some forms, death.
Hypodontia of upper lateral incisors	Upper lateral incisors are absent or only partially formed (peg-shaped). Pegged incisors are a partial expression of the allele.	Absence of permanent dentition	Failure of the permanent dentition to erupt. The primary dentition is not affected.
Cleft chin	Dimple or depression in the middle of the chin; less prominent in females than males.		
PTC tasting	The ability to taste the bitter substance phenylthiocarbamide (PTC). Tasting thresholds vary, suggesting that alleles at another locus may also exert an influence.		

The blood groups, like the ABO system, provide some of the best examples of Mendelian traits in humans. The ABO system is governed by three alleles, *A*, *B*, and *O*, found at the ABO locus on the ninth chromosome. These alleles determine which ABO blood type an individual has by coding for the production of molecules called **antigens** on the surface of red blood cells. If only antigen A is present, the blood type (phenotype) is A; if only B is present, the blood type is B; if both are present, the blood type is AB; and when neither is present, the blood type is O.

Dominance and recessiveness are clearly illustrated by the ABO system. The *O* allele is recessive to both *A* and *B*, so if a person has type O blood, he or she must be homozygous for (have two copies of) the *O* allele. But, since both *A* and *B* are dominant to *O*, an individual with blood type A can actually have one of two genotypes: *AA* or *AO*. The same is true of type B, which results from the genotypes *BB* and *BO* (Table 4-2). Type AB presents a slightly different situation and is an example of **codominance**.

Codominance is seen when a person has two different alleles but, instead of one having the ability to mask the expression of the other, the products of *both* alleles are expressed in the phenotype. So, when both *A* and *B* alleles are present, both A and B antigens can be detected on the surface of red blood cells.

MISCONCEPTIONS ABOUT DOMINANCE AND RECESSIVENESS

Traditional methods of teaching genetics have led to some misunderstanding of dominance and recessiveness. For example, some high school biology textbooks still teach that eye color is a Mendelian characteristic and that brown eyes are dominant to blue eyes. Actually, eye color isn't a Mendelian trait at all. Rather, it's influenced by alleles that occur not at just one locus, but at two or perhaps three. Another common claim found in many textbooks is that the ability to curl the tongue lengthwise (called tongue rolling) is a dominant trait, but it isn't. In fact, it's not a Mendelian trait. But, because of this type of misinformation, most people have the impression that dominance and recessiveness are all-or-nothing situations. This misconception especially pertains to recessive alleles. The general view is that when these alleles occur in heterozygotes (that is, carriers), they have absolutely no effect on the phenotype—that is, they're *completely* inactivated by the presence of another (dominant) allele. Certainly, this is how it appeared to Gregor Mendel and, until the last three decades or so, to most geneticists.

Still, various biochemical techniques available today show that many recessive alleles *do* influence the phenotype, although their effects can't usually be detected by simple observation. In fact, many recessive alleles only reduce the amount of whatever product they influence; they don't always eliminate it entirely. Indeed, it's clear that our *perception* of recessive alleles greatly depends on whether we examine them at the directly observable phenotypic level or the biochemical level.

Consider Tay-Sachs disease, a lethal condition resulting from the inability to produce an enzyme called hexosaminidase A (see Table 4-1). This inability, seen in people who are homozygous for a recessive allele (*ts*) on chromosome 15, invariably results in death by early childhood. Carriers don't have the disease; and practically speaking, they're unaffected. But Tay-Sachs carriers, although functionally normal, actually have only about 40 to 60 percent of the amount of the enzyme seen in people with normal amounts of the enzyme. This fact

TABLE 4-2	ABO Genotypes and Associated Phenotypes	
Genotypes	**Antigens on Red Blood Cells**	**ABO Blood Type (Phenotype)**
AA, AO	A	A
BB, BO	B	B
AB	A and B	AB
OO	None	O

antigens   Large molecules found on the surface of cells. Several different loci govern various antigens on red and white blood cells. (Foreign antigens provoke an immune response.)

codominance   The expression of two alleles in heterozygotes. In this situation, neither allele is dominant or recessive so they both influence the phenotype.

has led to the development of voluntary tests to screen carriers in populations at risk for Tay-Sachs disease.

There are also several misconceptions about dominant alleles. Most people think of dominant alleles as somehow stronger or even better. There's also the notion that dominant alleles are more common in populations because natural selection favors them. These misconceptions undoubtedly stem partly from the label "dominant" and its connotations of power and control. But in genetic usage, those connotations are misleading. Just think about it. If dominant alleles were always more common, then most people would have conditions such as achondroplasia and Marfan syndrome (see Table 4-1).

As you can see, the relationships between recessive and dominant alleles are more complicated than they first appear to be. Previously held views of dominance and recessiveness were guided by available technologies. But, as genetic technologies continue to change, new theories will emerge, and our perceptions will undoubtedly be further altered. In fact, it's possible that one day the concepts of dominance and recessiveness, as traditionally taught, will be obsolete.

PATTERNS OF INHERITANCE

It's obviously important to be able to establish the pattern of inheritance of genetic traits, especially those that cause serious disease. Also, in families with a history of inherited disorders, it's important to determine an individual's risk of inheriting harmful alleles or expressing symptoms. The principal technique traditionally used to assess risk of genetic disease has been the construction of a **pedigree chart**, or a diagram of matings and offspring in a family over the span of a few generations.

Pedigree analysis helps researchers determine if a trait is Mendelian. It also helps them establish the mode of inheritance. By ascertaining whether the locus that influences a particular trait is located on an autosome or sex chromosome and whether it's dominant or recessive, researchers have identified six different modes of Mendelian inheritance in humans: *autosomal dominant, autosomal recessive, X-linked recessive, X-linked dominant, Y-linked,* and *mitochondrial.* We'll discuss the first three of these in some detail.

Standardized symbols are used in pedigree charts. Squares and circles represent males and females, respectively. Horizontal lines connecting individuals indicate matings, and offspring are connected to horizontal mating lines by vertical lines. Siblings are joined by a horizontal line, connected to a vertical line, that descends from the parents (Fig. 4-6).

Autosomal Dominant Traits   As the term implies, autosomal dominant traits are governed by dominant alleles located on autosomes (that is, any chromosome except X or Y). One example of an autosomal dominant trait is brachydactyly, a condition characterized by malformed hands and shortened fingers (see Table 4-1).

Because brachydactyly is caused by a dominant allele, anyone who inherits just one copy of it will express the trait. (In this discussion, we'll use the symbol *B* to refer to the dominant allele that causes the condition and *b* for the recessive, normal allele.) Since the allele is rare, virtually everyone who has brachydactyly is a heterozygote (*Bb*). Unaffected individuals (that is, almost everybody) are homozygous recessive (*bb*).

Figure 4-7 is a partial pedigree for brachydactyly. It's apparent from this pedigree that all affected members have at least one affected parent, so the abnormality doesn't skip gen-

Parents

Offspring
(siblings)

FIGURE **4-6**
Typical symbols used in pedigree charts.

pedigree chart   A diagram showing family relationships; it's used to trace the hereditary pattern of particular genetic (usually Mendelian) traits.

FIGURE **4-7**
Inheritance of an autosomal dominant trait: a human pedigree for brachydactyly. How can individuals 5, 11, 14, 15, and 17 be unaffected? What is the genotype of all affected individuals?

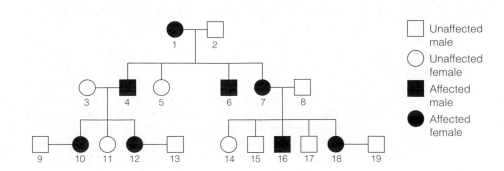

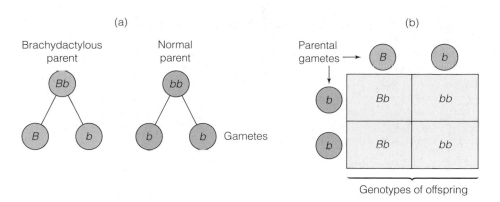

FIGURE 4-8
The pattern of inheritance of autosomal dominant traits is the direct result of the distribution of chromosomes, and the alleles they carry, into gametes during meiosis. (a) A diagram of possible gametes produced by two parents, one with brachydactyly and another with normal hands and fingers. The brachydactylous individual can produce two types of gametes: half with the dominant allele (*B*) and half with the recessive allele (*b*). All gametes produced by the normal parent will carry the recessive allele. (b) A Punnett square depicting the possible genotypes in the offspring of one parent with brachydactyly (*Bb*) and one with normal hands and fingers (*bb*). Statistically, we would expect half the offspring to have the *Bb* genotype and thus brachydactyly. The other half would be homozygous recessive (*bb*) and would be normal.

erations. This pattern is true of all autosomal dominant traits. Another characteristic of autosomal dominant traits is that there is no sex bias, and males and females are more or less equally affected.

One other fact illustrated by Figure 4-7 is that approximately half the offspring of affected parents are also affected. This proportion is what we would predict for an autosomal dominant trait where only one parent is affected, because half of that parent's gametes will have the dominant but harmful allele (Fig. 4-8).

Autosomal Recessive Traits   Autosomal recessive traits are also influenced by loci on autosomes but show a different pattern of inheritance. A good example is shown in Figure 4-9, a pedigree for albinism. Albinism is a metabolic disorder caused by an autosomal recessive allele that prevents the production of a pigment called melanin (see Chapter 16). People who inherit the most common variety of albinism have unusually light hair, skin, and eyes (Fig. 4-10). The frequency of this particular form of albinism varies widely among populations, with a prevalence of about 1 in 37,000 people of European ancestry. But approximately 1 in 200 Hopi Indians is affected.

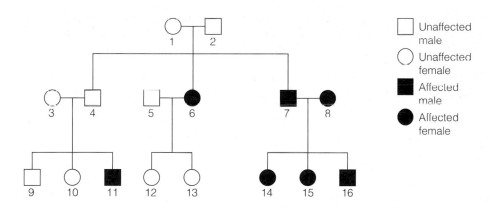

FIGURE 4-9
Partial pedigree for albinism, an autosomal recessive trait. Why are some of the offspring of affected individuals unaffected? Individuals 6 and 7, children of unaffected parents, are affected. Why? Four individuals are *definitely* unaffected carriers. Which ones are they?

Pedigrees for autosomal recessive traits show obvious differences from those for autosomal dominant characteristics. For one thing, an affected offspring can be produced by two phenotypically normal parents. In fact, most people who express recessive conditions have unaffected parents. In addition, the proportion of affected offspring from most matings is less than half. But when both parents have the trait, all the offspring will be affected. As in the pattern for autosomal dominant traits, males and females are equally affected.

The Mendelian principle of segregation explains the pattern of inheritance of autosomal recessive traits. In fact, this pattern is the very one Mendel first described in his pea experiments (look back to Fig. 4-3). Unaffected parents who produce an albino child *must both be carriers*, and their child is homozygous for the recessive allele that causes the abnormality. The Punnett square in Figure 4-11 shows how such a mating produces both unaffected and affected offspring in predictable proportions—the typical phenotypic ratio of 3:1.

FIGURE 4-10
An African albino. This young man has a greatly increased likelihood of developing skin cancer.

Parental genotypes $Aa \times Aa$

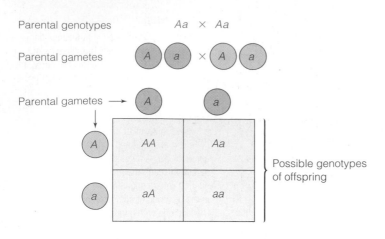

Possible genotypes
of offspring

FIGURE 4-11

A cross between two phenotypically normal parents, both of them carriers of the albinism allele. From a mating such as this between two carriers, we would expect the following possible proportions of genotypes and phenotypes in the offspring: homozygous dominants (*AA*) with normal phenotype, 25 percent; heterozygotes, or carriers (*Aa*) with normal phenotype, 50 percent; and homozygous recessives (*aa*) with albinism, 25 percent. This yields the phenotypic ratio of 3 normal to 1 albino.

SEX-LINKED TRAITS

Sex-linked traits are controlled by genes located on the X and Y chromosomes. Almost all of the more than 450 sex-linked traits listed in OMIM (see p. 68) are influenced by genes on the X chromosome (Table 4-3). Most of the coding sequences (that is, those segments that actually specify a protein) on the Y chromosome are involved in determining maleness and testis function. Although some Y-linked genes are expressed in areas other than the testes (Skaletsky et al., 2003), their functions aren't well known. For this reason, our discussion concerns only the X chromosome.

Hemophilia, one of the best known of the X-linked traits, is caused by a recessive allele on the X chromosome. This allele prevents the formation of a clotting factor in the blood, and affected individuals suffer bleeding episodes and may actually bleed to death from incidents that most of us would consider trivial.

The most famous pedigree illustrating this condition is that of Queen Victoria (1820–1901) of England and her descendants (Fig. 4-12). The most striking feature shown by this pattern of inheritance is that almost all affected people are males, because males have only one X chromosome and therefore, only one copy of X-linked genes. This means that *any* allele, even a recessive one, located on their X chromosome will be expressed, because there's no possibility of a dominant allele on a partner chromosome to block it.

Females, on the other hand, show the same pattern of expression of X-linked traits as for autosomal traits, because they have two X chromosomes. That is, just as with any other pair of chromosomes, the only way an X linked recessive allele can be expressed in a female is if she is homozygous for it. Females who have one copy of the hemophilia allele are carriers, however, and although they may have some tendency toward bleeding, they aren't severely affected.

TABLE 4-3	Some Mendelian Disorders Inherited as X-Linked Recessive Traits in Humans
Condition	**Manifestations**
G-6-PD (glucose-6-phosphate dehydrogenase) deficiency	Lack of an enzyme (G-6-PD) in red blood cells; produces severe, sometimes fatal anemia in the presence of certain foods (e.g., fava beans) and/or drugs (e.g., the antimalarial drug primaquin).
Muscular dystrophy	One form; other forms can be inherited as autosomal recessives; progressive weakness and atrophy of muscles beginning in early childhood; continues to progress throughout life; some female carriers may develop heart problems.
Red-green color blindness	Actually, there are two separate forms, one involving the perception of red and the other affecting only the perception of green. About 8 percent of European males have an impaired ability to distinguish green.
Lesch-Nyhan disease	Impaired motor development noticeable by 5 months; progressive motor impairment, diminished kidney function, self-mutilation, and early death.
Hemophilia	There are three forms; two (hemophilia A and B) are X-linked. In hemophilia A, a clotting factor is missing; hemophilia B is caused by a defective clotting factor. Both produce abnormal internal and external bleeding from minor injuries; severe pain is a frequent accompaniment; without treatment, death usually occurs before adulthood.
Ichthyosis	There are several forms; one is X-linked. A skin condition due to lack of an enzyme; characterized by scaly, brown lesions on the extremities and trunk. In the past, people with this condition were sometimes exhibited in circuses and sideshows as "the alligator man."

FIGURE 4-12
Pedigree for Queen Vic
descendants, showing inher
philia, an X-linked recessive trait

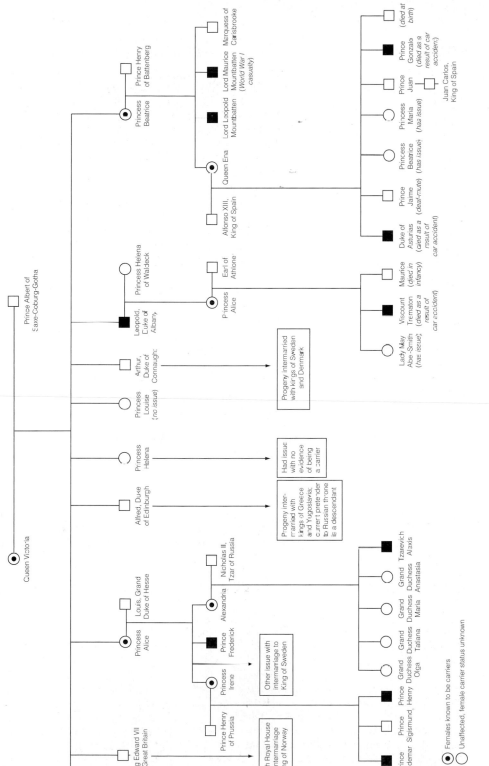

Non-Mendelian Inheritance

POLYGENIC INHERITANCE

Mendelian traits are described as *discrete,* or *discontinuous,* because their phenotypic expressions don't overlap; instead, they fall into clearly defined categories (Fig. 4-13a). For example, Mendel's pea plants were either short or tall, but none was intermediate in height. In the ABO system, the four phenotypes are completely distinct from one another; that is, there's no intermediate form between type A and type B to represent a gradation between the two. In other words, Mendelian traits don't show *continuous* variation.

However, many traits do have a wide range of phenotypic expressions that form a graded series. These are called **polygenic**, or *continuous,* traits (Fig. 4-13b and c). While Mendelian traits are governed by only one genetic locus, polygenic characteristics are influenced by alleles at two or more loci, and each locus contributes in some way to the pheno-

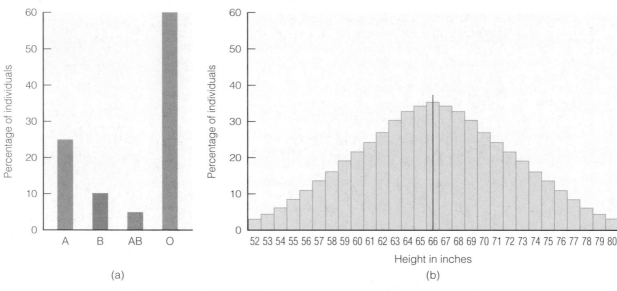

(a)   (b)

FIGURE **4-13**

(a) This bar chart shows the discontinuous distribution of a Mendelian trait (ABO blood type) in a hypothetical population. Expression of the trait is described in terms of frequencies.

(b) This histogram represents the continuous expression of a polygenic trait (height) in a large group of people. Notice that the percentage of extremely short or tall individuals is low; most people are closer to the mean, or average, height, represented by the vertical line at the center of the distribution.

(c) A group of male students arranged according to height. The most common height is 70 inches, which is the mean, or average, for this group.

polygenic   Referring to traits that are influenced by genes at two or more loci. Stature, skin color, eye color, and hair color are examples of polygenic traits. Many, but not all (eye color, for example), polygenic traits are influenced by environmental factors such as nutrition.

(c)

type. For example, one of the most frequently cited examples of polygenic inheritance in humans is skin color, and the single most important factor influencing it is the amount of the pigment melanin that is present.

Melanin production is believed to be influenced by between 3 and 6 genetic loci, with each locus having at least 2 alleles, neither of which is dominant. Since there are perhaps 6 loci and at least 12 alleles, these alleles can combine in many ways in individuals. If a person inherits 11 alleles coding for maximum pigmentation and only 1 for reduced melanin production, skin color will be very dark. A person who inherits a higher proportion of reduced pigmentation alleles will have lighter skin color. This is because in this system, as in some other polygenic systems, there is an *additive effect*—meaning that each allele that codes for melanin production makes a contribution to increased melanization (although for some characteristics, the contributions of the alleles aren't all equal). Likewise, each allele that codes for reduced melanin production contributes to less pigmentation. So the effect of multiple alleles at several loci, each making a contribution to individual phenotypes, is to produce continuous variation from very dark to very fair skin within the species. (Skin color is also discussed in Chapter 16.)

Polygenic traits actually account for most of the readily observable phenotypic variation in humans, and they've traditionally served as a basis for racial classification (see Chapter 15). Along with skin color, polygenic inheritance in humans is seen in hair color, weight, stature, eye color (Fig. 4-14), shape of face, shape of nose, and fingerprint pattern. Because they exhibit continuous variation, most polygenic traits can be measured on a scale composed of equal increments. For example, height (stature) can be measured in feet and inches (or meters and centimeters). If height in a large number of individuals were measured, the distribution of measurements would continue, uninterrupted, from the shortest extreme to the tallest. That's what is meant by *continuous traits*.

Because polygenic traits can usually be measured, biologists, geneticists, and physical anthropologists treat them statistically. Using simple summary statistics, such as the *mean* (average) or *standard deviation* (a measure of variation within a group), enables researchers to develop basic descriptions of and comparisons between populations. For example, a physical anthropologist might be interested in average height in two different populations and whether differences between the two are significant, and if so, why. (Incidentally, you should also note that *all* physical traits measured and statistically treated in fossils are polygenic.)

These particular statistical analyses aren't possible with Mendelian traits, simply because those traits can't be measured in the same way. But just because Mendelian traits aren't amenable to the same types of statistical tests that polygenic traits are doesn't mean that they provide less information about genetic processes. Mendelian characteristics can be described in terms of frequency within populations, and this makes it possible to compare groups for differences in prevalence. What's more, these traits can be analyzed for mode of inheritance (dominant or recessive) from pedigree data. Finally, for many Mendelian traits, the approximate or exact positions of genetic loci are known, and this makes it possible to examine the mechanisms and patterns of inheritance at these loci. This type of study isn't currently possible for polygenic traits; because they're influenced by several genes, they can't yet be traced to specific loci.

PLEIOTROPY

While polygenic traits are governed by the actions of several genes, **pleiotropy** is a situation where a single gene influences more than one phenotypic expression. Although this might seem unusual, pleiotropic effects are probably the rule rather than the exception.

The autosomal recessive disorder phenylketonuria (PKU) provides one example of pleiotropy (see Table 4-1). Individuals who are homozygous for the PKU allele don't produce phenylketonurase, the enzyme involved in the initial conversion of the amino acid phenylalanine to another amino acid, *tyrosine*. Because of this block in the metabolic pathway, phenylalanine breaks down into substances that accumulate in the central nervous system; and without dietary management, these substances lead to mental deficiencies and several other consequences. Because tyrosine is ultimately converted into several substances, including the pigment melanin, numerous other systems can also be affected. Consequently, another manifestation of PKU, owing to a diminished ability to produce melanin, is that affected people usually have blue eyes, fair skin, and light hair.

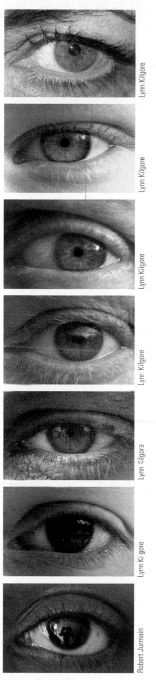

FIGURE 4-14
Examples of the continuous variation seen in human eye color.

pleiotropy A situation that occurs when the action of a single gene influences several seemingly unrelated phenotypic effects.

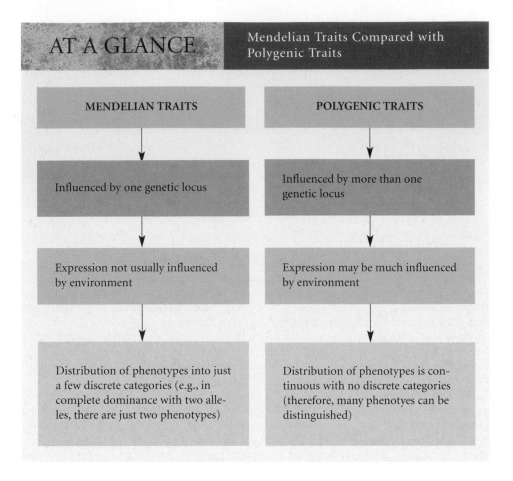

There are many examples of pleiotropic genes, including the allele that causes sickle-cell anemia (see p. 48). It isn't necessary to include a detailed discussion here, but it's clear that gene action may exert an influence over a number of seemingly unrelated phenotypic expressions.

MITOCHONDRIAL INHERITANCE

There's yet another component of inheritance that has gained much attention in recent years, and it involves the organelles called *mitochondria* (see p. 38). All cells contain several hundred of these oval-shaped structures, which convert energy (derived from the breakdown of nutrients) into a form that can be used by the cell.

Each mitochondrion contains several copies of a ring-shaped DNA molecule, or chromosome. While *mitochondrial DNA (mtDNA)* is distinct from the DNA found within cell nuclei, its molecular structure and functions are the same. The entire molecule has been sequenced and is known to contain around 40 genes that direct the conversion of energy within the cell.

Like nuclear DNA, mtDNA is subject to mutations, and some mutations can lead to disorders that result from impaired energy conversion. It's important to know that animals of both sexes inherit *all* their mtDNA, and thus all mitochondrial traits, from their mothers. Since mtDNA is inherited from only one parent, meiosis and recombination don't occur. This means that all the variation in mtDNA among individuals is caused by mutation, and therefore mtDNA is extremely useful for studying genetic change over time. So far, geneticists have used rates of mutation in mtDNA to investigate evolutionary relationships between species, to trace ancestral relationships within the human lineage, and to study genetic variability among individuals and/or populations. These techniques are still being refined, and it's clear that we have a lot to learn from mtDNA.

Genetic and Environmental Factors

From what we've said so far, you may have the impression that phenotypes are totally determined by genotypes; but that's not true. (Here the terms *genotype* and *phenotype* are used in a broader sense to refer to an individual's *entire* genetic makeup and *all* observable or detectable characteristics.) The genotype sets limits and potentials for development, but it also interacts with the environment; and this genetic-environmental interaction influences many aspects of the phenotype.

Many polygenic traits are quite obviously influenced by environmental conditions. Adult stature is a good example of a trait that's influenced by both genes and the environment because, even though maximum height is genetically determined, nutrition during childhood is also very important (see p. 426). One very well-known study showed that children of Japanese immigrants to Hawaii were, on average, 3 to 4 inches taller than their parents. This dramatic difference, seen in one generation, was attributed to environmental alteration—specifically to a change in diet (Froelich, 1970). For most traits, however, it's not possible to identify the *specific* environmental components that influence the phenotype.

Other important environmental factors include exposure to sunlight, altitude, and temperature—and unfortunately, increasing levels of exposure to toxic waste and airborne pollutants. These and many more factors contribute in complex ways to the continuous phenotypic variation seen in characteristics governed by multiple loci.

Mendelian traits are less likely to be influenced by environmental factors. For example, ABO blood type is determined at fertilization and remains fixed throughout the individual's lifetime, regardless of diet, exposure to ultraviolet radiation, temperature, and so forth.

While Mendelian and polygenic inheritance produce different kinds of phenotypic variation, it's important to understand that even for polygenic characteristics, Mendelian principles still apply at individual loci. In other words, if a trait is influenced by 7 loci, each one of those loci may have 2 or more alleles, with some perhaps being dominant to others or with the alleles being codominant. It's the combined action of the alleles at all seven loci, interacting with the environment, that results in observable phenotypic expression.

Modern Evolutionary Theory

By the beginning of the twentieth century, the foundations for evolutionary theory had already been developed. Darwin and Wallace had articulated the key principle of natural selection 40 years earlier, and the rediscovery of Mendelian genetics in 1900 contributed the other major component, namely, a mechanism for inheritance. We might expect that these two basic contributions would have been combined into a consistent theory of evolution, but they weren't. For the first 30 years of the twentieth century, rival explanations emphasized mutation *or* natural selection as the prime mover of evolutionary change. What was needed was a merger or synthesis of both views (not an either-or situation), but this didn't happen until the mid-1930s (see "A Closer Look," next page).

THE MODERN SYNTHESIS

Biologists working on mathematical models of evolutionary change in the late 1920s and early 1930s realized that mutation and natural selection weren't opposing processes and that both actually contributed to biological evolution. The two major foundations of the biological sciences had thus been brought together in what is called the Modern Synthesis. From such a "modern" (that is, the middle of the twentieth century onward) perspective, we define evolution as a two-stage process:

1. The production and redistribution of **variation** (inherited differences among individuals)

2. *Natural selection* acting on this variation, whereby inherited differences, or variation, among individuals differentially affect their ability to successfully reproduce.

variation (genetic)   Inherited differences among individuals; the basis of all evolutionary change.

A CLOSER LOOK   Development of Modern Evolutionary Theory

Our understanding of the evolutionary process came about through contributions of biologists in the United States, Great Britain, and Russia.

While "mutationists" were arguing with "selectionists" about the single primary mechanism in evolution, several population geneticists began to realize that small genetic changes and natural selection were both necessary ingredients in the evolutionary formula.

These population geneticists were largely concerned with mathematical reconstructions of evolution—in particular, they were measuring those small accumulations of genetic changes in populations over just a few generations. Central figures in these early theoretical developments included Ronald Fisher and J.B.S. Haldane in Great Britain, Sewall Wright in the United States, and Sergei Chetverikov in Russia.

While the work of these scientists often produced brilliant insights (see particularly Fisher's *The Genetical Theory of Natural Selection*, 1930), their conclusions were largely unknown to most evolutionary biologists, especially in North America. It remained, therefore, for someone to transcend these two worlds: the mathematical jargon of the population geneticists and the general constructs of theoretical evolutionary biologists. The scientist who performed this task (and who is credited as the first true synthesizer) was Theodosius Dobzhansky (Fig. 1). In his *Genetics and the Origin of Species* (1937), Dobzhansky skillfully integrated the mathematics of population genetics with overall evolutionary theory. His insights then became the basis for a period of tremendous activity in evolutionary thinking that directly led to major contributions by George Gaylord Simpson (who brought paleontology into the synthesis), Ernst Mayr, and others. In fact, the Modern Synthesis produced by these scientists stood basically unchallenged for an entire generation as *the* explanation of the evolutionary process. In recent years, however, some aspects of this theory have been brought under serious question (see Chapter 5).

FIGURE **1**
Theodosius Dobzhansky

A Current Definition of Evolution

As we discussed in Chapter 2, Charles Darwin saw evolution as the gradual unfolding of new varieties of life from previous forms. This is certainly one result of the evolutionary process. But these long-term effects can come about only through the accumulation of many small genetic changes occurring over the generations. Today, we can demonstrate how evolution works by examining some of these small genetic changes that occur between generations. From this modern genetic perspective, we define **evolution** as *a change in **allele frequency** from one generation to the next*.

Allele frequencies are indicators of the genetic makeup of a **population**, the members of which share a common **gene pool**. To show how allele frequencies change, we'll use a simplified example of an inherited trait, again the ABO blood groups (see p. 71). (*Note:* There are, in fact, several blood type systems, controlled by different loci that determine other properties of the red blood cells.)

Let's assume that the students in your anthropology class represent a population (an interbreeding group of individuals), and that we've identified the ABO blood type of each member. To be considered a population, individuals must choose mates more often from *within* the group than from outside it. Obviously, your class won't meet this requirement; but for our example, we'll overlook this point. The proportions of the *A*, *B*, and *O* alleles are the allele frequencies for this trait. For example, if 50 percent of all the ABO alleles in your class are *A*, 40 percent are *B*, and 10 percent are *O*, then the frequencies of these alleles are *A* = .50, *B* = .40, and *O* = .10.*

evolution   (modern genetic definition) A change in the frequency of alleles from one generation to the next.

allele frequency   In a population, the percentage of all the alleles at a locus accounted for by one specific allele.

population   Within a species, a community of individuals where mates are usually found.

gene pool   The total complement of genes shared by the reproductive members of a population.

---

*This is a simplified example. Because the ABO system is governed by three alleles, calculating allele frequencies is more complicated than for a two-allele system. In Chapter 15, we'll show how allele frequencies are calculated for a simple two-allele locus.

Since the frequencies for these alleles represent only proportions of a total, it's obvious that allele frequencies can refer only to groups or populations. Individuals don't have allele frequencies; they have either *A*, *B*, or *O* alleles in any combination of two (see p. 71). Individuals can't change alleles, either. From conception onward, a person's genetic composition is fixed. If you start out with blood type A, you'll always have type A. Individuals can't evolve over time; that's something only populations can do.

So, what happens when a population evolves? Assume that 25 years from now, we calculate the frequencies of the ABO alleles in the children of our classroom population and find the following: *A* = .30, *B* = .40, and *O* = .30. We can see that the frequencies, or relative proportions, have changed: *A* has decreased, *O* has increased, and *B* has remained the same. This simple and apparently minor change doesn't seem important; but still, it's an example of one kind of evolution. Over the short span of just a few generations, such changes in inherited traits may be only very small. But if they continue to happen, and particularly if they go in one direction (for example, the frequency of the *O* allele continues to increase) because of natural selection, they can produce new adaptations and even new species.

Whether we're talking about the short-term effects (as in our classroom population) from one generation to the next, which is sometimes called **microevolution**, or the long-term effects through time (speciation), also called **macroevolution**, the basic evolutionary mechanisms are similar. But, how do allele frequencies change, and what causes evolution? As we've already said, evolution is a two-stage process. Genetic variation must first be produced by mutation, and then it can be acted on by natural selection.

Factors That Produce and Redistribute Variation

MUTATION

You've already learned that change in the DNA molecule is one type of mutation and that many genes occur in two or more forms called alleles (*A*, *B*, or *O*, for example). If one allele changes to another—that is, if the gene itself is altered—a mutation has occurred. In fact, alleles are the results of mutations. Even the substitution of just one single DNA base for another, called a **point mutation**, can cause the allele to change. But, point mutations have to occur in sex cells if they're going to be important to the evolutionary process. This is because evolution occurs over time, so the mutation has to be passed from one generation to the next. In our classroom example, if a genetic change occurred in the sperm or egg of one of the students (*A* mutates to *B*, for example), the offspring's blood type will also be altered, causing a minute shift in allele frequencies of the next generation. In Chapter 3, we showed how a change in a single DNA base, a *point mutation*, could cause a change in hemoglobin structure (from normal to sickle-cell). Also in Chapter 3, we discussed how transposable elements and microsatellites can change the structure of a gene.

Actually, it would be rare to see evolution occurring by mutation alone, except in microorganisms. Mutation rates for any given trait are usually low, so we wouldn't really expect to see a mutation at the ABO locus in so small a population as your class. In larger populations, however, mutations might be observed (1 individual in 10,000, say); but by themselves, they'd have no effect on overall allele frequencies. When mutation is coupled with natural selection, however, evolutionary changes not only can occur, but they can occur more rapidly.

It's important to remember that mutation is the basic creative force in evolution because it's the *only* way to produce *new* genetic variation. Its key role in the production of variation represents the first stage of the evolutionary process.

GENE FLOW

The exchange of genes between populations is called **gene flow**. The term *migration* is frequently used instead; but strictly speaking, migration means "movement of people." In contrast, gene flow refers to the exchange of genes between groups, which can occur only if the migrants interbreed. Also, even if individuals move temporarily and mate in the new

microevolution   Small changes occurring within species, such as a change in allele frequencies.

macroevolution   Changes produced only after many generations, such as the appearance of a new species.

point mutation   A chemical change in a single base of a DNA sequence.

gene flow   Exchange of genes between populations

population (thus leaving a genetic contribution), they don't necessarily stay there. For example, the offspring of U.S. soldiers and Vietnamese women represent gene flow, even though the fathers returned to the United States after the Vietnam War.

In humans, social rules more than any other factor determine mating patterns, and cultural anthropologists can work closely with physical anthropologists to isolate and measure this aspect of evolutionary change. Population movements (particularly in the last 500 years) have reached enormous proportions, and few breeding isolates remain. But migration, on a smaller scale, has been a consistent feature of hominid evolution since the first dispersal of our genus, and gene flow between populations (even though sometimes limited) helps explain why, over the past million years, speciation has been rare. Of course, migration patterns are a manifestation of human cultural behavior, and this emphasizes once again the essential biocultural nature of human evolution.

An interesting example of how gene flow influences microevolutionary changes in modern human populations is seen in African Americans. African Americans are largely of West African descent, but there has also been considerable genetic admixture with European Americans. By measuring allele frequencies for specific genetic loci, we can estimate the amount of migration of European alleles into the African American gene pool. Data from northern and western U.S. cities (including New York, Detroit, and Oakland) have shown the migration rate (that is, the proportion of *non*-African genes in the African American gene pool) at 20 to 25 percent (Cummings, 2000). However, more restricted data from the southern United States (Charleston and rural Georgia) have suggested a lower degree of gene flow (4 to 11 percent).

It would be a misconception to think that gene flow can occur only through large-scale movements of entire groups. In fact, significant changes in allele frequencies can come about through long-term patterns of mate selection whereby members of a group obtain mates from one or more other groups. Especially, if mate exchange consistently occurs in one direction over a long period (for example, group A receives mates from group B but doesn't reciprocate) allele frequencies in group A may ultimately be altered.

Today, modern transportation plays a crucial role in determining the potential radius for finding mates. Throughout most of human history, humans found mates within a few miles of their home; but today it's not uncommon to marry someone from another continent. Of course, for most people, actual patterns are somewhat more restricted. For example, data from Ann Arbor, Michigan, indicate a mean marital distance (the average distance between birthplaces of partners) of about 160 miles. This isn't a huge distance, but it's still an area large enough to include a tremendous number of potential marriage partners.

GENETIC DRIFT

Genetic drift is the random factor in evolution, and it's a direct function of population size. *Drift occurs because the population is small.* If an allele is rare in a population comprised of, say, a few hundred individuals, then there's a chance it simply may not be passed on to offspring. In this type of situation, such an allele can eventually disappear altogether (Fig. 4-15). This may seem like a minor thing; but in effect, genetic variability in this population has been reduced.

Results of the particular kind of genetic drift called **founder effect** are seen in many modern human and nonhuman populations. Founder effect can occur when a small migrant band of "founders" leaves its parent group and forms a colony somewhere else. Over time, a new population will be established, and as long as mates are chosen only from within this population, all of its members will be descended from the founders. In effect, all the genes in the expanding group will have come from the few original colonists. In such a case, an allele that was rare in the founders' parent population but, just by chance, was carried by even one of the founders can eventually become common in that group's descendants. This is because a high proportion of members of later generations are all descended from that one founder (see Fig. 4-15).

Colonization isn't the only way founder effect can happen. Small founding groups may also consist of a few survivors of a large group that's been decimated by disaster (war, famine, disease, and so on). The founder population (the survivors) possesses only a sample of all the alleles that were present in the original group. By chance alone, some alleles

genetic drift   Evolutionary changes—that is, changes in allele frequencies—produced by random factors. Genetic drift is a result of small population size.

founder effect   A type of genetic drift in which allele frequencies are altered in small populations that are taken from, or are remnants of, larger populations.

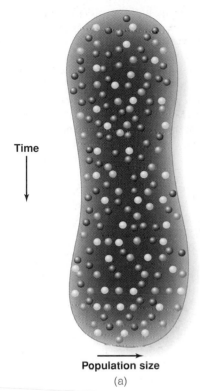

Time

A small population with considerable genetic variability. Note that the dark green and blue alleles are less common than the other alleles.

After just a few generations, the population is approximately the same size but genetic variation has been reduced. Both the dark green and blue alleles have been lost. Also, the red allele is less common and the frequency of the light green allele has increased.

Population size

(a)

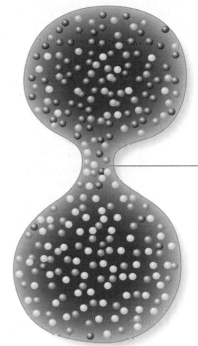

Original population with considerable genetic variation

A small group leaves to colonize a new area, or a bottleneck occurs, so that population size decreases and genetic variation is reduced.

Population size restored but the dark green and purple alleles have been lost. The frequencies of the red and yellow alleles have also changed.

Population size

(b)

FIGURE 4-15

Small populations are subject to genetic drift where rare alleles can be lost because, just by chance, they weren't passed to offspring. Also, although more common alleles may not be lost, their frequencies may change for the same reason. The first diagram (a) represents 6 alleles (different colored dots) that occur at one genetic locus in a small population. You can see that, in a fairly short period of time (3 or 4 generations), rare alleles can be lost and genetic diversity is consequently reduced. The second diagram (b) is an illustration of founder effect, a form of genetic drift, where diversity is lost because a large population is drastically reduced in size and it consequently passes through a genetic "bottleneck." Founder effect also happens when a small group leaves the larger group and "founds" a new population elsewhere. (In this case, the group of founders is represented by the bottleneck.) Those individuals that survive, or the founders, and the alleles they carry, represent only a sample of the variation that was present in the original population. And future generations, all descended from the survivors (founders), will therefore have less variability.

may be completely removed from the gene pool; other alleles may become "fixed" (that is, the only allele that exists) at a locus where originally there may have been two or more. Whatever the cause, the outcome is a reduction of genetic diversity, and the allele frequencies of succeeding generations may be substantially different from those of the original large population. The loss of genetic diversity in this type of situation is called a *genetic bottleneck*, and the effects can be extremely detrimental to a species.

There are many known examples (both human and nonhuman) of species or populations that have passed through genetic bottlenecks. Genetically, cheetahs (Fig. 4-16) are an extremely uniform species, and biologists believe that at some point in the past, these magnificent cats suffered a catastrophic decline in numbers. For reasons we don't know, but that are related to the species-wide loss of numerous alleles, male cheetahs produce a high percentage of defective sperm as compared to other cat species. Decreased reproductive potential, greatly reduced genetic diversity, and other factors (especially human hunting) have combined to jeopardize the continued existence of this species. Other species that have passed through genetic bottlenecks include California elephant seals, sea otters, and condors. Indeed, our own species is very uniform genetically, compared to chimpanzees, and it appears that all modern human populations are the descendants of a few small groups.

FIGURE 4-16

Cheetahs, like many other species, have passed through a genetic bottleneck. Consequently, as a species, they have little genetic variation.

Many examples of founder effect in human populations have been documented in small, usually isolated populations (such as island groups or small agricultural villages in New Guinea or South America). Even larger populations that are descended from fairly small groups of founders can show the effects of genetic drift many generations later. For example, French Canadians in Quebec, who currently number close to 6 million, are all descended from only about 8,500 founders who left France during the sixteenth and seventeenth centuries. Because the genes carried by the initial founders represented only a sample of the gene pool from which they were derived, strictly by chance, a number of alleles now occur in different frequencies from those of the current population of France. These differences include an increased prevalence of several harmful alleles (including those causing some of the diseases listed in Table 4-1), such as cystic fibrosis, a variety of Tay-Sachs, thalassemia, and PKU (Scriver, 2001).

One other example of genetic drift is provided by a fatal recessive condition called Amish microcephaly, in which a mutation results in abnormally small brains and heads in fetuses. The disorder is found only in the Old Order Amish community of Lancaster County, Pennsylvania, where it occurs in approximately 1 in 500 births (Kelley et al., 2002; Rosenberg et al., 2002). Genealogical research revealed that affected families have all been traced back nine generations to a single couple. One member of this couple carried the deleterious recessive allele that, because of customs promoting marriage within a small group, has greatly increased in frequency with very serious consequences. Indeed, much insight concerning the evolutionary factors that have acted in the past can be gained by understanding how such mechanisms continue to operate on human populations today. In small populations, drift plays a major evolutionary role because fairly sudden fluctuations in allele frequency can and do occur, solely because of small population size. Likewise, throughout a good deal of human evolution, at least the last 4–5 million years (my), hominids probably lived in small groups, and drift would have had significant impact.

While drift has contributed to evolutionary change in certain circumstances, the effects have been irregular and nondirectional. (Remember, drift is *random* in nature). Certainly, the pace of evolutionary change could have been accelerated if many small populations were isolated and thus subject to drift. By modifying the genetic makeup of such populations, drift can provide significantly greater opportunities for natural selection, the only truly directional force in evolution.

As we've seen, mutation, gene flow, and genetic drift can produce some evolutionary changes by themselves. These changes are usually *microevolutionary* ones, however; that is, they produce changes within species over the short term. To produce the kind of evolutionary changes that ultimately result in, for example, diversification of the first primates or appearance of the hominids, natural selection is necessary. But natural selection can't operate independently of the other evolutionary factors—mutation, gene flow, and genetic drift. All four factors (sometimes called the "four forces of evolution") work interactively.

Additional insight concerning the relative influences of the different evolutionary factors has emerged in recent studies of the early dispersal of modern *Homo sapiens* (discussed in Chapter 14). Evidence suggests that in the last 100,000 to 200,000 years, our species experienced a genetic bottleneck that considerably influenced the pattern of genetic variation seen in all human populations today. In this sense, modern humans can be seen as the fairly recent product of a form of genetic drift (founder effect) acting on a somewhat grand scale. Such evolutionary changes could be potentially significant over tens of thousands of years and could cause substantial genetic shifts within species.

RECOMBINATION

As we saw earlier in this chapter, in sexually reproducing species, both parents contribute genes to offspring, and during this process, maternal and paternal chromosomes exchange segments of DNA. By itself, recombination doesn't change allele frequencies (that is, it doesn't cause evolution). When paired chromosomes exchange DNA segments, however, genes sometimes find themselves in altered genetic environments (it's like they've moved to a new neighborhood). This fact can be important because the functions of some genes can be influenced simply by the alleles they're close to. Recombination thus not only changes the allelic composition of parts of chromosomes but also can affect how some genes act, and slight changes of gene function can become material for natural selection to act upon.

Natural Selection Acts on Variation

The evolutionary factors just discussed (mutation, gene flow, genetic drift, and recombination) interact to produce variation and to distribute genes within and between populations. But there's no long-term *direction* to any of these factors, and adaptation and evolution require that gene pools change in a specific direction. This means that some allele frequencies have to increase consistently, while others have to decrease, and natural selection is the factor that provides directional change in allele frequency relative to *specific environmental factors*. If the environment changes, then the selection pressures also change, and such a shift in allele frequencies is what we mean by *adaptation*. If there are long-term environmental changes in a consistent direction, then allele frequencies should also shift gradually over time. (The levels of organization in the evolutionary process are summarized in Table 4-4).

In Chapter 2, we discussed the general principles underlying natural selection and gave some nonhuman examples. Because biological anthropology is, of course, centrally concerned with human evolution, it's more relevant to show how natural selection operates in *human* populations. The best-documented example of natural selection in humans involves hemoglobin S, an altered form of hemoglobin that results from a point mutation in the gene that produces the hemoglobin beta chain (see p. 40). As you've already learned, if an individual inherits this allele (Hb^S) from both parents, he or she will suffer from sickle-cell anemia. Even with aggressive medical treatment, life expectancy in the United States today is less than 45 years for patients with sickle-cell anemia. Worldwide, sickle-cell anemia causes an estimated 100,000 deaths each year; in the United States, approximately 40,000 to 50,000 individuals, mostly of African descent, have this disease.

Hb^S is a mutation that occurs occasionally in all human populations, but the allele usually remains rare. In some populations, however, Hb^S is more common; this is especially true in western and central Africa, where its frequency approaches 20 percent. The frequency of the allele is also moderately high in parts of Greece and India (Fig. 4-17). Given the devastating effects of Hb^S in homozygotes, it seems strange that it's fairly common in these populations. One would think natural selection would have acted against it, but it hasn't. In fact, natural selection has actually increased its frequency, and the reason for this is malaria.

Malaria is a serious infectious disease caused by a single-celled, parasitic organism called a *Plasmodium*. This parasite is transmitted to humans by mosquitoes, and it kills an estimated 1 to 3 million people worldwide every year. Very briefly, after an infected mosquito bite, plasmodial parasites invade red blood cells, where they obtain the oxygen they need for reproduction (Fig. 4-18). The consequences of this infection to the human host include fever, chills, headache, nausea, vomiting, and frequently death. In parts of western and central Africa, where malaria is always present, as many as 50 to 75 percent of 2- to 9-year-olds are afflicted.

The geographical correlation between malaria and the distribution of the sickle-cell allele is indirect evidence of a biological relationship (Figs. 4-17 and 4-19). Today we know that individuals with one Hb^S and one Hb^A allele (that is, heterozygotes with sickle-cell trait), and thus some hemoglobin S, have greater resistance to malaria than do people who have only normal hemoglobin (people who are homozygous for the Hb^A allele). Heterozygotes resist infection because their red blood cells don't provide a suitable environment for the parasite to reproduce. So in areas where malaria is always present, individuals with sickle-cell trait have higher reproductive success than those with normal hemoglobin. Those with sickle-cell anemia, of course, have the lowest reproductive success; without treatment, most of them die before reaching adulthood.

The relationship between malaria and hemoglobin S provides one of the best examples we have of natural selection in contemporary humans. In this case, natural selection has

FIGURE **4-17**
The distribution of the sickle-cell allele in the Old World.

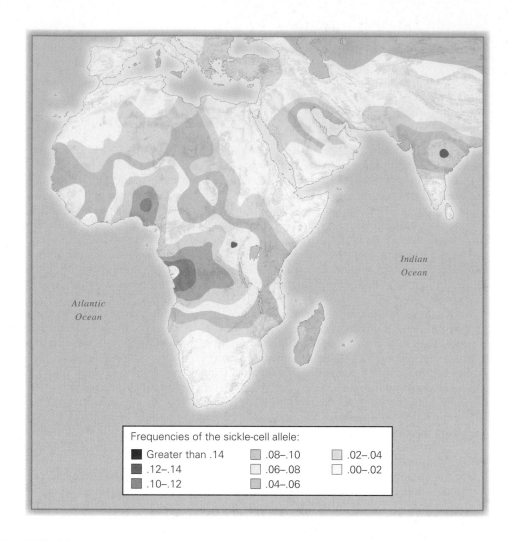

Frequencies of the sickle-cell allele:

■ Greater than .14	▨ .08–.10	▨ .02–.04
■ .12–.14	▢ .06–.08	□ .00–.02
▨ .10–.12	▨ .04–.06	

Atlantic Ocean

Indian Ocean

FIGURE **4-18**
The life cycle of the parasite that causes malaria.

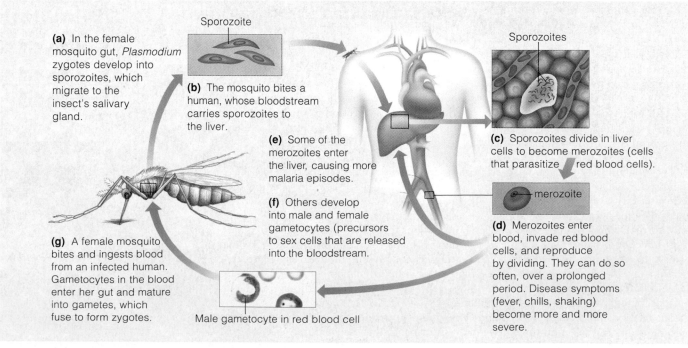

(a) In the female mosquito gut, *Plasmodium* zygotes develop into sporozoites, which migrate to the insect's salivary gland.

Sporozoite

(b) The mosquito bites a human, whose bloodstream carries sporozoites to the liver.

Sporozoites

(c) Sporozoites divide in liver cells to become merozoites (cells that parasitize red blood cells).

merozoite

(d) Merozoites enter blood, invade red blood cells, and reproduce by dividing. They can do so often, over a prolonged period. Disease symptoms (fever, chills, shaking) become more and more severe.

(e) Some of the merozoites enter the liver, causing more malaria episodes.

(f) Others develop into male and female gametocytes (precursors to sex cells that are released into the bloodstream.

(g) A female mosquito bites and ingests blood from an infected human. Gametocytes in the blood enter her gut and mature into gametes, which fuse to form zygotes.

Male gametocyte in red blood cell

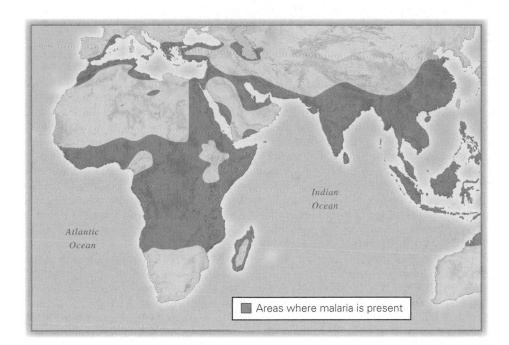

FIGURE **4-19**
The distribution of malaria in the Old World.

Areas where malaria is present

favored the heterozygous phenotype, which in turn has increased the frequency of the Hb^S allele. The benefit of this kind of selection is that more people in the population have greater resistance to malaria. The cost is that the Hb^S allele isn't being eliminated from the population, which means that there will always be some people with sickle-cell anemia.

Review of Genetics and Evolutionary Factors

In this chapter we discussed how genetic information is passed from individuals in one generation to those in the next. We also reviewed evolutionary theory and its current applications, emphasizing the crucial role of natural selection. The various levels—molecular, cellular, individual, and populational—are different aspects of the evolutionary process, and they're related to each other in a way that can eventually produce biological change over time. A step-by-step example will make this clear.

We begin with a hypothetical situation in which everyone in the population has the same hemoglobin type; therefore, initially no variation for this trait exists, and without some source of new variation, evolution isn't possible. But this situation can change with the substitution of a single base in the DNA sequence that can change the code enough to alter the protein product and ultimately the phenotype of the individual. Consider that in each generation, such an incident occurs in one or a few individuals. For a mutated allele to be passed on to succeeding offspring, the gametes must carry the alteration. Any new mutation, therefore, must be transmitted while sex cells are being formed.

Once a mutation has occurred in the DNA, it's packaged into chromosomes, and these chromosomes will assort during meiosis to be passed to offspring. The results of this process can be seen by looking at phenotypes (traits) in individuals, and the mode of inheritance is described simply by Mendel's principle of segregation. In other words, if our initial individual has a mutation in only one member of a pair of alleles on a set of paired chromosomes, there will be a 50 percent chance of passing this chromosome (with the new mutation) to an offspring.

But what does all this activity have to do with *evolution*? To repeat an earlier definition, evolution is a change in allele frequency in a *population* from one generation to the next.

The key point here is that we're considering entire groups of individuals, or populations, and it's populations that may change over time.

We know whether allele frequencies have changed in a population where sickle-cell hemoglobin is found by determining the percentage of individuals with the Hb^S allele versus those with the normal allele (Hb^A). If the relative proportions of these alleles change over time, evolution has occurred. But, in addition to discovering that evolution has occurred, it's important to know why; and there are several possible explanations. First, we know that the only way the new Hb^S allele could have arisen is by mutation, and we've shown how this can happen in a single individual. But this isn't an evolutionary change. For evolutionary change to happen, this new allele must *spread* in the population.

New alleles can spread rather quickly in small populations where mutations in just one or a few individuals can alter overall allele frequencies quite quickly. This case would be representative of genetic drift. As we discussed, drift acts in small populations, where random factors may cause significant changes in allele frequencies. Consequently, some alleles may be completely removed from the population, while others may become established as the only allele at that particular locus. (Such alleles are said to be fixed.)

In the course of human evolution, drift has probably played a significant role at times, and it's important to remember that at this microevolutionary level, drift and/or gene flow can (and will) produce evolutionary change, even in the absence of natural selection. However, directional evolutionary trends could only have been sustained by *natural selection*. The way this has worked in the past and still operates today is through differential reproduction. That is, individuals who carry a particular allele or combination of alleles produce more offspring than do other individuals with different alleles. So, the frequency of the new allele in the population increases slowly from generation to generation. When this process is compounded over hundreds of generations for numerous loci, the result is significant evolutionary change. The levels of organization in the evolutionary process are summarized in Table 4-4.

TABLE 4-4	Levels of Organization in the Evolutionary Process		
Evolutionary Factor	**Level**	**Evolutionary Process**	**Technique of Study**
Mutation	DNA	Storage of genetic information; ability to replicate; influences phenotype by production of proteins	Biochemistry, electron microscope, recombinant DNA
Mutation	Chromosomes	A vehicle for packaging and transmitting genetic material (DNA)	Light or electron microscope
Recombination (sex cells only)	Cell	The basic unit of life that contains the chromosomes and divides for growth and for production of sex cells	Light or electron microscope
Natural selection	Organism	The unit, composed of cells, that reproduces and which we observe for phenotypic traits	Visual study, biochemistry
Drift, gene flow	Population	A group of interbreeding organisms; changes in allele frequencies between generations; it's the population that evolves	Statistical analysis

VISUAL SUMMARY

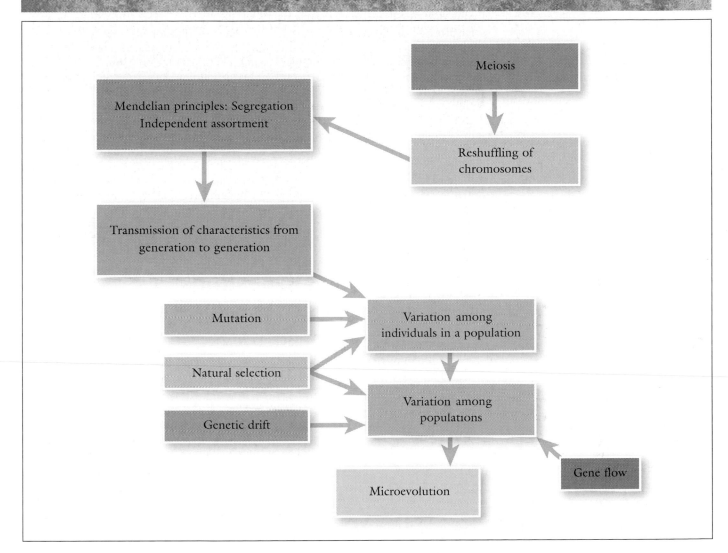

Summary: Putting It All Together

We've seen how Gregor Mendel discovered the principles of segregation, independent assortment, dominance and recessiveness by conducting experiments with pea plants. Even though the field of genetics progressed dramatically during the twentieth century, the concepts first put forth by Gregor Mendel are still the basis of our current knowledge of how traits are inherited.

Basic Mendelian principles are applied to the study of the various modes of inheritance we're familiar with today. We have presented three of these modes in some detail: autosomal dominant, autosomal recessive, and X-linked recessive. The most important factor in all the Mendelian modes of inheritance is the role of segregation of chromosomes, and the alleles they carry, during meiosis.

Building on fundamental nineteenth-century contributions by Charles Darwin and his contemporaries and the rediscovery 1900 of Mendel's work in 1900, advances in genetics throughout the twentieth century contributed to contemporary evolutionary thought. In particular, the combination of natural selection with Mendel's principles of inheritance and experimental evidence concerning the nature of mutation have all been synthesized into a modern understanding of evolutionary change, appropriately termed the Modern Synthesis. In this, the central contemporary theory of evolution, evolutionary change is seen as a two-stage process. The first stage is the production and redistribution of variation. The second stage is the process whereby natural selection acts on the accumulated genetic variation.

Mutation is crucial to all evolutionary change because it's the only source of completely new genetic material (which increases variation). In addition, the factors of recombination, genetic drift, and gene flow redistribute variation within individuals (recombination), within populations (genetic drift), and between populations (gene flow).

Natural selection is the central determining factor that influences the long-term direction of evolutionary change. How natural selection works can best be explained as differential reproductive success—in other words, how successful individuals are in leaving offspring to succeeding generations. For example, in malarial areas, people with sickle-cell trait are more successful at producing offspring than are people with normal hemoglobin or with sickle-cell anemia. Because it must be remembered that evolution is an integrated process, we've concluded this chapter with a discussion of how the various evolutionary factors can be integrated into a single, comprehensive view of evolutionary change.

Critical Thinking Questions

1. Has our discussion of dominance and recessiveness changed your understanding of these principles, and did the discussion differ from what you may have learned in the past?

2. Can you think of some examples of how selection, gene flow, genetic drift, and mutation have acted on populations or species in the past? Try to think of at least one human and one nonhuman example we didn't discuss. Why do you think genetic drift might be important today to endangered species?

3. Construct a pedigree chart for your family regarding some Mendelian trait such as blood type. If possible, include your siblings (if any), your parents, and your grandparents. If you're really ambitious, consider including aunts, uncles, and cousins.

Molecular Applications in Forensic Anthropology

No doubt you know of instances in which DNA analysis is used for forensic purposes to identify a criminal. Likewise, you've probably heard of cases in which mistakenly imprisoned individuals have been released when DNA evidence cleared them of criminal involvement—sometimes several years following conviction.

Since the 1980s, molecular applications have greatly assisted law enforcement agencies. In fact, immediately following development of the polymerase chain reaction (PCR) technique in the mid-1980s, the first widely applied examples of precise DNA genotyping were for forensic purposes.

Forensic anthropologists, from the outset, have been central contributors in these molecular applications. It must be emphasized that forensic science is a coordinated *team effort*. Thus, forensic anthropologists work in close collaboration with law enforcement agencies, medical examiners, forensic odontologists (i.e., dental experts), entomologists, and DNA identification laboratories.

The standard methods used in these laboratories include PCR and DNA fingerprinting (see p. 58). Both mitochondrial and nuclear DNA are used to identify individuals. PCR makes it possible to make a reliable identification of individuals from exceedingly small samples of tissue (e.g., blood, semen, teeth, and bone). Thus, even in cases where the remains have deteriorated badly over time or were crushed or burned in a mass disaster, proper collection and precise laboratory controls can often yield useful results. For example, a person missing for several years can be identified from just a small scrap of bone if the DNA fingerprint can be matched with that of a close relative. Because initial analysis of physical attributes of the skeleton (e.g., age, sex, stature) can greatly narrow the range of possible indentification (so that fewer potential relatives need to be tested for a match) anthropologists provide crucial assistance in the identification process. At present, existing data banks are insufficient to accomplish the task without such initial corroborating clues.

To successfully make a positive genetic ID, the DNA must be (1) extracted (from bone, by cutting a small section with a saw); (2) purified to remove chemicals that interfere with PCR; (3) amplified (i.e., replicated millions of times by PCR); and (4) sequenced (usually by use of "fingerprinting"—that is, characterizing for particular chromosomal regions unique repeated arrays of small DNA segments).

One renowned case of DNA identification from skeletal remains was that of the last tsar of Russia, Tsar Nicholas II. As is well known, Nicholas and all his immediate family were executed in July 1918. The bodies were long thought to have been completely destroyed, but the true location of the graves of the Russian royal family was discovered several years ago. Only after the fall of communism, however, were the skeletal remains finally exhumed in 1991.

A team led by the late William Maples was permitted to examine the remains and attempt to establish the exact identities of all the individuals (more than 1,000 bone fragments were mixed together) (Fig. 1). Anthropological analysis of the skeletons suggested that five members of the royal family were represented (Tsar Nicholas, Empress Alexandra, and their three oldest daughters). The absence of the remains of the two youngest children (Anastasia and Alexei) agrees with the evidence of documents from the time of the execution indicating that they had been buried elsewhere.

©Bettmann/CORBIS

Courtesy, Margaret Maples

FIGURE 1

Forensic anthropologist Bill Maples examines the cranium of Tsar Nicholas II (inset).

Molecular Applications in Forensic Anthropology CONTINUED

In 1992, the first DNA testing was done on small bone samples taken to England. Molecular results agreed with the anthropological findings (Gill et al., 1994), except that some lingering questions remained concerning the identification of the Tsar's mtDNA. To provide absolute confirmation, additional bone and tooth samples were taken and further DNA analysis was done at the Armed Forces DNA Identification Laboratory (AFDIL) in Washington, D.C. Moreover, because the DNA thought to come from the Tsar's skeleton showed a highly unusual pattern, permission was given by the Russian Orthodox Church to exhume the body of his younger brother (who had died in 1899) and compare the DNA with that taken from the presumed skeleton of Tsar Nicholas. The results showed beyond any doubt that the skeleton was indeed that of executed Tsar Nicholas II (Ivanov et al., 1996).

Scenes of mass disaster (such as fires, earthquakes, tsunamis, or plane crashes) are another context in which both forensic anthropology and DNA analysis play crucial roles. To respond quickly and effectively to such disasters, the federal government has organized regional disaster reaction work groups called DMORT (Disaster Mortuary Operational Response Team). A forensic anthropologist is included in all these teams, and sometimes the anthropologist is the team leader. In fact, following the tragic events of September 11, 2001, Paul Sledzik (a forensic anthropologist then at the Armed Forces Institute of Pathology) was the DMORT leader at the Pennsylvania crash site of United Flight 93.

During the recovery, the team followed strict procedures in the collection and analysis of the human remains and other evidence. It must be remembered that in addition to a site of immense personal tragedy this was also a crime scene. Accordingly, as in all such circumstances, close interaction with law enforcement agencies is essential; in this case, the FBI led the criminal investigation. (For a detailed documentation of the procedures followed at the Flight 93 crash site, see the website provided with other sources at the end of this feature.)

Forensic anthropologists also assisted in the recovery of human remains at the World Trade Center. Here procedures differed, as millions of tons of debris had to be sifted through, and the few human remains that were present were extremely fragmentary and severely burned.

In Pennsylvania, although broken and burned, the remains of victims were much more complete. Thus, the DMORT staff could select the material most likely to provide the best DNA results. Moreover, clothing and other personal items found with the remains could provide an exact identification (which could be further corroborated through basic anthropological observations of age, sex, etc.). Where identification was unambiguous, DNA analysis was not required.

From the World Trade Center, few remnants of associated clothing or personal effects were found. Moreover, since the bone and tooth fragments were so small and were often altered by intense heat, few of the standard anthropological skeletal observations were possible. As a result, basically all the presumed bone and dental remains are being analyzed for DNA.

More recently forensic anthropologists assisted in identifying remains of individuals killed during the tsunami that struck southern Asia in December 2004. Teams came from several countries, and up-to-date information on the tsunami assistance as well as forensic technical advances can be seen on the Environmental Sciences and Research (ESR) website (see Sources).

Major tragedies leading to large numbers of civilian deaths also occur during wars and ethnic conflicts. Forensic anthropologists are often asked to assist in these circumstances as well, since victims of atrocities sometimes are left in mass graves. When possible, these graves are intensively investigated, often revealing decomposed bodies as well as partial skeletons. Such work has sadly become more commonplace, keeping pace with the increase in brutality seen throughout the world. (Consider, for example, the tragedies of Argentina, Guatemala, Rwanda, the Balkans, and Iraq.)

Recovery efforts are concerned first with identifying the victims. Successful personal identification allows family members to learn the fate of missing loved ones. Second, the evidence obtained can be used in legal proceedings in which perpetrators are tried for genocide or other crimes against humanity. (Such trials are now being conducted in Africa, Iraq, and at the World Court.)

As with the circumstances at the 9/11 disaster sites, DNA analyses are sometimes required; but in other cases accurate personal identification can be done more quickly and more economically by using standard anthropological criteria and associated personal items (the latter corroborated by relatives of the deceased). Such methods are especially important in very poor, war-torn regions (where large-scale DNA testing is not affordable). However, international agencies have recently stepped up aid; for example, in Bosnia and Herzegovina, the International Commission on Missing Persons is overseeing large-scale DNA testing (Drukier et al., 2004; Klanowski, 2004). An analogous approach is also being implemented in the United States to identify bodies of hundreds of immigrants who died while trying to cross the Mexican-U.S. border (Baker and Baker, 2004).

In addition to the field collection and analysis contexts discussed above, forensic anthropologists are also becoming directly involved in molecular research in the laboratory. Several anthropologists working in cooperation with molecular biologists are investigating how to refine procedures to make DNA sequencing more accurate (Kontanis, 2004; Latham et al., 2004). For example, at AFDIL, anthropologist Heather Thew is a DNA analyst. Here she is directly involved in all steps of sample preparation and molecular analysis. Much of her work concerns the mtDNA testing of the remains of military personnel—some of whom have been missing since World War II; thus, the physical remains consist only of very fragmented bone pieces. Thew credits her anthropology training in human skeletal analysis and modern population biology for providing her with both a solid background and specialized skills that allow her to better perform many of the laboratory duties at AFDIL (Fig. 2.).

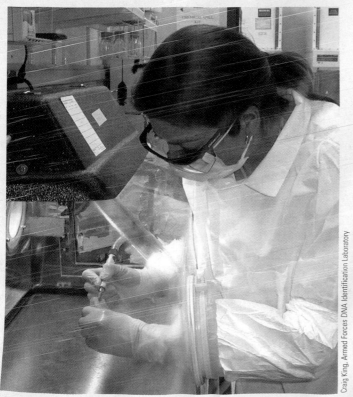

Craig King, Armed Forces DNA Identification Laboratory

FIGURE 2
DNA analyst Heather Thew prepares a bone sample at the Armed Forces DNA Identification Laboratory.

SOURCES

Baker, Lori E., and Erich Baker. 2004. "Reuniting Families: Using Phenotypic and Genotypic Forensic Evidence to Identify Unknown Immigrant Remains." Paper presented at Annual Meetings of the American Academy of Forensic Sciences, Dallas, February 2004.

Druikier, Piotr. 2004. "Anthropological Review of Remains from Srebrenica as Part of the Identification Process." Paper presented at Annual Meetings of the American Academy of Forensic Sciences, Dallas, February 2004.

Environmental Sciences and Research (ESR). See website: www.esr.cri.nz/competencies/forensicscience/dna/

Flight 93 Morgue Protocols. See website: www.dmort.org/FilesforDownload/Protocol_Flight_93.pdf

Gill, P., P.L. Ivanov, C. Kimpton, et al. 1994. "Identification of the Remains of the Romanov Family by DNA Analysis." Nature Genetics 6:130–135.

Ivanov, Pavel L., Mark J. Wadhams, Rhonda K. Roby, et al. 1996. "Mitochondrial DNA Sequence Heteroplasmy in the Grand Duke of Russia Georgij Romanov Establishes the Authenticity of the Remains of Tsar Nicholas II." Nature Genetics 12:417–420.

Klanowski, Eva. 2004. "Exhumation—and What After? ICMP Model in Bosnia and Herzegovina." Paper presented at Annual Meetings of the American Academy of Forensic Sciences, Dallas, February 2004.

Kotanis, Elias J. 2004. "Using Real-Time PCR Quantifications of Nuclear and Mitochondrial DNA to Develop Degradation Profiles for Various Tissues." Paper presented at Annual Meetings of the American Academy of Forensic Sciences, Dallas, February 2004.

Latham, Krista E. 2004. "The Ability to Amplify Skeletal DNA After Heat Exposure Due to Maceration." Paper presented at Annual Meetings of the American Academy of Forensic Sciences, Dallas, February 2004.

CHAPTER

Macroevolution: Processes of Verteb and Mammalian Evolu

© Shawn Gould

gists are investigating how to refine procedures to make DNA sequencing more accurate (Kontanis, 2004; Latham et al., 2004). For example, at AFDIL, anthropologist Heather Thew is a DNA analyst. Here she is directly involved in all steps of sample preparation and molecular analysis. Much of her work concerns the mtDNA testing of the remains of military personnel—some of whom have been missing since World War II; thus, the physical remains consist only of very fragmented bone pieces. Thew credits her anthropology training in human skeletal analysis and modern population biology for providing her with both a solid background and specialized skills that allow her to better perform many of the laboratory duties at AFDIL (Fig. 2.).

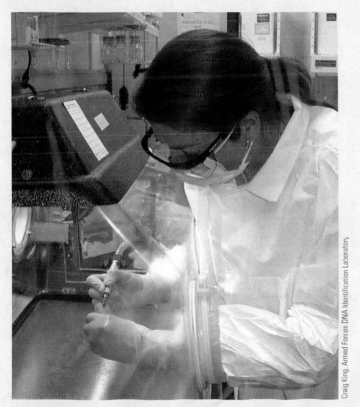

Craig King, Armed Forces DNA Identification Laboratory

FIGURE 2

DNA analyst Heather Thew prepares a bone sample at the Armed Forces DNA Identification Laboratory.

SOURCES

Baker, Lori E., and Erich Baker. 2004. "Reuniting Families: Using Phenotypic and Genotypic Forensic Evidence to Identify Unknown Immigrant Remains." Paper presented at Annual Meetings of the American Academy of Forensic Sciences, Dallas, February 2004.

Druikier, Piotr. 2004. "Anthropological Review of Remains from Srebrenica as Part of the Identification Process." Paper presented at Annual Meetings of the American Academy of Forensic Sciences, Dallas, February 2004.

Environmental Sciences and Research (ESR). See website: www.esr.cri.nz/competencies/forensicscience/dna/

Flight 93 Morgue Protocols. See website: www.dmort.org/FilesforDownload/Protocol_Flight_93.pdf

Gill, P., P.L. Ivanov, C. Kimpton, et al. 1994. "Identification of the Remains of the Romanov Family by DNA Analysis." *Nature Genetics* 6:130–135.

Ivanov, Pavel L., Mark J. Wadhams, Rhonda K. Roby, et al. 1996. "Mitochondrial DNA Sequence Heteroplasmy in the Grand Duke of Russia Georgij Romanov Establishes the Authenticity of the Remains of Tsar Nicholas II." *Nature Genetics* 12:417–420.

Klanowski, Eva. 2004. "Exhumation—and What After? ICMP Model in Bosnia and Herzegovina." Paper presented at Annual Meetings of the American Academy of Forensic Sciences, Dallas, February 2004.

Kotanis, Elias J. 2004. "Using Real-Time PCR Quantifications of Nuclear and Mitochondrial DNA to Develop Degradation Profiles for Various Tissues." Paper presented at Annual Meetings of the American Academy of Forensic Sciences, Dallas, February 2004.

Latham, Krista E. 2004. "The Ability to Amplify Skeletal DNA After Heat Exposure Due to Maceration." Paper presented at Annual Meetings of the American Academy of Forensic Sciences, Dallas, February 2004.

CHAPTER 5

Macroevolution: Processes of Vertebrate and Mammalian Evolution

© Shawn Gould

KEY QUESTIONS

In what ways do humans fit into a biological continuum (as vertebrates and as mammals)?

Introduction

Although paleontology is the study of extinct life, it's by no means a dusty subject. In recent years, cable programs have popularized the exciting world of paleontology, allowing viewers to experience worlds long gone. Shows such as *Walking with Dinosaurs* and *Walking with Cavemen* have given us glimpses of great ancient oceans teeming with brilliantly colored extinct fish and corals or of a dogged Neandertal hunting party that's pursuing a species of giant extinct Irish elk. Of course, the vibrant colors of long-dead fishes and the hairstyles of extinct humans are mostly conjecture, but the science underlying these choices is real.

The study of the history of life on earth is full of mystery and adventure. The bits and pieces of fossils are the remains of once living, breathing animals (some of them extremely large and dangerous). Searching for these fossils in remote corners of the globe is not a task for the faint of heart. Piecing together the tiny clues and ultimately reconstructing what *Tyrannosaurus rex* (or for that matter, a small, 50-million-year-old primate) looked like and how it might have behaved is really much like detective work. Sure, it can be serious; but it's also a lot of fun.

In this chapter we review the evolution of vertebrates and, more specifically, of mammals. It's important to understand these more general aspects of evolutionary history so that we can place our species in its proper biological context. *Homo sapiens* is only one of millions of species that have evolved. More than that, humans have been around for just an instant in the vast expanse of time that life has existed, and we want to know where we fit in this long and complex story of life on earth. To discover how humans relate in this continuum of evolving life on earth, we also discuss some contemporary issues relating to evolutionary theory. In particular, we emphasize concepts relating to large-scale evolutionary processes, that is, *macroevolution* (in contrast to the microevolutionary focus of Chapters 3 and 4). The fundamental perspectives reviewed here concern geological history, principles of classification, and modes of evolutionary change. These perspectives will serve as a basis for topics covered throughout much of the remainder of this book.

 Click!

Go to the following media for interactives and exercises on topics covered in this chapter

- Online Virtual Laboratories for Physical Anthropology, Fourth Edition

The Human Place in the Organic World

There are millions of species living today; if we were to include microorganisms, the total would likely exceed tens of millions. And if we added in the multitudes of species that are now extinct, the total would be staggering—perhaps *hundreds* of millions!

How do we deal scientifically with all this diversity? As humans, biologists approach complexity by simplifying it. One way to do this is to develop a system of **classification** that organizes diversity into categories and, at the same time, indicates evolutionary relationships.

Multicellular organisms that move about and ingest food (but don't photosynthesize, as do plants) are called animals (Fig. 5-1). Within the Kingdom Animalia there are more than 20 major groups termed *phyla* (*sing.*, phylum). One of these phyla is **Chordata**, containing animals with a nerve cord, gill slits (at some stage of development), and a supporting cord along the back. In turn, most (but not all) chordates are called **vertebrates**, because they have a vertebral column. Vertebrates also have a developed brain and paired sensory structures for sight, smell, and balance.

classification In biology, the ordering of organisms into categories, such as orders, families, and genera, to show evolutionary relationships.

Chordata The phylum of the animal kingdom that includes vertebrates.

vertebrates Animals with segmented, bony spinal columns; includes fishes, amphibians, reptiles, birds, and mammals.

FIGURE 5-1

In this classification chart, modified from Linnaeus, all animals are placed in certain categories based on structural similarities. Not all members of categories are shown; for example, there are up to 20 orders of placental mammals (8 are depicted). Chapter 6 presents a more comprehensive classification of the primate order.

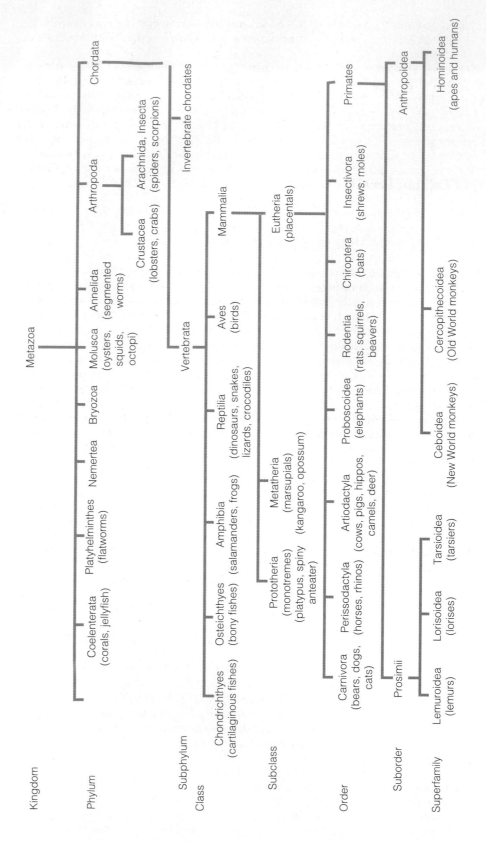

The vertebrates themselves are subdivided into six classes: cartilaginous fishes, bony fishes, amphibians, reptiles, birds, and mammals. We'll discuss mammalian classification later in this chapter.

By putting organisms into increasingly narrow groupings, this hierarchical arrangement organizes diversity into categories. It also makes statements about evolutionary and genetic relationships between species and groups of species. Further dividing mammals into orders makes the statement that, for example, all carnivores (Carnivora) are more closely related to each other than they are to any species placed in another order. Consequently, bears, dogs, and cats are more closely related to each other than they are to cattle, pigs, or deer (Artiodactyla). At each succeeding level (suborder, superfamily, family, subfamily, genus, and species), finer distinctions are made between categories until, at the species level, only those animals that can potentially interbreed and produce viable offspring are included.

Principles of Classification

Before we go any further, we need to discuss the basis of animal classification. The field that specializes in establishing the rules of classification is called *taxonomy*. Organisms are classified first, and most traditionally, according to their physical similarities. Such was the basis of the first systematic classification devised by Linnaeus in the eighteenth century (see Chapter 2).

Today, basic physical similarities are still considered a good starting point. But for similarities to be useful, they *must* reflect evolutionary descent. For example, the bones of the forelimb of all terrestrial air-breathing vertebrates (tetrapods) are so similar in number and form (Fig. 5-2) that the obvious explanation for the striking resemblance is that all four kinds of air-breathing vertebrates ultimately derived their forelimb structure from a common ancestor. What's more, recent discoveries of remarkably well-preserved fossils from Canada have provided exciting new evidence of how the transition from aquatic to land living took place and what the earliest tetrapods looked like (Daeschler et al., 2006; Shubin et al., 2006).

FIGURE 5-2
Homologies. Similarities in the forelimb bones of these animals can be most easily explained by descent from a common ancestor.

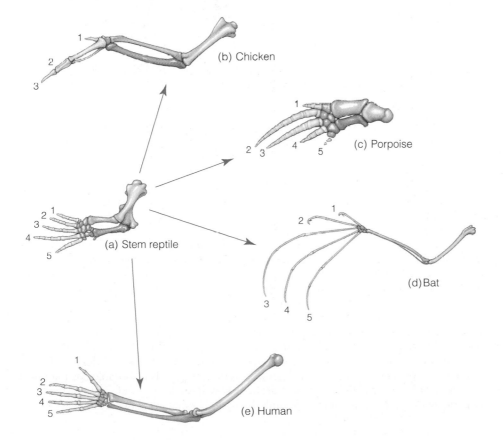

(b) Chicken

(c) Porpoise

(a) Stem reptile

(d) Bat

(e) Human

How could such seemingly major evolutionary modifications in structure occur? They quite likely began with only relatively minor genetic changes. For example, recent research shows that forelimb development in all vertebrates is directed by just a few regulatory genes, called *Hox* genes (see p. 46; Shublin et al., 1997; Riddle and Tabin, 1999). A few mutations in certain *Hox* genes among early vertebrates led to the basic limb plan seen in all subsequent vertebrates. With further additional, small mutations in these genes, or in the genes they regulate, the varied structures that make up the wing of a chicken, the flipper of a porpoise, or the upper limb of a human developed. You should recognize that *basic* genetic regulatory mechanisms are highly conserved in animals; that is, they've been maintained relatively unchanged for hundreds of millions of years. Like a musical score with a basic theme, small variations on the pattern can produce the different "tunes" that define one organism from another. This is the essential genetic foundation for most macroevolutionary change. Large anatomical modifications, therefore, don't always require major genetic rearrangements.

Structures that are shared by species on the basis of descent from a common ancestor are called **homologies**. Homologies, alone, are reliable indicators of evolutionary relationship, but we have to be careful not to draw hasty conclusions from superficial similarities. For example, both birds and butterflies have wings, but they shouldn't be grouped together on the basis of this single characteristic; butterflies (as insects) differ dramatically from birds in several other, even more fundamental ways. (For example, birds have an internal skeleton, central nervous system, and four limbs; insects don't.)

Here's what's happened in evolutionary history: From quite distant ancestors, both butterflies and birds have developed wings *independently*. So, their (superficial) similarities are a product of separate evolutionary responses to roughly similar functional demands. Such similarities, based on independent functional adaptation and not on shared evolutionary descent, are called **analogies**. The process that leads to the development of analogies (also called analogous structures) such as wings in birds and in butterflies is termed **homoplasy**. In the case of butterflies and birds, the homoplasy has occurred in evolutionary lines that share only very remote ancestry. Here, homoplasy has produced analogous structures separately from any homology. In some cases, however, homoplasy can occur in lineages that are more closely related (and share considerable homology as well). Examples of homoplasy in closely related lineages are evident among the primates (for example, New and Old World monkeys show considerable homoplasy and so do the great apes; see Chapter 6).

CONSTRUCTING CLASSIFICATIONS AND INTERPRETING EVOLUTIONARY RELATIONSHIPS

Evolutionary biologists typically use two major approaches, or "schools," when interpreting evolutionary relationships with the goal of producing classifications. The first approach, called **evolutionary systematics**, is the more traditional. The second, called **cladistics**, has emerged primarily in the last two decades. While aspects of both approaches are still used by most evolutionary biologists, in recent years cladistic methodologies have predominated among anthropologists. Indeed, one noted primate evolutionist commented that "virtually all current studies of primate phylogeny involve the methods and terminology" of cladistics (Fleagle, 1998, p. 1).

Before we begin drawing distinctions between these two approaches, it's first helpful to note features shared by both evolutionary systematics and cladistics. First, both schools are interested in tracing evolutionary relationships and in constructing classifications that reflect these relationships. Second, both schools recognize that organisms must be compared using specific features (called *characters*) and that some of these characters are more informative than others. And third (deriving directly from the previous two points), both approaches focus exclusively on homologies.

But these approaches also have some significant differences—in how characters are chosen, which groups are compared, and how the results are interpreted and eventually incorporated into evolutionary schemes and classifications. The primary difference is that cladistics more explicitly and more rigorously defines the kinds of homologies that yield the most useful information. For example, at a very basic level, all life (except for some viruses) shares DNA as the molecule underlying all organic processes. However, beyond

homologies Similarities between organisms based on descent from a common ancestor.

analogies Similarities between organisms based strictly on common function, with no assumed common evolutionary descent.

homoplasy (*homo*, meaning "same," and *plasy*, meaning "growth") The separate evolutionary development of similar characteristics in different groups of organisms.

evolutionary systematics A traditional approach to classification (and evolutionary interpretation) in which presumed ancestors and descendants are traced in time by analysis of homologous characters.

cladistics An approach to classification that attempts to make rigorous evolutionary interpretations based solely on analysis of certain types of homologous characters (those considered to be derived characters).

inferring that all life most likely derives from a single origin (a most intriguing point), the mere presence of DNA tells us nothing further regarding more specific relationships among different kinds of life-forms. To draw further conclusions, we need to look at particular characters that certain groups share as the result of more recent ancestry.

This perspective emphasizes an important point: Some homologous characters are much more informative than others. We saw earlier that all terrestrial vertebrates share homologies in the number and basic arrangement of bones in the forelimb. Even though these similarities are broadly useful in showing that these large evolutionary groups (amphibians, reptiles, birds, and mammals) are all related through a distant ancestor, they don't provide information we can use to distinguish one group from another (a reptile from a mammal, for example). These kinds of characters (also called traits) that are shared through such remote ancestry are said to be **ancestral** or primitive. We prefer the term *ancestral* because it doesn't reflect negatively on the evolutionary value of the character in question. In biological anthropology, the term *primitive* or *ancestral* simply means that a character seen in two organisms is inherited in both of them from a distant ancestor.

In most cases, analyzing ancestral characters doesn't supply enough information to make accurate evolutionary interpretations of relationships between different groups. In fact, misinterpretation of ancestral characters can easily lead to quite inaccurate evolutionary conclusions. Cladistics focuses on traits that distinguish particular evolutionary lineages; such traits are far more informative than ancestral traits. Lineages that share a common ancestor are called a **clade**, giving the name *cladistics* to the field that seeks to identify and interpret these groups. The characters of interest are said to be **derived**, or **modified**. Thus, while the general ancestral bony pattern of the forelimb in tetrapods doesn't allow us to distinguish among them, the further modification of this pattern in certain groups (as hooves, flippers, or wings, for instance) does.

A simplified example might help clarify the basic principles used in cladistic analysis. Figure 5-3a shows a hypothetical "lineage" of passenger vehicles. All of the "descendant" vehicles share a common ancestor, the prototype passenger vehicle. The first major division (I) differentiates passenger cars from trucks. The second split (that is, diversification) is between luxury cars and sports cars (you could, of course, imagine many other subcategories).

ancestral (primitive) Referring to characters inherited by a group of organisms from a remote ancestor and thus not diagnostic of groups (lineages) that diverged after the character first appeared.

clade A group of organisms sharing a common ancestor. The group includes the common ancestor and all descendants.

derived (modified) Referring to characters that are modified from the ancestral condition and thus *are* diagnostic of particular evolutionary lineages.

FIGURE 5-3
Evolutionary "trees" showing development of passenger vehicles.

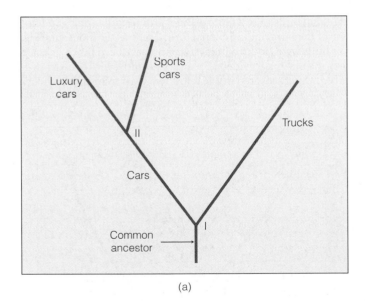

(a)

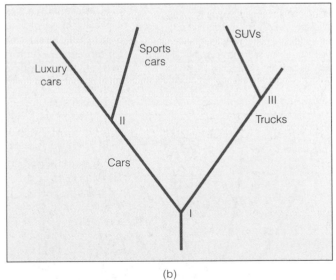

(b)

From a common ancestor of all passenger vehicles, the first major divergence is that between cars and trucks (I). A later divergence also occurs between luxury cars and sports cars (II). Derived features of each grouping ("lineage") appear only after its divergence from other groups (e.g., cargo beds are found only in trucks, cushioned suspension only in cars; likewise, only sports cars have a decorative racing stripe).

In this "tree," SUVs diverge from trucks, but like sports cars, they have a decorative racing stripe. This feature is a homoplasy and does *not* make SUVs sports cars. The message is that classifications based on just one characteristic that can appear independently in different groups can lead to an *incorrect* conclusion. **Note:** In (a), two clades are defined (I and II), while in (b), three clades (I, II, and III) are recognized.

Modified (derived) traits that distinguish trucks from cars might include type of frame, suspension, wheel size, and, in some forms, an open cargo bed. Derived characters that might distinguish sports cars from luxury cars could include engine size and type, wheel base size, and a decorative racing stripe.

Now let us assume that you're presented with an "unknown" vehicle (meaning one as yet unclassified). How do you decide what kind of vehicle it is? You might note such features as four wheels, a steering wheel, and a seat for the driver, but these are *ancestral* characters (found in the common ancestor) of all passenger vehicles. If, however, you note that the vehicle lacks a cargo bed and raised suspension (so it's not a truck) but has a racing stripe, you might conclude that it's a car, and more than that, a sports car (since it has a derived feature presumably of *only* that group).

All this seems fairly obvious, and you've probably noticed that this simple type of decision making characterizes much of human mental organization. Still, we frequently deal with complications that aren't so obvious. What if you're presented with a sports utility vehicle (SUV) with a racing stripe (Fig. 5-3b)? SUVs are basically trucks, but the presence of the racing stripe could be seen as a homoplasy with sports cars. The lesson here is that we need to be careful, look at several traits, decide which are ancestral and which are derived, and finally try to recognize the complexity (and confusion) introduced by homplasy.

Our example of passenger vehicles is useful up to a point. Because it concerns human inventions, the groupings possess characters that humans can add and delete in almost any combination. Naturally occurring organic systems are more limited in this respect. Any species can possess only characters that have been inherited from its ancestor or that have been subsequently modified (derived) from those shared with the ancestor. So any modification in *any* species is constrained by that species' evolutionary legacy—that is, what the species starts out with.

Another example, one drawn from paleontological (fossil) evidence of actual organisms, can help clarify these points. Most people know something about dinosaur evolution, and some of you may know about the recent controversies surrounding this topic. There are several intriguing issues concerning the evolutionary history of dinosaurs, and recent fossil discoveries have shed considerable light on them. We'll mention some of these issues later in the chapter, but here we consider one of the more fascinating: the relationship of dinosaurs to birds.

Traditionally, it was thought that birds were a quite distinct group from reptiles and not especially closely related to any of them (including extinct forms, such as the dinosaurs; Fig. 5-4a). Still, the early origins of birds were clouded in mystery and have been much debated for more than a century. In fact, the first fossil evidence of a very primitive bird (now known to be about 150 million years old) was discovered in 1861, just two years following Darwin's

FIGURE 5-4

Evolutionary relationships of birds and dinosaurs. (a) Traditional view, showing no close relationship. (b) Revised view, showing common ancestry of birds and dinosaurs.

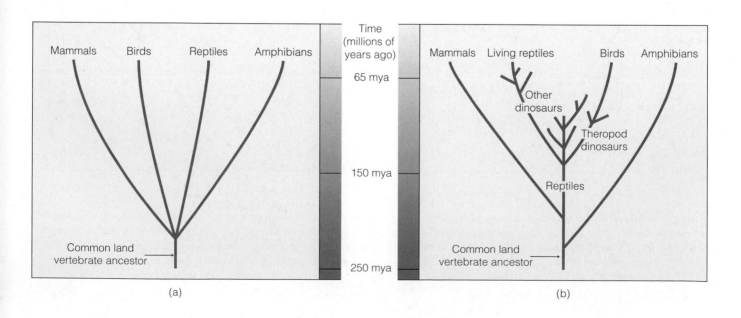

publication of *Origin of Species*. Despite some initial and quite remarkably accurate interpretations by Thomas Huxley linking these early birds to dinosaurs, most experts concluded that there was no close relationship. This view persisted through most of the twentieth century, but events of the last two decades have swung the consensus back to the hypothesis that birds *are* closely related to some dinosaurs. Two developments in particular have influenced this change of opinion: the remarkable discoveries in the 1990s from China, Madagascar, and elsewhere and the application of cladistic methods to the interpretation of these and other fossils.

Recent finds from Madagascar of chicken-sized, primitive birds dated to 70–65 million years ago (mya) show an elongated second toe (similar, in fact, to that in the dinosaur *Velociraptor*, made infamous in the film *Jurassic Park*). Indeed, these primitive birds from Madagascar show many other similarities to *Velociraptor* and its close cousins, which together comprise a group of small- to medium-sized ground-living, carnivorous dinosaurs called **theropods**. Even more extraordinary finds have been unearthed recently in China, where the traces of what were once *feathers* have been found embossed in fossilized sediments! For many researchers, these new finds have finally solved the mystery of bird origins (Fig. 5-4b), leading some experts to conclude that this evidence "shows that birds are not only *descended* from dinosaurs, they *are* dinosaurs (and reptiles)—just as humans are mammals, even though people are as different from other mammals as birds are from other reptiles" (Padian and Chiappe, 1998, p. 43).

There are some doubters who remain concerned that the presence of feathers in dinosaurs (145–125 mya) might simply be a homoplasy (that is, these creatures developed the trait independently from its appearance in birds). Certainly, the possibility of homoplasy must always be considered, as it can add considerably to the complexity of what seems like a straightforward evolutionary interpretation. Indeed, strict cladistic analysis assumes that homoplasy is not a common occurrence; if it were, perhaps no evolutionary interpretation could be very straightforward! In the case of the proposed relationship between some (theropod) dinosaurs and birds, the presence of feathers looks like an excellent example of a **shared derived** characteristic, which therefore *does* link the forms. What's more, cladistic analysis emphasizes that several characteristics should be examined, since homoplasy might muddle an interpretation based on just one or two shared traits. In the bird/dinosaur case, several other characteristics further suggest their evolutionary relationship.

One last point needs to be mentioned. Traditional evolutionary systematics illustrates the hypothesized evolutionary relationships using a *phylogeny,* more properly called a **phylogenetic tree**. Strict cladistic analysis, however, shows relationships in a **cladogram** (Fig. 5-5). If you examine the charts in Figures 5-4 and 5-5, you'll see some obvious differences. A phylogenetic tree incorporates the dimension of time, shown approximately in Figure 5-4 (you can find many other examples in this and upcoming chapters). A cladogram doesn't indicate time; all forms (fossil and modern) are shown along one dimension. Phylogenetic trees usually attempt to make some hypotheses regarding ancestor-descendant relationships (for example, theropods are ancestral to modern birds). Cladistic analysis (through cladograms)

theropods Small- to medium-sized ground-living dinosaurs, dated to approximately 150 mya and thought to be related to birds.

shared derived Relating to specific character traits shared in common between two life-forms and considered the most useful for making evolutionary interpretations.

phylogenetic tree A chart showing evolutionary relationships as determined by evolutionary systematics. It contains a time component and implies ancestor-descendant relationships.

cladogram A chart showing evolutionary relationships as determined by cladistic analysis. It's based solely on interpretation of shared derived characters. It contains no time component and does *not* imply ancestor-descendant relationships.

FIGURE 5-5

This cladogram shows relationships of birds, dinosaurs, and other terrestrial vertebrates. Notice that there's no time scale, and both living and fossil forms are shown along the same dimension—that is, ancestor-descendant relationships aren't indicated.

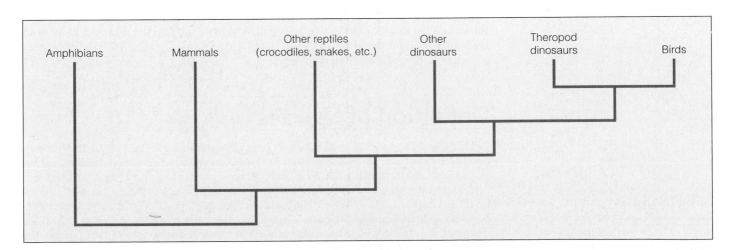

AT A GLANCE   Comparing Two Approaches to Interpretations of Evolutionary Relationships

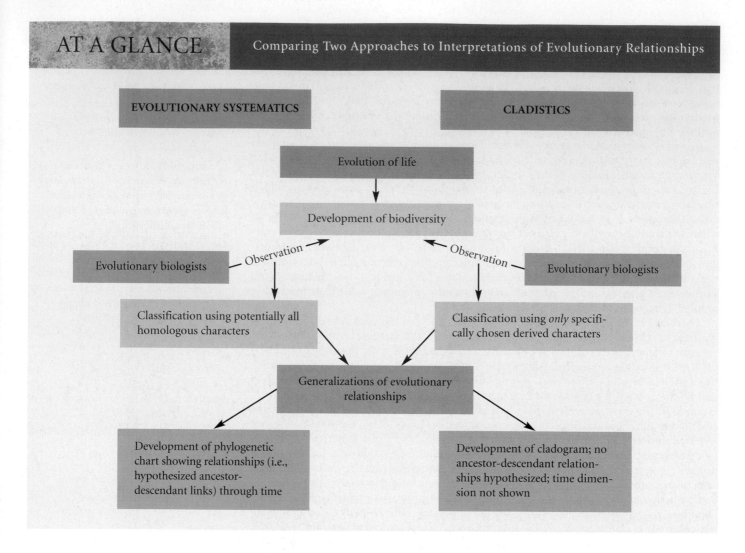

makes no attempt whatsoever to discern ancestor-descendant relationships. In fact, strict cladists are quite skeptical that the evidence really permits such specific evolutionary hypotheses to be scientifically confirmed (since there are many more extinct species than living ones).

In practice, most physical anthropologists (and other evolutionary biologists) utilize cladistic analysis to identify and assess the utility of traits and to make testable hypotheses regarding the relationships of groups of organisms. They also frequently extend this basic cladistic methodology to further hypothesize likely ancestor-descendant relationships shown relative to a time scale (that is, in a phylogenetic tree). In this way, aspects of both traditional evolutionary systematics and cladistic analysis are combined to produce a more complete picture of evolutionary history.

Definition of Species

Whether biologists are doing a cladistic or more traditional phylogenetic analysis, they're comparing groups of organisms—that is, different species, genera (*sing.*, genus), families, orders, and so forth. Fundamental to all these levels of classification is the most basic, the species.

It's appropriate, then, to ask, how do biologists define species? We addressed this issue briefly in Chapter 1, where we used the most common definition, one that emphasizes interbreeding and reproductive isolation. While it's not the only definition of species (others are discussed shortly), this view, called the **biological species concept** (Mayr, 1970), is the one preferred by most zoologists.

biological species concept A depiction of species as groups of individuals capable of fertile interbreeding but reproductively isolated from other such groups.

To understand what species are, you might consider how they come about in the first place—what Darwin called the "origin of species." This most fundamental of macroevolutionary processes is called **speciation**. According to the biological species concept, the way new species are first produced involves some form of isolation. Picture a single species (baboons, for example) composed of several populations distributed over a wide geographical area. Gene exchange between populations (gene flow) will be limited if a geographical barrier, such as an ocean or mountain range, effectively separates these populations. This extremely important form of isolating mechanism is called *geographical isolation* (see A, p. 105).

If one baboon population (A) is separated from another baboon population (B) by a mountain range, individual baboons of population A will not mate with individuals from B (Fig. 5-6). As time passes (perhaps hundreds or thousands of generations), genetic differences will accumulate in both populations. If population size is small, we can assume that genetic drift will also cause allele frequencies to change in both populations. Besides, since drift is *random*, we wouldn't expect the effects to be the same. Consequently, the two populations will begin to diverge genetically.

FIGURE **5-6**
This speciation model illustrates branching evolution, or cladogenesis.

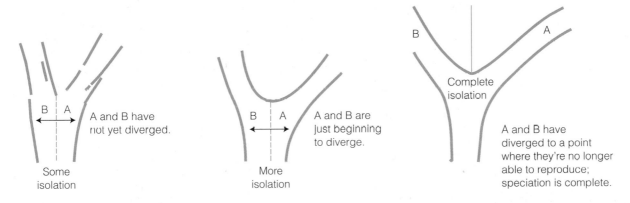

A and B have not yet diverged.

Some isolation

A and B are just beginning to diverge.

More isolation

Complete isolation

A and B have diverged to a point where they're no longer able to reproduce; speciation is complete.

As long as gene exchange is limited, the populations can only become more genetically different over time. What's more, further difference can be expected if the baboon groups are occupying slightly different habitats. These additional genetic differences would be incorporated through the process of natural selection. Certain individuals in population A would be more reproductively fit in their own environment, but they would show less reproductive success in the environment occupied by population B. So, allele frequencies will shift further; and the results, again, will be divergent in the two groups.

With the cumulative effects of genetic drift and natural selection acting over many generations, the result will be two populations that—even if they were to come back into geographical contact—could no longer interbreed. More than just geographical isolation might now apply. There may, for instance, be behavioral differences that interfere with courtship—what we call *behavioral isolation*. Using our *biological* definition of species, we would now recognize two distinct species where initially only one existed.

Another related process that can contribute to the further differentiation of populations into incipient species concerns mate recognition. This is sometimes called the **recognition species concept**, though the crucial process, again, concerns reproduction (that is, who's mating with whom; Ridley, 1993).

Assume in our baboon example that some isolation has already occurred and that phenotypic (and genotypic) differences are beginning to be established between two populations. In this situation, coloration patterns of faces or the size, location, coloration, or even smell of the female genital swelling might vary from group to group. If so, then a female from population A might not recognize a male from population B as an appropriate mate (and vice versa, of course). Natural selection would quickly favor such discrimination if hybrids were less reproductively successful than within-population crosses. Indeed, once such "selective breeding" became established, speciation would be accelerated considerably.

Another definition of species focuses primarily on natural selection and emphasizes that speciation is the result of influences of varied habitats. In this view, called the **ecological species concept**, a species is defined as a group of organisms exploiting a single niche.

speciation The process by which a new species evolves from an earlier species. Speciation is the most basic process in macroevolution.

recognition species concept A depiction of species in which the key aspect is the ability of individuals to identify members of their own species for purposes of mating (and to avoid mating with members of other species). In theory, this type of selective mating is a component of a species concept emphasizing mating and is therefore compatible with the biological species concept.

ecological species concept The concept that a species is a group of organisms exploiting a single niche. This view emphasizes the role of natural selection in separating species from one another.

A CLOSER LOOK   Small Changes, Big Impact

The phenomenon of island dwarfing, where body size changes can occur quite rapidly, is well recognized but not well understood. What are the precise mechanisms that cause large-bodied creatures to dwarf while other smaller creatures transform to gargantuan sizes? This occurrence has been observed and confirmed in a wide variety of animals (reptiles, birds, and some mammals), but it's only within the past few years that paleoanthropologists have been forced to confront the possibility that humans are not exempt.

The "island rule," as Van Valen (1973) called it, states that due to the unique adaptive pressures of islands, large-bodied vertebrates tend to become smaller over time, and smaller ones become bigger. The effects of the island rule tend to be inversely proportional to the island's size (Heaney, 1978) and positively correlated with the degree of isolation from the mainland (Foster, 1964). So, the smaller and more isolated the island, the bigger the size change.

Several mechanisms have been proposed to explain how evolution could produce such physical changes, though the most widely held is the "population and food availability" hypothesis. On islands or in other isolated areas, there's likely to be a decrease in resources due to reduced land area. Fewer animals can be supported by such limited resources, so mammals have fewer young and plants undergo slower growing cycles. Due to a general absence of large predators, we find a wider array of responses to the environment both within and between species. This variety is often expressed in complex and much-accelerated patterns of body size evolution (Grant, 1982).

Since larger-bodied individuals use more resources, natural selection favors smaller sizes (Lomolino, 2005). A micro-, though non-evolutionary example, is the well-known travels of the pioneers on the Oregon Trail. Often, most of the survivors who reached the West were the women and children as well as the smaller-bodied men. The large, burly men who would have been expected to "tough it out" were actually the first to succumb to the effects of dwindling food supplies. In isolated areas with finite resources, the selection for smaller individuals over time gives way to an overall smaller-bodied population. Because of their smaller size, a bigger population of these individuals can be maintained given a constant amount of resources (Anderson and Handley, 2002).

Though just hearing the words *elephant* and *mammoth* makes people think of large size, there are many well-known examples of island dwarfing in these vertebrates. British scientist Dorothea Bate (1879–1951) spent a good deal of her paleontological career studying such curiosities. Since she worked and traveled alone in the early twentieth century, she often dressed as a man while excavating previously unheard-of species like pygmy hippos, dwarf elephants, and giant dormice (just like in *Alice in Wonderland*). Among her finds were mainland Mediterranean elephant populations that had become isolated

on the islands of Crete and Cyprus, ultimately becoming dwarfed to only 6 feet tall at the shoulder.

Bate had such a gift for discovering island dwarfed species that one of the museum trustees who supported her wrote, "Only imagine the sensation you would make if you could walk down Piccadilly leading by a string your Pigmy [sic] Elephants, Hippopotami, *Myotragus,* Tortoises, etc. etc. all in one long queue, the little Elephant blowing his trumpet, and the Hippopotamus wagging its tail" (Shindler, 2006 p. 209).

Though she discovered numerous island curiosities of the Mediterranean, Bate would never see many of these animals appropriately placed in their evolutionary family tree. This is because mainland-to-island body size comparisons make no (or little) sense without a detailed phylogeny—it's only within such a framework that any pattern can be discerned. Such phylogenies are constantly under revision, with some evolutionary lineages only coming to light in recent years. What's more, it's crucial to recognize that both natural selection and genetic drift can become more intense in isolated settings, such as islands, thus accelerating the rate of evolutionary change. Such changes begin at a microevolutionary level; but over time, they may lead to macroevolutionary changes within a lineage, leading to speciation. It's within such a phylogenetic/evolutionary framework that we will be forced to confront an interesting variant within our own genus, *Homo*. In Chapter 14, we'll discuss a provocative find from the island of Flores, Indonesia, that brings the island rule shockingly close to home.

FIGURE 1
Scaled representation of the relative sizes of a dwarfed elephant when compared to a normal hippopotamus and Indian elephant. Redrawn from Attenborough (1987).

For each population, at first the habitats will vary slightly, and different phenotypes will be slightly more advantageous in each. For example, one population might be more arboreal and another more terrestrial; but there would not be an intermediate population equally successful on the ground and in the trees.

In recent years, the ecological species concept has attracted support from several evolutionary biologists, especially among physical anthropologists. While the biological species concept emphasizes gene flow and reproductive isolation, the ecological species concept stresses the role of natural selection. Clearly, our approach in this text has been to focus on the evolutionary contribution of natural selection; thus, the ecological species concept has much to offer here. Nevertheless, our understanding of species need not entail an either-or choice between the biological species concept and the ecological species concept. Some population isolation could indeed *begin* the process of speciation and, at this stage, the influence of genetic drift could be crucial. The process might then be reinforced by natural selection through habitat differentiation as well as mate recognition.

A final approach that biologists use to define species is primarily a practical one. How can species be defined when neither reproductive isolation nor ecological separation can be clearly tested? This type of difficulty plagues the interpretation of fossil organisms but sometimes crops up in discussions of contemporary species as well. For example, Colin Groves, of the Australian National University, has recently advocated splitting many populations of primates into separate species (Groves, 2001b). He utilizes a definition of species called the **phylogenetic species concept**, based on an identifiable parental pattern of ancestry.

For living species, characteristics that define a phylogenetic species could be phenotypic or more directly genotypic (identifying shared patterns in the karyotype or in specific DNA sequences). For extinct groups, with a few notable exceptions (from which ancient DNA has been extracted), the *only* evidence available comes from phenotypic characters that can be identified in fossil forms (see p. 107 for further discussion).

PROCESSES OF SPECIATION

Now that we've seen how species can be defined in somewhat varied ways, what are some of the more explicit theories developed by evolutionary biologists to account for *how* species originate? First, you should recognize that these hypotheses are quite abstract and thus difficult to test doing conventional field biology on contemporary species. Although rates of evolution vary widely among different groups of animals, the process is, by its very nature, a slow one. Some groups, such as fruit flies, members of genus *Drosophila*, seem to speciate especially slowly, taking a million years or more for a new species to be fully separate. The fastest rate of speciation in recent times may have occurred in freshwater fishes. Extreme isolation of cichlid fish populations (of which the angelfish is one of the most familiar forms) has periodically occurred in African lakes, producing "explosive speciation" in just the last few thousand years (Seehausen, 2002). We must emphasize, however, that such extreme isolation has likely never been a factor in the evolution of other vertebrates. Mammals seem to fall somewhere in between the slowly evolving fruit flies and the explosively speciating cichlids. As suggested by fossil evidence, it likely takes tens of thousands of years for speciation to occur in a free-ranging mammalian species.

Given the constraints of field testing in such a slowly occurring phenomenon as macroevolution, biologists have hypothesized that speciation could occur in three different ways: by allopatric speciation, parapatric speciation, or sympatric speciation.

By far, the most widely accepted view of speciation emphasizes an **allopatric** pattern. This model requires complete reproductive isolation within a population, leading to the formation of an incipient species separated (geographically) from its ancestral population.

In parapatric speciation, only *partial* reproductive isolation is required, so that the ranges of the populations may be partially overlapping. In this situation a hybrid zone would form in an area between the two partially separated populations. More complete separation could then occur through reinforcement of mate recognition and selective breeding.

Interestingly, in some areas of East Africa, there's good evidence that parapatric speciation might be currently (and slowly) taking place between populations of savanna baboons and hamadryas baboons. Long-term research by Jane Phillips-Conroy and Clifford Jolly has

phylogenetic species concept
Splitting many populations into separate species based on an identifiable parental pattern of ancestry.

allopatric Living in different areas; this pattern is important in the divergence of closely related species from each other and from their shared ancestral species because it leads to reproductive isolation.

carefully documented hybrid individuals produced by the mating of savanna baboons with hamadryas baboons. Traditionally, these two types of baboons have been placed in separate species (savanna as *Papio cynocephalus* and hamadryas as *Papio hamadryas*). Yet, the hybrids appear quite functional and are *fertile* (Phillips-Conroy et al., 1992; Jolly, 1993). So, what we're likely seeing here is speciation in process—and probably following a parapatric pattern. This means that we might regard these two types of baboons as incipient species. It's possible that some mate recognition differentiation may be operating as well, since male-female interactions differ considerably between savanna and hamadryas baboons.

The third type of speciation proposed, sympatric speciation, is theorized to occur completely within one population with *no* necessary reproductive isolation. In other words, two species result from one population that occupies the same geographic locality. However, this form of speciation, while possible, is not well supported by contemporary evidence and is thus considered the least significant of the three models.

A fourth type of speciation, sometimes recognized as a subset of sympatry, is called *instantaneous speciation*. In this pattern, chromosomal rearrangements occur (by chromosomal mutation), producing immediate reproductive barriers. This type of speciation, well documented in plants, can be rapid, and varieties can emerge with completely different numbers of chromosomes. Here, the process is one of multiplication of chromosome sets (due to mistakes in meiosis), producing a condition called *polyploidy* (the presence of more than two complete sets of chromosomes in an individual). While common in plants, such drastic reorganization of chromosome number is not a factor in the speciation of animals, where polyploidy is always lethal. However, somewhat less dramatic chromosomal alterations, could accelerate speciation in animals. Certainly, chromosomal alterations may be important in speciation, and some researchers have even suggested that such processes may be a central factor in macroevolution.

Even so, demonstration in animals of the systematic influence of such large-scale mutation has been difficult. In fact, theoretical models suggest that major mutational change could not *by itself* produce speciation in animals, but would require some further mechanism to help "fix" the genetic changes within populations. Inbreeding within small population segments has been suggested by some investigators as a possible mechanism that could reinforce rapid speciation by chromosomal mutation. What's more, some theoretical support for this process has been found in those species divided into small social groupings, such as in species of horses and primates.

INTERPRETING SPECIES AND OTHER GROUPS IN THE FOSSIL RECORD

Throughout much of this text, we'll be using various taxonomic terms for fossil primates (including fossil hominids). You'll be introduced to such terms as *Proconsul, Sivapithecus, Australopithecus,* and *Homo.* Of course, *Homo* is still a living primate. But it's especially complex to make these types of designations from remains of animals that are long dead (and only partially preserved as skeletal remains). In these contexts, what do such names mean in evolutionary terms?

Our goal when applying species, genus, or other taxonomic labels to groups of organisms is to make meaningful biological statements about the variation that's represented. When looking at populations of living or long-extinct animals, we certainly are going to see variation; this happens in *any* sexually reproducing organism due to the factors of recombination (see Chapter 3). As a result of recombination, each individual organism is a unique combination of genetic material, and the uniqueness is usually reflected to some extent in the phenotype.

Besides such *individual variation*, we see other kinds of systematic variation in all biological populations. *Age changes* alter overall body size, as well as shape, in many mammals. One pertinent example for fossil hominoid studies is the change in number, size, and shape of teeth from deciduous (also known as baby or milk) teeth (only 20 teeth are present) to the permanent dentition (32 are present). It would be an obvious error to differentiate fossil forms based solely on such age-dependent criteria. If one individual were represented just by milk teeth and another (seemingly very different) individual were represented just by adult teeth, they easily could be different-aged individuals from the *same* population.

Variation due to sex also plays an important role in influencing differences among individuals observed in biological populations. Differences in physical characteristics between males and females of the same species are called **sexual dimorphism**, and these can result in marked variation in body size and proportions in adults of the same species (in Chapter 6, we'll discuss this important topic in more detail).

Recognition of Fossil Species   Keeping in mind all the types of variation present within interbreeding groups of organisms, the minimum biological category we'd like to define in fossil primate samples is the *species*. As already defined (according to the biological species concept), a species is a group of interbreeding or potentially interbreeding organisms that is reproductively isolated from other such groups. In modern organisms, this concept is theoretically testable by observations of reproductive behavior. In animals long extinct, such observations are obviously impossible. Our only way, then, of getting a handle on the variation we see in fossil groups is to refer to living animals.

When studying a fossil group, we may observe without doubt that variation is present; the question is, what is its biological significance? Two immediate answers come to mind. Either the variation is accounted for by individual, age, and sex differences seen *within* every biological species (that is, it is **intraspecific**) or the variation represents differences *between* reproductively isolated groups (it is **interspecific**). How do we decide which answer is correct? To do this, we have to look at contemporary species.

If the amount of morphological variation we observe in fossil samples is comparable to that seen today *within species of closely related forms*, then we shouldn't "split" our sample into more than one species. We must, however, be careful in choosing modern analogues, because rates of morphological evolution vary among different groups of mammals. So, for example, when studying extinct fossil primates, we need to compare them with well-known modern primates that share important traits in common with the species of interest.

Even so, studies of living groups have shown that defining exactly where species boundaries begin and end is often difficult. In dealing with extinct species, the uncertainties are even greater. In addition to the overlapping patterns of variation *spatially* (over space), variation also occurs *temporally* (through time). In other words, even more variation will be seen in **paleospecies**, since individuals may be separated by thousands or even millions of years. Applying strict Linnaean taxonomy to such a situation presents an unavoidable dilemma. Standard Linnaean classification, designed to take account of variation present at any given time, describes a static situation. But when we deal with paleospecies, the time frame is expanded and the situation can be dynamic (that is, later forms might be different from earlier ones). In such a dynamic situation, taxonomic decisions (where to draw species boundaries) are ultimately going to be somewhat arbitrary.

Because the task of interpreting paleospecies is so difficult, paleoanthropologists have sought various solutions. Most researchers today define species using clusters of derived traits (identified cladistically). But, owing to the ambiguity of how many derived characters are required to identify a fully distinct species (as opposed to a subspecies), the frequent mixing of characters into novel combinations, and the always difficult problem of homoplasy, there continues to be disagreement. A good deal of the dispute is driven by philosophical orientation. Exactly how much diversity should one *expect* among fossil primates, especially among fossil hominids?

Some researchers, called "splitters," claim that speciation occurred frequently during hominid evolution, and they often identify numerous fossil hominid species in a sample being studied. As the nickname suggests, these scientists are inclined to split groups into many species. Others, called "lumpers," assume that speciation was less common and see much variation as being intraspecific. These scientists lump groups together, so that fewer hominid species are identified, named, and eventually plugged into evolutionary schemes. As you'll see in the following chapters, debates of this sort pervade paleoanthropology, perhaps more than in any other branch of evolutionary biology.

Recognition of Fossil Genera   The next and broader level of taxonomic classification, the **genus** (*pl.* genera), presents another problem. To have more than one genus, we obviously must have at least two species (reproductively isolated groups), and the species of one genus must differ in a basic way from the species of another genus. A genus is there-

sexual dimorphism   Differences in physical characteristics between males and females of the same species. For example, humans are slightly sexually dimorphic for body size, with males being taller, on average, than females of the same population.

intraspecific   Within species; refers to variation seen within the same species.

interspecific   Between species; refers to variation beyond that seen within the same species to include additional aspects seen between two different species.

paleospecies   Species defined from fossil evidence, often covering a long time span.

genus   (*pl.* genera) A group of closely related species.

fore defined as a group of species composed of members more closely related to each other than they are to species from any other genus.

Grouping species into genera can be quite subjective and is often much debated by biologists. One possible test for contemporary animals is to check for results of hybridization between individuals of different species—rare in nature, but quite common in captivity. If members of two normally separate species interbreed and produce live (though not necessarily fertile) offspring, the two parental species probably are not too different genetically and should therefore be grouped in the same genus. A well-known example of such a cross is horses with donkeys (*Equus caballus* × *Equus asinus*), which normally produces live but sterile offspring (mules).

As previously mentioned, we can't perform breeding experiments with extinct animals, which is why another definition of genus becomes highly relevant. Species that are members of the same genus share the same broad adaptive zone. An adaptive zone represents a general ecological lifestyle more basic than the narrower ecological niches characteristic of individual species. This ecological definition of genus can be an immense aid in interpreting fossil primates. Teeth are the most frequently preserved parts, and they often can provide excellent general ecological inferences. Cladistic analysis also helps scientists to make judgments about evolutionary relationships. That is, members of the same genus should all share derived characters not seen in members of other genera.

As a final comment, we should stress that classification by genus is not always a straightforward decision. For instance, in emphasizing the very close genetic similarities between humans (*Homo sapiens*) and chimpanzees (*Pan troglodytes*), some current researchers (Wildman et al., 2003) place both in the same genus (*Homo sapiens, Homo troglodytes*). This philosophy has even been argued by some to advocate extension of basic human rights to great apes (for instance, as proposed by members of the Great Ape Project). Such thinking likely makes you do a double take; this only underscores the point that when it gets this close to home, it's often difficult to remain objective!

Vertebrate Evolutionary History: A Brief Summary

Besides the staggering array of living and extinct life-forms, biologists must also contend with the vast amount of time that life has been evolving on earth. Again, scientists have devised simplified schemes—but in this case to organize *time*, not biological diversity.

To this end, geologists have formulated the **geological time scale** (Fig. 5-7), in which very large time spans are organized into eras that include one or more periods. Periods, in turn, can be broken down into epochs. For the time span encompassing vertebrate evolution, there are three eras: the Paleozoic, the Mesozoic, and the Cenozoic. The first vertebrates are present in the fossil record dating to early in the Paleozoic at 500 mya, and their origins probably go back considerably further. It's the vertebrates' capacity to form bone that accounts for their more complete fossil record *after* 500 mya.

During the Paleozoic, several varieties of fishes (including the ancestors of modern sharks and bony fishes), amphibians, and reptiles appeared. At the end of the Paleozoic, close to 250 mya, several varieties of mammal-like reptiles were also diversifying. It's generally thought that some of these forms ultimately gave rise to the mammals.

The evolutionary history of vertebrates and other organisms during the Paleozoic and Mesozoic was profoundly influenced by geographical events. We know that the positions of the earth's continents have dramatically shifted during the last several hundred million years. This process, called **continental drift**, is explained by the geological theory of *plate tectonics*, which states that the earth's crust is a series of gigantic moving and colliding plates. Such massive geological movements can induce volcanic activity (as, for example, all around the Pacific rim), mountain building (for example, the Himalayas), and earthquakes. Living on the juncture of the Pacific and North American plates, residents of the Pacific coast of the United States are acutely aware of some of these consequences, as illus-

geological time scale   The organization of earth history into eras, periods, and epochs; commonly used by geologists and paleoanthropologists.

continental drift   The movement of continents on sliding plates of the earth's surface. As a result, the positions of large landmasses have shifted drastically during the earth's history.

ERA	PERIOD	(Began mya)	EPOCH	(Began mya)
CENOZOIC	Quaternary	1.8	Holocene Pleistocene	0.01 1.8
	Tertiary	65	Pliocene Miocene Oligocene Eocene Paleocene	5 23 33 55 65
MESOZOIC	Cretaceous	136		
	Jurassic	190		
	Triassic	225		
PALEOZOIC	Permian	280		
	Carboniferous	345		
	Devonian	395		
	Silurian	430		
	Ordovician	500		
	Cambrian	570		
PRE-CAMBRIAN				

FIGURE 5-7
Geological time scale.

trated by the explosive volcanic eruption of Mt. St. Helens and the frequent earthquakes in Alaska and California.

While reconstructing the earth's physical history, geologists have established the prior, much altered, positions of major continental landmasses. During the late Paleozoic, the continents came together to form a single colossal landmass called *Pangea*. (In reality, the continents had been drifting on plates, coming together and separating, long before the end of the Paleozoic around 225 mya). During the early Mesozoic, the southern continents (South America, Africa, Antarctica, Australia, and India) began to split off from Pangea, forming a large southern continent called *Gondwanaland* (Fig. 5-8a). Similarly, the northern continents (North America, Greenland, Europe, and Asia) were consolidated into a northern landmass called *Laurasia*. During the Mesozoic, Gondwanaland and Laurasia continued to drift apart and to break up into smaller segments. By the end of the Mesozoic (about 65 mya), the continents were beginning to assume their current positions (Fig. 5-8b).

The evolutionary ramifications of this long-term continental drift were profound. Groups of land animals became effectively isolated from each other by oceans, significantly influencing the distribution of reptiles and mammals with each continental movement. These movements continued in the Cenozoic and indeed are still happening, although without such dramatic results.

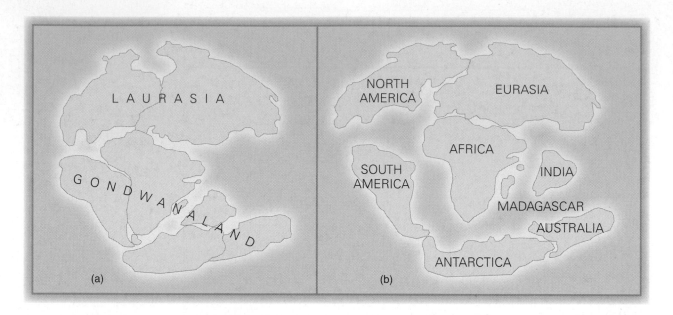

(a)   (b)

FIGURE 5-8

Continental drift. Changes in positions of the continental plates from the late Paleozoic to the early Cenozoic. (a) Positions of the continents during the Mesozoic (ca. 125 mya). Pangea is breaking up into a northern landmass (Laurasia) and a southern landmass (Gondwanaland). (b) Positions of the continents at the beginning of the Cenozoic (ca. 65 mya).

ecological niches   The positions of species within their physical and biological environments, together making up the *ecosystem*. A species' ecological niche is defined by such components as diet, terrain, vegetation, type of predators, relationships with other species, and activity patterns, and each niche is unique to a given species.

placental   A type (subclass) of mammal. During the Cenozoic, placentals became the most widespread and numerous mammals and today are represented by upwards of 20 orders, including the primates.

epochs   Categories of the geological time scale; subdivisions of periods. In the Cenozoic, epochs include the Paleocene, Eocene, Oligocene, Miocene, and Pliocene (from the Tertiary) and the Pleistocene and Holocene (from the Quaternary).

During most of the Mesozoic, reptiles were the dominant land vertebrates, and they exhibited a broad expansion into a variety of **ecological niches**, which included aerial and marine habitats. The most famous of these highly successful Mesozoic reptiles were the dinosaurs, which themselves evolved into a wide array of sizes and species and adapted to a variety of lifestyles. Dinosaur paleontology, never a boring field, has advanced several startling notions in recent years: that many dinosaurs were "warm-blooded" (see p. 113); that some varieties were quite social and probably also engaged in considerable parental care; that many forms became extinct because of major climatic changes to the earth's atmosphere from collisions with comets or asteroids; and finally, that not all dinosaurs became entirely extinct and have many descendants still living today (that is, all modern birds). (See Fig. 5-9 for a summary of major events in early vertebrate evolutionary history.)

The earliest mammals are known from traces of fossils from early in the Mesozoic, but the first **placental** mammals can't be positively identified until quite late in the Mesozoic, approximately 70 mya. This means that the highly successful mammalian diversification, portions of which we still see today, took place almost entirely within the most recent era of geological history, the Cenozoic.

The Cenozoic is divided into two periods, the Tertiary (about 63 million years duration) and the Quaternary, from about 1.8 mya up to and including the present (see Fig. 5-7). Paleontologists often refer to the next, more precise level of subdivision within the Cenozoic as the **epochs**. There are seven epochs within the Cenozoic: the Paleocene, Eocene, Oligocene, Miocene, Pliocene, Pleistocene, and Holocene, the last often referred to as the Recent epoch. As we'll see in Chapter 9, each epoch of the Cenozoic can be roughly assigned to a broad segment of primate evolution.

Mammalian Evolution

Following the extinction of the dinosaurs and many other Mesozoic forms (at the end of the Mesozoic), a wide array of ecological niches became available, and this allowed the rapid expansion and diversification of mammals. The Cenozoic was an opportunistic time for mammals, and it's known as the Age of Mammals. Mesozoic mammals were small animals about the size of mice, which they resembled superficially. The wide diversification of mammals in the Cenozoic saw the rise of the major lineages of all modern mammals. Indeed, mammals, along with birds, replaced reptiles as the dominant terrestrial vertebrates.

	PALEOZOIC						MESOZOIC		
Cambrian	Ordovician	Silurian	Devonian	Carbon-iferous	Permian		Triassic	Jurassic	Cretaceous
Trilobites abundant; also brachiopods, jellyfish, worms, and other invertebrates.	First fishes; trilobites still abundant; graptolites and corals become plentiful; possible land plants.	Jawed fishes appear; first air-breathing animals; definite land plants.	Age of Fish; first amphibians and first forests appear.	First reptiles; radiation of amphibians; modern insects diversify.	Reptile radiation; mammal-like reptiles appear.	Major extinction event	Reptiles further radiate; first dinosaurs; egg-laying mammals.	Great Age of Dinosaurs; flying and swimming dinosaurs appear; first toothed birds.	Placental and marsupial mammals appear; first modern birds.

570 mya   500 mya   430 mya   395 mya   345 mya   280 mya   225 mya   190 mya   136 mya   65 mya

How do we account for the rapid success of the mammals? Several characteristics relating to learning and general flexibility of behavior are of prime importance. To process more information, mammals were selected for larger brains than those typically found in reptiles. In particular, the cerebrum became generally enlarged, especially the outer covering, the neocortex, which controls higher brain functions (Fig. 5-10). In some mammals, the cerebrum expanded so much that it came to comprise most of the brain volume; the number of surface convolutions also increased, creating more surface area and thus providing space for even more nerve cells (neurons). As we'll soon see (in Chapter 6), this is a trend even further emphasized among the primates.

For such a large and complex organ as the mammalian brain to develop, a longer, more intense period of growth is required. Slower development can occur internally (*in utero*) as well as after birth. Internal fertilization and internal development aren't unique to mammals, but the latter is a major innovation among terrestrial vertebrates. Other forms (birds, most fishes, and reptiles) incubate their young externally by laying eggs, while mammals, with very few exceptions, give birth to live young. Even among mammals, however, there's considerable variation among the major groups in how mature the young are at birth. As you'll see, it is in mammals like us—the *placental* forms—that *in utero* development goes farthest.

FIGURE 5-9
This time line depicts major events in early vertebrate evolution.

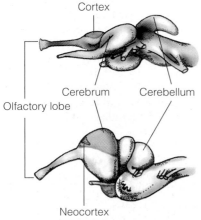

FISH BRAIN

Cortex

Cerebrum   Cerebellum

Olfactory lobe

Neocortex

REPTILE BRAIN

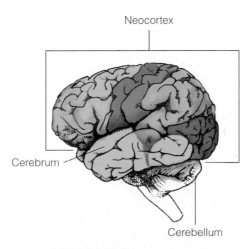

Neocortex

Cerebrum

Cerebellum

PRIMATE BRAIN

FIGURE 5-10
Lateral view of the brain in fishes, reptiles, and primates. You can see the increased size of the cerebral cortex of the primate brain. The cerebral cortex integrates sensory information and selects responses.

A CLOSER LOOK   Deep Time

The vast expanse of time during which evolution has occurred on earth staggers the imagination. Indeed, this fundamental notion of what John McPhee has termed "deep time" is not really understood or, in fact, widely believed. Of course, as we've emphasized beginning with Chapter 1, *belief*, as such, is not part of science. But observation, theory building, and testing are. Still, in a world populated mostly by nonscientists, the concept of deep time, crucial as it is to geology and anthropology, is resisted by many people. This situation really isn't surprising; as an idea that can be truly understood (that is, internalized and given some personal meaning), deep time is in many ways counterintuitive. As individuals, human beings measure their existence in months, years, or in the span of human lifetimes.

But what are these durations, measured against geological or galactic phenomena? In a real sense, these vast time expanses are beyond human comprehension. We can reasonably fathom the reaches of human history, stretching to about 5,000 years ago. In a leap of imagination, we can perhaps even begin to grasp the stretch of time back to the cave painters of France and Spain, approximately 17,000 to 25,000 years ago. How do we relate, then, to a temporal span that's 10 times this one, back to 250,000 years ago, about the time of the earliest *Homo sapiens*—or to 10 times this span to 2,500,000 years ago (about the time of the appearance of our genus, *Homo*)? We surely can respond that any of these time blocks are vast—and then *more* vast. But multiply this last duration another 1,000 times (to 2,500,000,000), and we're back to a time of fairly early life-forms. And we'd have to reach still further into earth's past, another 1.5 billion years, to approach the *earliest* documented life.

The dimensions of these intervals are humbling, to say the least. The discovery in the nineteenth century of deep time (as we documented in Chapter 2) in what the late Stephen Jay Gould called "geology's greatest contribution to human thought" plunged one more dagger into humanity's long-cherished special view of itself. Astronomers had previously established how puny our world was in the physical expanse of space, and then geologists showed that even on our own small planet, we were but residues dwarfed within a river of time "without a vestige of a beginning or prospect of an end" (from James Hutton, a founder of modern geology and one of the discoverers of deep time). It's no wonder that people resist the concept of deep time; it not only stupefies our reason, but implies a sense of collective meaninglessness and reinforces our individual mortality.

Geologists, astronomers, and other scholars have struggled for over a century, with modest success, to translate the tales told in rocks and hurtling stars in terms that everyone can understand. Various analogies have been attempted—metaphors, really—drawn from common experience. Among the most successful of these attempts is a "cosmic calendar" devised by eminent astronomer Carl Sagan in his book *Dragons of Eden* (1977). In this version of time's immensity, Sagan likens the passage of geological time to that of one calendar year. The year begins on January 1 with the "Big Bang," the cosmic explosion marking the beginning of the universe and the beginning of time. In this version, the Big Bang is set at 15 billion years ago,* with some of the major events in the geological past as follows:

(a) REPTILIAN (alligator): homodont

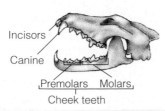

Incisors
Canine
Premolars Molars
Cheek teeth

(b) MAMMALIAN: heterodont

FIGURE 5-11
Reptilian and mammalian teeth.

Another distinctive feature of mammals is seen in the dentition. While living reptiles consistently have similarly shaped teeth (called a *homodont* dentition), mammals have differently shaped teeth (Fig. 5-11). This varied pattern, termed a **heterodont** dentition, is reflected in the ancestral (primitive) mammalian array of dental elements, which includes 3 incisors, 1 canine, 4 premolars, and 3 molars in each quarter of the mouth. Since the upper and lower jaws are usually the same and are symmetrical for both sides, the "dental formula" is conventionally illustrated by dental quarter (see p. 131 for a more complete discussion of dental patterns as they apply to primates). So, with 11 teeth in each quarter of the mouth, the ancestral mammalian dental complement includes a total of 44 teeth. Such a heterodont arrangement allows mammals to process a wide variety of foods. Incisors can be used for cutting, canines for grasping and piercing, and premolars and molars for crushing and grinding.

A final point regarding teeth relates to their disproportionate representation in the fossil record. As the hardest, most durable portion of a vertebrate skeleton, teeth have the greatest likelihood of becoming fossilized (that is, mineralized, since teeth are predominantly mineral to begin with). As a result, the vast majority of available fossil data (particularly early on) for most vertebrates, including primates, consists of teeth.

Another major adaptive complex that distinguishes contemporary mammals from reptiles is the maintenance of a constant internal body temperature. Known colloquially (and incorrectly) as warm-bloodedness, this crucial physiological adaptation is also seen in contemporary birds (and may have characterized many dinosaurs as well). In fact, many

Time Unit Conversion Using the Cosmic Calendar

1 year = 15,000,000,000 years	1 hour = 1,740,000 years
1 month = 1,250,000,000 years	1 minute = 29,000 years
1 day = 41,000,000 years	1 second = 475 years

			December 31 Events
Big Bang	January 1	Appearance of early hominoids (apes and humans)	12:30 P.M.
Formation of the earth	September 14		
Origin of life on earth (approx.)	September 25	First hominids	9:30 P.M.
		Extensive cave painting in Europe	11:59 P.M.
Significant oxygen atmosphere begins to develop	December 1	Invention of agriculture	11:59:20 P.M.
		Renaissance in Europe: Ming Dynasty in China; emergence of scientific method	11:59:59 P.M.
Precambrian ends; Paleozoic begins; invertebrates flourish	December 17		
Paleozoic ends and Mesozoic begins	December 25	Widespread development of science and technology; emergence of a global culture; first steps in space exploration	NOW: the first second of the New Year
Cretaceous period: first flowers; dinosaurs become extinct	December 28		
Mesozoic ends; Cenozoic begins; adaptive radiation of placental mammals	December 29		

*Recent evidence gathered by the Hubble Space Telescope has questioned the established date for the Big Bang. However, even the most recent data are somewhat contradictory, suggesting a date from as early as 16 billion years ago (indicated by the age of the oldest stars) to as recent as 8 billion years ago (indicated by the rate of expansion of the universe). Here, we'll follow the conventional dating of 15 billion years; if you apply the most conservative approximation (8 billion years), the calibrations shift as follows: 1 day = 22,000,000 years; 1 hour = 913,000 years; 1 minute = 15,000 years. Using these calculations, for example, the first hominids appear on December 31 at 7:37 P.M., and modern *Homo sapiens* are on the scene at 11:42 P.M.

contemporary reptiles are able to approximate a constant internal body temperature through behavioral means (especially by regulating activity and exposing the body to the sun). In this sense, reptiles (along with birds and mammals) could be said to be *homeothermic*. So a more useful distinction is to see how the energy to maintain body temperature is produced and channeled. In reptiles, it's obtained directly from exposure to the sun; reptiles are thus said to be *ectothermic*. In mammals and birds, however, the energy is generated *internally* through metabolic activity (by processing food or by muscle action); for this reason, mammals and birds are referred to as **endothermic**.

The Emergence of Major Mammalian Groups

There are three major subgroups of living mammals: the egg-laying mammals, or monotremes, the pouched mammals, or marsupials (Fig. 5-12), and the placental mammals. The monotremes (of which the platypus is one example) are extremely primitive and are considered more distinct from marsupials or placentals than these two subgroups are from each other.

heterodont Having different kinds of teeth; characteristic of mammals, whose teeth consist of incisors, canines, premolars, and molars.

endothermic (*endo*, meaning "within" or "internal") Able to maintain internal body temperature by producing energy through metabolic processes within cells; characteristic of mammals, birds, and perhaps some dinosaurs.

J. C. Stevenson/Animals Animals

FIGURE 5-12
A wallaby with an infant in the pouch (marsupials).

The most notable difference between marsupials and placentals concerns fetal development. In marsupials, the young are born extremely immature and must complete development in an external pouch. But placental mammals develop over a longer period of time *in utero*, made possible by the evolutionary development of a specialized tissue (the placenta) that provides for fetal nourishment.

With a longer gestation period, the central nervous system develops more completely in the placental fetus. What's more, after birth, the "bond of milk" between mother and young allows more time for complex neural structures to form. We should also emphasize that from a *biosocial* perspective, this dependency period not only allows for adequate physiological development but also provides for a wider range of learning stimuli. That is, a vast amount of information is channeled to the young mammalian brain through observation of the mother's behavior and through play with age-mates. It's not enough to have evolved a brain capable of learning. Collateral evolution of mammalian social systems has ensured that young mammal brains are provided with ample learning opportunities and are thus put to good use.

Processes of Macroevolution

As we noted earlier, evolution operates at both microevolutionary and macroevolutionary levels. We discussed evolution primarily from a microevolutionary perspective in Chapters 3 and 4; in this chapter, our focus is on macroevolution. Macroevolutionary mechanisms operate more on the whole species than on individuals or populations, and they take much longer than microevolutionary processes to have a noticeable impact.

ADAPTIVE RADIATION

As we mentioned in Chapter 2, the potential capacity of a group of organisms to multiply is practically unlimited, but its ability to increase its numbers is regulated largely by the availability of resources (food, water, shelter, and space). As population size increases, access to resources decreases, and the environment will ultimately prove inadequate. Depleted resources induce some members of a population to seek an environment in which competition is reduced and the opportunities for survival and reproductive success are increased. This evolutionary tendency to exploit unoccupied habitats may eventually produce an abundance of diverse species.

This story has been played out countless times during the history of life, and some groups have expanded extremely rapidly. This evolutionary process, known as **adaptive radiation**, can be seen in the divergence of the stem reptiles into the profusion of different forms of the late Paleozoic and especially those of the Mesozoic. It's a process that takes place when a life-form rapidly takes advantage, so to speak, of the many newly available ecological niches.

The principle of evolution illustrated by adaptive radiation is fairly simple, but important. It may be stated in this way: A species, or group of species, will diverge into as many variations as two factors allow. These factors are (1) its adaptive potential and (2) the adaptive opportunities of the available niches.

In the case of reptiles, there was little divergence in the very early stages of evolution, when the ancestral form was little more than one among a variety of amphibian water dwellers. Later, a more efficient egg (one that could incubate out of water), developed in reptiles; this new egg, with a hard, watertight shell, had great adaptive potential, but initially there were few zones to invade. When reptiles became fully terrestrial, however, a wide array of ecological niches became accessible to them. Once freed from their attachment to water, reptiles were able to exploit landmasses with no serious competition from any other animal. They moved into the many different ecological niches on land (and to some extent in the air and sea), and as they adapted to these areas, they diversified into a large number of species. This spectacular radiation burst forth with such evolutionary speed that it may well be termed an adaptive explosion.

Of course, the rapid expansion of placental mammals at the beginning of the Cenozoic is another excellent example of adaptive radiation.

adaptive radiation The relatively rapid expansion and diversification of life-forms into new ecological niches.

GENERALIZED AND SPECIALIZED CHARACTERISTICS

Another aspect of evolution closely related to adaptive radiation involves the transition from *generalized* characteristics to *specialized* characteristics. These two terms refer to the adaptive potential of a particular trait. A trait that's adapted for many functions is said to be generalized, while one that's limited to a narrow set of functions is said to be specialized.

For example, a generalized mammalian limb has five fairly flexible digits, adapted for many possible functions (grasping, weight support, and digging). In this respect, human hands are still quite generalized. On the other hand (or foot), there have been many structural modifications in our feet in order to make them suited for the specialized function of stable weight support in an upright posture.

The terms *generalized* and *specialized* are also sometimes used when speaking of the adaptive potential of whole organisms. Consider, for example, the aye-aye of Madagascar, an unusual primate species. The aye-aye is a highly specialized animal, structurally adapted to a narrow, rodent/woodpecker-like econiche—digging holes with prominent incisors and removing insect larvae with an elongated bony finger.

It's important to note that only a generalized ancestor can provide the flexible evolutionary basis for rapid diversification. Only a generalized species with potential for adaptation to varied ecological niches can lead to all the later diversification and specialization of forms into particular ecological niches.

An issue that we've already raised also bears on this discussion: the relationship of ancestral and derived characters. It's not always the case, but ancestral characters *usually* tend to be more generalized. And specialized characteristics are nearly always derived ones as well.

MODES OF EVOLUTIONARY CHANGE

Until fairly recently, evolutionary biologists generally agreed that microevolutionary mechanisms could be translated directly into the larger-scale macroevolutionary changes, especially the most central of all macroevolutionary processes, speciation. In the past two decades, this view has been seriously challenged. Many scientists now believe that macroevolution can't be explained solely in terms of accumulated microevolutionary changes. Consequently, these researchers are convinced that macroevolution is only partly understandable through microevolutionary models.

Gradualism versus Punctuated Equilibrium   The traditional view of evolution has emphasized that change accumulates gradually in evolving lineages, an idea called *phyletic gradualism*. Accordingly, the complete fossil record of an evolving group (if it could be recovered) would display a series of forms with finely graded transitional differences between each ancestor and its descendant; that is, many "missing links" will be present. The fact that such transitional forms are only rarely found is attributed to the incompleteness of the fossil record, or, as Darwin called it, "a history of the world, imperfectly kept, and written in changing dialect."

For more than a century, this perspective dominated evolutionary biology. But in the last 30 years, some biologists have called it into question. The evolutionary mechanisms operating on species over the long run aren't always gradual. In some cases species persist, basically unchanged, for thousands of generations. Then, rather suddenly (at least in geological terms) a "spurt" of speciation occurs. This uneven, nongradual process of long stasis and quick spurts has been termed **punctuated equilibrium** (Gould and Eldredge, 1977). In this model, there are no "missing links" between species; the gaps are real, not artifacts of an imperfect fossil record.

What the advocates of punctuated equilibrium are disputing are the tempo (rate) and mode (manner) of evolutionary change as commonly understood since Darwin's time. Rather than a slow, steady tempo, this alternate view postulates long periods of no change (that is, equilibrium) punctuated (interrupted) only occasionally by sudden bursts. From this observation, many researchers concluded that the mode of evolution, too, must be different from that suggested by classical Darwinists. Rather than gradual accumulation of small changes in a single lineage, advocates of punctuated equilibrium believe that an additional evolutionary mechanism is required to push the process along. Therefore, they postulate *speciation* as the major influence in bringing about rapid evolutionary change.

punctuated equilibrium The concept that evolutionary change proceeds through long periods of stasis punctuated by rapid periods of change.

How well does the paleontological record agree with the predictions of punctuated equilibrium? Considerable fossil data do, in fact, show long periods of stasis punctuated by occasional quite rapid changes (taking from about 10,000 to 50,000 years). The best supporting evidence for punctuated equilibrium has come from marine invertebrate fossils. Intermediate forms are rare, not so much because the fossil record is poor but because the speciation events and longevity of these transitional species were so short that we shouldn't expect to find them very often.

And while some of the fossil evidence of other animals, including primates (Gingerich, 1985; Brown and Rose, 1987; Rose, 1991), doesn't fit the expectations of punctuated equilibrium, it would be misleading to assume that evolutionary change in these groups must thus be taking place at a completely gradual tempo. Moreover, recent molecular evidence suggests that both gradual change and rapid punctuated change occurred in the evolution of both plants and animals (Pagel, et al. 2006). In all lineages, the pace assuredly speeds up and slows down due to factors that influence the size and relative isolation of populations. Environmental changes that influence the pace and direction of natural selection must also be considered. So, in general accordance with the Modern Synthesis, and as indicated by molecular evidence, microevolution and macroevolution don't need to be "decoupled," or considered separately, as some evolutionary biologists have suggested.

VISUAL SUMMARY

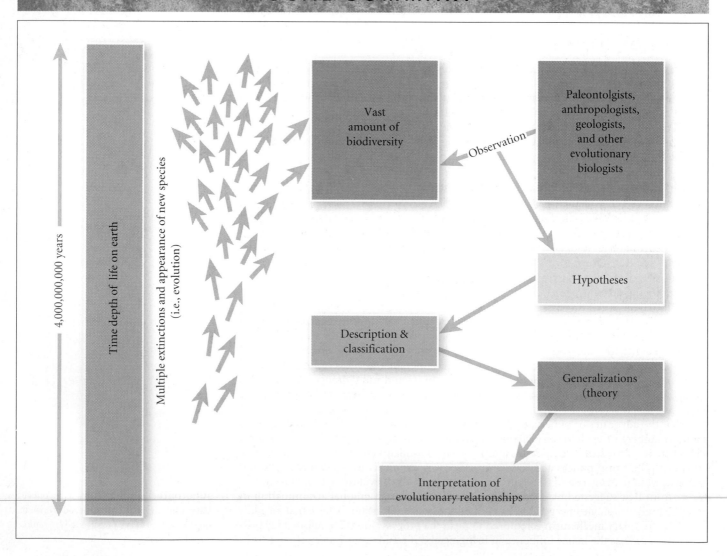

Summary: Putting It All Together

In this chapter, we've surveyed the basics of vertebrate and mammalian evolution, emphasizing a macroevolutionary perspective. Given the huge amount of organic diversity displayed, as well as the vast amount of time involved, two major organizing perspectives prove indispensable: (1) schemes of formal classification to organize organic diversity and (2) the geological time scale to organize geological time. We reviewed the principles of classification in some detail, contrasting two differing approaches: evolutionary systematics and cladistics. Because primates are vertebrates and, more specifically, mammals, we briefly reviewed these broader organic groups, emphasizing major evolutionary trends.

Theoretical perspectives relating to contemporary understanding of macroevolutionary processes (especially the concepts of species and speciation) are crucial to any interpretation of long-term aspects of evolutionary history, be it vertebrate, mammalian, or primate. Since genus and species designation is the common form of reference for both living and extinct organisms (and we use it frequently throughout the text), we discussed its biological significance in depth. From a more general theoretical perspective, evolutionary biologists have postulated two different modes of evolutionary change: gradualism and punctuated equilibrium. Currently, even though the available fossil record does not conform entirely to the predictions of punctuated equilibrium, we should not conclude that evolutionary tempo was necessarily strictly gradual (which it certainly was not).

Critical Thinking Questions

1. What are the two goals of classification? What happens when meeting both goals simultaneously becomes difficult or even impossible?

2. Remains of a fossil mammal have been found on your campus. If you adopt a cladistic approach, how would you determine (a) that it's a mammal rather than some other kind of vertebrate (discuss specific characters), (b) what kind of mammal it is (again, discuss specific characters), and (c) how it *might* be related to one or more living mammals (again, discuss specific characters)?

3. For the same fossil find (and your interpretation) in question 2, draw an interpretive figure using cladistic analysis (that is, draw a cladogram). Next, using more traditional evolutionary systematics, construct a phylogeny. Lastly, explain the differences between the cladogram and the phylogeny (be sure to emphasize the fundamental ways the two schemes differ).

4. a. Humans are fairly generalized mammals. What do we mean by this, and what specific features (characters) would you select to illustrate this statement?

   b. More precisely, humans are *placental* mammals. How do humans, and generally all other placental mammals, differ from the other two major groups of mammals?

Just When We Thought Things Couldn't Get Any Worse: Bushmeat and Ebola

Several major extinction events have occurred throughout the course of vertebrate evolution, and each of these decimated tens of thousands of species in a relatively short period of time. The best-documented of these extinction events occurred approximately 65 mya, at the end of the Mesozoic. Geological evidence indicates that at this time a large asteroid collided with the earth, causing major climatic changes and widespread extinctions of many life-forms, including the dinosaurs. Geologists have also found evidence of an earlier mass extinction, dating to the end of the Paleozoic (ca. 250 mya). That event, perhaps caused by a volcanic eruption or other geological forces, is estimated to have wiped out over 90 percent of all marine life.

Today, we're in the midst of another mass extinction crisis, one that could match the other two events of the last 250 million years. However, unlike the earlier mass extinctions, the current one is due to the environmentally destructive influence of a single expanding species. That species is, of course, *Homo sapiens*. Many primatologists and conservationists were taken off guard when, in the 1990s, they became aware of the devastating effects of a rapidly developing trade in *bushmeat* (meat derived from wild animals) in West and central Africa. (The problem has now expanded to East Africa.) Actually, as early as the 1960s and '70s, primatologists began reporting that monkeys in many West African forests were becoming scarce because of a developing commercial trade in monkey meat (Oates, 1999). But the current slaughter is unprecedented. In fact, some observers have likened the killing of primates and other species in parts of Africa to the near extermination of the American bison in the nineteenth century.

Wherever they occur, nonhuman primates have traditionally been an important source of food for people. In the past, subsistence hunting by indigenous peoples, armed with snares and bows and arrows, didn't usually constitute a serious threat to nonhuman primate populations, and certainly not to entire species. But now, hunters have greater access to firearms, and with shotguns and automatic rifles, they can wipe out an entire group of monkeys, gorillas, or chimpanzees in minutes.

The underlying factor that has produced the current bushmeat catastrophe is human population growth. The current human population of West and central Africa (approximately 24 million) increases at an annual rate of 2 to 4 percent. Traditionally, the people of these regions weren't pastoralists, and while today some households may keep a few cattle, goats, and chickens, the primary dietary source of animal protein is still meat from wild animals.

Another key factor in the rapidly developing bushmeat trade is logging, which occurs because of the high demand for tropical hardwoods in Europe and the United States. (We encourage you to consider this the next time you are tempted to buy anything made of wood from any tropical area.)

The construction of logging roads, mainly by French, German, and Belgian lumber companies, has opened up vast tracts of forest that, until recently, were inaccessible to local hunters. Once the roads are cut, hunters hitch rides to previously inaccessible areas. (Of course, the truck drivers receive a fee, ultimately derived from the sale of bushmeat.) Logging trucks also carry meat out of the forest, which allows hunters to kill more animals because they don't have to carry the meat. Lastly, the loggers themselves consume bushmeat. In one logging camp in Gabon, 1,200 loggers consumed an estimated 80 tons of bushmeat in just one year! In another camp in Congo, over 8,000 animals were consumed. What has emerged is a profitable trade in bushmeat, a trade in which logging company employees and local government officials participate with hunters, villagers, market vendors, and smugglers who cater to growing overseas markets.

As you can see, the hunting of wild animals for food, particularly in Africa, has quickly shifted from being a subsistence activity to a commercial enterprise of international scope. The carcasses of primates and other species are common sights in local African markets (Fig. 1). Gorilla and chimpanzee meat is considered a delicacy in the restaurants of some West African cities, and the trade extends beyond Africa. Wildlife carcasses are

FIGURE 1

Red-eared guenons (with red tails) and Preuss' guenons for sale in bushmeat market, Malabo, Equatorial Guinea.

Courtesy, John Oates

smuggled into European countries to be illegally sold at high prices, and chimpanzee and gorilla meat is reportedly sometimes served in some Belgian and French restaurants.

With unprecedented access to the forests, hunters currently take over 1 million metric tons of meat (equivalent to over 4 million cattle) from the forests annually. Most of this meat comes from elephants, duikers (small forest antelopes), monkeys, porcupines, reptiles, and rodents. About 1 percent comes from great ape carcasses, but much more comes from monkeys. Given the very slow reproductive rate of primates, and great apes in particular, this level of hunting far exceeds the replacement capacity of these species and also of many nonprimate species.

It's impossible to know how many animals are slaughtered each year. But estimates for monkeys and apes are in the thousands. In addition to those killed, hundreds of infants are orphaned and sold in the markets as pets (Fig. 2). Although a few of these traumatized orphans make it to sanctuaries, most die of injury, starvation, disease, and neglect within days or weeks of capture.

But it gets worse. About 80 percent of the world's remaining gorillas and most of the common chimpanzees are found in two west African countries, Gabon and the Republic of Congo (Walsh, et al., 2003; Leroy et al., 2004). Between 1983 and 2000, ape populations in Gabon declined by half, mostly because of hunting. But, these populations are now faced with another threat, the viral disease ebola. This severe disease, first recognized in 1976, is believed to be maintained in wild animals, most probably fruit bats (Leroy, et al., 2005). Furthermore, ebola is transmitted to humans through contact (butchering, eating) with infected animals. In humans, ebola is frequently fatal and symptoms include fever, vomiting, diarrhea, and sometimes, severe hemorrhaging.

Since 1994, there have been four outbreaks of ebola in Gabon, and ape carcasses were found near affected human settlements in three. In one area of Gabon where large-scale hunting hasn't occurred, ape populations declined by an estimated 90 percent between 1991 and 2000! Rouguet et al (2005) reported that ebola was the confirmed cause of death in great apes in the Republic of Congo in 2003 and 2004. But the worst news came in December, 2006, with a report that as many as 5000 gorillas had died of ebola in the Republic of Congo (Bermejo, 2006). Researchers now think the disease is being spread within and between gorilla groups and not through contact with reservoir species like bats; and this fact offers some slight hope that a vaccination program might be effective. But, it's obvious that, faced with the combination of ebola and commercial hunting, great ape populations in western Africa cannot

FIGURE 2

These orphaned chimpanzee infants are being bottle-fed at a sanctuary near Pointe Noir, Congo. Probably, they will never be returned to the wild and they face a very uncertain future.

be sustained and are now being diminished to small remnant populations.

The problems of deforestation, disease, and overhunting are overwhelming, and if solutions are to be found, they will need to focus on the needs of millions of people living in poverty and facing starvation. At the local level, it's nearly impossible to convince a poor farmer not to kill monkeys he can sell in the market for a higher price than his crops will bring. But selling primate carcasses represents only short-term gain because there can be no long-term profit.

Conservation organizations are encouraging logging companies to set aside refuges for threatened species. Logging companies are also being urged to stop employees from transporting hunters and to provide employees with sources of protein other than bushmeat. So far, one company has complied. Some governments are also considering ways to practice sustainable management of natural resources, including wildlife.

Locally, efforts are being directed at encouraging people to eat meat from domestic animals, but this transition will not be easy. Also, there are education programs that teach people about the substantial health risks (e.g., HIV/AIDS and ebola) associated with bushmeat.

Perhaps most encouraging is the establishment of the Great Ape Survival Project (GRASP) in 2001 by the United Nations

Just When We Thought Things Couldn't Get Any Worse: Bushmeat and Ebola CONTINUED

Environmental Program (UNEP). The GRASP Partnership is an alliance of governmental and nongovernmental agencies, great ape conservation groups, conservation groups, prominent scientists, and local communities in countries that are home to great apes. Because it has a position within the United Nations, GRASP can engage governments and organizations in ways that aren't possible for individual conservation groups. GRASP is also able to mobilize resources more effectively and can promote its conservation message internationally at the highest political levels.

In 2003, GRASP appealed for $25 million to be used in attempts to prevent all the great apes (including non-African orangutans) from going extinct. The money (in reality, a paltry sum) would be used to increase enforcement of laws that regulate hunting and illegal logging; and satellite surveillance would help monitor deforestation. Then, in 2005, the Intergovernmental Meeting on Great Apes and First GRASP Council Meeting convened in Kinshasha, Democratic Republic of the Congo (formerly Zaire). This meeting was attended by representatives of more than 200 governments and representatives of 18 of the 23 African and Asian countries where great apes live. At this conference, high-ranking delegates signed the Kinshasha Accord, which has as its goal the development of global strategies that will ensure the survival of the great apes.

It goes without saying that GRASP and other organizations must succeed. Unless deforestation, the spread of ebola, and the slaughter of nonhuman primates are curtailed *very, very, soon,* many species will certainly disappear. In fact, primatologists and conservationists fear that several primate species, certainly the great apes, could be exterminated from parts of Indonesia and West and central Africa by the year 2010. And by the year 2030, they could be extinct in the wild.

CRITICAL THINKING QUESTIONS

1. Can you suggest ways in which the bushmeat trade might be slowed? How would you suggest that the needs of the people be addressed while encouraging them not to kill or sell nonhuman primates and other animals?
2. How have industrialized nations contributed to the development of the bushmeat trade?
3. What are some things you can do that might help stop the bushmeat trade?
4. Can you think of other examples of trade in endangered species, including primates, in other parts of the world? Can you suggest ways in which these activities can be curtailed?

SOURCES

Bermejo, M., J.D. Rodríguez-Teijeiro, Germán Illera, et al. 2006. "Ebola Outbreak Killed 5000 Gorillas." *Science,* **314**:1564.

"Bushmeat. A Wildlife Crisis in West and Central Africa and Around the World." Bushmeat Crisis Task Force (BCTF). Online version at www.bushmeat.org.

"Bushmeat Factsheet." The Jane Goodall Institute. Online version at www.janegoodall.org/.

Hearn, Josephine. 2001. "Unfair Game. The Bushmeat Trade Is Wiping Out Large African Mammals." *Scientific American* June: 24–26.

Leroy, E.M., B. Kumulungui, X. Pourrot, et al. 2005. "Fruit Bats as Reservoirs of Ebola Virus." *Nature*. **438**:575-576.

Leroy, E.M., P. Rouquet, P. Formenty. et al. 2004. "Multiple Ebola Virus Transmission Events and Rapid Decline of Central African Wildlife." *Science*:**303**:387-390.

Strier, Karen B., 1999. *Primate Behavioral Ecology*. (2nd ed.) New York: Allyn & Bacon.

United Nations Environmental Program for Great Ape Survival Program website: www.unep.org/grasp

Walsh, Peter D., et al. 2003. "Catastrophic Ape Decline in Western Equatorial Africa." *Nature*. **422**: 611–614

CHAPTER 6

Survey of the Living Primates

David Haring/Duke Lemur Center

KEY QUESTIONS

What are the major characteristics of primates? Why are humans considered primates?

Why is it important to study nonhuman primates?

Introduction

 Click!

Go to the following media for interactives and exercises on topics covered in this chapter:

- Online Virtual Laboratories for Physical Anthropology, Fourth Edition

Chimpanzees aren't monkeys. Neither are gorillas and orangutans. They're apes, and even though most people think they're basically the same, they're not. Yet, how many times have you seen a greeting card or magazine ad with a picture of a chimpanzee and a phrase that says something like, "Don't monkey around" or "No more monkey business"? Or maybe you've noticed how people at zoos find captive primates especially funny, particularly when they tease them. While these issues may seem trivial, they aren't, because they illustrate how little most people know about our closest relatives. This is extremely unfortunate, because by better understanding these relatives, not only can we better know ourselves, but we can also try to preserve the many nonhuman primate species that are critically endangered.

One way to better understand any organism is to compare its anatomy and behavior with those of other, closely related species. This comparative approach helps explain how and why physiological and behavioral systems evolved as adaptive responses to various selective pressures throughout the course of evolution. This statement applies to *Homo sapiens* just as it does to any other species. So, if we want to identify the components that have shaped the evolution of our species, a good starting point is to compare ourselves to our closest living relatives, the approximately 230 species of nonhuman primates (**prosimians**, monkeys, and apes). (Groves, [2001b], suggests that there may be as many as 350 primate species.)

In this chapter we'll describe the physical characteristics that define the order **Primates**, give a brief overview of the major groups of living primates, and introduce some methods currently used to compare living primates genetically (For a comparison of human and nonhuman skeletons, see Appendix A). Before going further, we again want to call attention to a few common misunderstandings about evolutionary processes.

Evolution isn't a goal-directed process. Therefore, the fact that prosimians evolved before **anthropoids** doesn't mean that prosimians "progressed" or "advanced" to become anthropoids. Living primates aren't in any way "superior" to their evolutionary predecessors or to one another. Consequently, in discussions of major groupings of contemporary nonhuman primates, there's no implied superiority or inferiority of any of these groups. Each lineage or species has come to possess unique qualities that make it better suited to a particular habitat and lifestyle than others. Given that all contemporary organisms are "successful" results of the evolutionary process, it's best to completely avoid using such loaded terms as *superior* and *inferior*. Finally, you shouldn't make the mistake of thinking that contemporary primates (including humans) necessarily represent the final stage or apex of a lineage, because we continue to evolve as a lineage. The only species that represent final evolutionary stages of particular lineages are the ones that become extinct.

prosimians Members of a suborder of Primates, the Prosimii (pronounced "pro-sim´-ee-eye"). Traditionally, the suborder includes lemurs, lorises, and tarsiers.

primates Members of the order of mammals Primates (pronounced "pry-may´-tees"), which includes prosimians, monkeys, apes, and humans.

anthropoids Members of a suborder of Primates, the *Anthropoidea* (pronounced "ann-throw-poid´-ee-uh"). Traditionally, the suborder includes monkeys, apes, and humans.

Primate Characteristics

All primates share many characteristics with other placental mammals (see Chapter 5). Some of these traits are body hair, a relatively long gestation period followed by live birth, mammary glands (thus the term *mammal*), different types of teeth (incisors, canines, premolars, and molars), the ability to maintain a constant internal body temperature through physiological means or *endothermy* (see Chapter 5), increased brain size, and a considerable capacity for learning and behavioral flexibility. So, to differentiate primates as a group

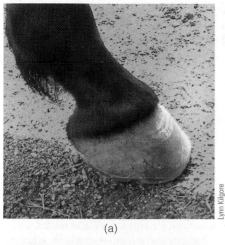

(a)

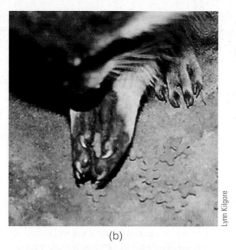

(b)

FIGURE **6-1**
(a) A horse's front foot, homologous with a human hand, has undergone reduction from 5 digits to one. (b) While raccoons are capable of considerable manual dexterity and can readily pick up small objects with one hand, they have no opposable thumb. (c) Many monkeys are able to grasp objects with an opposable thumb, while others have very reduced thumbs.
(d) Humans are capable of a "precision grip." (e) Chimpanzees with their reduced thumbs are capable of a precision grip but frequently use a modified form.

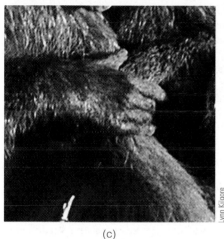

(c)

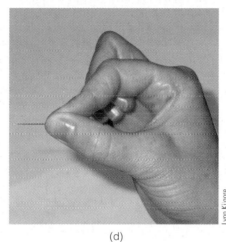

(d)

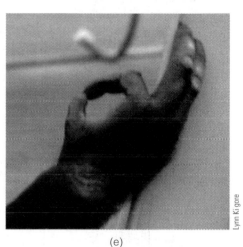

(e)

distinct from other mammals, we need to describe those characteristics that, taken together, set primates apart.

Identifying single traits that define the primate order isn't easy because, compared to most mammals, primates have remained quite *generalized*. That is, primates have retained many ancestral or primitive mammalian traits that many other mammals have lost over time. In response to particular selective pressures, many mammalian groups have become increasingly specialized or derived. For example, through the course of evolution, horses and cattle have undergone a reduction in the number of digits (fingers and toes) from the ancestral pattern of five, to one and two digits respectively. These species have also developed hard, protective coverings over their feet in the form of hooves (see Fig. 6-1a). This limb structure is adaptive in prey species, because their survival depends upon speed and stability, but it restricts the animal to only one type of locomotion (terrestrial quadrupedalism). It also limits limb function to support and movement, and the ability to manipulate objects is lost completely.

Because they're remarkably generalized, primates can't be defined by one or even a few traits they share in common. Therefore anthropologists have drawn attention to a group of characteristics that, when taken together, more or less characterize the entire Primate order. Still, these are a set of *general* tendencies that aren't all equally expressed in all primates. In addition, while some of these traits are unique to primates, many others are retained primitive mammalian characteristics. These latter traits are useful in contrasting the generalized primates with the more specialized varieties of some other placental mammals, but not for determining membership in a specific primate group. So, in the following list we intend to give you an overall structural and behavioral picture of that kind of animal we call "primate," focusing on those characteristics that tend to set primates apart from other mammals. Concentrating on certain ancestral mammalian traits along with more specific, derived ones has been the traditional approach of **primatologists**, and it's still used today. In their limbs and locomotion, teeth and diet, senses, brain, and behavior, primates reflect a common evolutionary history with adaptations to similar environmental challenges, primarily as highly social, arboreal beings.

A. *Limbs and Locomotion*

1. *A tendency toward an erect (orthograde) posture (especially in the upper body).* (Derived trait) All primates show this tendency to some degree, and it's variously associated with sitting, leaping, standing, and occasionally, bipedal walking.

2. *A flexible, generalized limb structure allows most primates to practice various locomotor behaviors.* (Ancestral trait) Primates have retained some bones (such as the clavicle, or collarbone) and certain abilities (like rotation of the forearm) that have been lost in more specialized mammals. Various aspects of hip and shoulder **morphology** also provide primates with a wide range of limb movement and function. Thus, by maintaining a generalized locomotor anatomy, primates aren't restricted to one form of movement, as are many other mammals. Primates also use their limbs for many activities besides locomotion.

3. *Hands and feet with a high degree of* **prehensility** *(grasping ability).* (Derived trait) Lots of animals can manipulate objects, but not as skillfully as primates can. All primates use their hands, and frequently their feet, to grasp and manipulate objects (Fig. 6-1b). This ability is variably expressed and is enhanced by several characteristics, including these:

   a. *Retention of five digits on the hands and feet.* (Ancestral trait) This trait varies somewhat throughout the order, with some species showing marked reduction of the thumb or of the second digit.

   b. *An opposable thumb, and in most species, a divergent and partially opposable big toe.* (Derived trait) Most primates are capable of moving the thumb so that it opposes or comes in contact (in some way) with the second digit or with the palm of the hand (Figs. 6-1c through 6-1e).

   c. *Nails instead of claws.* (Derived trait) This characteristic is seen in all primates except in some highly derived New World monkeys (marmosets and tamarins). All prosimians also possess a grooming claw on one digit.

   d. *Tactile pads enriched with sensory nerve fibers at the ends of digits.* (Derived trait) This characteristic enhances the sense of touch.

B. *Diet and Teeth*

1. *Lack of dietary specialization.* (Ancestral trait) This characteristic is typical of most primates, who tend to eat a wide assortment of food items. In general, primates are **omnivorous**.

2. *A generalized dentition.* (Ancestral trait) The teeth aren't specialized for processing only one type of food, a characteristic related to a general lack of dietary specialization.

C. *The senses and the brain.* (Derived trait) Primates (**diurnal** ones in particular) rely heavily on vision and less on **olfaction**, especially when compared to other mammals. This emphasis is reflected in evolutionary changes in the skull, eyes, and brain.

1. *Color vision.* (Derived trait) This is a characteristic of all diurnal primates. **Nocturnal** primates lack color vision.

2. *Depth perception.* (Derived trait) Primates have **stereoscopic vision**, or the ability to perceive objects in three dimensions. This is made possible through a variety of mechanisms, including

   a. *Eyes positioned toward the front of the face (not to the sides).* (Derived trait) This configuration provides for overlapping visual fields, or **binocular vision** (Fig. 6-2).

---

primatologists   Scientists who study the evolution, anatomy, and behavior of nonhuman primates. Those who study behavior in noncaptive animals are usually trained as physical anthropologists.

morphology   The form (shape, size) of anatomical structures; can also refer to the entire organism.

prehensility   Grasping, as by the hands and feet of primates.

omnivorous   Having a diet consisting of many food types (i.e., plant materials, meat, and insects).

diurnal   Active during the day.

olfaction   The sense of smell.

nocturnal   Active during the night.

stereoscopic vision   The condition whereby visual images are, to varying degrees, superimposed. This provides for depth perception, or viewing the external environment in three dimensions. Stereoscopic vision is partly a function of structures in the brain.

binocular vision   Vision characterized by overlapping visual fields provided by forward-facing eyes. Binocular vision is essential to depth perception.

b. *Visual information from each eye transmitted to visual centers in both **hemispheres** of the brain.* (Derived trait) In nonprimate mammals, most optic nerve fibers cross to the opposite hemisphere through a structure at the base of the brain. In primates, about 40 percent of the fibers remain on the same side (see Fig. 6-2), so that information is shared.

c. *Visual information organized into three-dimensional images by specialized structures in the brain itself.* (Derived trait) The capacity for stereoscopic vision depends on *each* hemisphere of the brain receiving visual information from *both* eyes and from overlapping visual fields.

3. *Decreased reliance on olfaction.* (Derived trait) This trend is expressed as an overall reduction in the size of olfactory structures in the brain (see p. 183–184). Corresponding reduction of the entire olfactory apparatus has also resulted in decreased size of the snout in most species. This is related to an increased reliance on vision. In some species, such as baboons, the large muzzle isn't related to olfaction, but to the need to accommodate large canine teeth. (See "A Closer Look," p. 127.)

4. *Expansion and increased complexity of the brain.* (Derived trait) This is a general trend among placental mammals, but it's especially true of primates. In primates, this expansion is most evident in the visual and association areas of the **neocortex** (portions of the brain where information from different **sensory modalities**

hemispheres Two halves of the cerebrum that are connected by a dense mass of fibers. (The cerebrum is the large, rounded, outer portion of the brain.)

neocortex The more recently evolved portions of the cortex of the brain that are involved with higher mental functions and composed of areas that integrate incoming information from different sensory organs.

sensory modalities Different forms of sensation (e.g., touch, pain, pressure, heat, cold, vision, taste, hearing, and smell)

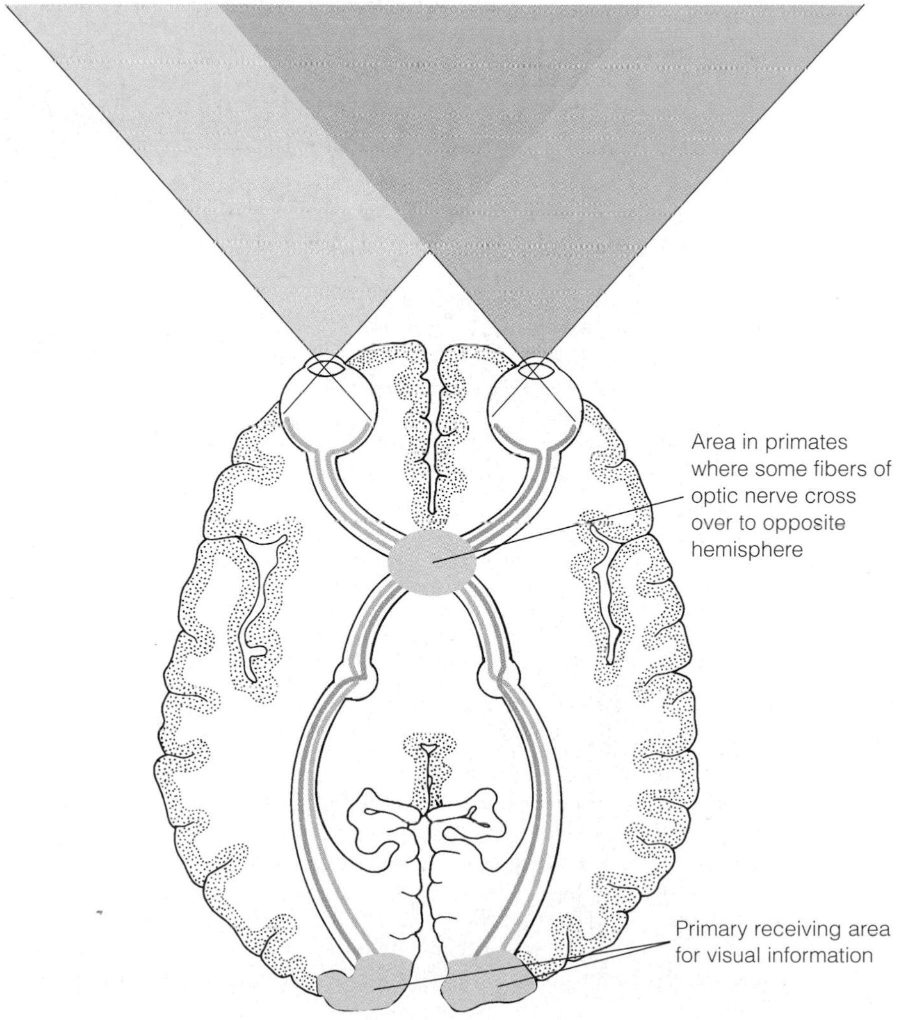

FIGURE **6-2**
Simplified diagram showing overlapping visual fields that permit binocular vision in primates with eyes positioned at the front of the face. (The green shaded area represents the area of overlap.) Stereoscopic vision (three-dimensional vision) is provided in part by binocular vision and in part by the transmission of visual stimuli from each eye to both hemispheres of the brain. (In nonprimate mammals, most, if not all, visual information crosses over to the hemisphere opposite the eye in which it was initially received.)

Area in primates where some fibers of optic nerve cross over to opposite hemisphere

Primary receiving area for visual information

125

A CLOSER LOOK   Primate Cranial Anatomy

Several significant anatomical features of the primate cranium help us distinguish primates from other mammals. The mammalian trend toward increased brain development has been further emphasized in primates, as shown by a relatively enlarged braincase. The primate emphasis on vision is further reflected in generally large eye sockets; the decreased dependence on olfaction is indicated by reduction of the snout and corresponding flattening of the face (Fig. 1).

Here are some of the specific anatomical details seen in modern and most fossil primate crania:

1. The primate face is shortened, and the size of the braincase, relative to that of the face, is enlarged compared to other mammals (see Fig. 1).

2. Eye sockets are enclosed at the sides by a ring of bone called the *postorbital bar* (see Fig. 1). In most other mammals, there is no postorbital bar. Also, in tarsiers, monkeys, apes, and humans, there is a plate of bone at the back of the eye orbit called the *postorbital plate*. The postorbital plate isn't present in lemurs and lorises. The functional significance of these structures hasn't been thoroughly explained, but it may be related to stresses on the eye orbits imposed by chewing (Fleagle, 1999).

3. The region of the skull that contains the structures of the middle ear is completely encircled by a bony structure called the *auditory bulla*. In primates, the floor of the auditory bulla is derived from a segment of the temporal bone (Fig. 2). Of the skeletal structures, most primate paleontologists consider the postorbital bar and the derivation of the auditory bulla to be the two best diagnostic traits of the primate order.

4. The base of the skull in primates is somewhat flexed, so that the muzzle (mouth and nose) is positioned lower relative to the braincase (Fig. 3). This arrangement provides for the exertion of greater force during chewing, particularly as needed for the crushing and grinding of tough vegetable fibers, seeds, and hard-shelled fruits.

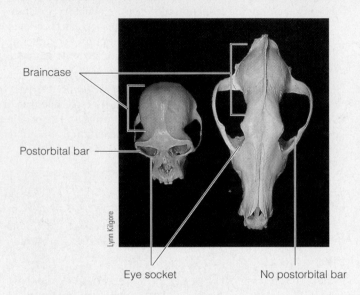

Braincase

Postorbital bar

Lynn Kilgore

Eye socket   No postorbital bar

FIGURE 1
The skull of a gibbon (left) compared to that of a red wolf (right). Note that the absolute size of the braincase in the gibbon is slightly larger than that of the wolf, even though the wolf (at about 80 to 100 pounds) is six times the size of the gibbon (about 15 pounds).

is integrated). Expansion in regions involved with the hand (both sensory and motor) is seen in many primate species, particularly humans.

D. *Maturation, learning, and behavior*
1. *A more efficient means of fetal nourishment, longer periods of gestation, reduced numbers of offspring (with single births the norm), delayed maturation, and extension of the entire life span.* (Derived trait)
2. *A greater dependence on flexible, learned behavior.* (Derived trait) This trend is correlated with delayed maturation and subsequently longer periods of infant and child dependency on at least one parent. As a result of both these trends, parental investment in each offspring is increased, so that although fewer offspring are born, they receive more intense and efficient rearing.
3. *The tendency to live in social groups and the permanent association of adult males with the group.* (Derived trait) Except for some nocturnal species, primates tend to associate with other individuals. The permanent association of adult males with the group is uncommon in mammals but widespread in primates.
4. *The tendency to diurnal activity patterns.* (Derived trait) This trend is seen in most primates; only one monkey species and some prosimians are nocturnal.

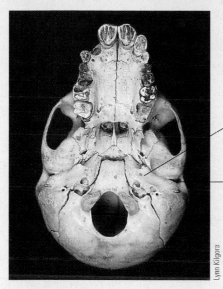

Portion of temporal bone enclosing auditory bulla

External opening to ear (external auditory meatus)

FIGURE 2
The base of an adolescent chimpanzee skull. (Note that in an adult animal, the bones of the skull would be fused together and would not appear as separate elements as shown here.)

FIGURE 3
The skull of a male baboon (a) compared to that of a red wolf (b). The angle at the base of the baboon skull is due to flexion. The corresponding area of the wolf skull is relatively flat. Note the forward-facing position of the eye orbits above the snout in the baboon. Also, be aware that, in the baboon, the enlarged muzzle does *not* reflect a heavy reliance on the sense of smell. Rather, it serves to support very large canine teeth, the roots of which curve back through the bone for as much as 1½ inches.

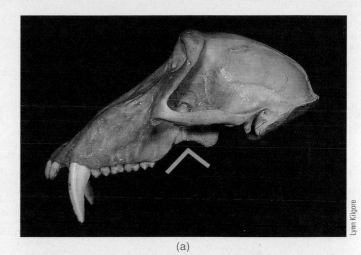

(a)

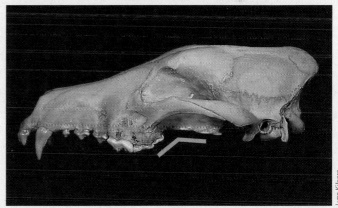

(b)

Primate Adaptations

In this section, we'll consider how primate anatomical traits evolved as adaptations to environmental circumstances. It's important to remember that when you see the phrase "environmental circumstances," it refers to several interrelated variables including climate, diet, habitat (woodland, grassland, forest, etc.), and predation.

EVOLUTIONARY FACTORS

Traditionally, the suite of characteristics shared by primates has been explained as the result of an adaptation to **arboreal** living. While other mammals were adapting to various ground-dwelling lifestyles and even marine environments, the primates found their **adaptive niche** in the trees. Many other mammals were also adapting to arboreal living; but while many of these nested in the trees, they continued to forage for food on the ground. Throughout the course of evolution, though, primates increasingly found foods (leaves, seeds, fruits, nuts, insects, and small mammals) in the trees themselves. Over time, this dietary shift enhanced a general trend toward *omnivory*; and correspondingly, it led to the retention of the generalized dentition that's characteristic of primates.

arboreal Tree-living; adapted to life in the trees.

adaptive niche An organism's entire way of life: where it lives, what it eats, how it gets food, how it avoids predators, and so on.

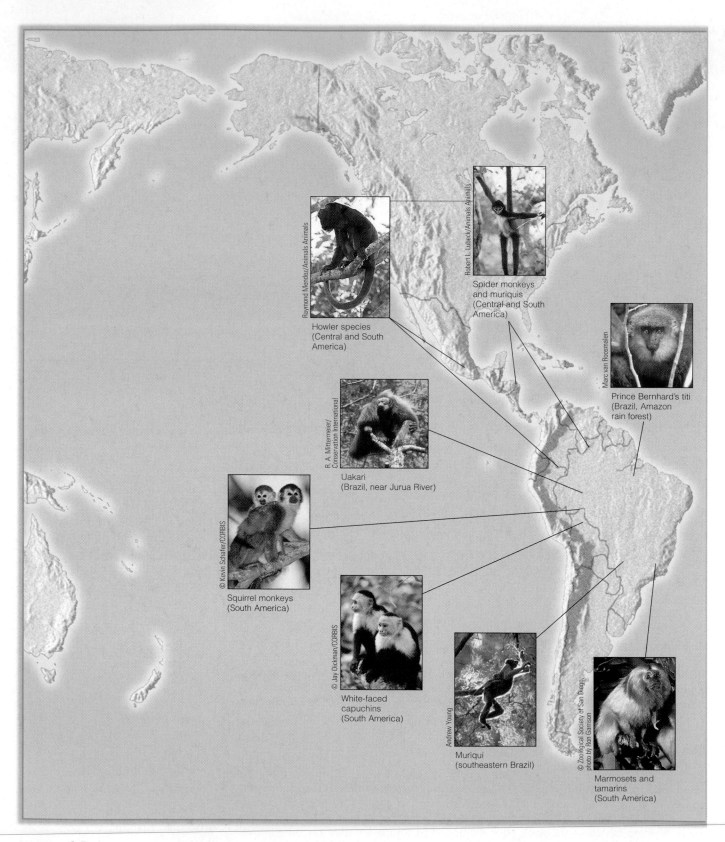

FIGURE 6-3
Geographical distribution of living nonhuman primates. Much original habitat is now very fragmented.

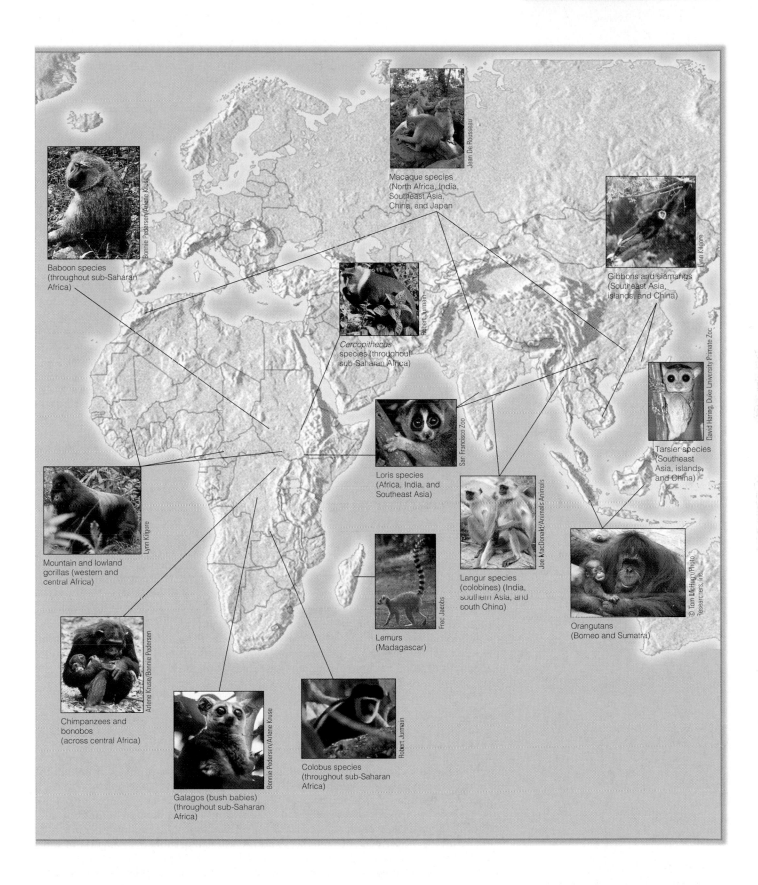

Macaque species (North Africa, India, Southeast Asia, China, and Japan

Gibbons and siamangs (Southeast Asia, islands, and China)

Baboon species (throughout sub-Saharan Africa)

Cercopithecus species (throughout sub-Saharan Africa)

Tarsier species (Southeast Asia, islands, and China)

Loris species (Africa, India, and Southeast Asia)

Mountain and lowland gorillas (western and central Africa)

Langur species (colobines) (India, southern Asia, and south China)

Orangutans (Borneo and Sumatra)

Lemurs (Madagascar)

Chimpanzees and bonobos (across central Africa)

Galagos (bush babies) (throughout sub-Saharan Africa)

Colobus species (throughout sub-Saharan Africa)

Increased reliance on vision, coupled with grasping hands and feet, are also adaptations to an arboreal lifestyle. In a complex, three-dimensional environment with uncertain footholds, acute color vision with depth perception is, for obvious reasons, extremely beneficial.

An alternative to this traditional *arboreal hypothesis*, called the *visual predation hypothesis* (Cartmill, 1972, 1992), points out that animals such as squirrels are also arboreal, yet they haven't evolved primate-like adaptations such as prehensile hands or forward-facing eyes. But visual predators, such as cats and owls, do have forward-facing eyes, and this fact may provide insight into an additional factor that could have shaped primate evolution.

Forward-facing eyes (which facilitate binocular vision), grasping hands and feet, and the presence of nails instead of claws need not have arisen as adaptive advantages in a purely arboreal setting, but they may be the hallmarks of an arboreal visual predator. So, early primates may first have adapted to shrubby forest undergrowth and the lowest tiers of the forest canopy, where they hunted insects and other small prey primarily through stealth.

A third scenario, the *angiosperm radiation hypothesis* (Sussman, 1991), suggests that the basic primate traits were developed in conjunction with another major evolutionary occurrence, the rise of the *angiosperms* (flowering plants) that began around 140 mya. Flowering plants provide numerous resources for primates, including nectar, seeds, and fruits. Sussman argues that since visual predation isn't common among modern primates, forward-facing eyes, grasping extremities, omnivory, and *color vision* may have arisen in response to the demand for fine visual and tactile discrimination, which is necessary when feeding on small food items such as fruits, berries, and seeds among branches and stems (Dominy and Lucas, 2001).

These hypotheses aren't mutually exclusive. The modern suite of primate characteristics might well have originated in non-arboreal settings and certainly may have been stimulated by the new econiches provided by evolving angiosperms. Still, at some point primates did take to the trees, and that's where most of them still live today. Even if the basic primate structural complexes originally facilitated visual predation and/or omnivory in shrubby undergrowth and terminal branches, they became ideally suited for the arboreal adaptations that followed.

Geographical Distribution and Habitats

With only a few exceptions (such as ourselves), nonhuman primates are relegated to the tropical or semitropical areas of the New and Old Worlds. In the New World, these areas include southern Mexico, Central America, and parts of South America. Old World primates are found in Africa, India, Southeast Asia (including numerous islands), and Japan (Fig. 6-3 see previous page).

As we've discussed, most primates are arboreal and live in forest or woodland habitats. But some Old World monkeys (such as baboons) have, to varying degrees, adapted to life on the ground in areas where trees are sparsely distributed. The African apes (gorillas, chimpanzees, and bonobos) also spend a great deal of time on the ground in forested and wooded habitats. Even so, no nonhuman primate species is fully adapted to a terrestrial lifestyle, and they all spend some time in the trees.

Diet and Teeth

Omnivory is one example of the overall lack of specialization in primates. Although the majority of primate species tend to emphasize some food items over others, most eat a combination of fruit, nuts, seeds, leaves, other plant materials, and insects. Many also get animal protein from birds and amphibians. Some (capuchins, baboons, bonobos, and especially chimpanzees) occasionally kill and eat small mammals, including other primates. Others, such as African colobus monkeys and the leaf-eating monkeys (langurs) of India and Southeast Asia, have become more specialized and subsist primarily on leaves.

This wide and varied menu is a good example of the advantages of having a generalized diet, especially in less-predictable environments: if one food source fails (for example, during drought or through human activities), other options may still be available. The downside of being generalized is that there may be competition for some resources with other species, including non-primate ones, that eat the same things. Specialization, where a species has a narrow ecological niche and eats only one or two things, can be advantageous in this regard because these species don't have much competition from others; but it can be catastrophic if the food supply disappears.

Like nearly all other mammals, primates have four kinds of teeth: incisors and canines for biting and cutting, and premolars and molars for chewing and grinding. Biologists use a kind of shorthand called a **dental formula** to describe the number of each type of tooth that typifies a species. A dental formula indicates the number of each tooth type in each quadrant of the mouth (Fig. 6-4). For example, all Old World *anthropoids* have two incisors, one canine, two premolars, and three molars on each side of the midline in both the upper and lower jaws, for a total of 32 teeth. This is represented as a dental formula of:

2.1.2.3 (upper)
2.1.2.3 (lower)

The dental formula for a generalized placental mammal is 3.1.4.3 (three incisors, one canine, four premolars, and three molars). Primates have fewer teeth than this ancestral pattern because of a general evolutionary trend toward a reduced number of teeth in many mammal groups. Consequently, the number of each type of tooth varies between lineages. For example, in most New World monkeys, the dental formula is 2.1.3.3 (two incisors, one canine, three premolars, and three molars). In contrast, humans, apes, and all Old World monkeys share a somewhat different dental formula: 2.1.2.3. This formula differs from that of the New World monkeys in that there's one less premolar.

The overall lack of dietary specialization in primates is correlated with minimal specialization in the size and shape of the teeth. This is because tooth form is directly related to diet. For example, carnivores typically have premolars and molars with high, pointed cusps adapted for tearing meat; herbivores, such as cattle and horses, have premolars with broad, flat surfaces suited to chewing tough grasses and other plant materials. Most primates have premolars and molars with low, rounded cusps, a molar morphology that enables them to process most types of foods. So, throughout their evolutionary history, the primates have developed a dentition adapted to a varied diet, and the capacity to exploit many foods has contributed to their overall success during the last 50 million years.

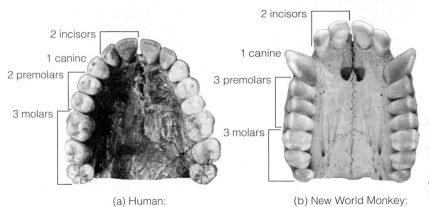

FIGURE 6-4

The human maxilla (a) illustrates a dental formula of $\frac{2.1.2.3}{2.1.2.3}$ characteristic of all Old World monkeys, apes, and humans. The *Cebus* maxilla (b) shows the $\frac{2.1.3.3}{2.1.3.3}$ dental formula that is typical of most New World monkeys.

Locomotion

Almost all primates are, at least to some degree, **quadrupedal**, meaning they use all four limbs to support the body during locomotion. Most primates use more than one form of locomotion, however, and they owe this important ability to their generalized anatomy.

Most of the quadrupedal primates are primarily arboreal, but terrestrial quadrupedalism is also common. The limbs of terrestrial quadrupeds are approximately the same length, with forelimbs being 90 percent (or more) as long as hind limbs (Fig. 6-5a). In arboreal quadrupeds, forelimbs are somewhat shorter (Fig. 6-5b).

Vertical clinging and leaping, another form of locomotion, is characteristic of many prosimians and tarsiers. As the term implies, vertical clingers and leapers support themselves vertically by grasping onto trunks of trees or other large plants while their knees and ankles are tightly flexed (Fig. 6-5c). By forcefully extending their long hind limbs, they can spring powerfully away either forwards or backwards.

dental formula Numerical device that indicates the number of each type of tooth in each side of the upper and lower jaws.

quadrupedal Using all four limbs to support the body during locomotion; the basic mammalian (and primate) form of locomotion.

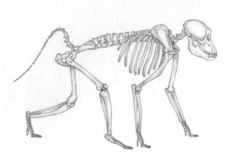

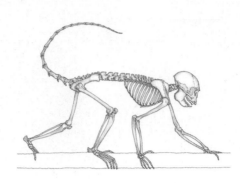

(a) Skeleton of a terrestrial quadruped (savanna baboon).

(b) Skeleton of an arboreal New World monkey (bearded saki).

(c) Skeleton of a vertical clinger and leaper (indri).

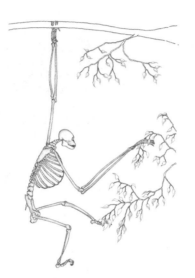

(d) Skeleton of a brachiator (gibbon).

FIGURE 6-5 (a–d)
Differences in skeletal anatomy and limb proportions reflect differences in locomotor patterns. (Redrawn by Stephen Nash from original art in John G. Fleagle, *Primate Adaptation and Evolution*, 2nd ed., 1999. Reprinted by permission of publisher and Stephen Nash.)

brachiation A form of locomotion used by some primates; the animal suspends itself from a branch or other handhold and moves by alternately swinging from one forelimb to the other; also called arm swinging.

lumbar Pertaining to the lower back. Monkeys have a longer lumbar area than that seen in apes and humans.

Brachiation, or arm swinging, is a suspensory form of locomotion in which the body moves by being alternatively supported under either forelimb. (You may have brachiated as a child on "monkey bars" in playgrounds.) Because of anatomical modifications at the shoulder joint, apes and humans are capable of true brachiation. However, only the small gibbons and siamangs of Southeast Asia use this form of locomotion almost exclusively (Fig. 6-5d).

Brachiation is seen in species characterized by arms longer than legs, a short, stable **lumbar** spine (lower back), long curved fingers, and reduced thumbs. As these are traits seen in all the apes, it's believed that, although none of the great apes (orangutans, gorillas, bonobos, and chimpanzees) habitually brachiates today, they may have inherited these characteristics from brachiating or perhaps climbing ancestors.

Some New World monkeys (such as spider monkeys) are called *semibrachiators*, since they practice a combination of leaping with some arm swinging. Some, though not all, New World species enhance arm swinging and other suspensory behaviors by using a *prehensile tail*, which in effect serves as an effective, grasping "fifth hand." Note that prehensile tails are exclusively a New World phenomenon; they aren't seen in any Old World primate species.

Primate Classification

The living primates are commonly categorized into their respective subgroups shown in Figure 6-6. This taxonomy is based on the system originally established by Linnaeus (see Chapter 2). Therefore, the primate order, which includes a diverse array of approximately 230 species, belongs to a larger group, the class *Mammalia*.

As you learned in Chapter 5, in any taxonomic system, animals are organized into increasingly specific categories. For example, the order Primates includes *all* primates. But at the next level down, the *suborder*, primates have traditionally been divided into two large categories, Prosimii (all prosimians: lemurs, lorises, and tarsiers) and Anthropoidea (all monkeys, apes, and humans). The suborder distinction is thus narrower or more specific than that of the order. At the suborder level, the prosimians are distinct as a group from all the other primates. This classification makes the biological and evolutionary statement that all the prosimian species are more closely related to one another than they are to any of the anthropoids. Likewise, all anthropoid species are more closely related to one another than they are to any of the prosimians.

The taxonomy shown in Figure 6-6 is the traditional one, and it's based on physical similarities between species and lineages. Unfortunately, this approach isn't always foolproof. For instance, two species that resemble each other anatomically (for example, some New and Old World monkeys) may in fact not be very closely related. By looking only at physical characteristics, it's possible to overlook the unknown effects of separate evolutionary history (see the discussion of homoplasy on p. 98). Genetic or biomolecular evidence avoids this problem and shows that Old and New World monkeys are quite distinct evolutionarily, meaning that they diverged from a common ancestor perhaps as long ago as 35 million years.

FIGURE **6-6**

Primate taxonomic classification. This abbreviated taxonomy illustrates how primates are grouped into increasingly specific categories. Only the more general categories are shown, except for the great apes and humans.

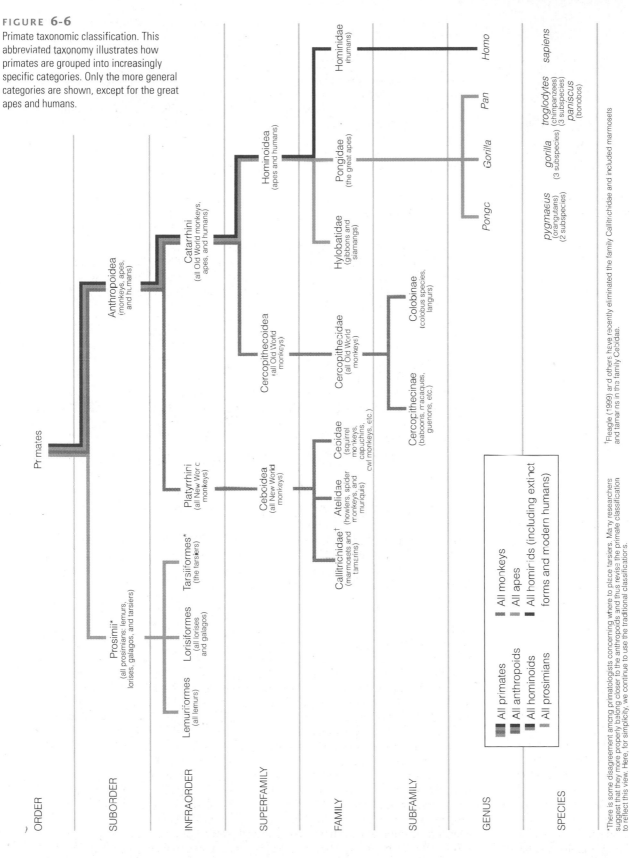

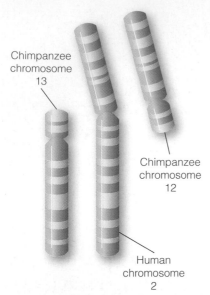

FIGURE 6-7

Human chromosome 2 has banding patterns that correspond to those of chimpanzee chromosomes 12 and 13. These similarities suggest that human chromosome 2 resulted from the fusion of these two ape chromosomes during the course of hominid evolution.

Chimpanzee chromosome 13

Chimpanzee chromosome 12

Human chromosome 2

Primate classification is currently in a state of transition, mainly because of biomolecular evidence that certain relationships (discussed later) are even closer than previously thought. Beginning in the 1970s, scientists began to apply biomolecular analysis to help identify biological and phylogenetic relationships between species. One early method was to compare the sequence of amino acids in particular proteins in different species. If the proteins were very similar, the species were closely related. For example, comparisons between human and African ape proteins show great similarity. In the 146 amino acids that make up the hemoglobin beta chain, there is only one difference between chimpanzees and humans.

Sibley and Alquist (1984) used another technique called *DNA hybridization* (where DNA from two species are matched to show how similar they are) to show that humans and chimpanzees are genetically closer than either is to the gorilla. (In fact, chimpanzees and humans share more genetic similarities than do zebras and horses or goats and sheep.) In the Sibley and Alquist study, 98.4 percent of the human and chimpanzee DNA base sequences that were studied were identical. Subsequent research hasn't substantially changed that figure since the time of that study, although the nature of the differences and similarities are now somewhat better understood.

Another way of making genetic comparisons between species has been to compare their karyotypes to identify similarities and differences in chromosome shape, size, number, and banding patterns (these banding patterns are formed when segments of DNA differentially take up certain stains. (These aren't the same patterns as those illustrated on page 58 in our discussion of DNA fingerprinting.) Humans and chimpanzees have 46 and 48 chromosomes, respectively. The banding patterns of human chromosome 2 correspond to those of two much smaller chimpanzee chromosomes (numbers 12 and 13). This finding led to the speculation that in some unknown ancestral hominoid, these two chromosomes fused to produce what became human chromosome 2 (Fig. 6-7).

Amino acid sequencing, DNA hybridization, and chromosomal comparisons have reaffirmed the basic tenets of traditional primate classification. But as useful as these techniques have been, they're *indirect* methods of comparing DNA sequences between species. Direct methods of DNA sequencing, such as those used in the Human Genome Project, have made it possible to make explicit between-species comparisons of DNA sequences, ushering in the field of *comparative genomics*.

A complete draft sequence of the chimpanzee genome, a major advance in comparative genomics, was completed in 2005 (The Chimpanzee Sequencing and Analysis Consortium, 2005). This research is a major milestone in comparative genomics, though prior to this achievement, molecular anthropologists had already compared the sequences of several chimpanzee and human genes or groups of genes.

These studies are vital because they reveal such differences in DNA as the number of nucleotide substitutions and/or deletions that have occurred since related species last shared a common ancestor. Geneticists calculate the rate of genetic change and use this information, combined with the degree of change, to estimate when related species diverged from a common ancestor. For example, Wildman et al. (2003) compared 97 human genes with their chimpanzee, gorilla, and orangutan counterparts, determining that humans are most closely related to chimpanzees and that the genes they studied are 98.4 to 99.4 percent identical. They calculated that humans and chimpanzees last shared a common ancestor with gorillas around 6-7 mya and that the chimpanzee and human lineages diverged between 5 and 6 mya. These results are consistent with the molecular findings of several other studies (Chen and Li, 2001; Clark, A.G., et al., 2003), prompting many primatologists to consider changing how the hominoids are classified (Goodman et al., 1998; Wildman et al., 2003). Although there's no formal acceptance of suggested changes, most anthropologists now support placing all great apes in the family Hominidae along with humans.

Taxonomic changes have also been suggested for tarsiers, which are highly specialized animals that have several unique physical characteristics (see p. 138). Because they share some similarities with prosimians, tarsiers have traditionally been classified as prosimians (with lemurs and lorises). But they also share certain anthropoid features and yet, for several anatomical traits, they're different from both groups.

Anthropologists who consider tarsiers to be more closely related to anthropoids have supported a reclassification. Instead of simply moving tarsiers into the suborder

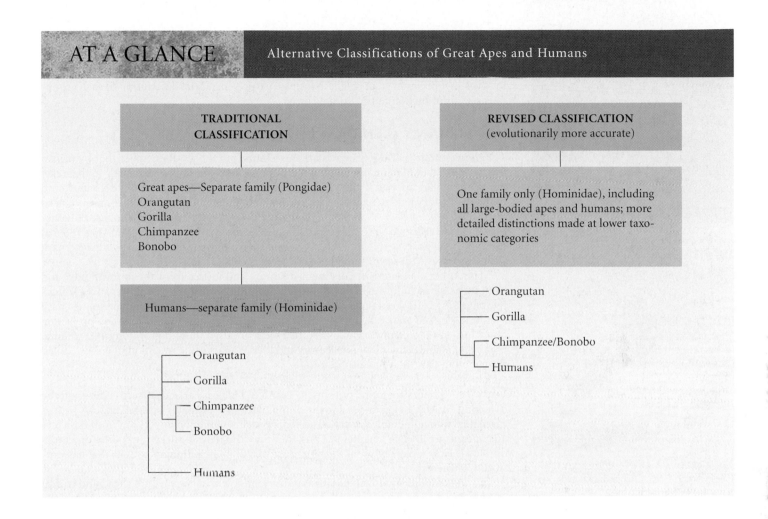

AT A GLANCE — Alternative Classifications of Great Apes and Humans

TRADITIONAL CLASSIFICATION

Great apes—Separate family (Pongidae)
Orangutan
Gorilla
Chimpanzee
Bonobo

Humans—separate family (Hominidae)

- Orangutan
- Gorilla
- Chimpanzee
- Bonobo
- Humans

REVISED CLASSIFICATION (evolutionarily more accurate)

One family only (Hominidae), including all large-bodied apes and humans; more detailed distinctions made at lower taxonomic categories

- Orangutan
- Gorilla
- Chimpanzee/Bonobo
- Humans

Anthropoidea, one scheme (Fig. 6-8) places lemurs and lorises in a different suborder, Strepsirhini (instead of Prosimii), while tarsiers are included with monkeys, apes, and humans in another suborder, Haplorhini (Szalay and Delson, 1979). In this classification, the conventionally named suborders Prosimii and Anthropoidea are replaced by Strepsirhini and Haplorhini, respectively. This designation hasn't been universally accepted. A recent cross-species comparison of almost 10,000 DNA base pairs in 64 species showed that tarsiers are genetically distinct from the anthropoids and are more closely related to lemurs (Murphy et al., 2001). Nevertheless, the terminology is now common, especially in technical publications. So if you see the term *strepsirhine*, you know that the author is referring specifically to lemurs and lorises.

The traditional system of primate classification is presented here, even though we acknowledge the need for modification particularly with regard to humans and the great apes. Until the new designations are formally adopted, we think it appropriate to use the standard taxonomy along with discussing proposed changes.

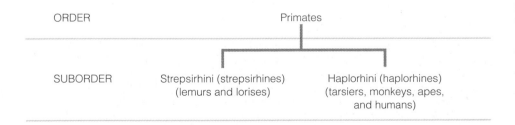

ORDER — Primates

SUBORDER — Strepsirhini (strepsirhines) (lemurs and lorises) — Haplorhini (haplorhines) (tarsiers, monkeys, apes, and humans)

FIGURE **6-8**
Revised partial classification of the primates. In this system, the terms Prosimii and Anthropoidea have been replaced by Strepsirhini and Haplorhini, respectively. The tarsier is included in the same suborder with monkeys, apes, and humans to reflect a closer relationship with these species than with lemurs and lorises. (Compare with Fig. 6-6.)

FIGURE 6-9

This cat's rhinarium enhances his sense of smell.

Lynn Kilgore

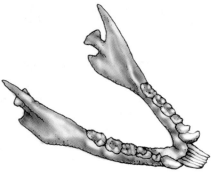

FIGURE 6-10

Prosimian dental comb, formed by forward-projecting incisors and canines.

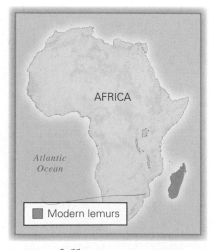

AFRICA

Atlantic Ocean

■ Modern lemurs

FIGURE 6-11

Geographical distribution of modern lemurs.

rhinarium   (rine-air´-ee-um) The moist, hairless pad at the end of the nose seen in most mammalian species. The rhinarium enhances an animal's ability to smell.

A Survey of the Living Primates

In this section we discuss the major primate subgroups. It's beyond the scope of this book to cover any species in great detail; so instead, we present a brief description of each grouping as an introduction to the Primate order.

PROSIMIANS (LEMURS, LORISES, AND TARSIERS)

The most primitive of the primates are the lemurs and lorises. Remember that by primitive we mean that prosimians, taken as a group, are more similar anatomically to their earlier mammalian ancestors than are the other primates (tarsiers, monkeys, apes, and humans). So, they tend to retain certain ancestral characteristics, such as a more pronounced reliance on *olfaction* (sense of smell). Their greater olfactory capabilities (compared to other primates) are reflected in the presence of a moist, fleshy pad, or **rhinarium** (Fig. 6-9), at the end of the nose, as well as a relatively long snout. Moreover, prosimians actively mark their territories with scent, something not seen in most other primates.

Many other characteristics distinguish lemurs and lorises from the anthropoids (and from tarsiers), including eyes placed more to the side of the face, differences in reproductive physiology, and shorter gestation and maturation periods. Lemurs and lorises also have a unique, derived trait called a "dental comb" (Fig. 6-10) formed by forward-projecting lower incisors and canines. These modified teeth are used in both grooming and feeding. One other characteristic that sets lemurs and lorises apart is the retention of a claw (called a "grooming claw") on the second toe.

Lemurs   Lemurs are found only on the island of Madagascar and adjacent islands off the east coast of Africa (Fig. 6-11). As the only nonhuman primates on Madagascar, lemurs diversified into numerous and varied ecological niches without competition from monkeys and apes, as we'll see in Chapter 9. Thus, the approximately 60 surviving species of lemurs on Madagascar today represent a kind of *Lost World*, an evolutionary pattern that has vanished elsewhere.

Lemurs range in size from the small mouse lemur, with a body length (head and trunk) of only 5 inches, to the indri, with a body length of 2 to 3 feet (Nowak, 1999). While the larger lemurs are diurnal and exploit a wide variety of dietary items, such as leaves, fruit, buds, bark, and shoots, the smaller forms (mouse and dwarf lemurs) are nocturnal and insectivorous.

Lemurs display considerable variation regarding several other aspects of behavior. While many are primarily arboreal, others, such as the ring-tailed lemur (Fig. 6-12), are more terrestrial. Some arboreal species are quadrupeds, and others (sifakas and indris) are vertical clingers and leapers (Fig. 6-13), meaning that they cling to a vertical substrate before thrusting off powerfully with their strong feet to leap toward another tree. Several species (for example, ring-tailed lemurs and sifakas) are gregarious, living in groups of 10 to 25 animals composed of males and females of all ages. Others (the indris) live in "family" units composed of a mated male-female pair and dependent offspring. Additionally, several nocturnal forms are mostly solitary (for example, pygmy mouse lemurs and aye-ayes).

Lorises   Lorises (Fig. 6-14), which resemble lemurs, were able to survive in mainland areas by adopting a nocturnal activity pattern at a time when most other prosimians, which were diurnal, became extinct. In this way, they were (and are) able to avoid competition with more recently evolved primates (the diurnal monkeys).

There are at least eight loris species, all of them found in tropical forest and woodland habitats of India, Sri Lanka, Southeast Asia, and Africa. Also included in the same general category are 6 to 9 (Bearder, 1987; Nowak, 1999) galago species (Fig. 6-15), which are widely distributed throughout most of the forested and woodland savanna areas of sub-Saharan Africa.

Locomotion in lorises is a slow, cautious, climbing form of quadrupedalism; their flexible hip joints permit suspension by hind limbs while using the hands in feeding. All galagos, however, are highly agile vertical clingers and leapers. Some lorises and galagos are almost entirely insectivorous, while others supplement their diet with various combinations of fruit, leaves, gums, and slugs. Lorises and galagos frequently forage alone, and unlike other primates, females leave young infants behind in nests in a practice called "infant parking." This sound dangerous, but lorises first bathe their young with saliva that can cause an allergic reaction sufficient to discourage most predators (Krane et al., 2003). Feeding ranges overlap, and two or more females occasionally forage together or share the same sleeping nest.

Lemurs and lorises represent the same general adaptive level. Both groups exhibit good grasping and climbing abilities and a well-developed visual apparatus; however, vision is not completely stereoscopic, and color vision may not be as well developed as in anthropoids. Most lemurs and lorises also have prolonged life spans as compared to most other small-bodied mammals, averaging about 14 years for lorises and 19 years for lemurs.

FIGURE **6-12**
Ring-tailed lemur.

Courtesy, Fred Jacobs

FIGURE **6-13**
Sifakas in their native habitat in Madagascar.

Courtesy, Fred Jacobs

Courtesy, San Francisco Zoo

FIGURE **6-14**
Slow loris.

Courtesy, Bonnie Pedersen/Arlene Kruse

FIGURE **6-15**
Galago, or "bush baby."

David Haring, Duke University Primate Zoo

FIGURE 6-16
Tarsier.

FIGURE 6-17
Geographical distribution of tarsiers.

Callitrichidae (kal-eh-trick´-eh-dee)

Cebidae (see´-bid´ee)

polyandry A mating system wherein a female continuously associates with more than one male (usually 2 or 3), with whom she mates. Among nonhuman primates, this pattern is seen only in marmosets and tamarins.

Tarsiers There are five recognized tarsier species (Nowak, 1999), all of which are restricted to island Southeast Asia, where they inhabit a wide range of forest types, from tropical forest to backyard gardens (Figs. 6-16 and 6-17). Tarsiers are nocturnal insectivores that use vertical clinging and leaping to surprise prey (which may also include small vertebrates) on lower branches and shrubs. They appear to form stable pair bonds, and the basic tarsier social unit is a mated pair and their young offspring (MacKinnon and MacKinnon, 1980).

As we've already mentioned, tarsiers present a complex blend of characteristics not seen in other primates. They're unique in that their enormous eyes, which dominate much of the face, are immobile within their sockets. To compensate for this inability to move their eyes, tarsiers, like owls, can rotate their heads 180°. Interestingly, each eye is about the size of a tarsier's brain (Beard, 2004).

ANTHROPOIDS: MONKEYS, APES, AND HUMANS

Although there is much variation among anthropoids, they share certain features that, when taken together, distinguish them as a group from prosimians (and most other placental mammals). Here's a partial list of these traits:

1. A larger average body size
2. Larger brain (in absolute terms and relative to body weight)
3. Reduced reliance on olfaction, indicated by absence of a rhinarium and other structures
4. Increased reliance on vision, with forward-facing eyes placed more to the front of the face
5. Greater degree of color vision
6. Back of eye socket protected by a bony plate
7. Blood supply to brain different from that of prosimians
8. Fusion of the two sides of the mandible at the midline to form one bone (in prosimians and tarsiers, they're joined by cartilage)
9. More generalized dentition, as seen in absence of a dental comb and some other features
10. Differences in female internal reproductive anatomy
11. Longer gestation and maturation periods
12. Increased parental care
13. More mutual grooming

Approximately 85 percent of all primates are monkeys (about 195 species). For this reason, it's frequently impossible to give precise numbers of species; the taxonomic status of some primates remains in doubt, and primatologists are still making new discoveries. (In fact, between 1990 and 2006, twenty-four species and subspecies of monkeys were discovered and described.) Monkeys are divided into two groups separated by geographical area (New World and Old World) as well as by several million years of separate evolutionary history, as we'll further appreciate in Chapter 9.

New World Monkeys The New World monkeys can be found in a wide range of arboreal environments throughout most forested areas in southern Mexico and Central and South America (see Fig. 6-18), and exhibit a wide range of size, diet, and ecological adaptations (Fig. 6-19). In size, they vary from the tiny marmosets and tamarins (about 12 ounces) to the 20-pound howler monkeys (Figs. 6-20 and 6-21). New World monkeys are almost exclusively arboreal, and some never come to the ground. Like the Old World monkeys, all except one species (the owl monkey) are diurnal.

One characteristic that distinguishes New and Old World monkeys is the shape of the nose. New World monkeys have broad noses with outward-facing nostrils. Conversely, Old World monkeys have narrower noses with downward-facing nostrils. To verify this, compare the white-faced capuchins in Figure 6-19 to the Sykes monkey in Figure 6-24, (p. 141) and to your own downward-facing nostrils. This difference in nose form has given rise to the terms *platyrrhine* (flat-nosed) and *catarrhine* (downward-facing nose) to refer to New and Old World anthropoids, respectively.

Platyrrhines have traditionally been divided into two families: **Callitrichidae** (marmosets and tamarins) and **Cebidae** (all others). But molecular data, along with recently reported fossil evidence, indicate that a major regrouping of New World monkeys is in order (Fleagle, 1999).*

Of the roughly 70 New World monkey species, marmosets and tamarins are the smallest. They have claws instead of nails and, unlike other primates, usually give birth to twins instead of one infant. They're mostly insectivorous, although the marmoset diet includes gums from trees, and tamarins also eat fruit. Locomotion is quadrupedal, and claws are used for climbing. These small monkeys live in social groups usually composed of a mated pair, or a female and two adult males, and their offspring—a condition called **polyandry**, which is rare, indeed. Marmosets and tamarins are among the few primate species in which males are extensively involved in infant care. (A truly progressive society!)

---

*One change is to create a new family, Atelidae, to include spider monkeys, howlers and muriquis (woolly spider monkeys). The other is to include marmosets and tamarins in the family Cebidae and to discard the family name Callitrichidae (Fig. 6-6), demoting it to a subfamily (Callitrichinae).

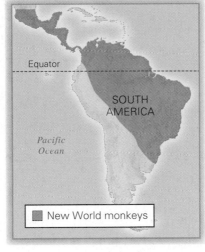

FIGURE 6-18
Geographical distribution of modern New World monkeys.

FIGURE 6-19
New World monkeys.

Prince Bernhard's titi monkey (discovered in 2002)

Female muriqui with infant

Male uakari

Squirrel monkeys

White-faced capuchins

FIGURE 6-20
A pair of golden lion tamarins.

FIGURE 6-21
Howler monkeys.

FIGURE 6-22
Spider monkey. Note the prehensile tail.

ischial callosities Patches of tough, hard skin on the buttocks of Old World monkeys and chimpanzees.

Cercopithecidae (serk-oh-pith´-eh-see-dee)

cercopithecines (serk-oh-pith´-eh-seens) The subfamily of Old World monkeys that includes baboons, macaques, and guenons.

colobines (kole´-uh-beans) Common name for members of the subfamily of Old World monkeys that includes the African colobus monkeys and Asian langurs.

Cebid and atelid species range in size from squirrel monkeys that weigh only 1.5 to 2.5 pounds and have a body length of 12 inches, to the larger howlers that are around 24 inches long and can weigh as much as 22 pounds (males). Their diet varies, with most relying on a combination of fruit and leaves supplemented to varying degrees with insects. Most are quadrupedal; but some, for example spider monkeys (Fig. 6-22), are semibrachiators. Howlers and spider monkeys also have powerful prehensile tails that they use not only in locomotion but also for suspending themselves from branches while feeding. Socially, most cebids and atelids are found in mixed-sex groups of all age categories. Some (such as titis) form monogamous pairs and live with their subadult offspring.

Old World Monkeys   Except for humans, Old World monkeys are the most widely distributed of all living primates. They're found throughout sub-Saharan Africa and southern Asia, ranging from tropical jungle habitats to semiarid desert and even to seasonally snow-covered areas in northern Japan (Fig. 6-23).

Most Old World monkeys are quadrupedal and primarily arboreal, but some (such as baboons) are also adapted to life on the ground. In general, they spend a good deal of time feeding, sleeping, and grooming. Old World monkeys also have areas of hardened skin on the buttocks called **ischial callosities** that serve as sitting pads.

Conveniently for students (and textbook authors), all Old World monkeys are placed in one taxonomic family, **Cercopithecidae**. In turn, this family is divided into two subfamilies: the **cercopithecines** and **colobines**.

The cercopithecines are the more generalized of the two groups, showing a more omnivorous dietary adaptation and cheek pouches for storing food (like hamsters). As a group, they eat almost anything, including fruit, seeds, leaves, grasses, tubers, roots, nuts, insects, birds' eggs, amphibians, small reptiles, and small mammals (the last seen in baboons).

The majority of cercopithecine species, such as the mostly arboreal guenons (Dutch for "clown"; Fig. 6-24), and the more terrestrial savanna (Fig. 6-25) and hamadryas baboons, are found in Africa. The many macaque species (including the well-known rhesus monkeys), however, are widely distributed in southern Asia and India.

Colobine species have a narrower range of food preferences and mainly eat mature leaves, which is why they're also called "leaf-eating monkeys." The colobines are found mainly in Asia, but both red colobus and black-and-white colobus are exclusively African (Fig. 6-26). Other colobines include several Asian langur species and the proboscis monkey of Borneo.

Locomotion in Old World monkeys includes arboreal quadrupedalism in guenons, macaques, and langurs; terrestrial quadrupedalism in baboons and macaques; and semibrachiation and acrobatic leaping in colobus monkeys.

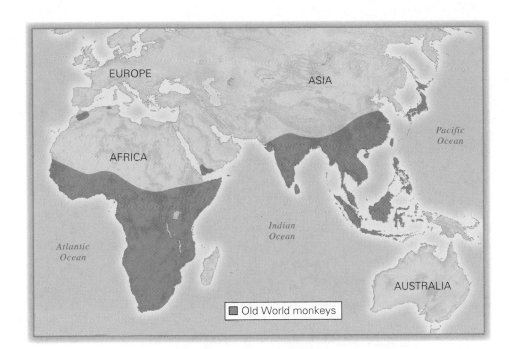

FIGURE 6-23
Geographical distribution of modern Old World monkeys.

FIGURE 6-24
Adult male sykes monkey, one of several guenon species.

Robert Jurmain

(a)

Courtesy, Bonnie Pedersen/Arlene Kruse

(b)

Courtesy, Bonnie Pedersen/Arlene Kruse

FIGURE 6-25
Savanna baboons. (a) Male. (b) Female.

FIGURE **6-26**
Black-and-white colobus monkey.

Lynn Kilgore

Marked differences in body size or shape between the sexes, referred to as **sexual dimor-phism**, are typical of some terrestrial species and are especially pronounced in baboons and patas monkeys. In these species, male body weight (up to 80 pounds in baboons) may be twice that of females.

Females of several species (especially baboons and some macaques) have pronounced cyclical changes of the external genitalia. These changes, which include swelling and red-ness, are associated with estrus, a hormonally initiated period of sexual receptivity in female nonhuman mammals correlated with ovulation. They serve as visual cues to males that females are sexually receptive.

Old World monkeys live in a few different kinds of social groups, though primatologists remain uncertain about social behavior in some species. Colobines tend to live in small groups, with only one or two adult males. Savanna baboons and most macaque species are found in large social units comprising several adults of both sexes and offspring of all ages. Monogamous pairing isn't common in Old World monkeys, but it's seen in a few langurs and possibly one or two guenon species.

Old and New World Monkeys: A Case of Homoplasy   We've mentioned several differences between New and Old World monkeys, but the fact remains that they're all monkeys. That is, they're all adapted to a similar (primarily arboreal) way of life. Except for South American owl monkeys, they're all diurnal. All live in social groupings, are omnivorous to varying degrees, and are quadrupedal (though there are variations of this general locomotor pattern).

These similarities are even more striking when you consider that New and Old World monkeys have followed separate evolutionary paths for at least 30 to 40 million years. It was once believed that both lineages evolved independently from separate prosimian ancestors; but today, the current consensus is that both New and Old World monkeys arose in Africa from a common monkey ancestor. The monkeys that gave rise to today's New World species reached South America by "rafting" over on chunks of land that had broken away from mainland areas (Hoffstetter, 1972; Ciochon and Chiarelli, 1980). This phenomenon, which we'll explain more fully in Chapter 9, probably happened many times over the course of several million years.

Whether the last common ancestor shared by New and Old World monkeys was a prosimian or, most likely, a monkey-like animal, what's most remarkable is that the two forms haven't become more different from one another than they have. The arboreal adaptations we see in the monkeys of *both* hemispheres are examples of *homoplasy* (see p. 98), result-ing from adaptation in geographically distinct populations that have responded to similar selective pressures.

sexual dimorphism   Differences in physical characteristics between males and females of the same species. For example, humans are slightly sexually dimorphic for body size, with males being taller, on aver-age, than females of the same population.

HOMINOIDS: APES AND HUMANS

The other large grouping of anthropoids (the hominoids) includes apes and humans. The superfamily **Hominoidea** includes the so-called lesser apes of the family **Hylobatidae** (gibbons and siamangs) and the great apes in the family Pongidae (orangutans, gorillas, bonobos, and chimpanzees), as well as humans in the family Hominidae. Apes and humans differ from monkeys in numerous ways:

1. Generally larger body size (except for gibbons and siamangs)
2. Absence of a tail
3. Shortened trunk (lumbar area shorter and more stable)
4. Arms that are longer than legs (only in apes)
5. Differences in position and musculature of the shoulder joint (related to an adaptation for suspensory feeding and locomotion)
6. More complex behavior
7. More complex brain and enhanced cognitive abilities
8. Increased period of infant development and dependency

Gibbons and Siamangs   The eight gibbon species and closely related siamangs are found in the southeastern tropical areas of Asia (Fig. 6-27). These are the smallest of the apes, with a long, slender body weighing 13 pounds in gibbons (Fig. 6-28) and around 25 pounds in the larger siamangs.

The most distinctive anatomical features of gibbons and siamangs are adaptations that facilitate brachiation. These include extremely long arms, long, permanently curved fingers, short thumbs, and powerful shoulder muscles. These highly derived adaptations may be related to feeding behavior while hanging beneath branches. The diet of both genera is largely composed of fruit, but both (especially siamangs) eat a variety of leaves, flowers, and insects.

The basic social unit of gibbons and siamangs is an adult male and female with dependent offspring. Although they've been described as monogamous, in reality, pair-bonded members sometimes mate with other individuals. As in marmosets and tamarins, male gibbons and siamangs are very much involved in rearing their young. Both males and females are highly **territorial** and protect their territories with elaborate whoops and siren-like "songs," lending them the name "the singing apes of Asia."

FIGURE **6-27**
Geographical distribution of modern Asian apes.

FIGURE **6-28**
White-handed gibbon.

Lynn Kilgore

Hominoidea   The formal designation for the superfamily of anthropoids that includes apes and humans.

Hylobatidae   (high-low-baht´-i-dee)

territorial   Pertaining to the protection of all or a part of the area occupied by an animal or group of animals. Territorial behaviors range from scent marking to outright attacks on intruders.

FIGURE **6-29**

Orangutans (a) Female; (b) Male

Noel Rowe

Lynn Kilgore

(a)   (b)

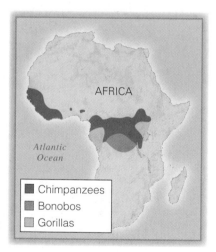

AFRICA

Atlantic Ocean

■ Chimpanzees
■ Bonobos
□ Gorillas

FIGURE **6-30**

Geographical distribution of modern African apes.

Orangutans   Orangutans (*Pongo pygmaeus*) (Fig. 6-29) are represented by two sub-species found today only in heavily forested areas on the Indonesian islands of Borneo and Sumatra (see Fig. 6-27). The name *orangutan* (which has no final *g* and should never be pronounced "orangutang") means "wise man of the forest" in the language of the local people. But, despite this somewhat affectionate-sounding label, orangutans are severely threatened with extinction in the wild due to poaching by humans and continuing habitat loss on both islands.

Orangutans are slow, cautious climbers whose locomotor behavior can best be described as four-handed—referring to their tendency to use all four limbs for grasping and support. Although they're almost completely arboreal, orangutans sometimes travel quadrupedally on the ground. Orangutans exhibit pronounced sexual dimorphism; males are quite large and may weigh more than 200 pounds, while females weigh less than 100 pounds.

In the wild, orangutans lead largely solitary lives, although adult females are usually accompanied by one or two dependent offspring. They're primarily **frugivorous** but may also eat bark, leaves, insects, and (rarely) meat.

Gorillas   The largest of all living primates, gorillas (*Gorilla gorilla*) are today confined to forested areas of western and eastern equatorial Africa (Fig. 6-30). There are three generally recognized subspecies, although molecular data suggest that one of these, the western lowland gorilla (Fig. 6-31), may be genetically distinct enough to be designated as a separate species (Ruvolo et al., 1994; Garner and Ryder, 1996). Western lowland gorillas, the most numerous of the three subspecies, are found in several countries of west-central Africa. Doran and McNeilage (1998) reported an estimated population size of perhaps 110,000. But, Walsh et al (2003) suggested their numbers were far lower. Now it's likely, due to human hunting and disease, that western lowland gorillas may be facing extinction in the wild (see pp. 118–119)." Eastern lowland gorillas live near the eastern border of the Democratic Republic of the Congo (DRC—formerly Zaire), and their population numbers about 12,000. Mountain gorillas (Fig. 6-32), the most extensively studied of the three subspecies, are restricted to the mountainous areas of central Africa in Rwanda, the DRC, and Uganda. There have probably never been many mountain gorillas, and today they're among the more endangered primates—numbering only about 600 in the wild.

Gorillas exhibit marked sexual dimorphism, with males weighing up to 400 pounds and females around 150 to 200 pounds. Since they're so heavy, adult gorillas, especially males, are primarily terrestrial, and like chimpanzees adopt a semiquadrupedal (knuckle-walking) posture when on the ground (Fig. 6-33).

frugivorous   (fru-give´-or-us) Having a diet composed primarily of fruit.

(a)

(b)

FIGURE 6-31
Western lowland gorillas.
(a) Male. (b) Female.

(a)

(b)

FIGURE 6-32
Mountain gorillas.
(a) Male. (b) Female.

FIGURE 6-33
Chimpanzee knuckle walking. Note how the weight of the upper body is supported on the knuckles and not on the palm of the hand.

Mountain gorillas live in groups consisting of one, or sometimes two, large silverback males, a variable number of adult females, and their subadult offspring. (The term *silverback* refers to the saddle of white hair across the back of fully adult males who are 12 or 13 years of age.) A silverback male may tolerate the presence of one or more young adult "blackback" males (probably his sons) in his group. Typically, but not always, both females and males leave their **natal group** as young adults. Females join other groups; and males, who appear to be less likely to emigrate, may live alone for a while or they may join up with other males before eventually forming their own group.

Systematic studies of free-ranging western lowland gorillas weren't begun until the mid-1980s, so even though they're the only gorillas you'll see in zoos, we don't know as much about them as we do about mountain gorillas. The social structure of western lowland gorillas is similar to that of mountain gorillas, but groups are smaller and somewhat less cohesive.

All gorillas are almost exclusively vegetarian: mountain and western lowland gorillas concentrate primarily on leaves, pith, and stalks, but western lowland gorillas eat more fruit. Recent studies also report that western lowland gorillas, unlike mountain gorillas (which avoid water), frequently wade through swamps while foraging on aquatic plants (Doran and McNeilage, 1998).

natal group The group in which animals are born and raised. (*Natal* pertains to birth.)

145

Perhaps because of their large body size and enormous strength, gorillas have long been considered ferocious, though in reality, they're usually shy and gentle. But this doesn't mean that gorillas aren't ever aggressive. In fact, among males, competition for females can be extremely violent. As might be expected, males will attack and defend their group from any perceived danger, whether it's another male gorilla or a human hunter. Still, the reputation of gorillas as murderous beasts is the result of uninformed myth making and little else.

Chimpanzees   Chimpanzees are probably the best known of all nonhuman primates, even though many people think they're monkeys (Fig. 6-34). Often misunderstood because of zoo exhibits, circus acts, television shows, and movies, the true nature of chimpanzees didn't become known until years of fieldwork with wild groups provided a more accurate picture. Today, chimpanzees are found in equatorial Africa, in a broad belt from the Atlantic Ocean in the west to Lake Tanganyika in the east. Their range, however, is patchy within this large geographical area, and it's becoming even more so with further habitat destruction.

In many ways, chimpanzees are anatomically similar to gorillas, with corresponding limb proportions and upper-body shape. However, the ecological adaptations and behaviors of chimpanzees and gorillas differ, with chimpanzees spending more time in the trees. Behavior observed in these species is quite different: Gorillas are typically placid and quiet; chimpanzees are often highly excitable, active, and noisy.

Chimpanzees are smaller than orangutans and gorillas. Although they're sexually dimorphic, sex differences aren't as pronounced as in these other species: male chimpanzees may weigh over 100 pounds, and females can weigh at least 80.

In addition to quadrupedal knuckle walking, chimpanzees (particularly youngsters) may brachiate while in the trees. When on the ground, they frequently walk bipedally for short distances when carrying food or other objects.

Chimpanzees eat a wide variety of foods, including fruit, leaves, insects, nuts, birds' eggs, berries, caterpillars, and small mammals. Both males and females occasionally take part in group hunting efforts to kill small mammals such as young bushpigs and antelope. Their prey frequently also includes monkeys, especially red colobus and young baboons (see p. 164). When these hunts are successful, the group (especially members of the hunting party) shares the prey.

Chimpanzees live in large, fluid communities ranging in size from 10 to as many as 100 individuals. A group of closely bonded males forms the core of chimpanzee communities in many locations, especially in East Africa (Wrangham and Smuts, 1980; Wrangham et al., 1992; Goodall, 1986). But, for some West African groups, females appear to be more central to the community (Boesch, 1996; Boesch and Boesch-Acherman, 2000; Vigilant et al., 2001). Relationships among closely bonded males aren't always peaceful or stable, yet these males cooperatively defend their territory and are highly intolerant of unfamiliar chimpanzees, especially males.

Even though chimpanzees are said to live in communities, it's rare for all members to be together at the same time. Rather, they tend to come and go, so that the individuals they encounter vary from day to day. Adult females usually forage either alone or in the com-

FIGURE **6-34**
Chimpanzees. (a) Male. (b) Female.

(a)   (b)

Courtesy, Ellen Ingmanson

FIGURE 6-35
Female bonobos with young.

pany of their offspring, a grouping that might include several animals since females with infants sometimes accompany their own mothers and their own siblings. These associations have been reported for the chimpanzees at Gombe, where about 40 percent of females remain in the group in which they were born (Williams, 1999). But, at most other localities, females leave their natal group to join another community. This behavioral pattern may reduce the risk of mating with close male relatives, because males apparently never leave the group in which they were born.

Chimpanzee social behavior is complex, and individuals form lifelong attachments with friends and relatives. If they continue to live in their natal group, the bond between mothers and infants can remain strong until one of them dies. This may be a considerable period, because many wild chimpanzees live well into their forties.

Bonobos Bonobos (*Pan paniscus*) are found only in an area south of the Zaire River in the DRC (see Fig. 6-30). Not officially recognized by European scientists until the 1920s, they remain among the least studied of the great apes. Although ongoing field studies have produced much information (Susman, 1984; Kano, 1992), research has been hampered by civil war in the region. There are currently no accurate counts of bonobos, though their numbers are believed to be between 10,000 and 20,000 (IUCN, 1996). These few are believed to be highly threatened by human hunting, warfare, and habitat loss.

Since bonobos bear a strong resemblance to chimpanzees, but are slightly smaller, they've been called "pygmy chimpanzees." The differences in body size aren't very striking, although bonobos are less stocky. They also have longer legs relative to arms, a relatively smaller head, and a dark face from birth (Fig. 6-35).

Bonobos are more arboreal than chimpanzees, and they're less excitable and aggressive. While aggression isn't unknown, it appears that physical violence both within and between groups is uncommon. Like chimpanzees, bonobos live in geographically based, fluid communities and eat many of the same foods, including occasional meat derived from small mammals (Badrian and Malinky, 1984). But male-female bonding is more important than in chimpanzees and most other nonhuman primates (Badrian and Badrian, 1984). This may be related to bonobo sexuality, which differs from that of other nonhuman primates in that copulation is frequent and occurs throughout a female's estrous cycle, so sex isn't linked solely to reproduction. In fact, bonobos are famous for their sexual behavior since they copulate frequently and seem to use sex to defuse potentially tense situations. Sexual behavior between members of the same sex is also common (Kano, 1992; de Waal and Lanting, 1997).

Given this aspect of bonobo behavior, it's perhaps not surprising that they've been called the "make love, not war" primate society.

Humans   Humans are the only living representatives of the habitually bipedal hominids (*Homo sapiens*). Our primate heritage is evident in our overall anatomy, genetic makeup, and in many behavioral aspects. Except for reduced canine size, human teeth are typical primate (especially ape) teeth. The human dependence on vision and decreased reliance on olfaction, as well as flexible limbs and grasping hands, are rooted in our primate, arboreal past. Humans can even brachiate (as many of us have demonstrated during childhood).

Humans in general are omnivorous, although all societies observe certain culturally based dietary restrictions. Even so, as a species with a rather generalized digestive system, we're physiologically adapted to digest an extremely wide assortment of foods. Perhaps to our detriment, we also share with our relatives a fondness for sweets that originates from the importance of high-energy fruits in the diets of many nonhuman primates.

Quite obviously, humans are unique among primates and indeed among all animals. For example, no member of any other species has the ability to write or think about issues such as how they differ from other life-forms. This ability is rooted in the fact that human evolution, during the last 800,000 years or so, has been characterized by dramatic increases in brain size and other neurological changes (see pp. 181–182).

Humans are also completely dependent on culture. Without cultural innovation, it would never have been possible for us to leave the tropics. As it is, humans inhabit every corner of the planet except for Antarctica, and we've even established outposts there—and lest we forget, a fortunate few have even walked on the moon! None of the technologies (indeed, none of the other aspects of culture) that humans have developed over the last several thousand years would have been possible without the highly developed cognitive abilities we alone possess. Nevertheless, the neurological basis for **intelligence** is rooted in our evolutionary past, and it's something we share with other primates. Indeed, research has demonstrated that several nonhuman primate species—most notably chimpanzees, bonobos, and gorillas—display a level of problem solving and insight that most people would have considered impossible 25 years ago (see Chapter 8).

Humans are uniquely predisposed to use spoken language, and for the last 5,000 years or so, we've also used written language. This ability exists because, during the course of human evolution, certain neurological and anatomical structures have been modified in ways not observed in any other species. But, while nonhuman primates aren't anatomically capable of producing speech, research has demonstrated that to varying degrees the great apes are able to communicate by using symbols, which is a foundation for language that humans and the great apes (to a limited degree) have in common.

Aside from cognitive abilities, the one other trait that sets humans apart from other primates is our unique form of striding, *habitual* bipedal locomotion. This particular trait appeared early in the evolution of our lineage, and over time, we've become more efficient at it because of related changes in the musculoskeletal anatomy of the pelvis, leg, and foot. But early hominids increasingly adopted bipedalism because they were already *preadapted* for it. That is, as primates, and especially as apelike primates, they were already behaviorally predisposed to, and anatomically capable of, at least short-term bipedal walking before they adopted it wholeheartedly. So, while it's certainly true that human beings are unique intellectually, and in some ways anatomically, we're still primates. As a matter of fact, humans are basically somewhat exaggerated African apes.

Endangered Primates

intelligence   Mental capacity; ability to learn, reason, or comprehend and interpret information, facts, relationships, and meanings; the capacity to solve problems, whether through the application of previously acquired knowledge or through insight.

In September 2000, scientists announced that a subspecies of red colobus, named Miss Waldron's red colobus, had officially been declared extinct. This announcement came after a 6-year search for the 20-pound monkey that hadn't yielded any results for 20 years (Oates et al., 2000). Sadly, this species, indigenous to the West African countries of Ghana and the Ivory Coast, has the distinction of being the first nonhuman primate to be declared

TABLE 6-1	African Primates in Danger of Extinction	
Species/Subspecies Common Name	Location	Estimating Size of Remaining Population
Barbary macaque	North Africa	23,000
Tana River mangabey	Tana River, Kenya	800–1,100
Sanje mangabey	Uzungwa Mts., Tanzania	1,800–3,000
Drill	Cameroon, Bioko	?
Preuss' guenon	Cameroon, Bioko	?
White-throated guenon	Southwest Nigeria	?
Pennant's red colobus	Bioko	?
Preuss' red colobus	Cameroon	8,000
Bouvier's red colobus	Congo Republic	?
Tana River red colobus	Tana River, Kenya	200–300
Uhehe red colobus	Uzungwa Mts., Tanzania	10,000
Zanzibar red colobus	Zanzibar	1,500
Mountain gorilla	Virunga Volcanoes (Rwanda, Uganda, and Democratic Republic of the Congo) and Impenetrable Forest (Uganda)	550–650

extinct in the twenty-first century, though it certainly won't be the last. In fact, as of this writing, over half of all nonhuman primate species are now in jeopardy, and some face almost immediate extinction in the wild (Table 6-1).

Population estimates of free-ranging primates are difficult to obtain, but some species (hapalemur, diadem sifaka, aye-aye, lion tamarin, muriqui, red colobus subspecies, lion-tailed macaque, and mountain gorilla) now number only in the hundreds. Others are believed to be represented in the wild by a few thousand (agile mangabey, mentawi langur, red colobus subspecies, moloch gibbon, Kloss' gibbon, orangutan, lowland gorilla, chimpanzee, and bonobo).

There are three basic reasons for the worldwide depletion of nonhuman primates: habitat destruction, human predation, and live capture for export or local trade. Underlying these three causes is one major factor, unprecedented human population growth, that's occurring at an even faster rate in developing countries than in the developed world. The developing nations of Africa, Asia, and Central and South America are home to over 90 percent of all nonhuman primate species; and these countries, aided in no small part by the

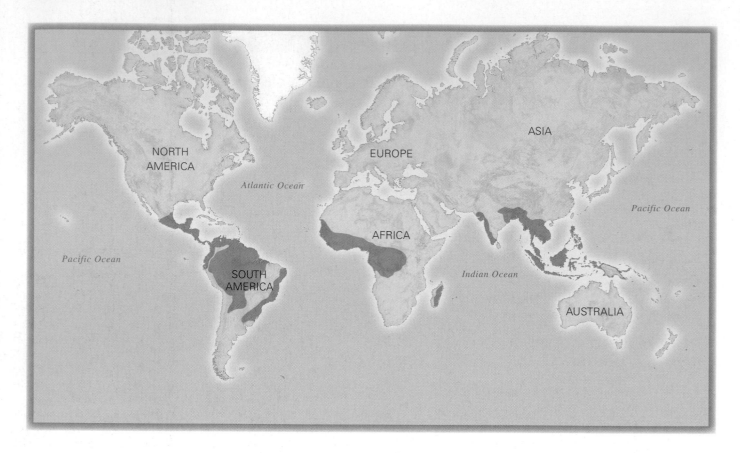

FIGURE **6-36**
Tropical rain forests of the world (distribution before recent massive destruction).

industrialized countries of Europe and the United States, are cutting their forests at a rate of about 30 million acres per year (Fig. 6-36). Unbelievably, in the year 2002, deforestation of the Amazon increased by 40 percent over that of 2001, due in large part to land clearing for the cultivation of soybeans to feed what seems to be an insatiable human appetite. In Brazil, the Atlantic rain forest originally covered some 385,000 square miles. Today, an estimated 7 percent is all that remains of what was once home to countless New World monkeys and thousands of other species. The tragedy of this situation literally cannot be overstated.

Much of the motivation behind the devastation of the rain forests is, of course, economic: the short-term gains from clearing forests to create immediately available (but poor) farm-land or ranchland; the use of trees for lumber and paper products; and large-scale mining operations (with their necessary roads, digging, and so on, all causing further habitat destruction). Regionally, the loss of rain forest ranks as a national disaster for some coun-tries. For example, the West African nation of Sierra Leone had an estimated 15,000 square miles of rain forest early in the twentieth century. Today, less than 530 square miles remain, and most of this destruction has occurred since World War II. People in many developing countries are also short of fuel and frequently use whatever firewood is obtainable. In addi-tion, the demand for tropical hardwoods (such as mahogany, teak, and rosewood) in the United States, Europe, and Japan continues unabated, creating an enormously profitable market for rain-forest products.

Primates have also been captured live for zoos, biomedical research, and the exotic pet trade. Live capture has declined since the Convention on International Trade in Endangered Species of Wild Flora and Fauna (CITES) was implemented in 1973. By August 2005 a total of 169 countries had signed this treaty, agreeing not to allow trade in species listed by CITES (see CITES Handbook, www.cites.org) as being endangered. However, even some CITES members are still occasionally involved in the illegal primate trade (Japan and Belgium, among others).

In many areas habitat loss has been, and continues to be, the single greatest cause of declining numbers of nonhuman primates. But everywhere primates occur, human hunt-ing for food now poses an even greater threat. This tragic turn of events occurred rather

A CLOSER LOOK

Ayes-Ayes: Victims of Derived Traits and Superstition

The primate order is filled with a variety of fascinating animals, although few seem as unusual as the aye-aye (*Daubentonia madagascariensis*). This is because most primates aren't as derived as aye-ayes are. Today, aye-ayes are the only members of their genus. A second species (a subfossil lemur) was exterminated by humans over the last few centuries, and the aye-aye was unknown (at least to Western science) until 1961. Like all lemurs, aye-ayes are found only on the island of Madagascar, where they occupy a niche similar to that of woodpeckers. Like woodpeckers, which aren't found on Madagascar, aye-ayes feed on insects and grubs that live in logs and tree bark. But, instead of using a long beak to drill for hidden prey, this nocturnal primate uses an extremely specialized, elongated, bony middle finger to tap, tap, tap along a tree trunk, listening for hollow spaces (Fig. 1). When an aye-aye finds a hollow space where a grub might be hiding, it tears through the bark with its continuously growing incisor teeth (a rodent trait) and scoops out the unlucky larva with the long nail at the end of its peculiar middle finger.

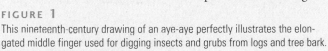

FIGURE 1

This nineteenth-century drawing of an aye-aye perfectly illustrates the elongated middle finger used for digging insects and grubs from logs and tree bark.

Aye-aye dentition is also quite derived and specialized for this particular dietary niche. The aye-aye dental formula of

$$\frac{1.0.1.3}{1.0.0.3}$$

isn't just unique among primates, it's unique among all mammals. As you can see, aye-ayes have no canine teeth and no lower premolars, although there's one upper premolar (Hershkovitz, 1977).

This perhaps strange-looking primate, which seems to have a permanent "bad hair day," is about the size of a small house cat and has little of the appeal of, say, a galago. Unfortunately, many Malagasy (the human inhabitants of Madagascar) find the aye-aye's appearance less than endearing and, in fact, they view them more as the stuff of nightmares. Many think aye-ayes are bad luck and don't realize that they're simply harmless primates making a living as best they can.

Sadly, the imagination of *Homo sapiens* may prove this primate's undoing. Aye-ayes are variously thought to be heralds of evil or murderers who creep into thatched huts and puncture their victims' aortas with their frightening middle fingers (Goodman and Schütz, 2000). Still others are superstitious that should an aye-aye point its long middle finger at a person, then he or she will die. So it seems that cruel fate and humans have pointed their own finger of condemnation at the aye-aye, for only about 2,500 live in the wild and only a dozen or so in captivity.

quickly; but during the 1990s, primatologists became increasingly aware of the immense scope of the slaughter, which now accounts for the loss of thousands of nonhuman primates and other species annually (see "Issue," pp. 118–119).

The slaughter may be most extreme in Africa, but it's by no means limited to that continent. In South America, for example, hunting nonhuman primates for food is common. One report documents that in less than two years, one family of Brazilian rubber tappers killed almost 500 members of various large-bodied primate species, including spider monkeys, woolly monkeys, and howler monkeys (Peres, 1990). What's more, live capture and (illegal) trade in endangered primate species continues unabated in China and Southeast Asia, where nonhuman primates are not only eaten but also funneled into the exotic pet trade. In Asia, another important factor is that primate body parts also figure prominently in traditional medicines, and with increasing human population size, the enormous demand for these products (and products from other, nonprimate species, such as tigers) has placed many species in extreme jeopardy.

Fortunately, steps are being taken to ensure the survival of some species. Many developing countries, such as Costa Rica and the Malagasy Republic (Madagascar), are designating national parks and other reserves for the protection of natural resources, including primates. Several private international efforts are aimed at curbing the "bushmeat" trade. It's only through such practices and through educational programs that many primate species have a chance of escaping extinction, at least in the immediate future.

If you're in your 20s or 30s, you will almost certainly live to hear about the extinction of some of our marvelously unique and clever evolutionary cousins. Many more will undoubtedly slip away unnoticed. Tragically, this will occur, in most cases, before we've even had the opportunity to get to know them.

Each species on earth is the current result of a unique set of evolutionary events that, over millions of years, has produced a finely adapted component of a diverse ecosystem. When that component disappears, that adaptation and that part of biodiversity are lost forever. What a tragedy it will be if, through our own mismanagement and greed, we awaken to a world without chimpanzees, mountain gorillas, or the tiny, exquisite lion tamarin. When that day comes, we truly will have lost a part of ourselves, and we will most certainly be the poorer for it.

VISUAL SUMMARY

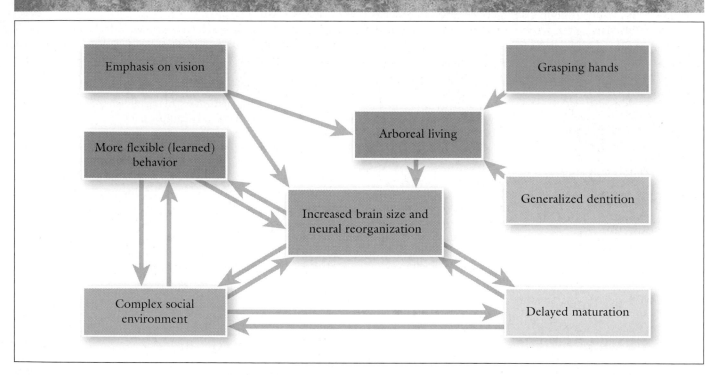

Summary: Putting It All Together

In this chapter, we've introduced you to the living primates: the mammalian order that includes prosimians, monkeys, apes, and humans. We discussed how primates, including humans, have retained some ancestral characteristics that have permitted them, as a group, to be generalized in their diet and locomotor patterns. You were also presented with a general outline of traits that differentiate primates from other mammals.

We also discussed primate classification and how primatologists are redefining relationships between some lineages, such as how chimpanzees, gorillas, and orangutans might be placed with humans in the family Hominidae. These changes reflect increasing knowledge of the genetic relationships between primate lineages, and in the case of tarsiers, reconsideration of various anatomical characteristics.

You also became acquainted with the major groups of nonhuman primates, especially regarding their basic social structure, diet, and locomotor patterns. Most primates are diurnal and live in social groups. The only nocturnal primates are lorises, some lemurs, tarsiers, and owl monkeys. Nocturnal species tend to forage for food alone, with offspring, or with one or two other animals. Diurnal primates live in a variety of social groupings including monogamous pairs; groups consisting of one male with several females and offspring; or groups composed of several males, females, and offspring.

Finally, we talked about the precarious existence of most nonhuman primates today as they face hunting, live capture, and habitat loss. These threats are all imposed by only one primate species (us) that arrived relatively late on the evolutionary stage. In the next two chapters, as we discuss various aspects of human and nonhuman primate behavior, you'll become better acquainted with this fairly recently evolved primate species, *Homo sapiens*, of which you are a member.

Critical Thinking Questions

1. How do you think continued advances in genetic research will influence how we look at our species' relationships with nonhuman primates in 10 years?

2. What factors are threatening the existence of nonhuman primates in the wild? Do you personally care? If so, what can you do to help save nonhuman primates from extinction?

3. How does a classification scheme reflect biological and evolutionary changes in a lineage? Can you give an example of suggested changes to how primates are classified? What do you think most people's reaction would be to hearing that scientists are placing the great apes into the same taxonomic family as humans?

CHAPTER 7

Primate Behavior

Lynn Kilgore

KEY QUESTIONS

How can behavior be a product of evolutionary processes?

What are the advantages and disadvantages of living in primate social groups?

Introduction

People are so intrigued by nonhuman animal **behavior** that nature shows are among the most popular television programs. You may watch some of them yourself. These shows perform a good service because for most people, they may be the only source of information about nonhuman animal behavior. Unfortunately, much of this information is doled out in short segments that are little more than sound bites crammed between commercials. That fact, coupled with the necessarily superficial presentation of scientific data, results in misleading narration that reinforces many misconceptions people have about other species.

In truth, behavior, especially in mammals and birds, is extremely complex because it's been shaped over evolutionary time by countless interactions between genetic and environmental processes. But not everyone has accepted this premise. Social scientists, in particular, have objected to the notion of genetic influences on human behavior because of concerns that it implies that behaviors are fixed and can't be modified by experience (that is, learning).

Furthermore, among the general public, there is the prevailing notion of a fundamental division between humans and all other animals. In some cultures, this view is fostered by religion; but even when religion isn't a factor, most people see themselves as uniquely set apart from all other species. This is unfortunate, because people judge other species from a human perspective, which of course isn't a valid thing to do. For example, many people think cats are cruel because they play with mice before they kill them. Horses are deliberately skittish if they leap aside when a breeze rattles the leaves of a shrub. But this kind of thinking is based on uninformed opinion, and the truth is that most people have no real understanding of why other species do what they do.

Sometimes cats do play with mice before killing them because that's how, as kittens, they learned to hunt small prey, and hunting small prey is how they survive in an undomesticated environment. Cruelty doesn't enter into it, because the cat has no concept of cruelty and no idea of what it's like to be the mouse. Likewise, the horse that tosses you onto a cactus doesn't do it deliberately. She does it because her behavior has been shaped by thousands of generations of horse ancestors who jumped first and asked questions later. Horses evolved as prey animals, and their evolutionary history is littered with unfortunate animals that didn't respond quickly to a sound in a shrub. In many cases they learned, too late, that the sound wasn't caused by a breeze at all. This is a mistake prey animals don't usually survive, and those that don't leap first leave few descendants.

Actually, this chapter isn't about cats and horses. It's about what we currently know and hypothesize about the individual and social behaviors of nonhuman primates. But we begin with the familiar examples of cats and horses because we want to point out that many basic behaviors have been shaped by the evolutionary history of particular species. Likewise, the same factors that have influenced many types of behavior in nonprimate animals also apply to primates. So, if we want to discover the underlying principles of behavioral evolution, we first need to identify the interactions between a number of environmental and physiological variables.

Click!

Go to the following media for interactives and exercises on topics covered in this chapter:

- Online Virtual Laboratories for Physical Anthropology, Fourth Edition

behavior Anything organisms do that involves action in response to internal or external stimuli. The response of an individual, group, or species to its environment. Such responses may or may not be deliberate, and they aren't necessarily the results of conscious decision making, as in single-celled organisms, insects, and many other species.

Primate Field Studies

The primary goal of primate field studies is to collect information on **free-ranging** animals, whose behavior is unaffected by human activities. Unfortunately, most, if not all primate populations have now been exposed to human activities that influence their behavior (Janson, 2000). What's more, wild primates aren't easy to study until they've been habituated to the presence of humans, whom they generally fear, and the habituation process can take a very long time. Also, habituation itself can change primate behavior. Until the last two decades, the most systematic information on free-ranging primates came from species that spend a lot of time on the ground (baboons, macaques, some lemurs, chimpanzees, and gorillas; Fig. 7-1a). This is because it's difficult to identify and observe arboreal primates as they flit through the forest canopy (Fig. 7-1b). Now, however, primatologists have accumulated a great deal of data on many arboreal species. Others have focused on nocturnal prosimians and tarsiers. Thanks to these efforts, many of the gaps in our knowledge of nonhuman primates are being filled. But with each new discovery come new questions, so the process will continue as long as there are wild primates to study.

The earliest studies of nonhuman primates in their natural habitats began with an American psychologist named Robert Yerkes who, in the late 1920s and 1930s, sent students into the field to study gorillas, chimpanzees, and howler monkeys. Japanese scientists began their pioneering work with Japanese macaques in 1948 (Sugiyama, 1965). In 1960, Jane Goodall began her now famous field study of chimpanzees at Gombe National Park, Tanzania. This project was closely followed by Dian Fossey's work with mountain gorillas in Rwanda and by Birute Galdikas' research on orangutans in Borneo.

These initial studies were, of necessity, largely descriptive in nature. However, some early studies of savanna baboons (DeVore and Washburn, 1963), hamadryas baboons (Kummer, 1968), and geladas (Crook and Gartlan, 1966) related aspects of **social structure** and individual behavior to ecological factors. Most early work emphasized male behaviors, partly because of the role of males in group defense. But by the late 1970s and early 1980s, primatologists were focusing more attention on females not only as mothers but also because they have an enormous influence on group dynamics.

free-ranging   Pertaining to non-captive animals living in their natural habitat. Ideally, the behavior of wild study groups would be free of human influence.

social structure   The composition, size, and sex ratio of a group of animals. Social structures are the results of natural selection in specific habitats, and they influence individual interactions and social relationships. In many species, social structure varies, depending on different environmental factors. Thus, in most primate species, social structure should be viewed as flexible, not fixed.

FIGURE **7-1**

(a) Rhesus macaques spend much of their time on the ground and are much easier to observe than black-and-white colobus. (b) Imagine trying to recognize the colobus monkeys as individuals. What tools and techniques would you use to identify them?

Courtesy, Jean De Rousseau

(a)

Courtesy, John Oates

(b)

Since then, primatologists have studied and continue to study well over 100 nonhuman primate species. Because most primates live in social groups, extensive research is devoted to primate social behavior, the costs and benefits of living in bisexual groupings, and the advantages and disadvantages of specific behaviors to individuals and groups. Behavioral research is done within an evolutionary framework, so primatologists test hypotheses relating to how behaviors have evolved. And now the application of genetic techniques to primate behavioral research is beginning to provide answers to many questions, especially those that relate to paternity and to reproductive success.

The Evolution of Behavior

Scientists who study behavior in free-ranging primates do so from an ecological and evolutionary perspective, meaning that they focus on the relationship between individual and social behaviors, the natural environment, and various physiological traits of the species in question. This approach is called **behavioral ecology**, and it's based on the underlying assumption that all of the biological components of ecological systems (animals, plants, and even microorganisms) evolved together. Behaviors are thus adaptations to environmental circumstances that existed in the past as well as in the present.

Briefly, the cornerstone of this perspective is that *behaviors have evolved through the operation of natural selection*. That is, if behaviors are influenced by genes, then they are subject to natural selection in the same way physical characteristics are. (Remember that within a specific environmental context, natural selection favors traits that provide a reproductive advantage to the individuals who possess them.) So behavior constitutes a phenotype, and those individuals whose behavioral phenotypes increase reproductive fitness will pass on their genes at a faster rate than others. But this doesn't mean that primatologists think that genes code for specific behaviors, such as a gene for aggression, another for cooperation, and so on. Studying complex behaviors from an evolutionary viewpoint doesn't imply a one gene-one behavior relationship, nor does it suggest that those behaviors that are influenced by genes can't be modified through learning.

Much of the behavior of insects and other invertebrates is largely under genetic control. In other words, most behavioral patterns in those species aren't learned. But in many vertebrates, especially birds and mammals, the proportion of behavior that's due to learning is substantially increased, while the proportion under genetic control is reduced. This is especially true of primates; and, in humans, who are so much a product of culture, most behavior is learned. But at the same time, we also know that in higher organisms, some behaviors are at least partly influenced by certain gene products such as hormones. You may be aware of studies showing that increased levels of testosterone increase aggression in many species. You may also have heard that some conditions such as depression, schizophrenia, and bipolar disorder are caused by abnormal levels of certain neurotransmitters. Neurotransmitters are chemicals produced by brain cells, and they're sent from one cell to another to cause a response (that is, they transmit information from cell to cell). These responses range from muscle activity to release of hormones elsewhere in the body.

Brain cells manufacture neurotransmitters due to the action of genes within them, and in this way, genes can influence aspects of behavior. But *behavioral genetics*, or the study of how genes affect behavior, is a relatively new field. So, we don't currently know the extent to which genes actually influence behavior in humans or other species. What we do know is that behavior must be viewed as the product of *complex interactions between genetic and environmental factors*. Between species, there's considerable variation in the limits and potentials for learning and for behavioral flexibility. In some species, the potentials are extremely broad; in others, they aren't. Ultimately, those limits and potentials are set by genetic factors that have been selected for throughout the evolutionary history of every species. That history, in turn, has been shaped by the ecological setting not only of living species *but also of their ancestors*.

A major goal of primatology is to determine how behaviors influence reproductive fitness and how ecological factors have influenced their development. While the actual mechanics of behavioral evolution aren't yet fully understood, new technologies and

behavioral ecology The study of the evolution of behavior, emphasizing the role of ecological factors as agents of natural selection. Behaviors and behavioral patterns have been selected for because they increase the reproductive fitness of individuals (i.e., they're adaptive) in specific environmental contexts.

methodologies are beginning to answer many questions. For example, genetic analysis has recently been used to establish paternity in a few primate groups, and this has helped support hypotheses about some behaviors (see p. 171). But in general, an evolutionary approach to the study of behavior doesn't provide definitive answers to many research questions. Rather, it provides a valuable framework within which primatologists analyze data to generate and test hypotheses concerning behavioral patterns.

Because primates are among the most social of animals, social behavior is a major topic in primate research. This is a broad subject that includes *all* aspects of behavior occurring in social groupings, even some you may not think of as social behaviors, like feeding or mating. To understand the function of one behavioral element, scientists need to determine how it's influenced by numerous interrelated factors. As an example, we'll consider some of the more important variables that influence social structure (see "A Closer Look," p. 160). But remember that we're discussing complex interactions and that social structure itself influences individual behavior, so in many cases, the distinctions between social and individual behaviors are blurred.

Russ Mittermeir

FIGURE 7-2
Dwarf mouse lemur

SOME FACTORS THAT INFLUENCE SOCIAL STRUCTURE

Body Size Among the living primates, body size is extremely diverse, ranging from dwarf mouse lemurs (Fig. 7-2) at about 2.5 ounces to gorillas at around 260 pounds. As a general rule, larger animals require fewer calories per unit of weight than smaller animals do. This is because larger animals have a smaller ratio of surface area to mass than do smaller animals. Since body heat is lost at the surface, larger animals can retain heat more efficiently, so they require less energy overall. It may seem strange, but two 10-pound monkeys require more food than one 22-pound monkey does (Fleagle, 1999).

Basal Metabolic Rate (BMR) The BMR concerns **metabolism**, the rate at which the body uses energy at a resting state to maintain all bodily functions. Metabolism is closely correlated with body size so, in general, smaller animals have a higher BMR than larger ones do. Consequently, smaller primates like galagos, tarsiers, marmosets, and tamarins require an energy-rich diet high in protein (insects), fats (nuts and seeds), and carbohydrates (fruits and seeds). Some larger primates, which tend to have a lower BMR and reduced energy requirements relative to body size, can benefit from less energy-rich foods such as leaves.

Diet The nutritional requirements of animals are related to the previous two factors, and all three have evolved together. When primatologists study the relationships between diet and behavior, they consider the benefits in terms of energy (calories) derived from various food items against the costs (energy expended) of obtaining and digesting them.

As we discussed in Chapter 6, most primates eat a wide variety of foods. But each species concentrates on some food types more than others; and almost all consume some animal protein, even if it's just in the form of insects and other invertebrates. While small-bodied primates focus on high-energy foods, larger-bodied species don't necessarily need to. For instance, mountain gorillas eat leaves, pith from bamboo stems, and other types of vegetation. Lowland gorillas do likewise, but they also exploit a wider range of materials that includes various water plants. These foods have less caloric value than fruits, nuts, and seeds, but they still serve these animals well because gorillas tend to spend much of the day eating. Besides, gorillas don't need to expend much energy searching for food since they're literally surrounded by it (Fig. 7-3).

Some monkeys, especially colobines (colobus and langur species), are primarily leaf eaters. Compared to many other monkeys, they're fairly large-bodied. They've also evolved elongated intestines and pouched stomachs that enable them, with the assistance of intestinal bacteria, to digest the tough fibers and cellulose in leaves. And, in at least two langur

metabolism The chemical processes within cells that break down nutrients and release energy for the body to use. (When nutrients are broken down into their component parts, such as amino acids, energy is released and made available for the cell to use.)

species, there's a duplicated gene that produces an enzyme which assists in the digestive process. Importantly, this gene duplication isn't found in other primates that have been studied, so the duplication event probably occurred after colobines and cercopithecines last shared a common ancestor (Zhang et al., 2002). Since having a second copy of the gene was advantageous to colobine ancestors who were probably already exploiting leaves, natural selection favored it to the point that it was established in the lineage.

Distribution of Resources Various kinds of foods are distributed in different ways. Food items such as leaves can be abundant and dense and so will support large groups of animals. (Think also of large herds of grazing animals that can be supported on large expanses of grassland.) Other foods, such as insects, may be widely scattered. For this reason, the animals that rely on them usually feed alone or perhaps in the company of one or two others.

Fruit and nuts in dispersed trees, or berries on shrubs, are foods that occur in clumps. These can most efficiently be exploited by smaller groups of animals, so large groups frequently break up into smaller subunits while feeding. Such subunits may consist of one-male groups (for example, hamadryas baboons) or **matrilines** (for example, macaques). Species that subsist on abundantly distributed resources may also live in one-male groups, and because food is plentiful, these one-male units are able to join with others to form large, stable communities (howlers and some colobines). To the casual observer, these communities can appear to be multimale-multifemale groups.

Some species that rely on foods distributed in small clumps tend to be protective of resources, especially if their feeding area is small enough to be defended. Some of these species live in small groups, composed of monogamous pairs (siamangs) or a female with one or two males (marmosets and tamarins). Naturally, dependent offspring are also included. Lastly, many kinds of food are only seasonally available. These include fruits, nuts, seeds, berries, and so on. Primates that rely on seasonally available foods must exploit several types and must move about to obtain food throughout the year. This is another factor that tends to favor smaller feeding groups.

The distribution and seasonality of water are also important variables. Water may be available year-round, as in continuously flowing rivers and streams or where there's abundant rainfall. But in areas that have a dry season, water may exist only in widely dispersed ponds that primates must share with other animals, including predators.

Predation Primates are vulnerable to many types of predators, including snakes, birds of prey, leopards, wild dogs, lions, and even other primates. Their responses to predation depend on the type of predator, body size, and social structure. Typically, where predation pressure is high and body size is small, large communities are advantageous. These may be multimale-multifemale groups or congregations of one-male groups (see "A Closer Look," p. 160).

Relationships with Other, Nonpredatory Species Many primate species associate with other primate and nonprimate species for various reasons including predator avoidance (see p. 164). When they do share habitats with other species, they exploit somewhat different resources (see p. 162).

Lynn Kilgore

FIGURE 7-3
This male mountain gorilla has only to reach out to find something to eat.

matrilines Groupings of females who are all descendants of one female (e.g., a female, her daughters, granddaughters, and their offpsring). Matrilines also include dependent male offspring. Among macaques, some matrilines are dominant to others, so that members of dominant matrilines have greater access to resources than do members of subordinate ones.

A CLOSER LOOK · Types of Nonhuman Primate Social Groups

1. *One male-multifemale.* A single adult male, several adult females, and their offspring. This is the most common primate mating structure, in which only one male actively breeds, and it's typically formed by a male joining a kin group of females. Females usually form the permanent nucleus of the group. Examples: guenons, gorillas, some pottos, some spider monkeys, patas, some langurs, and some colobus. In many species, several one-male groups may form large congregations.

2. *Multimale-multifemale* Several adult males, several adult females, and their young. Many of the males reproduce. The presence of several males in the group may lead to tension and to the formation of a dominance hierarchy. Examples: some lemurs, macaques, mangabeys, savanna baboons, vervets, squirrel monkeys, some spider monkeys, and chimpanzees. In some species (vervets, baboons and macaques), females are members of matrilines, or groups composed of a female, her female offspring, and their offspring. These kin groups are arranged in a hierarchy, so each matriline is dominant to some other matrilines and, at the same time, subordinate to others.

3. *Monogamous pair* A mated pair and its young. The term *monogamous* is somewhat misleading because extra-pair matings aren't uncommon. Species that form pairs are usu-ally arboreal, show minimal sexual dimorphism, and are frequently territorial. Adults don't normally tolerate other adults of the same sex. This grouping isn't found among the great apes, and it's the least common breeding structure among nonhuman primates. Examples: siamangs, gibbons, indris, titis, sakis, owl monkeys, and pottos. Males may directly participate in infant care.

4. *Polyandry:* one female and two males. This social group is seen only in some New World monkeys (marmosets and tamarins). Males participate in care of infants.

5. *Solitary:* individual forages for food alone. This group is seen in some nocturnal prosimians (aye-ayes, lorises, and galagos). In some species, adult females may forage in pairs or may be accompanied by offspring. Also seen in orang-utans.

There are also other groupings, such as foraging groups, hunting groups, all-female or all-male groups, and so on. Like humans, nonhuman primates don't always maintain one kind of group; single male-multifemale groups may sometimes form multimale-multifemale groups, and vice versa. Hamadryas baboons, for example, are described as living in one-male groups; but they form herds of 100 or more at night as they move to the safety of sleeping cliffs.

Dispersal Another factor that greatly influences social structure and relationships within groups is dispersal. As is true of most mammals (and indeed, most vertebrates), members of one sex leave the group in which they were born (their *natal group*) about the time they're sexually mature . There's considerable variability within and between species regarding which sex leaves, but male dispersal is the most common pattern in primates (ring-tailed lemurs, vervets, and macaques, to name a few). Female dispersal is seen in some colobus species, hamadryas baboons, chimpanzees, and mountain gorillas.

Dispersal may have more than one outcome. Typically, when females leave, they join another group. Males may do likewise, but in some species they may remain solitary for a time, or they may temporarily join an all-male "bachelor" group until they're able to establish a group of their own. But one common theme is that those individuals who disperse usually find mates outside their natal group. This commonality has led primatologists to conclude that the most valid explanations for dispersal are probably related to two major factors: reduced competition for mates (particularly between males) and, perhaps even more important, decreased likelihood of close inbreeding.

philopatric Remaining in one's natal group or home range as an adult. In most species, members of one sex disperse from their natal group as young adults, and members of the philopatric sex remain. In most of the nonhuman primate species, the philopatric sex is female.

Members of the **philopatric** sex enjoy certain advantages. Individuals (of either sex) who remain in their natal group are able to establish long-term bonds with relatives and other animals, with whom they cooperate to protect resources or enhance their social position. This is well illustrated by chimpanzee males, who permanently reside in their natal groups (see further discussion in Chapter 8). Also, because female macaques are philopatric, they form stable matrilineal subgroups. Larger matrilines can have greater access to foods, and these females support each other in conflict situations.

Because some individuals remain together over a long period of time, members of a primate group get to know each other well. They learn, as they must, how to respond to a variety of actions that may be threatening, friendly, or neutral. In such social groups, individuals must be able to evaluate situations before they act. Evolutionarily speaking, this ability would have placed selective pressure on social intelligence, which in turn would have selected for brains capable of assessing social situations and storing relevant information. One result of such selection would be the evolution of proportionately larger and more complex brains, especially among the higher primates (that is, anthropoids).

Life Histories   **Life history traits** are characteristics or developmental stages that typify members of a given species and therefore influence potential reproductive rates. These traits also influence primate social structure. Examples of life history traits are length of gestation, length of time between pregnancies (interbirth interval), period of infant dependency and age at weaning, age of sexual maturity, and life expectancy. But the importance of life history traits to social organization can't be analyzed in the absence of long-term data on primate groups, since primates have such long life spans. Fortunately, in addition to the Gombe chimpanzees, groups of many species have now been studied more or less continuously for more than 30 years.

Life history traits have important and complex consequences for many aspects of social life and social structure. They can also be critical to species survival. Shorter life spans are advantageous to species that live in marginal or unpredictable habitats (Strier, 2003). Since these species mature early and have short interbirth intervals, reproduction can occur at a relatively fast rate. Conversely, species with extended life spans are well suited to stable environmental conditions. The extended life spans of the great apes in particular, characterized by later sexual maturation and long interbirth intervals (3 to 5 years), means that most females will raise only 3 or 4 offspring to maturity. Today, this slow rate of reproduction increases the threat to great ape populations now being hunted at a devastating rate that far outpaces their replacement capacities (see "Issue," pp. 118–120).

Strategies   **Strategies** are behaviors that increase individual reproductive success. They also influence the structure and dynamics of primate social groups. We're accustomed to using the word *strategies* to mean deliberate schemes or plans purposefully designed to achieve goals. But in the context of nonhuman behavioral ecology, strategies are seen as products of natural selection, and no conscious planning or motivation is implied (Strier, 2003). Several kinds of strategies are discussed in behavioral studies, including *life history strategies, feeding strategies, social strategies, reproductive strategies,* and *predator avoidance strategies.*

Distribution and Types of Sleeping Sites   Gorillas are the only nonhuman primates that sleep on the ground. Primate sleeping sites can be in trees or on cliff faces, and their spacing can be related to social structure and to predator avoidance.

Activity Patterns   Most primates are diurnal, but several small-bodied prosimians and one New World monkey (the owl monkey) are nocturnal. Nocturnal species tend to forage for food alone or in groups of 2 or 3, and many use concealment to avoid predators.

Human Activities   We stated earlier that virtually all nonhuman primate populations are now affected by human hunting and forest clearing (see pp. 118–120). These activities severely disrupt and isolate groups, reduce numbers, reduce resource availability, and eventually can cause extinction.

Sympatric Species

Another issue that's basic to the behavioral ecology of primates is the differential exploitation of resources by **sympatric** species. This strategy provides a way to maximize access to food while at the same time reducing competition between different species.

life history traits   Characteristics and developmental stages that influence rates of reproduction. Examples include longevity; age at sexual maturity; length of time between births, etc.

strategies   Behaviors or behavioral complexes that have been favored by natural selection to increase individual reproductive fitness.

sympatric   Living in the same area; pertaining to two or more species whose habitats partly or largely overlap.

FIVE MONKEY SPECIES IN THE KIBALE FOREST, UGANDA

An early study of sympatric relationships between five monkey species was undertaken in the Kibale Forest (Fig. 7-4) of western Uganda (Struhsaker and Leyland, 1979). The five species were black-and-white colobus, red colobus, mangabey, blue monkey, and redtail monkey. In addition to these five, the Kibale Forest is home to two other monkey species as well as pottos, two galago species, and chimpanzees (for a discussion of the latter, see Ghiglieri, 1984). Altogether, 11 different nonhuman primate species coexist at Kibale.

The five species in the study differ in their anatomy, behavior, and dietary preferences. Body weights vary considerably, ranging from 3 to 4 kilograms for redtails up to 7 to 10 kilograms for mangabey and colobus species. Diet also differs: The two colobus species primarily eat leaves, and the other three species concentrate more on fruits supplemented by insects. These differences are important because, in order for two or more species to share the same habitat and get enough to eat, they need to exploit somewhat different resources in order to reduce competition for food.

More detailed analysis of feeding patterns showed still other differences. For instance, while both colobus species eat mostly leaves, black-and-white colobus mostly eat mature ones. As a way of avoiding competition, red colobus, on the other hand, eat a greater variety of leaves, usually immature ones, as well as fruits and shoots. Perhaps correlated with these dietary differences are the observations that black-and-white colobus spend less time feeding but more time resting; in contrast, red colobus range farther and live in higher density.

Several aspects of social organization also vary. For example, red colobus and mangabeys live in multimale-multifemale groups, while only one fully adult male is typically present in the other species. Among the mostly multimale-multifemale species, some aspects of social structure also differ. In mangabeys, females constitute the permanent core of the group, with males transferring out. In red colobus, it's the females who transfer and the males who are philopatric (Struhsaker and Leyland, 1987). There's so much variability, in fact, that researchers found little correlation between social organization and feeding ecology. The impression one gets from all this is that many primate species are exceedingly flexible regarding group composition, a fact that makes generalizing extremely tentative.

FIGURE **7-4**
Kibale Forest habitat, Uganda.

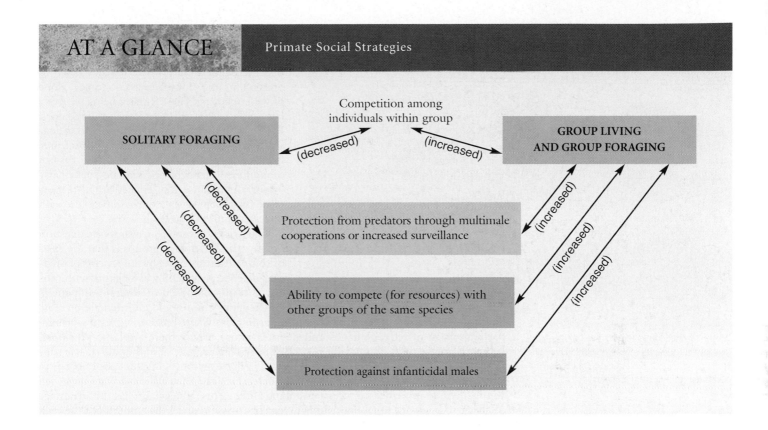

Still, the highly controlled nature of the Kibale study makes some comparisons and provisional generalizations possible:

1. The omnivores (mangabeys, redtail and blue monkeys) move about more than the folivores (the two colobus species).

2. Among the omnivores, there's an inverse relationship between body size and group size (that is, the smaller the body size, the larger the group tends to be). Also among the omnivores, there's a direct relationship between body size and **home range** size.

3. Omnivores are more spatially dispersed than folivores.

4. Female sexual swelling (see p. 170) is obvious only in those species (red colobus) that live in multimale-multifemale groups.

5. Feeding, spacing, group residency, dispersal, and reproductive strategies may be very different for males and females of the same species. These considerations have become a central focus of ecological and evolutionary research.

Why Be Social?

As you can see, the topic of primate behavior is complicated. Primatologists have to consider an animal's relative brain size, BMR, and reproductive physiology in addition to such ecological factors as the distribution of food resources and the nutritional value of foods and how they are selected and processed. (See Fleagle, 1999, and Strier, 2003, for detailed discussions of these factors.) What's more, the variability in ecological adaptations seen in closely related species, or even within the same species, must be understood. And it's important to know how primates interact with other species, including other primates.

But there's an even more basic question. Group living exposes primates to competition with other group members for resources, so why don't they live alone? After all, competition can lead to injury or even death, and it's costly in terms of energy expenditure. If they

home range The total area exploited by an animal or social group; usually given for 1 year—or for the entire lifetime—of an animal.

Time Life Pictures/Getty Images

FIGURE 7-5

When a baboon strays too far from its troop, as this one has done, it's more likely to fall prey to predators. Leopards are the most serious nonhuman threat to terrestrial primates.

conspecifics   Members of the same species.

lived alone, females would be free to forage without competition, and occasional encounters with males would still ensure reproductive success. Actually, some primate females (such as orangutans and chimpanzees) do forage, alone or with offspring. These females, being relatively large-bodied, have little to fear from predators. By feeding alone or with only one or two youngsters, they maximize their access to food, free from competition with others. In the case of orangutans, this behavior may be particularly important because the females are effectively removing themselves from competition with males who may be twice their size.

One widely accepted answer to the question of why primates live in groups is that the costs of competition are offset by the benefits of predator defense provided by associating with others. Groups composed of several adult males and females (multimale-multifemale groups) have traditionally been viewed as advantageous in areas where predation pressure is high, particularly in mixed woodlands and open savannas, where there are large predators. Leopards are the most significant predator of terrestrial primates, but they also take a substantial number of arboreal monkeys (Fig. 7-5). Where members of prey species occur in larger groups, the chances of early predator detection (and thus avoidance) are increased simply because more pairs of eyes are looking about. This strategy also has the advantage of giving individual animals more time to feed because it reduces the amount of time each one spends in surveillance (Janson, 1990; Isbell and Young, 1993).

Savanna baboons have long been cited as an example of this practice. Savanna baboons are found in semiarid grassland and broken woodland habitats throughout sub-Saharan Africa. During the day, they forage in large multimale-multifemale groups, and if they detect nonhuman predators, they flee to the safety of trees. But if they're at some distance from safety or if the predator is nearby, adult males may join forces to chase the intruder away. The effectiveness of male baboons in this regard shouldn't be underestimated, because they've been known to kill domestic dogs and even to attack leopards and lions.

Examples of increased group size as a defense against predators have been reported in vervets (Isbell, 1993) and capuchins (de Ruiter, 1986). In these species, vigilance was seen to increase as group size increased. Hamadryas baboons forage in small groups consisting of one male and a few females and offspring. But when predators are seen, such one-male units join with others to mobilize against the intruder.

The benefits of larger groups are also apparent in reports of polyspecific (more than one species) associations that function to reduce predation. In the Tai National Park, Ivory Coast, red colobus monkeys, a favorite prey of chimpanzees (see Chapter 8), frequently associate with Diana monkeys (a guenon species) as a predator avoidance strategy (Bshary and Noe, 1997; Noe and Bshary, 1997). Normally, these two species don't form close associations. But when chimpanzee predation increases, new groupings develop, and preexisting ones remain intact for longer than normal periods of time. McGraw and Bshary (2002) report that a third species, the sooty mangabey, sometimes provides additional support. The more terrestrial mangabeys live in multimale groups of up to 100 individuals, and they detect predators earlier than the other two species. Mangabeys are in proximity to red colobus and Diana monkeys only about 5 to 10 percent of the time, but when they're present, the other two species modify their foraging strategies. The normally arboreal red colobus monkeys even come to the ground (McGraw and Bshary, 2002). Consequently, through the strategy of interspecific associations, potential prey animals are able to spend more time feeding and increase their opportunities for foraging.

As effective as increased numbers can be in preventing predation, there are other explanations for primate sociality. One is that larger social groups can outcompete smaller groups of **conspecifics** when foraging in the same area (Wrangham, 1980). Wrangham also suggests that large multimale-multifemale groups evolved because males were attracted to related females living in association with one another. And lastly, females may tolerate familiar males since they can provide protection against other, potentially infanticidal males.

As you learned in the previous chapter, not all primates are found in large groups. Solitary foraging is typical of many species and is probably related to diet and distribution of resources. In the case of insectivorous lorises, solitary feeding reduces competition, which results in less distance traveled (and thus less energy expended) in the search for prey. Also, because insects usually don't occur in dense patches, they're more efficiently exploited by widely dispersed animals rather than by groups. Solitary foraging may also be related to predator avoidance in species that rely chiefly on concealment, rather than escape, for protection.

There's probably no single answer to the question of why primates live in groups. More than likely, predator avoidance is a major factor but not the only one. Group living evolved as an adaptive response to a number of ecological variables, and it has served primates well for a very long time.

Primate Social Behavior

Because primates solve their major adaptive problems in a social context, we might expect them to participate in various activities to reinforce the group's integrity. In the following sections, we describe the better known of these activities—and remember, all these behaviors have evolved as adaptive responses over more than 50 million years of primate evolution.

DOMINANCE

Many primate societies are organized into **dominance hierarchies**. Dominance hierarchies impose a certain degree of order within groups by establishing parameters of individual behavior. Although some animals often use aggression to increase their status, dominance usually serves to reduce the amount of actual physical violence. Not only are lower-ranking individuals unlikely to attack or even threaten a higher-ranking one, dominant animals can frequently exert control simply by making a threatening gesture. Individual rank or status may be measured by access to resources, including food items and mating partners. Dominant individuals are given priority by others, and they usually don't give way in confrontations.

Many primatologists think that the primary benefit of dominance is the increased reproductive success of high-ranking animals. This may be true for some species, but there's good evidence that lower-ranking males of some species also successfully mate. For example, subordinate baboon males frequently establish friendships with females and, simply because of this close association, they're able to mate surreptitiously with their female friend when she comes into estrus.

Low-ranking male orangutans also mate frequently. These young males don't develop certain secondary sex characteristics, such as wide cheek pads and heavier musculature, as long as they live near a dominant male (Fig. 7-6). One theory is that this arrested development protects them from the dominant male, who doesn't view them as a threat. But they are a threat in terms of reproductive success because their strategy is to force females to mate with them. In fact, primatologists use the term *rape* to describe the degree of force these young males use.

Increased reproductive success is also postulated for high-ranking females, who have greater access to food than subordinate females do. High-ranking females are provided with more energy for offspring production and care

dominance hierarchies Systems of social organization wherein individuals within a group are ranked relative to one another. Higher-ranking individuals have greater access to preferred food items and mating partners than do lower-ranking individuals. Dominance hierarchies are sometimes referred to as pecking orders.

FIGURE 7-6
Fully mature, breeding male orangutan with well-developed cheek pads (a) compared to a suppressed adult male without cheek pads (b).

© Chris Hellier/CORBIS
(a)

© Theo Allofs/CORBIS
(b)

(Fedigan, 1983), and presumably their reproductive success is greater. Altmann et al. (1988) reported that while dominant female yellow baboons in one study group didn't have higher birthrates than lower-ranking females did, they reached sexual maturity earlier (presumably because of their enhanced nutritional status), thus increasing their potential number of offspring throughout the course of their lives.

In one other example, during a drought in Kenya, dominant female vervets in two groups prevented a third group from gaining access to their water hole. The deprived third group resorted to licking dew from tree trunks; but even in this group, the higher-ranking members denied the lower-ranking members access to this resource. Consequently, over half of this group died, and all of those were either adolescents or low-ranking adults (Cheney et al., 1988).

Pusey et al. (1997) demonstrated that the offspring of high-ranking female chimpanzees at Gombe had significantly higher rates of infant survival. Their daughters also matured faster, which meant they had shorter interbirth intervals and thus produced more offspring.

An individual's rank isn't permanent, and it changes throughout life. It's influenced by many factors, including sex, age, level of aggression, amount of time spent in the group, intelligence, perhaps motivation, and sometimes the mother's social position (particularly true of macaques).

In species organized into groups containing a number of females associated with one or several adult males, the males are generally dominant to females. Within such groups, males and females have separate hierarchies, although very high-ranking females can dominate the lowest-ranking males (particularly young males). There are exceptions to this pattern of male dominance. Among many lemur species, females are the dominant sex. What's more, in species that form monogamous pairs (such as indris, gibbons), males and females are codominant.

All primates *learn* their position in the hierarchy. From birth, an infant is carried by its mother, and it observes how she responds to every member of the group. Just as important, it sees how others react to her. Dominance and subordination are indicated by gestures and behaviors, some of which are universal throughout the primate order (including humans), and this gestural repertoire is part of every youngster's learning experience.

Young primates also acquire social rank through play with age peers. As they spend more time with play groups, their social interactions widen. Competition and rough-and-tumble play allow them to learn the strengths and weaknesses of peers, and they carry this knowledge with them throughout their lives. So, through early contact with the mother and subsequent exposure to peers, young primates learn to negotiate their way through the complex web of social interactions that make up their daily lives.

COMMUNICATION

Communication is universal among animals and includes scents and unintentional, **autonomic** responses and behaviors that convey meaning. Such attributes as body posture convey information about an animal's emotional state. For example, a crouched position indicates a certain amount of insecurity or fear, while a purposeful, striding gait implies confidence. Autonomic responses to threatening or novel stimuli, such as raised body hair (most species) or enhanced body odor (gorillas), indicate excitement.

Many intentional behaviors also serve as communication. In primates, these include a wide variety of gestures, facial expressions, and vocalizations, some of which we humans share. Among many primates, an intense stare indicates a mild threat; and indeed, we humans find prolonged eye contact with strangers very uncomfortable. (For this reason, people should avoid eye contact with captive primates.) Other threat gestures include a quick yawn to expose canine teeth (baboons, macaques; Fig. 7-7); bobbing back and forth in a crouched position (patas monkeys); and branch shaking (many monkey species). High-ranking baboons *mount* the hindquarters of subordinates to express dominance (Fig. 7-8). Mounting may also serve to defuse potentially tense situations by indicating something like, "It's okay, I accept your apology, I know you didn't intend to offend me."

Primates also use a variety of behaviors to indicate submission, reassurance, or amicable intentions. Submission is indicated by a crouched position (most primates) or by presenting the hindquarters (baboons). Reassurance takes the form of touching, patting,

Lynn Kilgore

FIGURE 7-7

An adolescent male savanna baboon threatens the photographer with a characteristic "yawn" that shows the canine teeth. Note also that the eyes are closed briefly to expose light, cream-colored eyelids. This has been termed the "eyelid flash."

communication   Any act that conveys information, in the form of a message, to another individual. Frequently, the result of communication is a change in the recipient's behavior. Communication may not be deliberate, but may instead be the result of involuntary processes or a secondary consequence of an intentional action.

autonomic   Pertaining to physiological responses not under voluntary control. An example in chimpanzees would be the erection of body hair during excitement. An example in humans is blushing. Both convey information regarding emotional states; but neither behavior is deliberate, and communication is not intended.

FIGURE 7-8
One young male savanna baboon mounts another as an expression of dominance.

hugging, and holding hands. Grooming also serves in many situations to indicate submission or reassurance.

A wide variety of facial expressions indicating emotional state are seen in chimpanzees and, especially, in bonobos (Fig. 7-9). These include the well-known play face (also seen in several other primate and nonprimate species), associated with play behavior, and the fear grin (seen in *all* primates) to indicate fear and submission.

Primates also use a wide array of vocalizations for communication. Some, such as the bark of a baboon who's just spotted a leopard, are unintentional startled reactions. Others, such as the chimpanzee food grunt, are heard only in specific contexts. Even so, both vocalizations serve the same function: They inform others, although not necessarily deliberately, of the possible presence of predators or food.

Primates (and other animals) also communicate through **displays**, which are more complicated, frequently elaborate combinations of behaviors. For example, the exaggerated courtship dances of many male birds, often enhanced by colorful plumage, are displays. Common gorilla displays are chest slapping and the tearing of vegetation to indicate threat. Likewise, an angry chimpanzee, with hair bristling, may charge an opponent while screaming, waving its arms, and tearing vegetation.

By describing a few communicative behaviors shared by many primates (including humans), we don't mean that these gestures are dictated solely by genetic factors. Indeed, if primates aren't reared within a relatively normal social context, such behaviors may not be performed appropriately, because the contextual manifestations of communicatory actions are *learned*. But the underlying *predisposition* to learn and use them and the motor

displays Sequences of repetitious behaviors that serve to communicate emotional states. Nonhuman primate displays are most frequently associated with reproductive or agonistic behavior.

FIGURE 7-9
Chimpanzee facial expressions.

Relaxed

Relaxed with dropped lip

Horizontal pout face
(distress)

Fear grin
(fear/excitement)

Full play face

patterns involved in their execution are genetically influenced, and these factors do have adaptive significance. Theories about how such expressive devices evolved thus focus on motor patterns and the original context in which they occurred.

Over time, certain behaviors and motor patterns that originated in specific contexts have assumed increasing importance as communicatory signals. For example, crouching (seen also in many nonprimate species, such as dogs) initially helped avoid physical attack. But this behavior also conveyed that the individual was fearful, submissive, and nonaggressive. Crouching thus became valuable not only for its primary function but also for its role in communication, and natural selection increasingly favored it for this secondary role. In this way, over time, the expressions of specific behaviors may thus become elaborated or exaggerated because of their value in enhancing communication. Many complex displays also incorporate various combinations of **ritualized behaviors**.

Mounting, as seen in baboons, is a good example of a ritualized behavior. Higher-ranking individuals mount the hindquarters of more subordinate animals, not to mate but to express dominance. (When mounting serves a communicatory function, mounters and mountees may be members of the same sex.) In most anthropoid species that live in one-male or multimale groups, males (the mounters in the mating context) are socially dominant to females. So, in the context of communication, the mounter assumes the male reproductive role. Likewise, by presenting its hindquarters to solicit mounting, the mountee indicates submission or subordination. As communication, these behavior patterns are entirely removed from their original reproductive context, and they function instead to reinforce and clarify the respective social roles of individuals in specific interactions.

All nonhuman animals employ various vocalizations, body postures, and, to some degree, facial expressions that transmit information. The array of communicative devices is much richer among nonhuman primates, however, even though they don't use language the way humans do. Communication is important, for it's truly what makes social living possible. Through submissive gestures, aggression is reduced and physical violence is less likely. Likewise, friendly intentions and relationships are reinforced through physical contact and grooming. Indeed, we humans can see ourselves in other primate species most clearly in the familiar uses of nonverbal communication.

AGGRESSIVE AND AFFILIATIVE INTERACTIONS

Within primate societies, there's an interplay between **affiliative** behaviors, which promote group cohesion, and aggressive behaviors, which can lead to group disruption. Conflict within a group frequently develops out of competition for resources, including mating partners and food items. Instead of actual attacks or fighting, most intragroup aggression occurs in the form of various signals and displays, frequently within the context of a dominance hierarchy. Most of these situations are resolved through various submissive and appeasement behaviors.

But conflict isn't always resolved peacefully, and it can have serious consequences. For example, high-ranking female macaques frequently intimidate, harass, and even attack lower-ranking females in order to restrict their access to food. Dominant females consistently chase subordinates away from food and have even been observed to take food from their mouths. Eventually, these behaviors can result in weight loss and poorer nutrition in low-ranking females. Even more important, subordinate females exhibit lower reproductive success because they're less able to successfully rear offspring to maturity; this is partly because they're unable to obtain food (Silk et al., 2003).

Competition between males for mates frequently results in injury and occasionally in death. In species that have a distinct breeding season (such as squirrel monkeys), conflict between males is most common during that time. Male squirrel monkeys form coalitions to compete with other males, and when outright fighting occurs, injuries can be severe. In species not restricted to a mating season, competition between males can be an ongoing process. As you've seen, one-male social groups are common in primates, and a male who gains control of a group of females must constantly protect his own interests against the interests of other males attempting to displace him. Most of these conflicts don't result in death, but it can happen. In one well-known example, Dian Fossey once found the skull of an adult male mountain gorilla with a canine tooth of another male gorilla embedded in it.

ritualized behaviors   Behaviors removed from their original context and sometimes exaggerated to convey information.

affiliative   Pertaining to amicable associations between individuals. Affiliative behaviors, such as grooming, reinforce social bonds and promote group cohesion.

grooming   Picking through fur to remove dirt, parasites, and other materials that may be present. Social grooming is common among primates and reinforces social relationships.

Even though conflict can be destructive, a certain amount of aggression is useful in maintaining order within groups and protecting either individual or group resources. Fortunately, to reinforce bonds between individuals, promote group cohesion, minimize actual violence, and defuse potentially dangerous situations, an array of affiliative (friendly) behaviors serve to reinforce bonds between individuals and enhance group stability.

Common affiliative behaviors include reconciliation, consolation, and simple amicable interactions between friends and relatives. Most such behaviors involve various forms of physical contact, such as touching, hand-holding, hugging—and, among chimpanzees, kissing (Fig. 7-10). In fact, physical contact is one of the most important factors in primate development and is crucial in promoting peaceful relationships in many primate social groups.

Grooming is one of the most important affiliative behaviors in many primate species. Although grooming occurs in other animal species, social grooming is mostly a primate activity, and it plays an important role in day-to-day life (Fig. 7-11). Because grooming involves using the fingers to pick through the fur of another individual (or one's own) to remove insects, dirt, and other materials, it serves hygienic functions. But it's also a pleasurable activity that members of some species (especially chimpanzees) engage in for long periods of time.

FIGURE **7-10**
Adolescent savanna baboons holding hands.

Lynn Kilgore

FIGURE **7-11**
Grooming primates. (a) Patas monkeys; female grooming male. (b) Longtail macaques.
(c) Savanna baboons. (d) Chimpanzees.

Robert Jurma n

(a)

Courtesy, Meredith Small

(b)

Courtesy, Arlene Kruse/Bonnie Pedersen

(c)

Courtesy, Arlene Kruse/Bonnie Pedersen

(d)

Grooming occurs in a variety of contexts. Mothers groom infants. Males groom sexually receptive females. Subordinate animals groom dominant ones, sometimes to gain favor. Friends groom friends. In general, grooming is comforting. It restores peaceful relationships between animals who've quarreled, and it provides reassurance during tense situations. In short, grooming reinforces social bonds and consequently helps to maintain and strengthen a group's structure.

Conflict resolution through reconciliation is another important aspect of primate social behavior. Following a conflict, chimpanzee opponents frequently move, within minutes, to reconcile (de Waal, 1982). Reconciliation takes many forms, including hugging, kissing, and grooming. Even uninvolved individuals may take part, either grooming one or both participants or forming their own grooming parties. In addition, bonobos are unique in their use of sex to promote group cohesion, restore peace after conflicts, and relieve tension within the group (de Waal, 1987, 1989).

Social relationships are crucial to nonhuman primates, and the bonds between individuals can last a lifetime. These relationships serve a variety of functions. Individuals of many species form alliances in which one supports another against a third. Alliances, or coalitions, as they're also called, can be used to enhance the status of members. For example, at Gombe, the male chimpanzee Figan achieved alpha status because of his brother's support (Goodall, 1986, p. 424). In fact, chimpanzees so heavily rely on coalitions and are so skillful politically that an entire book, appropriately titled *Chimpanzee Politics* (de Waal, 1982), has been devoted to the topic.

Reproduction and Reproductive Strategies

In most primate species, sexual behavior is tied to the female's reproductive cycle, with females being sexually receptive to males only when they're in estrus. Estrus is characterized by behavioral changes that indicate a female is receptive. In Old World monkeys and apes that live in multimale groups, estrus is also accompanied by swelling and changes in color of the skin around the genital area. These changes serve as visual cues of a female's readiness to mate (Fig 7-12).

FIGURE 7-12

Estrous swelling of genital tissues in a female chimpanzee.

Lynn Kilgore

Permanent bonding between males and females isn't common among nonhuman primates. However, male and female savanna baboons sometimes form mating *consortships*. These temporary relationships last while the female is in estrus, and the two spend most of their time together, mating frequently. Also, as we mentioned earlier, lower-ranking baboon males often form "friendships" (Smuts, 1985) with females and occasionally may mate with them, although they may be driven away by high-ranking males when the female is most receptive.

Mating consortships are sometimes seen in chimpanzees and are particularly common among bonobos. In fact, a male and female bonobo may spend several weeks primarily in each other's company. During this time, they mate often, even when the female isn't in estrus. These relationships of longer duration aren't typical of chimpanzee (*Pan troglodytes*) males and females.

Such a male-female bond may result in increased reproductive success for both sexes. For the male, there's the increased likelihood that he will be the father of any infant the female conceives. At the same time, the female potentially gains protection from predators or other members of her group and perhaps assistance in caring for offspring she may already have.

FEMALE AND MALE REPRODUCTIVE STRATEGIES

Reproductive strategies, and especially how they differ between the sexes, have been a primary focus of primate research. The goal of such strategies is to produce and successfully rear to adulthood as many offspring as possible.

Primates are among the most **K-selected** of mammal species. By this we mean that individuals produce only a few young, in whom they invest a tremendous amount of parental care. Contrast this pattern with **r-selected** species, where individuals produce large numbers of offspring but invest little or no energy in parental care. Good examples of r-selected species include insects, most fishes, and among mammals, mice and rabbits.

Considering the degree of care required by young, dependent primate offspring, it's clear that enormous investment by at least one parent is necessary. In a majority of species, the mother carries most of the burden both before and after birth. Primates are totally helpless at birth. They develop slowly and are thus exposed to expanded learning opportunities within a *social* environment. This trend has been elaborated most dramatically in great apes and humans, especially in the latter. So, what we see in ourselves and our close primate kin (and presumably in our more recent ancestors as well) is a strategy in which at least one parent, usually the mother, makes an extraordinary investment to produce a few "high-quality," slowly maturing offspring.

Finding food and mates, avoiding predators, and caring for and protecting dependent young are difficult challenges for nonhuman primates. Moreover, in most species, males and females employ different strategies to meet these challenges.

Female primates spend almost their entire adult lives being pregnant, lactating, and/or caring for offspring, and the resulting metabolic demands are enormous. A pregnant or lactating female, although perhaps only half the size of her male counterpart, may require about the same number of calories per day. Even if these demands are met, her physical resources may be drained. For example, analysis of chimpanzee skeletons from Gombe National Park, in Tanzania, showed significant loss of bone and bone mineral in older females (Sumner et al., 1989).

Given these physiological costs, and the fact that her reproductive potential is limited by lengthy intervals between births, a female's best strategy is to maximize the amount of resources available to her and her offspring. Indeed, as we just discussed, females of many primate species (gibbons, marmosets, and macaques, to name a few) are extremely competitive with other females and aggressively protect resources and territories. In other species, as we've seen, females distance themselves from others to avoid competition. Males, however, face a separate set of challenges. Having little investment in the rearing of offspring, it's to the male's advantage to secure as many mates and produce as many offspring as possible.

SEXUAL SELECTION

One outcome of different mating strategies is **sexual selection**, a phenomenon first described by Charles Darwin. Sexual selection is a type of natural selection that operates on only one sex, usually males. The selective agent is male competition for mates and, in some species, mate choice by females. The long-term effect of sexual selection is to increase the frequency of traits that lead to greater success in acquiring mates.

In the animal kingdom, numerous male attributes result from sexual selection. For example, when mating, female birds of many species are attracted to males with more vividly colored plumage. Selection has thus increased the frequency of alleles that influence brighter coloration in males, and in these species (peacocks may be the best example) males are more colorful than females.

Sexual selection in primates is most important in species in which mating is polygynous and male competition for females is prominent. In these species, sexual selection produces dimorphism in several traits, most noticeably body size. As you've seen, the males of many primate species are considerably larger than females, and males have larger canine teeth. Conversely, in species that live in pairs (such as gibbons) or where male competition is reduced, sexual dimorphism in canine and body size is either reduced or nonexistent. For these reasons, the presence or absence of sexually dimorphic traits in a species can be a reasonably good indicator of mating structure.

reproductive strategies The complex of behavioral patterns that contributes to individual reproductive success. The behaviors need not be deliberate, and they often vary considerably between males and females.

K-selected Pertaining to an adaptive strategy (K-selection) whereby individuals produce relatively few offspring, in whom they invest increased parental care. Although only a few infants are born, chances of survival are increased for each individual because of parental investments in time and energy. Examples of nonprimate K-selected species are birds and canids (e.g., wolves, coyotes, and dogs).

r-selected Pertaining to an adaptive strategy (r-selection) that emphasizes relatively large numbers of offspring and reduced parental care (compared to K-selected species). *K-selection* and *r-selection* are relative terms (e.g., mice are r selected compared to primates but K-selected compared to many fish species).

sexual selection A type of natural selection that operates on only one sex within a species. It's the result of competition for mates, and it can lead to sexual dimorphism regarding one or more traits.

Joe MacDonald/Animals Animals

FIGURE 7-13
Hanuman langurs.

INFANTICIDE AS A REPRODUCTIVE STRATEGY?

One way males may increase their chances of reproducing is to kill infants fathered by other males. This explanation was first offered in an early study of Hanuman langurs in India (Hrdy, 1977). Hanuman langurs (Fig. 7-13) typically live in groups composed of one adult male, several females, and their offspring. Other males without mates form "bachelor" groups that frequently forage within sight of the one-male associations. These peripheral males occasionally attack and defeat a reproductive male and drive him from his group. Sometimes, following such takeovers, the new male kills some or all of the group's infants (fathered by the previous male).

Superficially, such behavior seems counterproductive, especially for a species as a whole. However, individual animals act to maximize their *own* reproductive success, no matter what effect their actions may have on the population or even the species. By killing infants fathered by other animals, male langurs may in fact increase their own chances of fathering offspring, albeit unknowingly. This is because, while a female is producing milk and nursing an infant, she doesn't come into estrus and therefore she isn't sexually available. But when an infant dies, its mother stops lactating; within two or three months, she resumes cycling and becomes sexually receptive again. So, by killing nursing infants, a new male avoids waiting 2 to 3 years for them to be weaned before he can mate with their mothers. This could be advantageous to him since chances are good that he won't even be in the group for 2 or 3 years. He also doesn't expend energy and put himself at risk by defending infants who don't carry his genes.

Hanuman langurs aren't the only primates that practice infanticide. It's been observed (or surmised) in many species, such as redtail monkeys, red colobus, blue monkeys, savanna baboons, howlers, orangutans, gorillas, chimpanzees (Struhsaker and Leyland, 1987), and humans. In the majority of reported nonhuman primate examples, infanticide coincides with the transfer of a new male into a group or, as in chimpanzees, an encounter with an unfamiliar female and infant. (It should also be noted that infanticide occurs in many nonprimate species, including rodents, cats, and horses.)

Numerous objections to this explanation of infanticide have been raised. Alternative explanations have included competition for resources (Rudran, 1973), aberrant behaviors related to human-induced overcrowding (Curtin and Dohlinow, 1978), and inadvertent killing during conflict between animals (Bartlett et al., 1993). Sussman and colleagues (1995), as well as others, have questioned the actual prevalence of infanticide, arguing that although it does occur, it's not particularly common. These authors have also suggested that if indeed male reproductive fitness is increased through the killing of infants, such increases are negligible. Other primatologists (Struhsaker and Leyland, 1987; Hrdy, 1995) maintain that both the incidence and patterning of infanticide by males are not only significant, but consistent with the assumptions established by theories of behavioral evolution.

FIGURE 7-14
An immigrant male chacma baboon chases a terrified female and her infant (clinging to her back). Resident males interceded to stop the chase.

© Peter Henzi

Henzi and Barrett (2003) reported that when chacma baboon males migrate into a new group, they "deliberately single out females with young infants and hunt them down" (Fig. 7-14). The importance of these findings is the conclusion that, at least in chacma baboons, the newly arrived males consistently make attempts at infanticide; and their attacks are highly aggressive and purposeful. These observations indicate that the incoming males are very motivated and are engaging in a goal-directed behavior, although they most certainly don't understand the possible reproductive advantages they may later gain.

Reports like these, however, don't prove that infanticide increases a male's reproductive fitness. To do this, primatologists must demonstrate two crucial facts:

1. Infanticidal males *don't* kill their own offspring.
2. Once a male has killed an infant, he subsequently fathers another infant with the victim's mother.

Borries et al. (1999) collected DNA samples from the feces of infanticidal males and their victims in several groups of free-ranging Hanuman langurs, specifically to determine if these males killed their own offspring. Their results showed that in all 16 cases where infant and male DNA was available, the males weren't related to the infants they either attacked or killed. Secondly, DNA analysis also showed that in 4 out of 5 cases where a victim's mother subsequently gave birth, the new infant was fathered by the infanticidal males. Although still more evidence is needed, this DNA evidence strongly suggests that infanticide may indeed give males an increased chance of fathering offspring.

polyandry A mating system wherein a female continuously associates with more than one male (usually 2 or 3), with whom she mates. Among nonhuman primates, this pattern is seen only in marmosets and tamarins.

FIGURE **7-15**
Primate mothers with young. (a) Sykes monkey. (b) Patas monkey. (c) Mongoose lemur. (d) Orangutan. (e) Chimpanzee.

Mothers, Fathers, and Infants

The basic social unit among all primates is the female and her infants (Fig. 7-15). Except in those species in which monogamy or **polyandry** occurs, males don't directly participate in the rearing of offspring. Observations both in the field and in captivity suggest that the mother-offspring core gives the social group its stability.

(a)

(b)

(c)

(d)

(e)

FIGURE **7-16**

Infant macaque clinging to cloth mother.

Harlow Primate Laboratory, University of Wisconsin

The mother-infant bond begins at birth. Although we don't fully understand the bonding process, there appear to be predisposing innate factors that strongly attract a female to her infant, so long as she has had sufficiently normal experience with her own mother. This doesn't mean that primate mothers possess innate knowledge of how to care for an infant. Monkeys and apes raised in captivity without contact with their own mothers not only don't know how to care for a newborn infant, but they may also be afraid of it and may attack and even kill it. For this reason, learning is essential to establishing a mother's attraction to her infant.

The crucial role of bonding between primate mothers and infants was clearly demonstrated in a famous series of experiments at the University of Wisconsin. Psychologist Harry Harlow (1959) raised some infant monkeys with surrogate mothers made of wire or a combination of wire and cloth, while other monkeys were raised with no mother at all. The first group of infants retained an attachment to their cloth-covered surrogate mother (Fig.7-16). But those raised with no mother were incapable of forming lasting attachments with other monkeys; they sat passively in their cages, staring vacantly into space. None of the motherless males ever successfully copulated, and those females who were (somewhat artificially) impregnated either paid little attention to offspring or reacted aggressively toward them (Harlow and Harlow, 1961). The point is that monkeys reared in isolation were denied opportunities to *learn* the rules of social and maternal behavior. Moreover, and just as essential, they were denied the all-important physical contact so necessary for normal primate psychological and emotional development.

The importance of a normal relationship with the mother is demonstrated by field studies as well. From birth, infant primates are able to cling to their mother's fur, and they're in more or less constant physical contact with her for several months. During this critical period, an infant develops closeness with its mother that doesn't always end with weaning. In fact, especially among some Old World monkeys, mothers and infants may remain close until one or the other dies.

In subsequent studies, Suomi and colleagues emphasized that social isolation initiated early in life could have devastating effects on subsequent development and behavior for many primate species. The primate deprivation syndrome that results from early isolation is characterized by displays of abnormal self-directed behavior, such as hugging oneself or rocking back and forth, and by gross deficits in all aspects of social behavior (Suomi et al., 1983, p. 190).

Although infants are mainly cared for by their mothers, in some species, presumed fathers also participate. Male siamangs are actively involved in the care of offspring, and among marmosets and tamarins, males provide most of the direct infant care. In fact, marmoset and tamarin offspring (frequently twins) are usually carried on the male's back and are transferred to their mother only for nursing.

Even in species where adult males aren't directly involved in infant care, they may take more than a casual interest in them; researchers have frequently noted this behavior in hamadryas and savanna baboons. But to establish that baboons exhibit paternal care, it's

Lynn Kilgore

FIGURE 7-17

Male savanna baboon carrying an infant. This is an example of alloparenting—or perhaps parental care.

necessary to establish paternity. Buchan et al. (2003) have done just that by analyzing the DNA of subadults and males. They showed that during disputes, the fathers intervened on behalf of their offspring significantly more often than for unrelated juveniles. Because disputes can lead to severe injury, Buchan and colleagues considered the male intervention an example of true paternal care. Although this study also demonstrates that nonhuman primates can recognize relatives, the exact mechanisms of kin recognition haven't been fully identified. Clues to how nonhuman primates recognize relatives may eventually come from new, molecular-based research.

What may be an extension of the mother-infant relationship has been called **alloparenting** (Fig. 7-17). This type of behavior occurs in many animal species but is most richly expressed in primates, and some researchers believe that it's found among all social primates. Usually, alloparents crowd around an infant and attempt to groom, hold, or touch it. Some species, langurs, for example, are well known for their "aunts," and as many as eight females may hold an infant during its first day of life. Occasionally, rough treatment by inexperienced or aggressive animals can result in an infant's injury or death. For this reason, mothers may attempt to shield infants from overly attentive individuals.

Several functions are suggested for alloparenting. If the mother dies, the infant stands a chance of being adopted by an alloparent or other individual. Also, it may simply be convenient for the mother to leave her infant occasionally with another female. Finally, alloparenting may help train young females in the skills of motherhood.

Because the survival of offspring is the key to individual reproductive success, parenting strategies have evolved throughout the animal kingdom. In many r-selected species such as fishes, parenting may involve nothing more than laying large numbers of eggs. But in birds and mammals, as you've seen, there's increased care of dependent young. Alloparenting is important in some mammalian species besides primates (for example, elephants), but even so, it's most highly developed in several primate species. Likewise, males provide group defense in many mammal species, but actual paternal care is most common in primates. And with further use of genetic technologies, the role of males and other related individuals in infant care will undoubtedly become clearer.

alloparenting A common behavior in many primate species whereby individuals other than the parent(s) hold, carry, and in general interact with infants.

VISUAL SUMMARY

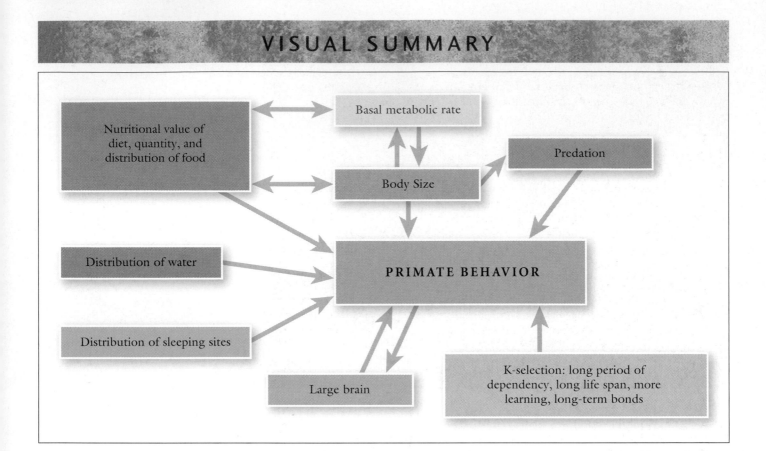

	Basal metabolic rate	
Nutritional value of diet, quantity, and distribution of food	Body Size	Predation
Distribution of water	**PRIMATE BEHAVIOR**	
Distribution of sleeping sites		
	Large brain	K-selection: long period of dependency, long life span, more learning, long-term bonds

Summary: Putting It All Together

In this chapter, we presented the major theoretical models for the evolution of behavior in primates. We also discussed some of the evidence, including the use of genetic analysis to support these models. The fundamental principle of behavioral evolution is that aspects of behavior (including social behavior) are influenced by genetic factors. And because some behavioral elements are therefore influenced by genes, natural selection can act on them in the same way it acts on physical and anatomical characteristics. We pointed out that in more primitive organisms, such as insects and most other invertebrates, the proportion of behavior that's directly influenced by genes is much greater than in mammals and birds.

Behavioral ecology is the discipline that examines behavior from the perspective of complex ecological relationships and the role of natural selection as it favors behaviors that increase reproductive fitness. This approach generates many models of behavioral evolution that can be applied to all species, including humans. Members of each species inherit a genome that is species-specific, and some part of that genome influences behaviors. But in more complex animals, the genome allows for greater degrees of behavioral flexibility and learning. In humans, who rely on cultural adaptations for survival, most behavior is learned.

Life history traits or strategies (developmental stages that characterize a species) are important to the reproductive success of individuals. These include length of gestation, number of offspring per birth, interbirth interval, age of sexual maturity, and longevity. Although these characters are strongly influenced by the genome of any species, they're also influenced by environmental and social factors such as nutrition and social status. In turn, nutritional requirements are affected by body size, diet, and basal metabolic rate (BMR).

We also described the various types of primate social groups: one male-multifemale groups; multimale-multifemale groups; so-called monogamous pairs; polyandry; and more or less solitary individuals. In addition, we presented various explanations for why primates live in social groups (for example, predator avoidance and competition for resources with other groups). There was also discussion of the various strategies primates have adopted to facilitate social living, including affiliative and aggressive interactions. Lastly, we talked about the relationships between mothers and infants and the increasing evidence that male primates provide more parental care than was previously thought.

Critical Thinking Questions

1. Apply some of the topics presented in this chapter to some nonprimate species that you're familiar with. Can you develop some hypotheses to explain the behavior of some domestic species? You might want to speculate on how behavior in domestic animals may differ from that of their wild ancestors. (Chapter 2 might help you here.)

2. In anticipation of the next chapter, can you speculate on how the behavioral ecology of nonhuman primates may be helpful in explaining human behavior?

3. We used birds as an example of sexual dimorphism resulting from sexual selection. But, there are some bird species in which males, not females, sit on the nest to warm and protect the eggs. These males are less colorful than the females. How would you explain this? (Hint: Sexual selection may not be the only factor involved in sexual dimorphism in bird coloration.)

Primates in Biomedical Research: Ethics and Concerns

Using nonhuman animals for experimentation is an established practice, long recognized for its benefits to human beings. An estimated 17 to 22 million animals are used annually in the United States to test new vaccines and other methods of treating or preventing disease, and to develop new surgical procedures. Nonhuman animals are also used in psychological experimentation and in the testing of consumer products.

Because of biological and behavioral similarities shared with humans, nonhuman primates are among the most desirable species for biomedical research. Therefore, about 50,000 nonhuman primates are used every year in the United States in biomedical research. Approximately 3,000 of these are involved in more than one study.

The most commonly used primates are baboons, vervets, several different macaque species, squirrel monkeys, marmosets, and tamarins. Because they are more expensive than other animals such as mice, rats, rabbits, cats, and dogs, primates are usually reserved for medical and behavioral studies and not for testing consumer goods such as cosmetics or household cleaners. (It should be noted that many cosmetic companies say they no longer perform tests on animals.)

Although work with primates has certainly benefited humankind, these benefits are expensive, not only monetarily but in terms of suffering and animal lives lost. The development of the polio vaccine in the 1950s serves as one example of the costs involved. Prior to the 1950s, polio had killed and crippled millions of people worldwide. Now this once feared disease is limited to India, Pakistan, Africa, and parts of Indonesia and the Middle East, and there are massive programs aimed at eliminating it altogether. It goes without saying that the near-eradication of polio has saved countless lives and reduced human suffering, but included in the price tag for the polio vaccine were the lives of 1.5 *million* rhesus macaques, mostly imported from India.

For this reason, serious questions have been raised about medical advances made at the expense of millions of nonhuman animals, many of whom are primates. Indeed, one well-known primatologist, speaking at a conference some years ago, questioned whether we can morally justify depleting populations of threatened species solely for the benefit of a single, highly overpopulated one. This question will seem outrageous and even offensive to many readers, especially in view of the fact that the majority of people would argue that *whatever* is necessary to promote human health and longevity is justified. However, it's a thought-provoking question, one that you might want to consider.

Leaving the broader ethical issues aside, one area of controversy regarding laboratory primates is housing. Traditionally, lab animals were kept, frequently in pairs, in small metal cages. These cages were usually bare, except for food and water, and they were frequently stacked one on top of another, so that their inhabitants found themselves in the unnatural situation of having animals above and below them, as well as on each side. (Unfortunately, this practice hasn't been entirely eliminated.)

The primary reason for small cage size is simple. Small cages are less expensive than large ones and they require less space, which is also costly. Moreover, sterile, unenriched cages (i.e., lacking objects for manipulation or play) are easier and therefore cheaper to clean. But for such curious, intelligent animals as primates, these easy-to-maintain facilities result in a deprivation that leads to depression, neurosis, and psychosis.

Chimpanzees, reserved primarily for AIDS and hepatitis B research, have perhaps suffered more than any other species from inadequate facilities. In 1990, Jane Goodall published a description of conditions she encountered in one lab she visited in Maryland. In this facility, she saw two-and three-year-old chimpanzees housed, two together, in cages measuring a mere 22 inches square and 24 inches high.

Obviously, it was virtually impossible for these youngsters to even move, and they'd been kept this way for over three months! At this same lab, adult chimpanzees, infected with HIV or hepatitis, were confined alone for several years in small isolation chambers about the size of a telephone booth. Their only view of their surroundings was through a small window, and a noisy ventilation system blocked most sound. Thus they spent years rocking back and forth, seeing little and hearing nothing of their surroundings.

Fortunately, conditions are improving. There has been increased public awareness of existing conditions; and among some members of the biomedical community, there's a growing sensitivity toward the special requirements of primates. In 1991, amendments to the Animal Welfare Act (first enacted in 1966) required all labs to provide minimum standards for the humane care of all "warm-blooded" animals. (For some reason, birds and rodents aren't included in this category.) These minimum standards provide specific requirements for cage size based on weight of the animal. For example, primates weighing less than 2.2 pounds must have 1.6 square feet of floor space per animal, and the cage must be at least 20 inches high. Those weighing more than 77 pounds are allotted at least 25 square feet of floor space per animal and at least 7 feet of vertical space.

Clearly, such cages aren't big enough for most activities and this restriction contributes to psychological stress. One method of reducing stress is to provide cages with objects and climbing structures (even part of a dead branch is an improvement and it costs nothing). Several facilities now provide environmental enrichment for their animals and many laboratory staff members are now trained to interact with the animals in their care in non-threatening ways. And, the Maryland lab that

Jane Goodall visited no longer keeps chimpanzees in isolation chambers.

Aside from the treatment of captive primates, there continues to be serious concern over the depletion of wild populations in order to provide research animals. Actually, the number of wild-caught animals used in research today is small compared to the numbers lost to habitat destruction and hunting for food. However, in the past, particularly in the 1950s and 1960s, the numbers of primates captured for research were staggering. In 1968, for example, 113,714 were received in the United States alone!

On average, the United States annually imports some 20,000 primates (some from breeding colonies in the country of origin). Although it would be best if no free-ranging primates were involved, at least these figures represent a substantial improvement since the 1960s. And there's mounting concern over primates provided by breeding colonies in countries where they occur naturally. For example, Chinese breeding centers get their breeding animals from free-ranging populations.

Undoubtedly, humans have much to gain by using nonhuman primates for experimentation, but we must provide them with humane treatment and enriched captive environments. We also have a moral obligation to ensure their survival in the wild. This means that existing laws that regulate the capture, treatment, and trade of wild-caught animals *must* be more strictly enforced.

In response to concerns for diminishing wild populations and regulations to protect them, in 1986 the National Institutes of Health (NIH) initiated the National Chimpanzee Breeding Program to provide chimpanzees primarily for AIDS and hepatitis B research. The breeding centers established under this program were so successful that, with a decline in demand for chimpanzees, there's actually a surplus of animals in need of housing.

One sign of progress is the establishment of sanctuaries for chimpanzees formerly used in biomedical research or surplus animals from breeding facilities. One such sanctuary built by Save the Chimps is located in Florida. Another is Chimp Haven, built on a 200-acre site donated by Caddo Parish in northern Louisiana, and partly funded by the National Institutes of Health (NIH), Phase I of Chimp Haven officially opened in 2005. By December, 2006, it was home to 77 chimpanzees and eventually it will have some 200 residents living in a natural outdoor setting with a summer climate similar to the humid tropics of chimpanzee habitat in Africa. In addition to being a sanctuary for chimpanzees, Chimp Haven is also open to tours for educational groups.

As might be expected, some critics have complained that the approximately 24 million dollars awarded by the NIH could have been better spent helping people. But actually, the Chimp Haven sanctuary is a far less expensive and more humane alternative than keeping these chimpanzees in research facilities. Also, it's even more important that we're obligated to them for the benefits we've derived from their lives as research animals. Surely part of this obligation is to provide them a cage-free retirement in outdoor enclosures with grass to walk on and trees to climb. But most of all, we owe them respect as complex, intelligent, and sensitive animals that are not so different from ourselves.

CRITICAL THINKING QUESTIONS

1. What do you see as the benefits derived from using non-human primates in biomedical research? Have you personally benefited from this type of research? If so, how?

2. Do you personally have concerns regarding the use of non-human primates in biomedical research? Explain your views.

3. Delineate the issues surrounding habitat enrichment for laboratory primates. Do you think enrichment is an important concern? Why or why not? If so, how would you address this issue, bearing in mind that there are constraints on funding?

SOURCES

Chimp Haven. www.chimphaven.org

Cyranoski, D. 2003. "China Launches Primate Centre to Broaden Medical Use of Monkeys." *Nature*, 424:239–240.

Goodall, Jane. 1990. *Through a Window*. Boston: Houghton-Mifflin.

Goodman, S. and E. Check, 2002. "The Great Primate Debate." *Nature*, 417:684–687.

Holden, Constance. 1988. "Academy Explores Use of Laboratory Animals." *Science* 242 (October): 185.

United States Department of Agriculture. Subchapter A—Animal Welfare. Washington, DC: U.S. Government Printing Office, Publication Number 311–364/60638, 1992.

CHAPTER 8

Primate Models for Human Behavioral Evolution

Courtesy, Tetsuro Matsuzawa

KEY QUESTIONS

Which patterns of nonhuman primate behavior are the most important for understanding human evolution?

How are humans unique among primates? In what ways are we not unique?

Introduction

In Chapter 1 we said that chimpanzees, in particular, are often used as models for early hominid behavior. But once the human and chimpanzee lineages diverged from a common ancestor, they traveled down different evolutionary paths and continued to evolve in response to different environmental pressures. Consequently, no living species, not even chimpanzees, can perfectly serve as a representative of early hominid adaptations.

Anyone who's even slightly curious about the beginnings of humankind would like to know more about our early ancestors. Drawings of early hominids, based on fossil remains, may give a fairly accurate depiction of what they looked like; but what did they *really* look like? What were their lives like? Did they have the same diseases people have today? What kinds of social groups did they form? What did they eat? How long did they live? How did they die? Can we answer these questions? No, not completely. But we can study the complex factors that influence many behaviors in nonhuman primates, and we can also continue to find and analyze fossil material. By combining what we learn from these two approaches, we can at least have a better understanding of how certain human behaviors evolved.

In the last chapter, we considered many of the factors that guided the evolutionary history of nonhuman primate behaviors. In the past two decades, primatologists have agreed that certain human behavioral predispositions reflect patterns also seen in other primates (Cartmill, 1990; King, 1994, 2004; de Waal, 1996). But even though chimpanzees and humans both exhibit a particular behavior, we still can't say for certain that it's a direct result of shared ancestry. What's important is to closely examine the *patterns of behavior* that have evolved as adaptive responses in nonhuman primates, while keeping in mind the enormous degree of flexibility in primate behavior. Then researchers can look for similar patterns in humans and try to draw conclusions about the ecological and genetic factors that may have produced similarities (and differences) between ourselves and our closest relatives. This approach places the study of human behavior firmly within an evolutionary context.

Certainly, human behavior is predominantly learned. But the *ability* to learn and behave in complex ways is ultimately rooted in biological factors, and natural selection has favored increased learning capacities and behavioral modification in the human lineage. This biological perspective doesn't propose that all human abilities and behaviors are genetically determined or unalterable. Rather, it helps explain *how* certain patterns may have come about and what their adaptive significance might be. Within this framework, the flexibility of human behavior is recognized and emphasized.

Human Origins and Behavior

What does it mean to be human? Clearly, certain aspects of behavior are what most dramatically set humans apart from other species. Long ago, culture became our strategy for coping with life's challenges. If suddenly stripped of all cultural attributes, modern humans wouldn't be able to survive year-round in many parts of the world; and no other primate even comes close to having the human ability to modify the environment.

Although we humans share more than 98 percent of our DNA sequences and many anatomical and behavioral characteristics with chimpanzees, we're undeniably quite different from them, physically as well as behaviorally. Humans have different limb proportions, flatter faces, smaller teeth, and, most important, relatively and absolutely bigger brains than

 Click!

Go to the following media for interactives and exercises on topics covered in this chapter:

- Online Virtual Laboratories for Physical Anthropology, Fourth Edition

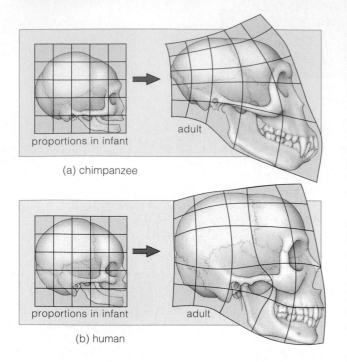

(a) chimpanzee

(b) human

FIGURE 8-1

Developmental changes in the skull of (a) chimpanzees and (b) humans illustrate morphological
variation between two closely related species.
These anatomical differences arise through
changes in regulatory genes in one or both
species. In turn, regulatory genes determine the
timing of development of structures.

any other primate. Anatomical differences, such as limb proportions, are the results of changes in the behavior of regulatory genes that guide the direction of embryonic development. These genes are highly conserved throughout the animal kingdom, and they govern the same developmental processes in all animals. But the length of time they operate to establish patterns and proportions of anatomical structures is determined by still other genes, and these genes do vary between species. Indeed, alterations in the activities of these developmental genes through the course of evolution may be the single most important factor in speciation. For example, chimpanzees have longer faces and larger teeth than humans because the genes that control the development of these structures cause them to develop at different rates (Fig. 8-1).

Despite these differences, humans and apes are sufficiently similar anatomically that we can identify many shared derived traits they both inherited from their last common ancestor. For example, human and ape shoulders are anatomically quite similar, but they're different from monkey shoulders. In humans, as in many species, some systems evolved at different times and rates than others. So, human hands are less derived than ape hands because our thumbs aren't as reduced and our fingers aren't as elongated. In fact, while humans have ape-like shoulders, we have the hands of a generalized cercopithecine monkey.

So what does all this mean in terms of behavior? It means that to some extent, we shouldn't limit our behavioral comparisons to chimpanzees, any more than we should limit anatomical comparisons. Rather, we should include many species in our behavioral analogies. The selective pressures that acted on ancestral monkeys have played a role in our evolution, too, and that's something we shouldn't forget.

In the 1970s, the prevailing theory was that early hominids diverged from the apes as they moved out of a forested environment and adapted to a savanna environment. Such a move meant that they were subjected to increased predation pressure, so they adopted bipedality partly out of the need to stand upright while looking for predators (see Chapter 10). The earliest hominids were already predisposed to adopting a bipedal stance because standing upright is something many earlier primates were able to do. The same principle applies to behavior. Although we now believe that early hominid ancestors probably exploited a more mixed woodland habitat rather than a savanna environment, they still had to have anatomical and behavioral capacities that allowed them to go there in the first place. But as a separate lineage, their own evolutionary story probably began with a behavioral shift to exploiting an econiche different from other hominoids, and this new adaptation required spending more time on the ground and exploiting different types of resources. These factors, in turn, selected for further behavioral and anatomical adaptations, while other hominoids were responding to different environmental pressures.

Modern terrestrial primates, such as baboons, live on the savanna, so researchers used them initially as a model for early hominid behavior and adaptation (Washburn and deVore, 1961). For example, because savanna baboons live in large multimale-multifemale groups partly as an adaptive response to predation, it was hypothesized that early hominids also had a similar social structure (and they probably did). But because we're closely related to chimpanzees, they too were used as an analogue for the development of many human behaviors, including tool use and competition for social rank. Thus several species have been chosen for comparison based on both behavioral ecology and biological relatedness (Dunbar, 2001).

Today, while primatologists still use nonhuman primate behavior to examine the evolution of human behavior, they now also use statistical tests to examine the relationships between two or more variables. For example, it's important to establish if there's a correlation between body size and basal metabolic rate (BMR; see p. 158). Then, having demonstrated a positive correlation, we might add another variable, such as diet. Subsequently, we could add other factors, such as increased brain size and social structure. In other words, we look for correlations between life history traits and sociality. Once positive (or negative) correlations are ascertained, we can propose certain principles to apply to the study of human behavioral evolution.

Brain and Body Size

The one characteristic that clearly differentiates humans from other animal species is *relative brain size*, by which we mean the proportion of some measure of body size, such as weight, that's accounted for by the brain. Brain size and body size are closely correlated. Clearly, an animal the size of a chimpanzee (about 100 to 150 pounds) has a larger brain than a squirrel monkey, which weighs about 2 pounds. But in cross-species comparisons, as body weight increases, brain size doesn't necessarily increase at the same rate.

The predictable relationship between body and brain size has been called the "index of **encephalization**" (Jerison, 1973). The degree of encephalization can be a powerful analytical tool, since it estimates the expected brain size for any given body size. Most primates are close to predicted ratios for brain-body size, but there's one notable exception: *Homo sapiens*. (Interestingly, squirrel monkeys also show a degree of encephalization that considerably exceeds predictions.) Modern humans have a brain size well beyond that expected for a primate of similar body weight. It's this degree of encephalization that must be explained as a unique and central component of recent human evolution. Using these same analytical perspectives as applied to the fossil materials in the next several chapters, you'll see that early members of the genus *Homo* as well as more primitive hominids (*Australopithecus*) weren't nearly as encephalized as modern humans are.

Carefully controlled comparisons are essential in making cross-species generalizations about animals of differing sizes (a point to keep in mind when we discuss early hominids, most of which varied notably from modern humans in body size). Such controls relate to considerations of what's called *scaling*, or (more technically) **allometry**. These allometric comparisons have become increasingly important in understanding contemporary primate life history variables and adaptations. Moreover, similar approaches, as directly borrowed from these primate models, are now also routinely applied to interpretation of the primate/hominid fossil record.

Beyond simple brain size comparisons between different species, it's more appropriate to emphasize the relative size of certain structures in the brain. Primitive (ancestral) brains, such as those of reptiles, are mostly composed of structures related to basic physiological functions, and there's a small **cortex** that receives sensory information (especially olfactory). As discussed in Chapter 5, in mammals, the relative size of the most recently evolved layer of the cortex, called the **neocortex**, has increased. This increase permits a more detailed and precise analysis and interpretation of incoming sensory information and therefore, more complex behavior. And in primates, expansion of the neocortex has accounted for much of the increase in brain size (Fig. 8-2). The primate neocortex comprises many complicated association areas. It's the part of the brain that, in humans, is associated with cognitive functions related to reasoning, complex problem solving, forethought, and language. In humans, the neocortex accounts for about 80 percent of total brain volume (Dunbar, 1998).

Timing of brain growth is also important. In nonhuman primates, the most rapid period of brain growth occurs shortly before birth; but in humans, it occurs after birth. This is because restraints on prenatal brain growth in humans are necessary if the infant is to pass through the birth canal. As it is, owing to the size of the head in human newborns, childbirth is more difficult in humans than in any other primate (see p. 428). Thus, human infants show considerable brain expansion for at least the first 5 years after birth. Because brain tissue is the most costly of all bodily tissues in terms of energy consumed, the metabolic costs of such rapid and sustained neurological growth are enormous, requiring more than 50 percent of an infant's metabolic output (Aiello, 1992).

In evolutionary terms, the metabolic costs of a large brain must be compensated for by benefits. That is, large brains wouldn't have evolved if they didn't offer some advantage (Dunbar, 1998). Various hypotheses have been proposed for the evolution of large brains in primates, and many scientists in the past focused on solutions to problems related to food getting and the kinds of foods a species eats. For example, some monkeys (with a smaller relative brain size) primarily eat leaves, which, although plentiful, aren't an energy-rich food. Primates also need a complex brain in order to be familiar with their home range; to be aware of when seasonal foods are available; and to solve the problem of extracting foods from shells, hard peels, and even underground roots. But one could argue that these are problems for all foraging species, squirrels and raccoons, for example, and yet these animals haven't evolved such relatively large brains.

encephalization The proportional size of the brain relative to some other measure, usually some estimate of overall body size, such as weight. More precisely, the term refers to increases in brain size beyond what would be expected given the body size of a particular species.

allometry Also called *scaling*; the differential proportion among various anatomical structures (for example, the size of the brain in proportion to overall body size changes during the development of an individual). Scaling effects must also be considered when comparing species.

cortex Layer. In the brain, the cortex is the layer that covers the cerebral hemispheres, which in turn cover more primitive or older structures related to bodily functions and the sense of smell. It's composed of nerve cells called neurons, which communicate with each other and send and receive messages to and from all parts of the body.

neocortex The more recently evolved portions of the cortex of the brain that are involved with higher mental functions and composed of areas that integrate incoming information from different sensory organs.

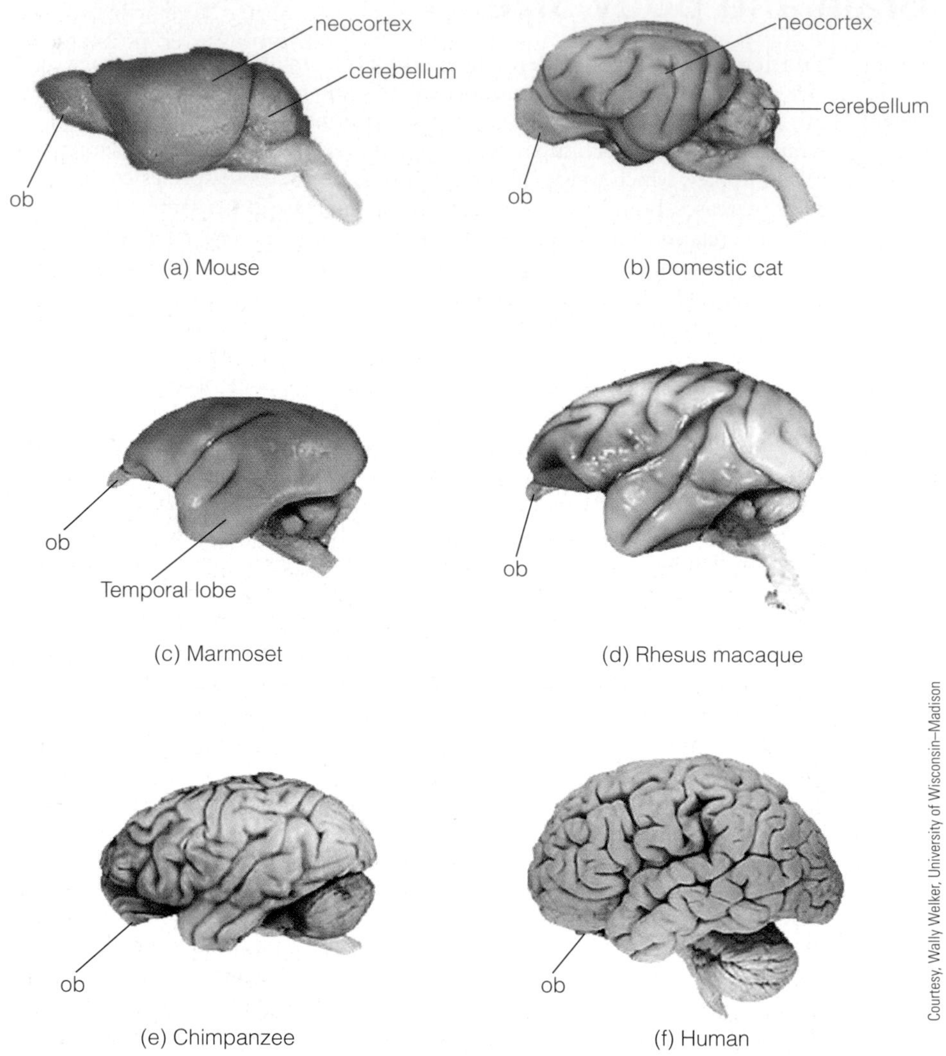

(a) Mouse

(b) Domestic cat

(c) Marmoset

(d) Rhesus macaque

(e) Chimpanzee

(f) Human

Courtesy, Wally Welker, University of Wisconsin–Madison

FIGURE 8-2

Comparisons of mammalian brains as seen in these left lateral views (front is to left). Expansion of the neocortex, the outer layers of the cerebral hemispheres, has been the most significant trend during the evolution of the mammalian brain. This is especially evident in the size of the neocortex relative to that of the olfactory bulb (ob) at the front of the brain. The olfactory bulb is the termination point of sensory fibers that send olfactory information from the nose to the brain. A relatively large olfactory bulb indicates a greater dependence on the sense of smell. Compare the size of this organ, relative to the neocortex, in these brains. In the mouse and cat it's particularly large, but it becomes smaller in primates. In humans, it's barely visible. In fact, in chimpanzees and humans, the neocortex is all that's visible from the top and sides except for the cerebellum. Also note the increasingly convoluted surface of the neocortex. This is due to cortical folding, which allows more neurons to be packed into a limited space. Increasing the number of neurons provides more interconnections between areas of the brain, allowing more information to be processed. The marmoset exhibits less cortical folding than the cat, but its temporal lobe (part of the neocortex) is better defined and brain size compared to body size is greater. As you can see, cortical folding is most pronounced in humans. (Illustrations are shown approximately the same size and not to scale.) (Photos provided by the University of Wisconsin–Madison Comparative Mammalian Brain Collection: http://brainmuseum.org. Preparation of these images and specimens was funded by the National Science Foundation and the National Institutes of Health.)

Another explanation, the *social brain hypothesis*, proposes that primate brains increased in relative size and complexity because primates live in social groups. The demands of social living are many, and primates must be able to negotiate a complex web of interactions including competition, alliance formation, forming and maintaining friendships, avoiding certain individuals, and so on. Barton and Dunbar (1997) thus suggest that intelligence evolved not only to solve physical problems (such as food getting and predator avoidance) but also to analyze and use social information such as which animals are dominant, who forms alliances with whom, whom to avoid, and so on.

In support of the social brain hypothesis, Bergman et al. (2003) showed that savanna baboons in a study group in Botswana recognized that the female social hierarchy is divided into matrilines and that the matrilines are ranked relative to one another. They also recognized dominance relationships within each matriline. In other words, these baboons understand the arrangement of hierarchies within hierarchies. So, interactions between individuals are influenced by the social position of individuals within matrilines and of matrilines within the entire group. Emphasizing the implications of such behavioral complexity for the evolution of increased intelligence in humans, these authors state, "The selective pressures imposed by complex societies may therefore have favored cognitive skills that constitute an evolutionary precursor to some components of human cognition" (Bergman et al., 2003, p. 1234).

But at the same time, group size is limited by brain size to the extent that a group can't be made up of more animals than individuals can recognize and interact with. Brain and group size therefore probably coevolved (Dunbar, 1998, 2001). Extrapolating from neocortical volume to the size of social groups, as seen in several nonhuman primate species, Dunbar (1998) speculates that large group size in some early members of the genus *Homo* is likely. This isn't to say that early humans always lived in large groups, but they may have formed large congregations by periodic associations of smaller groups.

Stanford (1999, 2001) proposes that meat eating was also important to the development of increased cognitive abilities in the human lineage. Hunting, especially of big game, was a topic of considerable interest in early hominid studies in the 1960s (Washburn and Lancaster, 1968). Those theories were eventually discounted for various reasons, one of which is that the earliest hominids weren't capable of hunting large prey.

Most nonhuman primates that do kill and eat small mammals don't actually hunt them. Chimpanzees, however, do hunt (Fig. 8-3); and their favorite prey is red colobus monkeys Stanford and others (Aiello and Wells, 2002) argue that if early hominids relied on a diet that increasingly contained a high proportion of meat, rich in protein and fats, such a diet would meet the nutritional demands of a lineage in which relatively large brains were becoming important. But as Stanford also points out, relatively large brain size hasn't developed in social carnivores such as wolves and lions. What's more, the percentage of meat in chimpanzee diets is small and may be similar to what early hominids obtained.

So, if meat was important in the evolution of large brains in hominids, some factor other than nutrition would have had to be important. Once chimpanzees (usually males) have made a kill, they often share the meat with relatives, allies, and females. Negotiating the complexities and strategies involved in the politics of sharing meat might be viewed as one aspect of the social brain hypothesis, which holds that neurological complexity evolved as a response to complicated behavioral challenges.

Compared to most humans, chimpanzees don't really eat much meat and there's some recent evidence that strongly suggests that meat became an important dietary component in human ancestors sometime after chimpanzees and humans went their separate ways. In a preliminary analysis of the chimpanzee genome, Clark et al. (2003) discovered that several of the genes responsible

FIGURE **8-3**
Male chimpanzees eating a red colobus monkey they have killed.

for producing enzymes involved in amino acid metabolism have changed over time in both species. (Animal protein is a major source of amino acids.) This finding adds support to theories that increased meat consumption may have been important for increased brain size in early humans (Penny, 2004). At the very least it indicates that as the two lineages diverged, both responded to different selective pressures; and selection favored enzyme mutations that enabled some hominids to digest meat more efficiently.

Language

One of the most significant events in human evolution was the development of language. In Chapter 7, we described several behaviors and autonomic responses that convey information among primates. But although we emphasized the importance of communication to nonhuman primate social life, we also said that nonhuman primates don't use language in the way that humans do.

The old, traditional view held by most linguists and behavioral psychologists was that nonhuman communication consists of mostly involuntary vocalizations and actions that convey information solely about an animal's emotional state (anger, fear, etc.). Nonhuman animals haven't been considered capable of communicating about external events, objects, or other animals, either in close proximity or removed in space or time. For example, when a startled baboon barks, other group members know only that it's startled. But they don't know why it barked, and they can determine this only by looking around. In general, then, it's been assumed that nonhuman animals, including primates, use a *closed system* of communication in which vocalizations, facial expressions, body postures and so on don't refer to specific external phenomena.

But many researchers have challenged these views for many years now (Steklis, 1985; King, 1994, 2004). For example, vervet monkeys (Fig. 8-4) use specific vocalizations to refer to particular categories of predators, such as snakes, birds of prey, and leopards (Struhsaker, 1967; Seyfarth, Cheney, and Marler, 1980a, 1980b). When researchers made tape recordings of vervet alarm calls and played them back within hearing distance of wild vervets, they saw different responses to various calls. When they heard leopard-alarm calls, the monkeys climbed trees; when they heard eagle-alarm calls, they looked up; and when they heard snake-alarm calls, they looked around at the ground nearby.

These results demonstrate that vervets use distinct vocalizations to refer to specific components of the external environment. These calls aren't involuntary, and they don't refer solely to the individual's emotional state (alarm), although this information is also conveyed.

FIGURE 8-4
Group of free-ranging vervets.

Lynn Kilgore

While these findings dispel certain long-held misconceptions about nonhuman communication (at least for some species), they also indicate certain limitations. Vervet communication is restricted to the present; as far as we know, no vervet can communicate about a predator it saw yesterday or one it might see in the future.

Other studies have demonstrated that numerous nonhuman primates, including cottontop tamarins (Cleveland and Snowdon, 1982), Goeldi's monkeys (Masataka, 1983), red colobus (Struhsaker, 1975), and gibbons (Tenaza and Tilson, 1977), produce distinct calls that have specific references. There's also growing evidence that many birds and some non-primate mammals use specific predator alarm calls (Seyfarth, 1987).

Humans use *language*, a set of written and/or spoken symbols that refer to concepts, other people, objects, and so on. This set of symbols is said to be *arbitrary* because the symbol itself has no inherent relationship with whatever it stands for. For example, the English word *flower*, when written or spoken, neither looks, sounds, smells, nor feels like the thing it represents. Humans can also recombine their linguistic symbols in an infinite number of ways to create new meanings, and we can use language to refer to events, places, objects, and people far removed in both space and time. For these reasons, language is described as an *open system* of communication, based on the human ability to think symbolically.

Language, as distinct from other forms of communication, has always been considered a uniquely human achievement, setting humans apart from the rest of the animal kingdom. But work with captive apes has changed this view. Although many researchers were skeptical about the capacity of nonhuman primates to use language, reports from psychologists, especially those who work with chimpanzees, leave little doubt that apes can learn to interpret visual signs and use them in communication. No mammal other than humans has the ability to speak. However, the fact that apes can't speak has less to do with lack of intelligence than with differences in the anatomy of the vocal tract and *language-related structures in the brain.*

Because of unsuccessful attempts by others to teach young chimpanzees to speak, psychologists Beatrice and Allen Gardner designed a study to test language capabilities in chimpanzees by teaching ASL (American Sign Language for the deaf) to an infant female named Washoe. The project began in 1966; and in 3 years, Washoe acquired at least 132 signs. "She asked for goods and services, and she also asked questions about the world of objects and events around her" (Gardner et al., 1989, p. 6).

Years later, when an infant chimpanzee named Loulis was placed in Washoe's care, she adopted him. Psychologist Roger Fouts and colleagues wanted to know if Loulis would spontaneously acquire signing skills through contact with Washoe and other chimpanzees in the study group. Within just 8 days, Loulis began to imitate the signs of others. Also, Washoe deliberately *taught* Loulis some signs. For example, when she wanted him to sit down, "Washoe placed a small plastic chair in front of Loulis, and then signed CHAIR/SIT to him several times in succession, watching him closely throughout" (Fouts et al., 1989, p. 290).

There have been other chimpanzee language experiments. A chimpanzee called Sara was taught to recognize plastic chips as symbols for various objects. Importantly, the chips didn't resemble the objects they represented. For example, the chip that represented an apple was neither round nor red. The fact that Sara was able to use the chips to communicate is significant because her ability to associate chips with concepts and objects to which they bore no similarity implies some degree of symbolic thought.

At the Yerkes Regional Primate Research Center in Atlanta, Georgia, another chimp, Lana, worked with a specially designed computer keyboard with chips attached to keys. After 6 months, Lana recognized symbols for 30 words and was able to ask for food and answer questions through the machine (Rumbaugh, 1977). Also at Yerkes, two male chimpanzees, Sherman and Austin, learned to communicate using a series of lexigrams, or geometric symbols, imprinted on a computer keyboard (Savage-Rumbaugh, 1986).

Dr. Francine Patterson, who taught ASL to a female lowland gorilla name Koko, reports that Koko uses more than 500 signs. Furthermore, Michael, an adult male gorilla who was also involved in the study until his death in 2000, had a considerable sign vocabulary, and the two gorillas regularly communicated with each other using signs.

In the late 1970s, a 2-year-old male orangutan named Chantek (also at Yerkes) began to use signs after 1 month of training. Eventually, he acquired approximately 140 signs, which he sometimes used to refer to objects and people not present. Chantek also invented signs and recombined them in novel ways, and he appeared to understand that his signs were *representations* of items, actions, and people (Miles, 1990).

Questions have been raised about this type of experimental work. Do the apes really understand the signs they learn, or are they merely imitating their trainers? Do they learn that a symbol is a name for an object, or do they only understand that making a symbol will produce that object? Other unanswered questions concern the apes' use of grammar, especially when they combine more than just a few "words" to communicate.

Partly in an effort to address some of these questions and criticisms, psychologist Sue Savage-Rumbaugh taught the two chimpanzees Sherman and Austin to use symbols to categorize *classes* of objects, such as "food" or "tool." She did this because in previous studies, apes had been taught symbols for *specific* items. Savage-Rumbaugh recognized that using

FIGURE 8-5
The bonobo Kanzi, as a youngster, using lexigrams to communicate with human observers.

Rose A. Sevcik, Language Research Center, Georgia State University; photo by Elizabeth Pugh

a symbol as a label isn't the same thing as understanding the *representational value* of the symbol. But if chimpanzees could classify things into groups, it would indicate that they can use symbols referentially.

Sherman and Austin were taught to recognize familiar food items, for which they routinely used symbols, as belonging to a broader category referred to by yet another symbol, "food." They were then introduced to unfamiliar food items, for which they had no symbols, to see if they would place them in the food category. They both had perfect or nearly perfect scores for this task, which further substantiated that they could categorize unfamiliar objects. More important, it was clear that they were capable of assigning to unknown objects symbols that denoted membership in a broad grouping. This ability strongly indicated that the chimpanzees understood that the symbols were being used referentially.

Throughout the relatively brief history of ape language studies, one often repeated criticism has been that young chimpanzees must be *taught* to use symbols. This pattern was contrasted with the ability of human children to learn language through exposure, without being deliberately taught. It was therefore significant when Savage-Rumbaugh and her colleagues reported that Kanzi, an infant male bonobo, was *spontaneously* acquiring and using symbols at the age of 2-1/2 years (Savage-Rumbaugh et al., 1986) (Fig. 8-5). In the same way, Kanzi's younger half sister began to use symbols spontaneously when she was only 11 months old. Both animals had been exposed to the use of lexigrams when they accompanied their mother to training sessions, but neither had actually been taught; in fact, they weren't directly involved in these sessions.

While Kanzi and his sister showed a remarkable degree of cognitive complexity, it nevertheless remains evident that apes don't acquire and use language in the same way humans do. It also appears that not all signing apes understand the referential relationship between symbol and object, person, or action. Even so, there's now abundant evidence that humans aren't the only species capable of some degree of symbolic thought and complex communication.

The Evolution of Language

From an evolutionary perspective, the ape language experiments may suggest clues to the origins of human language. It's also highly significant that free-ranging great apes use some gestures for communication (King, 2004). Therefore, it's quite possible that the last common ancestor we share with the living great apes had communication capabilities similar to those we see in these species. So, we need to identify the factors that enhanced the adaptive significance of these abilities in our own lineage. At the same time, it's equally important to explore why these pressures didn't operate to the same degree in our closest relatives.

While increased brain size played a crucial role in human evolution, it was changes in preexisting neurological structures that permitted the development of language. Current evidence suggests that *new* structures and novel connections haven't generally been the basis for most of the neurological differences we see among species. Rather, reorganization, elaboration, and/or reduction of existing structures, as well as shifts in the proportions of existing connections, have been far more important (Deacon, 1992). It's also important to understand that the neurological changes that enhanced language development in humans wouldn't have happened if early hominids hadn't already possessed the behavioral and neurological foundations that made them possible. For reasons we don't yet fully understand, communication became increasingly important during the course of human evolution, and natural selection favored anatomical and neurological changes that enhanced our ancestors' ability to use spoken language.

Some researchers argue that language capabilities appeared late in human evolution (that is, with the wide dispersal of modern *Homo sapiens* some 100,000 to 30,000 years ago). Others favor a much earlier origin, possibly with the appearance of the genus *Homo* some 2 million years ago (mya). Whichever scenario is correct, language came about as complex and efficient forms of communication gained selective value in our lineage.

As you've already learned, the metabolic costs of producing and maintaining brain tissues are high, and those costs must be offset by benefits. So we have to assume that there was intense selective pressure that favored the ability of early humans to communicate at increasingly precise levels.

In most people, language function is located in the left hemisphere, meaning it's **lateralized**. (The left hemisphere is the dominant hemisphere in most people and, since it controls motion on the right side of the body, most people are right-handed.) In particular two regions, *Broca's area* in the left frontal lobe and *Wernicke's area* in the left temporal lobe, are directly involved in the production and perception, respectively, of spoken language (Fig. 8-6).

Broca's area is located in the **motor cortex** immediately adjacent to a region that controls movement of muscles in the face, lips, larynx, and tongue. When a person is speaking, information is sent to Broca's area, where it's organized *specifically for communication*. Then it's transmitted to the adjacent motor areas, which in turn activate the muscles involved in speech. We know that Broca's area operates this way because when it's damaged, speech production is impaired patients can still make sounds but they can't speak. Also there's no muscle paralysis. Paralysis occurs only when there's damage to the nearby motor areas themselves.

Wernicke's area is an *association area* that lies near structures involved in the reception of sound. A lesion in Wernicke's area doesn't impair hearing, but it severely affects language comprehension. This, in turn, interferes with speech production because auditory information specifically related to language is sent from Wernicke's area to Broca's area by way of a bundle of nerve fibers connecting the two regions.

lateralized   Pertaining to lateralization, the functional specialization of the hemispheres of the brain for specific activities.

motor cortex   That portion of the cortex involved in sending outgoing signals involved in muscle use. The motor cortex is located at the rear of the frontal lobe.

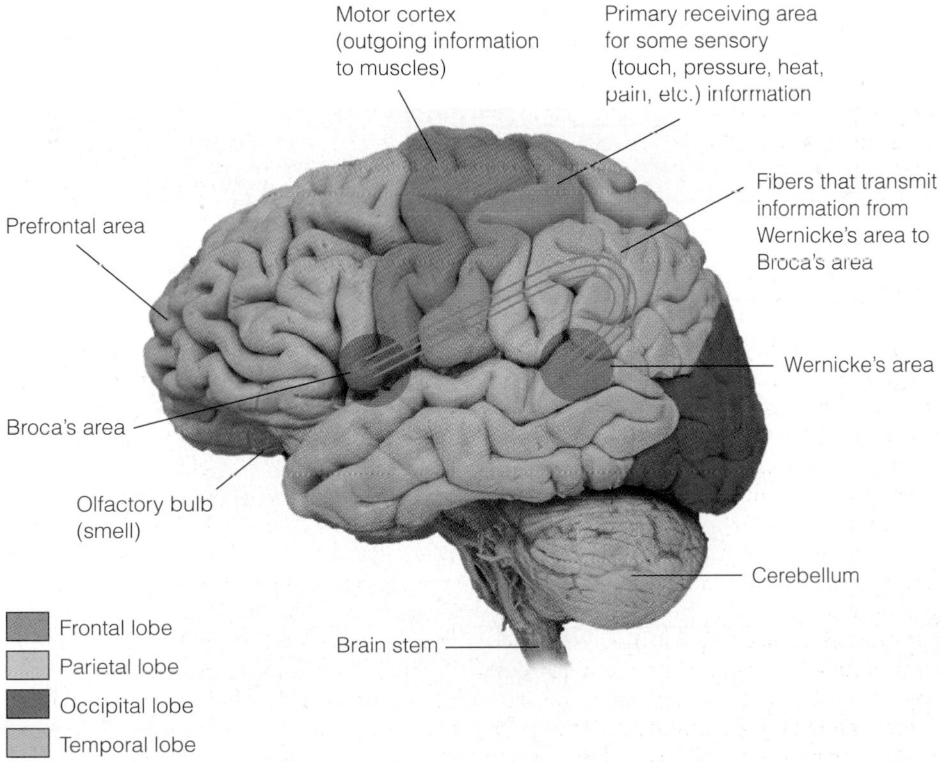

FIGURE 8-6
Left lateral view of the human brain, showing major regions and areas involved in language. Information that is to be used in speech is sent from Wernicke's area, via a bundle of nerve fibers, to Broca's area.

Motor cortex
(outgoing information
to muscles)

Primary receiving area
for some sensory
(touch, pressure, heat,
pain, etc.) information

Fibers that transmit
information from
Wernicke's area to
Broca's area

Prefrontal area

Wernicke's area

Broca's area

Olfactory bulb
(smell)

Cerebellum

Frontal lobe
Parietal lobe
Occipital lobe
Temporal lobe

Brain stem

© Royalty-Free/CORBIS

But the perception and production of speech involves much more than these two areas, and the use of written language requires still other neurological structures. Eventually, information relating to all the senses (visual, olfactory, tactile, and auditory) is combined and relayed to Broca's area, where it's translated for speech production. This uniquely human ability depends on the interconnections between receiving areas for all sensory stimuli. While the brains of other species have such areas, they don't have the ability to transform sensory information for the purpose of using language. Or maybe they do, at least to some degree.

Cantalupo and Hopkins (2001) report that magnetic resonance imaging of chimpanzee, bonobo, and gorilla brains demonstrates that in these species, a region analogous to part of Broca's area is larger on the left side than on the right. In humans, this particular area is involved in some of the motor aspects of speech production, and the report suggests that it also may have been important to the development of gestural language. These authors further note that in captive great ape studies, gestures are preferentially made by the right hand (controlled by the left hemisphere) most especially when gestures are combined with vocalizations. This study suggests, therefore, that perhaps the anatomical basis for the development of left-hemisphere dominance in speech production in humans was present, at least to an incipient degree, in the last common ancestor of humans and the African great apes.

Specialization of auditory centers of the left hemisphere for language may have preceded the evolutionary divergence of humans and apes; it may even have had its beginnings in the earliest mammals. A team of neuroscientists has shown that this type of lateralization is present in rhesus macaques (Poremba et al., 2004). These researchers demonstrated that, like humans and other species, rhesus macaques receive and process auditory information in the temporal lobes of both hemispheres. But these monkeys show greater metabolic activity in the left hemisphere *specifically when they hear vocalizations of other rhesus macaques.* This indicates that in macaques, the left temporal lobe is specialized for processing the vocalizations of conspecifics in particular.

But this specialization may have an evolutionary history that extends back to before the emergence of primates. Poremba et al. point to other studies indicating that mice and birds also analyze *conspecific* vocalizations in the left hemisphere (Ehret, 1987; George et al., 2002). These studies don't state that this trait is as developed in mice and birds as it is in macaques. And since the studies concern only the calls of members of the same species, they don't explain the origins of language in human ancestors. However, these discoveries do indicate that in human evolution, the development of *language-specific centers* in the left hemisphere occurred as an elaboration of a trend that has a very long evolutionary history.

AT A GLANCE   Evolution of Human Language

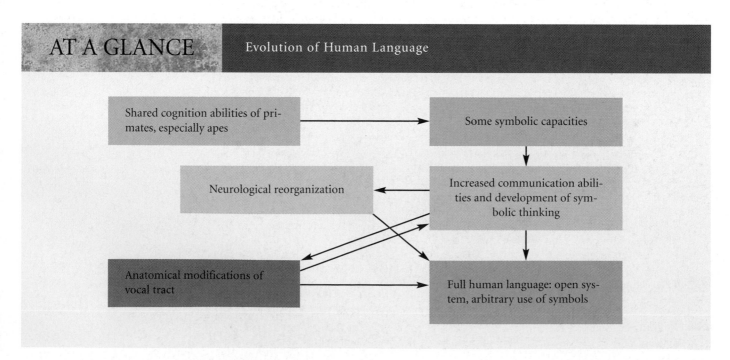

The recent identification of a gene that's involved in speech may provide another piece to the puzzle of the evolution of language in humans. The gene, called *FOXP2*, produces a protein that regulates the expression of other genes. These genes, in turn, influence the embryological development of circuits in the brain that relate to language in humans. People who inherit a particular *FOXP2* mutation are afflicted with developmental disorders in the brain that cause severe speech and language impairment (Lai et al., 2001).

The *FOXP2* gene isn't unique to humans. In fact, it's highly conserved; and since it's present in mice, all mammals probably have it. But, while *FOXP2* is important to neurological development in nonhuman mammals, it has nothing to do with language in these species. When researchers compared the human form of the FOXP2 protein to that of chimpanzees and gorillas, they found that the human protein differed from the two ape versions by two amino acid substitutions. This means that since humans last shared a common ancestor with chimpanzees and gorillas, the gene has undergone two point mutations during the course of human evolution. But in chimpanzees and gorillas, it hasn't changed.

The *FOXP2* gene is the first gene demonstrated to influence language development. It varies between humans and closely related species, indicating not only that natural selection has acted on it in our lineage, but also that the FOXP2 protein may have played a role in the development of language capacities in humans.

Primate Cultural Behavior

One important trait that makes primates, and especially chimpanzees and bonobos, attractive as models for behavior in early hominids may be called *cultural behavior*. Although many cultural anthropologists and others prefer to use the term *culture* to refer specifically to human activities, most biological anthropologists consider it appropriate to use *culture* in discussing nonhuman primates as well (McGrew, 1992, 1998; de Waal, 1999; Whiten et al., 1999). In fact, the term *cultural primatology* is now being used more frequently.

Undeniably, most aspects of culture are uniquely human, and we must be cautious when we try to interpret nonhuman animal behavior. But again, since humans are products of the same evolutionary forces that have produced other species, they can be expected to exhibit some of the same *behavioral patterns*, particularly of other primates. However, because of increased brain size and learning capacities, humans express many characteristics to a greater degree. We would argue that the *aptitude for culture* as a means of adapting to the natural environment is one such characteristic.

Among other things, cultural behavior is *learned*; it's passed from generation to generation not biologically, but through learning. Whereas humans deliberately teach their young, it appears that free-ranging nonhuman primates (except for a few reports) don't do so. But at the same time, like young nonhuman primates, human children acquire a tremendous amount of knowledge through observation rather than instruction (Fig. 8-7a). Nonhuman primate infants, through observing their mothers and others, learn about food items, appropriate behaviors, and how to use and modify objects to achieve certain ends (Fig. 8-7b). In turn, their own offspring will observe these activities. What emerges is a *cultural tradition* that may eventually come to typify an entire group or even a species.

The earliest reported example of cultural behavior concerned a study group of Japanese macaques on Koshima Island. In 1952, Japanese researchers began provisioning the macaque troop with sweet potatoes. The following year, a young female named Imo began washing her potatoes in a freshwater stream before eating them. Within 3 years, several monkeys had adopted the practice, but they had switched from using the stream to taking their potatoes to the ocean nearby. Maybe they liked the salt seasoning!

The researchers suggested that dietary habits and food preferences are learned and that potato washing was an example of nonhuman culture. Because the practice arose as an innovative solution to a problem (removing dirt) and gradually spread through the troop until it became a tradition, it was seen as containing elements of human culture.

A study of orangutans in 6 areas (4 Bornean and 2 Sumatran) listed 19 behaviors that showed sufficient regional variation to be classed as "very likely cultural variants" (van Schaik et al., 2003). Four activities in the "very likely" category involved the use of nests. In

(a)

(b)

FIGURE 8-7

(a) This little girl is learning the basic skills of computer use by watching her older sister. (b) A chimpanzee learns the art of termiting through intense observation.

five localities, nests were built exclusively for play activities and not for resting or sleeping. There was also variation in the construction of nests above resting nests (as in bunk beds) to provide shelter from bright sun or rain. While tool use didn't seem to be as elaborate as in chimpanzees, in one Bornean locality, orangutans used sticks to scratch themselves and leaves as "napkins." And in one Sumatran area, they pushed sticks into tree holes to obtain insects.

Chimpanzees exhibit somewhat more elaborate examples of *tool use*. This point is important, because traditionally, tool use (along with language) was said to set humans apart from other animals. Chimpanzees insert twigs and grass blades into termite mounds in a practice called "termite fishing." When termites seize the twig, the chimpanzee withdraws it and eats the attached insects. Chimpanzees modify some of their stems and twigs by stripping the leaves, in effect making a tool from the natural material. To some extent, chimpanzees even alter objects to a "regular and set pattern" and have been observed preparing objects for later use at an out-of-sight location (Goodall, 1986, p. 535). For example, a chimpanzee will carefully select a piece of vine, bark, twig, or palm frond and modify it by removing leaves or other extraneous material and then break off portions until it's the proper length. Chimpanzees have also been seen making these tools even before the termite mound is in sight.

All this preparation has several implications. First, the chimpanzees are engaged in an activity that prepares them for a future (not immediate) task at a somewhat distant location, and this action implies planning and forethought. Second, attention to the shape and size of the raw material indicates that chimpanzees have a preconceived idea of what the finished product needs to be in order to be useful. To produce a tool, even a simple tool, based on a concept is an extremely complex behavior that isn't the exclusive domain of humans.

Chimpanzees also crumple and chew handfuls of leaves, which they dip into tree hollows where water accumulates. Then they suck the water that would otherwise be inaccessible from their newly made "leaf sponges." They also use leaves to wipe substances from fur; twigs as toothpicks; and stones as weapons. They may drag or roll various objects, such as branches and stones, to enhance displays. Lastly, they use sticks or leaves to help process mammalian prey; but with one exception, these practices appear to be incidental. The one exception is in the Tai Forest (Ivory Coast), where chimpanzees use sticks to extract marrow from long bones (Boesch and Boesch, 1989).

In several West African study groups, chimpanzees use hammerstones with platform stones (Fig. 8-8) to crack nuts and hard-shelled fruits (Boesch et al., 1994). But it's important to note that neither the hammerstone nor the platform stone is deliberately manufactured.* Wild capuchin monkeys use leaves to extract water from cavities in trees (Phillips, 1998), they smash objects against stones (Izawa and Mizuno, 1977), and their use of stones in captivity (both as hammers and anvils) has been reported (Visalberghi, 1990). (Stones serve as anvils when fruit or other objects are bashed against the rock surface.) Chimpanzees are the only nonhuman animal to use stones both as hammers and anvils to obtain food. And they're the only nonhuman primate that consistently and habitually makes and uses tools (McGrew, 1992).

---

*Observers of nonhuman primates rarely distinguish natural objects used as tools from modified objects deliberately manufactured for specific purposes. In both cases, the term *tool* is normally applied.

It's significant that chimpanzees exhibit regional variation regarding the types and methods of tool use. Stone hammers and platforms are used only in West African groups. At sites in Central and East Africa, chimpanzees "fish" for termites with stems and sticks; but at some West African locations, they don't (McGrew, 1992).

Chimpanzees also show regional dietary preferences (Nishida et al., 1983; McGrew, 1992, 1998). For example, oil palms are exploited for their fruit and nuts at many locations, including Gombe; but even though these foods are present in the Mahale Mountains, the chimpanzees there don't eat them. Such regional patterns in tool use and food preferences that aren't related to environmental variation are reminiscent of the cultural variations characteristic of humans.

McGrew (1992) presents eight criteria for cultural behaviors in nonhuman species (Table 8-1). Of these, the first six were established by the pioneering cultural anthropologist Alfred Kroeber (1928); the last two were added by McGrew and Tutin (1978). McGrew (1992) demonstrated that Japanese macaques meet the first six criteria. However, all the macaque examples have developed within the context of human interference (which isn't to say they all resulted directly from human intervention). To avoid this difficulty, the last two criteria were added.

Chimpanzees unambiguously meet the first six criteria, although not all groups meet the last two because most study groups have been at least minimally provisioned. However, all criteria are met by at least some chimpanzees in some instances (McGrew, 1992). While it's obvious that chimpanzees don't possess human culture, we can't overlook the implications that tool use and local traditions of learned behavior have for early hominid evolution.

Using sticks, twigs, and stones enhances a chimpanzee's ability to exploit resources. Learning these behaviors occurs during infancy and childhood, partly as a result of prolonged contact with the mother. It's also important that exposure to others in social groupings provides additional learning opportunities. These statements also apply to early hominids. While sticks and unmodified stones don't remain to tell tales, our early ancestors surely used these same objects as tools in much the same ways as chimpanzees do today.

While chimpanzees in the wild haven't been observed modifying the stones they use, the male bonobo Kanzi (see p. 188) learned to strike two stones together to produce sharp-edged flakes. In a study conducted by Sue Savage-Rumbaugh and archaeologist Nicholas Toth, Kanzi was allowed to watch as Toth produced stone flakes, which were then used to

Courtesy, Tetsuro Matsuzawa

FIGURE 8-8
Chimpanzees in Bossou, Guinea, West Africa, use a pair of stones as hammer and anvil to crack oil-palm nuts. Although the youngster isn't being taught to use stone tools, it's learning about them through observation.

TABLE 8-1	Criteria for Cultural Acts in Other Species
Innovation	New pattern is invented or modified.
Dissemination	Pattern is acquired (through imitation) by another from an innovator.
Standardization	Form of pattern is consistent and stylized.
Durability	Pattern is performed without presence of demonstrator.
Diffusion	Pattern spreads from one group to another.
Tradition	Pattern persists from innovator's generation to the next.
Nonsubsistence	Pattern transcends subsistence.
Naturalness	Pattern is shown in absence of direct human influence.

Source: Adapted from Kroeber (1928), and McGrew and Tutin (1978). In McGrew (1992).

open a transparent plastic food container (Savage-Rumbaugh and Lewin, 1994). Bonobos apparently don't commonly use objects as tools in the wild, but Kanzi readily appreciated the usefulness of the flakes in obtaining food. What's more, he was able to master the basic technique of producing flakes without having been taught the various components of the process, although at first his progress was slow. Eventually, Kanzi realized that if he threw the stone onto a hard floor, it would shatter and he would have an abundance of cutting tools. Although his solution wasn't necessarily the one that Savage-Rumbaugh and Toth expected, it more importantly provided an excellent example of bonobo insight and problem-solving ability. Kanzi did eventually learn to produce flakes by striking two stones together, and he then used the flakes to obtain food. This behavior is not only an example of tool manufacture and tool use, albeit in a captive situation, but also a very sophisticated, goal-directed activity.

Human culture has become the environment in which modern humans live. Quite clearly, the use of sticks in termite fishing and hammerstones to crack nuts is hardly comparable to modern human technology. Even so, modern human technology had its beginnings in these very types of behaviors. But this doesn't mean that nonhuman primates are "on their way" to becoming human. Remember, evolution is not goal directed, and if it were, there's nothing to dictate that modern humans necessarily constitute an evolutionary goal. Such a conclusion is a purely **anthropocentric** view, and it has no validity in discussions of evolutionary processes.

In any case, nonhuman primates have probably practiced certain cultural behaviors for millions of years. As we've said, the common ancestor that humans share with chimpanzees undoubtedly used sticks and stones to exploit resources, and they may even have used these materials as weapons. We've only recently discovered and described these behaviors, but that doesn't mean our close relatives developed them recently. And, if we're to understand more clearly how cultural traditions emerged in our own lineage, we must continue to study these capabilities in nonhuman primates in their social and ecological context.

Aggressive Interactions Between Groups

Interactions between groups of conspecifics can be just as revealing as those that take place within groups. For many primate species, especially those whose ranges are small, contact with one or more other groups of the same species is a daily occurrence. And, as you read in Chapter 7, the nature of these encounters can vary from species to species.

Primate groups are associated with a *home range*, where they remain permanently. (Although individuals may leave their home range and join another community, the group itself remains in a particular area.) Within the home range is a portion called the **core area**. This area contains the highest concentration of predictable resources, and it's where the group most frequently may be found. Although portions of the home range may overlap with that of one or more other groups, core areas of adjacent groups don't overlap. The core area can also be said to be a group's **territory**, and it's the portion of the home range defended against intrusion. In some species, however, other areas of the home range may also be defended.

Not all primates are territorial. In general, territoriality is associated with species (such as gibbons and vervets) whose ranges are sufficiently small to permit patrolling and protection. But male chimpanzees are highly intolerant of unfamiliar chimpanzees, especially other males, and will fiercely defend their territories and resources. Therefore, chimpanzee intergroup interactions are almost always characterized by aggressive displays, chasing, and frequently, actual fighting.

Members of chimpanzee communities commonly travel to areas where their range borders or overlaps that of another community. These peripheral areas aren't entirely safe; and before entering them, chimpanzees usually hoot and display to determine if other animals are present. They then remain silent, listening for a response. If members of another community should appear, some form of aggression occurs until one group retreats.

Male chimpanzees (sometimes accompanied by one or two females) also patrol their borders. When patrolling, party members travel silently in compact groupings. They stop

anthropocentric Viewing nonhuman organisms in terms of human experience and capabilities; emphasizing the importance of humans over everything else.

core area The portion of a home range containing the highest concentration and most reliable supplies of food and water. The core area is frequently the area that will be defended.

territory The portions of an individual's or group's home range actively defended against intrusion, particularly by conspecifics.

frequently to sniff, look around, or climb tall trees, where they may sit for an hour or more surveying the region. During such times, individuals are tense; a sudden sound, such as a snapping twig, causes them to touch or embrace in reassurance (Goodall, 1986). It's apparent from their tension and very uncharacteristic silence that the chimpanzees are quite aware that they're venturing into a potentially dangerous situation.

If a border patrol happens to come upon one or two strangers, the patrollers most surely will attack. However, if they encounter a group larger than their own, they themselves may be attacked, or at least chased as they retreat.

Discussion among primatologists has focused on aggression between groups of conspecifics and whether the primary motivation is territoriality (that is, protection of resources in a given area) or whether other factors are also involved (Cheney, 1987; Manson and Wrangham, 1991; Nishida, 1991). Much of this discussion has centered on intergroup aggression and lethal raiding in chimpanzees and has emphasized implications for the evolution of human aggressive behavior (Fig. 8-9).

Beginning in 1974, Jane Goodall and her colleagues witnessed at least five unprovoked and extremely brutal attacks by groups of chimpanzees (usually, but not always, males) upon lone individuals. To explain these attacks, we must point out that by 1973, the original Gombe chimpanzee community had divided into two distinct groups, one in the north and the other in the south of what was once the original group's home range. In effect, the southern splinter group had denied the others access to part of their former home range.

By 1977, all seven males and one female of the splinter group were either known or suspected to have been killed. All observed incidents involved several animals, usually adult males, who brutally attacked lone individuals. It's impossible to know exactly what motivated the attackers, but it was clear that they intended to incapacitate their victims (Goodall, 1986). In fact, Goodall (1986) has suggested that the attacks strongly imply that although chimpanzees don't possess language and don't wage war as we know it, they do exhibit behaviors that, if present in early hominids, could have been precursors to war.

A situation similar to the one at Gombe was also reported for a group of chimpanzees in the Mahale Mountains south of Gombe. Over a 17-year period, all the males of a small community disappeared. Although no attacks were actually observed, there was circumstantial evidence that most of these males met the same fate as the Gombe attack victims (Nishida et al., 1985, 1990).

Primatologists have believed that lethal, unprovoked aggression between groups of conspecifics occurred in only two mammalian species: humans and chimpanzees. But a recent study has shown that it also happens in spider monkeys, although no killings have yet been seen (Aureli et al., 2006). Before its discovery in chimpanzees, such lethal aggression was thought to be an exclusively human endeavor, motivated by territoriality. In the past few years, some researchers have posed various questions within the theoretical framework that specific aggressive patterns may be explained by similar factors operating in both species. According to Manson and Wrangham (1991, p. 370), "These similarities between chimpanzees and humans suggest a common evolutionary background. Thus, they indicate that lethal male raiding could have had precultural origins and might be elicited by the same set of conditions among humans as among chimpanzees."

In chimpanzees and most traditional human cultures, males are *philopatric* and form lifelong bonds within their social group. Indeed, the core of a chimpanzee community is a group of closely bonded males who, because of their long-term association, act cooperatively in various endeavors, including hunting and attack. In most other primate species, females are the philopatric sex; and in some species (notably macaques and baboons),

FIGURE **8-9**

Members of a chimpanzee "border patrol" at Gombe survey their territory from a tree.

Curt Busse

females may cooperate in aggressive encounters against females from other groups. (Usually these conflicts develop as contests for resources, and they don't result in fatalities.) Generally, then, conflicts between groups of conspecifics involve members of the philopatric sex. In fact, Manson and Wrangham (1991) suggest that in chimpanzees, lethal aggression is a male activity because males are the philopatric sex. The fact that, among spider monkeys, males are philopatric may lend support to this hypothesis.

Efforts to identify the social and ecological factors that predispose males of some species to engage in lethal attacks have led to hypotheses that attempt to explain the function and adaptive value of these activities. In this context, the benefits and costs of extreme aggression must be identified. The principal benefit to aggressors is acquiring mating partners, food, and water. Costs include risk of injury or death and loss of energy expended in performing aggressive acts.

Although we may never have a precise explanation for lethal raiding, it appears that resource acquisition and protection are involved (Nishida et al., 1985, 1990; Goodall, 1986; Manson and Wrangham, 1991; Nishida, 1991; Aureli et al., 2006). Through careful examination of shared aspects of human and nonhuman primate social life, we can develop hypotheses regarding how intergroup conflict may have arisen in our own lineage.

Early hominids and chimpanzees may well have inherited from a common ancestor the predispositions that have resulted in shared patterns of strife between populations. It's impossible to draw direct comparisons between conflict in nonhuman primates and modern human warfare, owing to later human elaborations of culture, symbols (such as national flags), and language. But it's important and intriguing to speculate on the fundamental issues that may have led to the development of similar patterns in both species.

Affiliation, Altruism, and Cooperation

In Chapter 7, we briefly discussed affiliative behaviors and the role they play in maintaining group cohesion by reinforcing bonds between individuals. There are also behaviors that indicate just how important such bonds are, and some of them can perhaps be said to be examples of caregiving, or compassion.

It's a bit risky to use the term *compassion* because in humans, compassion is motivated by empathy for another. We don't know whether nonhuman primates can empathize with another's suffering or misfortune, but laboratory research has indicated that some of them do. Certainly there are many examples, mostly from chimpanzee studies, of caregiving actions that resemble compassionate behavior in humans. Examples include protecting victims during attacks, helping younger siblings, and staying near ill or dying relatives or friends.

In a poignant example from Gombe, the young adult female Little Bee brought food to her mother at least twice while the latter lay dying of wounds inflicted by attacking males (Goodall, 1986). When chimpanzees have been observed sitting near a dying relative, they were seen occasionally to shoo flies away or groom the other, as if trying to help in some way.

ALTRUISM

Altruism is behavior that benefits another while involving some risk or sacrifice to the performer. It's common in many primate species, and altruistic acts sometimes contain elements of compassion and cooperation. The most fundamental of altruistic behaviors, protecting dependent offspring, is ubiquitous among mammals and birds; and in most species, altruistic acts are confined to this context. However, among primates, recipients of altruistic acts may include individuals who aren't offspring and who may not even be closely related to the performer. Chimpanzees routinely come to the aid of relatives and friends; female langurs join forces to protect infants from infanticidal males; and male baboons protect infants and cooperate to chase predators. In fact, the primate literature abounds with examples of altruistic acts, when individuals place themselves at some risk to protect others from attacks by conspecifics or predators.

Adopting orphans is a form of altruism that has been reported for macaques and baboons, and it's common in chimpanzees. When chimpanzee youngsters are orphaned,

altruism Behavior that benefits another individual but at some potential risk or cost to oneself.

they're routinely adopted, usually by older siblings who are solicitous and highly protective. Adoption is crucial to the survival of orphans, who certainly wouldn't survive on their own. In fact, it's extremely rare for a chimpanzee orphan less than 3 years old to survive even if it is adopted.

One striking and poignant report concerns the attempted rescue of a young adult male baboon who, at some distance from his group, was being chased by a hyena. Suddenly, observers saw an adult female racing toward the hyena in what turned out to be a vain attempt to rescue the male (Stelzner and Strier, 1981; Strier, 2003). The female wasn't the victim's mother, and a female baboon is no match for a hyena. So we ask, "Why would she place herself in serious danger to help an animal to whom, as far as we know, she wasn't closely related?"

Evolutionary explanations of altruism are based on the premise that individuals are more likely to perform risky or self-sacrificing behaviors for the benefit of a relative, who shares genes with the performer. According to this hypothesis, known as *kin selection*, an individual may enhance his or her reproductive success by saving the life of a relative. Even if the performer's life is lost because of the act, the relative may survive to reproduce and pass on genes that both individuals share.

There's also the idea of *reciprocal altruism*, when the recipient of an altruistic act (that is, the one who benefits) may later return the favor (the debt to be paid in the future). Forming coalitions or alliances between two or more individuals is an often-cited example of reciprocal altruism, and it's common in baboons and chimpanzees. As we mentioned in Chapter 7, members of alliances support and defend one another in conflicts with others and/or to increase their status within the group hierarchy. In chimpanzees, members of coalitions are sometimes related, but this isn't always the case. Even though reciprocal altruism may occur, we still haven't explained it, so it's a hypothesis yet to be tested.

Group selection is another hypothesis that some primatologists have supported over the years. According to this model, an individual may act altruistically to benefit other group members because ultimately it's to the performer's benefit that the group be maintained. If the altruist dies, genes he or she shares with other group members may still be passed on (as in kin selection).

But there's a problem with group selection theory: According to natural selection theory, individual reproductive success is enhanced by acting selfishly, and the individual is the object of natural selection. Supporters of group selection explanations thus argue that natural selection acts, not only at the level of the individual, but at the species level as well. But, this is a point upon which there remains much disagreement.

This group selection issue hasn't been resolved, nor is it likely to be any time soon. But we do know that for various reasons discussed in Chapter 7, primates, including humans, have a better chance of surviving and reproducing if they live in groups. Given this important fact, any behavioral mechanism that reinforces the integrity and cohesion of social groupings is to the advantage of individual group members. These mechanisms include altruism, perhaps a form of compassion and a certain degree of empathy (de Waal, 2005) even if we don't accept all the premises of group selection. And we also know that, even though it isn't always obvious, people succeed better when using their highly developed communication skills to solve problems through cooperation instead of aggression.

The Primate Continuum

It's unfortunate that humans generally view themselves as separate from the rest of the animal kingdom. This perspective is, in no small measure, due to a prevailing lack of knowledge about other species' behaviors and abilities. To make matters worse, we're exposed to advertising, movies, and television that continuously reinforce these notions.

For decades, behavioral psychology taught that animal behavior represents nothing more than a series of conditioned responses to specific stimuli. (This perspective is convenient for those who wish to exploit nonhuman animals, for whatever purposes, and remain guilt-free.) Fortunately, this attitude has been changing in recent years to reflect a growing awareness that humans, although in many ways unquestionably unique, are nevertheless part of a biological continuum. Indeed, we're also a part of a behavioral continuum.

Where do humans fit, then, in this biological continuum? Are we at the top? The answer depends on the criteria used. Certainly, we're the most intelligent species if we define intelligence in terms of problem-solving abilities and abstract thought. But if we look more closely, we recognize that the differences between ourselves and our primate relatives, especially chimpanzees and bonobos, are primarily quantitative and not qualitative.

Although the human brain is absolutely and relatively larger than those of other primates, neurological processes are functionally the same. The need for close bonding with at least one parent and the need for physical contact are essentially the same. Developmental stages and dependence on learning are strikingly similar. Indeed, even in the capacity for cruelty and aggression combined with compassion, tenderness, and altruism exhibited by especially chimpanzees, we see a close parallel to the dichotomy between "evil" and "good" so long recognized in ourselves. The main difference between how chimpanzees and humans express these qualities (and thus the dichotomy) is one of degree. Humans are much more adept at cruelty and compassion, and we can reflect on our behavior in ways that chimpanzees can't. Like the cat that plays with a mouse, chimpanzees don't seem to understand the suffering they inflict on others; but humans do. Likewise, while an adult chimpanzee may sit next to and protect a dying relative or friend, it doesn't seem to feel intense grief and a sense of loss to the extent a human normally does.

To arrive at any understanding of what it is to be human, it's vastly important to recognize that many of our behaviors are but elaborate extensions of those of our hominid ancestors and close primate relatives. The fact that so many of us prefer to bask in the warmth of the "sun belt" with literally thousands of other people reflects our heritage as social animals adapted to life in the tropics. Likewise, the "sweet tooth" seen in so many humans is a direct result of our earlier primate ancestors' predilection for high-energy sugar contained in desirably sweet, ripe fruit. Recognizing our primate heritage is a significant aspect in our exploration of how humans came to be and how we continue to adapt.

VISUAL SUMMARY

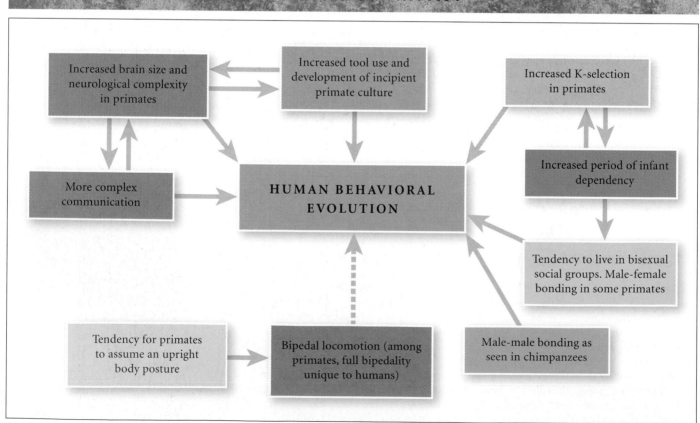

Summary: Putting It All Together

In this chapter, we discussed how biological anthropologists (including primatologists) apply what they've learned about nonhuman primate evolution, life history traits, and behavior to the study of early hominid behavior and adaptations. Although we humans share a common ancestry with all nonhuman primates, our complex behavior and language use are unique. This uniqueness is related to expansion of the neocortex of the brain since the divergence of the hominid lineage from that of the African great apes.

Due to the importance of neocortical expansion in human evolution, we emphasized some of the evolutionary changes that have occurred in the brain, particularly as they relate to language. Because the brain is such a metabolically expensive organ to maintain, selective pressures favoring increased behavioral complexity would have been enormous. An important source of these pressures may have been living in social groups.

We also described some of the evidence for cultural behavior in nonhuman primates, particularly regarding tool use in various populations. For example, while West African chimpanzees use stones to crack palm nuts, East African populations don't. Variation in cultural behavior and the transmission of these behaviors from one individual to another through observation and learning are hallmarks of human culture. Nonhuman primates exhibit certain aspects of culture, but so do several nonprimate species, although none of these species have adopted culture as an adaptive strategy the way humans have.

Critical Thinking Questions

1. Do you think that knowing about aggression between groups of chimpanzees is useful in understanding conflicts between human societies? Why or why not?

2. What are some examples of cultural behavior in nonprimate species that weren't mentioned in this chapter? Have you personally witnessed such behaviors?

Molecular Applications in Primatology

Primatologists have recently used molecular biological techniques to compare the DNA sequences of a wide range of contemporary primates. From these data, they've gained new insights concerning sensory perception, physiology, social relationships, and evolutionary relationships.

One crucial source of information concerns the precise identification of kin relationships within primate societies. Maternity is almost always obvious to primatologists studying primate social groups and probably to all members of these groups. Tracing paternity, however, has always been difficult, and without knowing who fathered whom, it's impossible to test hypotheses pertaining to such issues as kin selection, infanticide, and the selective advantage of dominance, etc. However, in the past several years, scientists have been using new techniques to overcome these difficulties.

Biologist Phillip Morin and anthropologist Jim Moore, of the University of California, San Diego, did the first molecular-based nonhuman primate behavior study by examining the Gombe chimpanzees (Morin et al., 1994). An important innovation of this research was that DNA samples were obtained from hair collected from sleeping nests (Fig. 1). This allowed researchers to avoid capturing the animals (usually by shooting them with a sedative dart) in order to draw blood samples (a potentially dangerous procedure for the chimpanzees). What's more, due to the development of PCR techniques (see p. 58), primatologists can now use much smaller DNA samples than before. For example, in the Gombe study, the researchers extracted small DNA samples from the chimpanzee hairs, made multiple copies of them, and then used DNA fingerprinting techniques to identify individual chimpanzees and close relatives.

Researchers at the Max Planck Institute for Evolutionary Anthropology (MPIEA) recently did a more complete study on West African chimpanzees from the Tai Forest. (The MPIEA, in Leipzig, Germany, has become the leading center for groundbreaking applications within anthropology.)

For example, MPIEA researchers found that most of the chimpanzee offspring within the Tai Forest community were fathered by resident males (Vigilant et al., 2001). Another DNA study of the Gombe chimpanzees demonstrated that *all* offspring were fathered by resident males (Constable, et al., 2001). These findings suggest that females generally choose mates from within their own group rather than from other groups. Detailed examination of social relationships within the Gombe community also showed that a variety of male strategies, such as dominance, possessiveness, opportunistic mating, and consortships, could increase reproductive success.

DNA can also be used to assess the degree of inbreeding in a community. At Gombe, 13 of 14 offspring weren't closely inbred. But, in one case, a male had successfully mated with his mother.

Jim Moore/Anthro Photo

FIGURE 1

Physical anthropologist Jim Moore collecting hair samples from a chimpanzee sleeping nest at Gombe.

Led by Dr. Leslie Knapp, the Primate Immunogenetics and Molecular Ecology Research Group at Cambridge University is investigating aspects of human and nonhuman primate genetic mechanisms and how these, in turn, might influence immunity, disease, and perhaps even social behavior. The focus of their investigations is a genetic system called the *major histocompatibility complex* or, more simply, the MHC (Grob et al., 1998). The group is currently studying MHC variation in chimpanzees, gorillas, mandrills, several New World monkeys, lemurs, and humans. Results are used to test hypotheses regarding the effects of natural selection on particular allele combinations, the antiquity of these genes in different primate groups, and the possible influences different genes may have on kin recognition, mate choice, and inbreeding avoidance (Knapp, personal communication).

As you can see, combining genetic and behavioral data is important because it permits explanations of behavior that previously weren't possible. For example, it's useful to know that two chimpanzees are brothers and, even more important, to examine how this biological relationship influences their behavior toward each other as compared toward other members of the group.

Primatologists still don't fully understand how nonhuman primates recognize relatives. Some studies propose that olfactory cues may be crucial, and as scientists test this hypothesis, they're discovering some genetic mechanisms that influence olfactory perception in primates, including humans.

Scientists have recently identified several genes that control olfactory reception in mammals. One of these, which is present and functional in prosimians and New World monkeys, directly influences a particular form of scent perception. However, it's completely dysfunctional in all Old World monkeys, apes, and humans. These facts were discovered separately by two pairs of investigators, one at the University of Southern California (Liman and Innan, 2003) and the other at the University of Michigan (Zhang and Webb, 2003). Moreover, both teams reached the same conclusions as to *when* in evolution this olfactory capability was lost in Old World anthropoids and *why*. The genetic mutations that led to reduced olfactory capabilities in the latter occurred after New and Old World primates diverged from one another but before the divergence of Old World monkeys and hominoids (that is, ca. 25–20 mya). Furthermore, the reason hypothesized for different selection forces in New and Old World forms is the parallel development of full color vision (which has also recently been investigated in different primates using molecular techniques). The researchers suggest that the advantages provided by full color vision relaxed the selection pressure that favored the detection of pheromones (chemicals produced by individuals that elicit a behavioral response in conspecifics). Eventually, this relaxed selection pressure led to deactivation of the genes that control this aspect of olfaction.

In yet another study, Yoav Gilad has shown that humans have far fewer genes that govern the function of olfactory receptors than any other primate, including the great apes (Gilad et al., 2003a, 2003b). But, when in hominid evolution this extreme reduction in the sense of smell occurred isn't known. However, a reduced sense of smell could be added to the list of characteristics that distinguish modern humans from the other primates.

Molecular approaches to the study of primate behavior are still relatively new, but they've already provided some important information that, in turn, will be used to develop hypotheses regarding many puzzling aspects of behavior. As these hypotheses are tested, and as new molecular techniques are developed, the evolution and functions of many complicated behavioral patterns will be better understood.

SOURCES

Constable, Julie L., Mary V. Ashley, Jane Goodall, and Anne E. Pusey. 2001. "Noninvasive Paternity Assignment in Gombe Chimpanzees." *Molecular Ecology* 10:1279–1300.

Gilad, Yoav, Orna Man, Svante Paabo, and Doran Lancet. 2003a. "Human Specific Loss of Receptor Genes." *Proceedings of the National Academy of Sciences* 100:3324–3327.

Gilad, Yoav, Carlos D. Bustamante, Doran Lancet, and Svante Paabo. 2003b. "Natural Selection on the Olfactory Receptor Gene Family in Humans and Chimpanzees." *American Journal of Human Genetics*, 73:489–501.

Grob, B., L. A. Knapp, R. D. Martin, and G. Anzenberger. 1998. "The Major Histocompatibility Complex and Mate Choice: Inbreeding Avoidance and Selection of Good Genes." *Exp. Clin. Immunogenet.* 15(3):119–129.

Liman, Emily R., and Hideki Innan. 2003. "Relaxed Selective Pressure on an Essential Component of Pheromone Transduction in Primate Evolution." *Proceedings of the National Academy of Sciences* 100:3328–3332.

Max Planck Institute for Evolutionary Anthropology website: www.eva.mpg.

de Morin, P. A., J. Wallis, J. Moore, and D. S. Woodruff. 1994. "Paternity Exclusion in a Community of Wild Chimpanzees Using Hypervariable Simple Sequence Repeats." *Molecular Evolution* 3:469–477.

Primate Immunogenetics and Molecular Ecology Research Group website: www-prime.bioanth.cam.ac.uk.

Vigilant, Linda, Michael Hofreiter, Heike Siedel, and Christophe Boesch. 2001. "Paternity and Relatedness in Wild Chimpanzee Communities." *Proceedings of the National Academy of Sciences* 98:12890–12895.

Zhang, Jianzhi, and David Webb. 2003. "Evolutionary Deterioration of the Vomeronasal Pheromone Transduction Pathway in Catarrrhine Primates." *Proceedings of the National Academy of Sciences* 100:8337–8341.

CHAPTER 9

Overview of the Fossil Primates

Ankarapithecus; Courtesy of John Kappelman, University of Texas

What were the oldest primates like and how do they compare to the most primitive of the living primates (the prosimians)?

Who are the oldest members of Hominoidea (apes and humans), and how do they compare with their modern counterparts? How do they fit into the primate family tree?

Introduction

When gazing into the eyes of a great ape, we see in them something unique that we feel inside ourselves. Often, however, when looking into the eyes of a galago ("bush baby"), we see nothing but a cuddly animal that we might like to take home as a pet (see Fig. 6-15 in Chapter 6). When most people think back to the origins of our own species, they generally stop once they've evoked the idea of an upright-walking ape ancestor. But have you ever considered extending your family tree to the baboons you may see in a wildlife park or to the lemurs or bush babies you see in the zoo? You might think, "How can a creature so small and, well, *animal*-like have anything to do with us or our evolutionary background?" In this chapter we focus on bridging the gap between these creatures and ourselves—between prosimian and anthropoid—to help us better understand our own evolutionary history.

As we've seen in Chapter 8, some of our primate cousins also have many of the traits we think of as uniquely human. Many of these similarities can be traced to shared origins in highly social groups living in the trees. We see these origins in the structure of our body and in the retention of many primitive features such as pentadactyly (five fingers and toes) and unfused lower arms, but also in more "derived" skeletal traits that came later. Among the most important of these derived primate traits are a more **orthograde** (upright) body position and forward-facing eyes. Distinguishing these uniquely primate features in the fossil record, as being different from those traits found in more distantly related mammalian cousins, is the first step in recognizing our own beginnings. As we move in time through the Cenozoic era (see Figure 5-7 in Chapter 5) we see in rough form the recapitulation of our own (Primate) order from "primitive" to highly derived. We'll also trace the development of mammals that resemble us more and more over time until we conclude this chapter in the Miocene (23 to 5 million years ago [mya]) with the emergence of the first hominoids (apes) and then the first possible hominids (humans). As you'll see, our ability to recognize primate families in the fossil record not only uses the same skills that allow us to discover our later human origins, but it also allows us to organize these mammals into meaningful groups.

This organization means that you'll face a multitude of taxonomic designations (Fig. 9-1). These names aren't meant to scare you, but they should impress upon you how successful past lineages of primates have been—in fact, much more so than they are now. As you'll see, learning about the past of our order can lend powerful perspective and meaning to our own origins, even though most of the fossil groups discussed in this chapter never led to any living forms and even fewer are related to our own hominid ancestors.

BACKGROUND TO PRIMATE EVOLUTION: LATE MESOZOIC

The exact origins of the earliest primates aren't well understood; in fact, they're shrouded in some amount of mystery. We *do* know that following the K-T (Cretaceous-Tertiary) extinction of the dinosaurs, the reign of the giant reptiles was over and the age of the mammals had begun. Primates were just one of the many groups of small mammals that were left to diversify and explore the many niches left vacant with the passing of the dinosaurs.

It was during the last period of the Mesozoic (the Cretaceous) that primates began to diverge from closely related mammalian lineages. Some scientists place these closely related (sister) lineages into a group known as **Archonta**. Archonta is the superorder designated

 Click!

Go to the following media for interactives and exercises on topics covered in this chapter:

- Online Virtual Laboratories for Physical Anthropology, Fourth Edition

orthograde An upright body position; this term relates to the position of the head and torso during sitting, climbing, etc., and doesn't necessarily mean an animal is bipedal.

Archonta The superorder designated for the sister orders of tree shrews, flying lemurs, plesiadapiforms, and primates.

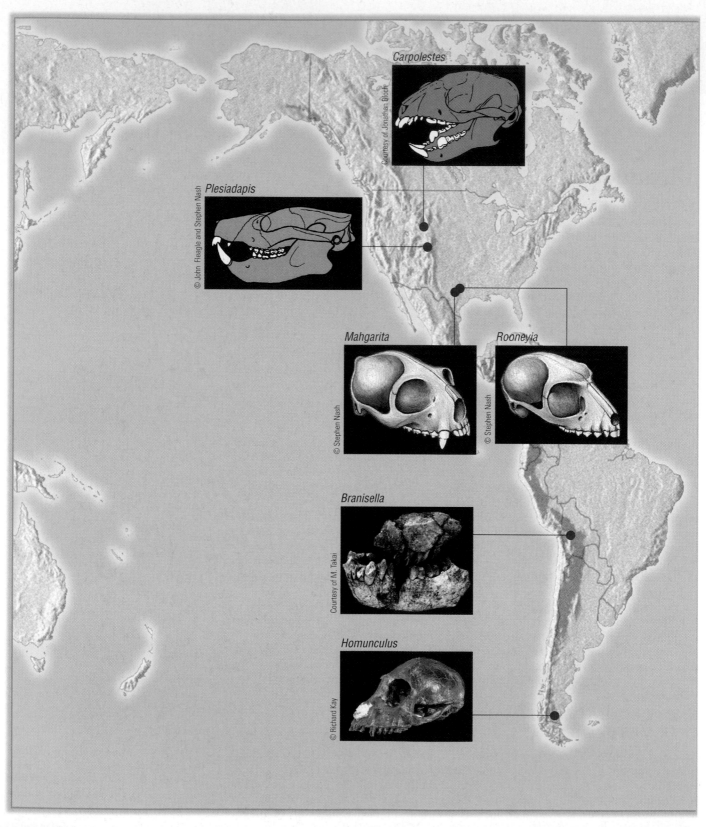

FIGURE 9-1
A map showing the location of the fossil primates discussed in this chapter.

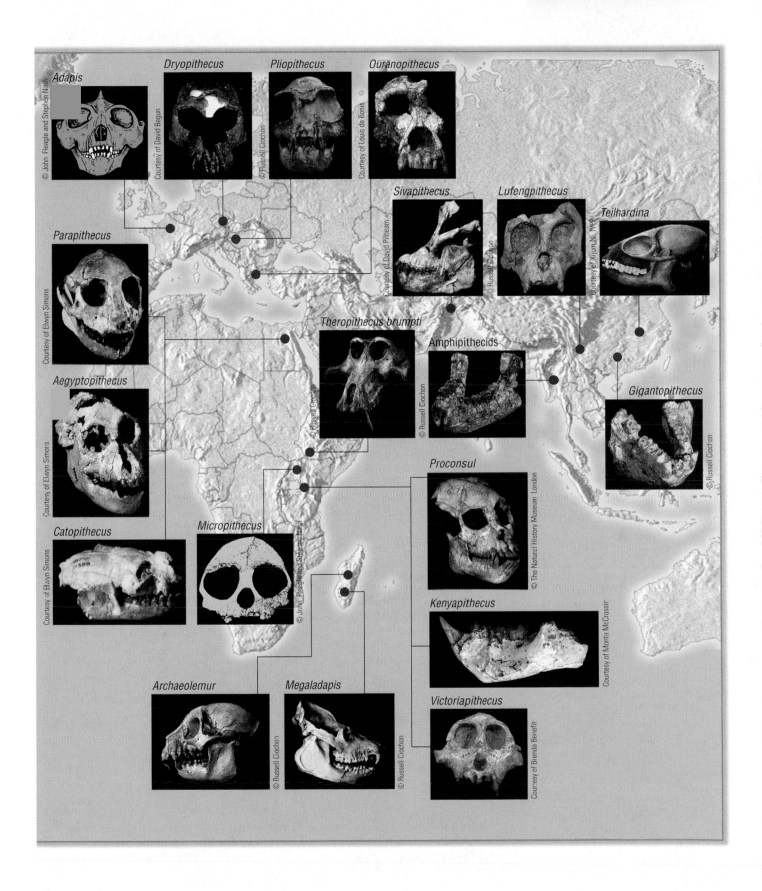

Adapis

Dryopithecus

Pliopithecus

Ouranopithecus

Sivapithecus

Lufengpithecus

Teilhardina

Parapithecus

Theropithecus brumpti

Amphipithecids

Gigantopithecus

Aegyptopithecus

Proconsul

Catopithecus

Micropithecus

Kenyapithecus

Archaeolemur

Megaladapis

Victoriapithecus

FIGURE 9-2

Archonta. The superorder designated for the sister orders of tree shrews, flying lemurs, plesiadapiforms, and primates.

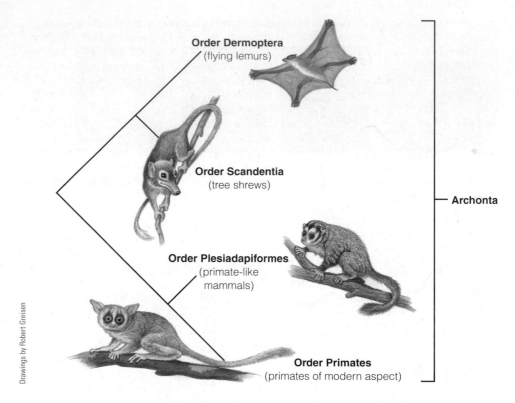

Order Dermoptera
(flying lemurs)

Order Scandentia
(tree shrews)

Order Plesiadapiformes
(primate-like
mammals)

Order Primates
(primates of modern aspect)

Archonta

Drawings by Robert Greisen

for the sister orders of tree shrews, flying lemurs (also known as the colugo, which don't fly and aren't lemurs), Plesiadapiformes (extinct primate-like mammals), and Primates (Fig. 9-2). This diversification of early mammals took place in a global, tropical climate that accompanied the emergence of modern plants—although neither the exact region where primates first evolved nor the precise pressures that molded their adaptations are known. These uncertainties continue to intrigue scientists.

Primate Origins

The Cenozoic is the broad time period during which primate evolution has unfolded (and continues to unfold). This time period is divided into seven epochs, the oldest of which is called the Paleocene (65 mya). As mentioned in Chapter 5, for each of these broad epochs, we can roughly attribute a particular phase of primate evolution and development. But evolution knows no temporal bounds, so the time line for these phases will always be imperfectly defined:

- Paleocene (65 mya; primate-like mammals, aka Plesiadapiformes)
- Eocene (55.8 mya; first true primates, Prosimians)
- Oligocene (33 mya; early Catarrhines, precursors to monkeys and apes, emerge)
- Miocene (23 mya; monkeys and apes emerge, also the first humanlike creatures appear)
- Pliocene (5.3 mya; early humans diversify)
- Pleistocene (1.8 mya; early *Homo* develops)
- Holocene (0.01 mya; the present epoch; modern humans)

Primate biologists have hypothesized that the initial radiation of primate-*like* animals occurred during the early Paleocene epoch (65 mya), with the first emergence of indisputable primates appearing in the earliest Eocene epoch (55.8 mya). New evidence has called this view into question, however; the results of new studies predict the origins of Primates to be as early as 90 mya, during the Cretaceous period (Miller et al., 2005). This disparity in dates arises from the difficulty in reconciling morphological and molecular data in our search for the key time of evolutionary divergence, or the time when the **last common ancestor (LCA)** between primates and their Archontan relatives lived. The last common ancestor is the hypothetical species that was the last to exist before it speciated into the myriad of sister orders related to primates. This critical species is difficult to pinpoint morphologically, and researchers often can't confidently associate it with any given fossil. Molecular data, on the other hand, can provide us with the estimated time of divergence, indicating the assumed date when the last common ancestor lived (Tavaré et al., 2002). Together, these two approaches (morphological and molecular) enable us to bracket the origins of indisputable primates at sometime between 90 mya and 55.8 mya—a very large swath of time, indeed! Until the more ancient date of 90 mya is more fully accepted, however, 55.8 mya remains the conservative estimate—although there are important implications related to either date one accepts.

Paleocene Primate-like Mammals

Fossil evidence indicates that between 64 and 52 mya, a major radiation of the plesiadapiforms (that is, primate-like mammals) occurred. Plesiadapiforms are members of an extinct group that's either closely related to Primates or is the actual precursor to our order. These creatures occupy a controversial position in primate phylogeny; sometimes they're even placed as a suborder of Primates, much as Prosimii and Anthropoidea are viewed today (Fig. 9-3).

Plesiadapiforms are best known from an array of fossil finds from the American West (especially Montana and Wyoming). Some of the more recent finds of these Paleocene mammals have been quite complete (including nearly complete skeletons). Some members of this group exhibit a striking continuity of traits with some of the earliest prosimians from the later Eocene epoch. Although as many as six families are commonly recognized within this group, we'll concentrate on the two families that are most pertinent for this discussion.

The first of these, the plesiadapids, were among the more successful plesiadapiforms. They were chipmunk- to marmot-sized mammals with large incisors similar to those of a rodent. However, unlike rodents, the plesiadapids had incisors that weren't continuously growing and didn't self-sharpen, suggesting that they used their incisors for a purpose other than gnawing. Some have suggested that this family subsisted on a vegetative diet of leaves supplemented with fruits. The best-known of this family is the genus *Plesiadapis*, which probably originated in North America but went on to colonize Europe via a land bridge across Greenland before eventually dying out.

The second family (the carpolestids) was quite common during the Paleocene in North America, although they were never as successful as the plesiadapids. These creatures were much smaller, generally mouse- to rat-sized, though they exhibit the typical enlarged incisors. They also have specialized dental traits that allow them to efficiently process fibrous vegetation as well as nuts and insects. For a long time, carpolestids were known only from fossil teeth and jaws, but our knowledge of them changed recently when a nearly complete skeleton of *Carpolestes* ("fruit stealer"; Fig. 9-4) was discovered in the Clarks Fork Basin of Wyoming (Bloch and Boyer, 2002). This specimen is estimated at about 3.5 ounces, the size of the average hamster, and its **postcranial** anatomy reveals many traits adapted to a highly arboreal environment (particularly since it had nails instead of claws; see Fig. 9-4). But unlike later true primates that were fully adapted to living in the trees, *Carpolestes* displays no adaptations for leaping. This combination of primitive and primate-like traits (nails were previously unknown outside true primates) has caused many to reassess all the plesiadapiforms and their position within primate evolutionary history. In fact, some primatologists now use these traits to link the plesiadapiforms with the later, more definite and more modern-looking primates. As we'll see, however, this interpretation does *not* mean these animals are considered primates themselves. At any rate, since the plesiadapiforms exhibit such tantalizing hints of connection to the true primates, they continue to be the source of great interest and may teach us much about homoplasy (see p. 98).

last common ancestor (LCA) The final evolutionary link between two related groups.

postcranial (*post*, meaning "after") In a quadruped, referring to that portion of the body behind the head; in a biped, referring to all parts of the body beneath the head (i.e., the neck down).

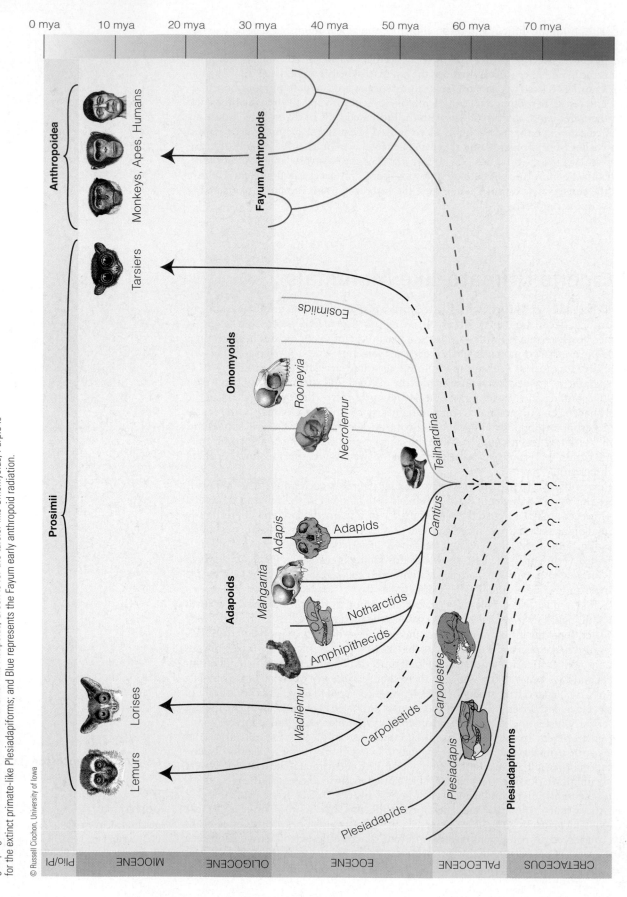

FIGURE 9-3

Family tree of early fossil primates and their relationships to modern prosimian groups. Colors represent major groupings within Primates. Red is for the lemur-like Adapoids; Green is for the tarsier-like Omomyoids; Purple is for the extinct primate-like Plesiadapiforms; and Blue represents the Fayum early anthropoid radiation.

(a)   (b)   (c)

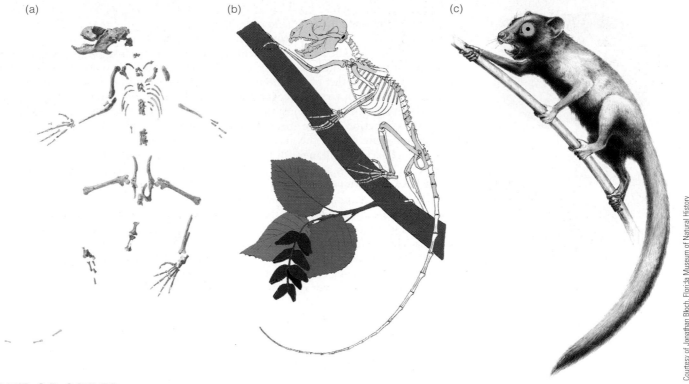

Courtesy of Jonathan Bloch, Florida Museum of Natural History

OUT OF ORDER

We've said the plesiadapiforms are primate-like, but for several decades, primate paleontologists had originally considered them as early members of the Primate order. What changed their view? A careful analysis of the more recently discovered fossils, using more rigorous cladistic methods, has resulted in a major reevaluation of this conclusion (Bloch and Silcox, 2001; Silcox, 2001; Bloch and Boyer, 2002). Although some plesiadapiforms such as *Plesiadapis* and *Carpolestes* do share some characteristics with true primates, these aren't enough for most researchers to put them in the primate order. In fact, these shared traits are more likely the result of primates retaining several ancestral mammalian characteristics. In other words, there are no *shared derived characteristics* (see p. 101)—other than the nails found in *Carpolestes*—that specifically link the plesiadapiforms with later primates. Even the presence of nails is likely due to homoplasy.

So, in light of these recent and major reinterpretations, which discard much of what had been assumed about the earliest primates, we're left with extremely meager evidence of the beginnings of the primate radiation. While fragmentary fossil remains from the Paleocene epoch of North Africa (discussed later) have been tentatively suggested as the earliest true primate, it appears that we'll have to await further, more complete discoveries on many continents before we can say much at all about the first primates.

Eocene Primates

During the Eocene epoch (55.8–34 mya), we see the gradual extinction of the plesiadapiforms and their replacement by the so-called primates of modern aspect, or the **euprimates**. These mammals, unlike the plesiadapiforms, have recognizable and modern derived primate traits such as forward-facing eyes, greater encephalization, a postorbital bar, nails instead of claws at the ends of their fingers and toes, and an opposable big toe (see pp. 124–125 for a discussion of basic primate characteristics). These features suggest an adaptation to environmental conditions that were fundamentally different from those experienced by the plesiadapiforms: a warmer climate with year-round rainfall and lush, broad-leaved evergreen forests.

FIGURE **9-4**
Nearly complete skeleton of *Carpolestes* discovered in the Clarks Fork Basin of Wyoming.
(a) *Carpolestes* as it was discovered.
(b) Reconstructed skeleton of *Carpolestes*
(c) Artist's rendering of *Carpolestes* as it might have looked in life.

euprimate The term *euprimate* means "true primate" and was coined by Elwyn Simons in 1972 (Conroy, 1990).

209

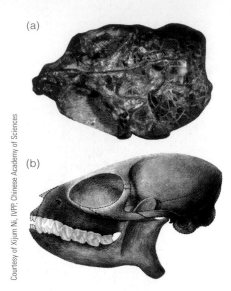

(a)

(b)

FIGURE 9-5

Teilhardina. (a) View of the skull of *Teilhardina* from the top. (b) An artist's reconstruction of *Teilhardina,* with areas in gray representing missing fragments.

At the beginning of the Eocene epoch, North America and Europe were connected; they didn't split apart until the middle Eocene. Meanwhile, during the middle to late Eocene, North America was sporadically connected to Asia via the Bering land bridge. These early connections between these three continents meant that they shared many species in common. In contrast, the continents of Africa, Antarctica, Australia, and South America were isolated from one another by large bodies of water. These connections and isolations led to a variety of animals of very different characters. In fact, the Eocene is a time of rapid diversification for all mammals, not just the primates. As a result, the variety of animals known from this time period is much greater than that known from the earlier Paleocene.

Euprimates are part of this wave of diversification. They came on the scene around 55.8 mya—nearly simultaneously, it seemed—in North America, Europe, and Asia. However, a closer look at the fossil record reveals that the earliest euprimates actually engaged in a rapid westward dispersal. These euprimates of the genus *Teilhardina* (Fig. 9-5) are found on three continents; however, because evidence points to Asia as the euprimates' starting point, Asia may be their cradle. Analysis of related species of *Teilhardina* shows that the oldest and most primitive members were from Asia, while the youngest were from North America. This evidence supports a westward migration of euprimates from Asia, through Europe, and eventually to North America (Smith et al., 2006; Fig. 9-6).

There are two main branches of euprimates, grouped into different superfamilies (Adapoidea and Omomyoidea). These two superfamilies include primitive primates that are described as being either more lemur-like (adapoid) or tarsier- or galago-like (omomyoid). Both groups are well known from cranial, dental, and postcranial remains from North America and Europe, as well as increasingly from Asia and Africa.

LEMUR-LIKE ADAPOIDS

The adapoids are the best known of the Eocene prosimians and include more than 35 genera. These are the most primitive of any known primate group, living or dead, as recognized by their dental anatomy. Their primitive **dental formula** (2.1.4.3; see Chapter 6) provided a generalized ancestral baseline from which many later, more derived varieties of dental specializations could evolve. The adapoids are divided into five families based mostly on biogeographic distinctions. The most prominent are the notharctids of North America (predominantly), the adapids of Europe, and the amphipithecids of Asia.

Cantius was the earliest notharctid, and one of the earliest adapoids, in general. This small- to medium-sized creature is known primarily from North America, with just two species from Europe. Cranial and skeletal remains indicate that it was a diurnal creature, foraging during the day. It also probably traveled very rapidly through the trees, leaping quadrupedally. Traits of its mandible and primitive dental formula of 2.1.4.3 indicate it was probably a fruit eater.

FIGURE 9-6

The rapid westward dispersal of euprimates of the genus *Teilhardina.* Analysis of related species of *Teilhardina* shows that the oldest and most primitive members were from Asia, while the youngest were from North America.

dental formula   Numerical shorthand for the number and kind of tooth found in one side of either the upper or lower jaw.

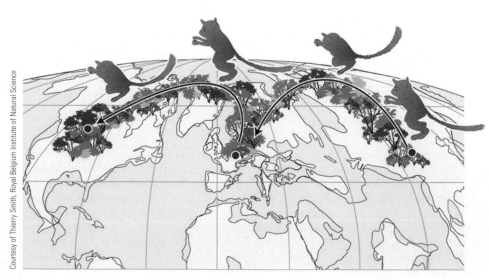

The second prominent family of adapoids, the adapids, abruptly appeared in Europe near the end of the Eocene and just as quickly became extinct. For this reason, phylogenetic relations for this group are not well understood, although they probably emigrated from another continent, most likely Asia. Perhaps the best known of this group is *Adapis*. Not only was it the first nonhuman fossil primate named, but it was also first described by the well-known nineteenth-century naturalist, Georges Cuvier. As you remember from Chapter 2, Cuvier didn't believe in evolving lineages, even going so far as to state in 1812, "*l'homme fossile n'existe pas*" ("fossil man does not exist"; by this he also meant fossil primates). So it's ironic that in 1822, it was Cuvier who described and named the first fossil primate. Unfortunately for him, he confused the remains for that of an ungulate (a hoofed mammal); shortly after his death in 1837, the fossil was correctly identified as a primate. *Adapis'* dental formula remains primitive (2.1.4.3), though some have argued that an incipient dental comb (a lemur feature; see p. 136) can be recognized in this fossil genus. (You may recall from Chapter 6 that a dental comb is a specialization of the front teeth in the lower jaw—the teeth are elongated and project forward like a small comb.) A slow, arboreal quadruped, *Adapis* most likely spent its time foraging for leaves during the daytime hours.

The third major adapoid family, the amphipithecids from Myanmar (Burma) and Thailand, doesn't fit neatly into any of the preconceived notions about early primates; but the amphipithecids do tell us much about primate adaptations. This curious family of animals from Asia has many challenging features that are difficult to interpret, with hazy evolutionary affiliations. Some say they're anthropoids of some kind; others say they're adapoids. Why the disagreement? Remember that in Chapter 5 we introduced the terms *homology* (similar traits based on descent) and *homoplasy* (similar traits that evolve independently in different groups) and talked about the example of theropod dinosaurs and birds sharing derived traits. Unlike dinosaurs and birds, however, the amphipithecids are a textbook example of convergent evolution: Their seemingly "anthropoid" traits are actually homoplasies, not shared derived traits. In this case, we see that these creatures' teeth can be somewhat deceiving. Since both early anthropoids and amphipithecids were exploiting the same dietary niche, they developed similar dental patterns. On the other hand, the postcranial skeleton and mandibles (Fig. 9-7) of amphipithecids betray their true affiliation as more primitive, but specialized adapoids that exploited a slow-moving arboreal niche (Ciochon and Gunnell, 2002). For many years the amphipithecid dental pattern confounded researchers; but with the discovery of more complete specimens, this mystery has now been solved. It seems that these remarkable adapoids, alone in Asia and in the absence of anthropoids, converged upon the anthropoid dental pattern.

EVOLUTION OF TRUE LEMURS AND LORISES

As we've mentioned, the adapoids were fairly lemur-like in their overall pattern, and they show distinctive primate tendencies. Although the ancient adapoids do resemble lemurs in overall anatomical body plan, this is mostly due to modern lemurs retaining some primitive traits. The adapoid fossils don't show the same specializations seen in contemporary lemurs, galagos, and lorises, such as development of the dental comb. For this reason, we may say that modern-day lemurs, galagos, and lorises have retained many primitive aspects of anatomy, but there's no clear evolutionary relationship between the Eocene adapoids and these latter-day creatures. Fossils of galagos and lorises have been found in late Eocene deposits of the Fayum Depression in Egypt, an area that we'll discuss in more detail next.

A recent non-adapoid late Eocene find (placed in the genus *Wadilemur*) from Egypt may have had the prosimian dental comb. This find postdates the loris-lemur split by some 10 million years. Scientists have placed it on the line leading to modern-day African lorises (Seiffert et al., 2005a). The existence of an early African loris in Egypt during this time supports the idea that their relatives, the lemurs, were also from the African mainland. It's thought that lemurs likely colonized Madagascar by crossing the

FIGURE 9-7
The teeth of the amphipithecids are misleading, but the mandibles betray their true phylogenetic affinity as lower primates.

© Russell Ciochon, University of Iowa

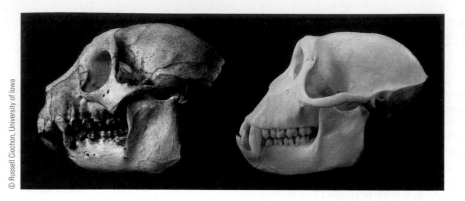

© Russell Ciochon, University of Iowa

FIGURE 9-8

Comparison of the skull of *Archaeolemur* (left) and a macaque monkey. Note how the lemur resembles the monkey in the shape of the jaw, teeth, and overall cranial form. This is an excellent example of convergent evolution.

subfossil   Bone not old enough to have become completely mineralized as a fossil.

bilophodonty   Molars that have 4 cusps, oriented in 2 parallel rows, that resemble ridges or "lophs." This is characteristic of Old World Monkeys.

Mozambique Channel, perhaps by unintentionally rafting over on drifting debris. This phenomenon of migration on drifting debris is described in "A Closer Look" on p. 220. This is also the suggested explanation for how monkeys originally colonized the New World.

There are few, if any, truly fossilized lemur remains in Madagascar; but, there are numerous **subfossil** lemurs. These unfossilized skeletal remains are too recent to have become completely mineralized into fossils. Many of these extinct subfossil lemurs were colossal compared to the lemurs of today—some of them were up to five times as big! Despite their large size, they were mostly tree dwelling and possibly even diurnal. Most interesting of all, many filled unusual environmental niches not shared by any living lemurs—an example of convergence upon other higher primate niches. For instance, the extinct *Archaeolemur* (Fig. 9-8), with its fused mandible and **bilophodont** molars, in many ways more closely resembled a monkey than the 37-pound lemur that it was (Fleagle, 1999). What's more, the sulcal (grooved) pattern of *Archaeolemur*'s brain was similar to that seen in higher primates (Martin, 1990). Based on this evidence, we can see this group as converging upon a monkey-like role on a monkey-less island.

The best known of the giant lemurs, however, was the 170-pound *Megaladapis*. Built more like a gorilla than a lemur (another incident of convergence), this specialized forest dweller lost its livelihood when the trees were cleared for farmland with the appearance of humans on the island. Sadly, the *Megaladapis* story isn't unusual; most of the 16 subfossil species discovered went extinct within the last 2,000 years—at the same time that humans began colonizing the island. Many believe that the predation and deforestation carried out

A CLOSER LOOK   Texas and the Last North American Prosimians

Today, the only "naturally" occurring primate species living in North America is *Homo sapiens*. But during the Eocene epoch (55.8–34 mya) two groups of early prosimians, the adapoids and the omomyoids, flourished across the entire North American continent. It was only toward the end of the Eocene that primates began slowly disappearing from the North American fossil record. This time period coincides with dramatic global cooling that would characterize the Oligocene epoch. As temperatures cooled at the end of the Eocene, primates living in what is today Canada and the northern United States began a slow retreat toward the southern end of the continent, making their final stand in the coastal plains of Texas.

The Texas environment these last American prosimians encountered during the Eocene was far different from that of Texas today (Fig. 1). Approximately 40 mya the body of water separating North and South America extended far beyond the current Texas coastline, pushing well into what's now central and west Texas. Today west Texas is known for its almost desertlike landscape; but during the Eocene, this part of Texas was a mix of mangrove swamps and lush tropical rain forests. Here, the last of the North American prosimians coexisted with many strange, now extinct creatures such as the mesonychids, carnivorous mammals that resembled wolves with hoofed feet; brontotheres, enormous rhino-like mammals with gigantic forked horns on

their snouts; and *Pterosphenus*, a giant marine snake measuring up to 17 feet long. The kinds of fossil tiger sharks and rays evident in these sediments reveal that this was a stressful environment like that where salt and freshwater mix (Westgate and Gee,

Courtesy of James Westgate, Lamar University

FIGURE 1

Coastal Texas during the Eocene. A tiny prosimian (left) clings to a shrub, safely out of reach of the giant rays and tiger sharks that prowl the brackish waters.

by these early peoples caused the extinction of these massive forms. Unfortunately, the remaining lemurs of Madagascar will meet the same fate, unless the continued destruction to their habitat ceases.

TARSIER-LIKE OMOMYOIDS

The tarsier-like omomyoids are more taxonomically diverse than the adapoids. They're often called tarsier-like because the European specimens of this group appear to be more closely related to the tarsier. They have a similar dental formula (1.1.3.3), large orbits, and small snouts (see Schmid, 1983, for a dissenting view). Earlier members of this group are somewhat more generalized than later ones, and some researchers believe they represent the stock for all later anthropoids—that is, New World monkeys, Old World monkeys, apes, and humans (Ross, 2000). **Paleoprimatologists** typically divide the omomyoids into three families—one restricted to North America, a second to Europe, and the third to Asia.

It's been suggested that some of the omomyoids from the late Eocene of Europe, such as *Necrolemur*, are closely related to the tarsier. However, many of the similarities noted are apparently superficial ones, not necessarily indicating any unique (that is, shared derived) relationship (Fleagle, 1999). Even so, at least one feature, the position of the olfactory portion of the brain that processes scent, links these Eocene forms with later tarsiers and anthropoids (sometimes called Haplorhini; see Chapter 6, p. 135).

One of these Oligocene tarsier-like omomyoids is the Texan, *Rooneyia*, which was about the size of the modern tarsier or galago (see "A Closer Look" on pp. 212–214). Only one specimen of *Rooneyia* (named for the Rooney Ranch on which it was found) has been discovered, and of that, only the skull was preserved. Without postcrania, it's difficult to determine what its locomotor pattern might have been; but we can assume that it was probably arboreally adapted, like the modern tarsiers it resembles. Unlike the nocturnal tarsier, however, the size of its orbits indicates a diurnal lifestyle. Its teeth, with their broad, flattened cusps, indicate a frugivorous (fruit) diet. One curiosity of this specimen is that it's preserved as a

paleoprimatologist   A person who specializes in the study of the nonhuman primate fossil record.

1990; Westgate, 1994). One can only imagine the perils a small primate might face when venturing to the shore for a drink!

So, who were the last of the North American prosimians (Fig. 2)? *Rooneyia,* apparently the lone survivor of the once abundant North American omomyoids, probably disappeared at the end of the Eocene. This tarsier-like primate had many omomyoid characteristics, including a tubular ear canal and large incisors, but also exhibits several characteristics, such as

an expanded brain and shortened face, that appear advanced in comparison to earlier omomyoids. Small eye orbits indicate that, unlike modern tarsiers and most other omomyoids, *Rooneyia* was most likely active during the day rather than at night. The last North American adapoid, *Mahgarita*, actually may have survived into the earliest part of the Oligocene. It appears likely that *Mahgarita* was a relatively late arrival to North America, probably migrating from Asia sometime during the middle Eocene. Like other lemur-like adapoids, *Mahgarita* exhibits relatively small eyes, a non-tubular ear canal, and relatively big canines. Some cranial features suggest that *Mahgarita* lived on a diet of leaves, which would have been plentiful in its dense rainforest environment (Wilson, 1966; Wilson and Szalay, 1976).

Although both *Rooneyia* and *Mahgarita* appear to have flourished in the tropical rainforests of Texas at the end of the Eocene, continually dropping temperatures eventually caused even these southernmost tropical rainforests to disappear. The disappearance of the Texas rain forests spelled the end for the North American prosimians. Following the Eocene extinction of the adapoids and omomyoids, North America would remain without primates for more than 30 million years, until the arrival of *Homo sapiens* between 10 to 20 thousand years ago.

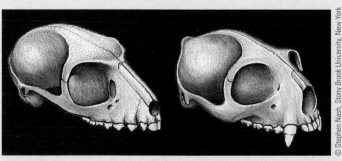

© Stephen Nash, Stony Brook University, New York

FIGURE 2

Artist's reconstruction of *Rooneyia* (right) and *Mahgarita* (left). Notice the difference in the size and shape of the incisors and canines, possibly denoting different feeding adaptations.

natural **endocast**. This type of fossil preservation occurs when the space left after the brain decays is filled with sediment, which then becomes solidified in the shape of the inside of the cranium. You can think of this as a kind of gelatin mold of the brain. It's a record of the brain's external features, which have impressed themselves upon the inside of the skull. Included in these details are the faint impressions of vessels and even the convolutions of the brain. These details have informed us about commonalities between the way that *Rooneyia* and modern tarsiers experience smells.

Another group of early primates (members of the eosimiid family), known from China and Burma, was at one time thought to be a front-runner for showing that the earliest anthropoid origins were in Asia. This group, however, encountered the same pitfalls that denied other candidates this coveted position. For one thing, the remains are fragmentary and show a mix of anthropoid and prosimian traits. Besides that, as we'll discuss next, their earliest known appearance at 47 mya already postdates anthropoid origins in northern Africa. At best, it seems that the eosimiids may represent an early Asian, dead-end anthropoid lineage, but it's more likely that they're instead another representative of a diverse Eocene radiation of tarsier-like primates.

EVOLUTION OF TRUE TARSIERS

For many years, "the 'living fossil' [had] no fossil record!" (Schwartz, 1984, p. 47). The situation has recently improved, but not by much. Fragmentary remains of fossil tarsiers are now known from the middle Eocene of Egypt and China, and the late Eocene of Thailand, demonstrating that modern tarsiers have retained essentially the same body plan that they had in the Eocene. Biomolecular evidence has shown that the five extant (currently existing) species of tarsiers diverged in the Miocene; and as you learned in Chapter 6, all living tarsiers are now limited in their distribution to islands of Southeast Asia.

Toward the end of the Eocene, there was a shift from tropical to drier and more seasonal climates. This change led to more diverse landscapes, opening many niches for the highly adaptable primates to exploit. This backdrop sets the stage for our next saga in primate origins—that of our own suborder, Anthropoidea. Of course, prosimian primates have continued to evolve since the Eocene, but we'll now focus on those primates most directly related to our own evolution as humans.

EOCENE AND OLIGOCENE EARLY ANTHROPOIDS

As you read this introduction to fossil forms, it's important to realize that when we're trying to interpret the past, things aren't as straightforward as they first seem. In addition to the debate about the earliest emergence of prosimians, and therefore the most primitive members of Primates, we're equally unsure about the origins of anthropoid primates—the ones that eventually led to our lineage as well as to apes and monkeys.

In recent years, new discoveries have led scientists to dispute an omomyoid or even an adapoid origin of anthropoids. Instead, recent molecular evidence indicates that anthropoid primates probably emerged *separately* from either of these two prosimian groups; and at 77 mya, they may have a time depth as ancient as either (Miller et al., 2005). Unfortunately, fossil anthropoid remains aren't known from that time, so the cradle of anthropoid origins remains hotly debated. Some paleoprimatologists suggest an Asian origin, while most support an African source.

As we've mentioned, the eosimiids were once thought to be a possible early anthropoid group, which would point to an Asian origin for Anthropoidea. But the earliest undisputed fossil anthropoid is dated to 50 mya, and it comes from the Middle Eocene of Algeria. This African specimen shows up 3 million years before the earliest eosimiids fossils in Asia, likely precluding Asia from being the cradle of anthropoid origins unless earlier finds emerge. Yet, this early African anthropoid is very small, and it's known only from a handful of teeth. So it's difficult to say much about it other than that its teeth are unmistakably "anthropoid" and foreshadow other early anthropoids from the late Eocene of Egypt.

The Fayum Depression in Egypt (see "A Closer Look" on p. 216), an arid region today, provides most of our early anthropoid record for the Eocene and Oligocene. Over the last five decades, paleoprimatologist Elwyn Simons and colleagues have excavated this rich area

endocast   A solid impression of the inside of the skull, often preserving details relating to the brain's size and surface features.

AT A GLANCE — Prosimian vs. Anthropoid Characteristics

General Prosimian Characteristics	General Anthropoid Characteristics
1. Smaller body size	1. Generally larger body size
2. Longer snouts with greater emphasis on smell	2. Shorter snouts with greater emphasis on vision
3. Eye sockets not completely enclosed in bone	3. Back of eye socket formed by bony plate
4. Dental comb	4. Less specialized dentition, as seen in absence of dental comb and some other features
5. Small simple premolars	5. Larger and more complex premolars
6. Primitive triangle-shaped molars	6. Derived square-shaped molars with new cusp
7. Grooming claw	7. Nails instead of claws on all digits
8. Artery running through the middle ear bone	8. Loss of the artery running through the middle ear bone
9. Unfused mandible	9. Fusion of the two sides of the mandible to form one bone
10. Unfused frontal bone	10. Fusion of the two sides of the frontal bone
11. Smaller brain size relative to body size	11. Larger brain (in absolute terms and relative to body weight)

See Appendix Fig. A-9a and A-9b for illustrations of these differences.

and found a remarkable array of fossil primates. One of the most recent discoveries, a new species of *Biretia*, is precisely dated to 37 mya and represents the most complete remains of an early African anthropoid. This small primate, weighing just under a pound, exhibits dental morphology typical of that expected for a basal (most primitive) anthropoid. Surprisingly, though, the structure of the upper molar tooth roots indicates that they had large orbits, implying that *Biretia* was nocturnal (Seiffert et al., 2005b). This is interesting because as discussed in Chapter 6 on p. 126, the general trend for Anthropoidea is toward a diurnal activity pattern. Simons has placed these fossils, based on their dental characters, into the extinct superfamily Parapithecoidea. This superfamily is significant as the root stock from which the later anthropoids evolved. Its Oligocene evolution (Seiffert et al., 2005b) is discussed in the next section. Somewhat younger (35 mya) Fayum primate genera are also known, including *Catopithecus* (Fig. 9-9), which clearly possessed anthropoid features (such as complete postorbital closure) and some derived catarrhine features (such as a 2.1.2.3 dental formula).

These Fayum discoveries help fill in the gap between later anthropoids and the middle Eocene anthropoids of Algeria. The earliest fossil anthropoids are known from Africa, and current molecular and biogeographic data agree that anthropoids had an African origin, much like the African origin of our own genus, *Homo* (Miller et al., 2005).

FIGURE 9-9

Three specimens of *Catopithecus*, the earliest anthropoid genus to preserve a skull. These elements give us our first view of early catarrhine cranial anatomy including fully enclosed orbits.

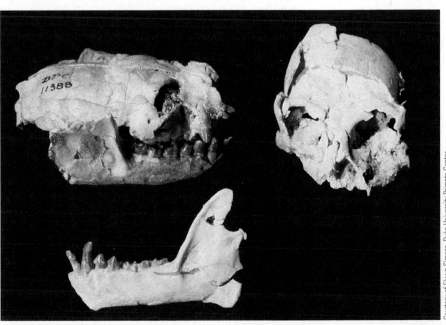

Oligocene Primates

The vast majority of Old World primate fossils of the Oligocene epoch (33–24 mya) come from just one region, the Fayum Depression in Egypt—the same area that has yielded abundant late Eocene remains. Altogether, well over 1,000 specimens have been retrieved from the Fayum, representing a paleontological record of what was once an extremely rich primate ecosystem.

A CLOSER LOOK   Primate Diversity in the Fayum

Today El-Fayuom, or the Fayum, is an Egyptian province about 40 miles southwest of Cairo. In the Eocene and Oligocene epochs (37–26 mya), it was a swampy forest playground for primates. Now all that's left of that primate Eden is chunks of petrified wood, flotsam adrift in the vast desert of the Sahara. The name, Fayum, probably comes from the ancient Egyptian word *Baym*, meaning "lake or sea" and referring to the area's proximity to a large lake near the Nile. Nowadays, though, the last thing anyone would associate with this arid region would be a body of water.

In 1906, the first primate ever discovered in Egypt was unearthed and later identified as *Apidium*. Many considered this discovery, hailed as a "dawn ape," to be the earliest relative of apes and monkeys. Though several primate fossils were discovered in the early 1900s, it wasn't until 1961 that the dogged persistence of Elwyn Simons led to the unearthing of the Fayum's true fossil primate abundance. Fifty years later, Simons still coaxes dry bones from the sand of the Fayum. Through the efforts of Simons and colleagues (Fig. 1), the Fayum primates are the best-studied fossils in the region, shaping much of our views regarding the diversification of prosimians, monkeys, and apes.

These fossils are often referred to as the "lower sequence primates" and "upper sequence primates" according to their placement in the stratigraphic section. From these Eocene (lower) and Oligocene (upper) sediments, over 17 genera are known, presenting us with a wide variety of dietary niches. What's most surprising, however, is that the prosimians and some anthropoids both exploit a frugivorous (fruit eating) lifestyle, challenging the idea that ecological changes might account for the emergence of the latter group (Kirk and Simons, 2000). So, for the time being, anthropoid origins remain as enigmatic as the sphinx. From this you can see that this region, well known for its pyramids and rich archaeological sites, has always been important in human history, even to our deepest roots.

FIGURE 1

Elwyn Simons and colleagues toil in the harsh heat of the Fayum in Egypt while collecting fossils of the earliest anthropoids. These fossils are so small that workers must excavate with their faces pressed close to the ground.

TRUE ANTHROPOIDS

The early primates of the Oligocene are generally placed into three families: the oligopithecids, parapithecids, and propliopithecids. Members of the oligopithecid family are among the earliest anthropoid primates, and they're known from key fossil discoveries from the late Eocene of the Fayum in Egypt. A slightly later primate from the early Oligocene (*Oligopithecus*) is estimated to have weighed approximately 3 pounds. Interestingly, its body size and dental proportions are similar to those seen in some contemporary small New World monkeys (marmosets and tamarins). Such general comparisons of these Oligocene primates to the New World (Fig. 9-10) provide support that the Fayum primate radiation is at the base of the entire New World anthropoid evolutionary group (that is, clade; see p. 99).

The most abundant of the Oligocene fossils from the Fayum are from the parapithecid family, and they belong to the genus *Apidium*. About the size of a squirrel, *Apidium* had several anthropoid-like features, but it also possessed some unusual dental features. *Apidium* fossils exhibit a dental formula of 2.1.3.3, indicating that *Apidium* probably appeared before the Old and New World anthropoids diverged. This makes it a candidate as an early ancestor of New World anthropoids (that is, platyrrhines). The teeth also suggest a diet composed of fruits and probably some seeds. Another interesting feature even suggests some-

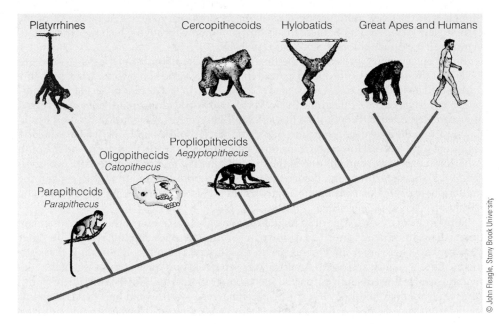

Platyrrhines   Cercopithecoids   Hylobatids   Great Apes and Humans

Propliopithecids
Aegyptopithecus

Oligopithecids
Catopithecus

Parapithecids
Parapithecus

FIGURE 9-10

Diagram of the phyletic relationships (clado-gram) of Fayum early anthropoids and living catarrhines (monkeys, apes, and humans) (Adapted from Fig. 13-18 in Fleagle, 1999, p. 418).

thing about this animal's social behavior; an unusually large degree of sexual dimorphism in canine size may indicate that *Apidium* lived in polygynous social groups of a single male and multiple females and offspring. Limb remains show that this creature was a small arboreal quadruped, adept at leaping and springing. We now know much more about the cranial anatomy of the parapithecids, due to the discovery of a complete skull of the genus, *Parapithecus* (Fig. 9-11), a close relative of *Apidium*.

The third major family, the propliopithecids, includes the most significant fossil genus from the Fayum, *Aegyptopithecus* (Fig. 9-12). This genus has been proposed as the ancestor of *both* later Old World monkeys and hominoids. *Aegyptopithecus* is known from several well-preserved crania, numerous jaw fragments, and a fair number of limb bones. The largest of the Fayum anthropoids, *Aegyptopithecus* was roughly the size of a modern howler monkey at 13 to 18 pounds. With a dental formula of 2.1.2.3, *Aegyptopithecus* shares the derived catarrhine (Old World anthropoid) dental formula. The skull was small and resembles a modern monkey skull in some details, while the brain size and morphology appear to have been somewhere between that of prosimians and that of anthropoids. Postcranial evidence reveals that *Aegyptopithecus* was likely a short-limbed, heavily muscled, slow-moving arboreal quadruped. So in most respects, *Aegyptopithecus* represents a primitive catarrhine; this makes it the best candidate from the Fayum to have given rise to Old World monkeys and hominoids.

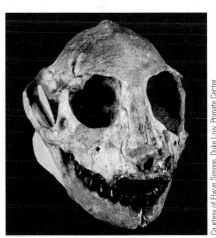

FIGURE 9-11

Parapithecus belongs to the group of Fayum anthropoids that are most closely related to the ancestry of New World monkeys.

EARLY PLATYRRHINES: NEW WORLD ANTHROPOIDS

The first primates found in the New World date to around 27 mya, about 10 million years *after* fossil evidence for the first anthropoids appears in the Fayum of Egypt. However, they probably evolved from ancestors similar to those seen within the Fayum primate radiation. The earliest platyrrhine or New World anthropoid fossils are found in the late Oligocene of Bolivia and have been placed into the genus *Branisella*. Members of this genus appear to have been small monkeys (about 2 pounds) with diets comprised primarily of fruit. The evolutionary relationships of these first fossil platyrrhines are still greatly debated. *Branisella* is thought to be so primitive that it's not placed into any living platyrrhine lineage; it may represent a remnant of the first platyrrhine radiation. Another member of this mysterious early radiation is picked up in the middle Miocene. A cranium of this creature, *Homunculus* (whose name means "miniature human"), was found in Argentina in 2004 embedded in volcanic ash dated to 16.5 mya (Fig. 9-13). *Branisella* and *Homunculus* both represent different side branches from the clade of living New World monkeys that includes the last common ancestor of extant platyrrhines and their extinct kin (Fig. 9-14). This doesn't mean,

FIGURE 9-12

Skull of *Aegyptopithecus*. This genus has been proposed as the ancestor of *both* Old World monkeys and hominoids.

FIGURE 9-13

Skull of *Homunculus,* a middle Miocene descendant of the earliest platyrrhine radiation.

FIGURE 9-14

Cladogram of extant groups of New World monkeys with fossils are plotted relative to their position regarding living groups. Note that only *Branisella* and *Homunculus* represent separate side branches. This shows the diversity of fossils within the New World, though this detail is not presented in the chapter (Adapted from Fig. 14.11 in Fleagle, 1999, p. 445).

though, that they have nothing to tell us about modern platyrrhines. As remnants of the earliest New World radiation, these fossils open a window through which we can begin to view the first primate colonizers of South America.

Based on the actual presence of the first platyrrhines in South America at 27 mya, it's likely that the very first anthropoids arrived in the New World somewhat earlier, probably during the late Eocene to early Oligocene (37 to 32 mya). In fact, recent molecular data indicate that the platyrrhine-catarrhine (New World–Old World anthropoid) lineages diverged approximately 35 mya (Schrago and Russo, 2003). This early transatlantic migration would have involved the crossing of some sort of oceanic barrier since South America was an island continent until 5 mya. How platyrrhines arrived in the New World in general, and in South America in particular, remains one of the most fascinating questions in primate evolution (Fig. 9-15). Several competing theories have been proposed in an attempt to explain the mysterious arrival of platyrrhines in South America: North American migration, Antarctic migration, and Atlantic "rafting."

Supporters of a North American migration route argue that one of the North American tarsier-like omomyoids journeyed down to South America, giving rise to the later platyrrhines. There are some problems with this theory. The most significant is that during the Eocene, North and South America were separated by a huge body of water, the currents of which flowed south to north. Such a migration from North America to South America would have been *against* strong ocean currents, so it would be a fantastic swimming feat for any primate. What's more, the complete absence of true anthropoid primates from the North American fossil record considerably weakens this argument.

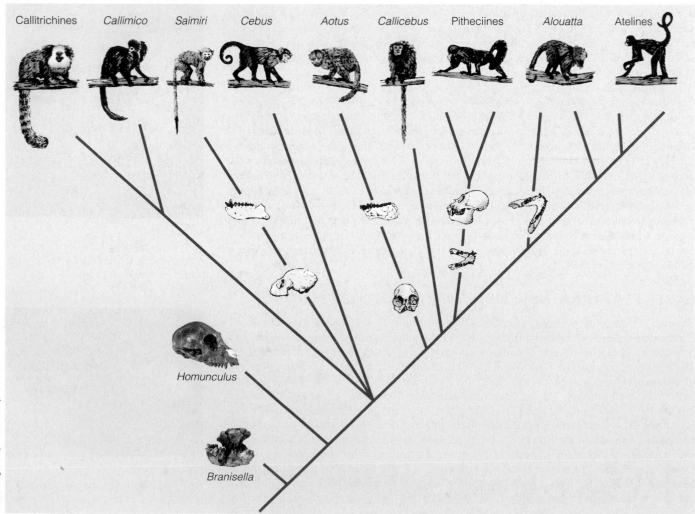

Callitrichines   *Callimico*   *Saimiri*   *Cebus*   *Aotus*   *Callicebus*   Pitheciines   *Alouatta*   Atelines

Homunculus

Branisella

Supporters of the alternative Antarctic migration route argue that early platyrrhines could have migrated to South America, first by crossing the water from Africa south to Antarctica and then by crossing a land bridge that linked Antarctica to South America. One weakness of this theory is that the distance of the ocean crossing between Africa and Antarctica at this time was nearly double (1,600 miles) the distance of a crossing between Africa and South America (870 miles; Houle, 1999). Another significant drawback to this theory is that not a single primate fossil has been recovered from the Antarctic continent, though it's not hard to understand why this has never been a popular excavation destination.

The most likely scenario for the arrival of platyrrhines to South America involves early platyrrhines floating across the Atlantic Ocean on rafts made of naturally formed mats of vegetation (see "A Closer Look" on p. 220). The rafting scenario is also supported by the fact that during the Eocene and Oligocene, South America and Africa were closer to each other than they are today. In addition, a great drop in Atlantic sea levels occurred during the middle Oligocene, just before the earliest platyrrhines appear in the fossil record of South America. This drop in sea level would have further decreased the distance between Africa and South America and may have exposed mid-Atlantic islands, allowing early platyrrhines to **island hop** their way to South America (Ciochon and Chiarelli, 1980a).

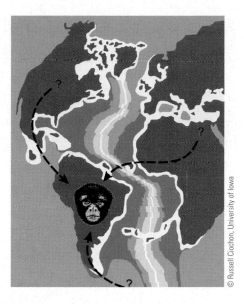

FIGURE **9-15**
Here are the continental relationships during the late Eocene. Several competing theories have been proposed in an attempt to explain the arrival of platyrrhines in South America: North American migration, Antarctic migration, and south Atlantic migration (by way of rafting or island hopping). The broken white line and surrounding shades of blue in the ocean represent seafloor spreading, which caused the continents to drift apart.

© Russell Ciochon, University of Iowa

AT A GLANCE	New World Monkey vs. Old World Monkey Characteristics	
General New World Monkey Characteristics	**General Old World Monkey Characteristics**
1. Sideways facing nostrils	1. Downward facing nostrils
2. Ring-like ear hole with no tube	2. Tube-like ear hole
3. Dental formula of 2.1.3.3	3. Dental formula of 2.1.2.3
4. Grasping tail	4. Ischial callosities
5. Distribution: Mexico and South America	5. Distribution: Africa, southern Asia and Japan
See Appendix Fig. A-10 for illustrations of these differences.	

Miocene Primates

Throughout the Miocene, we see diversification of the anthropoids into the groups we're familiar with today. The cercopithecoid monkeys and the hominoids compete for the dominant position on the primate landscape in the Old World, with the former finally emerging victorious. Today the number of ape groups is very limited compared to the diversity they enjoyed in the Miocene, while cercopithecoids remain relatively varied.

MONKEYING AROUND

Following the emergence of the Oligocene anthropoid *Aegyptopithecus* in the Fayum in Egypt, we have evidence of further diversification of later catarrhines—namely, the Old World monkeys and the hominoids. The cercopithecoids, as the Old World monkeys are

island hop To travel from one island to the next.

A CLOSER LOOK   Rafting and Primate Evolution

Despite the crazy images this statement might conjure in your head, rafting is actually a well-recognized method of animal migration for some vertebrates. In fact, there's documented evidence of such a natural raft carrying a crocodile 685 miles from Java to the Cocos Islands in 1930 (Ciochon and Chiarelli, 1980b). Admittedly, such instances of natural rafting are rare; but given the geologic span of time, even unlikely events (such as you winning the lottery or monkeys floating to South America) become likely. This idea is known as the sweepstakes model, and it was popularized by evolutionist G. G. Simpson (contributor to the Modern Synthesis, as discussed in Chapter 4).

As better information regarding the rare availability of land bridges or the implausibility of lost continents has been absorbed, scientists are relying more and more on sweepstakes models such as rafting to explain events that are essentially impossible to explain. Such is the case for the lemur population of Madagascar and the New World monkeys. In both circumstances, we have the relatively sudden appearance of primates in areas where no ancestor is present, and for which migration could only have been over a large body of water. Coincidentally, Africa is the apparent source of both the lemur and platyrrhine root stock.

The scenario goes as follows: A female primate and her mate live on the edge of a river. During one particularly nasty storm, their home is disconnected from the mainland, becoming a natural houseboat of sorts. The storm rages, and the entire raft is carried out to sea. Days later, the bedraggled primates wash ashore at their new home (Fig. 1). The rest is history. Or is it?

Recently, scientists reevaluated this sweepstakes model, exposing some serious flaws. To be a lucky ticket holder, the primates would have to actually survive the voyage, or the whole model is useless. In 1976, Simons calculated that it would take only 4–6 days for most small primates to succumb to the combined effects of lacking food and water as well as experiencing salt imbalance and exposure (Simons, 1976). The shortest distance today from the African mainland to Madagascar is 249 miles. Even with a stiff continuous wind, it would take 10 days to make the journey, so the migrant lemurs would be comatose days before. The first platyrrhines would've had to cross 870 miles—that's an intolerable amount of time for a thirsty primate.

Despite these shortcomings, rafting is still the best explanation that we have for these dispersals—short of

some even more obscure method of transportation. Combined with the probable existence of islands intermediate to Madagascar and the New World during the times of these voyages, it's quite possible that the primates were first washed upon one of these isles and only later rafted to their current residences. This would mean that they would not have to cross the entire span in one daunting voyage, but would instead engage in "island-hopping." In addition, Alain Houle (1998) has researched the idea of "floating islands" as a mode of distant dispersal of small- to medium-sized vertebrates. These vegetation rafts could have supported microhabitats that would have permitted small vertebrates, such as primates, to cross ocean barriers reaching far-distant islands. Additional random dispersals on vegetation rafts from these distant islands ultimately would have allowed primates to colonize the New World.

Incidentally, in 1947 a human rafting experiment, *Kon-Tiki*, was successfully undertaken to demonstrate the feasibility of a prehistoric balsa-wood vessel reaching Polynesia from South America. That raft, however, was not natural; the six crew members were able to provision for the 4,300-mile voyage, something our lemur and monkey cousins weren't able to do. Some earlier humans (presumably *H. erectus*) also must have found *some* way to cross open water, since we know they managed to get from one island (Java) in Indonesia to another (Flores) as long as 880 kya. This early, dangerous water crossing by *Homo erectus* led to the isolation and dwarfing of this species. It resulted in the evolution of the recently discovered little hominids, popularly referred to as "hobbits," who lived in splendid isolation on Flores until only 13 kya (see Chapter 14 for more details).

FIGURE 1

An artist's rendering of the south Atlantic populating scenario called rafting. The scene depicts a natural raft with primate passengers being swept into the sea. This raft might ultimately drift to the New World in one voyage but would more likely beach on a closer island. The latter scenario, called island-hopping, would allow primates to take their time in moving from one island to another before finally reaching South America.

© Russell Ciochon, University of Iowa/Drawing by Robert Greisen

known, fall into two families—one extinct (called the victoriapithecids) and the other being the living cercopithecids. The late Miocene was a highly successful time for the radiation of monkeys in the Old World. Their more immediate descendants from the Pliocene and the Pleistocene were much more varied in size, locomotion, and diet than their counterparts today.

The extinct family Victoriapithecidae represents the earliest members of the lineage leading to present-day Old World monkeys. The victoriapithecids were found throughout northern and eastern Africa as early as 19 mya, predating the split between the two extant *subfamilies* of Old World monkeys: the colobines (leaf-eating monkeys) and the cercopithecines (cheek-pouch monkeys), which occurred around 16 mya (Raaum et al., 2005). Since they're more primitive in many features than either colobines or cercopithecines, the victoriapithecids may represent the last common ancestors of all living Old World monkeys; but it's also possible that they represent an extinct **sister group**. The best known of the victoriapithecids is *Victoriapithecus* (Fig. 9-16), a small monkey whose cranium exhibits a mosaic of later colobine and cercopithecine features that place it close to the root of both subfamilies. The molars of *Victoriapithecus* exhibit bilophodonty, like all living Old World monkeys. The teeth of *Victoriapithecus* indicate a diet consisting of hard fruits and seeds, while postcranial skeletal features demonstrate similarities to living terrestrial monkeys (Benefit and McCrossin, 1997).

By 12 mya the victoriapithecids had been replaced by Old World forms that are still alive today, that is, cercopithecines (Old World monkeys that include baboons and macaques) and colobines (Old World monkeys that include the colobus and proboscis monkey). Fossils of the first true colobine are found in African deposits dating to approximately 9 mya. This form was smaller than most living forms, though at 8 to 9 pounds, it was no lightweight. The colobines quickly radiated into Europe and Asia following their first appearance in Africa. As we'll see, this was when Eurasian ape groups also began reentering Africa.

You may not know it, but you're probably already familiar with members of the Cercopithecinae, subfamily of the family Cercopithecidae. This subfamily includes monkeys such as today's macaques (for example, the rhesus monkeys used in labs) and baboons. Members of this group are often called the cheek-pouch monkeys, because of hamster-like pockets in their mouths that allow them to store food. In Asia, one of the most successful groups was the macaques (*Macaca*), which can also be found living in North Africa today. Although geographically widespread, most fossil macaques appear remarkably similar to each other and to living forms, indicating that primitive macaque morphology has been retained for more than 5 million years. This is bolstered by biomolecular evidence indicating that *Macaca* diverged from *Papio* (the modern baboon) about 10 mya (Raaum et al., 2005).

In East Africa, the baboon-like *Theropithecus* was the dominant cercopithecine genus of the Plio-Pleistocene (Fig. 9-17). Adaptations of the hands and teeth indicate that all species of *Theropithecus* exploited a dietary niche consisting almost exclusively of grasses—a unique diet among primates that feed on small objects. This group contains some notable fossil specimens, among them the largest monkey that ever lived (225 pounds). *Theropithecus* was an incredibly successful genus throughout much of the Pliocene and early Pleistocene; but sometime around the middle of the Pleistocene, most of its members went extinct, leaving a single remaining species—the gelada (*Theropithecus gelada*). While we don't completely understand exactly what caused these extinctions, many researchers hypothesize that competition with the closely related *Papio* baboons of today was a major factor. Today, the living gelada is confined to the high, wet grasslands of the Amhara plateau in Ethiopia, an ecological zone where no *Papio* baboons are found.

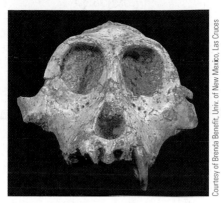

Courtesy of Brenda Benefit, Univ. of New Mexico, Las Cruces

FIGURE 9-16
Skull of *Victoriapithecus,* the first Old World monkey.

sister group Two lineages that diverged from a particular common ancestor. Since sister groups share a common ancestor, they are each other's closest relatives.

FIGURE 9-17
Skull of *Theropithecus brumpti,* the most bizarre fossil monkey (inset). An artist's rendering of *Theropithecus* on the landscape in the Omo Basin of Ethiopia about 3 mya.

© Russell Ciochon, University of Iowa

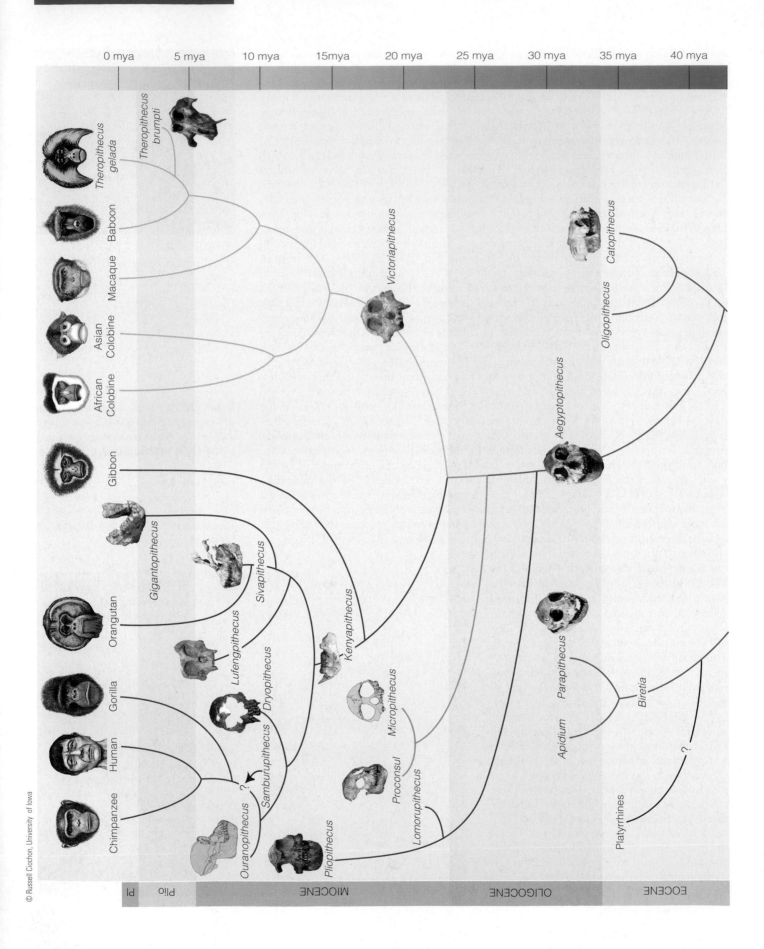

APING MONKEYS

By the end of the Oligocene, the world's major continents were located about where they are today. During the Miocene (23–5.3 mya), however, the drifting of South America and Australia away from Antarctica significantly altered ocean currents. At the same time, the South Asian plate continued to ram into Asia, producing the Himalayan plateau. Together, both of these major paleogeographical modifications significantly affected the climate, causing the early Miocene to be considerably warmer and wetter than the previous Oligocene. As a result, rain forests and dense woodlands became the dominant environments of Africa during the early Miocene. It was in this forested environment of Africa that the first apelike primates evolved.

Molecular evidence suggests that the evolutionary lineages leading to monkeys and apes diverged approximately 23 mya (Glazko and Nei, 2003; Fig. 9-18). Not surprisingly, the first apelike fossils share many anatomical characteristics with monkeys. In fact, in many of these early forms of the superfamily Proconsuloidea, the only apelike feature is the presence of the **Y-5 molar** pattern. As shown in Figure 9-19, the ape molars have 5 cusps separated by a "y" groove, as opposed to the monkey's typical 4 bilophodont cusps. Consequently, proconsuloids are commonly called **dental apes**, reflecting their apelike teeth but monkey-like postcranial skeleton.

Nearly all of the proconsuloid fossils come from East Africa, although some fossils have been recovered as far south and west as Namibia on the southern coast of Africa. The fossil record shows that these early apes were a highly diverse group, varying greatly in both size and in locomotor patterns. They ranged in size from that of a male orangutan (165–220 pounds) in *Proconsul* to the tiny *Micropithecus*, which probably weighed no more than 6–8 pounds, making it the smallest ape ever known to have lived (Fig. 9-20). The fossil record suggests a considerable diversity of locomotor patterns among the dental apes, including suspensory locomotion (swinging from their arms) as well as quadrupedalism either in trees or on the ground (Gebo et al., 1997; Fleagle, 1999).

The best known of the proconsuloids is *Proconsul*, who lived in Africa from 20 to 17 mya. It was long considered the first ape, but now that position has been challenged. This fruit-eating, apelike creature roamed a wide range of environments from rainforest to open woodlands. Though considered small-bodied, it actually ranged greatly in size from 10 to 150 pounds (Harrison, 2002). A typical dental ape, *Proconsul* exhibits a generalized cranium (Fig. 9-21) and an apelike Y-5 dental pattern, but postcranial remains show *Proconsul*'s limbs

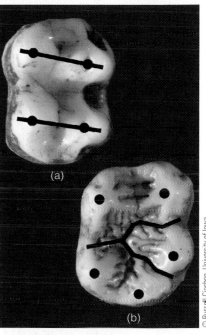

FIGURE 9-18 (OPPOSITE)

Family tree of early catarrhines and their relationships to modern Old World monkeys and apes. Red is for living apes and their immediate ancestors (Hominoidea); Green is for the Old World monkeys and their immediate ancestors (Cercopithecoidea); Orange is for dental apes (Proconsuloidea); Purple is for the primitive catarrhines (Pliopithecoidea); and Blue represents the Fayum early anthropoid radiation.

FIGURE 9-19

Comparison of bilophodont molars as found in cercopithecoids and Y-5 molars as seen in hominoids. (a) Notice that the 4 cusps are positioned in 2 parallel rows or lobes. (b) See how the 5 cusps are arranged so that a Y-shaped valley runs between them.

Y-5 molar Molars that have 5 cusps with grooves running between them, forming a Y shape. This is characteristic of hominoids.

dental ape An early ape that postcranially resembles a monkey, but dentally is hominoid (i.e., has a Y-5 molar configuration).

FIGURE 9-20

Diversity of early Miocene ape mandibles. The shapes and sizes of these mandibles and teeth illustrates the adaptive diversity of apes during this time. They ranged in size from that of a male orangutan through half the size of a modern gibbon and ate foods as varied as hard roots and soft fruit.

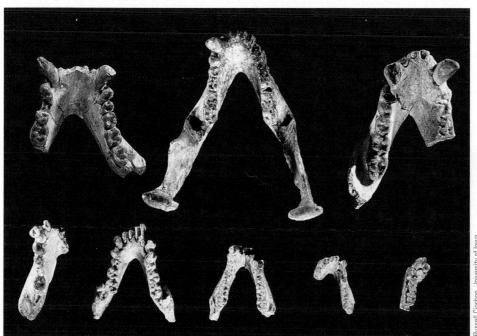

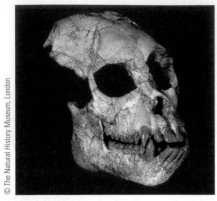

FIGURE 9-21

Skull of *Proconsul,* the best known of the early Miocene dental apes.

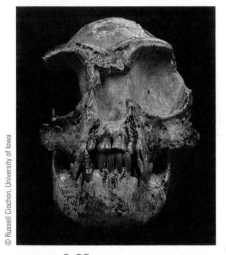

FIGURE 9-22

Pliopithecus, from the middle Miocene of Europe. The pliopithecoids were the first catarrhines to leave Africa. Since this skull is of a female, no sagittal crest is present, though strong temporal lines indicate that this individual enjoyed a diet of hard plant items.

and long torso retained adaptations for quadrupedal locomotion similar to that of monkeys. Curiously enough, some scientists believe that *Proconsul* might not have had a tail, which could indicate that this particular hominoid characteristic had a relatively ancient origin (Begun, 2003; Nakatsukasa et al., 2004; Ward, 2005). However, the proconsuloids' position as a mere dental ape has caused many researchers to place them outside of Hominoidea (in Proconsuloidea), just prior to the divergence of hominoids and cercopithecoids. This would mean not only that *Proconsul's* lack of tail was due to convergence but also that the time depth of taillessness within Hominoidea, itself, is still unknown.

Members of the superfamily Pliopithecoidea, like the proconsuloids, also date to the early Miocene of Africa, though they're more primitive than all other catarrhines. Most evidence indicates that the pliopithecoids were an early, small-bodied offshoot of the ape family tree; but in their time they appear to have been a highly successful group, undergoing a rapid adaptive radiation in the Miocene.

Toward the end of the early Miocene, around 19 mya, the Arabian plate moved into its current location, forming a land bridge between Africa and Eurasia. Major animal migrations could then take place between the two previously separated landmasses. It's thought that African pliopithecoids were among the first transcontinental migrants and, importantly, represent the first anthropoids to colonize both Asia *and* Europe. Researchers thus commonly agree that the pliopithecoids were the first catarrhines to leave Africa. Until recently, however, this migration was only *assumed,* since pliopithecoid fossil remains were known only from Eurasia. However, a newly discovered pliopithecoid, *Lomorupithecus,* has proven to be the earliest member of this group; dating to the early Miocene (nearly 20 mya), it's from Uganda in Africa, as predicted (Rossie and MacLatchy, 2006). This find provides the proof that pliopithecoids had their roots in Africa, bringing this idea from the realm of conjecture into reality.

Dating to the middle Miocene, *Pliopithecus* is the best-known pliopithecoid from Europe. Robust features of the mandible and the presence of a **sagittal crest** on the cranium indicate that *Pliopithecus* probably ate a diet consisting of relatively tough foods, most likely leaves (Fig. 9-22). Postcranially, it appears that *Pliopithecus* possessed some features for suspensory locomotion (arm hanging) similar to that of some large platyrrhines, although it clearly lacked the grasping prehensile tail of New World monkeys. There are some indications that *Pliopithecus* may have possessed a short tail (decidedly *un-*apelike), but this feature is still greatly debated (Ankel, 1965).

Despite the intensity of their radiation early on, it appears that later, during the Pliocene, the success of the pliopithecoids ended. All forms went extinct with no living descendants.

HOMINOIDS, THE TRUE APES

The first true apes, those belonging to the superfamily Hominoidea, appear in Africa during the middle Miocene, approximately 16 mya. Probably the best known of these early African hominoids is *Kenyapithecus*. Anatomical evidence indicates that *Kenyapithecus* was a large-bodied terrestrial quadruped, possibly the first to adapt to life on the ground, with specialized adaptations in the humerus, wrist, and hands (McCrossin et al., 1998). In par-

AT A GLANCE   Old World Monkey vs. Ape Characteristics

General Old World Monkey Characteristics	General Ape Characteristics
1. Narrow nose and palate	1. Broad nose and palate
2. Smaller brain (in absolute terms and relative to body weight)	2. Even larger brain (in absolute terms and relative to body weight)
3. Bilophodont molars	3. Y-5 molars
4. Smaller average body size	4. Larger average body size
5. Longer torso	5. Shorter torso
6. Shorter arms	6. Longer arms
7. Tail	7. No tail

See Appendix Fig. A-11 for illustrations of these differences.

ticular, the hand bones indicate that *Kenyapithecus* may have employed a form of locomotion similar to the knuckle-walking typical of living gorillas and chimpanzees. The jaw and dentition of *Kenyapithecus* also exhibit greater similarities to extant great apes than to earlier Miocene forms such as *Proconsul*.

Soon after the pliopithecoids became the first anthropoids to leave Africa, the hominoids also began to migrate out of Africa. Like the pliopithecoids, the hominoids rapidly colonized the Old World and quickly experienced two highly successful adaptive radiations in Europe and in Asia.

European Radiation Europe was likely the first stop on the hominoid radiation outside of Africa at around 16 mya; the colonization of Asia actually occurred later, at around 15 mya (Heizmann and Begun, 2001). Although this radiation was widespread geographically, so far we've found only scant evidence of it from scattered localities in France, Spain, Italy, Greece, Austria, Germany, and Hungary.

The best-known middle Miocene hominoid from Europe is *Dryopithecus*, from southern France and northern Spain (Fig. 9-23). *Dryopithecus* resembles modern hominoids in many cranial and postcranial features, including long arms, large hands, and long fingers—all signifying an ability to brachiate, or swing through the trees. The teeth of *Dryopithecus* imply an unusual diet of both fruit and leaves (Begun, 1994). The combination of skeletal and dental remains suggests that *Dryopithecus* was a highly arboreal species, rarely descending from its high-canopy forested habitat.

One late Miocene European fossil hominoid is *Ouranopithecus*, unique in that the first fossils were discovered in Greece during World War I when Allied soldiers dug trenches to protect themselves from enemy troops. The abundance of the fossils found within these trenches led Camille Arambourg, a French commander (and paleontologist), to order his machine-gun-toting soldiers to unearth fossils until they were redeployed elsewhere (de Bonis and Koufos, 1994).

The result of these amateur and, later, professional excavations was an abundance of *Ouranopithecus* fossils that appear to have been deposited when a flood drowned a large local population. The face of *Ouranopithecus* shares many features with living African great apes, including large browridges and a wide distance between the eye orbits (Fig. 9-24). Some of these traits are even like some early fossil hominids. *Ouranopithecus'* powerful jaws, with small canines and extremely thick molar enamel, led some researchers to postulate that these hominoids subsisted on a diet consisting of relatively hard foods such as nuts (Ungar and Kay, 1995). The variation in both body and canine size indicates a range of sexual size dimorphism comparable to that of the modern gorilla, which they resemble in size.

Asian Radiation The hominoids of the middle and late Miocene of Asia represent one of the most varied Miocene fossil ape assemblages. These Asian fossil apes are geographically dispersed from Turkey in the west to China in the east.

Sivapithecus dates to the middle and late Miocene and has been recovered from southern Asia, in the Siwalik Hills of India and Pakistan. Over the last 30 years, paleoanthropologists led by David Pilbeam have recovered numerous specimens from the Potwar Plateau of Pakistan. Included in this large collection are a multitude of mandibles, many postcranial remains, and a partial cranium including most of the face. *Sivapithecus* was a large hominoid, ranging from 70 to 150 pounds, and probably inhabited a mostly arboreal niche. The most characteristic anatomical aspects of *Sivapithecus* are seen in the face, which exhibits a concave profile (dished face), broad **zygomatics** (cheekbones), and procumbent (projecting) maxilla and incisors, remarkably resembling that of the modern orangutan (Pilbeam, 1982; Fig. 9-25). It's important to note that the body of *Sivapithecus* is distinctively *unlike* living orangutans or any other known hominoid, for that matter. For example, the forelimb exhibits a unique mixture of traits, probably indicating some mode of arboreal quadrupedalism with no ability for brachiation (Pilbeam et al., 1990).

One of *Sivapithecus'* descendants from the late Miocene through Pleistocene, *Gigantopithecus* ("Giganto"), was discovered in a rather unconventional way. For thousands of years, Chinese pharmacists have used fossils as ingredients in potions intended to cure ailments ranging from backache to sexual impotence. In 1935, German paleoanthropologist Ralph von Koenigswald came across a large fossil primate molar in a Hong Kong apothecary

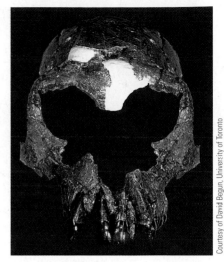

FIGURE 9-23
Skull of *Dryopithecus*, the earliest European ape. The left side is reconstructed as a mirror image of the complete right side.

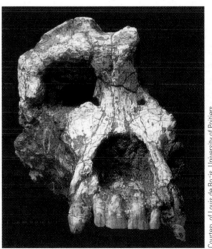

FIGURE 9-24
Ouranopithecus, possible ancestor of the African apes. Notice that the face shares many features with living African great apes, including large browridges and a wide distance between the eye orbits.

sagittal crest A ridge of bone that runs down the middle of the cranium like a short Mohawk. This serves as the attachment for the large temporal muscles, indicating strong chewing.

zygomatic Cheekbone.

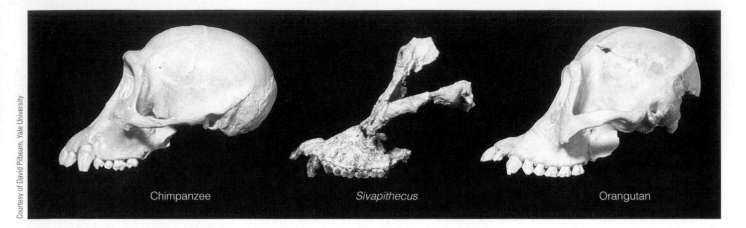

Courtesy of David Pilbeam, Yale University

Chimpanzee   *Sivapithecus*   Orangutan

FIGURE 9-25
Comparison of a modern chimpanzee (left), *Sivapithecus* (middle), and a modern orangutan (right). Notice that both *Sivapithecus* and the orangutan exhibit a dished face, broad cheekbones, and projecting maxilla and incisors.

FIGURE 9-26
An artist's rendering of *Gigantopithecus* enjoying a meal of the tasty, but tough, tropical fruit known as durian.

© Russell Ciochon, University of Iowa, drawing by Stephen Nash

shop. He named the fossil tooth *Gigantopithecus*, meaning "gigantic ape," and the species *blacki*, in honor of his late friend and colleague Davidson Black (the discoverer of "Peking Man"). Subsequent researchers were able to source the teeth to China's southernmost Guangxi Province, a karstic (eroded limestone) region of great rock towers riddled with caves.

While 4 lower jaws and 1,500 isolated teeth of the extinct ape have been found, no other bones have turned up. Based only on the jaws and teeth, however, researchers can attempt to reconstruct both the animal and its way of life. Estimates based on these massive mandibles indicate that the Chinese species of Giganto likely weighed more than 900 pounds and was possibly 10 feet tall when standing erect on its hind legs. This makes *Gigantopithecus* the largest primate that ever lived. With its size and ape affiliation, we can infer that it was probably a ground-dwelling, fist-walking creature.

The small incisors and canines, as well as very thick enamel on the cheek teeth—combined with the massive, robust jaws—lead to the inevitable conclusion that the animal was adapted to the consumption of tough, fibrous foods by cutting, crushing, and grinding them. Some researchers have argued that Giganto's huge mandible and dentition were an adaptation for a diet consisting primarily of bamboo, much like that of the giant panda. More current research has supported this claim asn also concludes that their diet may have included the durian, a tropical fruit with a tough outer skin (Ciochon et al., 1990a; Fig. 9-26).

One intriguing question is what contact our remote ancestor, *Homo erectus*, may have had with the giant ape; there's direct evidence indicating that the two coexisted in Vietnam and China (Fig. 9-27). Following the remake of *King Kong* and the History Channel special, *Giganto: The Real King Kong*, there have been reports from U.S. war veterans who say that they came face to face with huge, hairy apes in the Southeast Asian jungle when they were posted in Vietnam. These contemporary reports are likely fanciful; still, we can contemplate the time when our remote ancestors did encounter the giant of all apes in the tropical rainforests of Southeast Asia (Fig. 9-28). Sadly, sometime near the end of the middle Pleistocene, around 200 thousand years ago (kya), Giganto went extinct. The animal had flourished for more than 8.5 million years (see "A Closer Look" on p. 228), but human predation and/or environmental change may have proven too much for the vegetarian giant.

FIGURE 9-27

Comparison of the mandibles and teeth of *Gigantopithecus* and *Homo sapiens*. Notice that Giganto's jaw is almost three times the size of the human's, as are the teeth.

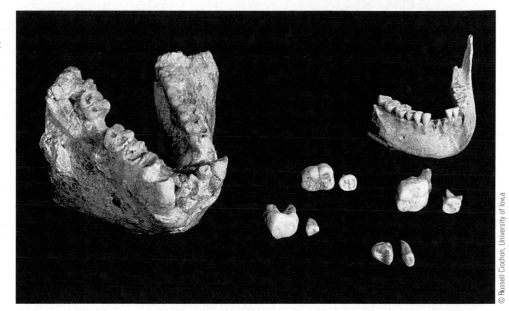

FIGURE 9-28

Homo erectus (left) observing a Giganto family group. The artist has accurately reconstructed the habitat of Pleistocene southern China, including the plants and animals.

A CLOSER LOOK   Discovery of the Other *Gigantopithecus*

As discussed in this chapter, we can consider *Gigantopithecus* as the fifth great ape and very possibly the only great ape to go extinct in the Pleistocene around 200 mya. But did you know that *Gigantopithecus* is the only great ape to have a lineage extending back to the Miocene (8.5 mya)? Evidence shows that this great ape increased in size as the genus evolved, which follows a trend seen in other large Pleistocene mammals such as the mammoth. The discovery of India's *Gigantopithecus giganteus*, which was found near the northern Indian city of Bilaspur in Himachael Pradesh Province in 1968, is a striking corroboration of this hypothesis. On the fateful day of March 17, 1968, a peasant named Sunkha Ram (Fig. 1) dug up a piece of a Giganto jaw from the base of his mud fence, where he had buried it 24 years before, and sold it to Grant Meyer, a member of Elwyn Simons' Yale University India Primate Expedition. How the jaw of *Gigantopithecus giganteus* came to be buried in this peasant's mud fence is a tale straight out of pulp fiction.

In 1944, when Sunkha Ram was a boy of 12, he often helped his father tend the fields of *gram*, a pealike vegetable that's cultivated throughout northern India. One day, while wandering through the fields right after the *gram* had been harvested, the boy found among the rubble three pieces of a huge jawbone. He took them home and asked his father what they might be. His father replied, "The bones of devils." The boy asked his father what he should do with them, and his father told him to keep them, because "they might come in handy some day." So the child took the jawbone fragments back to the field where he had found them, and he buried them carefully at the base of his father's mud-rock fence.

More than two decades later, when Sunkha Ram was 36, he heard about the Yale paleoanthropological expedition and Simons' search for fossils. On that March morning, he slipped one of the jawbone fragments into his pocket and went to his road crew job in the valley of Haritalyangar. Later in the day, he found paleoanthropologist Grant Meyer and showed him the specimen (Fig. 2). Meyer immediately gave him some rupees for his "devil bone." In the evening, Meyer and other expedition members eagerly visited Sunkha Ram at his home in the village of Domera. After much discussion and persuasion, they convinced him to sell them the other two pieces of the mandible, and finally the jaw was restored to its original, complete form. They asked Sunkha Ram to lead them to the spot where the mandible had been found and conducted extensive excavations in the *gram* field for a period of 6 weeks, but found no more evidence of Giganto (Ciochon et al., 1990b, pp. 100–101).

There's even an interesting twist in the naming of this remarkable fossil. In 1968 Elwyn Simons and his colleague, S. R. K. Chopra, named the fossil *Gigantopithecus* "*bilaspurensis*" ("giant ape of Bilaspur"). They were pleased with this name, but later had to change it to *Gigantopithecus giganteus* since the species had actually been named in 1915 by paleontologist Guy Pilgrim from the Geological Survey of India in Calcutta. Pilgrim had found a single, oversized, lower second molar tooth near the village of Alipur in northern India in 1915. He named it *Dryopithecus giganteus*. Subsequent researchers compared this single tooth, now in the Calcutta Museum, with the second molar of the complete jaw discovered by Simons' team and found them to be identical. Since the jaw clearly belonged to the genus *Gigantopithecus*, the priority for naming the species was given to Pilgrim's species name of *giganteus*, proposed in 1915, instead of the later "*bilaspurensis*." This meant Guy Pilgrim was actually the first paleontologist to discover the giant ape, but he was never aware of it. *Gigantopithecus giganteus* was about half the size of the later *Gigantopithecus blacki*. It had all of the characteristic giant ape features (including a deep and robustly thick jaw), though the two species are separated by about 6 million years in time. *Gigantopithecus giganteus* was found in sediments that date to the end of the Miocene epoch, about 8.5 mya. Clearly, the Indian species was adapted to a different environment and probably had a different diet, yet it was unmistakably *Gigantopithecus* (Miller et al., 2007).

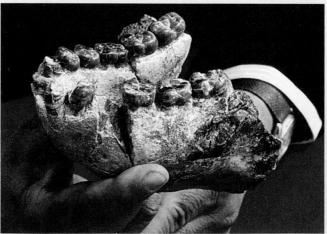

FIGURE 1

Sunkha Ram in 1982, the man who discovered the *Gigantopithecus giganteus* jaw as a 12-year-old boy in India.

FIGURE 2

The mandible of *Gigantopithecus giganteus* from northern India.

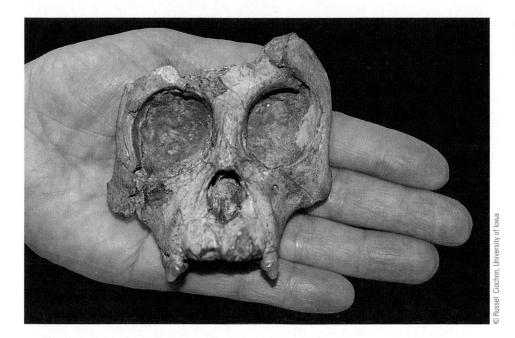

FIGURE 9-29
Skull of a *Lufengpithecus* juvenile from the late Miocene of Yunnan Province, China.

A final ape from Asia, *Lufengpithecus*, may represent a relic species: a previously unidentified sixth great ape. Fossils of *Lufengpithecus* have been recovered from four localities in Yunnan Province, southern China, and date to the late Miocene/early Pliocene (10–5 mya). This medium-sized ape, with an estimated adult body weight of about 110 pounds, is known from several skulls and thousands of isolated teeth (Fig. 9-29). Based on features of the midface and the tall, slender incisors, some researchers have argued that *Lufengpithecus* is related to European *Dryopithecus*, while others think it may be a distant relative of *Sivapithecus*.

If not for its advantageous location in southern China, *Lufengpithecus* would just be another of the many apes that faced extinction at the end of the Miocene. This ape is found within a protected area created by the uplift of the Tibetan Plateau—the result of Himalayan mountain building (Harrison et al., 2002). Within this refuge, a sort of "lost world," *Lufengpithecus* survived until at least 5 mya—or at least, that's what conventional wisdom leads us to believe. In recent years, however, Pleistocene cave sites in southern China that have long yielded teeth belonging to *Gigantopithecus* have now also produced teeth identified as those of a previously unknown, chimpanzee-sized ape. The teeth are too small to be those of either Giganto or the orangutan, *Pongo*. Could these mystery ape teeth be a descendant of *Lufengpithecus*? If this proves true, it would demonstrate the existence of three distinct great ape lineages in Asia: the massive *Gigantopithecus*, the large-bodied *Pongo*, and the chimpanzee-sized *Lufengpithecus* descendant. As you've seen in Chapter 6, though, this Asian hominoid diversity has dwindled, just as it has in Africa and elsewhere in the world.

EVOLUTION OF EXTANT HOMINOIDS

Hylobatids: The Lesser Apes
Biomolecular evidence indicates that the gibbon-great ape split occurred approximately 15–18 mya, placing this divergence around the time the first migration into Eurasia from Africa became geographically possible (Pilbeam, 1996; Raaum et al., 2005). The molecular evidence also shows that the radiation of the current hylobatids (lesser apes such as gibbons) occurred only 10.5 mya, although the scant fossil record of gibbons leaves us little anatomical evidence to reconstruct the ensuing diversification (Chatterjee, 2006). Various researchers have pointed out that some pliopithecoids exhibit gibbon-like features in the shape of the face and thus might represent gibbon ancestors. But pliopithecoids and Oligocene catarrhines actually share numerous primitive features, including the lack of a tubelike middle ear, the presence of a small tail, and an elbow

joint that's strikingly similar to those of various Fayum primates. These features, as well as their monkey-like limb proportions, clearly remove pliopithecoids from consideration as the ancestors of modern gibbons. From molecular evidence, however, we can glean that the gibbon radiation began 10.5 mya in the northern part of Southeast Asia before moving southward to Malaysia and Sumatra. Once in Sumatra, gibbons differentiated into two taxa, including the modern *Hylobates,* which eventually made its way into Borneo and Java around 3–5 mya (Chatterjee, 2006). Unfortunately, this molecular evidence has no anatomical counterpart, so the fossil record of the gibbons remains somewhat of a mystery.

Pongids: The Great Apes As with the gibbons, there's little conclusive evidence linking fossil hominoids to the nonhuman hominoids living in Africa today—gorillas, chimpanzees, and bonobos. Strangely, after beginning their migration into Asia and Europe, hominoids disappear from the African fossil record around 13 mya and reappear during the late Miocene around 9.5 mya. This gap in the hominoid fossil record has led some researchers to conclude that the reappearance of hominoids in Africa during the late Miocene was the result of Eurasian hominoids migrating back into Africa at the same time the colobine monkeys were leaving.

One candidate for African ape/human ancestor is *Ouranopithecus,* the large-bodied hominoid from Greece. Based primarily on the facial similarities discussed earlier, *Ouranopithecus* is often argued as a possible ancestor to the extant African apes. This makes an ape that's similar to *Ouranopithecus* a kind of prodigal son who returned to Africa from a long stay (and evolution) in Europe. This pongid line would later diverge in the late Miocene, producing our own family, Hominidae (see Chapter 11). It's possible that the late Miocene *Samburupithecus,* since it is found *in* Africa, may represent the actual root stock that led to both humans and the African apes after the hominoid return from Europe. Represented only by a maxillary fragment and a few teeth, its dentition shows clear similarities to that of the living African great apes, especially gorillas, though its evolutionary relationships are still debated (Pickford and Ishida, 1998; Sawada et al., 1998). In 2005, researchers discovered several teeth of a fossil chimpanzee at a site near Lake Baringo in Kenya. This discovery adds some fossil time depth to at least the *Pan* lineage. These fossil chimpanzee teeth date to approximately 500 kya and represent the first and only fossils belonging to the genus *Pan* (these are rare because tropical forest environments aren't conducive to preserving organic remains). Although currently not placed in a particular chimpanzee species, the fossil teeth exhibit greater similarities to the comman chimpanzee (*P. troglodytes*) than to bonobos (*P. paniscus*) (McBrearty and Jablonski, 2005).

Of all the living hominoids, the orangutan's ancestry is probably the best understood. It's generally accepted that *Sivapithecus* gave rise to both *Gigantopithecus* (sometime before 9 mya) as well as to orangutans (*Pongo*) sometime in the Miocene. Since the earliest *Sivapithecus* fossils date to more than 12 mya, it's clear that the branching event separating orangutans and the lineage leading to the African great apes and humans must have occurred before then. In fact, biomolecular evidence indicates that this divergence took place approximately 14 mya (Raaum et al., 2005). The relationship between *Sivapithecus* and *Pongo* is based primarily on cranial similarities, and there's still some debate about the evolutionary proximity of *Sivapithecus* to *Pongo* due to vastly differing postcranial anatomies. Most researchers now agree, however, that the postcrania could have evolved convergently with that seen in African apes. Several other Asian hominoids have been suggested as more recent orangutan ancestors, but there's little evidence to support these assertions.

AT A GLANCE

Biomolecular Family Tree

Molecular anthropology is the branch of anthropology that systematically studies primate taxa using comparative genomics. It can follow several lines of biological evidence, including proteins, amino acids, chromosomes, and genes.

A *biomolecular phylogeny* is a family tree that shows the degree of relatedness among taxonomic groupings based on a gene or protein. Since evolution involves genetic change, these changes can be studied through comparative genomics. This tree is compiled from the research of Raaum et al. (2005), Sterner et al. (2006), Schrago and Russo (2003), and Glazko and Nei (2003).

Scientists now believe that most evolutionary changes in proteins are nonadaptive, meaning they are exempt from natural selection. Their changes are thus neutral results of genetic drift. Since we know that genetic drift is a statistical process, one with a near-constant rate of change over a long period of time, the number of genetic differences between two species is a measure of how long they've been separated from one another. Each protein has its own rate of mutation (for instance, histones change very slowly; globins, like hemoglobin, change more

quickly). In the same way, so-called junk DNA (noncoding DNA) can actually inform us about mutational distances since it's also not subject to natural selection.

The statistical rate of change is measured using a *molecular clock*. This is a theoretical clock that assumes the amount of difference between two samples is proportional to the amount of time elapsed since their last common ancestor existed. Researchers can use this time to estimate the date when two species diverged, where more differences means more time has elapsed.

It's important to point out that since biomolecular clocks, and thus biomolecular phylogenies, are based on statistical inference and not on direct evidence, they can only support but never prove a hypothesis. So, we must use the fossil record to test these hypotheses and to calibrate the clock accordingly.

FIGURE 1

Biomolecular primate family tree based on the work of various researchers (see text).

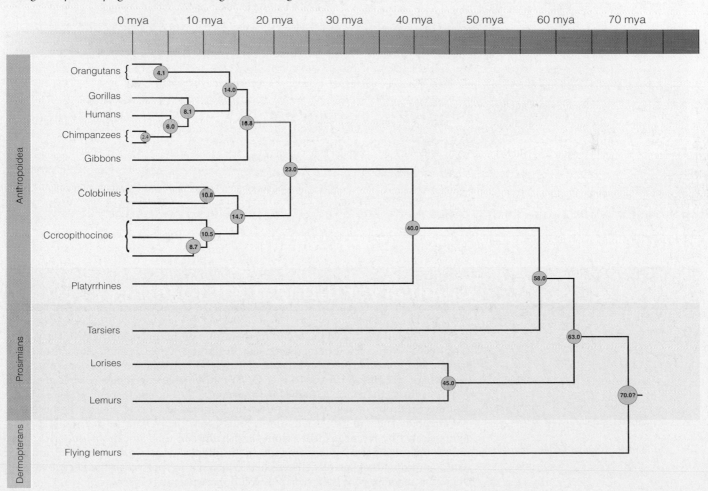

VISUAL SUMMARY

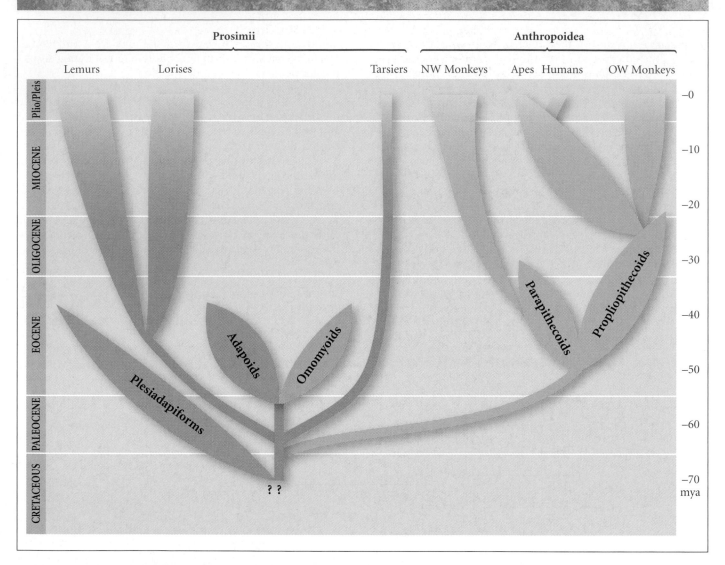

Prosimii

Anthropoidea

Lemurs   Lorises   Tarsiers   NW Monkeys   Apes   Humans   OW Monkeys

Plio/Pleis
MIOCENE
OLIGOCENE
EOCENE
PALEOCENE
CRETACEOUS

−0
−10
−20
−30
−40
−50
−60
−70
mya

Plesiadapiforms
Adapoids
Omomyoids
Parapithecoids
Propliopithecoids

? ?

Summary: Putting It All Together

In this chapter, we've traced the evolutionary history of our primate origins from as early as 65 mya down to a few thousand years ago. Beginning in the late Cretaceous, the earliest primate ancestors were probably little more than arboreally adapted insectivores much like the modern tree shrews. In the Paleocene, no indisputable euprimates are yet apparent, despite claims to the contrary. In the following epoch, the Eocene, we begin to see an abundant diversification of primates that are readily identifiable. During this epoch, the lemur-like adapoids and the tarsier-like omomyoids begin their evolutionary radiations. As demonstrated by recent evidence from the Fayum and other locations in Africa, early anthropoid origins also date to sometime in the middle Eocene. In addition, Old and New World anthropoids apparently shared their last common ancestry in the Eocene or early Oligocene and have gone their separate evolutionary pathways ever since.

In the Old World, the Oligocene reveals numerous possible early anthropoid ancestors, again at the Fayum. By and large, they're all primitive Old World anthropoids, and none of the modern lineages (Old World monkeys, gibbons, large-bodied hominoids) can definitely be traced into the Oligocene. The Miocene reveals the first Old World monkeys and a highly complex array of hominoid forms, many of large-bodied varieties. More than 30 different genera and probably dozens of species are represented in those remains discovered in Africa, Asia, and Europe. Some early forms from Kenya and Uganda (the proconsuloids) are more primitive than all of the hominoids from Eurasia. Though there's little firm evidence tying these fossil forms to living apes or to humans, good cladistic evidence suggests that *Sivapithecus* is closely related to the ancestors of the orangutan. Where, then, are the ancestors of the African apes—or, even more relevant, of ourselves? In the next part of your text, we'll seek to answer this question.

Critical Thinking Questions

1. Why is it difficult to distinguish the earliest members of the primate order from other placental mammals? If you found a nearly complete skeleton of an early Paleocene mammal, what structural traits might lead you to determine that it was a primate?

2. Compare and contrast the adapoids and omomyoids with living members of the primate order. Why do we call them lemur- or tarsier-like and not lemurs and tarsiers?

3. What are some of the ways in which monkeys are thought to have colonized the New World? How likely do you find each of the explanations, and why?

4. Where is the Fayum Depression, and why is it significant in primate evolution? Are there any other sites where so many fossil primates have been found? Why or why not?

5. What is meant by "dental apes" compared to true hominoids? If you were given a jaw to study of a supposed dental ape, what particular features would you look for first?

6. Compare *Gigantopithecus* in Asia with the modern gorilla in Africa. How do their dietary niches differ?

CHAPTER 10

Paleoanthropology: Reconstructing Early Hominid Behavior and Ecology

KEY QUESTIONS

What are the central aspects of paleoanthropology?

Why, from a biocultural perspective, do we want to learn about both the behavior and the anatomy of ancient hominids?

Introduction

A portion of a pig's tusk, a small sample of volcanic sediment, a battered rock, a primate's molar: What do these seemingly unremarkable remains have in common, and more to the point, why are they of interest to paleoanthropologists? First of all, if they're all discovered at certain sites in Africa or Eurasia, they *may* be quite ancient—indeed, perhaps millions of years old. Further, some of these materials actually inform scientists directly of quite precise dating of the finds—in this case, 2.2 million years old. Last, and most exciting, some of these finds may have been modified, used, and discarded by bipedal creatures who looked and behaved in some ways like ourselves (but were, in other respects, very different). And what of that molar? Is it a fossilized remnant of an ancient hominid? These are the kinds of questions asked by paleoanthropologists, and to answer them, these researchers travel to remote locales across the Old World.

How do we identify possible hominids from other types of animals (and importantly, from other primates), especially when all we have are fragmentary fossil remains from just a small portion of a skeleton? How do humans and our most distant ancestors compare with other animals? In the last four chapters, we've seen how humans are classified as primates, both structurally and behaviorally, and how our evolutionary history coincides with that of other mammals and, specifically, other primates. Even so, we're a unique kind of primate, and our ancestors have been adapted to a particular lifestyle for several million years. Some primitive hominoid probably began this process close to 7 million years ago (mya), though better-preserved fossil discoveries reveal more definitive evidence of hominids shortly after 5 mya.

We're able to determine the hominid nature of these remains by more than the structure of teeth and bones; we know that these animals are hominids also because of the way they behaved—emphasizing once again the *biocultural* nature of human evolution. In this chapter, we'll discuss the methods scientists use to explore the secrets of early hominid behavior and ecology, and we'll demonstrate these methods through the example of the best-known early hominid site in the world: Olduvai Gorge, in East Africa.

 Click!

Go to the following media for interactives and exercises on topics covered in this chapter:

- Online Virtual Laboratories for Physical Anthropology, Fourth Edition
- Hominid Fossils CD-ROM: An Interactive Atlas

Definition of Hominid

The earliest evidence of hominids that has been found dates to the end of the Miocene and mainly includes dental and cranial pieces. But dental features alone don't describe the special features of hominids, and they certainly aren't distinctive of the later stages of human evolution. Modern humans, as well as our most immediate hominid ancestors, are distinguished from the great apes by more obvious features than tooth and jaw dimensions. For example, various scientists have pointed to such distinctive hominid characteristics as bipedal locomotion, large brain size, and toolmaking behavior as being significant (at some stage) in defining what makes a hominid a hominid.

It's important to recognize that not all these characteristics developed simultaneously or at the same pace. In fact, over the last several million years of hominid evolution, quite a different pattern has been evident, in which each of the components (dentition, locomotion, brain size, and toolmaking) have developed at quite different rates. This pattern, in which physiological and behavioral systems evolve at different rates, is called **mosaic evolution**. As we first pointed out in Chapter 1 and will emphasize in this and the next chapter,

mosaic evolution A pattern of evolution in which the rates of evolution in one functional system vary from those in other systems. For example, in hominid evolution, the dental system, locomotor system, and neurological system (especially the brain) all evolved at markedly different rates.

235

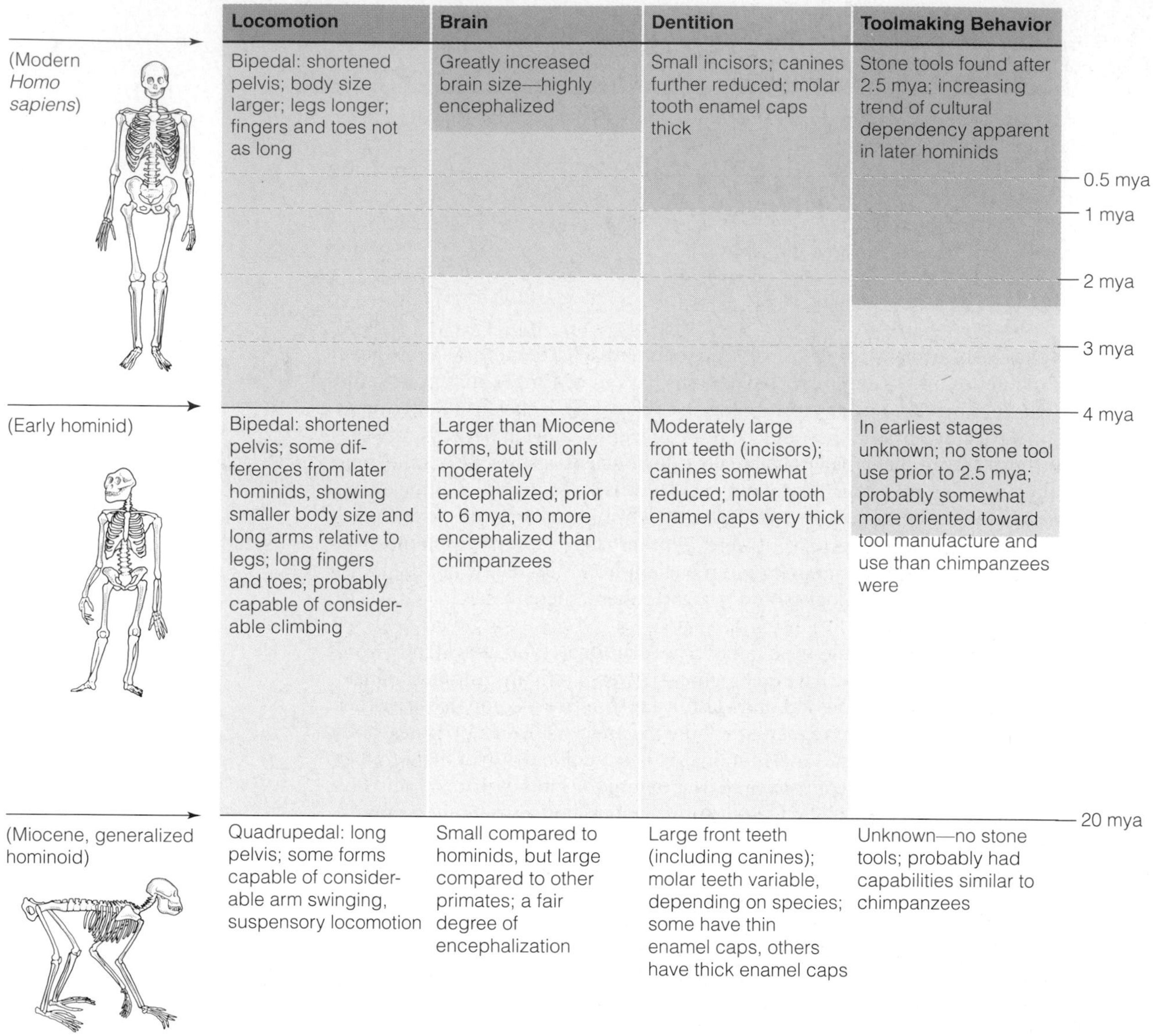

	Locomotion	Brain	Dentition	Toolmaking Behavior
(Modern *Homo sapiens*)	Bipedal: shortened pelvis; body size larger; legs longer; fingers and toes not as long	Greatly increased brain size—highly encephalized	Small incisors; canines further reduced; molar tooth enamel caps thick	Stone tools found after 2.5 mya; increasing trend of cultural dependency apparent in later hominids
(Early hominid)	Bipedal: shortened pelvis; some differences from later hominids, showing smaller body size and long arms relative to legs; long fingers and toes; probably capable of considerable climbing	Larger than Miocene forms, but still only moderately encephalized; prior to 6 mya, no more encephalized than chimpanzees	Moderately large front teeth (incisors); canines somewhat reduced; molar tooth enamel caps very thick	In earliest stages unknown; no stone tool use prior to 2.5 mya; probably somewhat more oriented toward tool manufacture and use than chimpanzees were
(Miocene, generalized hominoid)	Quadrupedal: long pelvis; some forms capable of considerable arm swinging, suspensory locomotion	Small compared to hominids, but large compared to other primates; a fair degree of encephalization	Large front teeth (including canines); molar teeth variable, depending on species; some have thin enamel caps, others have thick enamel caps	Unknown—no stone tools; probably had capabilities similar to chimpanzees

Time scale (right margin): 0.5 mya, 1 mya, 2 mya, 3 mya, 4 mya, 20 mya

FIGURE 10-1
Mosaic evolution of hominid characteristics: a postulated time line.

culture Extrasomatic (non-bodily) adaptations to the environment. This includes systematic learned behaviors that can be communicated to others. Aspects of this capacity have been identified among our closest ape relatives.

the single most important defining characteristic for the full course of hominid evolution is bipedal locomotion. In the earliest stages of hominid emergence, skeletal evidence indicating bipedal locomotion is the only truly reliable indicator that these fossils were indeed hominids. But in later stages of hominid evolution, other features, especially those relating to brain development and behavior, become highly significant (Fig. 10-1).

These behavioral aspects of hominid emergence—particularly toolmaking—are what we'd like to emphasize in this chapter. Important structural attributes of the hominid brain, teeth, and especially locomotor apparatus are discussed in the next chapter, where we investigate early hominid anatomical adaptations in greater detail.

BIOCULTURAL EVOLUTION: THE HUMAN CAPACITY FOR CULTURE

One of the most distinctive behavioral features of humans is our extraordinary elaboration of and dependence on **culture**. Certainly other primates, and many other animals, for that matter, modify their environments. As we saw in Chapter 8, chimpanzees especially are now known for such behaviors as using termite sticks, and some even carry rocks to use for crushing nuts. Because of such observations, we're on shaky ground when it comes to drawing sharp lines between early hominid toolmaking behavior and that exhibited by other animals. In fact, when Jane Goodall wrote Louis Leakey to tell him of a Gombe chimp's use of tools, he responded, "Now we must redefine tool, redefine Man, or accept chimpanzees as humans." For many people, scientists and laypeople alike, it's been easier to simply redefine what makes us unique. This approach may remind you of the famous retort made by Supreme Court Justice Stewart Potter in response to his inability to exactly define what is obscene: "I know it when I see it" (*Jacobellis v. Ohio*, 378 U.S. 184, 197 [1964]). Many have taken this same casual approach to defining hominids, with similarly disheartening results.

Another point to remember is that human culture, at least as it's defined in contemporary contexts, involves much more than toolmaking capacity. For humans, culture integrates an entire adaptive strategy involving cognitive, political, social, and economic components. *Material culture*—or the tools humans use—is but a small portion of this cultural complex.

Still, when we examine the archaeological record of earlier hominids, what's available for study is almost exclusively limited to material culture, especially the residues of stone tool manufacture (debris; called debitage). This is why it's extremely difficult to learn anything about the earliest stages of hominid cultural development before the regular manufacture of stone tools. As you'll see, this most crucial cultural development has been traced to approximately 2.5 mya (Semaw et al., 1997). Yet because of our contemporary primate models, we can assume that hominids were undoubtedly using other kinds of tools (made of perishable materials) and displaying a whole array of other cultural behaviors long before then. But with no "hard" evidence preserved in the archaeological record, our understanding of the early development of these nonmaterial cultural components remains elusive.

The fundamental basis for human cultural success relates directly to our cognitive abilities. Again, we're not dealing with an absolute distinction, but a relative one. As you've already learned, other primates, as documented in the great apes, have some of the language capabilities exhibited by humans. Even so, modern humans display these abilities in a complexity several orders of magnitude beyond that of any other animal. And only humans are so completely dependent on symbolic communication and its cultural by-products that contemporary *Homo sapiens* could not survive without them.

At this point you may be wondering when the unique combination of cognitive, social, and material cultural adaptations became prominent in human evolution. In answering that question, we must be careful to recognize the manifold nature of culture; we can't expect it to always contain the same elements across species (as when comparing ourselves to nonhuman primates) or through time (when trying to reconstruct ancient hominid behavior). Richard Potts (1993) has critiqued such overly simplistic perspectives and suggests instead a more dynamic approach, one that incorporates many subcomponents (including aspects of behavior, cognition, and social interaction).

We know that the earliest hominids almost certainly didn't regularly manufacture stone tools (at least, none that have been found and identified as such). These earliest members of the hominid lineage, dating back to approximately 7–5 mya, may have carried objects such as naturally sharp stones or stone flakes, parts of carcasses, and pieces of wood around their home ranges. At the very least, we would expect them to have displayed these behaviors to at least the same degree as that exhibited in living chimpanzees.

Also, as you'll see in the next chapter, by 6 mya—and perhaps as early as 7 mya—hominids had developed one crucial advantage: They were bipedal and so could more easily carry all kinds of objects from place to place. Ultimately, the efficient exploitation of resources widely distributed in time and space would most likely have led to using "central" spots where key components—especially stone objects—were cached, or collected (Potts, 1991; see "A Closer Look" on pp. 248–249).

What we know for sure is that over a period of several million years, during the formative stages of hominid emergence, many components interacted, but not all of them developed simultaneously. As cognitive abilities developed, more efficient means of communication and learning resulted. Largely because of consequent neurological reorganization, more elaborate tools and social relationships also emerged. These, in turn, selected for greater intelligence, which in turn selected for further neural elaboration. Quite clearly, these mutual dynamic interactions are at the very heart of what we call hominid *biocultural* evolution.

A CLOSER LOOK   What Is a Hominid?

At first glance, this is a simple question, and so far our discussion has provided a straightforward answer: A hominid is a bipedal primate—more specifically, a bipedal hominoid. But who are our closest relatives? This, too, at least superficially, is pretty easy: The great apes are our closest relatives.

But which apes? Now things get a bit stickier. Traditionally, classifications contrasted humans (and our immediate predecessors) in the hominid family (technically called the Hominidae) with the pongid family of great apes (including chimpanzees, bonobos, gorillas, and orangutans, all technically called the Pongidae). We discussed this classification in Chapter 6 (see p. 135) but also noted that there were some serious problems with it. In particular, the *African great apes* are considerably more closely related to humans than is the orangutan. More specifically yet, accumulating genetic evidence has shown that chimpanzees and bonobos are slightly more closely related to humans than gorillas are.

This order of relationships, most particularly the extremely close genetic/evolutionary relationship of the human line to other African large-bodied hominoids, is exceedingly important to recognize. Indeed, no other observation in this text more clearly illuminates the human place in a biological continuum. It wouldn't be an overstatement, in fact, to describe hominids as "bipedal African apes." We could show the order of relationships in a chart, using simple terminology:

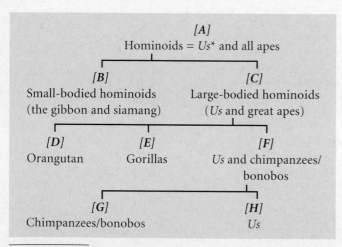

*Us = bipedal hominoids, including *H. sapiens* and all our predecessors, back to the split with our closest relatives, the chimpanzee/bonobo lineage.

Scientists, of course, use standardized terminology, and this is especially rigorous for names used in formal classifications. The rules followed in naming make good sense. But unfortunately, nobody considered the burden on introductory students when these names were first suggested. Here is how the preceding classification appears using the technical names now preferred by a growing number of paleoanthropologists (for example, Wood and Richmond, 2000):[†]

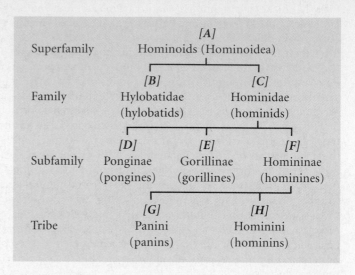

In this scheme, a hominid includes us (and our immediate predecessors) but *also* all the great apes (and their immediate predecessors, back to a common ancestor). What we call "hominid" in this book ("us") is now (following this new system) technically referred to as hominin.

Two final points can be made. First, classification *must* accurately reflect evolutionary relationships, so the traditionally recognized family of great apes (Pongidae) should be scrapped. That will, in turn, require a major reshuffling of the entire hominoid superfamily. But, evolutionary biologists haven't yet agreed on the best way to do this.[‡] Consequently, in this book we continue to refer to "us" as hominids. If you see the term *hominin* in other publications, recognize that it's being used synonymously with our use of the term *hominid*.

[†]Even this seemingly highly detailed classification fails to make an important distinction (between the Asian and the African large-bodied hominids, a distinction emphasized in Chapter 9). The classification shown isn't inaccurate; it's simply incomplete and probably will need further refining.

[‡]The recent annual meetings of the American Association of Physical Anthropologists (2007) give evidence as to how little consensus there is regarding terminology. Three different sessions dealt with fossil evidence of our immediate precursors—and were entitled (for the first time at these meetings) as "Hominin Evolution." A total of 29 of the presentations in these sessions used either "hominid" or "hominin" in their titles, and these were nearly equally split (16 preferred "hominid" and 13 used "hominin").

The Strategy of Paleoanthropology

To adequately understand human evolution, we obviously need a broad base of information. It's the paleoanthropologist's task to recover and interpret all the clues left by early hominids. *Paleoanthropology* is defined as "the study of ancient humans." As such, it's a diverse **multidisciplinary** pursuit seeking to reconstruct every possible bit of information concerning the dating, anatomy, behavior, and ecology of our hominid ancestors. In the past few decades, the study of early humans has marshaled the specialized skills of many different kinds of scientists. This growing and exciting adventure includes, but is not limited to, geologists, vertebrate paleontologists, archaeologists, physical anthropologists, and paleoecologists (Table 10-1).

Geologists, usually working with other paleoanthropologists, do the initial surveys to locate potential early hominid sites. Many sophisticated techniques aid in this search, including the analysis of aerial and satellite imagery, though the most common way to find these sites is to simply trip over fossil remains. Vertebrate paleontologists are usually involved in this early survey work, helping find fossil beds containing faunal (animal) remains, because where conditions are favorable for the preservation of bone from such species as pigs and elephants, hominid remains may also be preserved. Paleontologists also can (through comparison with known faunal sequences) give quick and dirty approximate age estimates of fossil sites in the field without having to wait for the results of more time-consuming (though more accurate) analyses that will later be performed in a lab.

Once identified, fossil beds likely to contain hominid finds are subjected to extensive field surveying. For some sites, generally those postdating 2.5 mya (roughly the age of the oldest identified human artifacts), archaeologists take over in the search for hominid material traces. We don't necessarily have to find remains of early hominids themselves to know that they consistently occupied a particular area. Such material clues as **artifacts** inform us directly about early hominid activities. Modifying rocks according to a consistent plan, or simply carrying them around from one place to another (over fairly long distances in a manner not explicable by natural means, like streams or glaciers) is characteristic of no other animal but a hominid. So, when we see such material evidence at a site, we know without a doubt that hominids were present.

Because organic materials such as wood or fiber aren't usually preserved in the archaeological record of the oldest hominids, we have no solid evidence of the earliest stages of hominid cultural modifications. On the other hand, our ancestors at some point around 2.5 mya started showing a veritable fascination with stones, because they provided not only easily accessible and transportable materials (to use as convenient objects for throwing or for holding down other objects, such as skins and windbreaks) but also the most durable and sharpest cutting edges available at that time. Luckily for us, stone is almost indestructible, and some early hominid sites are strewn with thousands of stone artifacts. The earliest artifact sites now documented are from the Gona and Bouri areas in northeastern Ethiopia, dating to 2.5 mya (Semaw et al., 1997; de Heinzelin et al., 1999). Other contenders

TABLE 10-1	Subdisciplines of Paleoanthropology	
Physical Sciences	**Biological Sciences**	**Social Sciences**
Geology	Physical anthropology	Archaeology
Stratigraphy	Paleoecology	Ethnoarchaeology
Petrology	Paleontology (fossil	Cultural anthropology
(rocks, minerals)	animals)	Ethnography
Pedology (soils)	Palynology (fossil pollen)	Psychology
Geomorphology	Primatology	
Geophysics		
Chemistry		
Taphonomy		

multidisciplinary Refers to research involving mutual contributions and cooperation of experts from various scientific fields (i.e., disciplines).

artifacts Objects or materials made or modified for use by hominids. The earliest artifacts are usually made of stone or, occasionally, bone.

for the "earliest" stone assemblage come from the adjacent Hadar and Middle Awash areas, immediately to the south in Ethiopia, dated 2.5–2 mya.

If an area is clearly demonstrated to be a hominid site, much more concentrated research will then begin. We should point out that a more mundane but significant aspect of paleoanthropology not reflected in Table 10-1 is the financial one. Just the initial survey work in usually remote areas costs many thousands of dollars, and mounting a concentrated research project costs several hundred thousand dollars more. This is why many projects are engaged in areas where promising surface finds have been made; massive financial support is required from government agencies and private donations, and it's unrealistic to simply dig at random. A great deal of a paleoanthropologist's efforts and time is necessarily devoted to writing grant proposals or speaking on the lecture circuit to raise the required funds for this work.

Once the financial hurdle has been cleared, a coordinated research project can begin. Usually headed by an archaeologist or physical anthropologist, the field crew continues to survey and map the target area in great detail. In addition, field crew members begin searching carefully for bones and artifacts eroding out of the soil, taking pollen and soil samples for ecological analysis, and carefully collecting rock and other samples for use in various dating techniques. If, in this early stage of exploration, members of the field crew find fossil hominid remains, they will feel very lucky indeed. The international press usually considers human fossils the most exciting kind of discovery, a fortunate circumstance that produces wide publicity and often ensures future financial support. More likely, the crew will accumulate much information on geological setting, ecological data (particularly faunal remains), and, with some luck, artifacts and other archaeological traces.

Although paleoanthropological fieldwork is typically a long and arduous process, the detailed analyses of collected samples and other data back in the laboratory are even more time-consuming. Archaeologists must clean, sort, label, and identify all artifacts, and vertebrate paleontologists must do the same for all faunal remains. Knowing the kinds of animals represented—whether forest browsers, woodland species, or open-country forms—greatly helps in reconstructing the local *paleoecological* settings in which early hominids lived. Analyzing the fossil pollen collected from hominid sites by a scientist—called a palynologist—further aids in developing a detailed environmental reconstruction. All these paleoecological analyses can assist in reconstructing the diet of early humans. Also, the **taphonomy** of the site must be worked out in order to understand its depositional history—that is, how the site formed over time, and if its present state is in a *primary* or *secondary* **context**.

In the concluding stages of interpretation, the paleoanthropologist draws together these essentials:

1. *Dating*
   geological
   paleontological
   geophysical

2. *Paleoecology*
   paleontology
   palynology
   geomorphology
   taphonomy

3. *Archaeological traces of behavior*

4. *Anatomical evidence from hominid remains*

By analyzing all this information, scientists try to "flesh out" the kind of creature that may have been our direct ancestor, or at least a very close relative. Primatologists may assist here by showing the detailed relationships between the anatomical structure and behavior of humans and that of contemporary nonhuman primates (see Chapters 6–8). Cultural anthropologists and ethnoarchaeologists (who study the "archaeology" of living groups by examining their material remains) may contribute ethnographic information concerning the varied nature of modern human behavior, particularly ecological adaptations of those contemporary hunter-gatherer groups exploiting roughly similar environmental settings as those reconstructed for a hominid site.

taphonomy   (*taphos*, meaning "dead") The study of how bones and other materials came to be buried in the earth and preserved as fossils. Taphonomists study the processes of sedimentation, the action of streams, preservation properties of bone, and carnivore disturbance factors.

context   The environmental setting where an archaeological trace is found. *Primary* context is the setting in which the archaeological trace was originally deposited. A *secondary* context is one to which it has been moved (such as by the action of a stream).

The end result of years of research by dozens of scientists will (we hope) produce a more complete and accurate understanding of human evolution—how we came to be the way we are. Both biological and cultural aspects of our ancestors contribute to this investigation, each process developing in relation to the other.

Paleoanthropology in Action— Olduvai Gorge

Several paleoanthropological projects of the scope just discussed have recently been pursued in diverse places in the Old World, including East and South Africa, Indonesia, and the Republic of Georgia in eastern Europe. Of all these localities, the one that has yielded the finest quality and greatest abundance of paleoanthropological information concerning early hominid behavior has been Olduvai Gorge.

First "discovered" in the early twentieth century by a German butterfly collector, Olduvai was soon scientifically surveyed and its wealth of paleontological evidence recognized. In 1931, Louis Leakey made his first trip to Olduvai Gorge and almost immediately realized its significance for studying early humans. From 1935, when she first worked there, until she retired in 1984, Mary Leakey directed the archaeological excavations at Olduvai.

Located in the Serengeti Plain of northern Tanzania, Olduvai is a steep-sided valley resembling a miniature version of the Grand Canyon. A deep ravine cut into an almost mile-high grassland plateau of East Africa, Olduvai extends more than 25 miles in total length. Climatically, the semiarid pattern of present-day Olduvai is believed to be similar to what it has been for the last 2 million years. The surrounding countryside is a grassland savanna broken occasionally by scrub bushes and acacia trees.

Geographically, Olduvai is located on the eastern branch of the Great Rift Valley of Africa. The geological processes associated with the formation of the Rift Valley make Olduvai (and other East African sites) extremely important to paleoanthropological investigation. Three of these results of geological rifting are most significant:

1. Faulting, or earth movement, exposes geological beds near the surface that are normally hidden by hundreds of feet of accumulated sediment called overburden.

2. Active volcanic processes cause rapid sedimentation, which often yields excellent preservation of bone and artifacts that normally would be scattered by carnivore activity and erosion forces.

3. Volcanic activity provides a wealth of radiometrically datable material.

As a result, Olduvai is the site of superb preservation of ancient hominids, portions of their environment, and their behavioral patterns in datable contexts, all of which are readily accessible.

The greatest contribution Olduvai has made to paleoanthropological research is the establishment of an extremely well-documented and correlated *sequence* of geological, paleontological, archaeological, and hominid remains over the last 2 million years. At the very foundation of all paleoanthropological research is a well-established geological context. At Olduvai, the geological and paleogeographical context is known in minute detail. Today, Olduvai is a geologist's delight, containing sediments in some places 350 feet thick, accumulated from lava flows (basalts), tuffs (windblown or waterborne fine deposits from nearby volcanoes), sandstones, claystones, and limestone conglomerates, all neatly stratified like a layer cake (Fig. 10-2). A hominid site can therefore be accurately dated relative to other sites in the Olduvai Gorge by cross-correlating known marker beds that have already been dated and can be quite quickly identified by geologists in the field. At the most general geological level, the stratigraphic sequence at Olduvai is broken down into four major geological strata called beds (Beds I–IV).

Paleontological evidence of fossilized animal bones also has come from Olduvai in great abundance. More than 150 species of extinct animals have been recognized, including fish, turtles, crocodiles, pigs, giraffes, horses, and many birds, rodents, and antelopes. Careful analysis of such remains has yielded voluminous information concerning the ecological

FIGURE **10-2**

FIGURE **10-2**

View of the main gorge at Olduvai. Notice the clear sequence of geological beds. The discontinuity to the right is a major fault line.

Robert Jurmain

conditions of early human habitats. What's more, the precise analysis of bones directly associated with artifacts can sometimes tell us about the diets and ways bone was handled and modified by early hominids. (There are some reservations, however; see "A Closer Look," pp. 248–249.)

The archaeological sequence is also well documented for the last 2 million years. Beginning at the earliest hominid site in Olduvai (ca. 1.85 mya), there is already a well-developed stone tool kit, including primarily numerous small flake tools (Leakey, 1971). Such a tool industry is called *Oldowan* (after Olduvai), and it continues into later beds with some small modifications.

Finally, partial remains of several fossilized hominids have been found at Olduvai, ranging in time from the earliest occupation levels to fairly recent *Homo sapiens*. Of the more than 40 individuals represented, many are quite fragmentary, but a few are excellently preserved. While the center of hominid discoveries has now shifted to other areas of East Africa, it was the initial discovery by Mary Leakey of the *Zinjanthropus* (nicknamed "Zinj") skull at Olduvai in July 1959 that focused the world's attention on this remarkably rich area (Fig. 10-3).

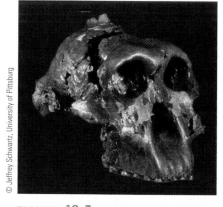

© Jeffrey Schwartz, University of Pittsburg

FIGURE **10-3**

Zinjanthropus cranium, discovered by Mary Leakey at Olduvai Gorge in 1959. As we will see in Chapter 11, this fossil is now included as part of the genus *Paranthropus*.

Dating Methods

An essential objective of paleoanthropology is placing sites and fossils into a time frame. In other words, we want to know how old they are. How, then, do we date sites—or more precisely, the geological strata or layers, in which sites are found? The question is both reasonable and important, so let's examine the dating techniques used by paleontologists, archaeologists, and other scientists involved in paleoanthropological research.

Scientists use two kinds of dating for this purpose: relative dating and **chronometric dating** (also known as *absolute dating*). Relative dating methods tell us that something is older or younger than something else, but not by how much. If, for example, a cranium is found at a depth of 50 feet and another cranium at 70 feet at the same site, we usually assume that the specimen discovered at 70 feet is older. We may not know the date (in years) of either one, but we'd know that one is older (or younger) than the other. Although this may not satisfy our curiosity about the actual number of years involved, it would give some idea of the evolutionary changes in cranial morphology (structure), especially if we found several crania at different levels and compared them.

This method of relative dating is based on **stratigraphy** and was one of the first techniques to be used by scientists working with the vast period of geological time. Stratigraphy,

chronometric dating   (*chrono*, meaning "time," and *metric*, meaning "measure") A dating technique that gives an estimate in actual numbers of years.

stratigraphy   Study of the sequential layering of deposits.

in turn, is based on the **principle of superposition**, which states that a lower stratum (layer) is older than a higher stratum. Because much of the earth's crust has been laid down by layer after layer of sedimentary rock, much like the layers of a cake, stratigraphy has been a valuable aid in reconstructing the history of the earth and the life upon it.

Stratigraphic dating does, however, have some problems. Earth disturbances, such as volcanic activity, river activity, and mountain building, may shift strata and the objects within them, and the chronology of the material may be difficult or even impossible to reconstruct. What's more, it's impossible to accurately determine the time period of a particular stratum—that is, how long it took to accumulate.

Another method of relative dating is *fluorine analysis*, which applies only to bones (Oakley, 1963). Bones in the earth are exposed to the seepage of groundwater that usually contains fluorine. The longer a bone lies in the earth, the more fluorine it will incorporate during the fossilization process. Bones deposited at the same time in the same location thus should contain the same amount of fluorine. Professor Oakley of the British Museum used this technique in the early 1950s to expose the Piltdown (England) hoax by demonstrating that a human skull was considerably older than the jaw (ostensibly also human) found with it (Weiner, 1955). When a discrepancy in fluorine content led Oakley and others to more closely examine the bones, they found that the jaw was not that of a hominid at all but of a young adult orangutan! (See Issue, pp. 260–261.)

Unfortunately, fluorine analysis is useful only with bones found at the same location. Because the amount of fluorine in groundwater is based on local conditions, it varies from place to place. Also, some groundwater may not contain any fluorine. For these reasons, it's impossible to use fluorine analysis when comparing bones from different localities.

In both stratigraphy and fluorine analysis, it's impossible to calculate the actual age of the rock stratum and the objects in it. To determine the age in years, scientists have developed various chronometric techniques based on the phenomenon of radioactive decay. Actually, the theory is pretty simple: Certain radioactive isotopes of elements are unstable, causing them to decay and form an isotopic variation of another element. Since the rate of decay follows a definite mathematical pattern, the radioactive material forms an accurate geological time clock of sorts. By measuring the amount of decay in a particular sample, scientists can calculate the number of years it took for that amount of decay to accumulate. Chronometric techniques have been used for dating the immense age of the earth as well as artifacts less than 1,000 years old. Several techniques have been employed for a number of years and are now quite well known.

The most important chronometric technique used to date early hominids involves potassium-40 (^{40}K), which has a **half-life** of 1.25 billion years and produces argon-40 (^{40}Ar). Known as the K/Ar or potassium-argon method, this procedure has been extensively used by paleoanthropologists in dating materials in the 1- to 5-million-year range, especially in East Africa where past volcanic activity makes this dating technique possible. A variant of this technique, the $^{40}Ar/^{39}Ar$ method, also has recently been used to date several hominid localities. The $^{40}Ar/^{39}Ar$ method allows analysis of smaller samples (even single crystals), reduces experimental error, and is more precise than standard K/Ar dating. Consequently, it can be used to date a wide chronological range—indeed, the entire hominid record, even up to modern times. Recent applications have provided excellent dates for several early hominid sites in East Africa (discussed in Chapter 11) as well as somewhat later sites in Java (discussed in Chapter 12). In fact, the technique was recently used to date the famous Mt. Vesuvius eruption of A.D. 79, which destroyed the city of Pompeii as documented by ancient historians. Remarkably, the midrange date obtained by the $^{40}Ar/^{39}Ar$ technique was A.D. 73, just 6 years from the known date (Renne et al., 1997)! Organic material, such as bone, can't be measured by these techniques; but the rock matrix in which the bone is found can be. Scientists used K/Ar dating to obtain a minimum date for the deposit containing the *Zinjanthropus* cranium by dating a volcanic layer above the fossil.

Rocks that provide the best samples for K/Ar and $^{40}Ar/^{39}Ar$ are those heated to an extremely high temperature, such as that generated by volcanic activity. When the rock is in a molten state, argon, a gas, is driven off. As the rock cools and solidifies, potassium-40 continues to break down to argon; but now the gas is physically trapped in the cooled rock. To obtain the date of the rock, scientists reheat it and measure the escaping gas. Because the rock must in the past have been exposed to extreme heat, this limits these techniques

principle of superposition   In a stratigraphic sequence, the lower layers were deposited before the upper layers. Or, simply put, the stuff on top of a heap was put there last.

half-life   The time period in which one-half the amount of a radioactive isotope is converted chemically (into a daughter product). For example, after 1.25 billion years, half the ^{40}K remains; after 2.5 billion years, one-fourth remains.

to areas where sediments have been superheated, such as regions of past volcanic activity or meteorite falls.

A well-known radiometric method popular with archaeologists makes use of carbon-14 (^{14}C), with a half-life of 5,730 years. Carbon-14 has been used to date material from less than 1,000 years to as old as 75,000 years, although accuracy is reduced for materials more than 40,000 years old. Since this technique applies to the latter stages of hominid evolution, its applications relate to material discussed in Chapters 13 and 14. Some inorganic artifacts can be directly dated through the use of **thermoluminescence (TL)**. This method, too, relies on the principle of radiometric decay. Stone material used in manufacturing tools invariably contains trace amounts of radioactive elements, such as uranium or thorium. As the rock gets heated (perhaps by accidentally falling into a campfire, or by deliberately being heated to help in its production), the rapid heating releases displaced beta particles trapped within the rock. As the particles escape, they emit a dull glow known as thermoluminescence. After that, radioactive decay resumes within the fired stone, again building up electrons at a steady rate. To determine the age of an archaeological sample, the researcher must heat the sample to 500°C and measure its thermoluminescence; from that, the date can be calculated. Used especially by archaeologists to date ceramic pots from recent sites, TL can also be used to date burned flint tools from earlier hominid sites. Like TL, two other techniques also used to date sites from the latter phases of hominid evolution (where neither K/Ar nor radiocarbon is possible), are uranium-series dating and electron spin resonance (ESR) dating. Uranium series dating relies on radioactive decay of short-lived uranium isotopes, and ESR is similar to TL because it's based on measuring trapped electrons. However, while TL is used on heated materials such as clay or stone tools, ESR is used on dental enamel of animals. All three of these dating methods have been used to provide key dating controls for hominid sites discussed in Chapters 12–14.

You should realize that none of these methods is precise. Each one has problems that must be carefully considered during laboratory measurement and when collecting material to be analyzed. Because the methods aren't perfectly accurate, approximate dates are given as probability statements with an error range. For example, a date given as 1.75 ± 0.2 million years should be read as having a 67 percent chance that the actual date lies somewhere between 1.55 and 1.95 million years (see "A Closer Look," p. 245).

thermoluminiscence (TL) (thermo-loo-min-ess´-ence) Technique for dating certain archaeological materials, such as stone tools, heated in the past, that release stored energy of radioactive decay as light upon reheating.

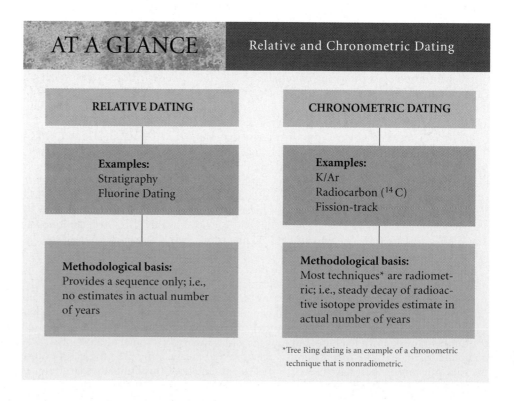

Chronometric dates are usually determined after testing several geological samples. The dates that result from such testing are combined and expressed statistically. For example, say that five different samples are used to give the K/Ar date 1.75 ± 0.2 my for a particular geological bed. The individual results from all five samples are totaled together to give an average date (here, 1.75 mya), and the standard deviation is calculated (here, 0.20 mya; that is, 200,000 years). The dating estimate is then reported as the mean plus or minus (±) one standard deviation. Those of you who have taken statistics will realize that (assuming a normal distribution) 67 percent of a distribution of dates is included within 1 standard deviation (±) of the mean. Thus, the chronometric result, as shown in the reported range, is simply a probability statement that 67 percent of the dates from all the samples tested fell within the range of dates from 1.55 to 1.95 mya. You should carefully read chronometric dates and study the reported ranges. It's likely that the smaller the range, the more samples were analyzed. Smaller ranges mean more precise estimates; better laboratory controls will also increase precision.

To sum up, there are two ways of answering the question of age. We can say that a particular fossil is x number of years old, a date determined usually by chronometric dating techniques. Or we can say that fossil X lived before or after fossil Y, a relative dating technique.

APPLICATIONS OF DATING METHODS: EXAMPLES FROM OLDUVAI

Olduvai has been a rich proving ground for numerous dating techniques. As a result, it has some of the best-documented chronology for any hominid site in the Lower or Middle Pleistocene.

As we've noted, the potassium-argon (K/Ar) method is an extremely valuable tool for dating early hominid sites and has been widely used in areas containing suitable volcanic deposits (mainly in East Africa) or superheated debris from meteorites (mainly in Indonesia). At Olduvai, K/Ar has given several reliable dates of the underlying basalt and several tuffs in Bed I, including the one associated with the "Zinj" find (now dated at 1.79 ± 0.03 mya).

Due to several potential sources of error, K/Ar dating must be cross-checked using other independent methods. Once again, the sediments at Olduvai provide some excellent examples of the use of many of these other dating techniques.

Fission-track dating is one of the most important techniques for cross checking K/Ar determinations. The key to fission-track dating is that uranium238 (^{238}U) decays regularly by spontaneous fission. By counting the proportion of uranium atoms that have fissioned or split apart (shown as microscopic tracks caused by explosive fission of ^{238}U nuclei), researchers can estimate the age of a mineral or natural glass sample. One of the earliest applications of this technique was on volcanic pumice from Olduvai, giving a date of 2.30 (±0.28 mya)—in good agreement with K/Ar dates. Fission-track dating has also been used to date baked earth and pottery from contexts as recently as 5,000 years ago from a site in Iran (Wagner, 1996).

Another important means of cross-checking dates is called **paleomagnetism**. This technique is based on the constantly shifting nature of the earth's magnetic pole. Of course, the earth's magnetic pole is now oriented in a northerly direction, but this hasn't always been so. In fact, the orientation and intensity of the geomagnetic field have undergone numerous documented changes in the last few million years. From our current viewpoint, we call a northern orientation "normal" and a southern one "reversed." Major epochs (also called "chrons") of recent geomagnetic time are

0.7 mya–present	Normal
2.6–0.7 mya	Reversed
3.4–2.6 mya	Normal
?–3.4 mya	Reversed

paleomagnetism Dating method based on the earth's shifting magnetic pole.

245

Paleomagnetic dating is accomplished by carefully taking samples of sediments that contain magnetically charged particles. Since these particles maintain the magnetic orientation they had when they were consolidated into rock (millions of years ago), we have a kind of "fossil compass." Then the paleomagnetic *sequence* is compared against the K/Ar dates to see if they agree. Some complications may arise, for during an epoch, a relatively long period of time can occur when the geomagnetic orientation is the opposite of what's expected. For example, during the reversed epoch from 2.6 to 0.7 mya (the Matuyama epoch), there was an *event* lasting about 210,000 years when orientations were normal. (Because this phenomenon was first conclusively demonstrated at Olduvai, it's appropriately called the *Olduvai event*.) But, once these oscillations in the geomagnetic pole are worked out, the sequence of paleomagnetic orientations can provide a valuable cross-check for K/Ar and fission-track age determinations.

A final dating technique used at Olduvai and other African sites is based on the regular evolutionary changes in well-known groups of mammals. This technique, called *faunal correlation* or **biostratigraphy**, provides yet another means of cross-checking the other methods. This technique employs some of the same methods used in relative stratigraphic dating, but it incorporates information on sequences of faunal remains from chronometrically dated sites across space. For instance, presence of particular fossil pigs, elephants, antelopes, rodents, and carnivores in areas where dates are known (by K/Ar, for example) can be used to extrapolate an approximate age by noting which genera and species are present in other areas not otherwise possible to accurately date.

All these methods—potassium-argon, fission-track, paleomagnetism, and biostratigraphy—have been used in dating sites at Olduvai. So many different dating techniques are necessary because no single one is perfectly reliable by itself. Sampling error, contamination, and experimental error can all introduce ambiguities into our so-called absolute dates. Because the sources of error are different for each technique, however, cross-checking among several independent methods is the most reliable way of authenticating the chronology for early hominid sites.

Excavations at Olduvai

Because the vertical cut of the Olduvai Gorge provides a cross section of 2 million years of earth history, sites can be excavated by digging "straight in" rather than first having to remove tons of overlying dirt (Fig. 10-4). In fact, as mentioned before, sites are usually discovered by merely walking the exposures and observing what bones, stones, and so forth, are eroding out.

Robert Jurmain

biostratigraphy   A relative dating technique based on regular changes seen in evolving groups of animals as well as presence or absence of particular species.

Several dozen hominid sites (at a minimum, they are bone and tool scatters) have been surveyed at Olduvai, and Mary Leakey extensively excavated close to 20 of these. An incredible amount of paleoanthropological information has come from these excavated areas. The data generally can be grouped into three broad categories of site types, depending on implied function:

1. *"Butchering" localities*, areas containing one or only a few individuals of a single species of large mammal associated with a scatter of archaeological traces. Two butchering sites, one containing an elephant and another containing a *Deinotherium* (a large extinct relative of the elephant), have been found at levels approximately 1.7 mya at Olduvai. Both sites contain parts of only a single animal, and it's impossible to ascertain whether the hominids actually killed these animals or exploited them after they were already dead. A third butchering locality dated at approximately 1.2 mya shows more consistent and efficient exploitation of large mammals by this time.

2. *Quarry localities*, areas where early hominids extracted stone to make tools. At such sites, thousands of small stone fragments of only one type of rock are found, usually associated with no or very little bone refuse. At Olduvai, a 1.6- to 1.7-million-year-old area was apparently a chert (a rock resembling flint) factory site, where hominids came repeatedly to obtain this material.

3. *Multipurpose localities* (also called "home bases" or "campsites"), general-purpose areas where hominids possibly ate, slept, and put the finishing touches on their tools. The accumulation of living debris, including broken bones of many animals of several different species and many broken stones (some complete tools, some waste flakes), is a basic human pattern. As Glynn Isaac noted:

> The fact that discarded artifacts tend to be concentrated in restricted areas is itself highly suggestive. It seems likely that such patches of material reflect the organization of movement around a camp or home base, with recurrent dispersal and reuniting of the group at the chosen locality. Among living primates this pattern in its full expression is distinctive of man. The coincidence of bone and food refuse with the artifacts strongly implies that meat was carried back—presumably for sharing. (Isaac, 1976, pp. 27–28)

(See "A Closer Look," pp. 248–249, for a different interpretation.)

Several multipurpose areas have been excavated at Olduvai, including one that is over 1.8 million years old. This site has a circle of large stones forming what at one time was thought to be a base for a windbreak; however, this interpretation is now considered unlikely. Whatever its function, without the meticulous excavation and recording of modern archaeological techniques, the presence of such an archaeological **feature** would never have been recognized. It's important to recognize that although many people think archaeologists obtain their information simply by analyzing objects (stone tools, gold statues, or whatever), it's actually the *context* and **association** of objects (that is, precisely where the objects are found and what is found associated with them) that give archaeologists the information they need in order to understand the behavioral patterns of ancient human populations. Once pot hunters or looters pilfer a site, proper archaeological interpretation is never again possible.

The types of activities carried out at these multipurpose sites remain open to speculation (see Fig. 10-5). Archaeologists had thought, as Glynn

feature In archaeology, an immovable residue of human occupation, such as an ash pit.

association Relationships between components of an archaeological site. All the things artifacts are found with.

FIGURE **10-5**

A dense scatter of stone and some fossilized animal bone from a site at Olduvai, dated at approximately 1.6 mya. Some of these remains are the result of hominid activities.

Robert Jurmain

247

A CLOSER LOOK   Who Was Doing What at Olduvai and the Other Plio-Pleistocene Sites?

The long-held interpretation of the bone refuse and stone tools discovered at Olduvai has been that most, if not all, of these materials result from hominid activities. More recently, however, a comprehensive reanalysis of the bone remains from Olduvai localities has challenged this view (Binford, 1981, 1983). Archaeologist Lewis Binford criticizes those drawn too quickly to concluding that these bone scatters are the remnants of hominid behavior patterns while simultaneously ignoring the possibility of other explanations.

From information concerning the kinds of animals present, which body parts were found, and the differences in preservation among these skeletal elements, Binford has concluded that much of what's preserved can be explained by carnivore activity. This conclusion has been reinforced by certain details observed by Binford himself in Alaska—details on animal kills, scavenging, the transportation of elements, and preservation that are the result of wolf and dog behaviors. Binford describes his approach:

> I took as "known," then, the structure of bone assemblages produced in various settings by animal predators and scavengers; and as "unknown" the bone deposits excavated by the Leakeys at Olduvai Gorge. Using mathematical and statistical techniques I considered to what degree the finds from Olduvai Gorge could be accounted for in terms of the results of predator behavior and how much was "left over." (Binford, 1983, pp. 56–57)

Binford isn't arguing that all of the remains found at Olduvai resulted from nonhominid activity. In fact, he recognizes that "residual material" was consistently found on surfaces with high tool concentration "which could not be explained by what we know about African animals" (Binford, 1983).

Support for the idea that early hominids utilized at least some of the bone refuse has come from a totally different perspective. Researchers have analyzed (both macroscopically and microscopically) the cut marks left on fossilized bones. By experimenting with modern materials, they've been able to delineate more clearly the differences between marks left by stone tools and those left by animal teeth or other factors (Bunn, 1981; Potts and Shipman, 1981). Analyses of bones from several early localities at Olduvai have shown unambiguously that hominids used these specimens and left telltale cut marks from their stone tools. The sites investigated so far reveal a somewhat haphazard cutting and chopping, apparently unrelated to deliberate disarticulation. So the conclusion (Shipman, 1983) is that hominids scavenged carcasses, probably of carnivore kills, and did *not* hunt large animals themselves.

Following and expanding on the experimental approaches pioneered by Binford, Bunn, and others, Robert Blumenschine of Rutgers University has recently conducted a more detailed analysis of the Olduvai material. Like his predecessors, Blumenschine has also concluded that the cut marks on animal bones are the result of hominid processing (Blumenschine, 1995). Blumenschine and colleagues further surmise that most meat acquisition (virtually all from large animals) was the result of scavenging (from remains of carnivore kills or from animals that died from natural causes). In fact, these researchers suggest

Isaac's quote indicates (and as Mary Leakey argued), that the sites functioned as "campsites." Lewis Binford has forcefully critiqued this view and has alternatively suggested that much of the refuse accumulated is the result of nonhominid (that is, predator) activities. Another possibility, suggested by Richards Potts (1984), is that these areas served as collecting points (caches) for some tools. This last interpretation has received considerable support from other archaeologists in recent years.

A final interpretation, incorporating aspects of the hypotheses proposed by Binford and Potts, has been suggested by Robert Blumenschine. He argued that early hominids were gatherers and scavengers, and the bone and stone scatters reflect these activities (Blumenschine, 1986; Blumenschine and Cavallo, 1992).

.

blank   In archaeology, a stone suitably sized and shaped to be further worked into a tool.

flake   Thin-edged fragment removed from a core.

core   Stone reduced by flake removal; a core may or may not be used as a tool itself.

Experimental Archaeology

Simply classifying artifacts into categories and types is not enough. We can learn considerably more about our ancestors by understanding how they made and used their tools. It is, after all, the artifactual traces of prehistoric tools of stone (and, to a lesser degree, bone) that provide much of our information concerning early human behavior. Tons of stone debris

that scavenging was a crucial adaptive strategy for early hominids and considerably influenced their habitat usage, diet, and stone tool utilization (Blumenschine and Cavallo, 1992; Blumenschine and Peters, 1998). What's more, Blumenschine and colleagues have developed a model detailing how scavenging and other early hominid adaptive strategies integrate into patterns of land use (that is, differential utilization of various niches in and around Olduvai). From this model they formulated specific hypotheses concerning the predicted distribution of artifacts and animal remains in different areas at Olduvai. Ongoing excavations at Olduvai are now aimed specifically at *testing* these hypotheses.

If early hominids (close to 2 mya) weren't hunting consistently, what did they obtain from scavenging the kills of other animals? One obvious answer is, whatever meat was left behind. However, the position of the cut marks suggests that early hominids were often hacking at non-meat-bearing portions of the skeletons. Perhaps they were after bone marrow and brain, substances not fully exploited by other predators and scavengers (Binford, 1981; Blumenschine and Cavallo, 1992).

Exciting new discoveries from the Bouri Peninsula of the Middle Awash of Ethiopia provide the best evidence yet for meat and marrow exploitation by early hominids. Dated to 2.5 mya (that is, as old as the oldest known artifacts), antelope and horse fossils from Bouri show telltale incisions and breaks indicating that bones were not only smashed to extract marrow but also cut, ostensibly to retrieve meat (de Heinzelin et al., 1999). The researchers who analyzed these materials have suggested that the greater dietary reliance on animal products may have been important in stimulating brain enlargement in the lineage leading to genus *Homo*.

Another new research twist relating to the reconstruction of early hominid diets has come from biochemical analysis of hominid teeth from South Africa (dating to about the same time range as hominids from Olduvai—or perhaps slightly earlier). In an innovative application of stable carbon isotope analysis (see p. 252), Matt Sponheimer and Julia Lee-Thorp found that these early hominid teeth revealed telltale chemical signatures relating to diet (Sponheimer and Lee-Thorp, 1999). In particular, the proportions of stable carbon isotopes indicated that these early hominids either ate grass products (such as seeds) or ate meat/marrow from animals that in turn had eaten grass products (that is, the hominids might well have derived a significant portion of their diet from meat or other animal products). This evidence comes from an exciting new perspective that provides a more *direct* indicator of early hominid diets. While it's not clear how much meat these early hominids consumed, these new data do suggest they were consistently exploiting more open regions of their environment. Moreover, a new laser technology makes it possible to detect from a single tooth indications of what sorts of foods were eaten from year to year and even seasonally within the same year. Drs. Sponheimer, Thorpe, and colleagues have used this exciting new approach to show some early hominids were able to flexibly move between different environments and exploit seasonally available foods (Sponheimer et al., 2006).

litter archaeological sites worldwide. A casual walk along the bottom of Olduvai Gorge could well be interrupted every few seconds by tripping over prehistoric tools!

So, archaeologists are presented with a wealth of information revealing at least one part of human material culture. What do these artifacts tell us about our ancestors? How were these tools made, and how were they used? To answer these questions, contemporary archaeologists have tried to reconstruct prehistoric techniques of stone toolmaking, butchering, and so forth. In this way, experimental archaeologists are, in a sense, trying to re-create the past.

STONE TOOL (LITHIC) TECHNOLOGY

Stone is by far the most common residue of prehistoric cultural behavior. For this reason, archaeologists have long been keenly interested in this material.

When struck properly, certain types of stone will fracture in a controlled way; these nodules are called **blanks**. The smaller piece that comes off is called a **flake**, while the larger remaining chunk is called a **core** (Fig. 10-6). Both core and flake have sharp edges useful for cutting, sawing, or scraping. The earliest hominid cultural inventions probably used nondurable materials that didn't survive archaeologically (such as a digging stick or an ostrich eggshell used as a watertight container). Still, a basic human invention was the recognition that stone can be fractured to produce sharp edges.

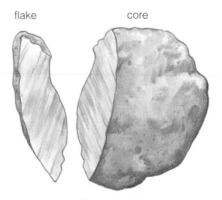

flake   core

FIGURE **10-6**
Flake and core.

FIGURE 10-7
Direct percussion.

FIGURE 10-8
Pressure flaking.

FIGURE 10-9
Microwear: the polish left on an experimental flint implement after scraping wood for 10 minutes. Bright, smooth areas are the microwear polish; dark, grainy areas are the unworn flint surface. Arrows indicate implement edge. (Magnification 200×).

lithic (*lith*, meaning "stone") Referring to stone tools.

knappers People (frequently archaeologists) who make stone tools.

direct percussion Striking a core or flake with a hammerstone.

microliths (*micro*, meaning "small," and *lith*, meaning "stone") Small stone tools usually produced from narrow blades punched from a core; found especially in Africa during the latter part of the Pleistocene.

pressure flaking A method of removing flakes from a core by pressing a pointed implement (e.g., bone or antler) against the stone.

For many years, it's been assumed that in the earliest known stone tool industry (that is, the Oldowan), both core and flake tools were deliberately manufactured as final, desired products. Such core implements as "choppers" were thought to be central artifactual components of these early **lithic** assemblages (in fact, the Oldowan is often depicted as a "chopping tool industry"). However, detailed reevaluation of these artifacts has thrown these traditional assumptions into doubt. By carefully analyzing the attributes of Oldowan artifacts from Olduvai, Potts (1991, 1993) concluded that the so-called core tools really weren't tools after all. He suggests instead that early hominids were deliberately producing flake tools, and the various stone nodules (choppers) were simply "incidental stopping points in the process of removing flakes from cores" (Potts, 1993, p. 60). As Potts summarizes his reevaluation, "The flaked stones of the Oldowan thus cannot be demonstrated to constitute discrete target designs, but can be shown to represent simple by-products of the repetitive act of producing sharp flakes" (Potts, 1993, pp. 60–61).

Breaking rocks by bashing them together is one thing. Producing consistent results, even apparently simple flakes, is quite another. You might want to give it a try, just to appreciate how difficult making a stone tool can be. It takes years of practice before modern stone **knappers** learn the intricacies—the type of rock to choose, the kind of hammer to employ, the angle and velocity with which to strike, and so on. Such experience allows us to appreciate how skilled in stoneworking our ancestors truly were.

Flakes can be removed from cores in various ways. The object in making a tool, however, is to produce a usable cutting surface. By reproducing results similar to those of earlier stoneworkers, experimental archaeologists can infer which kinds of techniques *might* have been employed.

For example, the nodules (now thought to be blanks) found in sites in Bed I at Olduvai (ca. 1.85–1.2 mya) are flaked on one side only (that is, *unifacially*). It's possible, but by no means easy, to produce such implements by hitting one stone—the hammerstone—against another—the core—in a method called **direct percussion** (Fig. 10-7).

In Bed IV sites (ca. 400 kya*), however, most of the tools are flaked on both sides (that is, *bifacially*) and have long rippled edges. Such a result can't be reproduced by direct percussion with just a hammerstone. The edges must have been straightened ("retouched") with a "soft" hammer, such as bone or antler.

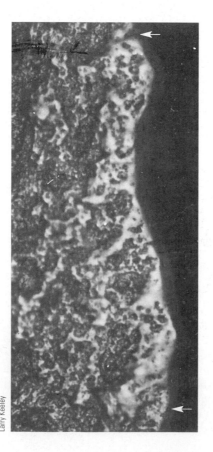

Larry Keeley

Reproducing implements similar to those found in later stages of human cultural development calls for even more sophisticated techniques. Tools such as the delicate **microlith**s found in the uppermost beds at Olduvai (ca. 17 kya), the superb Solutrean blades from Europe (ca. 20 kya), and the expertly crafted Folsom projectile points from the New World (ca. 10 kya) all require a mastery of stone matched by few knappers today.

To reproduce implements like those just mentioned, the knapper must remove extremely thin flakes. This can be done only through **pressure flaking**—for example, using a pointed piece of bone, antler, or hard wood and pressing firmly against the stone (Fig. 10-8).

Once the tools were manufactured, our ancestors used them in ways that we can infer through further experimentation. For example, archaeologists from the Smithsonian Institution successfully butchered an entire elephant (which had died in a zoo) using stone tools they had made for that purpose (Park, 1978). Other archaeologists have cut down (small) trees using stone axes they had made.

Ancient tools themselves may carry telltale signs of how they were used. Lawrence Keeley per-

---

*kya = thousand years ago.

formed a series of experiments in which he manufactured flint tools and then used them in diverse ways—whittling wood, cutting bone, cutting meat, and scraping skins. Viewing those implements under a microscope at fairly high magnification revealed patterns of polishes, striations, and other kinds of **microwear** (Fig. 10-9). What's most intriguing is that these patterns varied, depending on how the tool was used and which material was worked. For example, Keeley was able to distinguish among tools used on bone, antler, meat, plant materials, and hides. In the latter case, he was even able to determine if the hides were fresh or dried! Orientations of microwear markings also give some indication of how the tool was used (such as for cutting or scraping). Evidence of microwear polish has been examined on even the extremely early hominid stone tools from Koobi Fora (East Lake Turkana), in Kenya (Keeley and Toth, 1981).

Recent advances in tool use studies include the application of scanning electron microscopy (SEM). Working at 10,000× magnification, researchers have found that the edges of stone implements sometimes retain plant fibers and amino acids, as well as nonorganic residues, including **phytoliths**. Because phytoliths produced by different plant species are morphologically distinctive, there is good potential for identifying the botanical materials that came in contact with the tool during use (Rovner, 1983). Such work is most exciting—for the first time, we may be able to make definite statements concerning the uses of ancient tools.

ANALYSIS OF BONE

Experimental archaeologists are also interested in the ways bone is altered by human and natural forces. Other scientists are vitally concerned with this process as well; in fact, it has produced an entire new branch of paleoecology—taphonomy. Taphonomists have carried out comprehensive research on how natural factors influence bone deposition and preservation. In South Africa, C. K. Brain collected data on contemporary African butchering practices, carnivore (dog) disturbances, and so forth, and then correlated these factors with the kinds and numbers of elements usually found in bone accumulations (Brain, 1981). In this way, he was able to account for the accumulation of most (if not all) of the bones in South African cave sites. Likewise, in East African game parks, observations have been made on decaying animals to measure the effects of weathering, predator chewing, and trampling (Behrensmeyer et al., 1979; Perkins, 2003).

Further insight into the many ways bone is altered by natural factors has come from experimental work in the laboratory (Boaz and Behrensmeyer, 1976). In an experiment conducted at the University of California, Berkeley, human bones were put into a running-water trough. Researchers observed how far the water carried different pieces and recorded how much and what kind of damage was done. Such information is extremely useful in interpreting early hominid sites. For example, the distribution of hominid fossils at Olduvai suggests that active water transport was less prevalent there than in the Omo River Valley.

Detailed examination of bones may also provide evidence of butchering and bone breakage by hominids, including cut marks and percussion marks left by stone tools. Great care must be taken to distinguish marks left on bone by carnivore or rodent gnawing, weathering processes, hoof marks, or even normal growth. High magnification of a cut made by a stone tool may reveal a minutely striated and roughened groove scored into the bone's surface. Many such finds have been recognized at early hominid sites, including Olduvai Gorge (Bunn et al., 1980; Bunn, 1981; Potts and Shipman, 1981) (see "A Closer Look" on pp. 248–249).

Reconstruction of Early Hominid Environments and Behavior

Now that we've reviewed the various methods used by paleoanthropologists to *collect* their varied data, we can look at the intriguing ways this information is *interpreted*. Be aware that much of this interpretation is quite speculative and not as amenable to scientific verification as are more concrete sources of data (for example, that relating to dating, geology, or

microwear   Polishes, striations, and other diagnostic microscopic changes on the edges of stone tools.

phytoliths   (*phyto*, meaning "hidden," and *lith*, meaning "stone") Microscopic silica structures formed in the cells of many plants, particularly grasses.

hominid anatomy). (In Chapter 1, we discussed how hypotheses are developed and tested by scientists, noting the requirement that *scientific* explanations must be falsifiable.)

Paleoanthropologists are keenly interested not just in *how* early hominids evolved but also in *why* the process occurred the way that it did. Accordingly, they frequently use the data available as a basis for broad, speculative scenarios that try to explain both early hominid adaptations to a changing environment and the new behaviors that these hominids adopted. Such scenarios are fascinating, and paleoanthropologists enjoy constructing them (and certainly many in the general public enjoy reading them). Without doubt, for scientists and laypersons alike, our curiosity inevitably leads to intriguing and sweeping generalizations. Still, in the following discussion, we'll focus on what is *known* from the paleoanthropological record itself and separate that from the more speculative conclusions. You, too, should evaluate these explanations with a critical eye and try to identify the empirical basis for each type of reconstruction. It's important to go beyond accepting views merely because they are appealing (often because they're simple) or just because they seem *plausible*. We always need to ask ourselves what kinds of evidence support a particular contention, how generally the explanation fits the evidence (that is, how consistent it is with different types of data from varied sources), and what types of *new* evidence might either help to verify or potentially falsify the interpretation.

ENVIRONMENTAL EXPLANATIONS FOR HOMINID ORIGINS

As we'll discuss in the next chapter, the earliest hominids evolved late in the Miocene or very early in the Pliocene (7–5 mya). What were the environmental conditions at that time? Can these general ecological patterns help explain the origins of the first hominids (as they diversified from other kinds of hominoids)?

Before continuing, we'll give you one more word of caution. Many students have the common misconception that a single large environmental change is related clearly to a major adaptive change in a type of organism (in other words, environmental change X produced adaptation Y in a particular life form). This oversimplification is a form of **environmental determinism**, and it grossly underestimates the true complexity of the evolutionary process. It's clear that the environment does influence evolutionary change, as seen in the process of natural selection; but organisms are highly complex systems, composed of thousands of genes, and any adaptive shift to changing environmental circumstances is likely to be a compromise, balancing several selective factors simultaneously (such as temperature requirements, amount and distribution of food and water, predators, and safe sleeping sites). In our discussion of the socioecological dynamics of nonhuman primate adaptations in Chapter 7, we made this same point.

There's some evidence that at about the same time the earliest hominids were diverging, some major ecological changes *may* have been occurring in Africa. Could these ecological and evolutionary changes be related to each other? As we'll see, such a sweeping generalization has produced much debate. For most of the Miocene, Africa was generally tropical, with heavy rainfall persisting for most of the year; consequently, most of the continent was heavily forested. However, beginning later in the Miocene and intensifying up to the end of the epoch (about 5 mya), the climate became cooler, drier, and more seasonal.

We should also mention that in other regions of the world, paleoecological evidence reveals a distinct cooling trend at the end of the Miocene. But our focus is on Africa, particularly eastern and central Africa, for it's from these regions that we have the earliest evidence of hominid diversification. We've already noted that one method paleoanthropologists use to reconstruct environments is to analyze animal remains and fossilized pollen. Using another innovative technique, scientists study the chemical pathways utilized by different plants. In particular, **stable carbon isotopes** are produced by plants in differing proportions, depending partly on temperature and aridity (plants adapted to warmer, wetter climates—such as most trees, shrubs, and tubers—versus plants requiring hotter, drier conditions, as typified by many types of grasses). Animals eat the plants, and the differing concentrations of the stable isotopes of carbon are incorporated into their bones and teeth, thus providing a "signature" of the general type of environment in which they lived.

environmental determinism An interpretation that links simple environmental changes directly to a major evolutionary shift in an organism. Such explanations tend to extremely oversimplify the evolutionary process.

stable carbon isotopes Isotopes of carbon that are produced in plants in differing proportions, depending on environmental conditions. By analyzing the proportions of the isotopes contained in fossil remains of animals (who ate the plants), it's possible to reconstruct aspects of ancient environments (particularly temperature and aridity).

Through a combination of these analytical techniques, paleoecologists have gained a reasonably good handle on worldwide and continent-wide environmental patterns of the past. For example, one model postulates that as climates grew cooler in East Africa 12–5 mya, forests became less continuous. As a result, forest "fringe" habitats and transitional zones between forests and grasslands became more widespread. It's hypothesized that in such transitional environments, some of the late Miocene hominoids may have more intensively exploited the drier grassland portions of the fringe (these would be the earliest hominids); conversely, other hominoids concentrated more on the wetter portions of the fringe (these presumably were the ancestors of African great apes). In the incipient hominids, further adaptive strategies would have followed, including bipedalism, increased tool use, dietary specialization (perhaps on hard items such as seeds and nuts), and changes in social organization.

Such assertions concerning interactions of habitat, locomotion, dietary changes, and social organization are not really testable (since we don't know which changes came first). Still, some of the more restricted contentions of this "climatic forcing" theory are amenable to testing, though some of the model's more basic predictions haven't been confirmed. Most notably, further analyses using stable carbon isotopes from several East African localities suggest that during the late Miocene, environments across the area were consistently quite densely forested (that is, grasslands never predominated, except perhaps at a local level).

You should be aware that at the local level, there can be wide fluctuations in temperature, rainfall, and vegetation, and in the animals exploiting the vegetation. For example, local uplift, like a mountain, can produce a rain shadow, dramatically altering rainfall and temperature in a region. River and related lake drainages also have major impacts in some areas, and these topographical features are often influenced by highly localized geological factors. To generalize about climates in Africa, good data from several regions are required.

So it would seem, given current evidence and available analytical techniques, that our knowledge of the factors influencing the appearance of the *earliest* hominids is very limited. Considering the constraints, most hypotheses relating to potential factors are best kept restricted in scope and directly related to actual data. In this way, scientists can more easily evaluate the usefulness of these hypotheses, and they can be modified and built upon.

Other environmentally oriented hypotheses have been proposed for somewhat later stages of hominid evolution in Africa. Analysis of faunal remains from South African sites led Elizabeth Vrba of Yale University to suggest an *evolutionary pulse theory*. In this view, at various times during the Pliocene and early Pleistocene, the environment all across Africa became notably more arid. Vrba hypothesized that these major climatic shifts may have played a central role in stimulating hominid evolutionary development at key stages.

At one group of later hominid sites in Java, Indonesia, researchers are seeking to illuminate the flora and fauna that may have *enticed* our ancestors away from Africa, rather than thinking that harsh environments drove them out. The long sedimentary sequence of this region, known as the Sangiran Dome, allows for stable isotope analyses of the large and varied fossil assemblage—from mammals to clams and snails, to fossil pollen and other plant remains. It's here, in these favorable circumstances, that nearly 100 fossils of the extinct human, *Homo erectus*, have been found, spanning a 700 kya time range from 1.6 to 0.9 mya. This unique co-occurrence makes Sangiran an outstanding locality to test the effects of climate change on the evolving human lineage. The surrounding sites provide a wealth of information about climatic conditions and the environment that attracted and sustained *H. erectus* in Central Java. This region offers scientists a rare opportunity to determine just how flexible the adaptations of our hominid cousins might have been. (See "A Closer Look," p. 254).

This new view of humans—as just one of many animals attracted out of Africa by the promise of open niches—is more in line with additional data derived from thousands of fossils in East Africa (Behrensmeyer et al., 1997) that have failed to show that the environmental transitions Vrba (1992) invokes were as widespread as initially proposed. Further detailed analysis by Richard Potts of the Smithsonian Institution has, in fact, shown that ecosystems changed rapidly and often unpredictably throughout various areas of Africa (Bower, 2003; Potts, 2003). Rather than large-scale environmental changes "forcing" hominids into new adaptive strategies, perhaps our ancestors flourished and evolved because they were flexible opportunists.

A CLOSER LOOK

In Search of Ancient Human Ancestors— and a Little Shade

"Whoops!" Upon hearing this exclamation, my colleagues halt their progress along the narrow earthen walkways that outline the flooded rice paddies and make an emerald patchwork quilt on the Java landscape. They turn around and see that I've slipped. Again. Each misstep comes with some good-hearted ribbing as my comrades heave me back onto dry land. Each day we traverse the paddies by way of the thin dikes en route to our research site in central Java. Around us rise great cliffs of ancient soil, striated like an intricately layered cake. Rich green jewel tones dazzle the eye as we pass by peasants laboring in the fields under the hot sun. We, too, are in Java to work, but we toil for a different kind of produce—we seek answers about our early ancestor, Homo erectus. *As we tread across the paddies to a dusty oxcart path, our eyes comb the adjacent outcrops for darkened silhouettes of fossils—carefully, we note their locations. By the time we reach our destination, our backpacks are filled with curious remains—this one a tooth of a fossil deer, that one a piece of ancient crocodile bone—but no humans. All the fossils are stained crimson or black by the very soils in which they have lain for nearly a million years. As we begin to examine the exposed sediments, we resume our search for more fossils, our sweat-soaked shirts sticking to our skin. It's 9 A.M. and we're already tired and hot, but we quickly brush these distractions away. Our search has just begun.*

For the past 8 years, my colleagues and I have been conducting fieldwork in the rice paddies of Central Java. You might think it unusual to conduct scientific research in a rice paddy, but you have to "follow the fossils." Ancient sediments in our field area, the Sangiran Dome, were forced to the surface by the pressure of subterranean mud volcanoes about 120,000 years ago. What attracts us to the Sangiran Dome? It's the 1- to 2-million-year-old fossils and sediments that have been unearthed by erosion and other natural processes. This special series of events means that the Sangiran Dome is prime for both discovering the fossils of early humans in their original environmental context and for radiometrically dating them using volcanic sediments— a common occurrence in Java, an island formed by volcanoes.

If the cradle of human origins is Africa, then Asia was one of the playgrounds where our species grew and matured. Around 2 million years ago, *Homo erectus*, our first widely traveled ancestor, left the African savanna homeland to expand its horizons in the larger world (*Homo erectus* will be the main topic of Chapter 12). The first stop on this species' journey was in what is now the Republic of Georgia in southeastern Europe, where four skulls and a partial skeleton have been found. From here, we know that *Homo erectus* ventured onward to East Asia and eventually Java. We know little about the features that attracted them to the Javanese landscape, or when the first immigration to this island occurred. We do know that over time, the descendants of original *Homo erectus* immigrants evolved, giving us both full-sized primitive peoples with thick skulls and projecting browridges and later the diminutive "Hobbits" on the island of Flores (you'll meet them in Chapter 14).

Every good realtor will tell you that it's "location, location, location!" What was it about this Asian setting—particularly the island of Java—that drew these ancient immigrants to colonize, as evidenced by the nearly 100 fossils of *Homo erectus* that have been unearthed there over the past 70 years? Was it, perhaps, the rich volcanic soils and the vegetation they fostered that attracted our distant relatives to the Sangiran Dome, or did *Homo erectus* simply follow land-loving animals to the newly emergent environment of Central Java? Our research centers on this very issue, using visual and geochemical clues from soils and plant and animal fossils to reconstruct the landscape of Java when *Homo erectus* first arrived millions of years ago.

As the sun dips low on the horizon, the valley of the Sangiran Dome dims. At the end of the day, our team reassembles for the trek back to our van, joking and chatting about the day's finds. Our packs are heavy with samples of ancient soils, fossil shells and teeth, and rocks from ancient volcanic eruptions, all being hauled back for analysis. We watch our shadowy likenesses in the murky water of the paddies as we trudge out of the mists of time. In an hour we'll return to the hustle and bustle of Solo and wash away the dirt of ages. But before reentering civilization, we cast one last look into the past and wonder—"What was this place like during the time of our very ancient ancestors?" Was the landscape dominated by palms, mahogany, and cashew-bearing trees, as it is today, or was the countryside completely foreign? The full answers are just beyond our grasp. Perhaps today we carry in our backpacks the answers to these questions. Some day soon we'll be able to look at this landscape as our ancestors did, linking our common histories with modern technology.

—Russell L. Ciochon

© Russell Ciochon, University of Iowa

FIGURE 1

The Sangiran research team carefully negotiates the narrow dikes that lead to fossil-rich geological beds intricately layered like a cake.

WHY DID HOMINIDS BECOME BIPEDAL?

As we've noted several times, the adaptation of hominids to bipedal locomotion was *the* most fundamental adaptive shift among the early members of our family. But what were the factors that initiated this crucial change? Ecological theories, similar to some of those just discussed, have long been thought to be central to the development of bipedalism. Clearly, however, environmental influences would have to occur *before* documented evidence of well-adapted bipedal behavior. In other words, the major shift would have been at the end of the Miocene. Although the evidence indicates that no *sudden* wide ecological change took place at that time, locally forests probably did become patchier as rainfall became more seasonal. Given the changing environmental conditions, did hominids come to the ground to seize the opportunities offered in these more open habitats? Did bipedalism quickly ensue, stimulated somehow by this new way of life? At a very general level, the answer to these questions is yes. Obviously, hominids did at some point become bipedal, and this adaptation took place on the ground. Likewise, hominids are more adapted to mixed and open-country habitats than are our closest modern ape cousins. Successful terrestrial bipedalism probably made possible the further adaptation to more arid, open-country terrain. Still, this rendition simply tells us *where* hominids found their niche, not *why*.

As always, it's wise to be cautious when speculating about causation in evolution. It is all too easy to draw superficial conclusions. For example, scientists often surmise that the mere fact that ground niches were available (and perhaps lacked direct competitors) inevitably led the earliest hominids to terrestrial bipedalism. But consider this: Plenty of mammalian species, including some nonhuman primates, also live mostly on the ground in open country—and they aren't bipedal. Clearly, beyond such simplistic environmental determinism, some more complex explanation for hominid bipedalism is required. There must have been something *more* than just an environmental opportunity to explain this adaptation to such a unique lifestyle.

Another issue sometimes overlooked in the discussion of early hominid bipedal adaptation is that these creatures did not suddenly become *completely* terrestrial; but they also didn't slouch about, as illustrations of a linear progression of human evolution would suggest. As Tim White has pointed out, "You don't gradually go from being a quadruped to being a biped. What would the intermediate stage be—a triped? I've never seen one of those." His joke rings true, for the gradual transition would not be to a hunched-over, lolloping thing—a creature like that would be quickly eaten on the savanna—but would occur more as a time-sharing arrangement where early hominids spent some of their time as competent bipeds on the ground and some of their time safely concealed in the trees. We know, for example, that all terrestrial species of nonhuman primates (including savanna baboons, hamadryas baboons, patas monkeys; see Chapter 7) regularly seek out "safe sleeping sites" off the ground. These safe havens help protect against predation and are usually found in trees or on cliff faces. Likewise, early hominids almost certainly sought safety at night *in the trees*, even after they became well adapted to terrestrial bipedalism during daytime foraging. What's more, the continued opportunities for feeding in the trees would most likely have remained significant to early hominids, well after they were also utilizing ground-based resources.

Various hypotheses explaining why hominids initially became bipedal have been suggested and are summarized in Table 10-2. The primary influences claimed to have stimulated the shift to bipedalism include acquiring the ability to carry objects (and offspring); hunting on the ground; gathering of seeds and nuts; feeding from bushes; improving thermoregulation (that is, keeping cooler on the open savanna); having a better view of open country (to spot predators); walking long distances; and provisioning by males of females with dependent offspring.

These are all creative scenarios, but once again they're not very conducive to rigorous testing and verification. Still, two of the more ambitious scenarios proposed by Clifford Jolly (1970) and Owen Lovejoy (1981) deserve further mention. Both of these views sought to link several aspects of early hominid ecology, feeding, and social behavior, and both utilized models derived from studies of contemporary nonhuman primates.

Jolly's seed-eating hypothesis used the feeding behavior and ecology of gelada baboons as an analogy for very early hominids. Seed eating is an activity that requires keen hand-eye coordination, with bipedal shuffling improving efficiency of foraging. In this view, early

TABLE 10-2	Possible Factors Influencing the Initial Evolution of Bipedal Locomotion in Hominids	
Factor	**Speculated Influence**	**Comments**
Carrying (objects, tools, weapons, infants)	Upright posture freed the arms to carry various objects (including offspring).	Charles Darwin emphasized this view, particularly relating to tools and weapons; however, evidence of stone tools is found much later in record than first evidence of bipedalism.
Hunting	Systematic hunting is now thought not to have been practiced until after the origin of bipedal hominids.	Systematic hunting is now thought not to have been practiced until after the origin of bipedal hominids (see Issue, Chapter 12).
Seed and nut gathering	Feeding on seeds and nuts occurred while standing upright.	Model initially drawn from analogy with gelada baboons (see text).
Feeding from bushes	Upright posture provided access to seeds, berries, etc., in lower branches; analogous to adaptation seen in some specialized antelope.	Climbing adaptation already existed as prior ancestral trait in earliest hominids (i.e., bush and tree feeding already was established prior to bipedal adaptation).
Thermoregulation (cooling)	Vertical posture exposes less of the body to direct sun; increased distance from ground facilitates cooling by increased exposure to breezes.	Works best for animals active midday on savanna; moreover, adaptation to bipedalism may have initially occurred in woodlands, not on savanna.
Visual surveillance	Standing up provided better view of surrounding countryside (view of potential predators as well as other group members).	Behavior seen occasionally in terrestrial primates (e.g., baboons); probably a contributing factor, but unlikely as "prime mover."
Long-distance walking	Covering long distances was more efficient for a biped than for a quadruped (during hunting or foraging); mechanical reconstructions show that bipedal walking is less energetically costly than quadrupedalism (this is not the case for bipedal *running*).	Same difficulties as with hunting explanation; long-distance foraging on ground also appears unlikely adaptation in *earliest* hominids.
Male provisioning	Males carried back resources to dependent females and young.	Monogamous bond suggested; however, most skeletal data appear to falsify this part of the hypothesis (see text).

hominids are hypothesized to have adapted to open country and bipedalism as a result of their *primary* adaptation to eating seeds and nuts (found on the ground). The key assumption is that early hominids were eating seeds acquired in similar ecological conditions to those of contemporary gelada baboons.

Lovejoy, meanwhile, has combined *presumed* aspects of early hominid ecology, feeding, pair bonding, infant care, and food sharing to devise his creative scenario. This view hinges on these assumptions: (1) that the earliest hominids had offspring at least as K-selected (see p. 171) as other large-bodied hominoids; (2) that hominid males ranged widely and provisioned females and their young, who remained more tied to a "home base"; and (3) that males were paired *monogamously* with females.

As we've noted, while not strictly testable, such scenarios do make certain predictions (which can be potentially falsified or upheld). Accordingly, aspects of each scenario can be evaluated in light of more specific data (obtained from the paleoanthropological record). Regarding the seed-eating hypothesis, predictions relating to size of the back teeth in most early hominids are met, but the proportions of the front teeth in many forms aren't what we'd expect to see in a committed seed eater. Besides, the analogy with gelada baboons is not as informative as once thought; these animals actually don't eat that many seeds and certainly aren't habitual bipeds. Finally, many of the characteristics that Jolly suggested were restricted to hominids (and geladas) are also found in several late Miocene hominoids (who weren't hominids). Thus, regarding the seed-eating hypothesis, the proposed dental and dietary adaptations don't appear to be linked specifically to hominid origins or bipedalism.

Further detailed analyses of data have also questioned crucial elements of Lovejoy's male-provisioning scenario. The evidence that appears to most contradict this view is that *all* early hominids were quite sexually dimorphic (McHenry, 1992). According to Lovejoy's model (and analogies with contemporary monogamous nonhuman primates such as gibbons), there shouldn't be such dramatic differences in body size between males and females. Recent studies (Reno et al., 2003, 2005) have questioned this view, suggesting, at least for one species (*Australopithecus afarensis*), that sexual dimorphism was only very moderate. This conclusion appears at odds with most of the evidence regarding early hominids. What's more, the notions of food sharing (presumably including considerable meat), home bases, and long-distance provisioning are questioned by more controlled interpretations of the archaeological record (see "A Closer Look", pp. 248–249).

Another imaginative view is also relevant to this discussion of early hominid evolution, since it relates the adaptation to bipedalism (which was first) to increased brain expansion (which came later). This interpretation, proposed by Dean Falk, suggests that an upright posture put severe constraints on brain size (since blood circulation and drainage would have been altered and cooling would consequently have been more limited than in quadrupeds). Falk thus hypothesizes that new brain-cooling mechanisms must have coevolved with bipedalism, articulated in what she calls the "radiator theory" (Falk, 1990). Falk further surmises that the requirements for better brain cooling would have been particularly marked as hominids adapted to open-country ground living on the hot African savanna. Another interesting pattern observed by Falk concerns two different cooling adaptations found in different early hominid species. She thus suggests that the type of "radiator" adapted in the genus *Homo* was particularly significant in reducing constraints on brain size—which presumably limited some other early hominids. The radiator theory works well, since it not only helps explain the relationship of bipedalism to later brain expansion but also explains why only some hominids became dramatically encephalized.

The radiator theory, too, has been criticized by some paleoanthropologists. Most notably, the presumed species distinction concerning varying cooling mechanisms is not as obvious as suggested by the hypothesis. Both types of venous drainage systems can be found in contemporary *Homo sapiens* as well as within various early hominid species (that is, the variation is intraspecific, not just interspecific). Indeed, in some early hominid specimens, both systems can be found in the *same* individual (expressed on either side of the skull). Besides, as Falk herself has noted, the radiator itself didn't lead to larger brains; it simply helped reduce constraints on increased encephalization among hominids. It thus requires some *further* mechanism (prime mover) to explain why, in some hominid species, brain size increased the way it did.

CHAPTER 11

Hominid Origins in Africa

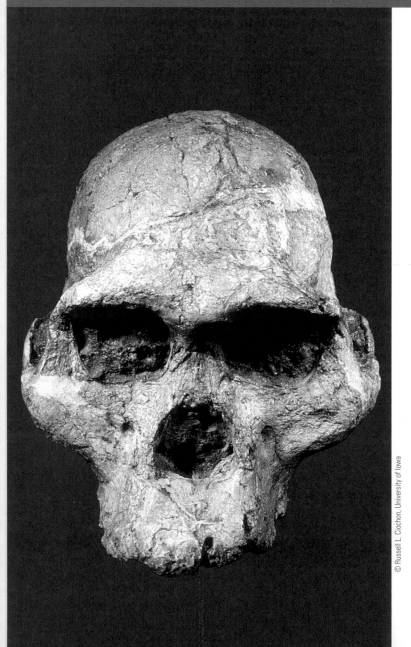

© Russell L. Ciochon, University of Iowa

KEY QUESTION

Who are the oldest members of the human family, and how do these early hominids compare with modern humans and with modern apes? How do they fit within a biological continuum?

Introduction

Today, our species dominates the planet, using our brains and cultural inventions to invade every corner of the earth. Yet, 5 million years ago (mya), our ancestors were little more than bipedal apes, confined to a few regions in Africa. What were these creatures like? When and how did they begin their evolutionary journey?

In Chapter 10, we discussed the techniques paleoanthropologists use to locate and excavate sites, as well as the multidisciplinary approaches used to interpret discoveries. In this chapter, we turn to the physical evidence of the hominid fossils themselves. The earliest fossils identifiable as hominids are all from Africa. During the early Pliocene (by 4 mya), the fossil discoveries are fairly abundant, and paleoanthropologists consider them as unambiguously members of the hominid family. Indeed, the fossil evidence becomes more complete over the next several million years, encompassing the Pliocene and the first half of the Pleistocene epochs. This time period is usually referred to as the **Plio-Pleistocene**.

Hominids, of course, evolved from earlier primates (dating from the Eocene to late Miocene), and in Chapter 9 we discussed the fossil evidence of prehominid primates. These fossils provide us with context within which to understand the subsequent evolution of the human family. In fact, from quite recent discoveries, the earliest hominids are now thought to date as far back as the end of the Miocene (7–5 mya). This fossil material is extremely exciting, extending the evidence of the human family back a further 2 million years into prehistory. What's more, these discoveries have all been made very recently—just in the last eight years. As a result, detailed evaluations are still in process, and conclusions must remain tentative.

One thing is certain, however. The earliest members of the human family were confined to Africa. Only much later do their descendants disperse from the African continent to other areas of the Old World (this "out of Africa" saga will be the topic of the next chapter).

The Bipedal Adaptation

In our overview in Chapter 10 of behavioral reconstructions of early hominids, we highlighted several hypotheses that attempt to explain *why* bipedal locomotion first evolved in the hominids. Here we turn to the specific anatomical (that is, **morphological**) evidence that shows us when, where, and how hominid bipedal locomotion evolved.

In our discussion of primate anatomical trends in Chapter 6, we noted a general tendency in all primates for erect body posture and some bipedalism. Of all living primates, however, efficient bipedalism as the primary (habitual) form of locomotion is seen *only* in hominids. Functionally, the human mode of locomotion is most clearly shown in our *striding* gait, where weight is alternately placed on a single fully extended hind limb. This specialized form of locomotion has developed to a point where energy levels are used to near peak efficiency. This is far from the case in nonhuman primates, who move bipedally with hips and knees bent and maintain balance clumsily and inefficiently, toddling along rather than striding.

Our mode of locomotion is extraordinary when you think about it, where "the body, step by step, teeters on the edge of catastrophe" (Napier, 1967, p. 56). In this way, the act of human walking is the act of *almost falling* repeatedly! The problem is to maintain balance on the "stance" leg while the "swing" leg is off the ground. In fact, during normal walking, both feet are simultaneously on the ground only about 25 percent of the time, with this figure diminishing as speed of locomotion increases.

 Click!

Go to the following media for interactives and exercises on topics covered in this chapter:

- Online Virtual Laboratories for Physical Anthropology, Fourth Edition
- Hominid Fossils CD-ROM: An Interactive Atlas

Plio-Pleistocene Pertaining to the Pliocene and first half of the Pleistocene, a time range of 5–1 mya. For this time period, numerous fossil hominids have been found in Africa.

morphological Pertaining to the form and structure of organisms.

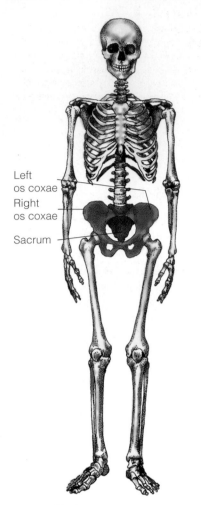

Left os coxae
Right os coxae
Sacrum

FIGURE 11-1

The human pelvis: various elements shown on a modern skeleton.

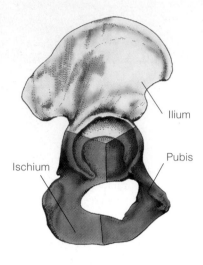

Ilium
Ischium
Pubis

FIGURE 11-2

The human os coxae, composed of three bones (right side shown).

FIGURE 11-3

Ossa coxae. (a) *Homo sapiens.* (b) Early hominid (*Australopithecus*) from South Africa. (c) Great ape. Note especially the length and breadth of the iliac blade (boxed) and the line of weight transmission (shown in red).

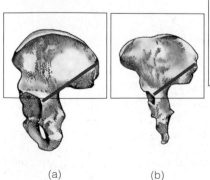

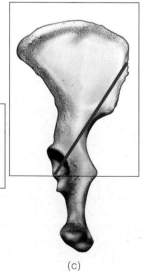

(a)   (b)   (c)

Maintaining a stable center of balance in this complex form of locomotion calls for many drastic structural/anatomical alterations in the basic primate quadrupedal pattern. The most dramatic changes are seen in the pelvis. The pelvis is composed of three elements: two *ossa coxae* (*sing.,* os coxae—hip bones), joined at the back to the sacrum (Fig. 11-1). In a quadruped, the ossa coxae are vertically elongated bones positioned along each side of the lower portion of the spine and oriented more or less parallel to it. In hominids, the pelvis is comparatively much shorter and broader and extends around to the side (Fig. 11-2). This configuration helps to stabilize the **line of weight transmission** in a bipedal posture from the lower back to the hip joint (Fig. 11-3).

Several consequences resulted from the remodeling of the pelvis during early hominid evolution. Broadening the two sides and extending them around to the side and front of the body produced a basin-shaped structure that helps support the abdominal organs (*pelvis* means "basin" in Latin). These alterations also repositioned the attachments of several key muscles that act on the hip and leg, changing their mechanical function. Probably the most important of these altered relationships is that involving the *gluteus maximus,* the largest muscle in the body, which in humans forms the bulk of the buttocks. In quadrupeds, the gluteus maximus is positioned to the side of the hip and functions to pull the thigh to the side and away from the body. In humans, this muscle is positioned behind the hip; this arrangement allows it, along with the hamstrings, to extend the thigh, pulling it to the rear during walking and running (Fig. 11-4). The gluteus maximus is a truly powerful extensor of the thigh and provides additional force, particularly during running and climbing.

Modifications also occurred in other parts of the skeleton because of the shift to bipedalism. The most significant of these, summarized in "A Closer Look" on pages 266–267, include (1) repositioning of the foramen magnum, the opening at the base of the skull through which the spinal cord emerges; (2) the addition of spinal curves that help to transmit the weight of the upper body to the hips in an upright posture; (3) shortening and broadening of the pelvis and the stabilization of weight transmission (discussed earlier); (4) lengthening of the hind limb, thus increasing stride length; (5) angling of the femur (thighbone) inward to bring the knees and feet closer together under the body; and (6) several structural changes in the foot, including the development of a longitudinal arch and realignment of the big toe in parallel with the other toes (that is, it was no longer divergent).

As you can appreciate, the evolution of hominid bipedalism required complex anatomical reorganization. For natural selection to produce anatomical change of the magnitude seen in hominids, the benefits of bipedal locomotion must have been significant, indeed! We mentioned in Chapter 10 several possible adaptive advantages that bipedal locomotion *may* have conferred upon early hominids. But these all remain hypotheses (even more accurately, they could be called scenarios), and we have inadequate data for testing the various proposed alternatives.

Still, given the anatomical alterations required for efficient bipedalism, some major behavioral stimuli must have been influencing its development. When interpreting evolutionary history, biologists are fond of saying that form follows function. In other words, during evolution, organisms don't undergo significant

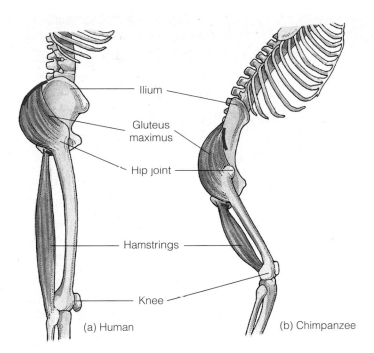

Ilium

Gluteus
maximus

Hip joint

Hamstrings

Knee

(a) Human   (b) Chimpanzee

FIGURE 11-4
Comparisons of important muscles that act to
extend the hip. Note that the attachment surface (origin, shown in red) of the gluteus maximus in humans (a) is farther in back of the hip
joint than in a chimpanzee standing bipedally.
(b) Conversely, in chimpanzees, the hamstrings
are farther in back of the knee.

reorganization in structure *unless* these changes—over many generations—assist individuals in some functional capacity (and in so doing, increase their reproductive success). Such
changes didn't necessarily occur all at once, but probably evolved over a fairly long period
of time. Even so, once behavioral influences initiated certain structural modifications, the
process gained momentum and proceeded irreversibly.

We say that hominid bipedalism is habitual and obligate. By *habitual*, we mean that
hominids, unlike any other primate, move bipedally as their standard and most efficient
mode of locomotion. By *obligate*, we mean that hominids are committed to bipedalism and
cannot locomote efficiently in any other way. For example, the loss of grasping ability in
the foot makes climbing much more difficult for humans (although by no means impossible). The central task, then, in trying to understand the earliest members of the hominid
family is to identify anatomical features that indicate bipedalism and to interpret to what
degree these organisms were committed to this form of locomotion (that is, was it habitual and was it obligate?).

What structural patterns are observable in early hominids, and what do they imply
regarding locomotor function? All the major structural changes required for bipedalism
are seen in early hominids from Africa (at least as far as the evidence permits conclusions
to be made). In particular, the pelvis, as clearly documented by several excellently preserved specimens, was dramatically remodeled to support weight in a bipedal stance (see
Fig. 11-3b).

Other structural changes shown after 4 mya in the earliest relatively complete hominid
postcranial remains also further confirm the pattern seen in the pelvis. For example, the vertebral column (as known from specimens in East and South Africa) shows the same curves
as in modern hominids. The lower limbs were also elongated, and they seemed to be proportionately about as long as in modern humans (although the arms were longer). Further,
the carrying angle of weight support from the hip to the knee was very similar to that seen
in *Homo sapiens*.

Fossil evidence of early hominid foot structure has come from two sites in South Africa;
especially important are some recently announced new fossils from **Sterkfontein** (Clarke
and Tobias, 1995). These specimens, consisting of four articulating elements from the ankle
and big toe, indicate that the heel and longitudinal arch were both well adapted for a bipedal
gait. But the paleoanthropologists (Ron Clarke and Phillip Tobias) who analyzed these
remains also suggest that the large toe was *divergent*, unlike the hominid pattern shown in

line of weight transmission The
line over which a significant weight load is
carried; in a bone structure, the portion of
the bone carrying the load will usually be
reinforced (i.e., thicker/buttressed).

Sterkfontein (sterk'-fon-tane)

A CLOSER LOOK   Major Features of Bipedal Locomotion

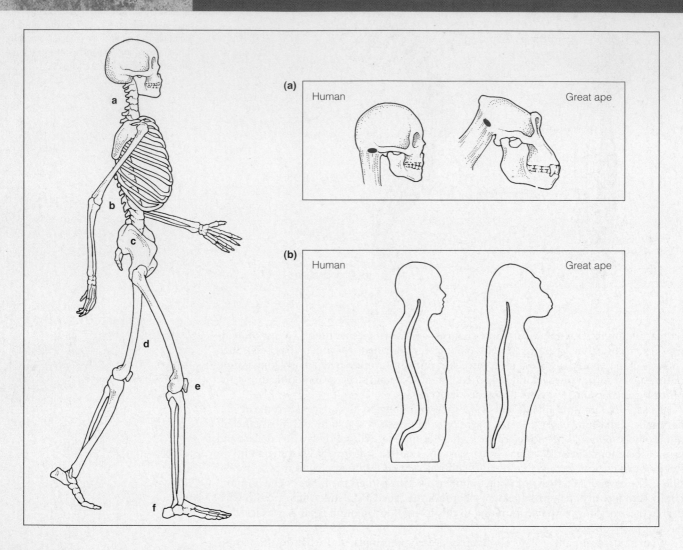

During hominid evolution, several major structural features throughout the body have been reorganized (from that seen in other primates) to facilitate efficient bipedal locomotion. These are illustrated here, beginning with the head and progressing to the foot: (a) The foramen magnum (shown in red) is repositioned farther underneath the skull, so that the head is more or less balanced on the spine (and thus requires less-robust neck muscles to hold the head upright). (b) The spine has two distinctive curves—a backward (thoracic) one and a forward (lumbar) one—that keep the trunk (and weight) centered above the pelvis. (c) The pelvis is shaped more in the form of a basin to support internal organs; the ossa coxae (specifically, iliac blades)

"A Closer Look" on pages 266–267. If the large toe really did possess this anatomical position, it most likely would have aided the foot in grasping. In turn, this grasping ability (as in other primates) would have enabled early hominids to more effectively exploit arboreal habitats. Finally, since anatomical remodeling is always constrained by a set of complex functional compromises, a foot highly capable of grasping and climbing is *less* capable as a stable platform during bipedal locomotion. So, some researchers see early hominids as not necessarily obligate bipeds. Further investigation of the cave site in 1998 revealed a remarkable find—the remains of a nearly complete skeleton belonging to the same individual from which the foot came—affectionately nicknamed "Little Foot" (see p. 290).

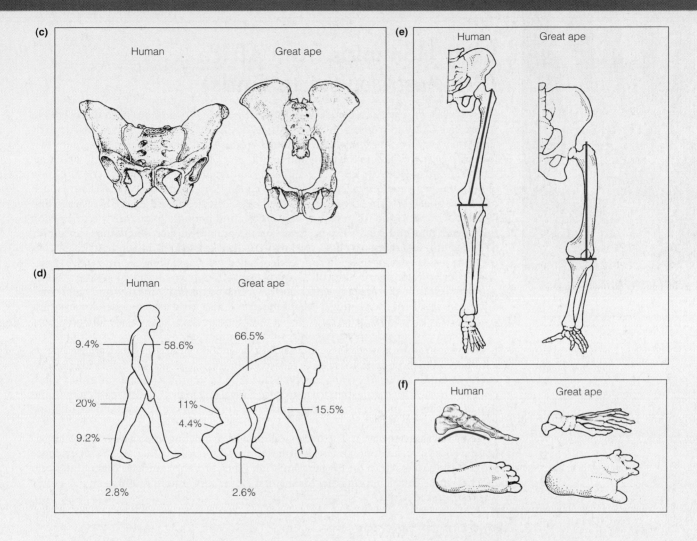

arc also shorter and broader, thus stabilizing weight transmission. (d) Lower limbs are elongated, as shown by the proportional lengths of various body segments (for example, in humans the thigh comprises 20 percent of body height, while in gorillas it comprises only 11 percent). (e) The femur is angled inward, keeping the legs more directly under the body; modified knee anatomy also permits full extension of this joint. (f) The big toe is enlarged and brought in line with the other toes; a distinctive longitudinal arch also forms, helping absorb shock and adding propulsive spring.

More evidence for evolutionary changes in the pedal (foot) skeleton comes from Olduvai Gorge in Tanzania, where a nearly complete hominid foot is preserved (Fig. 11-5), and from Hadar in Ethiopia, where numerous foot elements have been recovered. As in the remains from South Africa, the East African fossils suggest a well-adapted bipedal gait. The arches are developed, but some differences in the ankle also imply that considerable flexibility was possible (again, suggested for continued adaptation to climbing). As we'll see, some researchers have recently concluded that many early forms of hominids probably spent considerable time in the trees. What's more, they may not have been quite as efficient bipedally, as has previously been suggested. Still, to this point, most researchers think that *all* the early hominids that have been identified from Africa were both habitual and obligate bipeds (despite the new evidence from South Africa and the earliest traces from central and East Africa, all of which will require further study).

Early Hominids from Africa (Pre-*Australopithecus* Finds)

Over the last 80 years, a tremendous number of hominid fossils have been discovered in Africa. The first finds came from South Africa, but by the 1970s East Africa (particularly along the Rift Valley in Ethiopia, Kenya, and Tanzania) had taken preeminence. Many factors influenced this shift in the focus and significance of discovery. The geological circumstances found in East Africa produce a clearer stratigraphic picture and better association of hominids with archaeological artifacts, and equally important, these materials are much more easily datable (using chronometric methods). Also, fossils are generally easier to find in East Africa, although it's never any easy task to find hominid fossils anywhere! Erosion from wind, rain, and gravity expose fossils on the ground surface, where they can simply be picked up—assuming, of course, you know exactly *where* to look. In South Africa, by contrast, the fossils are embedded in rock matrix called *breccia*, making delicate archaeological recovery extraordinarily difficult. Even so, excavations have continued at several South African sites. From this ongoing work, researchers have explored some new and highly productive locales; as of this writing, perhaps the most intact early hominid skeleton ever discovered ("Little Foot") is being excavated at Sterkfontein Cave, just outside Johannesburg.

The saga of new and more intriguing African hominid discoveries is not yet completed; in fact, it hasn't even slowed. As recently as 2002, from a site in central Chad, archaeologists announced the most remarkable discovery made in the last 75 years. What made this discovery (from Chad) so surprising was (1) its location (in central Africa, *not* in either South or East Africa), (2) its age (estimated at close to 7 mya, making it by far the earliest hominid found anywhere), and (3) its physical appearance (quite unexpected and unlike anything discovered previously).

So, if we accept the latest discoveries and provisional dating as accurate, hominid origins go back in Africa approximately 7 million years. Hominids, as far as current evidence indicates, stayed in Africa for the next 5 million years, first emigrating to other Old World locales 2 mya. Thus it appears that for the first 70 percent of hominid history, our family was restricted to Africa.

EARLIEST TRACES

The distinction of being designated "the earliest hominid" is one that draws worldwide media coverage, but it's a notoriously fickle title. When this textbook was first published in 1979, the earliest hominid was dated at between 3 and 4 mya. By the seventh edition (1997), based on some Ethiopian fossils, the date had been pushed back to 4.4 mya. By 2000 (based on Kenyan material), the date was further extended to close to 6 mya. And in 2002, the startling find from Chad suggested that the current bearer of the "earliest" title is 7 million years old.

This brief history is not intended to force unsuspecting students to memorize exactly what was found and when. Our point is to illustrate how rapidly discoveries have taken place; in just the last decade, the reported span of hominid existence has increased by 60 percent.

Central Africa From our latest information, the earliest known hominid is a nearly complete cranium discovered in 2001 at a site called Toros-Menalla in northern Chad (Brunet et al., 2002; Fig. 11-6). Provisional dating using faunal correlation (biostratigraphy; see p. 246) suggests a date nearly 7 mya (Vignaud et al., 2002). Surprisingly, the very early suggested age of this fossil places it at almost 1 million years earlier than *any* of the other proposed early hominids (and close to 3 million years earlier than the oldest well-established hominid discoveries).

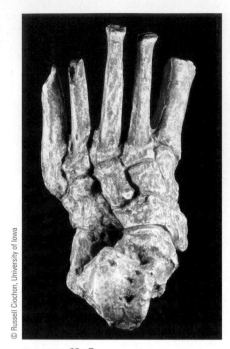

FIGURE 11-5
A nearly complete hominid foot (OH 8) from Olduvai Gorge, Tanzania.

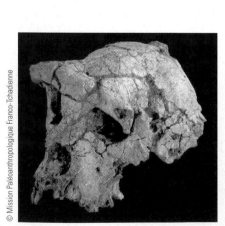

FIGURE 11-6
A nearly complete cranium of *Sahelanthropus* from Chad, dating to 7 mya.

The morphology of the fossil is unusual, with a combination of characteristics unlike that found in other early hominids. The braincase is small, estimated at no larger than a modern chimpanzee's (preliminary estimate in the range of 320 to 380 cm^3), and it's massively built, with huge browridges in front, a crest on top, and large muscle attachments in the rear (Fig. 11-7). Yet, combined with these apelike features is a smallish vertical face containing front teeth very unlike an ape's. In fact, a lower face more tucked in under the brain vault (and not protruding, as in most other early hominids) is more of a *derived* feature more commonly expressed in much later hominids (especially members of genus *Homo*). What's more, unlike the dentition seen in apes (and some early hominids), the upper canine is reduced and is worn down from the tip (rather than shearing along its side against the first lower premolar).

In recognition of this unique combination of characteristics, the lead researcher, Michael Brunet (of the University of Poitiers, in France), has placed the Toros-Menalla remains into a new genus and species of hominid, *Sahelanthropus tchadensis* (Sahel being the region of the southern Sahara in North Africa).

These new finds from Chad have forced an immediate and significant reassessment of early hominid evolution. Two cautionary comments, however, are in order. First, the dating is only approximate, because it's based on biostratigraphic correlation with sites in Kenya (1,500 miles to the east). The faunal sequences, nevertheless, seem to be clearly bracketed by two very well-dated sequences in Kenya. Second, and perhaps more serious, is the hominid status of the Chad fossil. Given the facial structure and dentition, it's difficult to see how *Sahelanthropus* could be anything but a hominid. Still, some researchers (Wolpoff et al., 2002) have raised questions regarding the evolutionary interpretation of *Sahelanthropus*, suggesting that this fossil may represent an ape rather than a hominid. As we said earlier, the best-defining anatomical characteristics of hominids relate to bipedal locomotion. Unfortunately, no **postcranial** elements have been recovered from Chad—at least not yet. Consequently, we don't yet know the locomotor behavior of *Sahelanthropus*, and this raises even more fundamental questions: What if further finds show this form not to be bipedal? Should we still consider it a hominid? What, then, are the defining characteristics of our family?

East Africa Two areas in East Africa, one in central Kenya and the other from the Middle Awash area of northeastern Ethiopia, have also quite recently yielded very early hominid remains. The oldest of these finds come from sites in the Tugen Hills of central Kenya, near Lake Baringo (Pickford and Senut, 2001; Senut et al., 2001). Good radiometric determinations place the age of the remains at close to 6 mya.

The fossil remains are a mixed assortment, with a couple of pieces of lower jaw and several isolated teeth. Most intriguing, however, are a few pieces of limb bone, including two excellently preserved femora. From these latter fossils especially, French paleontologist Brigitte Senut (of the Museum of Natural History in Paris) and her colleagues are convinced that these 6-million-year-old primates walked *bipedally* and are thus hominids (Senut et al., 2001; Galik et al., 2004). But there are also some unusual aspects of the teeth, mostly suggesting a primitive, apelike morphology. This curious combination of features has led the French scientists to assign the remains to a completely new genus and species (*Orrorin tugenensis*).

Coming from a few hundred miles north of the Tugen Hills, in the Middle Awash region of Ethiopia, another group of quite early fossils was also first described in 2001. Yohannes Haile-Selassie, an anthropology graduate student at the University of California, Berkeley, discovered the first remains in 1997, with further discoveries extending to 2001 and 2002 (Haile-Selassie, 2001; Haile-Selassie et al., 2004). Well-controlled radiometric dating determinations place the fossils in the late Miocene (at 5.8–5.2 mya), just a little later than the Tugen Hills finds. These latter fossil remains are quite fragmentary, including mostly teeth, a jaw fragment, and just a few pieces of the limb skeleton, the latter including one toe bone, a phalanx from the middle of the foot (see Appendix A, Fig. A-8). From suggestive clues seen in this toe bone, Haile-Selassie concludes that this primate was a well-adapted *biped* (once again, the best supporting evidence of hominid status).

Other, more complete remains from the Middle Awash area were discovered at the Aramis site (discussed shortly) and originate a little later in time. These remains have been

postcranial (*post*, meaning "after") In a quadruped, referring to that portion of the body behind the head; in a biped, referring to all parts of the body beneath the head (i.e., the neck down).

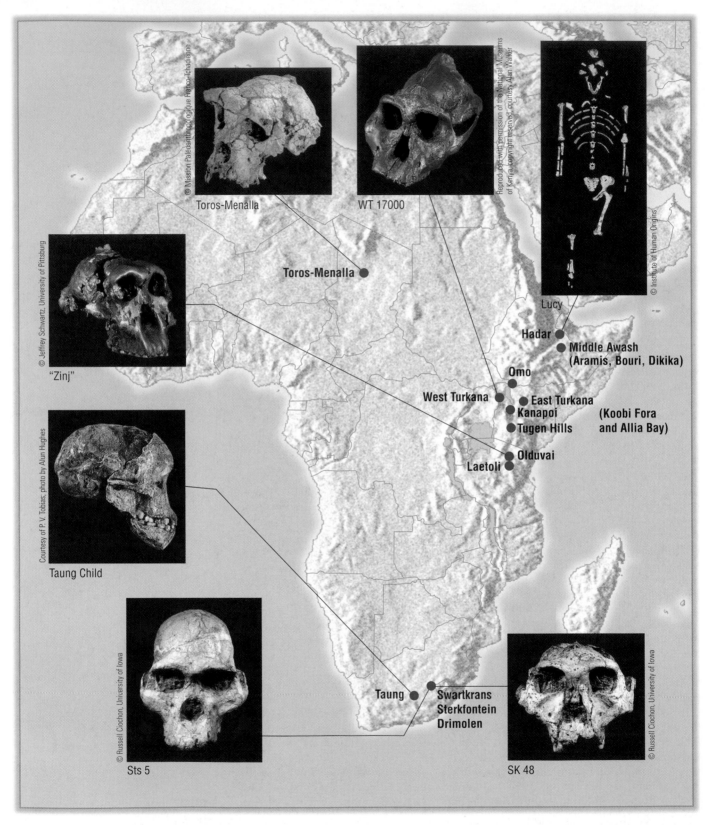

Toros-Menalla

WT 17000

Lucy

"Zinj"

Hadar

Middle Awash
(Aramis, Bouri, Dikika)

Omo

West Turkana   **East Turkana**

Kanapoi   **(Koobi Fora**

Tugen Hills   **and Allia Bay)**

Olduvai

Laetoli

Taung Child

Taung   **Swartkrans**
Sterkfontein
Drimolen

Sts 5   SK 48

FIGURE 11-7
Early hominid fossil finds and localities (pre-*Australopithecus*,
Australopithecus, and *Paranthropus* localities).

assigned to the genus *Ardipithecus*, and Haile-Selassie and colleagues (Haile-Selassie et al., 2004) have determined that the earlier fossils from this same region should be placed in this same genus (but a different species) from the later fossils.

In addition to the reasonably complete remains from the Tugen Hills and the Middle Awash, there are several scattered finds of what many researchers think may be other very early hominids. In the time range 5–4 mya, there are three additional localities (two from central Kenya and one from Ethiopia). None of this further material is particularly informative (or diagnostic), however, since only a single (fragmentary) specimen has been recovered from each locality.

ARDIPITHECUS FROM ARAMIS (ETHIOPIA)

The Middle Awash sites are in one of the most exciting areas for future research in East Africa—the Afar Triangle of northeastern Ethiopia, where the Red Sea, Rift Valley, and Gulf of Aden all intersect. From this region have come many of the most important recent discoveries providing insight into human origins. Several areas have yielded fossil remains in recent decades, and researchers are currently exploring many potentially very rich sites. One of these quite recently discovered sites, located in the Middle Awash (along the banks of the Awash River), is called **Aramis**. Initial radiometric dating of the sediments places the hominid remains at 4.4 mya, making this the earliest substantial *collection* of hominids yet discovered.

Beginning with excavations in the 1990s, the fossil hominids from Aramis include up to 50 different individuals (Wolpoff, 1999). This crucial and quite large fossil assortment includes several dental specimens as well as an upper arm bone (humerus) and some fragmentary cranial remains. Most exciting of all, in 1995, researchers discovered 40 percent of a skeleton. Unfortunately, the bones are all encased in limestone matrix, and it's a long and tedious process to remove the fossils intact from the cementlike material surrounding them. In fact, as of this writing, the Aramis remains (including the skeleton) have not yet been fully scientifically described. Still, details from initial reports are highly suggestive that these remains are, in fact, very early hominids (White et al., 2006).

What makes researchers think these are early hominid fossils? First of all, in an Aramis partial cranium, the *foramen magnum* is positioned farther forward in the base of the skull than is the case in quadrupeds (Fig. 11-8). Second, features of the humerus also differ from those seen in quadrupeds, indicating that the Aramis humerus did not function in locomotion to support weight (that is, the upper limbs were free). From these two features, the provisional interpretation by Tim White, of the University of California, Berkeley, and his colleagues was that the Aramis individuals were *bipedal*. Initial interpretation of the partial skeleton (while not yet fully cleaned and reported) also suggests obligate bipedalism (Wolpoff, 1999).

Still, these were definitely quite primitive hominids, displaying an array of characteristics clearly distinct from other members of our family. These primitive characteristics include flattening of the cranial base and relatively thin enamel caps on the molar teeth. From measurements of the humerus head, Wolpoff (1999) estimates a body weight of 42 kg (93 pounds); if this humerus comes from a male individual, this weight estimate is very similar to that hypothesized for other Plio-Pleistocene hominids (see Table 11-1, p. 272).

So, current conclusions (which will be either unambiguously confirmed or falsified as the skeleton is fully cleaned and studied) interpret the Aramis remains as among the earliest hominids yet known. These primitive hominids from Aramis were apparently bipedal, although not necessarily in the same way that later hominids were.

Based on their analyses, Tim White and colleagues have concluded (White et al., 1995) that the fossil hominids from Aramis are so primitive and so different from other early hominids that they should be assigned to a new genus (and, necessarily, a new species as well): *Ardipithecus ramidus*. Most especially, the thin enamel caps on the molars are in dramatic contrast to all other confirmed early hominids, who show quite thick enamel caps. These other early hominid forms (all somewhat later than *Ardipithecus*) are placed in the genus **Australopithecus**. White and his associates have further suggested that as the earliest and most primitive hominid yet discovered, *Ardipithecus* may possibly be the root species for all later hominids.

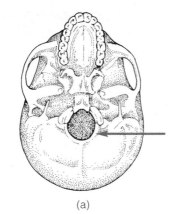

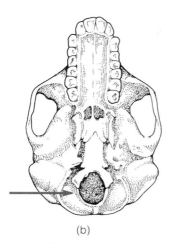

FIGURE 11-8
Position of the foramen magnum in (a) a human and (b) a chimpanzee. Note the more forward position in the human cranium.

Aramis (air´-ah-miss)

Australopithecus An early hominid genus, known from the Plio-Pleistocene of Africa, characterized by bipedal locomotion, a relatively small brain, and large back teeth.

TABLE 11-1	Estimated Body Weights and Stature in Plio-Pleistocene Hominids			
	Body Weight		**Stature**	
	Male	**Female**	**Male**	**Female**
A. afarensis	45 kg (99 lb)	29 kg (64 lb)	151 cm (59 in.)	105 cm (41 in.)
A. africanus	41 kg (90 lb)	30 kg (65 lb)	138 cm (54 in.)	115 cm (45 in.)
A. robustus	40 kg (88 lb)	32 kg (70 lb)	132 cm (52 in.)	110 cm (43 in.)
A. boisei	49 kg (108 lb)	34 kg (75 lb)	137 cm (54 in.)	124 cm (49 in.)
H. habilis	52 kg (114 lb)	32 kg (70 lb)	157 cm (62 in.)	125 cm (49 in.)

Source: After McHenry, 1992. *Note:* Reno et. al (2003) conclude that sexual dimorphism in *A. afarensis* was considerably less than shown here.

This view doesn't take into account the recently discovered fossils from Toros-Menalla and the Tugen Hills, which are each provisionally assigned to other early hominid genera (*Sahelanthropus* and *Orrorin,* respectively). However, this interpretation does encompass the earlier remains from the Middle Awash—which, for the moment, are also included within *Ardipithecus.*

Another intriguing aspect of all these late Miocene/early Pliocene locales (that is, Tugen Hills, early Middle Awash sites, and Aramis) relates to the ancient environments associated with the suggested earliest of hominids. Rather than the more open grassland savanna habitats so characteristic of most later hominid sites, the environments at these early locales are more heavily forested. The oldest of the hominid localities, Toros-Menalla, shows (from initial analysis) a mosaic of environments (Vignaud et al., 2002). The hominids almost certainly died near a lakeshore, but apparently forest and grassland habitats were also nearby. The general ecological association of the very early hominids with forested habitats isn't surprising. After all, hominids almost certainly diverged from a line of forest-living hominoids—and likely did so not long before these late Miocene hominids came on the scene.

sectorial   Adapted for cutting or shearing; among primates, refers to the compressed (side-to-side) first lower premolar, which functions as a shearing surface with the upper canine.

Australopithecus/Paranthropus from East Africa

Several sites in Ethiopia, Kenya, and Tanzania have yielded remains of somewhat later hominids than the *Ardipithecus* remains from Aramis. Dating from 4.2 mya to approximately 1.4 mya, most of these later East African fossils are included either in the genus *Australopithecus* or in a closely related genus called *Paranthropus.** Note, however, that many paleoanthropologists place some other specimens from the later half of this time span in the genus *Homo.*

The earliest members of *Australopithecus* found to date come from a total of four sites, two located near Lake Turkana in northern Kenya (Allia Bay and Kanapoi) and two from the Middle Awash of Ethiopia. Not as many specimens have been found at these sites as the large collection of *Ardipithecus,* but from what has been discovered, researchers have detected some interesting patterns. First, as with the *Ardipithecus* specimens, limb bones indicate that these individuals were bipedal. What's more, the molar teeth have thick enamel, as seen in other members of *Australopithecus.* But these still quite early hominid specimens (dated 4.2–3.9 mya) also have some primitive characteristics. For example, Meave Leakey and colleagues point to such primitive features as a large canine, a **sectorial** lower first premolar (Fig. 11-9), and a small opening for the ear canal (Leakey et al., 1995).

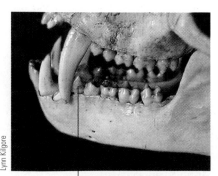

Lynn Kilgore

Sectorial lower first premolar

FIGURE 11-9

Left lateral view of the teeth of a male patas monkey. Note how the large upper canine shears against the elongated surface of the *sectorial* lower first premolar.

---

*Most, but not all, paleoanthropologists make this genus-level distinction; but some researchers still favor including *Paranthropus* as part of *Australopithecus.* All experts do agree that *Paranthropus* is a separate lineage.

AT A GLANCE

Key Very Early Fossil Hominid Discoveries (pre-*Australopithecus*; prior to 4 mya)

	Site	Dates (mya)	Hominids
East Africa	Middle Awash (Ethiopia; five localities)	5.8–5.2	*Ardipithecus*
	Aramis (Ethiopia)	4.4	*Ardipithecus ramidus*
	Tugen Hills	~6.0	*Orrorin tugenensis*
Central Africa	Toros-Menalla	~7.0	*Sahelanthropus tchadensis*

Newer discoveries from Ethiopia (one also from the Aramis site and the other nearby in the Middle Awash) further confirm the earlier interpretations made from the Kenyan fossils. Detailed comparisons with other fossils suggest to Tim White and associates that this fossil species may be transitional between *Ardipithecus* and later *Australopithecus* (discussed in a moment) (White et al., 2006). Since these particular *Australopithecus* individuals have initially been interpreted as more primitive than all the later members of the genus, paleoanthropologists have assigned them to a separate species (*Australopithecus anamensis*).

Slightly later and much more complete remains of *Australopithecus* have come from the sites of Hadar (in Ethiopia) and Laetoli (in Tanzania). Much of this material has been known for some time (since the mid-1970s), and the fossils have been very well studied; in fact, in some cases they're quite famous. For example, the Lucy skeleton was discovered at Hadar in 1974, and the Laetoli footprints were first found in 1978.

Literally thousands of footprints have been found at Laetoli, representing more than 20 different kinds of animals (Pliocene elephants, horses, pigs, giraffes, antelope, hyenas, and an abundance of hares). Several hominid footprints have also been found, including a trail more than 75 feet long (Fig. 11-10), made by at least two—and perhaps three—individuals (Leakey and Hay, 1979). Such discoveries of well-preserved hominid footprints are extremely important in furthering our understanding of human evolution. For the first time, we can make *definite* statements regarding the locomotor pattern and stature of early hominids. Analyses of these Pliocene footprints suggest a stature of about 4 feet 9 inches for the larger individual and 4 feet 1 inch for the smaller individual.

Courtesy Peter Jones

FIGURE 11-10

Hominid footprint from Laetoli, Tanzania. Note the deep impression of the heel and the large toe (arrow) in line (adducted) with the other toes.

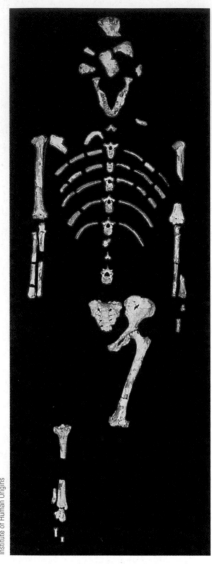

FIGURE 11-11

"Lucy," a partial hominid skeleton, discovered at Hadar in 1974. This individual is assigned to *Australopithecus afarensis*.

australopithecine (os-tra-loh-pith´-e-seen) The colloquial name for members of the genus *Australopithecus* and *Paranthropus*. The term was first used as a subfamily designation, but it's now most often used informally.

Studies of these impression patterns clearly show that these individuals used a bipedal mode of locomotion (Day and Wickens, 1980). As we've discussed, the development of bipedal locomotion is the most important defining characteristic of early hominid evolution. Some researchers, however, have concluded that these early hominids weren't bipedal in quite the same way that modern humans are. From detailed comparisons with modern humans, researchers have estimated stride length, cadence, and speed of walking in the Laetoli hominids; results indicate that these individuals traveled in a slow-moving ("strolling") fashion with a rather short stride (Charteris et al., 1981).

Some extraordinary discoveries at Hadar are most noteworthy. In particular, there's the Lucy skeleton (Fig. 11-11), which Don Johanson found eroding out of a hillside. This fossil is scientifically designated as Afar Locality (AL) 288-1, but is usually just called Lucy (after the Beatles' song, "Lucy in the Sky with Diamonds"). Representing almost 40 percent of a skeleton, this is one of the three most complete individuals from anywhere in the world for the entire period before about 100,000 years ago.*

Because the Laetoli area was covered periodically by ashfalls from nearby volcanic eruptions, accurate dating is possible and has provided dates of 3.7–3.5 mya. Dating from the Hadar region hasn't been as straightforward; however, more complete dating calibration, using various techniques (see Chapter 10), has determined a range of 3.9–3.0 mya for the hominid discoveries from this area.

AUSTRALOPITHECUS AFARENSIS FROM LAETOLI AND HADAR

Several hundred specimens, representing a minimum of 60 individuals (and perhaps as many as 100), have been removed from Laetoli and Hadar. These materials currently represent the largest *well-studied* collection of early hominids, and we've already met a couple of the "rock" stars. It's also been suggested that fragmentary specimens from other locales in East Africa are remains of the same species as that found at Laetoli and Hadar. Most anthropologists refer to this species as *Australopithecus afarensis*.

Without question, *A. afarensis* is more primitive and less derived than the later **australopithecine** fossils from South or East Africa (discussed below), although the recently described late Miocene hominids as well as *Australopithecus anamensis* are even more primitive. By *primitive*, we mean that *A. afarensis* is less evolved in any particular direction than are later-occurring hominid species. That is, *A. afarensis* shares more primitive features with other early homin*oids* and with living great apes than do later hominids, who display more derived characteristics.

For example, the teeth of *A. afarensis* are quite primitive. The canines are often large, pointed teeth. Moreover, the lower first premolar is semisectorial (that is, it provides a shearing surface for the upper canine), and the tooth rows are parallel, even converging somewhat toward the back of the mouth (Fig. 11-12).

The cranial portions that are preserved, including a more recently discovered specimen, also display several primitive hominoid characteristics, including a compound crest in the back as well as several primitive features of the cranial base. Cranial capacity estimates for *A. afarensis* show a mixed pattern when compared to later hominids. A provisional estimate for the one partially complete cranium—apparently a large individual—gives a figure of 500 cm³; but another, even more fragmentary cranium is apparently quite a bit smaller and has been estimated at about 375 cm³ (Holloway, 1983). So, for some individuals (males?), *A. afarensis* is well within the range of other australopithecine species (see "A Closer Look"), but others (females?) may have a significantly smaller cranial capacity. A detailed depiction of cranial size for *A. afarensis* isn't currently possible, however; this part of the skeleton is unfortunately too poorly represented in the fossil record. One thing is clear: *A. afarensis* had a small brain, probably averaging for the whole species not much over 420 cm³.

---

*The others are a specimen from Sterkfontein in South Africa (p. 285), a newly discovered infant skeleton from Dikika (also from the Middle Awash), and an *H. erectus* skeleton from W. Turkana.

On the other hand, many postcranial remains have been found at Hadar. Initial impressions suggest that relative to lower limbs, the upper limbs are longer than in modern humans (also a primitive hominoid condition). (By this, we don't mean that the arms of *A. afarensis* were longer than the legs.) In addition, the wrist, hand, and foot bones show several differences from modern humans (Susman et al., 1985). Stature can now be confidently estimated: *A. afarensis* was a short hominid. From her partial skeleton, Lucy is figured to be only 3 ½ to 4 feet tall. But Lucy—as demonstrated by her pelvis—was probably a female, and at Hadar and Laetoli, there is evidence of larger individuals as well. The most economical hypothesis explaining this variation is that *A. afarensis* was quite sexually dimorphic: The larger individuals are male and the smaller ones, such as Lucy, are female. Estimates of male stature can be approximated from the larger footprints at Laetoli, inferring a height of not quite 5 feet. If we accept this interpretation, *A. afarensis* was a very sexually dimorphic form indeed. In fact, for overall body size, this species may have been as dimorphic as *any* living primate (that is, as much as gorillas, orangutans, or baboons). A recent reanalysis of the *A. afarensis* fossils (Reno et al., 2003) has come to a dramatically different conclusion. Phillip Reno and colleagues at Kent State University used a larger sample

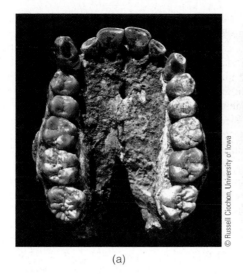
(a)

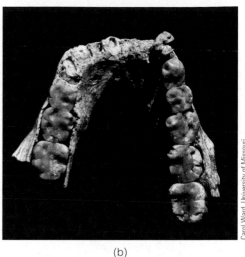
(b)

FIGURE **11-12**

Jaws of *Australopithecus afarensis*.
(a) Maxilla, AL 200-1a, from Hadar, Ethiopia. (Note the parallel tooth rows and large canines.)
(b) Mandible, LH 4, from Laetoli, Tanzania. This fossil is the type specimen for the species *Australopithecus afarensis*.

A CLOSER LOOK Cranial Capacity

Cranial capacity, usually reported in cubic centimeters, is a measure of brain size, or volume. The brain itself, of course, doesn't fossilize. However, the space once occupied by brain tissue (the inside of the cranial vault) does sometimes preserve, at least in those cases where fairly complete crania are recovered.

For purposes of comparison, it's easy to obtain cranial capacity estimates for contemporary species (including humans) from analyses of skeletonized specimens in museum collections. From studies of this nature, estimated cranial capacities for modern hominoids have been determined as follows (Tobias, 1971, 1983):

	Range (cm³)	Average (cm³)
Human	1150–1750*	1325
Chimpanzee	285–500	395
Gorilla	340–752	506
Orangutan	276–540	411
Bonobo	—	350

*The range of cranial capacity for modern humans is very large—in fact, even greater than that shown (which approximates cranial capacity for the *majority* of contemporary *H. sapiens*).

These data for living hominoids can then be compared with those obtained from early hominids:

	Average (cm³)
Sahelanthropus	~350
Orrorin	Not currently known
Ardipithecus	Not currently known
Australopithecus anamensis	Not currently known
Australopithecus afarensis	438
Later australopithecines	410–530
Early members of genus *Homo*	631

As the tabulations indicate, cranial capacity estimates for australopithecines fall within the range of most modern great apes, and gorillas actually average slightly more than *A. afarensis*. It's important to remember, however, that gorillas are very large animals, whereas australopithecines probably weighed on the order of 100 pounds (see Table 11-1, p. 272). Since brain size is partially correlated with body size, comparing such different-sized animals can't be justified. Compared to living chimpanzees (most of which are slightly larger than early hominids) and bonobos (which are somewhat smaller), australopithecines had *proportionately* about 10 percent bigger brains, and so we would say that these early hominids were more *encephalized*.

Abbreviations Used for Fossil Hominid Specimens

For those hominid sites where a number of specimens have been recovered, standard abbreviations are used to designate the site as well as the specimen number (and occasionally museum accession information as well). In this chapter, the following abbreviations are used.

Abbreviation	Explanation	Example
AL	Afar locality	AL-288-1
LH	Laetoli hominid	LH 4
OH	Olduvai hominid	OH 5
KNM-ER (or simply ER)	Kenya National Museums, East Rudolf*	ER 1470
KNM-WT (or simply WT)	Kenya National Museums, West Turkana	WT 17000
Sts	Sterkfontein, main site	Sts 5
Stw	Sterkfontein, west extension	Stw 53
SK	Swartkrans	SK 48

*East Rudolf is the former name for Lake Turkana; the abbreviation was first used before the lake's name was changed. All these fossils (as well as others from sites throughout Kenya) are housed in Nairobi at the National Museums of Kenya.

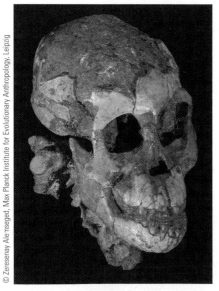

© Zeresenay Alemseged, Max Planck Institute for Evolutionary Anthropology, Leipzig

FIGURE 11-13

Complete skull with attached vertebral column of the infant skeleton from Dikika, Ethiopia, (estimated age, 3.3 mya).

and a different statistical approach from that of other researchers. This new study concluded that *A. afarensis* was not very sexually dimorphic at all—finding, in fact, about the same degree of male-female body size difference as seen in modern *H. sapiens*. It's important to note, however, that this revised interpretation is inconsistent not just with prior consensus views of *A. afarensis*, but with those of virtually all early hominids (see Table 11-1, p. 272).

An important new find of a mostly complete infant *A. afarensis* skeleton was announced in 2006 (Fig. 11-13). The discovery was made at the Dikika locale in northeastern Ethiopia, very near the Hadar sites mentioned earlier. What's more, the infant comes from the same geological horizon as Hadar, with the same dating (3.3 mya). Although the initial discovery of the fossil was back in 2000, it has taken several years and thousands of hours of preparation by lead researcher Zeresenay Alemseged, of the Max Planck Institute of Evolutionary Anthropology, to remove portions of the skeleton from the surrounding cemented matrix (full preparation will likely take several more years; Alemseged et al., 2006).

What makes this find of a 3-year-old infant so remarkable is that, for the first time in hominid evolution prior to about 100,000 years ago, we have a very well preserved immature individual. From the infant's extremely well preserved teeth, scientists hypothesize that she was female. A comprehensive study of her developmental biology has already begun, and many more revelations are surely in store as the Dikika infant is more completely cleaned and studied. For now, and accounting for her immature age, the skeletal pattern appears to be quite similar to adult *A. afarensis*. What's more, the limb proportions, anatomy of the hands and feet, and shape of the scapula (shoulder blade) reveal a similar "mixed" pattern of locomotion. The foot and lower limb indicate this infant would have been a terrestrial biped; yet, the shoulder and (curved) fingers suggest she was also capable of climbing about quite ably in the trees.

What makes *A. afarensis* a hominid? The answer is revealed by its manner of locomotion. From the abundant limb bones recovered from Hadar and those beautiful footprints from Laetoli, we know without question that *A. afarensis* walked bipedally when on the ground. Whether Lucy and her contemporaries still spent considerable time in the trees, and just how efficiently they walked, have become topics of some controversy. Most researchers, however, agree that *A. afarensis* was an efficient habitual biped while on the ground. These hominids were also clearly obligate bipeds, which would have hampered their climbing abilities but would not necessarily have kept them from climbing at all. As one physical anthropologist has surmised:

> One could imagine these diminutive early hominids making maximum use of *both* terrestrial and arboreal resources in spite of their commitment to exclusive bipedalism when on the ground. The contention of a mixed arboreal and terrestrial behavioral repertoire would make adaptive sense of the Hadar australopithecine forelimb, hand, and foot morphology without contradicting the evidence of the pelvis. (Wolpoff, 1983b, p. 451)

ANOTHER EAST AFRICAN HOMINID

The pace of hominid discoveries in East Africa has dramatically increased in recent years, and many of these new discoveries have revealed a different combination of anatomical features from those recognized in remains discovered previously. Among the most distinctive and intriguing of these new finds is a cranium unearthed in 1999 on the west side of Lake Turkana in northern Kenya (Leakey et al., 2001).

Dated to 3.5 mya, this fossil hominid is thus contemporaneous with *Australopithecus afarensis*. Yet, it shows a quite distinctive combination of facial and dental features (most especially, a flat lower face and fairly small molar teeth). In these respects, this newly discovered Kenyan hominid is different from *A. afarensis*—and in fact, from *all* known australopithecines. Because the skull has been severely distorted, its overall morphology, including the crucial placement of the face relative to the cranial vault as well as cranial capacity, is difficult to establish clearly. But the best estimates suggest that the cranial capacity is similar to that of *Australopithecus* (that is, in the range of 400 to 500 cm^3).

Because of its unusual anatomical features, Meave Leakey and her colleagues have proposed an entirely new hominid genus (*Kenyanthropus*) for this exceptional cranium. Due to the great degree of distortion, White (2003) has argued that the remains cannot be reliably identified and that it may be an early Kenyan version of *Australopithecus afarensis*, not a new genus at all. Whether the separate (*Kenyanthropus*) designation will be substantiated by further, more detailed analysis remains to be seen. At minimum, this and all the other discoveries from recent years are forcing a major reassessment of the early stages of hominid evolution (see Appendix B).

LATER EAST AFRICAN FINDS

At several localities in East Africa, researchers have recovered an assortment of fossil hominids, including many specimens of later members of *Australopithecus* as well as the first representatives of *Paranthropus*, from geological contexts with dates after 3 mya. Up to 10 different such sites are now known (in the time range of 3–1 mya), but here we'll concentrate on the three most significant ones: East Lake Turkana, West Lake Turkana (both in northern Kenya), and Olduvai Gorge (in northern Tanzania).

Located very near the considerably older Allia Bay site on the east shore of Lake Turkana is Koobi Fora (Fig. 11-14). With sediments dating to 1.8–1.3 mya, Koobi Fora has provided specimens representing at least 100 individuals, and this fine sample includes several complete crania, many jaws, and an assortment of postcranial bones. Next to Olduvai, Koobi Fora has yielded the most information concerning early hominid behavior. More than 20 archaeological sites have been discovered, and excavation or testing has been done at 10 localities.

Across the lake, on the west side of Lake Turkana, are other deposits that recently have yielded new and exciting discoveries—including the earlier *Kenyanthropus* finds (discussed earlier). Olduvai Gorge (discussed in detail in Chapter 10) has also yielded a considerable collection of early hominid fossils.

FIGURE 11-14

Excavations in progress at Koobi Fora, in East Lake Turkana, northern Kenya..

National Museums of Kenya

AUSTRALOPITHECUS AND *PARANTHROPUS* FROM OLDUVAI AND LAKE TURKANA

Most fossil hominids from Olduvai, West Lake Turkana, and especially Koobi Fora are later in time than the *A. afarensis* remains from Laetoli and Hadar (by at least 500,000 years). So it's not surprising that they are more derived, in some cases dramatically so. These later hominids are also considerably more diverse. Most researchers accept the interpretation that all the hominids from Laetoli and Hadar are members of a single taxon, *A. afarensis*. But it's clear that the remains from the Turkana area and Olduvai collectively represent multiple taxa—two different genera and perhaps up to 5 or 6 different species. Current discussion on how best to sort this complex material is among the most vehement in paleoanthropology. Here we summarize the broad patterns of physical morphology. At the end of this chapter, we'll take up the various schemes that attempt to interpret the fossil remains in a broader evolutionary context.

FIGURE 11-15

The "Black Skull," WT 17000, discovered at West Lake Turkana in 1985. This specimen is provisionally assigned to *Paranthropus aethiopicus*. It's called the Black Skull due to its dark color from the fossilization (mineralization) process.

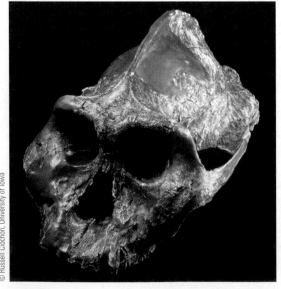

© Russell Ciochon, University of Iowa

Following 2.5 mya, later (and more derived) hominids are found in East Africa. This is a most distinctive group that had popularly been known for some time as "robust" australopithecines; but as we've said, they are now thought distinct enough to be placed in a separate genus (*Paranthropus*). By *robust*, it has traditionally been meant that these forms—when compared to *Australopithecus*—were larger in body size. However, more recent and better controlled studies (Jungers, 1988; McHenry, 1988, 1992) have shown that all these species of early hominid overlapped considerably in body size. As you'll soon see, "robust" forms have also been found in South Africa.

These new weight estimates have prompted many researchers either to drop the use of the term **robust** (along with its opposite, **gracile**) or to present it in quotation marks to emphasize its conditional application. We believe that *robust* can be used in this latter sense because it still emphasizes important differences between *Australopithecus* and *Paranthropus* in the scaling of craniodental traits. In other words, even if not larger overall, robust forms are clearly robust in the skull and dentition.

Dating to approximately 2.5 mya, the earliest representative of *Paranthropus* comes from northern Kenya on the west side of Lake Turkana. A complete cranium (WT 17000—"the Black Skull": due to rich magnesium deposits, the fossil was dyed black during fossilization) was unearthed there in 1985 and has turned out to be a most important discovery (Fig. 11-15). This skull, with a cranial capacity of only 410 cm³, is among the smallest for any hominid known, and it has other primitive traits reminiscent of *A. afarensis*. For example, there's a compound crest in the back of the skull, the upper face projects considerably, the upper dental row converges in back, and the cranial base is extensively pneumatized—that is, it has air pockets (Kimbel et al., 1988).

But here's what makes the Black Skull so fascinating: Mixed into this array of distinctively primitive traits are a host of derived ones that link it to other members of the robust group (including a broad face, a very large palate, and a large area for the back teeth). This mosaic of features seems to place skull WT 17000 between earlier *A. afarensis* on the one hand and the later robust species on the other. Because of its unique position in hominid evolution, WT 17000 (and the population it represents) has been placed in a new species, *Paranthropus aethiopicus*.

Around 2 mya, different varieties of even more derived members of the robust lineage were on the scene in East Africa. As well documented by finds at Olduvai and Koobi Fora, *Paranthropus* has relatively small cranial capacities (ranging from 510 to 530 cm³) and very large, broad faces with massive back teeth and lower jaws. The larger (probably male) individuals also show a raised ridge, called a **sagittal crest**, along the midline of the cranium. The first find of a recognized Plio-Pleistocene hominid in East Africa, in fact, was of a nearly complete *Paranthropus* cranium, which Mary Leakey discovered in 1959 at Olduvai Gorge (see p. 242). Louis Leakey originally named the fossil *Zinjanthropus*, and it's still popularly referred to as "Zinj." However, it and other members of the same species in East Africa are now usually classified as *Paranthropus boisei*.

Early *Homo*

In addition to the *Paranthropus* remains in East Africa, another contemporaneous Plio-Pleistocene hominid is quite distinctive. Most paleoanthropologists have placed these materials (as best documented by fossil discoveries from Olduvai and Koobi Fora) in the genus *Homo*. For this reason, they're seen as different from all species assigned to *Australopithecus* or *Paranthropus*.*

The earliest appearance of genus *Homo* in East Africa may be as ancient as that of the *Paranthropus*. (As we've discussed, the Black Skull from West Turkana has been dated to

robust Referring to large, heavily built body/anatomical structure.

gracile Referring to smaller, more lightly built body/anatomical structure.

sagittal crest A ridge of bone that runs down the middle of the cranium like a short Mohawk. This serves as the attachment for the large temporal muscles, indicating strong chewing.

*As we'll discuss shortly, several paleoanthropologists have recently reevaluated the status of "early *Homo*."

AT A GLANCE	Key East African Australopithecine* and Early *Homo* Discoveries	
Site	**Dates (mya)**	**Hominids**
Olduvai (N. Tanzania)	1.85–1.0	Australopithecines, early *Homo*
Turkana (N. Kenya; eastern side of Lake Turkana)	1.9–1.3	Many australopithecines; several early *Homo*
(west side of Lake Turkana)	(3.5–1.6)	*Paranthropus* (*P. aethiopicus*); also *Kenyanthropus** 2 nearly complete crania; 3 jaw fragments, isolated teeth; 1 nearly complete skeleton (*H. erectus*)
Bouri (N.E. Ethiopia)	2.5	Australopithecines (*A. garhi*)
Hadar (N.E. Ethiopia)	3.5–3.0	Many early australopithecines (*A. afarensis*);
Laetoli (N. Tanzania)	3.6–3.4	Early australopithecines (*A. afarensis*); also, well-preserved footprints

*Australopithecine: This designation includes both genera, *Australopithecus* and *Paranthropus*.

approximately 2.5 mya.) Reinterpretations of a temporal fragment from the Lake Baringo region of central Kenya have suggested that early *Homo* may also be close to this same antiquity, with an estimated age of 2.4 mya (Hill et al., 1992). Remains more clearly diagnostic of early *Homo* (including a lower jaw) have more recently been reported from Hadar, in Ethiopia; they are also dated to 2.3 mya (Kimbel et al., 1996). Because the robust (*Paranthropus*) lineage was probably diverging at this time, it's not surprising to find the earliest representatives of the genus *Homo* also beginning to diversify.

Based on the discovery of fragmentary remains at Olduvai Gorge, Louis Leakey was first to suggest (in the early 1960s) the presence of a Plio-Pleistocene hominid with a significantly larger brain than seen in other hominids. Leakey and his colleagues gave a new species designation to these fossil remains, naming them **Homo habilis.**

The *Homo habilis* material at Olduvai ranges in time from 1.85 mya for the earliest to about 1.6 mya for the latest. Due to the fragmentary nature of the fossil remains, interpretations have been difficult and much disputed. The most immediately obvious feature distinguishing the *H. habilis* material from the australopithecines is cranial capacity. For all the measurable *H. habilis* skulls, the estimated average cranial capacity is 631 cm^3, compared to 520 cm^3 for all measurable *Paranthropus* specimens and 442 cm^3 for *Australopithecus* crania (McHenry, 1988; see "A Closer Look" on p. 275). *Homo habilis*, therefore, shows an increase in cranial size of about 20 percent over *Paranthropus* and an even greater increase over some of the smaller-brained forms (*Australopithecus* from South Africa, discussed shortly). In their initial description of *H. habilis*, Leakey and his associates also pointed to differences from australopithecines in cranial shape and in tooth proportions (larger front teeth relative to back teeth and narrower premolars).

The naming of this fossil material as *Homo habilis* ("handy man") was meaningful from two perspectives. First of all, Leakey inferred that members of this group were the early Olduvai toolmakers. If that's true, how do we account for a *Paranthropus* individual like Zinj lying in the middle of the largest excavated area known at Olduvai? What was he doing there? Leakey suggested that he was the remains of a *habilis* meal! Except in cases where cut marks are left behind (see pp. 248–249), we must point out again that there's no clear way archaeologically to establish the validity of such a claim. However, as the debate over Leakey's assertion demonstrates, cultural factors as well as physical morphology must be considered in interpreting hominids as biocultural organisms. Secondly, and most significantly, by calling this group *Homo*, Leakey was arguing for at least *two separate branches* of hominid evolution in the Plio-Pleistocene. Clearly, only one group could be on the main branch eventually leading to *Homo sapiens*. By labeling this new group *Homo* rather than *Australopithecus,* Leakey was guessing that he had found our ancestors.

Because the initial evidence was so fragmentary, most paleoanthropologists were reluctant to accept *H. habilis* as a valid taxon distinct from *all* other early hominids. Later discoveries, especially from Lake Turkana, of better-preserved fossil material have shed further light on early *Homo* in the Plio-Pleistocene. The most important of this additional material is a nearly complete cranium (ER 1470) discovered at Koobi Fora (Fig. 11-16). With a cranial capacity of 775 cm^3, this individual is well outside the known range for australopithecines and actually overlaps the lower boundary for *Homo erectus*. In addition, the shape of the skull vault is in many respects unlike that of australopithecines. The face is still quite robust (Walker, 1976), however, and the fragments of tooth crowns that are preserved indicate that the back teeth in this individual were quite large. Dating of the Koobi Fora early *Homo* material places it contemporaneous with the Olduvai remains—that is, about 1.8–1.6 mya.

Based on evidence from Olduvai and particularly from Koobi Fora, we can reasonably postulate that one or more species of early *Homo* were present in East Africa probably by 2.4 mya, developing in parallel with at least one other line of hominids (Fig. 11-17). These two very different hominid lineages lived contemporaneously for a minimum of 1 million years, after which the australopithecines apparently disappeared forever.

REDEFINING THE GENUS *HOMO*?

Recently, this widely supported interpretation of early *Homo* has been significantly challenged. Most notably, Bernard Wood (of George Washington University) and colleague Mark Collard (of University College, London) have argued that all the early *Homo* specimens are

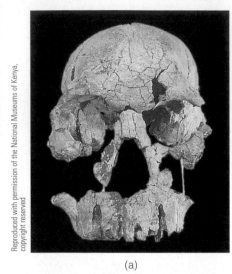

(a)

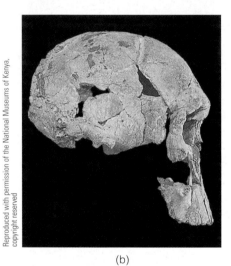

(b)

FIGURE 11-16

A nearly complete early *Homo* cranium from East Lake Turkana (ER 1470), one of the most important single fossil hominid discoveries from East Africa. (a) Frontal view; (b) lateral view.

Homo habilis (hab´-ih-liss) A species of early *Homo*, well known from East Africa but perhaps also found in other regions.

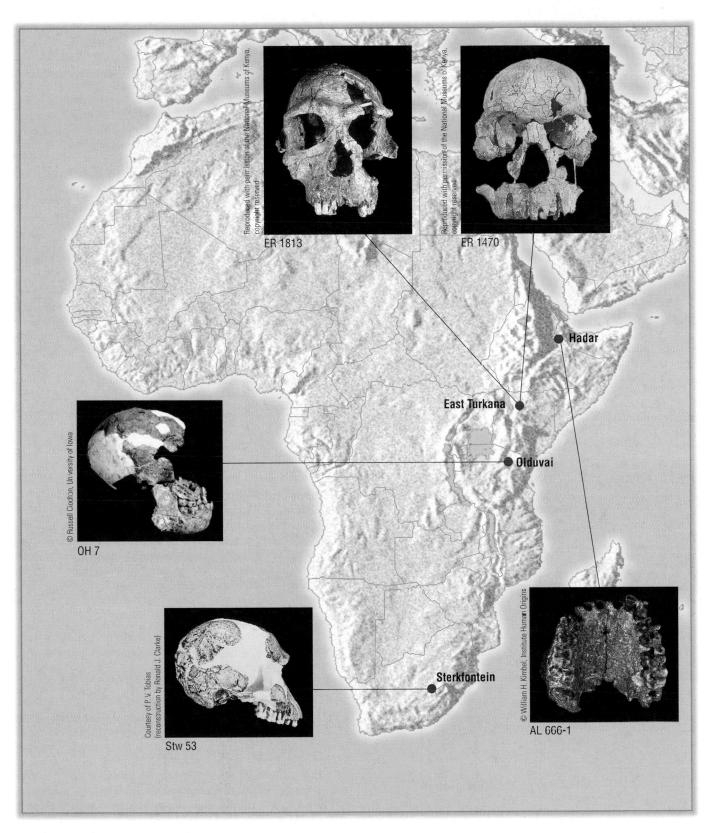

ER 1813

ER 1470

Hadar

East Turkana

Olduvai

OH 7

Stw 53

Sterkfontein

AL 666-1

FIGURE **11-17**
Early *Homo* fossil finds.

very different from other (later) members of *Homo*. Pointing to primitive features of the face and limb proportions, these researchers have reassigned everything previously assigned as early *Homo* back into *Australopithecus*.

This radical reinterpretation of the status of early *Homo* is highly controversial. Many paleoanthropologists flatly disagree (Walker, 2002; Cela-Conde and Ayala, 2003), while others remain cautious (for example, Foley, 2002). Such differences in interpretation of variation in the fossil record are not unusual (quite the opposite, in fact). The problems are in the first place due to the considerable variation present in what has been called early *Homo*. The specimens collectively lumped into early *Homo* are indeed a mixed bag, and some of the fossils might well belong to an australopithecine. This difficulty is heightened when attempting to relate one part of the body to another. A key aspect of Wood and Collard's reinterpretation is based on the apparent primitive limb proportions (that is, proportionately long arms). But it's not at all certain which fossil limb bones go with which cranial remains. For this reason, it's possible to assign a cranium like ER 1470 to early *Homo*, while unassociated limb bones *might* come from the same species—or they could just as easily have belonged to a contemporaneous *Paranthropus boisei* individual (explaining why the limbs would be proportioned like those of an australopithecine).

Based on the degree of encephalization shown by the early *Homo* cranial remains, at least some of these specimens don't belong in *Australopithecus* (indeed, Wood and Collard concede that their placement of these fossils into *Australopithecus* is tentative and probably will need to be revised further). For the moment, then, it seems prudent to continue including those specimens with good cranial preservation from Olduvai, Koobi Fora, and elsewhere as early *Homo*. Even so, we should always recognize that as in any such decision, a classification is merely a hypothesis—and one easily prone to eventual falsification.

South African Sites

EARLIEST DISCOVERIES

The first quarter of the twentieth century saw the discipline of paleoanthropology in its scientific infancy. Informed opinions considered the likely origins of the human family to be in Asia, where fossil forms of a primitive kind of *Homo* had been found in Indonesia in the 1890s. Europe was also considered a center of hominid evolution, for spectacular discoveries there of premodern humans (including the famous Neandertals) and millions of stone tools had come to light, particularly in the early 1900s. In addition, it was very satisfying for European scientists to believe that humans originated on their own continent.

Few scholars would have given much credence to Darwin's prediction:

> In each region of the world the living mammals are closely related to the extinct species of the same region. It is, therefore, probable that Africa was formally inhabited by extinct apes closely allied to the gorilla and chimpanzee, and as these two species are now man's nearest allies, it is somewhat more probable that our early progenitors lived on the African continent than elsewhere. (Darwin, *The Descent of Man*, 1871)

And in fact, it would be many more decades before the East African discoveries would come to light. It was in such an atmosphere of preconceived biases that the discoveries of a young Australian-born anatomist were to jolt the foundations of the scientific community in the 1920s. Raymond Dart (Fig. 11-18) arrived in South Africa in 1923 at the age of 30 to take up a teaching position in Johannesburg. Fresh from his evolution-oriented training in England, Dart had developed a keen interest in human evolution. So, when startling new evidence began appearing at his very doorstep, he was well prepared.

The first clue came in 1924, when Dart received a shipment of fossils from the commercial limeworks quarry at Taung (200 miles southwest of Johannesburg). He immediately recognized something that was quite unusual—a natural **endocast** of a higher primate. The endocast fit into another limestone block containing the fossilized front portion of the skull,

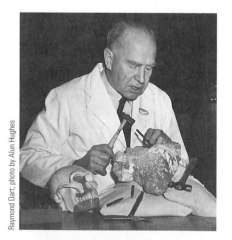

FIGURE 11-18

Raymond Dart, shown working in his laboratory.

endocast   A solid impression of the inside of the skull, often preserving details relating to the brain's size and surface features.

face, and lower jaw (Fig. 11-19). These were difficult to see clearly, however, for the bone was hardened into a cemented limestone matrix. Dart patiently chiseled away for weeks, later describing the task:

> No diamond cutter ever worked more lovingly or with such care on a precious jewel—nor, I am sure, with such inadequate tools. But on the seventy-third day, December 23, the rock parted. I could view the face from the front, although the right side was still imbedded. . . . What emerged was a baby's face, an infant with a full set of milk teeth and its permanent molars just in the process of erupting. I doubt if there was any parent prouder of his offspring than I was of my Taung baby on that Christmas. (Dart, 1959, p. 10)

As indicated by the formation and eruption of the teeth, the Taung child was probably about 3 to 4 years old. Interestingly, the rate of development of this and many other Plio-Pleistocene hominids was more like that of apes than of modern *Homo* (Bromage and Dean, 1985). Dart's initial impression that this form was a hominoid was confirmed when he could observe the face and teeth more clearly. But as it turned out, it took considerably more effort before the teeth could be seen completely; Dart worked for 4 years to separate the upper and lower jaws.

Still, long before he had an unimpeded view of the dentition, Dart was convinced that this discovery was a remarkable one—an early hominoid from South Africa. The question was, what kind of hominoid? Dart realized that it was extremely improbable that this specimen could have been a forest ape, for the climate of South Africa has been relatively dry for millions of years. Even though the climate at Taung may not have been as dry as Dart initially speculated (Butzer, 1974), it was still an unlikely spot to find an ape.

If it wasn't an ape, then what was it? Features of the skull and teeth of this small child held clues that Dart seized on almost immediately. The entrance of the spinal cord into the brain (the *foramen magnum* at the base of the skull; see Fig. 11-8) was farther forward in the Taung skull than in modern great apes, though not as much as in modern humans. From this fact Dart concluded that the head was balanced *above* the spine, indicating erect posture. He also observed that the slant of the forehead was not as receding as in apes, the milk canines were exceedingly small, and the newly erupted permanent molars were very large, broad teeth. In all these respects, the Taung fossil was more akin to hominids than to apes. There was, however, a disturbing feature that was to confuse many scientists for several years: The brain was quite small. More recent studies have estimated the Taung child's brain size at approximately 405 cm³ (which translates to a full adult estimate of 440 cm³), not very large (for a hominid) when compared to modern great apes (see "A Closer Look" on p. 275).

The estimated cranial capacity of the Taung fossil falls within the range of modern great apes, and gorillas actually average about 10 percent more capacity. But remember that gorillas are very large animals, while the Taung specimen derives from a population in which adults may have averaged less than 80 pounds. Since brain size is partially correlated with body size, comparing such differently sized animals is unjustified. A more meaningful comparison would be with the bonobo (*Pan paniscus*), whose body weight is similar to that estimated for the Taung fossil. Bonobos have adult cranial capacities averaging 356 cm³ for males and 329 cm³ for females, and so the Taung child, versus a *comparably sized* ape, displays 25 percent more cranial capacity.

Despite the relatively small size of the fossil's brain, Dart saw that it was no ape. Realizing the immense importance of his findings, he promptly reported them in the British scientific weekly *Nature* on February 7, 1925. It was a bold venture since Dart, only 32, was presumptuously proposing a whole new view of human evolution. He named the small-brained Taung child **Australopithecus africanus** (southern ape of Africa) and explained that he saw it as a kind of halfway "missing link" between modern apes and humans. This concept of there being just one missing link was a fallacious one, but Dart did correctly emphasize the fossil's hominid-like features.

Not all scientists were ready for such a theory from such an "unlikely" place. Many received Dart's report with indifference, disbelief, and even scorn. Dart realized that more complete remains were needed. The skeptical world would not accept the evidence of one

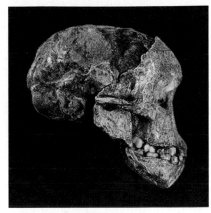

Alun Hughes, reproduced by permission of Professor P. V. Tobias

FIGURE 11-19

The Taung child, discovered in 1924. The endocast is in back, with the fossilized bone mandible and face in front.

Australopithecus africanus
(os-tral-oh-pith´-e-kus af-ri-kan´-us)

AP/Wide World Photos

FIGURE 11-20
Robert Broom.

partial immature individual, no matter how suggestive the clues. Most scientists in the 1920s regarded this little Taung child as an interesting, aberrant form of ape. Clearly, more fossil evidence was needed, particularly adult crania (since these would show more diagnostic features). Not an experienced fossil hunter himself, Dart sought further assistance in the search for more australopithecines.

FURTHER DISCOVERIES OF SOUTH AFRICAN HOMINIDS

Soon after publication of his controversial theories, Dart found a strong ally in Robert Broom (Fig. 11-20). A Scottish physician and part-time paleontologist, Broom already had established his credentials as a fossil hunter with his highly successful paleontological work on early mammal-like reptiles in South Africa.

Although he was interested in Dart's work, Broom was unable to participate actively in the search for more australopithecines until 1936. From two of Dart's students, Broom learned of another commercial limeworks site, called Sterkfontein, not far from Johannesburg. Here, as at Taung, the quarrying involved blasting out large sections with dynamite, leaving piles of debris that often contained fossilized remains. Accordingly, Broom asked the quarry manager to keep his eyes open for fossils, and when Broom returned to the site in August 1936, the manager asked, "Is this what you are looking for?" Indeed it was, for Broom held in his hand the endocast of an adult australopithecine— exactly what he had set out to find! Looking further over the scattered debris, Broom was able to find nearly all of the remaining skull for that individual.

Such remarkable success, just a few months after beginning his search, was not the end of Broom's luck; his magical touch was to continue unabated for several more years. In the 1930s and 1940s, Broom discovered two more hominid sites, including **Swartkrans**, the second to only Sterkfontein as the most prolific of all South African Plio-Pleistocene locales (each site has yielded hundreds of fossils). In the 1940s, Raymond Dart discovered another hominid site, bringing the total to five.

From these additional sites came many extremely important discoveries that would eventually swing the tide of intellectual thought to the views that Dart expressed back in 1925. Particularly important was the discovery of a nearly complete cranium and pelvis at Sterkfontein in 1947. As the number of discoveries increased, it became more and more difficult to simply write off the australopithecines as aberrant apes.

By 1949, at least 30 hominid individuals were represented from five South African sites, and leading scientists were coming to accept the australopithecines as hominids. With this acceptance came the necessary recognition that hominid brains had their greatest expansion *after* earlier changes in teeth and locomotor systems. In other words, once again we see that the rate of evolution in one functional system of the body varies from that of other systems, thus displaying the *mosaic* nature of human evolution.

Since the 1950s, exploration of the South African hominid sites has continued, and many important discoveries were made in the 1970s and 1980s. The most spectacular new find was in 1998 at Sterkfontein, where Ron Clarke and his associates from the University of Witwatersrand found the remains of a virtually complete australopithecine skeleton (Little Foot). Most of the remains are still embedded in the surrounding limestone matrix, and it may take years to remove, clean, and reconstruct them (Fig. 11-21).

As we'll discuss in more detail shortly, dating of all the South African Plio-Pleistocene sites has been difficult; estimates for the Sterkfontein australopithecine skeleton are approximately 2.2 mya. Even though the remains have yet to be fully excavated, this is recognized as an unusually significant find. Because such complete individuals are so rare in the hominid fossil record, this discovery has tremendous potential to shed more light on the precise nature of early hominid locomotion. For example, will the rest of the skeleton confirm what foot bones of the same individual have implied about tree climbing in this bipedal hominid (see p. 265)? What's more, analyzing such a completely preserved skeleton enables scientists to more accurately assess relative proportion of brain size compared to body size as well as to develop better estimates of overall body size, relative proportions of the limbs, and much more.*

Swartkrans (swart´-kranz)

*It's the lack of association of cranial with postcranial remains that makes it so difficult to interpret early *Homo* (see p. 292).

REVIEW OF HOMINIDS FROM SOUTH AFRICA

The Plio-Pleistocene hominid discoveries from South Africa are most significant. First, they were the initial hominid discoveries in Africa and helped point the way to later finds in East and central Africa. Second, morphology of the South African hominids shows broad similarities to the forms in East Africa, but with several distinctive features, which argues for separation at least at the species level. Finally, there's a large assemblage of hominid fossils from South Africa, and exciting discoveries are still being made (see Fig. 11-21).

Further discoveries are also coming from entirely new sites. In the 1990s, the site known as Drimolen was found in South Africa, very near to Sterkfontein and Swartkrans (Keyser, 2000). So far, the findings are only provisionally published; but we do know that up to 80 specimens have been recovered, including the most complete *Paranthropus* cranium found anywhere in Africa.

A truly remarkable collection of early hominids, the remains from South Africa coming from nine different caves, exceed 1,000 (counting all teeth as separate items), and the number of individuals is now more than 200. From an evolutionary point of view, the most meaningful remains are those of the pelvis, which now include portions of nine ossa coxae (see p. 264). Remains of the pelvis are so important because, better than any other area of the body, this structure displays the unique requirements of a bipedal animal (as in modern humans *and* in our hominid forebears).

Paranthropus   In addition to the discoveries of *P. aethiopicus* and *P. boisei* in East Africa, there are numerous finds of *Paranthropus* in South Africa. Like their East African cousins, the South African robust forms also have small cranial capacities, large broad faces and **megadont** back teeth (although not as massive as in East Africa). (The only measurable specimen equals 530 cm^3; the Drimolen cranium is smaller and might come from a female, but no cranial measurements have as yet been published.) They also possess large, broad faces and very large premolars and molars (although not as massive as those found in East Africa). Owing to differences in dental proportions, as well as important differences in facial features (Rak, 1983), most researchers now agree that there is a species-level difference between the later East African robust variety (*P. boisei*) and the South African group (*P. robustus*).

Despite these differences, all members of the robust lineage appear to be specialized for a diet made up of hard food items, such as seeds and nuts. For many years, paleoanthropologists (for example, Robinson, 1972) had speculated that *Paranthropus* concentrated

FIGURE 11-21
Paleoanthropologist Ronald Clarke carefully excavates an australopithecine skeleton, nicknamed "Little Foot," from the limestone matrix at Sterkfontein cave. Clearly seen are the cranium (with articulated mandible) and the upper arm bone.

megadont   Big toothed.

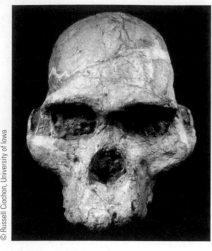

FIGURE 11-22

A gracile australopithecine cranium from Sterkfontein (Sts 5). Discovered in 1947, this specimen is the best-preserved gracile skull yet found in South Africa.

their diet on heavier vegetable foods than those seen in the diet of other early hominids. More recent research that included examining microscopic polishes and scratches on the teeth (Kay and Grine, 1988) confirms this view.

Australopithecus Another variety of hominid (also small-brained, but not as large-toothed as the robust varieties) is known from Africa. However, while the *Paranthropus* lineage is represented in both East and South Africa, this other (gracile) australopithecine form is known only from the southern part of the continent. First named *A. africanus* by Dart for the single individual at Taung, this australopithecine is also found at other sites, especially Sterkfontein (Fig. 11-22).

Traditionally, it had been thought that there was a significant variation in body size between the gracile and robust forms. But as mentioned earlier and shown in Table 11-1, there isn't much difference in body size among these hominids. In fact, most of the differences between the *Paranthropus* and *Australopithecus* are found in the face and dentition.

The facial structure of the South African gracile australopithecines is more lightly built and somewhat dish-shaped compared to the more vertical configuration seen in *Paranthropus*. As we noted earlier, in these robust individuals, a raised ridge along the midline of the skull is occasionally observed. This structure provides additional attachment area for the large temporal muscle, which is the primary muscle operating the massive jaw below. These differences in the relative proportions of the teeth and jaws best define *Paranthropus* as compared to *Australopithecus*, not only in South Africa but in East Africa as well. In fact, most of the differences in skull shape we've discussed can be directly attributed to contrasting jaw function in the two forms. Both the sagittal crest and broad vertical face of the robust form are related to the muscles and biomechanical requirements of the heavy back-tooth chewing adaptation seen in this specialized hominid (see Fig. 11-23).

Early *Homo* in South Africa

As in East Africa, early members of the genus *Homo* have also been found in South Africa, apparently living contemporaneously with other hominids. At both Sterkfontein and Swartkrans, and perhaps Drimolen as well, fragmentary remains have been recognized as most likely belonging to *Homo*. In fact, Ron Clarke (1985) has shown that the key fossil of early *Homo* from Sterkfontein (Stw 53) is very similar to a cranium from Olduvai (see Fig. 11-17).

However, a problem with both the Olduvai specimen and Stw 53 is that while many (but not all) experts agree that they belong to the genus *Homo*, they strongly disagree on whether these early *Homo* fossils should be included in the species *habilis*. In the following sections, we'll discuss the relationships of the Plio-Pleistocene fossil hominids to one another and the difficulties of such genus and species interpretation.

GEOLOGY AND DATING PROBLEMS IN SOUTH AFRICA

While the geological and archaeological context in East Africa is often straightforward, the South African early hominid sites are much more complex geologically. Except for the newly discovered sites, all the sites were found following commercial quarrying activity, which greatly disrupted the geological picture and, in the case of Taung, completely destroyed the site.

The hominid remains are found with thousands of other fossilized bones embedded in limestone cliffs, caves, fissures, and sinkholes. The limestone was formed by millions of generations of shells of marine organisms during the Precambrian—more than 2 billion years ago—when South Africa was submerged under a shallow sea. Once deposited, the limestones were cut through by percolating groundwater from below and rainwater from above, forming a maze of caves and fissures often connected to the surface by narrow shafts (Fig. 11-24). Through these vertical shafts and horizontal cave openings, bones either fell or were carried in, where they conglomerated with sand, pebbles, and soil into a cementlike matrix called breccia.

As the cave fissures filled in, they were constantly subjected to further erosion forces from above and below, so that caves would be partially filled, then closed to the surface for a considerable time, then reopened again to recommence accumulation thousands of years later. All this activity yields an incredibly complex geological situation that can be worked out

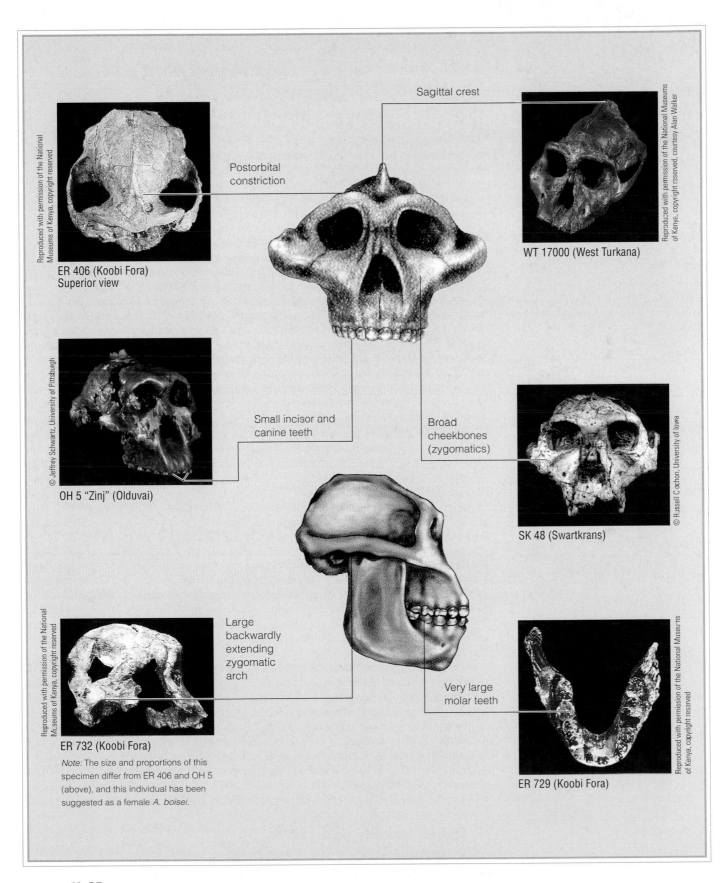

Sagittal crest

Postorbital constriction

ER 406 (Koobi Fora)
Superior view

WT 17000 (West Turkana)

OH 5 "Zinj" (Olduvai)

Small incisor and canine teeth

Broad cheekbones (zygomatics)

SK 48 (Swartkrans)

ER 732 (Koobi Fora)

Note: The size and proportions of this specimen differ from ER 406 and OH 5 (above), and this individual has been suggested as a female *A. boisei*.

Large backwardly extending zygomatic arch

Very large molar teeth

ER 729 (Koobi Fora)

FIGURE **11-23**

Morphology and variation of the robust australopithecines (*Paranthropus*). (Note both typical features and range of variation as shown in different specimens.)

AT A GLANCE   Key South African Pliocene and Early Pleistocene Hominid Discoveries

Site	Dates (mya)	Hominids
Swartkrans	1.8–1.0	*Paranthropus robustus;* early *Homo?*
Drimolen	2.0–1.5	*Paranthropus robustus*
Taung	2.5–2.0??	*Australopithecus africanus*
Sterkfontein	2.2?	*Australopithecus africanus;* early *Homo?*

only after the most detailed kind of paleoecological analysis. Since bones accumulated in these caves and fissures largely by accidental processes, it seems likely that none of the South African sites are *primary* hominid localities. In other words, unlike the East African sites, these aren't areas where hominids organized activities, scavenged food, and so on.

Just how did all the fossilized bone accumulate? And most particularly, what were the ancient hominids doing there? At Swartkrans and Sterkfontein, the bones probably accumulated through the combined activities of carnivorous leopards, saber-toothed cats, and hyenas. The unexpectedly high proportion of primate (baboon and hominid) remains also suggests that these sites were the location (or very near the location) of primate sleeping sites, thus providing ready primate prey for various predators (Brain, 1981).

Owing to the complex geological picture as well as a lack of appropriate material (such as volcanic deposits) for chronometric techniques, dating the South African early hominid sites has posed tremendous problems. Without chronometric dating, the best that can be done is to correlate the faunal sequences in South Africa with areas in East Africa where dates are better known (this approach is called biostratigraphy; see p. 246). Faunal sequencing of this sort on pigs, bovids such as antelope, and Old World monkeys has provided some broad estimates for dates of the key South African sites (see "At a Glance," above).

Interpretations: What Does It All Mean?

By this time, you may think that anthropologists are obsessed with finding small scraps buried in the ground and then assigning them confusing numbers and taxonomic labels impossible to remember. But it's important to realize that the collection of all the basic fossil data is the foundation of human evolutionary research. Without fossils, our speculations would be completely hollow. Several large, ongoing paleoanthropological projects are now collecting additional data in an attempt to answer some of the more perplexing questions about our evolutionary history.

The numbering of specimens, which may at times seem somewhat confusing, is an effort to keep the designations neutral and to make reference to each individual fossil as clear as possible. The formal naming of finds as *Australopithecus, Paranthropus,* or *Homo habilis* should come much later, since it involves a lengthy series of complex interpretations. Assigning generic and specific names to fossil finds is more than just a convenience; when we attach a particular label, such as *A. africanus,* to a particular fossil, we should be fully aware of the biological implications of such an interpretation.

From the time that fossil sites are first located until the eventual interpretation of hominid evolutionary events, several steps take place. Ideally, they should follow a logical order, for if interpretations are made too hastily, they confuse important issues for many years. Here's a reasonable sequence:

1. Selecting and surveying sites
2. Excavating sites and recovering fossil hominids
3. Designating individual finds with specimen numbers for clear reference

4. Cleaning, preparing, studying, and describing fossils

5. Comparing with other fossil material—in chronological framework if possible

6. Comparing fossil variation with known ranges of variation in closely related groups of living primates and analyzing ancestral and derived characteristics

7. Assigning taxonomic names to fossil material

But the task of interpretation still isn't complete, for what we really want to know in the long run is what happened to the populations represented by the fossil remains. In looking at the fossil hominid record, we're actually looking for our ancestors. In the process of eventually determining those populations that are our most likely antecedents, we may conclude that some hominids are on evolutionary side branches. If this conclusion is accurate, those hominids necessarily must have become extinct. It's both interesting and relevant to us as hominids to try to find out what influenced some earlier members of our family to continue evolving while others died out.

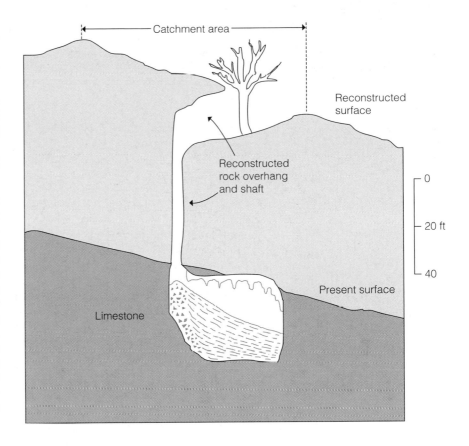

FIGURE 11-24

Swartkrans, geological section. The upper (reconstructed) part has been removed by erosion since the accumulation of the fossil-bearing deposit. (After Brain, 1970.)

CONTINUING UNCERTAINTIES—TAXONOMIC ISSUES

As we mentioned earlier, paleoanthropologists are concerned with making biological interpretations of variation found in the hominid fossil record. Most especially, researchers try to assign extinct forms to particular genera and species. We saw in Chapter 9 that for the diverse array of Miocene hominoids, the evolutionary picture is exceptionally complex. As new finds accumulate, there's continued uncertainty even about family assignment, to say nothing of genus and species!

For the very end of the Miocene and for the Plio-Pleistocene, the situation is much clearer. First, there's a larger fossil sample from a more restricted geographical area (South, Central, and East Africa) and from a more concentrated time period (spanning about 6 million years, from 7 to 1 mya). Second, more complete specimens exist (such as Lucy and the newly found Dikika infant), so we have good evidence for most parts of the body. Accordingly, there's considerable consensus on several basic aspects of evolutionary development during the Plio-Pleistocene. Not all paleoanthropologists are fully convinced of the clear hominid status for the earliest finds; but as more detailed analyses are completed, the strong consensus is emerging that these forms are indeed hominids (White et al., 2006). What's more, for fossils dating later than 4 mya, researchers agree unanimously that these forms are hominids (members of the family Hominidae or an equivalent taxon; see p. 238). And as support for this point, all these forms are seen as habitual, well-adapted bipeds, at least partially committed to a terrestrial niche. Researchers also generally agree as to genus-level assignments for most of the forms, although *Sahelanthropus*, *Orrorin*, *Kenyanthropus*, and *Ardipithecus* have all been so recently named that they haven't yet been fully evaluated and accepted (there's also some disagreement regarding the status of early *Homo*).

As for species-level designations, little consensus can be found. Indeed, as new fossils have been discovered, the picture seems to muddy further. Once again, we're faced with a complex evolutionary process. In attempts to deal with it, we impose varying degrees of simplicity. In so doing, we hope that the evolutionary processes will become clearer—not just for introductory students, but for professional paleoanthropologists and textbook authors

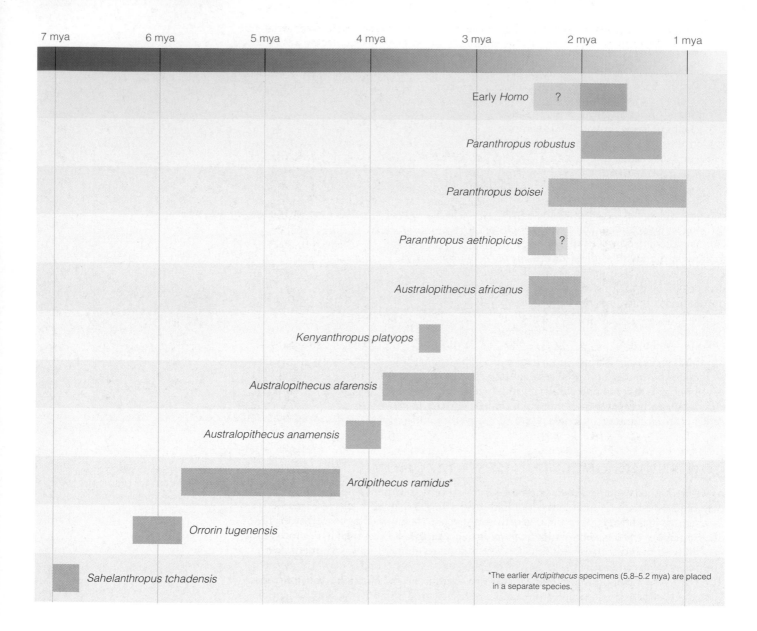

7 mya	6 mya	5 mya	4 mya	3 mya	2 mya	1 mya

Early *Homo* ?

Paranthropus robustus

Paranthropus boisei

Paranthropus aethiopicus ?

Australopithecus africanus

Kenyanthropus platyops

Australopithecus afarensis

Australopithecus anamensis

Ardipithecus ramidus*

Orrorin tugenensis

Sahelanthropus tchadensis

*The earlier *Ardipithecus* specimens (5.8–5.2 mya) are placed in a separate species.

Time line of Plio-Pleistocene hominids. Note that most dates are approximations. Question marks indicate those estimates that are most tentative.

as well. Even so, evolution is not a simple process, and disputes and disagreements are bound to arise, especially in making such fine-tuned interpretations as species-level designations.

It may prove impossible to work out clear patterns of relationships among the early hominids. Despite our best attempts, the number and complexity of hominid groups (more technically called *taxa*), which seem to increase monthly, may frustrate all attempts at simplification.

One particularly difficult obstacle is the varied combination of anatomical characteristics, seen especially in the earliest-suggested members of the hominid family. For example, *Sahelanthropus* has a very primitive-looking braincase (especially in the back) combined with a fairly advanced hominid-looking face and canine teeth. *Orrorin*, on the other hand, combines what some claim are very chimpanzee-looking teeth with a highly efficient bipedal gait. And *Ardipithecus* shows yet another pattern, combining some aspects of primitive-looking teeth with other components of a suggested bipedal gait.

Fueled by all these admittedly confusing combinations of characteristics is the suspicion by some researchers (for example, Bernard Wood, 2002) that roughly similar characteristics (like some form of bipedality or reduction of the canine teeth) could have evolved more than once—that is, separately in different lineages of hominids (or possibly even in other hominoids closely related to hominids). This evolutionary process results from what we have called *homoplasy* (see p. 98). If this inherently messy evolutionary factor was in fact widespread among our late Miocene and Pliocene relatives, it may prove almost impossible to discern which forms are related to others and which ones are more closely related to us. Worse yet, it may prove extremely tricky to identify some of these forms as hominids at all.

SEEING THE BIGGER PICTURE

Despite all the difficulties, paleoanthropologists still want to understand the broad patterns of early hominid evolution. The interpretation of our paleontological past in terms of which fossils are related to other fossils and how they might be related to modern humans is usually shown diagrammatically in the form of a *phylogeny*. Such a diagram is a family tree of fossil evolution. You should note, though, that strict practitioners of cladistics prefer to use cladograms; see p. 101. This kind of interpretation is the eventual goal of evolutionary studies; but it's the final goal, only after enough data are available to understand what's going on.

Another, more basic way to handle these data is to divide the fossil material into subsets. This avoids (for the moment) what are still problematic phylogenetic relationships. Accordingly, for the Plio-Pleistocene hominid material from Africa, we can divide the data into three broad groupings:

Set I. Pre-*Australopithecus*/basal hominids (7.0–4.4 mya) The earliest (and most primitive) collection of remains that have been classified as hominids are those from Toros-Menalla, the Tugen Hills, and the Middle Awash, the latter area also including the site of Aramis. These fossils have, for the moment, been assigned to three separate (and newly proposed) genera—*Sahelanthropus*, *Orrorin*, and *Ardipithecus*—so are each provisionally interpreted as being generically distinct from all the other early hominid forms (listed in sets II and III). Analysis thus far indicates that at least for the later Aramis fossils, these forms were likely bipedal, but with a primitive dentition. Brain size of *Ardipithecus* is not yet known, but was almost certainly quite small.

Set II. *Australopithecus*/*Paranthropus*
Subset A. Early primitive forms (4.2–3.0 mya) This grouping comprises one well-known species, A. afarensis, especially well documented at Laetoli and Hadar. Slightly earlier, closely related forms (probably representing a distinct second species) come from four other sites and are provisionally called Australopithecus anamensis. Best known from analysis of the A. afarensis material, the hominids in this set are characterized by a small brain, large teeth (front and back), and a bipedal gait (probably still allowing for considerable climbing).
Subset B. Later, more derived forms (2.4–1.0 mya) This group is composed of at least two genera including a total of several species. (Most experts recognize at least three; some subdivide this material into five or more species.) Remains have come from several sites in both South and East Africa. All of these forms have very large back teeth and show no appreciable brain enlargement (that is, encephalization) compared to *A. afarensis*. A growing majority of researchers view the robust lineage as more specialized and showing a greater dependence on a diet of coarse vegetable foods. As such, these early hominids reflect a different adaptation than other contemporaneous hominids and are thus best placed in a separate genus (*Paranthropus*).

Set III. Early *Homo* (2.4–1.8 mya) The best-known specimens are from East Africa (East Turkana and Olduvai), but early remains of *Homo* have also been found in South Africa (Swartkrans and possibly Sterkfontein and Drimolen). This group is composed of possibly just one, but probably more than one, species. Early *Homo* is characterized (compared to *Australopithecus* and *Paranthropus*) by greater encephalization, altered cranial shape, and smaller (especially molars) and narrower (especially premolars) teeth. As discussed on p. 282, considerable variation is seen among different specimens, so much so that some paleoanthropologists have removed this group from *Homo* altogether and temporarily reassigned it to *Australopithecus*.

Although hominid fossil evidence has accumulated in great abundance, the fact that so much of the material has been discovered so recently makes any firm judgments concerning the route of human evolution premature. Paleoanthropologists certainly aren't deterred from making their "best guesses," however, and diverse hypotheses have abounded in recent years. The vast majority of the hundreds of recently discovered fossils from Africa is still in the descriptive and early analytical stages. Right now, constructing the phylogenies of human evolution is like building a house with only a partial blueprint. We're not even sure how many rooms there are! Until the existing fossil evidence has been adequately studied, to say nothing about possible new finds, speculative hypotheses must be viewed with a critical eye.

Seeing the Very Big Picture: Adaptive Patterns of Early African Hominids

As you're by now aware, there are several different African hominid genera and certainly lots of species. This, in itself, is interesting. Speciation was occurring quite frequently among the various lineages of early hominids—more frequently, in fact, than among later hominids. What explains this pattern?

Evidence has been accumulating at a furious pace in the last decade, but it's still far from complete. What's clear is that we'll never have anything approaching a complete record of early hominid evolution—so significant gaps will remain. After all, we're able to discover hominids only in those special environmental contexts where fossilization was likely. All the other potential habitats they might have exploited are now invisible to us.

Still, patterns are emerging from the fascinating data we do have. First, it appears that early hominid species (pre-*Australopithecus*, *Australopithecus*, *Paranthropus*, and early *Homo*) all had restricted ranges. It's therefore likely that each hominid species exploited a relatively small area and could easily have become separated from other populations of its own species. So, genetic drift (and to some extent, natural selection as well) could have led to rapid genetic divergence and eventual speciation.

Second, most of these species appear to be at least partially tied to arboreal habitats, although there's disagreement on this point regarding early *Homo* (see Wood and Collard, 1999b; Foley 2002). Also, robust forms (*Paranthropus*) were probably somewhat less arboreal than *Ardipithecus* or *Australopithecus*. These highly megadont hominids apparently concentrated on a diet of coarse, fibrous plant foods, such as roots. Exploiting such resources may have routinely taken these hominids farther away from the trees than their dentally more gracile—and perhaps more omnivorous—cousins.

Third, except for some early *Homo* individuals, there's very little in the way of an evolutionary trend of increased body size or of markedly greater encephalization. Beginning with *Sahelanthropus*, brain size was no more than that in chimpanzees—although when controlling for body size, this earliest of all known hominids may have had a proportionately larger brain than any living ape. Close to 6 million years later (that is, the time of the last surviving australopithecine species), relative brain size increased by no more than 10 to 15 percent. Perhaps, tied to this relative stasis in brain capacity, there's no absolute association of any of these hominids with patterned stone tool manufacture (see Chapter 10).

Although conclusions are becoming increasingly controversial, for the moment, early *Homo* appears to be a partial exception. This group shows both increased encephalization and numerous occurrences of likely association with stone tools (though at many of the sites, australopithecine fossils were *also* found).

Lastly, all of these early African hominids show an accelerated developmental pattern (similar to that seen in African apes), one quite different from the *delayed* developmental pattern characteristic of *Homo sapiens* (and our immediate precursors). This apelike development is also seen in some early *Homo* individuals (Wood and Collard, 1999a). Rates of development can be accurately reconstructed by examining dental growth markers (Bromage and Dean, 1985), and these data may provide a crucial window into understanding this early stage of hominid evolution.

These African hominid predecessors were rather small, able bipeds, but still closely tied to arboreal and/or climbing niches. They had fairly small brains and, compared to later *Homo*, matured rapidly. It would take a major evolutionary jump to push one of their descendants in a more human direction. For the next chapter in this more human saga, read on.

VISUAL SUMMARY

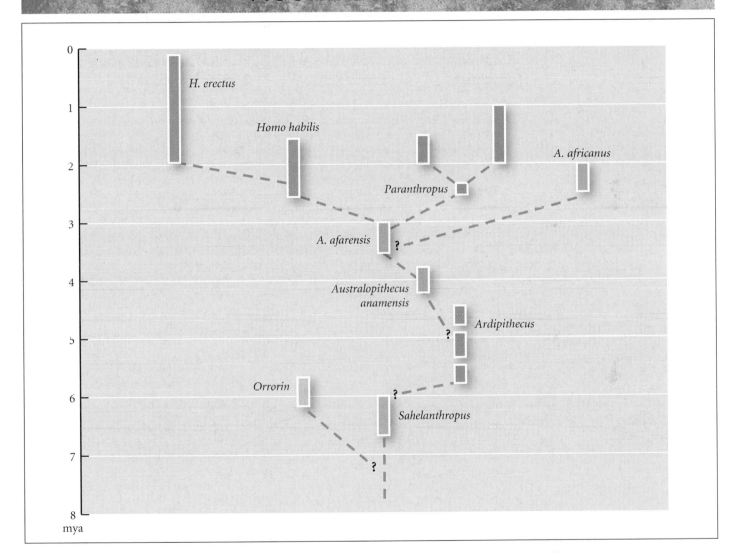

Summary: Putting It All Together

In the "Visual Summary," we present a simplified scheme showing tentative relationships among the early African fossil hominids discussed in this chapter. Question marks indicate those relationships that are most tentative, particularly obvious for all the earliest material (the pre-*Australopithecus* fossils, dated prior to 4 mya). Indeed, right now, with all this material so recently discovered and seemingly displaying highly complex patterns of hominid evolution, it's unwise to make anything but the most general of hypotheses.

The picture after 4 mya is somewhat clearer. It appears, for the moment, that *Australopithecus afarensis* still can be viewed as a good potential common ancestor of most (if not all) later hominids. Although *Paranthropus* looks like a quite separate and specialized evolutionary branch that was a dead end, the relationships among many of the other later australopithecines are not as clear, nor is it certain which of the earlier Pliocene fossils is most closely related to *Homo*. As a further study aid, Table 11-2 presents the early hominid materials we consider the most significant. Those who'd like to pursue a more detailed evaluation of the early hominids can see Appendix B.

Science is a journey of discovery, seeking to find as many documented facts as possible. Science is also a search for clarity. The last few years of paleoanthropological research have immensely enriched our record of facts. The search for clarity continues. No doubt, more discoveries are in the offing. We certainly live in interesting times.

TABLE 11-2	Chronological Summary of Most Significant Hominid Fossils Discussed in this Chapter			
Epoch	**Sites**	**Dates (mya)**	**Taxonomic Designation**	**Comments**
Plio-Pleistocene	East Turkana (Koobi Fora) and Olduvai	1.8–1.0	Derived australopithecine and early *Homo*	Highly derived australopithecine and first relatively complete fossils of early *Homo*
	Taung and Sterkfontein	2.5–2.0?	*Australopithecus africanus*	Best-known early hominid from South Africa; many well-preserved fossils
	Hadar and Laetoli	3.6–3.0	*Australopithecus afarensis*	Earliest well-documented group of early hominids; potentially ancestral to later *Australopithecus* and early *Homo*
	Aramis	4.4	*Ardipithecus ramidus*	Earliest large sample of hominid fossils; not yet well described; likely shows very unusual mosaic of characteristics (some highly derived)
Miocene	Toros-Menalla	~7.0	*Sahelanthropus*	Earliest proposed hominid fossils; unusual mosaic of characteristics

Critical Thinking Questions

1. (a) Why is postcranial evidence (particularly the lower limb) so crucial in showing the australopithecines (or other early forms) as definite hominids? (b) What particular aspects of the australopithecine pelvis and lower limb are hominid-like?

2. In what ways are the remains of *Sahelanthropus* and *Ardipithecus* primitive? How do we know that these forms are hominids? How sure are we?

3. Assume that you're in the laboratory analyzing the "Lucy" *A. afarensis* skeleton. You also have complete skeletons from a chimpanzee and a modern human. (a) Which parts of the Lucy skeleton are more similar to the chimpanzee? Which are more similar to the human? (b) Which parts of the Lucy skeleton are *most* informative?

4. Why are some Plio-Pleistocene hominids from East Africa called early *Homo*? What does this imply for the evolutionary relationships of the australopithecines? What alternative interpretations have been proposed, and why?

5. What's the first thing you'd do if you found an early hominid fossil and were responsible for its formal description and publication? Describe what you'd include in your publication.

6. Discuss two current disputes regarding taxonomic issues concerning early hominids. Try to give support for alternative positions.

7. Why would one use the taxonomic term *Paranthropus* instead of *Australopithecus*?

8. What is a phylogeny? Construct one for early hominids (7.0–1 mya). Make sure you can describe what conclusions your scheme makes. Also, try to defend it.

9. What are the most recently discovered of the earliest hominid materials, and how are they, for the moment, incorporated into a phylogenetic scheme? How secure do you think this interpretation is?

CHAPTER 12

The Earliest Dispersal of the Genus *Homo:* *Homo Erectus* and Contemporaries

© Russell Ciochon, University of Iowa

KEY QUESTION

Who were the first members of the human family to disperse out of Africa, and what were they like (behaviorally and anatomically)?

Introduction

Along the lakeshores of East Africa about 2.0 million years ago, there arose a new and decidedly distinct human ancestor. Ambling along the beach, a large male may have stood close to 6 feet tall; what's more, he and his kin had larger and quicker brains than their African precursors and could no doubt process more information more quickly. This hominid was different from any that came before it. For the first 5 million years of evolution, hominids had been restricted to Africa, but this species quickly found its way out of Africa, traveling as far as Southeast Asia, discovering new tools, foods, and technologies.

There's some morphological variation among the different geographical groups of these highly successful hominids, and paleoanthropologists are still debating how to classify them. New discoveries are being announced every year. In particular, new finds from the Caucasus region in eastern Europe are forcing a major reevaluation of exactly what the first hominid emigrants looked like (Fig. 12-1).

After 2 million years ago (mya), there's universal agreement that the hominids found outside of Africa are all members of genus *Homo*, since there seems to be less diversity in these hominids than we can see in their predecessors. Therefore, taxonomic debates focus solely on how many species are represented. The species for which we have the most evidence is called *Homo erectus*. What's more, this is the one group that almost all paleoanthropologists agree upon; for these reasons, we'll concentrate our discussion on *Homo erectus*. We will, however, also discuss alternative interpretations that call for splitting the fossil sample into more species.

The Life and Times of *Homo erectus*

The oldest specimens of *H. erectus* have been found in East Africa, and they're dated to approximately 1.8 mya. These new East African hominids used the same stone tools as their ancestors. They lived in many environments, including lakeshores, riversides, forests, and grasslands. These early *H. erectus* populations also scavenged and ate at least some meat, as evidenced by cut-marked bone. They weren't the first hominid to do any of these things, but they were the first to travel widely.

Whether they were following their prey, the shifting environment, or the population had expanded enough to force migration, *Homo erectus* left Africa about 1.8 mya. From Kenya they headed north, where we find them first in the Republic of Georgia, at a site named **Dmanisi**, within the Caucasus region (dated to about 1.7 mya). After the Caucasus region, the next earliest fossil sites are found far away on the island of Java, Indonesia. At about 1.6 mya, *H. erectus* seems to have had a well-established population on the island. They were most likely still using Oldowan-style tools, just as the earliest of their species had done in Kenya, although no conclusive evidence of tools has yet been found in Java. So, as you can see, about 1.6 mya *H. erectus* was living in three geographically divided regions: East Africa, eastern Europe, and Southeast Asia. Paleoanthropologists recognize *H. erectus* as a grade of evolution different from that of their more ancient African predecessors. A **grade** is an evolutionary grouping of organisms showing a similar adaptive pattern. Increases in body size and robustness, changes in limb proportions, and greater encephalization all indicate that these hominids were more like modern humans in their adaptive pattern than their African ancestors were. We should point out that a grade only implies general adaptive aspects of

Click!

Go to the following media for interactives and exercises on topics covered in this chapter:

- Online Virtual Laboratories for Physical Anthropology, Fourth Edition
- Hominid Fossils CD ROM: An Interactive Atlas

Dmanisi (dim´-an-eese´-ee)

grade A grouping of organisms sharing a similar adaptive pattern. Grade isn't necessarily based on closeness of evolutionary relationship, but it does contrast organisms in a useful way (e.g., *Homo erectus* with *Homo sapiens*).

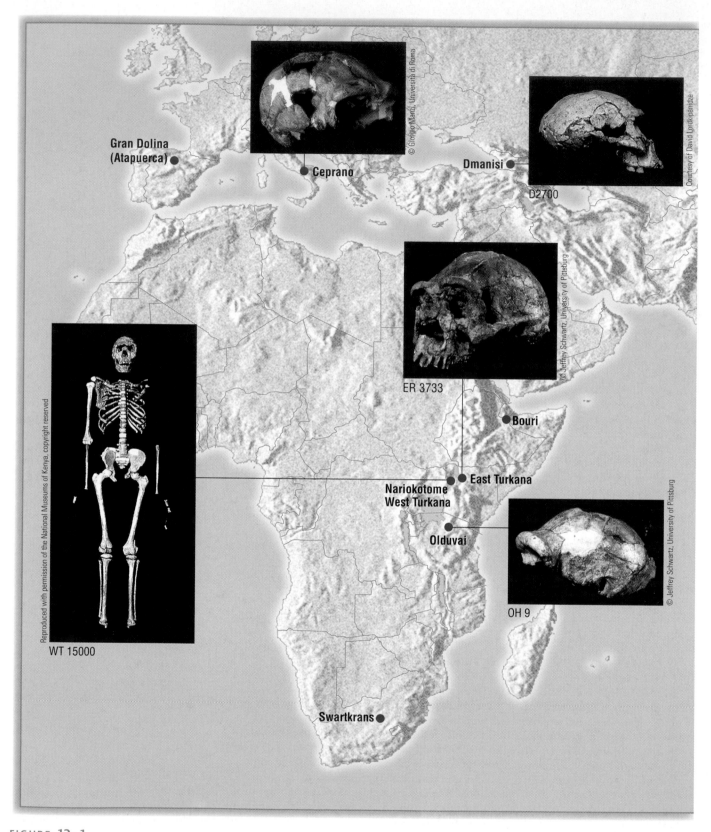

FIGURE 12–1

Major *Homo erectus* sites and localities of other contemporaneous hominids.

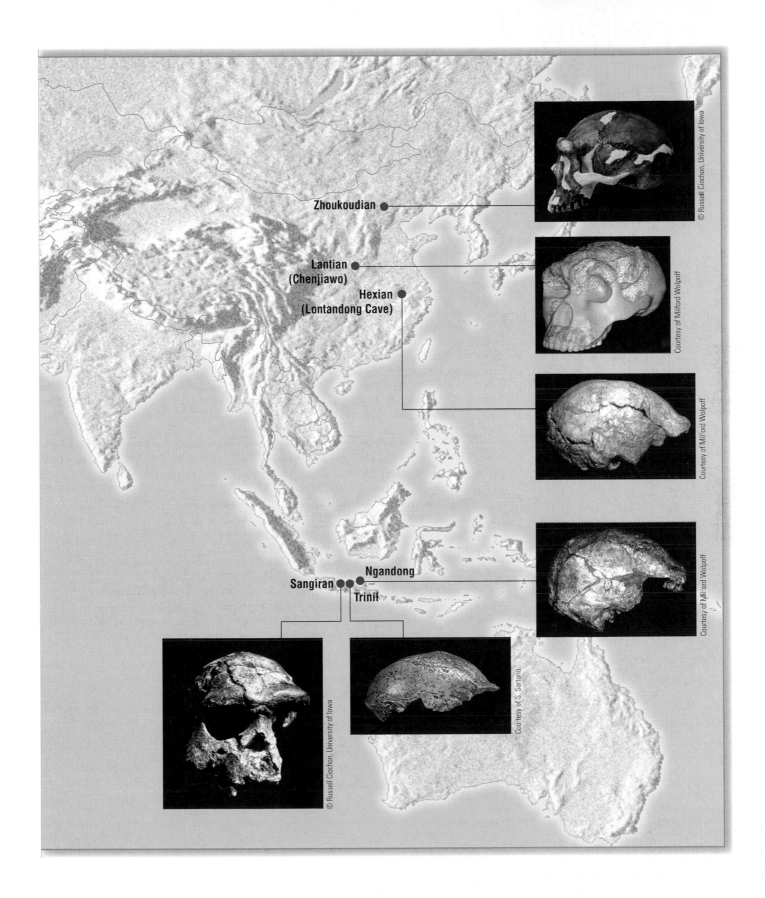

Zhoukoudian

Lantian
(Chenjiawo)

Hexian
(Lontandong Cave)

Ngandong

Sangiran

Trinil

© Russell Ciochon, University of Iowa

Courtesy of Milford Wolpoff

Courtesy of Milford Wolpoff

Courtesy of Milford Wolpoff

© Russell Ciochon, University of Iowa

Courtesy of S. Sartono

a group of animals; it tells us nothing directly about shared ancestry (organisms that share common ancestry are said to be in the same *clade*; see p. 99). For example, orangutans and African great apes could be said to be in the same grade, but they are not in the same clade (see p. 135).

The hominids discussed in this chapter are not only members of a new and distinct grade of human evolution, they're also closely related to each other. Whether they all belong to the same clade is debatable. Even so, it's clear from these fossils that a major adaptive shift had taken place—one setting hominid evolution in a distinctly more human direction.

The Morphology of *Homo erectus*

These *Homo erectus* populations lived far across the world from one another. They are, however, united by common traits that we'll now summarize briefly.

BODY SIZE

As conclusively shown by the discovery of the nearly complete skeleton of "**Nariokotome** Boy" (on the west side of Lake Turkana in Kenya), we know that *H. erectus* was larger than earlier hominids. From this and other less-complete specimens, anthropologists estimate that some *Homo erectus* adults weighed well over 100 pounds, with an average adult height of about 5 feet 6 inches (McHenry, 1992; Ruff and Walker, 1993; Walker and Leakey, 1993). Another point to keep in mind is that *Homo erectus* was quite sexually dimorphic—at least as indicated by the East African specimens. For adult males, weight and height in some individuals may have been considerably greater than 100 pounds. In fact, if the Nariokotome Boy had lived to adulthood, he probably would have grown to an adult height of over 6 feet (Walker, 1993).

Increased height and weight in *H. erectus* are also associated with a dramatic increase in robusticity. In fact, a heavily built body was to dominate hominid evolution not just during *H. erectus* times, but through the long transitional era of premodern forms as well. Only with the appearance of anatomically modern *H. sapiens* did a more gracile skeletal structure emerge, and it still characterizes most modern populations.

BRAIN SIZE

While *Homo erectus* differs in several respects from both early *Homo* and *Homo sapiens*, the most obvious feature is its cranial size—which is closely related to brain size. Early *Homo* had cranial capacities ranging from as small as 500 cm^3 to as large as 800 cm^3. *H. erectus*, on the other hand, shows considerable brain enlargement, with a cranial capacity of 750* to 1,250 cm^3 (and a mean of approximately 900 cm^3). However, in making such comparisons, we must bear in mind two key questions: What is the comparative sample, and what were the overall body sizes of the species being compared?

As for the first question, you may recall that many anthropologists are now convinced that more than one species of early *Homo* existed in East Africa around 2 mya. If so, only one of them could have been the ancestor of *H. erectus*. If we choose the smaller-bodied sample of early *Homo* as our presumed ancestral group, then *H. erectus* shows as much as a 40 percent increase in cranial capacity. But, if the comparative sample we use is the larger-bodied group of early *Homo* (for example, skull 1470, from East Turkana), then *H. erectus* shows a 25 percent increase in cranial capacity.

As we've discussed, brain size is closely tied to overall body size. We've focused on the increase in *H. erectus* brain size, but *H. erectus* was also considerably larger overall than earlier members of the genus *Homo*. In fact, when we compare *H. erectus* with the larger-bodied early *Homo* sample, their *relative* brain size is about the same (Walker, 1991). What's more, when you compare the relative brain size of *H. erectus* with that of *H. sapiens*, you'll note that *H. erectus* was considerably less encephalized than later members of the genus *Homo*.

post-orbital constriction

Nariokotome (nar´-ee-oh-koh´-tow-may)

---

*Considerably smaller cranial capacities have been found in recently discovered fossils from the Caucasus region.

CRANIAL SHAPE

Homo erectus crania display a highly distinctive shape, partly because of increased brain size, but probably more correlated with increased body size. The ramifications of this heavily built cranium are reflected in thick cranial bone and large browridges (supraorbital tori) above the eyes, and a projecting **nuchal torus** at the rear of the skull (Fig. 12-2).

nuchal torus   (nuke´-ul, pertaining to the neck) A projection of bone in the back of the cranium where neck muscles attach; used to hold up the head.

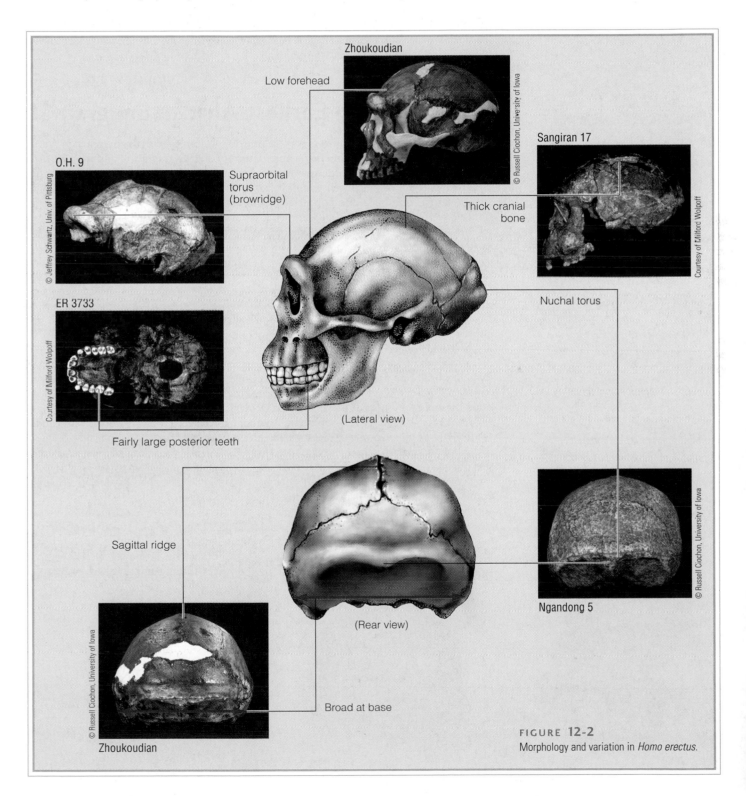

Zhoukoudian

Low forehead

© Russell Ciochon, University of Iowa

Sangiran 17

O.H. 9

Supraorbital torus (browridge)

© Jeffrey Schwartz, Univ. of Pittsburg

Thick cranial bone

Courtesy of Milford Wolpoff

ER 3733

Courtesy of Milford Wolpoff

Nuchal torus

(Lateral view)

Fairly large posterior teeth

Sagittal ridge

Ngandong 5

© Russell Ciochon, University of Iowa

(Rear view)

© Russell Ciochon, University of Iowa

Broad at base

Zhoukoudian

FIGURE **12-2**
Morphology and variation in *Homo erectus*.

The braincase is long and low, receding from the large browridges with little forehead development. Also, the cranium is wider at the base compared with earlier *and* later species of genus *Homo*. The maximum cranial breadth is below the ear opening, giving the cranium a pentagonal shape (when viewed from behind). In contrast, the skulls of early *Homo* and *H. sapiens* have more vertical sides, and the maximum width is *above* the ear openings.

Most specimens also have a sagittal ridge (also called a sagittal keel) running along the midline of the skull. Very different from a sagittal crest, the keel is a small ridge that runs front to back along the sagittal suture. The sagittal keel, along with the supraorbital tori and the nuchal torus, don't seem to have served an obvious function in the life of *H. erectus*— but most likely reflect bone buttressing in a very robust skull.

Who Were the Earliest African Emigrants?

When working with fossils, every new piece of evidence can potentially overturn previous views. We have presented a concise reconstruction of *erectus*' migration and morphology, but there's new evidence that the species may not be so simply depicted.

First, while 1.8 mya is a well-established date for the appearance of *H. erectus* in East Africa, similar hominids also appear at just about the same time in Indonesia and the Caucasus region (see Fig. 12-1). Radiometric dates of sediments on the island of Java have recently placed *H. erectus* at a site called Mojokerto 1.8 million years ago. It's possible for us to explain these hominids in Asia at this early date *if* we assume that *H. erectus* evolved in East Africa by 1.8 mya (or slightly earlier) and, in just a few thousand years, expanded rapidly to other regions.

At an almost equally early date, hominids were also present in the Caucasus region of easternmost Europe. Newly discovered fossils from the Dmanisi site in the Republic of Georgia (see Fig. 12-1) have been radiometrically dated to 1.75 mya. Not only do the Dmanisi hominids show up early, but they also look different from the usual *H. erectus* we've just briefly described.

In some respects, the Dmanisi crania are similar to those of *H. erectus* (for example, the long, low braincase, wide base, and sagittal keeling; see especially Fig. 12-3b, and compare with Fig. 12-2). However, other characteristics of the Dmanisi individuals are different from other hominid finds outside of Africa. In particular, the most complete specimen (specimen 2700; see Fig. 12-3c) has a less-robust and thinner browridge, a projecting lower face, and a relatively large upper canine. At least when viewed from the front, this skull is more reminiscent of the smaller early *Homo* specimens from East Africa than it is of *Homo erectus*. Also, specimen 2700's cranial capacity is very small—estimated at only 600 cm³, well within the range of early *Homo*. In fact, the four Dmanisi crania so far described have relatively small cranial capacities—the other three were estimated at 630 cm³, 650 cm³ and 780 cm³.

Probably the most remarkable discovery yet from Dmanisi is a fourth skull that researchers excavated in 2002 (and published in 2005). This nearly complete cranium is of an older adult male; and surprisingly for such an ancient find, he died with only one tooth remaining in his jaws(Lordkipanidze et al., 2006). Because his jawbones show advanced resorption of bone, it seems that he lived for several years without being able to chew his food

FIGURE 12-3

Dmanisi crania discovered in 1999 and 2001 and dated to 1.8–1.7 mya. (a) Specimen 2282. (b) Specimen 2280. (c) Specimen 2700.

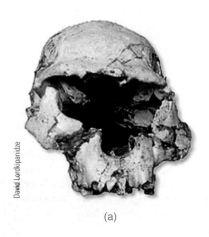

(a)

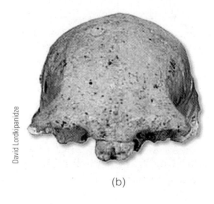

(b)

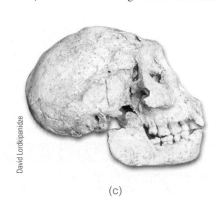

(c)

(Fig. 12-4). David Lordkipanidze, who leads the excavations at Dmanisi, and his colleagues have suggested that this individual required a fair amount of assistance to survive in an era when the only way to process food was to use your teeth (Lordkipanidze et al., 2005, 2006). However, this contention requires more detailed investigation before it can be further confirmed.

Researchers have also recovered some stone tools at Dmanisi. The tools are similar to early ones from Africa, and they're quite different from the seemingly more advanced technology of the **Acheulian** industry broadly associated with African *H. erectus* after 1.4 mya (see p. 314).

Based on these recent, startling revelations from Dmanisi, we can ask several questions:

1. Was *Homo erectus* the first hominid to leave Africa—or did an earlier form of *Homo* get out even earlier?

2. Did hominids require a large brain and sophisticated stone tool culture to disperse out of Africa?

3. Was the large, robust body build of *H. erectus* a necessary adaptation for the initial occupation of Eurasia?

Of course, since the Dmanisi discoveries are very new, it's important to view any conclusions as highly tentative. But in any case, the recent evidence raises important and exciting possibilities. The Dmanisi findings suggest that the first hominids to leave Africa were quite possibly a very early form of *H. erectus*, possessing smaller brains than later *erectus* and carrying with them a typical African Oldowan stone tool culture. Several postcranial bones, from at least two individuals, have been recovered at Dmanisi. Although only provisionally published (Fischman, 2005), it appears that these hominids were not especially tall, with an estimated height of barely over 4½ feet. Certainly, based on this evidence, they seem much smaller than the full *H. erectus* from East Africa or from Asia. Yet, it's quite possible that most of the crania so far known, and perhaps all the postcranial pieces, might come from female individuals, though the mostly toothless skull represents a more robust male individual; crucially, however, his cranial capacity is no greater than the others. It's possible the Dmanisi hominids were quite sexually dimorphic, like other populations of *H. erectus*. If so, further finds may show that, overall, the population was bigger-sized than current evidence leads us to believe. Nevertheless, what we do have shows the Dmanisi hominids were just generally very short and small brained, having none of the adaptations believed to be essential to hominid migration—that is, being tall and having relatively large brains. It's possible we may find that there were *two* migrations out of Africa at this time: one consisting of the small-brained, diminutive Dmanisi hominids, and an almost immediate second one that founded the well-recognized *erectus* populations of Java and China. All this evidence is so new, however, that it's too soon even to predict what further revisions may be required.

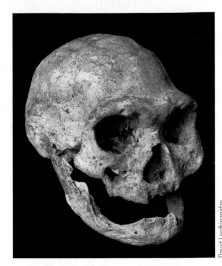

David Lordkipanidze

FIGURE 12-4
Most recently discovered cranium from Dmanisi, almost totally lacking in teeth (with both upper and lower jaws showing advanced bone resorption).

Historical Overview of *Homo erectus* Discoveries

Because it was the first recognized human ancestor to be found, *Homo erectus* has been embroiled in every new discovery related to the study of human evolution. Since the Java find of 1891, *Homo erectus* has been considered our ancestor. The story of *Homo erectus* starts with a Dutch anatomist, lured to Indonesia by the ideas of Alfred Russel Wallace, who believed that human ancestors had evolved in Asia. The resulting story takes us through more than a century of evolutionary thought and across three continents.

It's important to realize that in the early years of paleoanthropology, taxonomic *splitting* (naming every new fossil a different species and genus) was quite common. When there are few known specimens of a species, no one can really understand the true range of variation encompassed within the species. We'll mention the historical names in the following sections, but these fossils are all now considered as members of *Homo erectus*.

Acheulian (ash´-oo-lay-en) Pertaining to a stone tool industry from the Lower and Middle Pleistocene; characterized by a large proportion of bifacial tools (flaked on both sides). Acheulian tool kits are common in Africa, Southwest Asia, and western Europe, but they're thought to be less common elsewhere. Also spelled *Acheulean*.

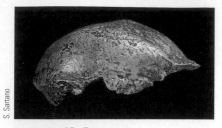

S. Sartano

The famous Trinil skullcap discovered by Eugene Dubois near the Solo River in Java. This is the first time a fossil human was found outside of Europe or Africa.

JAVA

After the publication of *On the Origin of Species*, as well as the attention paid to the ideas of Alfred Russel Wallace, debates about evolution were prevalent throughout Europe. While many theorists simply stayed home and debated the merits of natural selection and the likely course of human evolution, one young Dutch anatomist decided to go find evidence of it. Eugene Dubois (1858–1940) enlisted in the Dutch East Indian Army and was shipped to the island of Sumatra, Indonesia, to look for what he called "the missing link."

In October 1891, after moving his search to the neighboring island of Java, Dubois' field crew unearthed along the Solo River near the town of Trinil a skullcap that was to become internationally famous (Fig. 12-5). The following year, a human femur was recovered about 15 yards upstream in what Dubois claimed was the same level as the skullcap, and he assumed that the skullcap (with a cranial capacity of slightly over 900 cm^3) and the femur belonged to the same individual.

After studying these discoveries for a few years, Dubois startled the world in 1894 with a paper titled "*Pithecanthropus erectus*, A Manlike Species of Transitional Anthropoid from Java." Dubois' views were harshly criticized, but eventually there was general acceptance that he had been correct in identifying the skull as representing a previously undescribed species; that his estimates of cranial capacity were reasonably accurate; and that *Pithecanthropus erectus*, or *H. erectus* as we call it today, is a close relative and perhaps an ancestor of *H. sapiens*.

By 1930 the controversy had faded, especially in light of important new discoveries near Peking (Beijing), China, in the late 1920s (discussed shortly). Similarities between the Beijing skulls and Dubois' *Pithecanthropus* were obvious. Scientists pointed out that the Java form was not an "apeman," as Dubois contended, but instead was closely related to modern *Homo sapiens*. You might think that Dubois would welcome the finds from China and the support they provided for the human status of *Pithecanthropus*, but he didn't. In fact, he refused to recognize any connection between the Beijing and Java materials, eventually suggesting that the Trinil skullcap was that of a giant extinct gibbon.

HOMO ERECTUS FROM JAVA

Six sites in eastern Java have yielded all the *H. erectus* fossil remains found to date on that island. The dating of these fossils has been hampered by the complex nature of Javanese geology, but it's been generally accepted that most of the fossils belong to the Early to Middle **Pleistocene** and are between 1.6 and 1 million years old. But as we noted earlier, more precise chronometric dating estimates have suggested that the site of Mojokerto may be close to 1.8 million years old, and very late *H. erectus* survivors (from Ngandong) may be as young as 27,000 years old.

The Ngandong specimens were the next group to be found in Java. An excavation of a fossil-rich deposit within an ancient river terrace produced 11 mostly complete hominid crania. Two specialized dating techniques, discussed in Chapter 10, have determined that animal bones found at the site—and presumably associated with the hominids—are only about 50,000 to 25,000 years old (Swisher et al., 1996). These dates are controversial, but further evidence is now establishing a *very* late survival of *Homo erectus* in Java, long after the species had disappeared elsewhere. So, these individuals would be contemporary with *Homo sapiens*—which, by this time, had expanded widely throughout the Old World, even into Australia around 40 to 60 thousand years ago (kya). As we'll see in Chapter 14, even later—and very unusual—hominids have been found elsewhere, apparently evolving while isolated on another Indonesian island.

At Sangiran Dome (see "A Closer Look," p. 306), west of Trinil and Ngandong, over 80 different fossils have been found. The Sangiran Dome specimens represent a long-thriving population that has been preserved in an area of about 5 miles long by 2.5 miles wide. The geology of the area shows evidence first of a lakeshore, but as that lake receded, rivers were left to snake across the grasslands. *H. erectus* most likely lived through seasonal monsoon-like conditions marked by alternating wet and dry seasons—just like the seasons of southeast Asia today. The Sangiran Dome specimens also display some of the largest cranial capacities among *H. erectus* individuals, ranging from 813 cm^3 to 1,059 cm^3.

Pleistocene   The epoch of the Cenozoic from 1.8 mya until 10,000 ya. Frequently referred to as the Ice Age, this epoch is associated with continental glaciations in northern latitudes.

Zhoukoudian   (Zhoh´-koh-dee´-en)

One of the eleven Ngandong *Homo erectus* crania excavated from the terraces of the Solo River in Java.

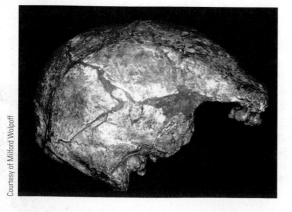

Courtesy of Milford Wolpoff

From further detailed analysis of the local geology, we know that the earliest *Homo erectus* groups arrived at the coastal swamps of south-central Java about 1.6 mya (see Fig. 12-7). About 800 kya, the hominids and most other contemporary large mammals seem to have left the area. In the meantime, volcanic debris has continued to accumulate up to the present era.

We can't say much about the *H. erectus* way of life in Java. Very few artifacts have been found, and those have come mainly from river terraces, not from primary sites: "On Java there is still not a single site where artifacts can be associated with *H. erectus*" (Bartstra, 1982, p. 319).

PEKING (BEIJING)

The story of Peking *H. erectus* is another saga filled with excitement, hard work, luck, and misfortune. Europeans had known for a long time that "dragon bones," used by the Chinese as medicine and aphrodisiacs, were actually ancient mammal bones. Scientists eventually located one of the sources of these bones near Beijing at a site called **Zhoukoudian**. Serious excavations were begun there in the 1920s under the direction of a young Chinese geologist named Pei Wenshong. In 1929 a fossil skull was discovered, and Pei brought the specimen to anatomist Davidson Black. The result was worth the labor. The skull turned out to be a juvenile's, and although it was thick, low, and relatively small, Black was sure it belonged to an early hominid. The response to this discovery, quite unlike that which greeted Dubois almost 40 years earlier, was enthusiastically favorable.

Franz Weidenreich (Fig. 12-8), a distinguished anatomist well known for his work on European fossil hominids, succeeded Black. After Japan invaded China in 1933, Weidenreich decided to move the fossils. He left China in 1941, taking plaster casts, photographs, and drawings of the material with him. After he left, the bones were packed, and arrangements were made for the U.S. Marine Corps in Beijing to take them to the United States. But the bones never reached the United States, and they've never been found. To this day, no one knows what happened to them.

ZHOUKOUDIAN *HOMO ERECTUS*

The fossil remains of *H. erectus* discovered in the 1920s and 1930s, as well as some more recent excavations at Zhoukoudian (Fig. 12-9), are by far the largest collection of *H. erectus* material found anywhere. This excellent sample includes 14 skullcaps (Fig. 12-10), other cranial pieces, and more than 100 isolated teeth, but only a scattering of postcranial elements (Jia and Huang, 1990). Various interpretations to account for this unusual pattern of preservation have been offered, ranging from ritualistic treatment or cannibalism by the hominids themselves to the more mundane suggestion that the *H. erectus* remains are simply the leftovers of the meals of giant hyenas.

At any rate, the hominid remains belong to upward of 40 adults and children and together provide much evidence. Because of Weidenreich's meticulous work, the Zhoukoudian fossils have led to a good overall picture of Chinese *H. erectus*. Like the materials from Java, they have typical *H. erectus* features, including a supraorbital torus in front and a nuchal torus behind. Also, the skull has thick bones, a sagittal keel, and a protruding face and, like the Javanese forms, is broadest near the bottom. These specimens have been dated at various times to be between 670,000 and 410,000 years old.

FIGURE 12-7
The Sangiran Dome Team, composed of researchers from the University of Iowa and the Bandung Institute of Technology, shown here during a paleoecological analysis of the ancient strata of the Dome.

FIGURE 12-8
Franz Weidenreich.

12-9
Zhoukoudian cave.

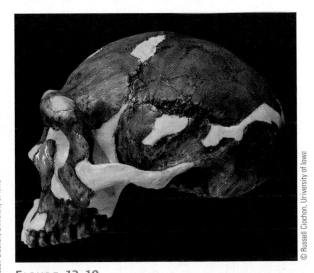

FIGURE 12-10
Composite cranium of Zhoukoudian *Homo erectus*, reconstructed by Ian Tattersall and Gary Sawyer of the American Museum of Natural History in New York.

305

A CLOSER LOOK   Dragon Bone Hill: Cave Home or Hyena Den?

About 30 miles southwest of Beijing, near Zhoukoudian, is the locality known as Dragon Bone Hill. In the 1920s and 1930s, this cave site yielded the first (and still the largest) cache of fossils of *Homo erectus*, historically known as Peking Man. The remains of about 45 individuals, along with thousands of stone tools, debris from tool manufacture, and thousands of animal bones, were contained within the 100-foot-thick deposits that once completely filled the original cave. Some evidence unearthed at the site suggests to many researchers that these creatures, who lived from about 670 to 410 kya, had mastered the use of fire and practiced cannibalism. Still, despite years of excavation and analysis, little is certain about what occurred here long ago.

To most of the early excavators, the likely scenario was that these particular early humans lived in the cave where their bones and stone tools were found. The animal bones were likely the remains of meals—proof of their hunting expertise. A more sensational view, first advanced in 1929, was that the cave contained evidence of cannibalism. Skulls were conspicuous among the remains, suggesting to Chinese paleoanthropologist Jia Lanpo that these might be the trophies of headhunters.

But another Chinese paleoanthropologist—Pei Wenzhong, who codirected the early Zhoukoudian excavations—believed that the skulls and accompanying damage were due to hyena chewing, not human killers. In 1939, his views were bolstered by

Zhoukoudian Museum, China and © Russell Ciochon, University of Iowa

(a)

(b)

FIGURE 1

These illustrations demonstrate the two interpretations of the remains from Dragon Bone Hill: the more traditional, Cave Home model (a) vs. the newer, and probably more accurate, Hyena Den model (b).

FIGURE 12-11

Chinese tools from Middle Pleistocene sites. (Adapted from Wu and Olsen, 1985.)

Cultural Remains   More than 100,000 artifacts have been recovered from this vast site, which was occupied intermittently for many thousands of years. Early on, tools are generally crude and shapeless, but they become more refined over time. Common tools at the site are choppers and chopping tools, but retouched flakes were fashioned into scrapers, points, burins, and awls (Fig. 12-11).

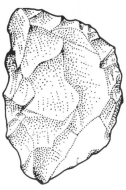

Quartzite chopper

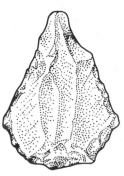

Flint point

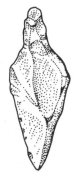

Flint awl

Graver, or burin

the emerging science of taphonomy, which is the study of how, after death, animal and plant remains become modified, moved, buried, and fossilized (see Chapter 10, p. 240). Published observations on the way hyenas at the Vienna zoo fed on cow bones led later scientists to reject the idea of cannibalism, although they continued to look upon the cave as a shelter used by early humans equipped with stone tools and fire (as reflected in the title of *The Cave Home of Peking Man*, published in 1975).

In the mid- to late 1970s, however, Western scientists began to better appreciate and develop the field of taphonomy. One assumption of taphonomy is that the most common species at a fossil site and/or the best-preserved animal remains at the site are most likely the ones to have inhabited the area in life. Of all the mammal fossils from the cave, very few belonged to *H. erectus*—perhaps only 0.5 percent, suggesting that most of the time, this species did not live in the cave. What's more, none of the *H. erectus* skeletons is complete. There's a lack of limb bones—especially of forearms, hands, lower leg bones, and feet—indicating that these individuals died somewhere else and that their partial remains were later carried to the cave. But how?

The answer is suggested by the remains of the most common and complete animal skeletons in the cave deposit—those of the giant hyena, *Pachycrocuta brevirostris*. Had *H. erectus*, instead of being the mighty hunters of anthropological lore, simply met the same unhappy fate as the deer and other prey species in the cave? To test the giant hyena hypothesis, scientists reexamined the fossil casts and a few actual fossils of *H. erectus* from Zhoukoudian for evidence of carnivore damage. Surprisingly, two thirds of the *H. erectus* fossils displayed puncture marks from a carnivore's large, pointed front teeth, most likely the canines of a hyena. What's more, there were long, scraping bite marks, typified by U-shaped grooves along the bone, and fracture patterns comparable to those modern

hyenas make when they chew bone. One of the *H. erectus* bones, part of a femur, even reveals telltale surface etchings from stomach acid, indicating it was swallowed and then regurgitated.

Cut marks (made by stone tools) observed on several mammal bones from the cave suggest that early humans did sometimes make use of Zhoukoudian, even if they weren't responsible for accumulating most of the bones. Stone tools left near the cave entrance also attest to their presence. Given its long history, the cave may have served a variety of occupants or at times have been configured as several separate, smaller shelters. Another possibility is that, in a form of time sharing, early humans ventured partway into the cave during the day to scavenge on what the hyenas had not eaten and to find temporary shelter. They might not have realized that the animals, which roamed at twilight and at night, were sleeping in the dark recesses a couple of hundred feet away.

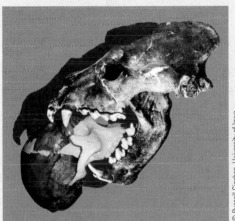

FIGURE 2
A composite image of the skulls of *Pachycrocuta* and *Homo erectus* that shows how the giant hyena may have attacked the face. Recent studies have shown that many of the *Homo erectus* remains from Zhoukoudian show hyena damage.

© Russell Ciochon, University of Iowa

The way of life at Zhoukoudian has traditionally been described as that of hunter-gatherers who killed deer, horses, and other animals and gathered fruits, berries, and ostrich eggs. Fragments of charred ostrich eggshells and abundant deposits of hackberry seeds unearthed in the cave suggest that these hominids supplemented their diet of meat by gathering herbs, wild fruits, tubers, and eggs. Layers of what has long been thought to be ash in the cave (over 18 feet deep at one point) have been interpreted as indicating the use of fire by *H. erectus*; but as we'll see, researchers don't really know whether Beijing hominids could actually make fire.

More recently, several researchers have challenged this picture of Zhoukoudian life. Lewis Binford and colleagues (Binford and Ho, 1985; Binford and Stone, 1986a, 1986b) reject the description of Beijing *H. erectus* as hunters and argue that the evidence clearly points more accurately to scavenging. Using advanced archaeological techniques of analysis, Noel Boaz and colleagues have even questioned whether the *H. erectus* remains at Zhoukoudian represent evidence of hominid habitation of the cave. By comparing the types of bones, as well as the damage to the bones, with that seen in contemporary carnivore dens, Boaz and Ciochon (2001) have suggested that much of the material in the cave likely accumulated through the activities of a giant extinct hyena. In fact, they hypothesize that most of the *H. erectus* remains, too, are the food refuse of hyena meals.

Boaz and his colleagues do recognize that the tools in the cave, and possibly the cut marks on some of the animal bones, provide evidence of hominid activities at Zhoukoudian. They also recognize that more detailed analysis is required to test their hypotheses and to "determine the nature and scope" of the *H. erectus* presence at Zhoukoudian (see "A Closer Look," p. 306).

Probably the most intriguing archaeological aspect of the presumed hominid behavior at Zhoukoudian has been the long-held assumption that *H. erectus* deliberately used fire inside the cave. Controlling fire was one of the major cultural breakthroughs of all prehistory. By providing warmth, a means of cooking, an aid to further modify tools, and so forth, controlled fire would have been a giant technological innovation. While some potential early African sites have yielded evidence that to some have suggested hominid control of fire, it's long been concluded that the first *definite* evidence of hominid fire use comes from Zhoukoudian.

Now, more recent evidence has also radically altered this assumption. Much more detailed excavations at Zhoukoudian were carried out in 1996 and 1997 by biologist Steve Weiner and colleagues. These researchers also carefully analyzed soil samples for distinctive chemical signatures that would show whether fire had occurred in the cave (Weiner et al., 1998). They found that burnt bone was only rarely found in association with tools. And in most cases, the burning appeared to have taken place *after* fossilization—that is, the bones were not cooked. In fact, it turns out that the "ash" layers mentioned earlier aren't actually ash, but naturally accumulated organic sediment. This last conclusion was derived from chemical testing that showed absolutely no sign of wood having been burnt inside the cave. Finally, the "hearths" that have figured so prominently in archaeological reconstructions of presumed fire control at this site are apparently not hearths at all. They are simply round depressions formed in the past by water.

Another provisional interpretation of the cave's geology suggests that the cave wasn't open to the outside like a habitation site, but was accessed only through a vertical shaft. This theory has led archaeologist Alison Brooks to remark, "It wouldn't have been a shelter, it would have been a trap" (quoted in Wuethrich, 1998). These serious doubts about control of fire, coupled with the suggestive evidence of bone accumulation by carnivores, have led anthropologists Noel Boaz and Russell Ciochon to conclude that "Zhoukoudian cave was neither hearth nor home" (Boaz and Ciochon, 2001).

OTHER CHINESE SITES

More work has been done at Zhoukoudian than at any other Chinese site. Even so, there are other paleoanthropological sites worth mentioning. Four of the more important sites outside of Zhoukoudian are Majuangou, two in Lantian County (often simply referred to as Lantian), Yunxian, and several finds in Hexian County (usually referred to as the Hexian find).

Majuangou is an archaeological site found on the eastern boundary of the Nihewan Basin in northern China. While no hominid fossils have been found there, this site preserves indisputable evidence of stone tools that can be identified as choppers and scrapers. These tools are directly comparable to those found in the African Plio-Pleistocene, except that in China tools were made from chert, sandstone, and quartz rather than from the lava cobbles used at places like Olduvai Gorge. Many of these tools are found on actual living floors, so it's possible to refit the tools to reconstruct the original core from which they were made. Accompanying these tools are numerous remains of elephants, horses, hyenas, deer, and gazelle, many of which show clear evidence of modification ("cut marks") by *Homo erectus*. Dating of the site using paleomagnetism (see p. 245) has yielded an age of 1.66 mya, making this the oldest instance of stone tool processing of fauna and the earliest definitive hominid occupation in China (Zhu et al., 2004).

Before the excavation of two sites in Lantian County, Shaanxi Province, in the mid-1960s, Zhoukoudian was widely believed to be the oldest hominid site in China. Dated to 1.15 mya, Lantian is older than Zhoukoudian (Zhu et al., 2003), though Majuangou has now surpassed it in antiquity (though here, we don't yet have any evidence of *H. erectus* fossils). From the Lantian sites, the cranial remains of two adult female *Homo erectus* have been found in association with fire-treated pebbles and flakes, as well as ash (Woo, 1966) (see Fig. 12-12a). One of the specimens, an almost complete mandible containing several teeth, is quite similar to those from Zhoukoudian.

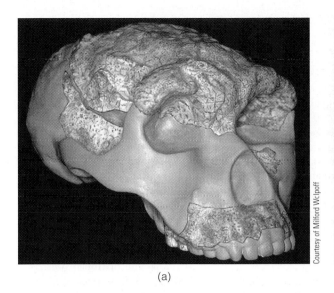

(a)

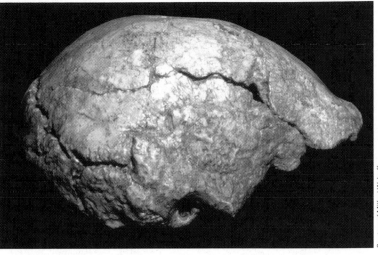

(b)

Two badly distorted crania were discovered in Yunxian County, Hubei Province, in 1989 and 1990 (Li and Etler, 1992). A combination of ESR and paleomagnetism dating methods gives us an average dating estimate of 580–800 kya. If the dates are correct, this would place Yunxian intermediately between Lantian and Zhoukoudian in the Chinese sequence. Due to extensive distortion of the crania from ground pressure, it was very difficult to compare these crania with other *Homo erectus* fossils; recently, however, French paleoanthropologist Amélie Vialet has restored the crania using sophisticated imaging techniques (Vialet et al., 2005). A reassessment of the fauna and paleoenvironment of the site also has been undertaken, showing that Yunxian *erectus* still employed relatively primitive hunting methods since they favored those prey with limited defensive capabilities, such as young and old animals.

In 1980 and 1981 the remains of several individuals, all bearing some resemblance to similar fossils from Zhoukoudian, were recovered from Hexian County in South China (Wu and Poirier, 1995) (see Fig. 12-12b). A close relationship has been postulated between the *Homo erectus* specimens from the Hexian find and from Zhoukoudian (Wu and Dong, 1985). Indeed, some date the remains to 400 kya (Wu et al., 2006), making it contemporaneous with Zhoukoudian; these dates are disputed, and others experts place the age at only 190 kya. Either way, the remains of *Homo erectus* from Hexian still rank as one of the more recent of their species in the world. As such, their importance should not be underestimated.

The Asian crania from both Java and China share many similar features, which may be explained by *H. erectus* migration from Java to China perhaps around 1 million years ago.

FIGURE **12-12**

(a) Reconstructed cranium of *Homo erectus* from Lantian, China, dated to approximately 1.15 mya. (b) Hexian cranium.

AT A GLANCE	Key *Homo erectus* Discoveries from Asia	
Site	**Dates**	**Human Remains**
Ngandong (Java, Indonesia)	50–25 ky	11 crania
Zhoukoudian (N. China)	670–410 ky	40 individuals; includes 14 skullcaps, but very few postcranial remains
Lantian (2 sites; C. China)	1.15 my	2 crania
Sangiran (Java, Indonesia)	1.6 my	At least 5 individuals; crania and a few postcranial remains

FIGURE 12-13

Nearly complete skull of *Homo erectus* from East Lake Turkana, Kenya; dated to approximately 1.8 mya.

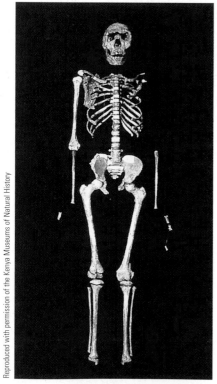

FIGURE 12-14

WT 15000 from Nariokotome, Kenya: the most complete *H. erectus* specimen yet found.

African *H. erectus* forms are generally older than most Asian forms, and they're different from them in several ways.

EAST AFRICA

Olduvai   Back in 1960, Louis Leakey unearthed a fossil skull at Olduvai that he identified as *H. erectus*. (see Chapter 10 for a comprehensive discussion of Olduvai). Skull OH 9, as it's called, came from Upper Bed II and is dated at 1.4 mya. It preserves a massive cranium, but the fossil is faceless except for a bit of nose below the supraorbital torus. Estimated at 1,067 cm^3, the cranial capacity of OH 9 is the largest of all the African *Homo erectus* specimens. The supraorbital torus is huge, the largest known for any hominid, but the walls of the braincase are thin. This latter characteristic is seen in most East African *H. erectus* specimens; in this respect they differ from Asian *H. erectus*, in which cranial bones are thick. This and other differences have led some researchers to place East African specimens in a separate species, called *Homo ergaster*.

East Turkana   Some 400 miles north of Olduvai Gorge, at the northern border of Kenya, is Lake Turkana—a long, alkaline, and salty lake. The badlands to the east of the lake, first explored by Richard Leakey and colleagues in 1969, have been a virtual gold mine of Plio-Pleistocene hominid finds, including *Paranthropus*, *Homo habilis*, and *Homo erectus*.

The most significant *H. erectus* discovery from East Turkana is a nearly complete skull (Fig. 12-13). Dated at 1.8 mya, this specimen is the oldest *Homo erectus* ever found. The cranial capacity is estimated at 848 cm^3, at the lower end of the range for *H. erectus* (750 to 1,250 cm^3), which isn't surprising considering its early date. It generally resembles Asian *H. erectus*—but with some important differences, which we'll soon discuss. Researchers have unearthed Oldowan flakes, cobbles, and core tools at various sites ranging from lake lagoons to dry grasslands. Acheulian tools are introduced to the area about 1.4 mya, adding bifacially flaked "hand axes" to the tool kit.

West Turkana   In August 1984, Kamoya Kimeu, a member of Richard Leakey's team, enhanced his reputation as an outstanding fossil hunter when he discovered a small piece of skull on the west side of Lake Turkana. Leakey and his colleague, Alan Walker of Pennsylvania State University, excavated the site now known as Nariokotome.

The dig was a resounding success and produced the most complete *H. erectus* skeleton ever found (Fig. 12-14). Known properly as WT 15000, the almost complete skeleton includes facial bones and most of the limb bones, ribs, vertebrae, and pelvis. Such well-preserved postcranial elements make for a very unusual discovery, because these elements are scarce at other *H. erectus* sites. The Nariokotome skeleton is quite ancient, dated chronometrically to about 1.6 mya. The skeleton is that of a boy about 12 years of age with an estimated height of about 5 feet 3 inches. Had he grown to maturity, it's estimated that his height would have been more than 6 feet—taller than *H. erectus* was previously thought to have been. The postcranial bones look very similar, though not quite identical, to those of modern humans. The cranial capacity of WT 15000 is estimated at 880 cm^3; brain growth was nearly complete, and the boy's adult cranial capacity would have been approximately 909 cm^3 (Begun and Walker, 1993). (See "A Closer Look," p. 311.)

Bouri   Two sites from Ethiopia have yielded *H. erectus* fossils, the most significant coming from the Bouri locale in the Middle Awash region. As you've seen, numerous remains of earlier hominids have come from this area (see Chapter 11 and Appendix B). The recent discovery of a mostly complete cranium from Bouri is important because this individual (dated at approximately 1 mya) is more like Asian *H. erectus* than are most of the earlier East African remains we've discussed (Asfaw et al., 2002). Consequently, the suggestion by several researchers that East African fossils are a different species from (Asian) *Homo erectus* isn't supported by the morphology of the Bouri cranium.

A CLOSER LOOK   The Nariokotome Skeleton

Discovering the spectacularly well-preserved skeleton from Nariokotome on the west side of Lake Turkana has given anthropologists considerable new insight into key anatomical features of *Homo erectus*. Since its recovery in 1984 and 1985, detailed studies have been undertaken, and the published results (Walker, 1993; Walker and Leakey, 1993) have allowed researchers to draw some initial conclusions. In addition, the extraordinary quality of the remains has allowed anthropologists to speculate on some major behavioral traits of *H. erectus* in Africa—and, more generally, of the entire species.

The remains comprise an almost complete skeleton, lacking only most of the small bones of the hands and feet and the unfused ends of long bones. This degree of preservation is remarkable. It makes this individual the most complete skeleton of *any* fossil hominid yet found from before about 100,000 ya (after that time, deliberate burial greatly improved preservation). This superior preservation may well have been aided by rapid sedimentation in what's thought to have been an ancient, shallow swamp. Once the individual died, his skeleton would have been quickly covered up, but even then some disturbance and breakage occurred—from chewing by catfish, but most especially from trampling by large animals wading in the swamp 1.6 mya.

As we've said, the individual was not fully grown when he died. His age (11 to 13 years; Walker, 1993) is determined by the stage of dental eruption—his permanent canines aren't yet erupted—and by union of the ends of long bones. Also, as we have noted, this young *Homo erectus* male was quite tall (5 feet 3 inches), and using modern growth curve approximations, his adult height would have been over 6 feet if he'd lived to full maturity.

More than simply being tall, the body proportions of this boy's skeleton are intriguing. Reconstructions suggest that he had a linear build with long appendages, conforming to predictions of *Allen's rule* for inhabitants of hot climates (see Chapter 16). Further extrapolating from this observation, Alan Walker suggests that *H. erectus* must have had a high sweating capacity in order to dissipate heat in the modern human fashion. (See p. 408 for a discussion of heat adaptation in humans.)

The boy's limb proportions suggest that mean annual temperature (90°F/30°C) in East Africa was quite warm 1.6 mya. Paleoecological reconstructions confirm this estimate of tropical conditions; indeed, they were much like the climate today in northern Kenya.

We can observe a final interesting feature in the pelvis of this adolescent skeleton. It's very narrow and is thus correlated with a narrow, bony birth canal. Walker (1993) again draws a behavioral inference from this anatomical feature. He estimates that a newborn with a cranial capacity no greater than a mere 200 cm^3 could have passed through a female pelvis this size. As we showed elsewhere, the adult cranial capacity estimate for this individual was slightly greater than 900 cm^3—thus arguing for significant postnatal growth of the brain (exceeding 75 percent of its eventual size) and again mirroring the modern human pattern. Walker speculates that this slow neural expansion (compared to other primates) leads to delayed development of motor skills and thus a prolonged period of infant-child dependency (what Walker terms secondary altriciality). This conclusion, however, is not supported by more recently analyzed dental data, which show an accelerated, australopithecine-like rate of maturation (Dean et al., 2001).

AT A GLANCE — Key *Homo erectus* Discoveries from Africa

Site	Dates	Human Remains
Bouri (Ethiopia)	1.0 my	Well-preserved cranium
Olduvai (Tanzania)	1.4 my	Partial cranium and a few postcranial pieces
Nariokotome (W. Turkana, Kenya)	1.6 my	Mostly complete adolescent skeleton
E. Lake Turkana (Kenya)	1.8 my	One nearly complete cranium and a few postcranial pieces

SUMMARY OF EAST AFRICAN *HOMO ERECTUS*

The *Homo erectus* remains from East Africa show several differences from the Javanese and Chinese fossils. Some African cranial specimens—particularly ER 3733, presumably a female, and WT 15000, presumably a male—aren't as strongly buttressed at the supraorbital and nuchal tori, and their cranial bones aren't as thick. Indeed, some researchers are so impressed by these differences, as well as others in the postcranial skeleton, that they're arguing for a *separate* species status for the African material, to distinguish it from the Asian samples. Bernard Wood, the leading proponent of this view, has suggested that the name *Homo ergaster* be used for the African remains and that *H. erectus* be reserved solely for the Asian material (Wood, 1991). In addition, the very early dates now postulated for the dispersal of *H. erectus* into Asia (Java) would argue for a more than 1-million-year separate history for Asian and African populations.

In any case, this species division has not been fully accepted, and the current consensus (and the one we prefer) is to continue referring to all these hominids as *Homo erectus* (Kramer, 1993; Conroy, 1997; Rightmire, 1998; Asfaw et al., 2002). So, as with some earlier hominids, we'll have to accommodate a considerable degree of intraspecific variation within this species. Wood has concluded, regarding variation within such a broadly defined *H. erectus* species, that "It is a species which manifestly embraces an unusually wide degree of variation in both the cranium and postcranial skeleton" (Wood, 1992a, p. 329).

EUROPE

Because of the recent discoveries from Dmanisi (see p. 302), the time frame for the earliest hominid occupation of Europe is being dramatically pushed back. For several decades, researchers assumed that hominids didn't reach Europe until late in the Middle Pleistocene (after 400,000 ya) and were already identifiable as a form very similar to *Homo sapiens*. So, they concluded that *H. erectus* (and contemporaries) never got there. But, as the new discoveries are evaluated, these assumptions are being discarded, and radical revisions concerning hominid evolution in Europe are becoming necessary.

While not as old as the Dmanisi material, fossils from the Gran Dolina site in northern Spain are extending the antiquity of hominids in western Europe. (Gran Dolina is located in the very productive region called Atapuerca, where later hominid fossils have also been found.) The dating of Gran Dolina, based on specialized techniques discussed in Chapter 10 (see p. 244), is approximately 850–780 kya (Parés and Pérez-González, 1995; Falguéres et al., 1999). These early Spanish finds are thus *at least* 250,000 years older than any other hominid yet discovered in western Europe. Because all the remains so far identified are fragmentary, assigning these fossils to particular species poses something of a problem; but initial analysis suggests that these fossils aren't *H. erectus*. Spanish paleoanthropologists who have studied the Gran Dolina fossils have decided to place these hominids into another (separate) species, one they call *Homo antecessor* (Bermúdez de Castro et al., 1997; Arsuaga et al., 1999). However, it remains to be seen whether this newly proposed species will prove to be distinct from other species of *Homo* (see p. 316 for further discussion).

AT A GLANCE	Key *Homo erectus* (or Contemporaries) Discoveries from Europe	
Site	**Dates**	**Human Remains**
Ceprano (Italy)	900–800 ky	Well-preserved cranium
Gran Dolina (Atapuerca, N. Spain)	850–780 ky	Fragmentary remains
Dmanisi (Republic of Georgia)	1.75my	4 crania plus a few postcranial remains

Finally, the southern European discovery of a well-preserved cranium from the Ceprano site in central Italy may be the best evidence yet of *H. erectus* (strictly defined) in Europe (Ascenzi et al., 1996). Provisional dating of a partial cranium from this important site suggests a date between 800 and 900 kya (Fig. 12-15). Phillip Rightmire (1998) has concluded that cranial morphology places this specimen quite close to *H. erectus*. Italian researchers have proposed other views. The exact relationship of Ceprano to *Homo erectus* remains to be fully determined.

After about 400,000 ya, the European fossil hominid record becomes increasingly abundant. More fossils mean more variation, so it's not surprising that interpretations regarding the proper taxonomic assessment of many of these remains have been debated, in some cases for decades. In recent years, several of these somewhat later "premodern" specimens have been considered either as early representatives of *Homo sapiens* or as a separate species, one immediately preceding *H. sapiens*. These enigmatic premodern humans are discussed in Chapter 13. A time line for the *H. erectus* discoveries discussed in this chapter as well as other finds of more uncertain status is shown in Figure 12-16.

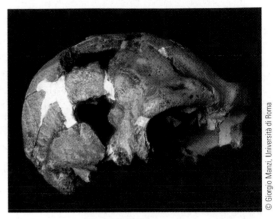

FIGURE 12-15

The Ceprano *Homo erectus* cranium from central Italy, provisionally dated to 800–900 kya. This is the best evidence for *Homo erectus* in Europe.

FIGURE 12-16

Time line for *Homo erectus* discoveries and other contemporary hominids. Note that most dates are approximations. *Note:* Most dates are only imprecise estimates. However, the dates from East African sites are chronometrically determined and are thus much more secure. The early dates from Java are also radiometric and are gaining wide acceptance.

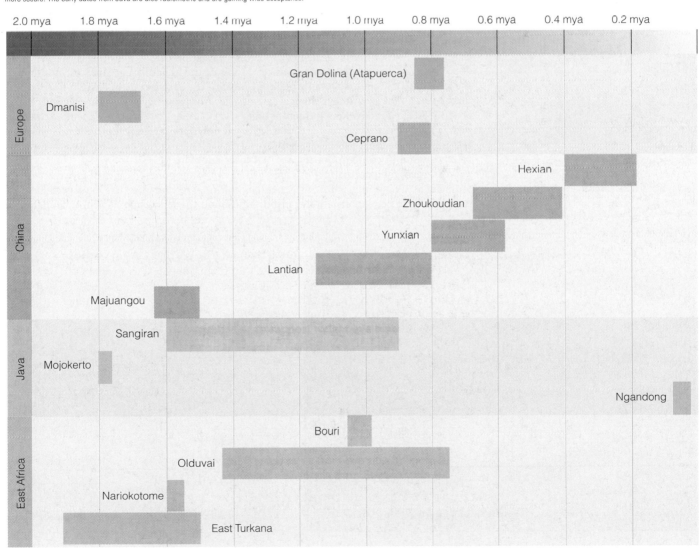

FIGURE 12-17

Acheulian biface ("hand axe"), a basic tool of the Acheulian tradition.

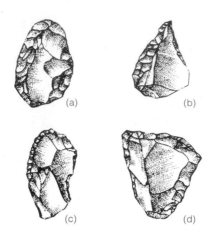

FIGURE 12-18

Small tools of the Acheulian industry. (a) Side scraper. (b) Point. (c) End scraper. (d) Burin.

FIGURE 12-19

(a) A Middle Pleistocene butchering site at Olorgesailie, Kenya, excavated by Louis and Mary Leakey, who had the catwalk built for observers.
(b) A close-up of numerous Acheulian tools, mainly hand axes, found at Olorgesailie in Kenya. Thousands of similar tools were found at this site.

Technological Trends in *Homo erectus*

During the existence of *H. erectus* in Africa, a new tool kit was developed. The important change in this kit was a core worked on both sides, called a *biface* (known widely as a hand axe or cleaver; Fig. 12-17). The biface had a flatter core than seen in the roundish, earlier Oldowan pebble core (which in fact probably wasn't a tool at all, but a blank from which flakes were removed; see p. 250). Using the biface as a basic part of what's called an Acheulian tool industry, this stone tool technology spread from Africa after 1.4 mya and became standardized as the basic *H. erectus* all-purpose lithic tool kit for more than a million years. With the biface as a kind of "Acheulian Swiss army knife," these tools served to cut, scrape, pound, and dig. This most useful tool has been found in Africa, parts of Asia, and later in Europe. Note that Acheulian tool kits also included several types of small tools (Fig. 12-18).

For many years, scientists thought that a cultural "divide" separated the Old World, with Acheulian technology made *only* in Africa, the Middle East, and parts of Europe (elsewhere, the Acheulian was presumed to be absent). But recently reported excavations from more than 20 sites in southern China have forced reevaluation of this hypothesis (Yamei et al., 2000). As we've noted, the most distinctive tools of the Acheulian are bifaces, and they're the very tools thought lacking throughout most of the Pleistocene in eastern Europe and most of Asia. The new archaeological assemblages from southern China are securely dated at about 800 kya and contain numerous bifaces, very similar to contemporaneous Acheulian bifaces from Africa (see Figs. 12-17 and 12-19). It now appears likely that cultural traditions relating to stone tool technology were largely equivalent over the *full* geographical range of *H. erectus* and its contemporaries (see "A Closer Look," p. 315).

While geographical distinctions aren't so obvious, temporal changes in tool technology are evident. Beginning with the Acheulian culture, we find the first evidence that raw materials were being constantly transported around the landscape. When Acheulian tool

(a)

(b)

A CLOSER LOOK　　The Sky Is Falling

The blazing red soil of Guangxi in southwest China is all that remains of a powerful conflagration in the wake of a violent meteor impact some 800 kya. As it struck the ground somewhere in Indochina, the asteroid liquefied the terrain and sent it spewing skyward in a hailstorm of fire that scarred land as far south as Australia. The remnants of this event can be found scattered across China, Indonesia, and Australia and are known collectively as the Australasian Tektite Strewn Field (Paine, 2001). The tektites themselves are the fragments of ejecta fused in the furnace of the impact and flung across the landscape. These onyx spheroids resemble miniature meteorites; and, most crucially for paleoanthropology, they allow us to date the appearance of bifacial tools (that is, the Acheulian industry) in China. Because tektites are superheated, as in volcanic eruptions, they can be radiometrically dated using the potassium-argon technique (see Chapter 10, p. 243). Consequently, we can then also get a date for the stone tools lying alongside them in the Bose Basin of China.

The "Movius Line" (named after Harvard archaeologist Hallum Movius) was long believed to represent an imaginary, though very real, technological barrier separating the primitive residents of Asia from the western makers of bifacial hand axes.

Underlying this dichotomy was the implicit conviction that a lack of Acheulian-type tools throughout eastern Eurasia was more a function of reduced intelligence than resource scarcity. Recent excavations in the Bose Basin, Guangxi, have thrown this scheme into doubt with the revelation that at least some Asian *H. erectus* were fully capable of making bifacial tools and were doing so as early as 800 kya (Yamei et al., 2000).

More important still, the tektites represent an underlying reason that these tools exist at all. As molten earth showered the region, it scoured the landscape of the dense and impenetrable forest that had long excluded habitation by *Homo erectus* populations, previously restricting them to more open river valleys. A cataclysmic natural event opened a new world for human hands to exploit. Outcroppings of stone materials ideal for biface manufacture were left bare and steaming. An event that so nearly ended life in the region—a small-scale version of the asteroid impact that ended the reign of dinosaurs—became a reason for it to prosper. Far from dim-witted country cousins, *Homo erectus* in Asia represents a population of savvy opportunists who turned a potential doomsday into the heyday of stone tool manufacture in the region.

FIGURE 1
The red laterite soils of Guangxi in southwest China, from which many important Acheulian-style handaxes have been discovered alongside tektites used to date the site to 800 kya.

© Russell Ciochon, University of Iowa

users found a good piece of stone, they would take that chunk with them as they traveled around the landscape. This behavior suggests foresight, because they likely knew they may need to use a tool in the future—and this rock in front of them would be handy later. This is a recognized change from the Oldowan, where all stone tools are found very close to their raw material sources.

Evidence of butchering is widespread at *H. erectus* sites and, in the past, such evidence has been cited in arguments for consistent hunting. Researchers formerly interpreted any association of bones and tools as evidence of hunting, but many studies now suggest that cut marks on bones from the *H. erectus* time period often overlay carnivore tooth marks. This means that hominids were gaining access to the carcasses after the carnivores and were therefore scavenging the meat, not hunting the animals. It's also crucial to mention that these hominids were gaining a large amount of their daily calories from gathering wild plants, tubers, and fruits. Like hunter-gatherers of modern times, *H. erectus* individuals were most likely consuming 80 percent of their daily calories from plant materials.

Seeing the Big Picture: Interpretations of *Homo erectus*

Several aspects of the geographical, physical, and behavioral patterns shown by *H. erectus* (broadly defined) seem clear. But new discoveries and more in-depth analyses are helping us to reevaluate our prior ideas. The fascinating fossil hominids discovered at Dmanisi are perhaps the most challenging piece of this puzzle.

Past theories suggest that *Homo erectus* was able to emigrate from Africa owing to more advanced culture and a more modern anatomy as compared to earlier African predecessors. Yet, the Dmanisi cranial remains show that these very early Europeans still had small brains; what's more, *Homo erectus* has been found in Java at 1.6 mya, and these hominids were still using Oldowan-style tools.

So it seems that some key parts of earlier hypothesis are not fully accurate. At least some of the earliest emigrants from Africa didn't yet show the entire suite of *Homo erectus* physical and behavioral traits. How different the Dmanisi hominids are from the full *H. erectus* pattern remains to be seen, and the discovery of more complete postcranial remains will be most illuminating.

Going a step further, the four crania from Dmanisi are extremely variable; one of them, in fact, does look more like *Homo erectus*. It would be tempting to conclude that more than one type of hominid is represented here—but they're all found in the same geological context. The archaeologists who excavated the site conclude that all the fossils are closely associated with each other. The simplest hypothesis is that they all are members of the *same* species. This degree of apparent intraspecific variation is biologically noteworthy, and it's influencing how paleoanthropologists interpret all of these fossil samples.

This growing awareness of the broad limits of intraspecific variation among some hominids brings us to our second consideration: Is *Homo ergaster* in Africa a separate species from *Homo erectus*, as strictly defined in Asia? While this interpretation was popular in the last decade, it now is losing support. The finds from Dmanisi raise fundamental issues of interpretation. Among these four crania from one locality (see Fig. 12-3), we see more variation than between the African and Asian forms, which many researchers have interpreted as different species. Also, the new discovery from Bouri (Ethiopia) of a more *erectus*-looking cranium further weakens the separate-species interpretation of *Homo ergaster*.

The separate-species status of the early European fossils from Spain (Gran Dolina) is also not yet clearly established. We still don't have much good fossil evidence from this site; but an early date, prior to 750 kya, is well confirmed. Recall also that no other western European hominid fossils are known until at least 150,000 years later, and a seemingly almost contemporaneous find from Italy looks like *Homo erectus* (Bischoff et al., 2006). It's quite apparent that later in the Pleistocene, the possible descendants of these hominids are well established both in Africa and in Europe. These later premodern humans are the topic of the next chapter.

When looking back at the evolution of *H. erectus*, we realize how significant this early human's achievements were. It was *H. erectus* who increased in body size with more efficient bipedalism; who embraced culture wholeheartedly as an adaptive strategy; whose brain was reshaped and increased in size to within the range of *H. sapiens*; who became a more efficient scavenger and likely hunter with a greater dependence on meat; and who apparently established more permanent living sites. In short, it was *H. erectus*, committed to a cultural way of life, who transformed hominid evolution to human evolution. As Richard Foley states, "The appearance and expansion of *H. erectus* represented a major change in adaptive strategy that influenced the subsequent process and pattern of human evolution" (1991, p. 425).

VISUAL SUMMARY

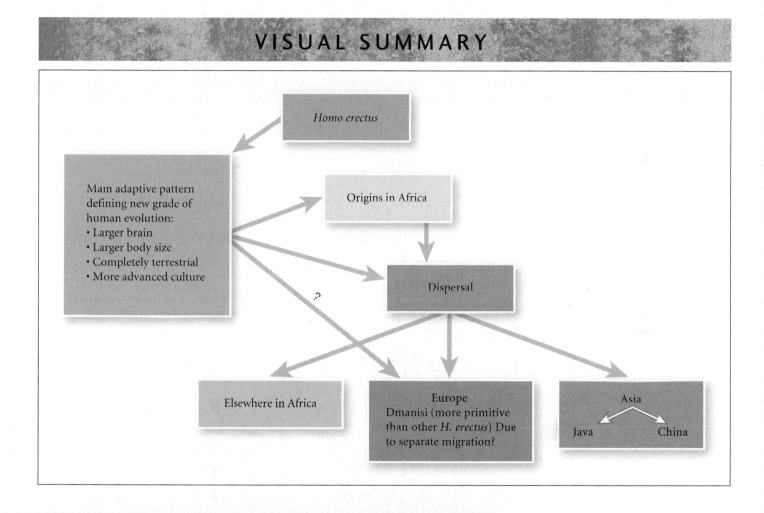

Summary: Putting It All Together

Homo erectus remains are found in geological contexts dating from about 1.8 mya to at least 200 kya—and probably much later—and spanning a period of more than 1.5 million years. While the nature and timing of migrations are uncertain, it's likely that *H. erectus* first appeared in East Africa and later migrated to other areas. This widespread and highly successful hominid defines a new and more modern grade of human evolution.

Historically, the first finds were made by Dubois in Java, and later discoveries came from China and Africa. Differences from early *Homo* are notable in *H. erectus*' larger brain, taller stature, robust build, and changes in facial structure and cranial buttressing.

The long period of *H. erectus* existence was marked by a remarkably uniform technology over space and time. Even so, compared to earlier hominids, *H. erectus* and contemporaries introduced more sophisticated tools and probably ate novel and/or differently processed foods. By using these new tools and—at later sites—possibly fire as well, they were also able to move into different environments and successfully adapt to new conditions.

It's generally assumed that certain *H. erectus* populations evolved into later premodern humans, some of which, in turn, evolved into *Homo sapiens*. Evidence supporting such a series of transitions is seen in the Ngandong fossils (and others discussed in Chapter 13), which display both *H. erectus* and *H. sapiens* features. There are still many questions about *H. erectus* behavior—for example, did they hunt, and did they control fire? We also wonder about their relationship to later hominids. Was the mode of evolution gradual or rapid, and which *H. erectus* populations contributed genes? The search for answers continues.

In Table 12-1 you'll find a useful summary of the most significant hominid fossils discussed in this chapter.

TABLE 12-1	Key Hominid Fossils Discussed in This Chapter			
	Site	Dates (ya)	Taxonomic Designation	Comments
Asia	Java (6 locales)	1,8000,000–25,000	*Homo erectus*	First *H. erectus* discovery; most finds in disturbed river terrace contexts
	China (6 locales; most significant is Zhoukoudian)	400,000+–1200,000+	*Homo erectus*	Up to 40 individuals at Zhoukoudian; also, many artifacts; Zhoukoudian, however, probably not primary living site
Europe	Ceprano	900,000–800,000	*Homo erectus*	One individual; well-preserved cranium; Similar to Asian *H. erectus*
	Gran Dolina (Atapuerca, Spain)	780,000	Quite likely not *H. erectus*; referred to by discoverers as *Homo antecessor*	Remains quite incomplete; oldest W. European fossil hominid discovery
	Dmanisi (Republic of Georgia)	1,800,000–1,700,000	*Homo erectus* (very primitive example—or could be classified as early *Homo*)	4 well-preserved crania plus partial mandible and a few postcranial bones; among oldest *H. erectus* found anywhere
Africa	Bouri (Ethiopia)	1,000,000	*Homo erectus*	Well-preserved cranium plus postcranial bones; morphology quite similar to Asian *H. erectus*
	Nariokotome (West Turkana, Kenya)	1,600,000	*Homo erectus*, also frequently referred to as *Homo ergaster*	Nearly complete adolescent skeleton, probably of a male; shows some differences from Asian *H. erectus*
	East Turkana (Kenya)	1,800,000	*Homo erectus*, also frequently referred to as *Homo ergaster*	Well-preserved cranium plus several other postcranial remains likely coming from same group; cranium likely of female; shows several differences from Asian *H. erectus*

Critical Thinking Questions

1. Why is the nearly complete skeleton from Nariokotome so important? What kinds of evidence does it provide?

2. Assume that you're in the laboratory and have the Nariokotome skeleton, as well as a skeleton of a modern human. First, given a choice, what age and sex would you choose for the human skeleton, and why? Second, what similarities and differences do the two skeletons show?

3. What fundamental questions of interpretation do the fossil hominids from Dmanisi raise? Does this evidence completely overturn the hypothesis concerning *H. erectus* dispersal from Africa? Explain why or why not.

4. How has the interpretation of Dragon Bone Hill been revised in recent years? What kinds of new evidence from this site have been used in this reevaluation, and what does that tell you about modern archaeological techniques and approaches?

5. You're interpreting the hominid fossils from three sites in East Africa (Nariokotome, Olduvai, and Bouri)—all considered possible members of *H. erectus*. What sorts of evidence would lead you to conclude that there was more than one species? What would convince you that there was just one species? Why do you think some paleoanthropologists (splitters) would tend to see more than one species, while others (lumpers) would generally not? What kind of approach would you take, and why?

Ancient DNA

An exciting and potentially highly informative new direction of research has focused on extracting and analyzing DNA samples from ancient remains. Some of these finds can be extremely ancient, most notably insect tissue embedded in amber (that is, fossilized tree resin). Some of the insect DNA derived from these sources is upward of 120 million years old, and these discoveries, first reported in 1992, were the inspiration for Michael Crichton's *Jurassic Park*.

Amber provides an unusual and favorable environment for long-term preservation of small organisms—a situation, unfortunately, not applicable to larger organisms such as vertebrates. Even so, following the introduction of PCR technology, scientists were able to look for *very* small amounts of DNA that just might still linger in ancient human remains.

In 1986, researchers reported results of sequenced brain DNA obtained from mummified remains found in a Florida bog and dated at 7,000–8,000 years ago (Doran et al., 1986). The famous "Iceman" mummy discovered in the Alps in 1991 also yielded widely publicized DNA information about his population origins, shown to be not far from where he died (Fig. 1). More recently, a group of Italian biologists led by Franco Rollo of the Molecular Anthropology/Ancient DNA Laboratory of the University of Camerino has analyzed the Iceman's intestinal contents using molecular techniques. Their results show that the Iceman's last meal was composed of red deer and possibly cereal grains, and that his preceding meal contained ibex, cereals, and other plant food (Rollo et al., 2002). He apparently ate his next-to-last meal at a lower altitude than the 10,500-foot locale where he died. This observation is supported by other DNA studies of pollen found in his lungs, showing that he had recently passed through a midaltitude carboniferous forest.

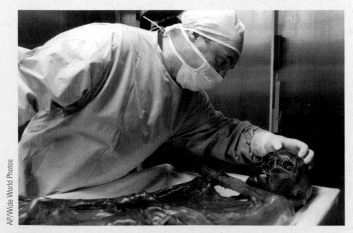

FIGURE 1
Iceman.

Another intriguing line of evidence has come from mtDNA analysis of early European farmers from a 7,500-year-old site in Germany (Haak et al., 2005). The most interesting aspects of these new data concern these questions: How did farming first spread to Europe? And who are the ancestors of contemporary Europeans? So far, the new molecular information hasn't fully answered these questions (and conflicts with some earlier data from the Y chromosome). Still, this kind of information is very exciting and opens vast new opportunities for understanding ancient population migrations.

No nuclear DNA was identified in any of the examples just discussed, so researchers used the more plentiful mitochondrial DNA. Their successes gave hope that they could analyze even more ancient remains containing preserved human DNA.

And indeed, in 1997, Matthias Krings and associates from the University of Munich and the Max Planck Institute of Evolutionary Anthropology (see p. 200) made a startling breakthrough. They successfully extracted, amplified, and sequenced DNA from a Neandertal skeleton. As discussed in the next chapter (p. 343), seven other Neandertals (ranging in date from 50,000 to 29,000 ya) have since yielded enough mtDNA for analysis.

As we've noted, the place of Neandertals in human evolution has been and continues to be a topic of fascination and contention. This is why the Neandertal DNA evidence is so important. Besides, comparing Neandertal DNA patterns with those of early modern humans would be extremely illuminating. Certainly, numerous early *H. sapiens* skeletons from Europe and elsewhere are still likely to contain some DNA. And indeed, as we'll see in Chapter 14, in just the last 3 years, nine early modern *H. sapiens* individuals have had their DNA sequenced (Caramelli et al., 2003; Serre, et al, 2004; Kulikov et al., 2004).

These new finds, all coming from Europe or easternmost Asia, extending from France in the west to Russia in the east, support the view that Neandertal DNA is quite distinct from living people *as well as* from the first modern *H. sapiens* finds in Europe. But questions remain concerning possible contamination of the ancient samples. With PCR, even the tiniest amounts of extraneous DNA (even a single molecule) can be replicated millions of times; so there's always a chance of contamination from handling by excavators or lab investigators. In fact, one researcher has estimated that the few skin cells shed by researchers in the lab contain more DNA than most fossils do! Even with the best attempts at contamination control, inadvertent contamination can never be ruled out.

As a result, *any* ancient human shown to be a very close genetic match to living people is immediately suspicious. The DNA of one early modern *sapiens* (from Italy) was essentially identical to that of living people—thus increasing the need for scrutiny even further. In fact, the eminent molecular biologist Svante Pääbo (who is a director at the Max Planck Institute for

Evolutionary Anthropology) has concluded that "Cro-Magnon [early modern] DNA is so similar to modern human DNA that there is no way to say whether what has been seen is real" (Pääbo, quoted in Abbott, 2003, p. 468).

Similar difficulties have surrounded the analysis of a potentially older early modern human from the Lake Mungo site in Australia (see Chapter 14, p. 363, for further discussion). In addition to possible recent contamination, there are potential problems caused by mutant mtDNA insertions into nuclear DNA (forming "pseudogenes"). Any molecular analysis using mtDNA may actually be getting readings from these altered/inserted genes rather than from "real" mtDNA.

By analyzing nuclear DNA from ancient specimens, researchers can alleviate some of these difficulties, although until recently no nuclear DNA has been sequenced from any hominid older than a few thousand years. Significant technological advances in 2005 allowed much faster analysis of small fragments of ancient DNA; with these powerful new molecular tools teams of researchers obtained considerable nuclear DNA sequence information from an ancient mammoth (Poinar et al., 2005) and from a cave bear (Noonan et al., 2005). But, by far the most startling breakthrough came in late 2006 when two teams of researchers simultaneously announced remarkably successful nuclear DNA sequencing of a 38,000-year-old Neandertal. One group of researchers from California (Noonan et al., 2006) had previously analyzed the mammoth DNA and the other (from the Max Planck Institute) used a completely new method to obtain amazing results (Green et al., 2006). The California researchers sequenced an impressive 65,000 Neandertal base pairs, and the Max Planck team, led by Svante Pääbo, sequenced approximately one million Neandertal base pairs! With further refinements, the Max Planck team is predicting a complete genome sequence for Neandertals within two years; that is, they are confident they can determine all three billion base pairs from a tiny sample from one bone of this 38,000-year-old hominid. Even a few months ago this would have seemed more like science fiction than an actually attainable scientific goal.

These results will be extraordinarily important because they provide a database from which to learn a vast amount about Neandertal biology and behavior. For example, are there particular gene differences in Neandertals as compared to modern humans that help explain alterations in brain organization? And, even more intriguing, will genetic changes be discovered that help account for the development of particular fully human behaviors, such as language? Anthropologists have wondered for more than a century just how different were the Neandertals from modern people and exactly what became of them. The extraordinary new window the DNA evidence provides will go a long way towards answering these questions (for more discussion, see the next chapter).

SOURCES

Abbott, Alison. 2003. "Anthropologists Cast Doubt on Human DNA Evidence." *Nature* (News) 423:468.

Caramelli, David, Carlos Lalueza-Fox, Cristano Vernesi, et al. 2003. "Evidence for a Genetic Discontinuity between Neandertals and 24,000-Year-Old Anatomically Modern Europeans." *Proceedings of the National Academy of Sciences* 100:6593–6597.

Doran, G. H., D. N. Dickel, W. E. Ballinger, Jr., et al. 1986. "Anatomical, Cellular, and Molecular Analysis of 8,000-Yr-Old Human Brain Tissue from the Windover Archaeological Site." *Nature* 323:803–806.

Green, Richard E., Johannes Krause, Susan E. Ptak, et al. 2006. "Analysis of One Million Base Pairs of Neanderthal DNA." *Nature* 444:330–336.

Haak, Wolfgang, Peter Forster, Barbara Bramanti, et al. 2005. "Ancient DNA from the First European Farmers in 7500-Year-Old Neolithic Sites." *Science* 310:1016–1018.

Krings, M., A. Stone, R. W. Schmitz, et al. 1997. "Neandertal DNA Sequences and the Origin of Modern Humans." *Cell* 90:19–30.

Kulikov, Eugene E., Audrey B. Poltaraus, and Irina A. Lebedeva 2004. "DNA Analysis of Sunghir Remains." Poster Presentation, European Paleopathology Association Meetings, Durham, U.K., August 2004.

Noonan, James P., Michael Hofreiter, Doug Smith, et al. 2005. "Genomic Sequencing of Pleistocene Cave Bears." *Science* 309:597–600.

Noonan, James P.M., Graham Coop, Sridhar Kudaravalli, et al. 2006. "Sequencing and Analysis of Neanderthal Genomic DNA." *Science* 314:1113–1118.

O'Rourke, Dennis H., M. Geoffrey Hayes, and Shawn W. Carlyle. 2000. "Ancient DNA Studies in Physical Anthropology." Annual Reviews of Anthropology 29:217–242.

Poinar, Hendrik N., Carsten Schwarz, Ji Qi, et al. 2005. "Metagenomics to Paleogenomics: Large-Scale Sequencing of Mammoth DNA." *Science Express*, December 20, 2005. www.scienceexpress.org/20 December 2005/

Rollo, Franco, Massimo Ubaldi, Lucca Ermini, and Isolina Marota. 2002. "Otzi's Last Meals: DNA Analysis of the Intestinal Content of the Neolithic Glacier Mummy from the Alps." *Proceedings of the National Academy of Sciences* 99:12594–12599.

Schmitz, Ralf W., David Serre, Georges Bonani, et al. 2002. "The Neandertal Type Site Revisited: Interdisciplinary Investigations of Skeletal Remains from the Neander Valley, Germany." *Proceedings of the National Academy of Sciences* 99:13342–13347.

CHAPTER 13

Premodern Humans

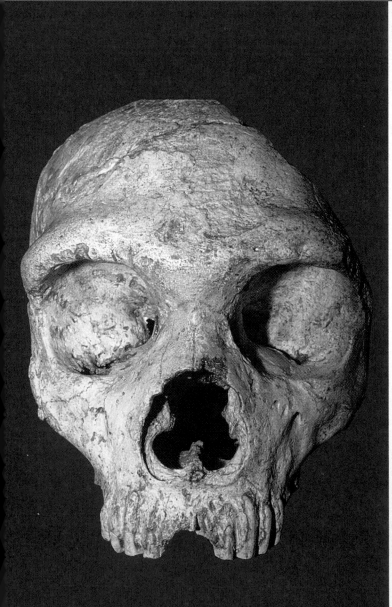

© Robert Franciscus, University of Iowa

KEY QUESTION

Who were the immediate precursors to modern *Homo sapiens,* and how do they compare with modern humans?

Introduction

What do you think of when you hear the term *Neandertal*? Most people think of imbecilic, bent-over brutes. Yet, Neandertals were quite advanced; they had brains at least as large as ours, and they showed many sophisticated cultural capabilities. What's more, they definitely weren't bent over, but fully erect (as hominids had been for millions of years previously). In fact, Neandertals and their immediate predecessors could easily be called human.

That brings us to possibly the most basic of all questions: What does it mean to be human? The meaning of this term is highly varied, encompassing religious, philosophical, and biological considerations. As you know, physical anthropologists primarily concentrate on the biological aspects of the human organism. All living people today are members of one species, sharing a common anatomical pattern and similar behavioral potentials. We call hominids like us "modern *Homo sapiens,*" and in the next chapter we'll discuss the origin of forms that were essentially identical to living people.

When in our evolutionary past can we say that our predecessors were obviously human? Certainly, the further back we go in time, the less hominids look like modern *Homo sapiens*. This is, of course, exactly what we'd expect in an evolutionary sequence.

We saw in Chapter 12 that *Homo erectus* took crucial steps in the human direction, and defined a new *grade* of human evolution. In this chapter, we'll discuss the hominids who continued this journey. Both physically and behaviorally, they're much like modern *Homo sapiens*; though they still show several significant differences. So, while most paleoanthropologists are comfortable referring to these hominids as "human," we need to qualify this recognition a bit in order to set them apart from fully modern people. Thus, in this text, we'll refer to these fascinating immediate predecessors as "premodern humans."

▶ Click!

Go to the following media for interactives and exercises on topics covered in this chapter:

- Hominid Fossils CD-ROM: An Interactive Atlas
- Online Virtual Laboratories for Physical Anthropology, Fourth Edition

When, Where, and What

Most of the hominids discussed in this chapter lived during the **Middle Pleistocene**, a period beginning 780,000 years ago (ya) and ending 125,000 ya. In addition, some of the later premodern humans, especially the Neandertals, lived well into the **Late Pleistocene** (125,000–10,000 ya).

THE PLEISTOCENE

The Pleistocene has been called the Ice Age because, as had occurred before in geological history, it was marked by periodic advances and retreats of massive continental glaciations. During glacial periods, temperatures dropped dramatically; ice accumulated as a result of more snow falling each year than melting. The spaces of time between these cold glacial periods are commonly known as **interglacial** periods. Considerably warmer temperatures during interglacial periods caused ice built up during glacial periods to melt, resulting in glaciers retreating back toward the earth's polar regions. The Pleistocene was characterized by numerous advances and retreats of ice, with at least 15 major and 50 minor glacial advances documented in Europe alone (Tattersall et al., 1988).

It's important to remember that these **glaciations**, which enveloped huge swaths of Europe, Asia, and North America as well as Antarctica, were mostly confined to northern

Middle Pleistocene The portion of the Pleistocene epoch beginning 780,000 ya and ending 125,000 ya.

Late Pleistocene The portion of the Pleistocene epoch beginning 125,000 ya and ending approximately 10,000 ya.

interglacials Climatic intervals when continental ice sheets are retreating, eventually becoming much reduced in size. Interglacials in northern latitudes are associated with warmer temperatures, while in southern latitudes the climate becomes wetter.

glaciations Climatic intervals when continental ice sheets cover much of the northern continents. Glaciations are associated with colder temperatures in northern latitudes and more arid conditions in southern latitudes, most notably in Africa.

latitudes. As a result, hominids—at the time, all still restricted to the Old World—were severely affected as the climate, flora, and animal life shifted during these Pleistocene oscillations. For hominids living during this time, the most dramatic of these effects were in Europe and northern Asia—less so in southern Asia and in Africa.

While as we've said, glaciers were primarily restricted to the northern latitudes, the climate also fluctuated in the south. In Africa, the main effects were related to changing rainfall patterns. During glacial periods, the climate in Africa became more arid, while during interglacials, rainfall increased. The changing availability of food resources certainly affected hominids in Africa; but probably even more importantly, migration routes also swung back and forth. For example, during glacial periods (Fig. 13-1), the Sahara Desert expanded, blocking migration in and out of sub-Saharan Africa (Lahr and Foley, 1998).

In Eurasia, glacial advances also greatly affected migration routes. As the ice sheets expanded, sea levels dropped, more northern regions became uninhabitable, and some key passages between areas became blocked by glaciers. For example, during glacial peaks, much of western Europe would have been cut off from the rest of Eurasia (Fig. 13-2).

FIGURE 13-1
Changing Pleistocene environments in Africa.

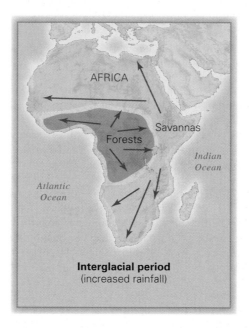
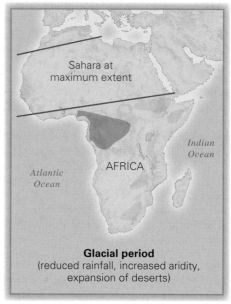

FIGURE 13-2
Changing Pleistocene environments in Eurasia. Green areas show regions of likely hominid occupation. Blue areas are major glaciers. Arrows indicate likely migration routes.

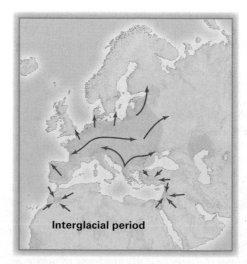

During the warmer—and, in the south, wetter—interglacials, the ice sheets shrank, sea levels rose, and certain migration routes reopened (for example, from central into western Europe). Clearly, to understand Middle Pleistocene hominids, it's crucial to view them within their shifting Pleistocene world.

DISPERSAL OF MIDDLE PLEISTOCENE HOMINIDS

Like their *Homo erectus* predecessors, later hominids were widely distributed in the Old World, with discoveries coming from three continents—Africa, Asia, and Europe. For the first time it appears that Europe became more permanently and densely occupied, as Middle Pleistocene hominids have been discovered widely from England, France, Spain, Germany, Italy, Hungary, and Greece. Africa, as well, probably continued as a central area of hominid occupation, and finds have come from North, East, and South Africa. Finally, Asia has yielded several important finds, most especially from China (see Fig. 13-6 on pp. 328–329). We should point out, though, that these Middle Pleistocene premodern humans didn't vastly extend the geographical range of *Homo erectus*, but largely replaced the earlier hominids in previously exploited habitats. One exception appears to be the more successful occupation of Europe, a region where earlier hominids have only sporadically been found.

MIDDLE PLEISTOCENE HOMINIDS: TERMINOLOGY

The premodern humans of the Middle Pleistocene (that is, after 780,000 ya) generally suc ceeded *H. erectus*. Still, in some areas—especially in Asia—there apparently was a long period of coexistence, lasting 300,000 years or longer; you'll recall the very late dates for the Javanese Ngandong *H. erectus* (see p. 304).

The earliest premodern humans exhibit several *H. erectus* characteristics: the face is large, the brows are projected, the forehead is low, and in some cases the cranial vault is still thick. Even so, some of their other features show that they were more derived toward the modern condition than were their *Homo erectus* predecessors. Compared to *Homo erectus*, these premodern humans possessed an increased brain size, a more rounded braincase (that is, maximum breadth is higher up on the sides), a more vertical nose, and a less-angled back of the skull (occipital). We should note that the maximum span of time encompassed by Middle Pleistocene premodern humans is at least 500,000 years, so it's no surprise that over time, we can observe certain trends. Later Middle Pleistocene hominids, for example, show even more brain expansion and an even less-angled occipital than do earlier forms.

Accordingly, we know that premodern humans were a diverse group dispersed over three continents. Deciding how to classify them has been in dispute for decades, and anthropologists still have disagreements. However, a growing consensus has recently emerged. Beginning perhaps as early as 850,000 ya and extending to about 200,000 ya, the fossils from Africa and Europe are placed within *Homo heidelbergensis*, named after a fossil found in Germany in 1907. What's more, some Asian specimens possibly represent a regional variant of *H. heidelbergensis*.

Until recently, many researchers regarded these fossils as early, but more primitive, members of *Homo sapiens*. In recognition of this somewhat transitional status, the fossils were called "archaic *Homo sapiens*," with all later humans also belonging to the species *Homo sapiens*. However, most paleoanthropologists now find this terminology unsatisfactory. For example, Phillip Rightmire concludes that "simply lumping diverse ancient groups with living populations obscures their differences" (1998, p. 226). In our own discussion, we recognize *Homo heidelbergensis* as a transitional species between *Homo erectus* and later hominids (that is, primarily, *Homo sapiens*). Keep in mind, however, that this species was probably an ancestor of both modern humans and Neandertals. It's debatable whether *Homo heidelbergensis* actually represents a fully separate species in the *biological* sense, that is, following the biological species concept (see p. 102). Still, it's useful to give this group of premodern humans a separate name to make this important stage of human evolution more easily identifiable. (We'll return to this issue later in the chapter, when we discuss the theoretical implications in more detail.)

FIGURE 13-3

The Kabwe (Broken Hill) *Homo heidelbergensis* skull from Zambia. Note the very heavy supraorbital torus.

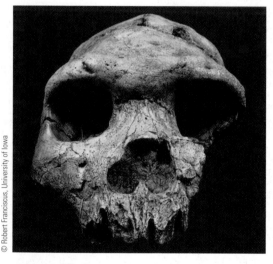

FIGURE 13-4

Bodo cranium, the earliest evidence of *Homo heidelbergensis* in Africa.

Premodern Humans of the Middle Pleistocene

AFRICA

In Africa, premodern fossils have been found at several sites (Figs. 13-3 and 13-4). One of the best known is Kabwe (Broken Hill). At this site in Zambia, fieldworkers discovered a complete cranium, together with other cranial and postcranial elements belonging to several individuals. In this and other African premodern specimens, we can see a mixture of older and more recent traits. The skull's massive supraorbital torus (one of the largest of any hominid), low vault, and prominent occipital torus recall those of *H. erectus*. On the other hand, the occipital region is less angulated, the cranial vault bones are thinner, and the cranial base is essentially modern. Dating estimates of Kabwe and most of the other premodern fossils from Africa have ranged throughout the Middle and Late Pleistocene, but recent estimates have given dates for most of the sites in the range of 600,000–125,000 ya.

A total of eight other crania from South and East Africa also show a combination of retained ancestral with more derived (modern) characteristics, and they're all mentioned in the literature as being similar to Kabwe. The most important of these African finds come from the sites of Florisbad and Elandsfontein in South Africa, Laetoli in Tanzania, and Bodo in Ethiopia (see Fig. 13-6 pp. 328–329).

Bodo is one of the most significant of these other African fossils. A nearly complete cranium, Bodo has been dated to relatively early in the Middle Pleistocene (estimated at 600,000 ya), making it one of the oldest specimens of *Homo heidelbergensis* from the African continent. The Bodo cranium is particularly interesting because it shows a distinctive pattern of cut marks, similar to modifications seen in butchered animal bones. Researchers have thus hypothesized that the Bodo individual was defleshed by other hominids, but for what purpose is not clear. The defleshing may have been related to cannibalism, though it also may have been for some other purpose, such as ritual. In any case, this is the earliest evidence of deliberate bone processing of hominids *by* hominids (White, 1986).

The general similarities in all these African premodern fossils indicate a close relationship between them, almost certainly representing a single species (most commonly referred to as *H. heidelbergensis*). These African premodern humans also are quite similar to those found in Europe.

EUROPE

More fossil hominids of Middle Pleistocene age have been found in Europe than in any other region. Maybe it's because more archaeologists have been searching longer in Europe than elsewhere. In any case, during the Middle Pleistocene, Europe was more widely and consistently occupied than it was earlier in human evolution.

AT A GLANCE	Key Middle Pleistocene Premodern Human *(H. heidelbergensis)* Fossils from Africa	
Site	**Dates (ya)**	**Human Remains** *Homo heidelbergensis*
Bodo (Ethiopia)	Middle Pleistocene (600,000)	Incomplete skull, part of braincase
Kabwe (Broken Hill, Zambia)	Late Middle Pleistocene; (130,000 or older)	Nearly complete cranium, cranial fragments of second individual, miscellaneous postcranial bones

The time range of European premodern humans extends the full length of the Middle Pleistocene and beyond. At the earlier end, the Gran Dolina finds from northern Spain (discussed in Chapter 12; see p. 312) are definitely not *Homo erectus*. The Gran Dolina remains may, as proposed by Spanish researchers, be members of a new hominid species. However, Rightmire (1998) has suggested that the Gran Dolina hominids may simply represent the earliest well-dated occurrence of *H. heidelbergensis*, possibly dating as early as 850,000 ya.

More recent and more completely studied *H. heidelbergensis* fossils have been found throughout much of Europe. Examples of these finds come from Steinheim (Germany), Petralona (Greece), Swanscombe (England), Arago (France), and another cave at Atapuerca (Spain). Like their African counterparts, these European premoderns have retained certain *H. erectus* traits, but they're mixed with more derived ones—for example, increased cranial capacity, more rounded occiput, parietal expansion, and reduced tooth size (Fig. 13-5).

The hominids from Atapuerca are especially interesting. These finds come from another cave in the same area as the Gran Dolina discoveries. Dated to between 600,000 and 530,000 (Bischoff et al., 2006), a total of at least 28 individuals have been recovered from a site called Sima de los Huesos, literally meaning "pit of bones." In fact, with more than 4,000 fossil fragments recovered, Sima de los Huesos contains more than 80 percent of all Middle Pleistocene hominid remains in the world (Bermudez de Castro et al., 2004). Excavations continue at this remarkable site, where bones have somehow accumulated within a deep chamber inside a cave. From initial descriptions, paleoanthropologists interpret the hominid morphology as showing several indications of an early Neandertal-like pattern, with arching browridges, projecting midface, and other features (Rightmire, 1998).

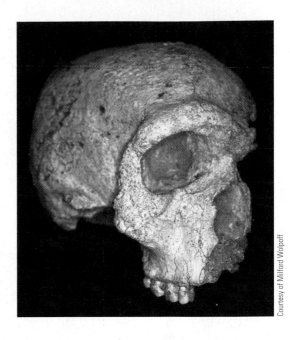

Courtesy of Milford Wolpoff

FIGURE 13-5

Steinheim cranium, a representative of *H. heidelbergensis* from Germany.

AT A GLANCE	Key Middle Pleistocene Premodern Human *(H. heidelbergensis)* Fossils from Europe	
Site	**Dates (ya)**	**Human Remains**
Arago (Tautavel, France)	400,000–300,000; date uncertain	Face; parietal perhaps from same person; many cranial fragments; up to 23 individuals represented
Atapuerca (Sima de los Huesos, northern Spain)	600,000–530,000	Minimum of 28 individuals, including some nearly complete crania
Steinheim (Germany)	300,000–250,000; date uncertain	Nearly complete skull, lacking mandible
Swanscombe (England)	300,000–250,000; date uncertain	Occipital and parietals

ASIA

Like their contemporaries in Europe and Africa, Asian premodern specimens discovered in China also display both earlier and later characteristics. Chinese paleoanthropologists suggest that the more ancestral traits, such as a sagittal ridge (see p. 301) and flattened nasal bones, are shared with *H. erectus* fossils from Zhoukoudian. They also point out that some of these features can be found in modern *H. sapiens* in China today, indicating substantial genetic continuity. That is, some Chinese researchers have argued that anatomically, modern Chinese didn't evolve from *H. sapiens* in either Europe or Africa; instead, they evolved specifically in China from a separate *H. erectus* lineage. Whether such regional evolution occurred or whether anatomically modern migrants from Africa displaced local populations is the subject of a major ongoing debate in paleoanthropology. This important controversy will be the central focus of the next chapter.

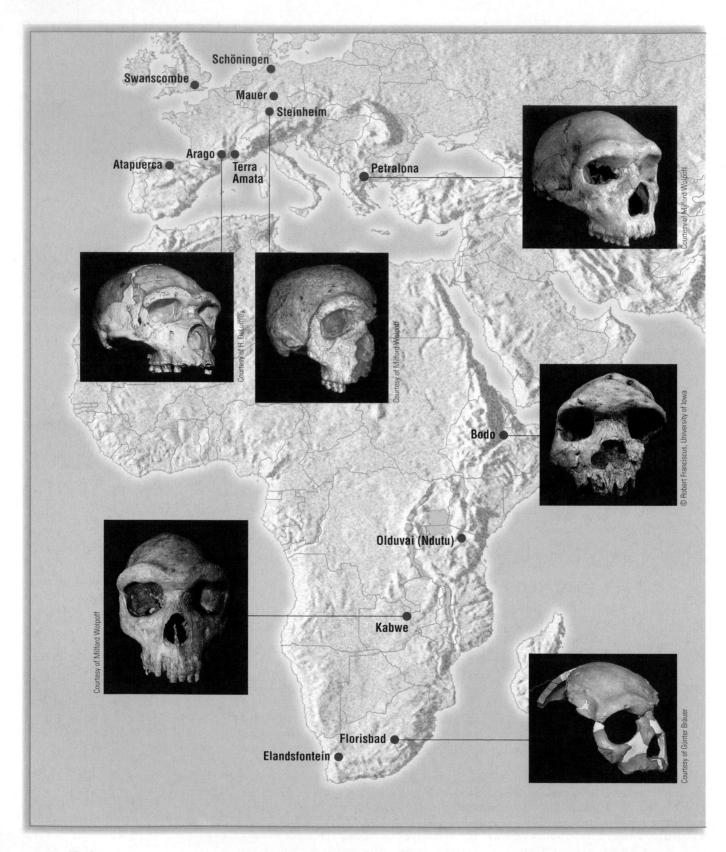

FIGURE 13-6

Fossil discoveries and archaeological localities of Middle Pleistocene premodern hominids.

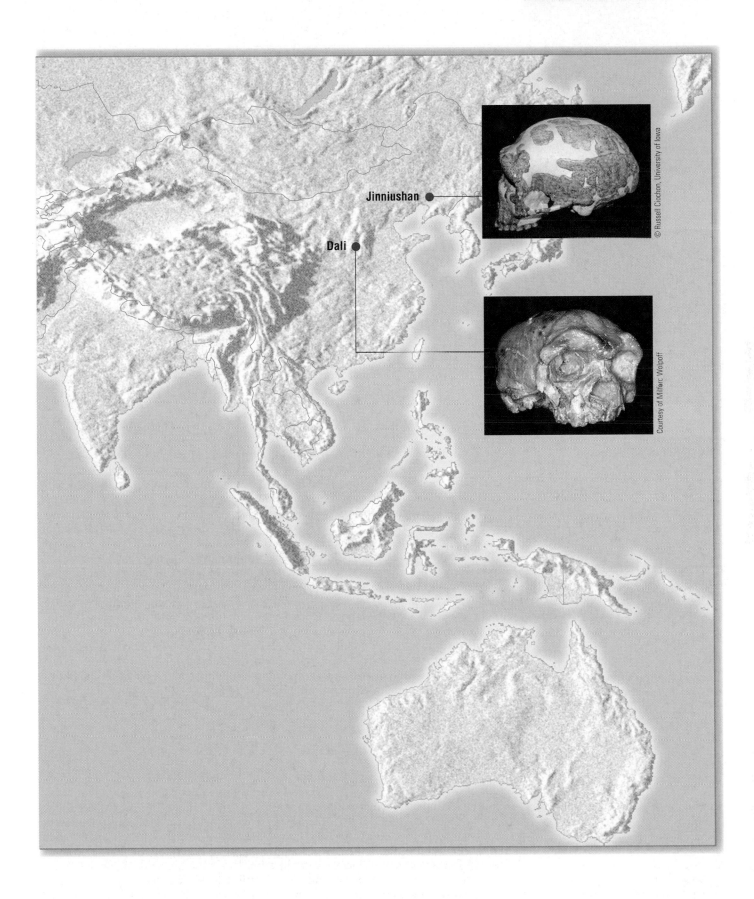

AT A GLANCE	Key Middle Pleistocene Premodern Human *(H. heidelbergensis)* Fossils from Asia	
Site	**Dates (ya)**	**Human Remains**
Dali (China)	Late Middle Pleistocene (230,000–180,000)	Nearly complete skull
Jinniushan (China)	Late Middle Pleistocene (200,000)	Partial skeleton, including a cranium

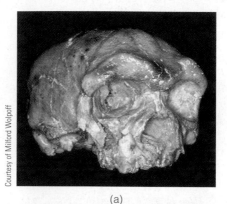

Courtesy of Milford Wolpoff

(a)

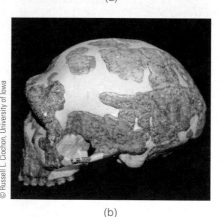

© Russell L. Ciochon, University of Iowa

(b)

FIGURE 13-7

(a) Dali skull and (b) Jinniushan skull, both from China. These two crania are considered by some to be Asian representatives of *Homo heidelbergensis.*

Dali, the most complete skull of the latter Middle or beginning of the Late Pleistocene fossils in China, displays *H. erectus* and *H. sapiens* traits, with a cranial capacity of 1,120 cm³ (Fig. 13-7). Like Dali, several other Chinese specimens combine both earlier and later traits. In addition, a partial skeleton from Jinniushan, in northeast China, has been given a provisional date of 200,000 ya (Tiemel et al., 1994). The cranial capacity is fairly large (approximately 1,260 cm³), and the walls of the braincase are thin. These are both modern features, and they're somewhat unexpected in an individual this ancient—if the dating estimate is indeed correct. Just how to classify these Chinese Middle Pleistocene hominids has been a subject of debate and controversy. Recently, though, a leading paleoanthropologist has concluded that they're regional variants of *Homo heidelbergensis* (Rightmire, 2004).

A Review of Middle Pleistocene Evolution

Premodern human fossils from Africa and Europe resemble each other more than they do the hominids from Asia. The mix of some ancestral characteristics—retained from *Homo erectus* ancestors—with more derived features gives the African and European fossils a distinctive look; thus, Middle Pleistocene hominids from these two continents are usually referred to as *H. heidelbergensis.*

The situation in Asia isn't so tidy. To some researchers, the remains, especially those from Jinniushan, seem more modern than do contemporary fossils from either Europe or Africa. This observation explains why Chinese paleoanthropologists and some American colleagues conclude that the Jinniushan remains are early members of *H. sapiens.* Other researchers (e.g., Rightmire, 1998, 2004) suggest that they represent a regional branch of *H. heidelbergensis.*

The Pleistocene world forced many small populations into geographical isolation. Most of these regional populations no doubt died out. Some, however, did evolve, and their descendants are likely a major part of the later hominid fossil record. In Africa, *H. heidelbergensis* is hypothesized to have evolved into modern *H. sapiens.* In Europe, *H. heidelbergensis* evolved into Neandertals. Meanwhile, the Chinese premodern populations may all have met with extinction. Right now, though, there's no consensus on the status or the likely fate of these enigmatic Asian Middle Pleistocene hominids (Fig. 13-8).

Middle Pleistocene Culture

The Acheulian technology of *H. erectus* carried over into the Middle Pleistocene with relatively little change until near the end of the period, when it became slightly more sophisticated. Bone, a very useful tool material, was apparently practically unused during this time. Stone flake tools similar to those of the earlier era persisted, possibly in greater variety. Some of the later premodern humans in Africa and Europe invented a method—the Levallois technique (Fig. 13-9)—for controlling flake size and shape. Requiring several coordinated steps, this was no easy feat, and it suggests increased cognitive abilities in later premodern populations.

Interpreting the distribution of artifacts during the later Middle Pleistocene has generated considerable discussion among archaeologists. As we noted in Chapter 12, a general geograph-

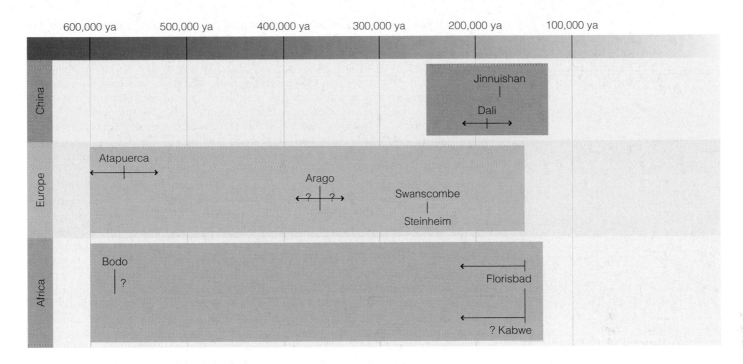

	600,000 ya	500,000 ya	400,000 ya	300,000 ya	200,000 ya	100,000 ya

China: Jinnuishan, Dali

Europe: Atapuerca, Arago (? ?), Swanscombe, Steinheim

Africa: Bodo ?, Florisbad, ? Kabwe

FIGURE 13-8
Time line of Middle Pleistocene hominids. Note that most dates are approximations. Question marks indicate those estimates that are most tentative.

ical distribution characterizes the Early Pleistocene, with bifaces (mostly hand axes) found quite often at sites in Africa, only rarely at sites in most of Asia, and not at all among the rich assemblage at Zhoukoudian. Also, where hand axes proliferate, the stone tool industry is referred to as Acheulian. At localities without hand axes, various other terms are used—for example, *chopper/chopping tool*, which is a misnomer since most of the tools are actually flakes.

Acheulian assemblages have been found at many African sites as well as numerous European ones—for example, Swanscombe in England and Arago in France. Even though there are broad geographical patterns in the distribution of what we call Acheulian, this shouldn't blind us to the considerable intraregional diversity in stone tool industries. Clearly, a variety of European sites do show a typical Acheulian complex, rich in bifacial hand axes and cleavers. However, at other contemporaneous sites in Germany and Hungary, fieldworkers found a variety of small retouched flake tools and flaked pebbles of various sizes, but no hand axes. So it seems that different stone tool industries coexisted in some areas for long periods, and various explanations (Villa, 1983) have been offered to account for this apparent diversity. Some say that different groups of hominids may have produced the tool industries; others suggest that the same group may have produced them when performing varied activities at different sites. The type of stone tool manufactured was also affected by the amount and quality of workable rock in the area (also see "A Closer Look," p. 315). In an area without large cores, it's harder to produce hand axes since the material to make them has to be brought in from another area.

Premodern human populations continued to live both in caves and in open-air sites, but they may have increased their use of caves. Did these hominids control fire? Klein (1999), in interpreting archaeological evidence from France, Germany, and Hungary, suggests that

FIGURE 13-9
The Levallois technique.

Nodule

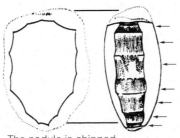

The nodule is chipped on the perimeter.

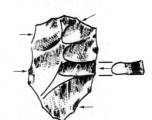

Flakes are radially removed from top surface.

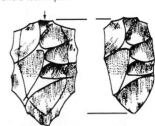

A final blow at one end removes a large flake.

they did. What's more, Chinese archaeologists insist that many Middle Pleistocene sites in China contain evidence of human-controlled fire. Still, not everyone is convinced.

We know that Middle Pleistocene hominids built temporary structures, because researchers have found concentrations of bones, stones, and artifacts at several sites. We also have evidence that they exploited many different food sources—fruits, vegetables, fish, seeds, nuts, and bird eggs, each in its own season. Importantly, they also exploited marine life, a new innovation in human evolution. The most detailed reconstruction of Middle Pleistocene life in Europe comes from Terra Amata, a site in what is now the city of Nice, in southern France (de Lumley and de Lumley, 1973; Villa, 1983). This site provides fascinating evidence relating to short-term, seasonal visits by hominid groups, who built flimsy shelters, gathered plants, ate food from the ocean, and possibly hunted medium- to large-sized mammals.

The hunting capabilities of premodern humans, as for earlier hominids, are still greatly disputed. So far, the evidence doesn't clearly establish widely practiced advanced abilities. A recent and exceptional find, however, is once again challenging some assumptions about hunting capabilities of premodern humans in Europe. In 1995, from the site of Schöningen in Germany, researchers discovered three remarkably well-preserved wooden spears (Thieme, 1997). As we've noted before, fragile organic remains, such as wood, are rarely preserved more than a few hundred years; yet these beautifully crafted implements are provisionally dated to 400,000–380,000 ya. Beyond this surprisingly ancient date, the spears are intriguing for several other reasons. First, they're all large (about 6 feet long), finely made of hard spruce wood, and expertly balanced. Each spear would have required considerable planning, time, and skill to manufacture. Additionally, the weapons were most likely used as throwing spears, presumably to hunt large animals. Also interesting in this context, the bones of numerous horses were recovered at Schöningen. Archaeologist Hartmut Thieme has thus concluded that "the spears strongly suggest that systematic hunting, involving foresight, planning and the use of appropriate technology, was part of the behavioural repertoire of pre-modern hominids" (1997, p. 807). These extraordinary spears from Schöningen make a strong case that at least some Middle Pleistocene populations had advanced hunting skills.

As documented by the fossil remains as well as artifactual evidence from archaeological sites, the long period of transitional hominids in Europe continued well into the Late Pleistocene (after 125,000 ya), though, with the appearance and expansion of the Neandertals, the evolution of premodern humans took a unique turn.

Neandertals: Premodern Humans of the Late Pleistocene

Since their discovery more than a century ago, the Neandertals have haunted the minds and foiled the best-laid theories of paleoanthropologists. They fit into the general scheme of human evolution, and yet they're misfits. Classified variously as either *H. sapiens neanderthalensis* or *Homo neanderthalensis*, they are like us and yet different. It's not easy to put them in their place. Many anthropologists classify Neandertals as *H. sapiens*, but as a subspecies, *Homo sapiens neanderthalensis**, with modern *H. sapiens* designated as *Homo sapiens sapiens*. However, not all experts agree with this interpretation. The wide use of *Homo heidelbergensis* in reference to the ancestor of both Neandertals and modern *Homo sapiens* has led to the increasingly common placement of Neandertals into a separate species: *Homo neanderthalensis*.

Neandertal fossil remains have been found at dates approaching 130,000 ya; but in the following discussion of Neandertals, we'll focus on those populations that lived especially during the last major glaciation, which began about 75,000 ya and ended about 10,000 ya (Fig. 13-10). We should also note that the evolutionary roots of Neandertals apparently

Thal, meaning "valley," is the old spelling; but due to rules of taxonomic naming, this spelling is retained in the formal species designation *Homo neanderthalensis* (although the *h* was *never* pronounced). The modern spelling, *tal*, is now used this way in Germany; we follow contemporary usage in the text with the spelling of the colloquial *Neandertal*.

reach quite far back in western Europe, as evidenced by the 500,000+ year-old remains from Sima de los Huesos, Atapuerca, in northern Spain. The majority of fossils have been found in Europe, where they've been most studied. Our description of Neandertals is based primarily on those specimens, usually called *classic* Neandertals, from western Europe. Not all Neandertals—including others from eastern Europe and western Asia and those from the interglacial period just before the last glacial one—exactly fit our description of the classic morphology. They tend to be less robust, possibly because the climate in which they lived was not as cold as in western Europe during the last glaciation.

One striking feature of Neandertals is brain size, which in these hominids actually was larger than that of *H. sapiens* today. The average for contemporary *H. sapiens* is between

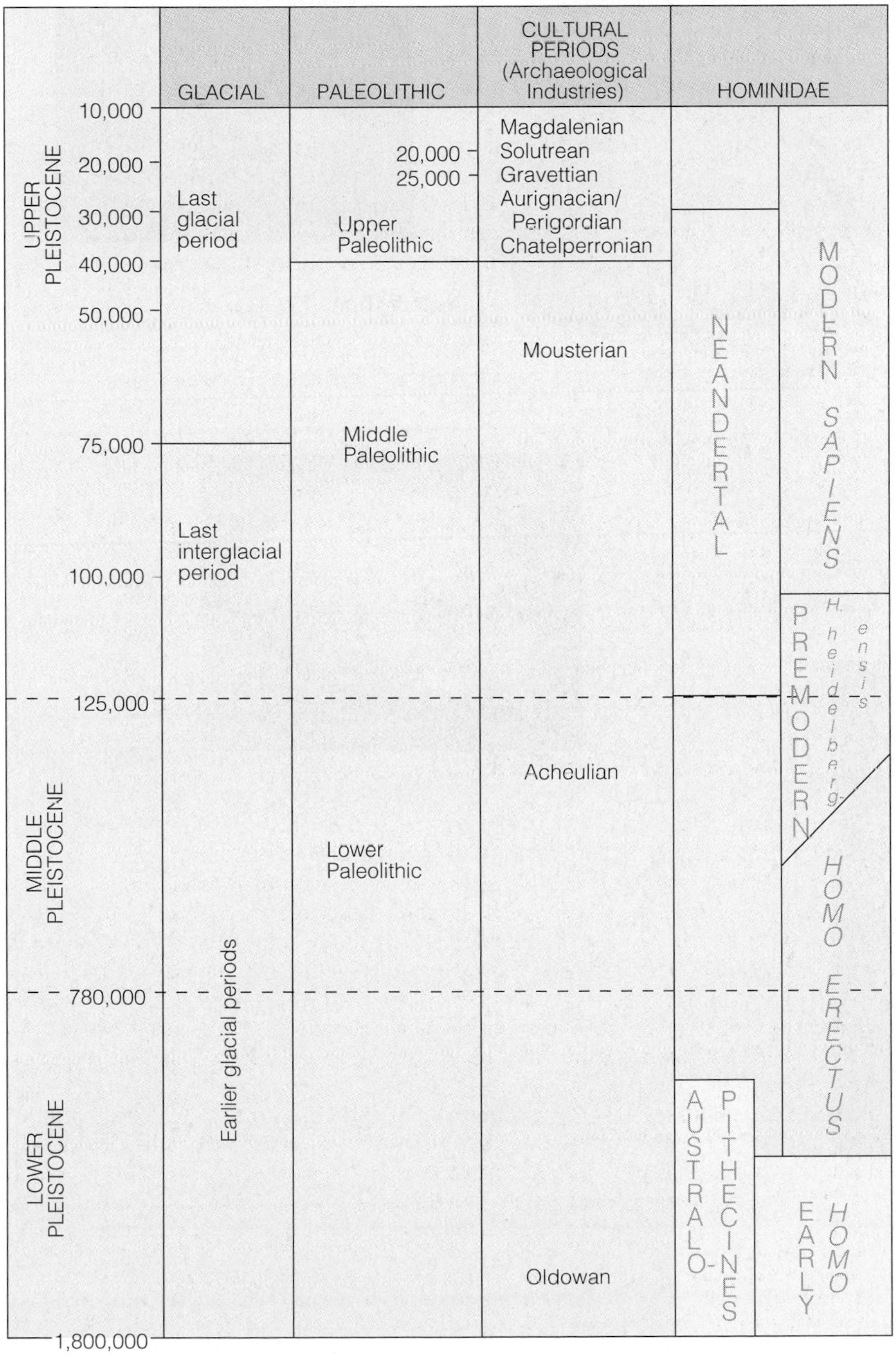

	GLACIAL	PALEOLITHIC	CULTURAL PERIODS (Archaeological Industries)	HOMINIDAE	
UPPER PLEISTOCENE 10,000 20,000 30,000 40,000 50,000 75,000 100,000	Last glacial period / Last interglacial period	Upper Paleolithic (20,000 / 25,000) / Middle Paleolithic	Magdalenian Solutrean Gravettian Aurignacian/ Perigordian Chatelperronian / Mousterian	NEANDERTAL	MODERN SAPIENS
125,000				PREMODERN	*H. heidelbergensis*
MIDDLE PLEISTOCENE 780,000	Earlier glacial periods	Lower Paleolithic	Acheulian		*HOMO ERECTUS*
LOWER PLEISTOCENE 1,800,000			Oldowan	AUSTRALO-PITHECINES	EARLY *HOMO*

FIGURE **13-10**
Correlation of Pleistocene subdivisions with archaeological industries and hominids. Note that the geological divisions are separate and different from the archaeological stages (e.g., Upper Pleistocene is *not* synonymous with Upper Paleolithic).

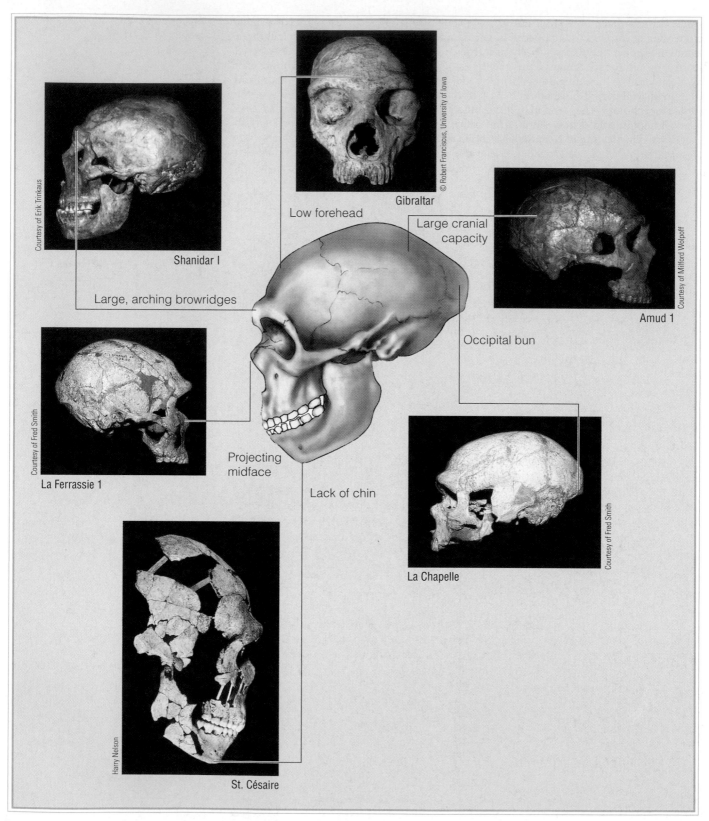

Courtesy of Erik Trinkaus

Shanidar I

© Robert Franciscus, University of Iowa

Gibraltar

Low forehead

Large cranial capacity

Courtesy of Milford Wolpoff

Amud 1

Large, arching browridges

Courtesy of Fred Smith

La Ferrassie 1

Occipital bun

Projecting midface

Lack of chin

Courtesy of Fred Smith

La Chapelle

Harry Nelson

St. Césaire

FIGURE 13-11

Morphology and variation in Neandertal crania.

1,300 and 1,400 cm³, while for Neandertals it was 1,520 cm³. The larger size may be associated with the metabolic efficiency of a larger brain in cold weather. The Inuit (Eskimo), also living in very cold areas, have a larger average brain size than most other modern human populations do. We should also point out that the larger brain size in both premodern and contemporary human populations adapted to *cold* climates is partially correlated with larger body size, which has also evolved among these groups (see Chapter 16).

The classic Neandertal cranium is large, long, low, and bulging at the sides. Viewed from the side, the occipital bone is somewhat bun shaped, but the marked occipital angle typical of many *H. erectus* crania is absent. The forehead rises more vertically than that of *H. erectus*, and the browridges arch over the orbits instead of forming a straight bar (Fig. 13-11).

Compared with anatomically modern humans, the Neandertal face stands out. It projects almost as if it were pulled forward. This feature can be seen by comparing the distance of the nose and teeth from the eye orbits with that seen in modern *H. sapiens*. Postcranially, Neandertals were very robust, barrel-chested, and powerfully muscled. This robust skeletal structure, in fact, dominates hominid evolution from *H. erectus* through all premodern forms. Still, the Neandertals appear particularly robust, with shorter limbs than seen in most modern *H. sapiens* populations. Both the facial anatomy and the robust postcranial structure of Neandertals have been interpreted by Erik Trinkaus, of Washington University in St. Louis, as adaptations to rigorous living in a cold climate.

For about 100,000 years, Neandertals lived in Europe and western Asia (see Fig. 13-12 on p. 336), and their coming and going have raised more questions and controversies than for any other hominid group. As we've noted, Neandertal forebears were transitional forms dating to the later Middle Pleistocene. However, it's not until the Late Pleistocene that Neandertals become fully recognizable.

WESTERN EUROPE

One of the most important Neandertal discoveries was made in 1908 at La Chapelle-aux-Saints in southwestern France. A nearly complete skeleton was found buried in a shallow grave in a **flexed** position. Several fragments of nonhuman long bones had been placed over the head, and over them, a bison leg. Around the body were flint tools and broken animal bones.

The skeleton was turned over for study to a well-known French paleontologist, Marcellin Boule, who depicted the La Chapelle Neandertal as a brutish, bent-kneed, not fully erect biped. Because of this exaggerated interpretation, some scholars, and certainly the general public, concluded that all Neandertals were highly primitive creatures.

Why did Boule draw these conclusions from the La Chapelle skeleton? Today, we think he misjudged the Neandertal posture because this adult male skeleton had osteoarthritis of the spine. Also, and probably more important, Boule and his contemporaries found it difficult to fully accept as a human ancestor an individual who appeared in any way to depart from the modern pattern.

The skull of this male, who was possibly at least 40 years of age when he died, is very large, with a cranial capacity of 1,620 cm³. Typical of western European classic forms, the vault is low and long; the supraorbital ridges are immense, with the typical Neandertal arched shape; the forehead is low and retreating; and the face is long and projecting. The back of the skull is protuberant and bun shaped (Figs. 13-11 and 13-13).

The La Chapelle skeleton isn't a typical Neandertal, but an unusually robust male who "evidently represents an extreme in the Neandertal range of variation" (Brace et al., 1979, p. 117). Unfortunately, this skeleton, which Boule claimed didn't even walk completely erect, was widely accepted as "Mr. Neandertal." But not all Neandertal individuals express the suite of classic Neandertal traits to the degree seen in this one (see Fig. 13-11).

Another Neandertal site excavated recently in southern France has revealed further fascinating details about Neandertal behavior. From the 100,000- to 120,000-year-old Moula-Guercy Cave site, Alban Defleur, Tim White, and colleagues have analyzed 78 broken skeletal fragments from probably 6 individuals (Defleur et al., 1999). The intriguing aspect of these remains concerns *how* they were broken. Detailed analysis of cut marks, pits, scars, and other features clearly suggests that these individuals were *processed*—that is, they "were defleshed and disarticulated. After this, the marrow cavity was exposed by a hammer-on-anvil

flexed The position of the body in a bent orientation, with arms and legs drawn up to the chest.

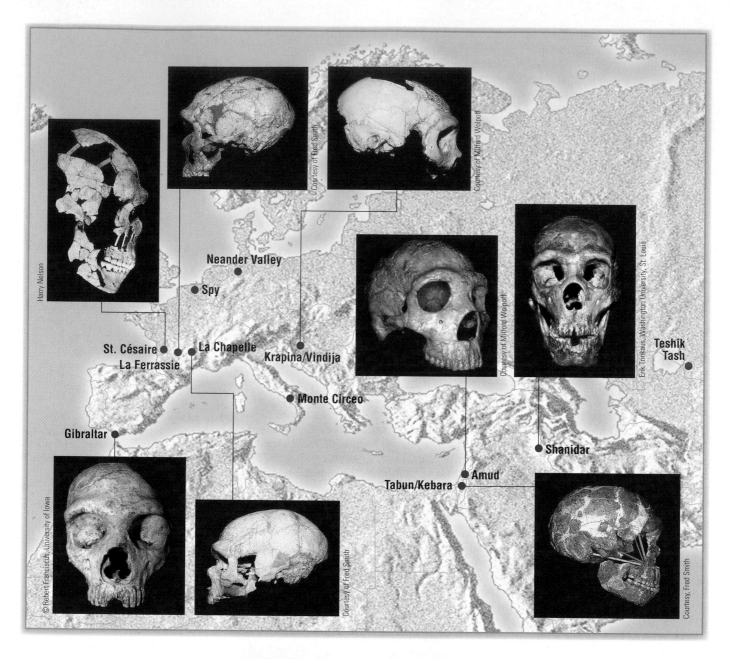

FIGURE **13-12**
Fossil discoveries of Neandertals.

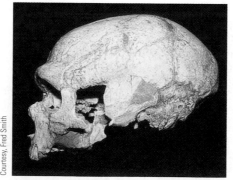

Courtesy, Fred Smith

FIGURE **13-13**
La Chapelle-aux-Saints. Note the occipital bun, projecting face, and low vault.

Upper Paleolithic A cultural period usually associated with modern humans, but also found with some Neandertals, and distinguished by technological innovation in various stone tool industries. Best known from western Europe, similar industries are also known from central and eastern Europe and Africa.

technique" (Defleur et al., 1999, p. 131). What's more, the nonhuman bones at this site, especially the deer remains, were processed in an identical way. In other words, the Moula-Guercy Neandertals provide the best-documented evidence thus far of Neandertal *cannibalism*.

Some of the most recent of the western European Neandertals come from St. Césaire in southwestern France and are dated at about 35,000 ya (Fig. 13-14). The bones were recovered from a bed including discarded chipped blades, hand axes, and other stone tools of an **Upper Paleolithic** tool industry associated with Neandertals. There's another late site in central Europe, where radiocarbon dating has indicated that the most recent Neandertal remains at Vindija, in Croatia (discussed shortly), are about 32,000 to 33,000 years old (Smith et al., 1999).

The St. Césaire and Vindija sites are important for several reasons. Anatomically modern humans were living in central and western Europe by about 35,000 ya or a bit earlier. So, it's possible that Neandertals and modern *H. sapiens* were living quite close to each other for several thousand years (Fig. 13-15). How did these two groups interact? Evidence from a number of French sites indicates that Neandertals may have borrowed technological methods and tools (such as blades) from the anatomically modern populations and thereby modified their own tools, creating a new industry, the **Chatelperronian**.

CENTRAL EUROPE

There are quite a few other European classic Neandertals, including significant finds in central Europe (see Fig. 13-12). At Krapina, Croatia, researchers have recovered an abundance of bones—1,000 fragments representing up to 70 individuals—and 1,000 stone tools or flakes (Trinkaus and Shipman, 1992). Krapina is an old site, possibly the earliest showing the full classic Neandertal morphology, dating back to the beginning of the Late Pleistocene (estimated at 130,000–110,000 ya). And, despite the relatively early date, the characteristic Neandertal features of the Krapina specimens, although less robust, are similar to the western European finds (Fig. 13-16). Krapina is also important as an intentional burial site—one of the oldest on record.

About 30 miles from Krapina, Neandertal fossils have also been discovered at Vindija. The site is an excellent source of faunal, cultural, and hominid materials stratified in *sequence* throughout much of the Late Pleistocene. Neandertal fossils consisting of some 35 specimens are dated between about 42,000 and 32,000 ya. (The latter date would be the best verified of the more recent Neandertal discoveries; Higham et al., 2006.) While the overall anatomical pattern is definitely Neandertal, some features of the Vindija individuals, such as smaller browridges and slight chin development, approach the morphology seen in early modern south-central European *H. sapiens*. These similarities have led some researchers to suggest a possible evolutionary link between the late Vindija Neandertals and modern *H. sapiens*.

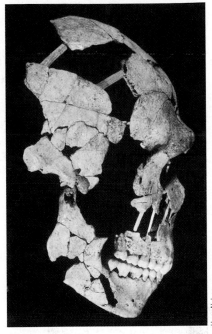

FIGURE 13-14
St. Césaire, among the "last" Neandertals.

Chatelperronian Pertaining to an Upper Paleolithic industry found in France and Spain, containing blade tools and associated with Neandertals.

FIGURE **13-15**
Time line for Neandertal fossil discoveries.

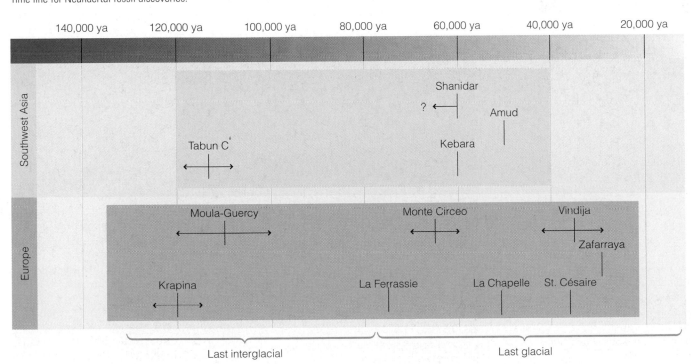

FIGURE 13-16
Krapina C. (a) Lateral view showing
characteristic Neandertal traits. (b) Three-
quarters view.

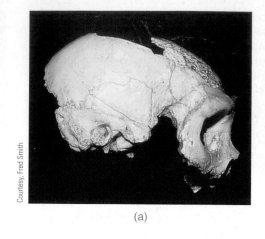

Courtesy, Fred Smith

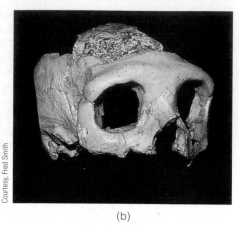

Courtesy, Fred Smith

(a)   (b)

WESTERN ASIA

Israel   In addition to European Neandertals, many important discoveries have been made in southwest Asia. Several specimens from Israel display some modern features and are less robust than the classic Neandertals of Europe, though again, the overall pattern is Neandertal. The best known of these discoveries is from Tabun—short for Mugharet-et-Tabun, meaning "cave of the oven"—at Mt. Carmel, a short drive south from Haifa (Fig. 13-17). Tabun, excavated in the early 1930s, yielded a female skeleton, recently dated by thermoluminescence (TL) at about 120,000–110,000 ya. If this dating is accurate, Neandertals at Tabun were generally contemporary with early modern *H. sapiens* found in nearby caves. (TL dating is discussed on p. 244.)

A more recent Neandertal burial, a male discovered in 1983, comes from Kebara, a neighboring cave of Tabun at Mt. Carmel. A partial skeleton, dated to 60,000 ya, contains the most complete Neandertal pelvis so far recovered. Also recovered at Kebara is a hyoid—a small bone located in the throat, and the first ever found from a Neandertal; this bone is especially important because of its usefulness in reconstructing language capabilities.*

---

*The Kebara hyoid is identical to that of modern humans, suggesting that Neandertals did not differ from modern *H. sapiens* in this key element.

FIGURE 13-17
Excavation of the Tabun Cave, Mt. Carmel, Israel.

Harry Nelson

Iraq   A most remarkable site is Shanidar cave, in the Zagros Mountains of northeastern Iraq, where fieldworkers found partial skeletons of 9 individuals, 4 of them deliberately buried. Among these individuals is a particularly interesting one called Shanidar 1. This is a skeleton of a male who lived to be approximately 30 to 45 years old, a considerable age for a prehistoric human (Fig. 13-18). His height is estimated at 5 feet 7 inches, and his cranial capacity is 1,600 cm^3. Shanidar 1 also exhibits several other fascinating features:

> There had been a crushing blow to the left side of the head, fracturing the eye socket, displacing the left eye, and probably causing blindness on that side. He also sustained a massive blow to the right side of the body that so badly damaged the right arm that it became withered and useless; the bones of the shoulder blade, collar bone, and upper arm are much smaller and thinner than those on the left. The right lower arm and hand are missing, probably not because of poor preservation . . . but because they either atrophied and dropped off or because they were amputated. (Trinkaus and Shipman, 1992, p. 340)

Besides these injuries, the man had further trauma to both legs, and he probably limped. It's hard to imagine how he could have performed day-to-day activities. Both Ralph Solecki, who supervised the work at Shanidar Cave, and Erik Trinkaus, who has studied the Shanidar remains, believe that to survive, Shanidar 1 must have been helped by others: "A one-armed, partially blind, crippled man could have made no pretense of hunting or gathering his own food. That he survived for years after his trauma was a testament to Neandertal compassion and humanity" (Trinkaus and Shipman, 1992, p. 341).

CENTRAL ASIA

About 1,600 miles east of Shanidar in Uzbekistan, inside a cave at Teshik Tash, researchers found what may be the easternmost Neandertal discovery. Actually, new analyses suggest that the Teshik Tash skeleton may be that of a modern human, and not a Neandertal at all (Glantz et al., 2004). The skeleton is that of a 9-year-old boy who appears to have been deliberately buried. It was reported that five pairs of wild goat horns surrounded him, suggesting a burial ritual or perhaps a religious cult, but owing to inadequate published documentation of the excavation, this interpretation has been seriously questioned. The Teshik Tash individual, like some specimens from Croatia and southwest Asia, also shows a mixture of Neandertal traits (heavy browridges and occipital bun) and modern traits (high vault and definite signs of a chin), though expression of these traits in a child would've been minimized.

In sum, Teshik Tash may or may not be the easternmost location for Neandertals. Based on the assumption that Teshik Tash is a Neandertal, geographical distribution of the Neandertals extended from France eastward, possibly extending to central Asia—a distance of about 4,000 miles.

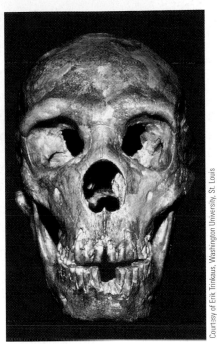

FIGURE 13-18
Shanidar 1. Does he represent Neandertal compassion for the disabled?

Courtesy of Erik Trinkaus, Washington University, St. Louis

Culture of Neandertals

Anthropologists almost always associate Neandertals, who lived in the cultural period known as the Middle Paleolithic, with the **Mousterian** industry—although they don't always associate the Mousterian industry with Neandertals. Early in the last glacial period, Mousterian culture extended across Europe and North Africa into the former Soviet Union, Israel, Iran, and as far east as Uzbekistan and possibly even China. Also, in sub-Saharan Africa, the contemporaneous Middle Stone Age industry is broadly similar to the Mousterian.

TECHNOLOGY

Neandertals improved on previous prepared-core techniques—that is, the Levallois—by inventing a new variation. They trimmed a flint nodule around the edges to form a disk-shaped core. Each time they struck the edge, they produced a flake, and they kept at it until

Mousterian   Pertaining to the stone tool industry associated with Neandertals and some modern *H. sapiens* groups. Also called Middle Paleolithic. This industry is characterized by a larger proportion of flake tools than found in Acheulian tool kits.

AT A GLANCE   Key Neandertal Fossil Discoveries

Site	Dates (ya)	Human Remains
Vindija (Croatia)	42,000–32,000	35 specimens; almost entirely cranial fragments
La Chapelle (France)	50,000	Nearly complete adult male skeleton
Shanidar (Iraq)	70,000–60,000	9 individuals (partial skeletons)
Tabun (Israel)	110,000 date uncertain	2 (perhaps 3) individuals, including almost complete skeleton of adult female
Krapina (Croatia)	125,000–120,000	Up to 40 individuals, but very fragmentary

the core became too small and was discarded. In this way, they produced more flakes per core than their predecessors did. They then reworked the flakes into various forms including scrapers, points, and knives (Fig. 13-19).

Neandertal craftspeople elaborated and diversified traditional methods, and there's some indication that they developed specialized tools for skinning and preparing meat, hunting, woodworking, and hafting. Even so, in strong contrast to the next cultural period, the Upper Paleolithic, there's almost no evidence that they used bone tools. Still, Neandertals advanced their technology well beyond that of earlier hominids. It's quite possible that their technological advances helped provide a basis for the remarkable changes of the Upper Paleolithic, which we'll discuss in the next chapter.

SUBSISTENCE

We know, from the abundant remains of animal bones at their sites, that Neandertals were successful hunters. But while it's clear that Neandertals could hunt large mammals, they may not have been as efficient at this task as were Upper Paleolithic hunters. For example, it wasn't until the beginning of the Upper Paleolithic that the spear-thrower, or atlatl, came into use (see p. 370). Soon after that, the bow and arrow greatly increased efficiency (and safety) in hunting large mammals. Because they had no long-distance weaponry and were

(see p. 370)

FIGURE **13-19**

Examples of the Mousterian toolkit, including from left to right, a Levallois point, a perforator, and a side scraper.

© Randall White, New York University

mostly limited to thrusting spears, Neandertals may have been more prone to serious injury—a hypothesis supported by paleoanthropologists Thomas Berger and Erik Trinkaus. Berger and Trinkaus (1995) analyzed the pattern of trauma, particularly fractures, in Neandertals and compared it with that seen in contemporary human samples. Interestingly, the pattern in Neandertals, especially the relatively high proportion of head and neck injuries, was most similar to that seen in contemporary rodeo performers. Berger and Trinkaus concluded that "The similarity to the rodeo distribution suggests frequent close encounters with large ungulates unkindly disposed to the humans involved" (Berger and Trinkaus, 1995, p. 841).

We know much more about European Middle Paleolithic culture than any earlier period, because it's been studied longer and by more scholars. Recently, however, Africa has been a target not only of physical anthropologists but also of archaeologists, who have added considerably to our knowledge of African Pleistocene hominid history. In many cases, the technology and assumed cultural adaptations in Africa were similar to those in Europe and southwest Asia. We'll see in the next chapter that the African technological achievements also kept pace with, or even preceded, those in western Europe.

SPEECH AND SYMBOLIC BEHAVIOR

There are a variety of hypotheses concerning the speech capacities of Neandertals, and many of these views are contradictory. Some researchers argue that Neandertals were incapable of human speech. But the prevailing consensus has been that they *were* capable of articulate speech, maybe even fully competent in the range of sounds produced by modern humans.

However, recent genetic evidence may call for a reassessment of just when fully human language first emerged (Enard et al., 2002). In humans today, mutations in a particular gene (locus) are known to produce serious language impairments. From an evolutionary perspective, what's perhaps most significant concerns the greater variability seen in the alleles at this locus in modern humans as compared to other primates. One explanation for this increased variation is intensified selection acting on human populations, perhaps quite recently—and thus potentially after the evolutionary divergence of the Neandertals.

But even if we conclude that Neandertals *could* speak, it doesn't necessarily mean their abilities were at the level of modern *Homo sapiens*. Today, paleoanthropologists are quite interested in the apparently sudden expansion of modern *H. sapiens* (discussed in Chapter 14), and they've proposed various explanations for this group's rapid success. Also, as we attempt to explain how and why modern *H. sapiens* expanded its geographical range, we're left with the problem of explaining what happened to the Neandertals. In making these types of interpretations, a growing number of paleoanthropologists suggest that *behavioral* differences are the key. Further confirmation of a recent evolutionary shift, resulting from the mutation of a crucial gene that influences language capacity, will help support this view.

Researchers believe that Upper Paleolithic *H. sapiens* had some significant behavioral advantages over Neandertals and other premodern humans. Was it some kind of new and expanded ability to symbolize, communicate, organize social activities, elaborate technology, obtain a wider range of food resources, or care for the sick or injured—or, was it some other factor? Compared with modern *H. sapiens*, were the Neandertals limited by neurological differences that may have contributed to their demise?

The direct anatomical evidence derived from Neandertal fossils isn't much help in answering these questions. Ralph Holloway (1985) has maintained that Neandertal brains—at least as far as the fossil evidence suggests—aren't significantly different from those of modern *H. sapiens*. What's more, as we've seen, Neandertal vocal tracts (as well as other morphological features), compared with our own, don't appear to have seriously limited them.

Most of the reservations about advanced cognitive abilities in Neandertals are based on archaeological data. Interpretation of Neandertal sites, when compared with succeeding Upper Paleolithic sites—especially those documented in western Europe—have led to several intriguing contrasts, as shown in Table 13-1.

Due to this type of behavioral and anatomical evidence, Neandertals in recent years have increasingly been viewed as an evolutionary dead end. Right now, we can't say whether their disappearance and ultimate replacement by anatomically modern Upper Paleolithic

TABLE 13-1	Cultural Contrasts* Between Neandertals and Upper Paleolithic Modern Humans
Neandertals	**Upper Paleolithic Modern Humans**
Tool Technology Numerous flake tools; few, however, apparently for highly specialized functions; use of bone, antler, or ivory very rare; relatively few tools with more than one or two parts	Many more varieties of stone tools; many apparently for specialized functions; frequent use of bone, antler, and ivory; many more tools comprised of two or more component parts
Hunting Efficiency and Weapons No long-distance hunting weapons; close-proximity weapons used (thus, more likelihood of injury)	Use of spear-thrower and bow and arrow; wider range of social contacts, perhaps permitting larger, more organized hunting parties (including game drives)
Stone Material Transport Stone materials transported only short distances—just "a few kilometers" (Klein, 1989)	Stone tool raw materials transported over much longer distances, implying wider social networks and perhaps trade
Art Artwork uncommon; usually small; probably mostly of a personal nature; some items perhaps misinterpreted as "art"; others may be intrusive from overlying Upper Paleolithic contexts; cave art absent	Artwork much more common, including transportable objects as well as elaborate cave art; well executed, using a variety of materials and techniques; stylistic sophistication
Burial Deliberate burial at several sites; graves unelaborated; graves frequently lack artifacts	Burials much more complex, frequently including both tools and remains of animals

*Note: The contrasts are more apparent in some areas (particularly western Europe) than others (eastern Europe, Near East). Elsewhere (Africa, eastern Asia), where there were no Neandertals, the cultural situation is quite different. Even in western Europe, the cultural transformations weren't necessarily abrupt but may have developed more gradually from Mousterian to Upper Paleolithic times. For example, Straus (1995) argues that many of the Upper Paleolithic features weren't consistently manifested until after 20,000 ya.

peoples—with their presumably "superior" culture—was the result of cultural differences alone, or whether it was also influenced by biological variation.

BURIALS

Anthropologists have known for some time that Neandertals deliberately buried their dead. Undeniably, the spectacular discoveries at La Chapelle, Shanidar, and elsewhere were the direct results of ancient burial, which permits preservation that's much more complete. Such deliberate burial treatment goes back at least 90,000 years at Tabun. From a much older site, some form of consistent "disposal" of the dead—not necessarily belowground burial—is evidenced: At Atapuerca, Spain, more than 700 fossilized elements (representing at least 28 different individuals) were found in a cave at the end of a deep vertical shaft. From the nature of the site and the accumulation of hominid remains, Spanish researchers are convinced that the site demonstrates some form of human activity involving deliberate disposal of the dead (Arsuaga et al., 1997).

The recent re-dating of Atapuerca to more than 500,000 years ago suggests that Neandertals—more precisely, their immediate precursors—were, by quite early in the Middle Pleistocene, handling their dead in special ways. Such behavior was previously thought to have emerged only much later, in the Late Pleistocene. As far as current data indicate, this practice is seen in western European contexts well before it appears in Africa or in eastern Asia. For example, in the premodern sites at Kabwe and Florisbad (discussed earlier), deliberate disposal of the dead is not documented. Nor is it seen in African early modern sites—for example, the Klasies River Mouth, dated at 120,000–100,000 ya (see p. 357).

Yet, in later contexts (after 35,000 ya), where modern *H. sapiens* remains are found in clear burial contexts, their treatment is considerably more complex than in Neandertal burials. In these later (Upper Paleolithic) sites, grave goods, including bone and stone tools as well as animal bones, are found more consistently and in greater concentrations. Because many Neandertal sites were excavated in the nineteenth or early twentieth century before more rigorous archaeological methods had been developed, many of these supposed burials are now in question. Still, the evidence seems quite clear that deliberate burial was practiced not only at La Chapelle, La Ferrassie (eight graves), Tabun, Amud, Kebara, Shanidar, and Teshik Tash but also at several other localities, especially in France. In many cases, the body's *position* was deliberately modified and placed in the grave in a flexed posture (see p. 335). This flexed position has been found in 16 of the 20 best-documented Neandertal burial contexts (Klein, 1999).

Finally, as further evidence of Neandertal symbolic behavior, researchers point to the placement of supposed grave goods in burials, including stone tools, animal bones (such as cave bear), and even arrangements of flowers, together with stone slabs on top of the burials. Unfortunately, in many instances, again due to poorly documented excavation, these finds are questionable. Placement of stone tools, for example, is occasionally seen, but it apparently wasn't done consistently. In those 33 Neandertal burials for which we have adequate data, only 14 show definite association of stone tools and/or animal bones with the deceased (Klein, 1989). It's not until the next cultural period, the Upper Paleolithic, that we see a major behavioral shift, as demonstrated in more elaborate burials and development of art.

Genetic Evidence

With the revolutionary advances in molecular biology (discussed in Chapter 3), fascinating new avenues of research have become possible in the study of earlier hominids. It's becoming fairly commonplace to extract, amplify, and sequence ancient DNA from contexts spanning the last 10,000 years or so. For example, researchers have analyzed DNA from the 5,000-year-old "Iceman" found in the Italian Alps.

It's much harder to find usable DNA in even more ancient remains, since the organic components, often including the DNA, have been destroyed during the mineralization process. Still, in the past few years, exciting results have been announced about DNA found in 12 different Neandertal fossils dated between 32,000 and 50,000 ya. These fossils come from sites in France (including La Chapelle), Germany (from the original Neander Valley locality), Belgium, Italy, Spain, Croatia, and Russia (Krings et al., 1997, 2000; Ovchinnikov et al., 2000; Schmitz et al., 2002; Serre et al., 2004; Green et al., 2006).

The technique used in studying the Neandertal fossils involves extracting mitochondrial DNA (mtDNA), amplifying it through polymerase chain reaction, or PCR (see p. 58), and sequencing nucleotides in parts of the molecule. Results from the Neandertal specimens show that these individuals are genetically more different from contemporary *Homo sapiens* populations than modern human populations are from each other—in fact, about three times as much. Consequently, Krings and colleagues (1997) have hypothesized that the Neandertal lineage separated from that of our modern *H. sapiens* ancestors sometime between 690,000 and 550,000 ya.

New advances have allowed much more of the Neandertal genetic pattern to be determined with the ability to now sequence big chunks of the nuclear DNA (see p. 320). One immediate application of these remarkable new data allows the suggested divergence dates derived from mitochondrial DNA to be more thoroughly confirmed. From the two studies published in 2006 (Green et al. 2006; Noonan et al., 2006), the origins of the Neandertals have been traced to approximately 700-500 kya. Moreover, the much more extensive Neandertal nuclear DNA patterns are as distinct from those of modern humans as are the differences seen in mtDNA. Considering both the length of time that Neandertals were likely separate from the lineage of modern humans as well as their distinct genetic patterning, it looks more probable they should be considered a separate species—or, at least, a population well on its way to becoming separate (see p. 344).

Trends in Human Evolution: Understanding Premodern Humans

As you can see, the Middle Pleistocene hominids are a very diverse group, broadly dispersed through time and space. There is considerable variation among them, and it's not easy to get a clear evolutionary picture. Because we know that regional populations were small and frequently isolated, many of them probably died out and left no descendants. So it's a mistake to see an "ancestor" in every fossil find.

Still, as a group, these Middle Pleistocene premoderns do reveal some general trends. In many ways, for example, it seems they were *transitional* between the hominid grade that came before them (*H. erectus*) and the one that followed them (modern *H. sapiens*). It's not a stretch to say that all the Middle Pleistocene premoderns derived from *H. erectus* forebears and that some of them, in turn, were probably ancestors of the earliest fully modern humans.

Paleoanthropologists are certainly concerned with such broad generalities as these, but they also want to focus on meaningful anatomical, environmental, and behavioral details as well as underlying processes. So they consider the regional variability displayed by particular fossil samples as significant—but just *how* significant is up for debate. In addition, increasingly sophisticated theoretical approaches are being used to better understand the processes that shaped the evolution of later *Homo*, at both macroevolutionary and microevolutionary levels.

Scientists, like all humans, assign names or labels to phenomena, a point we addressed in discussing classification in Chapter 5. Paleoanthropologists are certainly no exception. Yet, working from a common evolutionary foundation, paleoanthropologists still come to different conclusions about the most appropriate way to interpret the Middle/Late Pleistocene hominids. Consequently, a variety of species names have been proposed in recent years.

At the extreme lumping end of the spectrum, only one species is recognized for all the premodern fossils. They are called *Homo sapiens* and are thus further lumped with modern humans, although they're partly distinguished by such terminology as "archaic *H. sapiens*" (see Fig. 13-20a).

At the other end of the spectrum, paleontological splitters have identified at least three species, all distinct from *H. sapiens*. Two of these, *H. heidelbergensis* and *H. neanderthalensis*, were discussed earlier; and a third species, called *Homo helmei*, has recently been proposed (Foley and Lahr, 1997; Lahr and Foley, 1998). It's been suggested that this last group is a possible African ancestor of *both* modern humans and Neandertals, but one that appears fairly late in the Middle Pleistocene (300,000–250,000 ya) and so comes largely after *H. heidelbergensis*. This more complex evolutionary interpretation is shown in Figure 13-20b.

We addressed similar differences of interpretation in Chapters 11 and 12, and we know that disparities like these can be frustrating to students who are new to paleoanthropology. The proliferation of new names is confusing, and it might seem that experts in the field are endlessly arguing about what to call the fossils.

Fortunately, it's not quite that bad. There's actually more agreement than you might think. No one doubts that all these hominids are closely related to each other as well as to modern humans. And everyone agrees that only some of the fossil samples represent populations that left descendants. Where paleoanthropologists disagree is when they start discussing which hominids are the most likely to be closely related to later hominids. The grouping of hominids into evolutionary clusters (clades) and assigning of different names to them is a reflection of differing interpretations—and, more fundamentally, of somewhat differing philosophies.

But we shouldn't emphasize these naming and classification debates too much. Most paleoanthropologists recognize that a great deal of these disagreements result from simple, practical considerations. Even the most enthusiastic splitters acknowledge that the fossil "species" are not true species as defined by the biological species concept (see p. 102). As prominent paleoanthropologist Robert Foley puts it, "It is unlikely they are all biological species. . . . These are probably a mixture of real biological species and evolving lineages of subspecies. In other words, they could potentially have interbred, but owing to

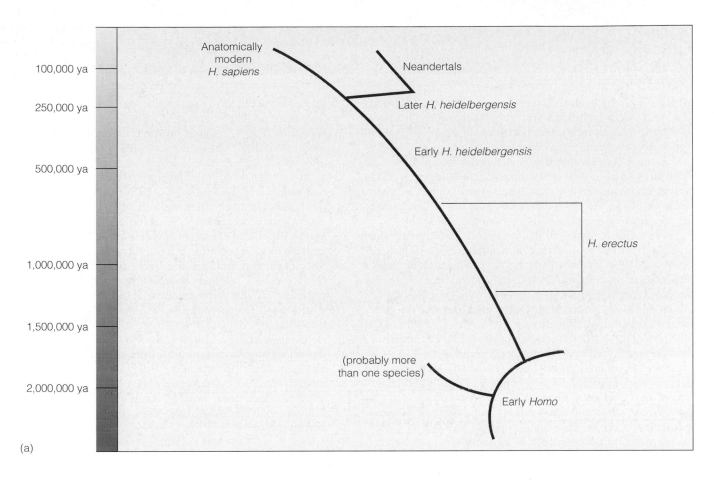

(a)

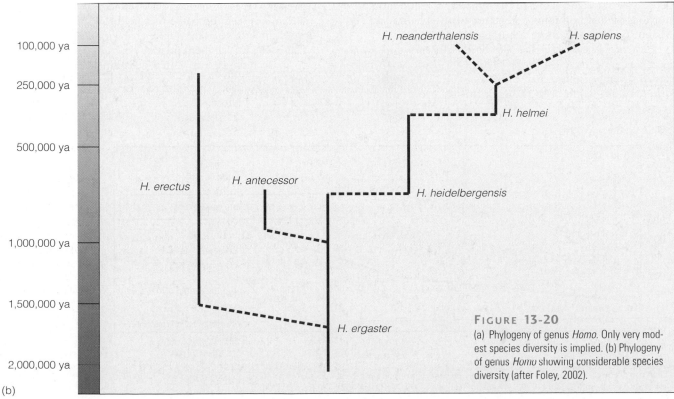

(b)

FIGURE 13-20

(a) Phylogeny of genus *Homo*. Only very modest species diversity is implied. (b) Phylogeny of genus *Homo* showing considerable species diversity (after Foley, 2002).

A CLOSER LOOK   Are They Human?

At the beginning of this chapter we posed the question, What does it mean to be human? Applying this term to our extinct hominid predecessors is somewhat tricky. Various prior hominid species share with contemporary *Homo sapiens* a mosaic of physical features. For example, they're all bipedal, most (but not all) have fairly small canine teeth, some are completely terrestrial, and some are moderately encephalized (while others are much more so). Thus, the *physical* characteristics that define humanity appear at different times during hominid evolution.

Even more tenuous are the *behavioral* characteristics frequently identified as signifying human status. The most significant of these proposed behavioral traits include major dependence on culture, innovation, cooperation in acquiring food, full language, and elaboration of symbolic representations in art and body adornment. Once again, the characteristics become apparent at different stages of hominid evolution. But distinguishing when and how these behavioral characteristics became established in our ancestors is even more problematic than analyzing anatomical traits. While the archaeological record provides considerable information regarding stone tool technology, it's mostly silent on other aspects of material culture. The social organization and language capabilities of earlier hominids are as yet almost completely invisible.

From the available evidence, we can conclude that *H. erectus* took significant steps in the human direction—well beyond that of earlier hominids. *H. erectus* vastly expanded hominid geographical ranges, achieved the full body size and limb proportions of later hominids, had increased encephalization, and became considerably more culturally dependent.

H. heidelbergensis (in the Middle Pleistocene) and, to an even greater degree, Neandertals (in the Late Pleistocene), maintained several of these characteristics—such as body size and proportions—while also showing further evolution in the human direction. Most particularly, relative brain size increased further, expanding on average about 22 percent beyond that of *H. erectus* (Fig. 1). Notice, however, that the largest jump in proportional brain size occurs very late in hominid evolution—only with the appearance of fully modern humans.

In addition to brain enlargement, cranial shape also was remodeled in *H. heidelbergensis* and Neandertals, producing a more globular shape of the vault as well as suggesting further neurological reorganization. Stone tool technology also became more sophisticated during the Middle Pleistocene, with the manufacture of tools requiring a more complicated series of steps. Also, for the first time, fire was definitely controlled and widely used; caves were routinely occupied; hominid ranges were successfully expanded throughout much of Europe as well as into northern Asia (that is, colder habitats were more fully exploited); structures were built; and more systematic hunting took place.

Some premoderns also were like modern humans in another significant way. Analysis of teeth from a Neandertal shows that these hominids had the same *delayed maturation* found in modern *H. sapiens* (Dean et al., 2001). We don't yet have similar data for earlier *H. heidelbergensis* individuals, but it's possible that they, too, showed this distinctively human pattern of development.

Did these Middle and Late Pleistocene hominids have the full language capabilities and other symbolic and social skills of living peoples? It's impossible to answer this question completely, given the types of fossil and archaeological evidence available. Yet, it does seem probable that neither *H. heidelbergensis* nor the Neandertals had this entire array of *fully* human attributes. That's why we call them premodern humans.

So, to rephrase our initial question, Were these hominids human? We could answer conditionally: They *were* human—at least, mostly so.

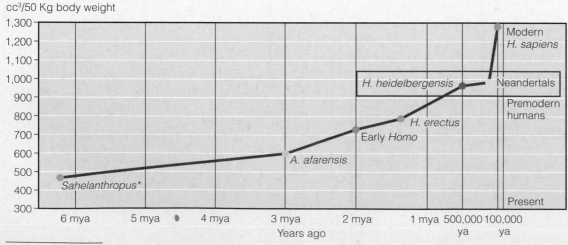

cc³/50 Kg body weight

FIGURE 1

Relative brain size in hominids. The scale shows brain size as cm³ per 50 kg of body weight. Premodern humans have a more than 20% increase in relative brain size compared to *H. erectus*, but modern humans show another 30% expansion beyond that in premodern humans.

*There are no direct current data for body size in *Sahelanthropus*. Body size is estimated from tooth size in comparison with *A. afarensis*.
Data abstracted from McHenry (1992), Wood and Collard (1999), Brunet (2002), and Carroll (2003).

allopatry [that is, geographical separation] were unlikely to have had the opportunity" (Foley, 2002, p. 33).

Even so, Foley, along with an increasing number of other professionals, distinguishes these different fossil samples with species names to highlight their distinct position in hominid evolution. That is, these hominid groups are more loosely defined as a type of paleospecies (see p. 107) rather than as fully biological species. Giving distinct hominid samples a separate (species) name makes them more easily identifiable to other researchers and makes various cladistic hypotheses more explicit—and equally important, more directly testable. Eminent paleoanthropologist F. Clark Howell of the University of California, Berkeley, also recognizes these advantages; but he's less emphatic about species designations. Howell recommends the term *paleo-deme* for referring to either a species or subspecies classification (Howell, 1999).

The hominids that best illustrate these issues are the Neandertals. Fortunately, they're also the best known, represented by dozens of well-preserved individuals. With all this evidence, researchers can systematically test and evaluate many of the differing hypotheses.

Are Neandertals very closely related to modern *H. sapiens*? Certainly. Are they physically and behaviorally distinct from both ancient and fully modern humans? Yes. Does this mean Neandertals are a fully separate biological species from modern humans and therefore theoretically incapable of fertily interbreeding with modern people? Probably not. Finally, then, should Neandertals really be placed in a separate species from *H. sapiens*? For most purposes, it doesn't matter, since the distinction at some point is arbitrary. Speciation is, after all, a *dynamic* process. Fossil groups like the Neandertals represent just one point in this process (see Fig. 5-6, p. 103, and this chapter's "Visual Summary").

We can view Neandertals as a distinctive side branch of later hominid evolution. Similar to the situation among contemporary baboons—comparing savanna to hamadryas—we could say that Neandertals were an incipient species. Given enough time and enough

VISUAL SUMMARY

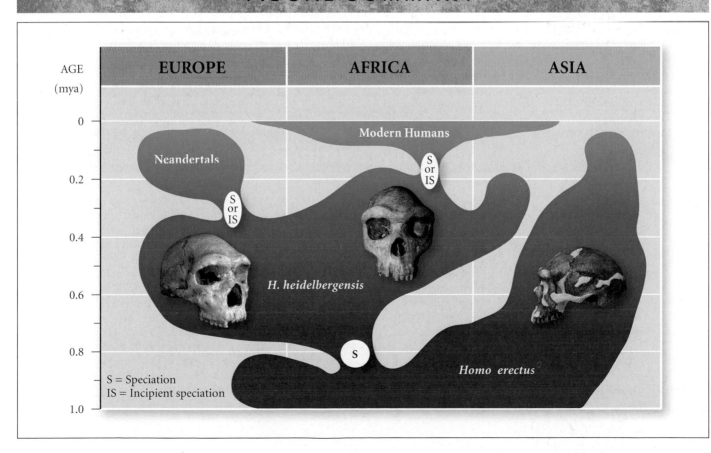

isolation, they likely would have separated completely from their modern human contemporaries. The new DNA evidence suggests they were well on their way. But as fossil, archaeological, and some genetic data* are making increasingly clear, Neandertals never quite got that far. Their fate, in a sense, was decided for them as more successful competitors expanded into Neandertal habitats. These highly successful hominids were fully modern humans, and in the next chapter we'll focus on their story.

---

*The genetic data are controversial. Ancient DNA studies seem to point to a fairly distinct difference and thus likely speciation of Neandertals; however, when considering genetic diversity within contemporary species (such as baboons, chimpanzees or gorillas), the likelihood of speciation appears much less certain.

TABLE 13-2   Most Significant Premodern Human Discoveries Discussed in this Chapter

Site	Dates (ya)	Taxonomic Designation	Comments
La Chapelle	50,000	Neandertal *Homo neanderthalensis*	Historically most important site in France in description of Neandertal morphology
Tabun	110,000	Neandertal *Homo neanderthalensis*	Important early Neandertal site; shows clear presence of Neandertals in Near East
Atapuerca (Sima de los Huesos)	600,000–530,000	*Homo heidelbergensis*	Large sample; earliest evidence in Europe of Neandertal morphology; evidence of disposal of the dead
Steinheim	300,000–250,000?	*Homo heidelbergensis*	Transitional-looking fossil
Jinniushan	200,000?	*Homo heidelbergensis* Early *Homo sapiens*, as termed by the Chinese	Possibly oldest example of *H. sapiens* in China, but status uncertain
Kabwe (Broken Hill)	130,000+?	*Homo heidelbergensis*	Transitional-looking fossil; similar to Bodo
Bodo	600,000	*Homo heidelbergensis*	Earliest evidence of *H. heidelbergensis* in Africa and perhaps anywhere

Summary: Putting It All Together

The Middle Pleistocene (780,000–125,000 ya) was a period of transition in human evolution. Fossil hominids from this period show similarities both with their predecessors (*H. erectus*) and with their successors (*H. sapiens*). They've also been found in many areas of the Old World, in Africa, Asia, and Europe—in the latter case, being the first truly successful occupants of that continent. Because these transitional hominids are more derived—and advanced in the human direction—than *H. erectus*, we can refer to them as premodern humans. With this terminology, we also recognize that these hominids display several significant anatomical and behavioral differences from modern humans.

Although there's some dispute about the best way to formally classify the majority of Middle Pleistocene hominids, most paleoanthropologists now prefer to call them *H. heidelbergensis*. Similarities between the African and European Middle Pleistocene hominid samples suggest that they all can be reasonably seen as part of this same species. The contemporaneous Asian fossils, however, don't fit as neatly into this model, and conclusions regarding these premodern humans remain less definite.

Some of the later *H. heidelbergensis* populations in Europe likely evolved into Neandertals. Abundant Neandertal fossil and archaeological evidence has been collected from the Late Pleistocene time span of Neandertal existence, about 130,000–29,000 ya. But unlike their Middle Pleistocene (*H. heidelbergensis*) predecessors, Neandertals are more geographically restricted; they're found only in Europe and southwest Asia. Various lines of evidence—anatomical, archaeological, and genetic—also suggest that they were isolated and distinct from other hominids.

These observations have led to a growing consensus among paleoanthropologists that the Neandertals were largely a side branch of later hominid evolution. Still, there remain significant differences in theoretical approaches regarding how best to deal with the Neandertals; that is, should they be considered as a separate species or as a subspecies of *H. sapiens*? We suggest that the best way to view the Neandertals is within a dynamic process of speciation. Neandertals can thus be interpreted as an incipient species—one in the process of splitting from early *H. sapiens* populations.

In Table 13-2 you'll find a useful summary of the most significant premodern human fossils discussed in this chapter.

Critical Thinking Questions

1. Why are the Middle Pleistocene hominids called premodern humans? In what ways are they human?

2. What is the general popular conception of Neandertals? Do you agree with this view? (Cite both anatomical and archaeological evidence to support your conclusion.)

3. Compare the skeleton of a Neandertal with that of a modern human. In which ways are they most alike? In which ways are they most different?

4. What evidence suggests that Neandertals deliberately buried their dead? Do you think the fact that they buried their dead is important? Why? How would you interpret this behavior (remembering that Neandertals were not identical to us)?

5. How are species defined, both for living animals and for extinct ones? Use the Neandertals to illustrate the problems encountered in distinguishing species among extinct hominids. Contrast specifically the interpretation of Neandertals as a distinct species with the interpretation of Neandertals as a subspecies of *H. sapiens*.

CHAPTER 14

The Origin and Dispersal of Modern Humans

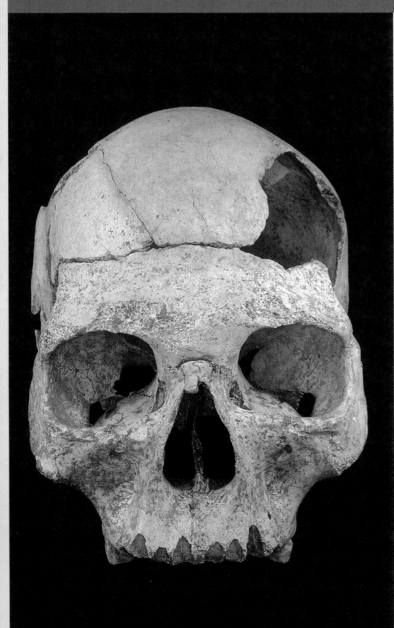

© Erik Trinkaus, Washington University, St. Louis

KEY QUESTION

Is it possible to determine when and where modern people first appeared?

Introduction

Sometime, probably close to 200,000 years ago (ya), the first modern *Homo sapiens* evolved in Africa. Within 150,000 years or so, their descendants had spread across most of the Old World, even expanding as far as Australia (and somewhat later to the Americas).

Who were they, and why were these early modern people so successful? What was the fate of the other hominids, such as the Neandertals, who were already long established in areas outside Africa? Did they evolve as well, leaving descendants among some living human populations? Or were they completely swept aside and replaced by African emigrants?

In this chapter, we'll discuss the origin and dispersal of modern *H. sapiens*. All contemporary populations—more than 6 billion living humans—are placed within this species (and the same subspecies as well). Most paleoanthropologists agree that several fossil forms, dating back as far as 100,000 ya, should also be included in the same group. In addition, some recently discovered fossils from Africa also are clearly *H. sapiens*, but they show some (minor) differences from living people and could thus be described as near modern. Still, we can think of these early African humans as well as their somewhat later relatives as "us."

These first modern humans, who evolved by 195,000 ya, are probably descendants of some of the premodern humans we discussed in Chapter 13. In particular, African populations of *H. heidelbergensis* are the most likely ancestors of the earliest modern *H. sapiens*. The evolutionary events that took place as modern humans made the transition from more ancient premodern forms and then dispersed throughout most of the Old World were relatively rapid, and they raise several basic questions:

1. When (approximately) did modern humans first appear?
2. Where did the transition take place? Did it occur in just one region or in several?
3. What was the pace of evolutionary change? How quickly did the transition occur?
4. How did the dispersal of modern humans to other areas of the Old World (outside their area of origin) take place?

These questions concerning the origins and early dispersal of modern *Homo sapiens* continue to fuel much controversy among paleoanthropologists. And it's no wonder, for members of early *Homo sapiens* are our *direct* ancestors, which makes them close relatives of all contemporary humans. They were much like us skeletally, genetically, and (most likely) behaviorally, too. In fact, it's the various hypotheses regarding the behaviors and abilities of our most immediate predecessors that have most fired the imaginations of scientists and laypeople alike. In every major respect, these are the first hominids that we can confidently refer to as *fully* human.

In this chapter, we'll also discuss archaeological evidence from the Upper Paleolithic (see p. 336). This evidence will give us a better understanding of the technological and social developments during the period when modern humans arose and quickly came to dominate the planet.

The evolutionary story of *Homo sapiens* is really the biological autobiography of all of us. It's a story that still has many unanswered questions; but several theories can help us organize the diverse information that's now available.

Click!

Go to the following media for interactives and exercises on topics covered in this chapter:

- Online Virtual Laboratories for Physical Anthropology, Fourth Edition
- Hominid Fossils CD-ROM: An Interactive Atlas

Approaches to Understanding Modern Human Origins

In attempting to organize and explain modern human origins, paleoanthropologists have developed two major theories: the complete replacement model and the regional continuity model. These two views are quite distinct, and in some ways they're completely opposed to each other. What's more, the popular press has further contributed to a wide and incorrect perception of irreconcilable argument on these points by "opposing" scientists. In fact there's a third theory, which we call the partial replacement model, that's a kind of compromise, incorporating some aspects of the two major theories. Since so much of our contemporary view of modern human origins is influenced by the debates linked to these differing theories, let's start by briefly reviewing each one. Then we'll turn to the fossil evidence itself to see what it can contribute to answering the four questions we've posed.

THE COMPLETE REPLACEMENT MODEL: RECENT AFRICAN EVOLUTION

The *complete replacement model* was developed by British paleoanthropologists Christopher Stringer and Peter Andrews (1988). It's based on the origin of modern humans in Africa and later replacement of populations in Europe and Asia (Fig. 14-1). This theory proposes that anatomically modern populations arose in Africa within the last 200,000 years and then migrated from Africa, *completely replacing* populations in Europe and Asia. It's important to note that this model doesn't account for a transition from premodern forms to modern *H. sapiens* anywhere in the world except Africa. A critical deduction of the Stringer and Andrews theory is that anatomically modern humans appeared as the result of a biological speciation event. So in this view, migrating African modern *H. sapiens* could not have interbred with local non-African populations, because the African modern humans were a *biologically* different species. Taxonomically, all of the premodern populations outside Africa would, in this view, be classified as belonging to different species of *Homo*. For example, the Neandertals would be classified as *H. neanderthalensis* (see p. 347 for further discussion). This speciation explanation fits nicely with, and in fact helps explain, *complete* replacement; but Stringer has more recently stated that he isn't dogmatic on this issue. He does suggest that even though there may have been potential for interbreeding, apparently very little actually took place.

Interpretations of the latter phases of human evolution have recently been greatly extended by newly available genetic techniques. As we emphasized elsewhere, advances in molecular biology have revolutionized the biological sciences, including physical anthropology, and they've recently been applied to the question of modern human origins. Using numerous contemporary human populations as a data source, geneticists have precisely determined and compared a wide variety of DNA sequences. The theoretical basis of this approach assumes that at least some of the genetic patterning seen today can act as a kind of window on the past. In particular, the genetic patterns observed today between geographically widely dispersed humans are thought to partly reflect migrations occurring in the late Pleistocene. This hypothesis can be further tested as various types of contemporary population genetic patterning are better documented.

To get a clearer picture of these genetic patterns, geneticists have studied both nuclear and mitochondrial DNA (see p. 38). They consider Y chromosome and mtDNA patterns particularly informative, since neither is significantly recombined during sexual reproduction. As a result, mitochondrial inheritance follows a strictly maternal pattern (inherited through females), while the Y chromosome follows a paternal pattern (transmitted only from father to son).

As these new data have accumulated, consistent relationships are emerging, especially in showing that indigenous African populations have far greater diversity than do populations from elsewhere in the world. The consistency of the results is highly significant, because it strongly supports an African origin for modern humans and some mode of replacement elsewhere.

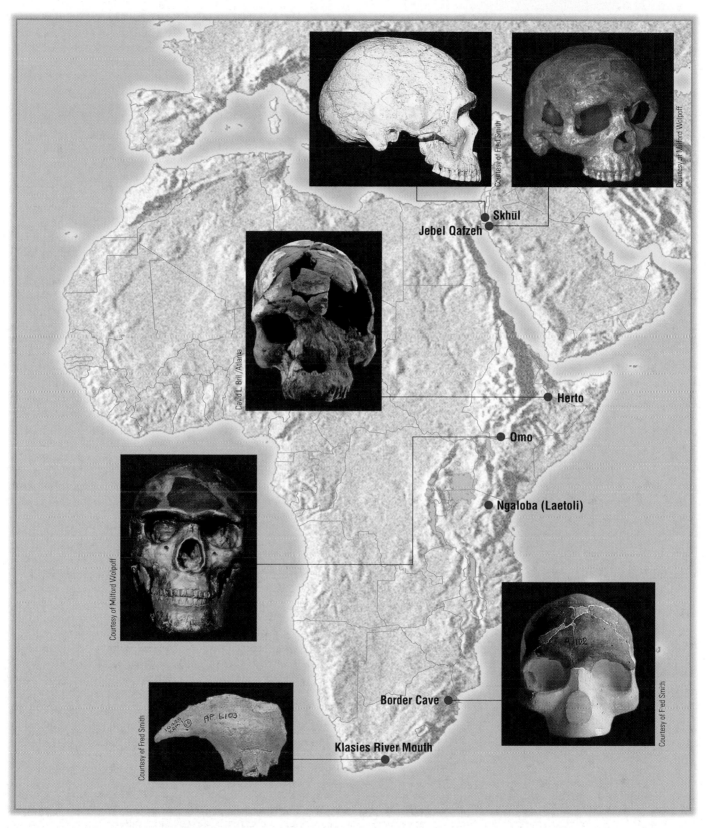

FIGURE 14-1
Modern humans from Africa and the Near East.

Certainly, most molecular data come from contemporary species, since DNA is not *usually* preserved in long-dead individuals. Even so, exceptions do occur, and these cases open another genetic window—one that can directly illuminate the past. As discussed in Chapter 13 (see p. 343), Neandertal DNA has been recovered from eight Neandertal fossils.

In addition, nine ancient fully modern *H. sapiens* skeletons from sites in Italy, France, the Czech Republic, and Russia have recently had their mtDNA sequenced (Caramelli et al., 2003, 2006; Kulikov et al., 2004; Serre et al., 2004). The results show mtDNA sequence patterns very similar to the patterns seen in living humans—and thus significantly different from the mtDNA patterns found in the eight Neandertals so far analyzed.

If these results are further confirmed, they provide strong *direct* evidence of a genetic discontinuity between Neandertals and these early fully modern humans. In other words, these data suggest that no—or very little—interbreeding took place between Neandertals and anatomically modern humans.

Still, there's a potentially serious problem with these latest DNA results from the early modern skeletons. The mtDNA sequences are so similar to those of modern humans that they could, in fact, be the result of contamination—that is, the amplified and sequenced DNA could belong to some person who recently handled the fossil. The molecular biologists who did this research took many experimental precautions, following standard practices used by other laboratories. But there's currently no way to rule out such contamination, which would likely have occurred during excavation. Still, the results do fit with an emerging overall agreement on the likely distinctions between Neandertals and modern humans.

PARTIAL REPLACEMENT MODELS

Various alternative perspectives also suggest that modern humans originated in Africa and then, when their population increased, expanded out of Africa into other areas of the Old World. But unlike those who subscribe to the complete replacement hypothesis, supporters of these partial replacement models claim that some interbreeding occurred between emigrating Africans and resident premodern populations elsewhere. So, partial replacement assumes that *no* speciation event occurred, and all these hominids should be considered members of *H. sapiens*. Günter Bräuer, of the University of Hamburg, suggests that very little interbreeding occurred—a view supported recently by John Relethford (2001) in what he describes as "mostly out of Africa." Fred Smith, of Loyola University, also favors an African origin of modern humans; but his "assimilation" model hypothesizes that in some regions, more interbreeding took place (Smith, 2002).

THE REGIONAL CONTINUITY MODEL: MULTIREGIONAL EVOLUTION

The regional continuity model is most closely associated with paleoanthropologist Milford Wolpoff, of the University of Michigan, and his associates (Wolpoff et al., 1994, 2001). They suggest that local populations—not all, of course—in Europe, Asia, and Africa continued their indigenous evolutionary development from premodern Middle Pleistocene forms to anatomically modern humans. But if that's true, then we have to ask how so many different local populations around the globe happened to evolve with such similar morphology. In other words, how could anatomically modern humans arise separately in different continents and end up so much alike, both physically and genetically? The multiregional model answers this question by (1) denying that the earliest modern *H. sapiens* populations originated *exclusively* in Africa, challenging the notion of complete replacement; and (2) asserting that significant levels of gene flow (migration) between premodern populations was extremely likely.

Through gene flow and natural selection, according to the multiregional hypothesis, local populations would *not* have evolved totally independently from one another, and such mixing would have "prevented speciation between the regional lineages and thus maintained human beings as a *single*, although obviously *polytypic* (see p. 381), species throughout the Pleistocene" (Smith et al., 1989). Thus, under a multiregional model there are no taxonomic distinctions between modern and premodern hominids. That is, all hominids from *H. erectus* though modern humans are classified as *H. sapiens*.

Advocates of the multiregional model aren't dogmatic about the degree of regional continuity. They recognize that a likely strong influence of African migrants existed throughout the world—and is still detectable today. Agreeing with Smith's assimilation model, this modified multiregionalism suggests that perhaps only minimal gene continuity existed in several regions (for example, western Europe) and that most modern genes are the result of large African migrations and/or more incremental gene flow (Relethford, 2001; Wolpoff et al., 2001).

SEEING THE BIG PICTURE

Looking beyond the arguments concerning modern human origins—which the popular media often overstates and overdramatizes—most paleoanthropologists now recognize an emerging consensus view. In fact, new evidence from fossils and especially from molecular comparisons is providing even more clarity. Data from sequenced ancient DNA, various patterns of contemporary human DNA, and the newest fossil finds from Ethiopia all suggest that a "strong" multiregional model is extremely unlikely. Supporters of this more extreme form of multiregionalism claim that modern human populations in Asia and Europe evolved *mostly* from local premodern ancestors—with only minor influence coming from African population expansion. But with the breadth and consistency of the latest research, for practical purposes, this strong version of multiregionalism is falsified.

Also, as various investigators integrate these new data, views are beginning to converge even further. Several researchers suggest an out-of-Africa model that leads to virtually complete replacement elsewhere. At the moment, this complete replacement rendition can't be falsified. Still, even devoted advocates of this strong replacement version recognize the potential for at least *some* interbreeding, although they believe it was likely very minor. We can conclude, then, that during the latter Pleistocene, one or more major migrations from Africa fueled the worldwide dispersal of modern humans. However, the African migrants might well have interbred with resident populations outside Africa. In a sense, it's all the same, whether we see this process either as very minimal multiregional continuity or as not quite complete replacement.

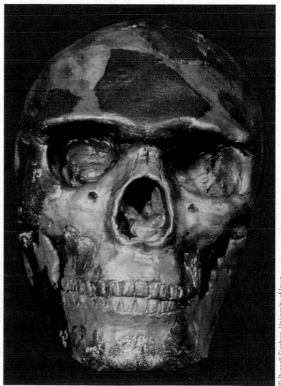

FIGURE 14-2

Reconstructed skull of Omo I, an early modern human from Ethiopia, dated to 195 kya. Note the clear presence of a chin.

The Earliest Discoveries of Modern Humans

AFRICA

In Africa, several early fossil finds have been interpreted as fully anatomically modern forms (see Fig. 14-1). The earliest of these specimens comes from Omo Kibish in southernmost Ethiopia. Recent redating of a fragmentary skull (Omo 1) demonstrates this is the earliest modern human yet found in Africa—or, for that matter, anywhere. Using ^{40}Ar/^{39}Ar and corroborating relative dating methods, the age for the Omo site is estimated at 195,000 ya (McDougall et al., 2005). A perplexing aspect of fossil finds at this site concerns the variation shown between the individuals. Omo 1 (see Fig. 14-2) is essentially modern in most respects (note the presence of a chin; Fig. 14-3), but another ostensibly contemporary cranium (Omo 2) is much more robust and less modern in morphology. Somewhat later African modern human fossils come from the Klasies River Mouth on the south coast and Border Cave, just slightly to the north. Using relatively new techniques, paleoanthropologists have dated both sites to about 120,000–80,000 ya. The original geological context at Border Cave is uncertain, and the fossils may be younger than those at Klasies River Mouth. Although recent reevaluation of the Omo site has provided much more dependable dating, there are still questions remaining about some of the other early African modern fossils. Nevertheless, it now seems very likely that early modern humans appeared in East Africa by shortly after

© Russell Ciochon, University of Iowa

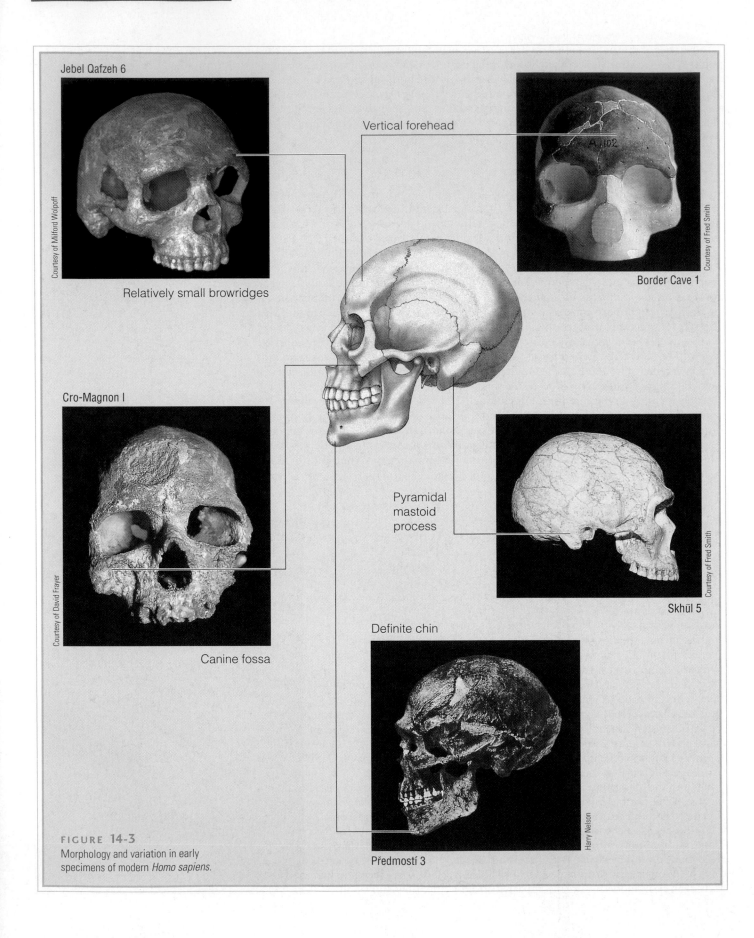

Jebel Qafzeh 6

Courtesy of Milford Wolpoff

Relatively small browridges

Vertical forehead

A.1102

Border Cave 1

Courtesy of Fred Smith

Cro-Magnon I

Courtesy of David Frayer

Canine fossa

Pyramidal
mastoid
process

Skhūl 5

Courtesy of Fred Smith

Definite chin

Předmostí 3

Harry Nelson

FIGURE 14-3
Morphology and variation in early
specimens of modern *Homo sapiens*.

200,000 ya and had migrated to southern Africa by approximately 100,000 ya. New fossil finds are helping confirm this view. Because either good preservation and/or accurate dating were lacking, scientists have been unsure whether even the earliest modern human fossil remains actually were from Africa (since some finds from the Middle East were perhaps as ancient).

Herto   The announcement in June 2003 of well-preserved *and* well-dated *H. sapiens* fossils from Ethiopia has now gone a long way toward filling these gaps in the African fossil record. As a result, these fossils are helping to resolve key issues regarding modern human origins. Tim White of the University of California, Berkeley, and his colleagues have been working for over a decade in the Middle Awash area of Ethiopia. They've discovered a remarkable array of early fossil hominids (*Ardipithecus, Australopithecus garhi,* and *Australopithecus anamensis*) as well as somewhat later forms (*H. erectus*). From this same area in the Middle Awash—in the Herto member of the Bouri formation—highly significant new discoveries came to light in 1997. For simplicity, these new hominids are referred to as the Herto remains.

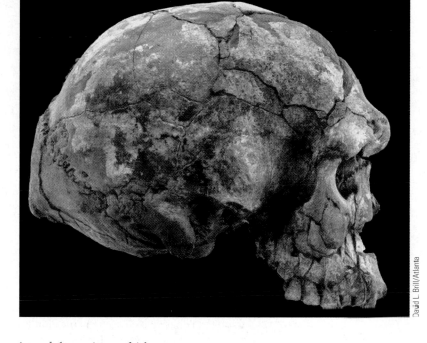

David L. Brill/Atlanta

FIGURE **14-4**
Herto cranium from Ethiopia, dated 160,000–154,000 ya. This is the best-preserved early modern *H. sapiens* cranium yet found.

These exciting new Herto fossils include a mostly complete adult cranium, a fairly complete (but heavily reconstructed) child's cranium, and another adult incomplete cranium as well as a few other cranial fragments. Following lengthy reconstruction and detailed comparative studies, White and colleagues were prepared to announce their findings in 2003.

What they found caused quite a sensation among paleoanthropologists, and it was reported in the popular press as well. First, well-controlled radiometric dating ($^{40}Ar/^{39}Ar$) securely places the remains at between 160,000 and 154,000 ya, making these the best-dated hominid fossils from this time period from anywhere in the world. And note, especially, that this date is clearly *older* than any other equally modern *Homo sapiens* from anywhere else in the world. Second, the preservation and morphology of the remains leave little doubt about their relationship to modern humans. The mostly complete adult cranium (Fig. 14-4) is very large, with an extremely long cranial vault. The cranial capacity is 1,450 cm³, well within the range of contemporary *H. sapiens* populations. The skull is also in some respects heavily built, with a large, arching browridge in front and a large, projecting occipital protuberance in back. The face does not project, in stark contrast to Eurasian Neandertals.

The overall impression is that this individual—as well as the child, aged 6 to 7 years, and the incomplete adult cranium—are clearly *Homo sapiens*. White and his team performed comprehensive statistical studies, comparing these fossils with other early *H. sapiens* remains as well as with a large series (over 3,000 crania) from modern populations. They concluded that while not identical to modern people, the Herto fossils are near modern. That is to say, these fossils "sample a population that is on the verge of anatomical modernity but not yet fully modern." (White et al., 2003, p. 745) To distinguish these individuals from fully modern humans (*H. sapiens sapiens*), the researchers have placed them in a newly defined subspecies: *Homo sapiens idaltu*. The word *idaltu*, from the Afar language, means "elder" (White et al., 2003).

Further analysis has shown that the morphological patterning of the crania doesn't specifically match that of *any* contemporary group of modern humans. What can we then conclude? First, we can say that these new finds strongly support an African origin of modern humans. The Herto fossils are the right age, and they come from the right place. Besides that, they look much like what we might have predicted. These new Herto finds are the most conclusive fossil evidence yet supporting an African origin of modern humans. They're thus compatible with an array of genetic data indicating some form of replacement model for human origins.

AT A GLANCE   Key Early Modern *Homo sapiens* Discoveries from Africa and the Near East

Site	Dates (ya)	Human Remains
Qafzeh (Israel)	110,000	Minimum of 20 individuals (*H. sapiens sapiens*)
Skhūl (Israel)	115,000	Minimum of 10 individuals (*H. sapiens sapiens*)
Omo (Ethiopia)	195,000	Two partial crania; one is more robust than the other (*H. sapiens sapiens*)
Herto (Ethiopia)	160,000–154,000	Dental and cranial remains of 4 individuals (*H. sapiens idaltu*)

THE NEAR EAST

In Israel, researchers found early modern *H. sapiens* fossils, including the remains of at least 10 individuals, in the Skhūl Cave at Mt. Carmel (Figs. 14-5 and 14-6a). This is very near the Neandertal site of Tabun, also located at Mt. Carmel. Also from Israel, the Qafzeh Cave has yielded the remains of at least 20 individuals (Fig. 14-6b). Although their overall configuration is definitely modern, some specimens show certain premodern features. Skhūl has been dated to between 100,000 and 130,000 ya (Grün et al., 2005) while Qafzeh has been dated to around 92,000–120,000 ya (Grün and Stringer, 1991). The time line for these fossil discoveries is shown in Figure 14-7.

Such early dates for modern specimens pose some problems for those advocating the influence of local evolution, as proposed by the multiregional model. How early do the premodern *H. sapiens* populations—that is, Neandertals—appear in the Near East? A recent chronometric calibration for the Tabun Cave suggests a date as early as 120,000 ya. This date for Tabun suggests that there's considerable overlap in the timing and occupation of the Near East by Neandertals and modern humans. This chronology runs counter to what would be predicted by the multiregional model. So, while Neandertals may *slightly* precede modern forms in the Near East, there still seems to be considerable overlap in the timing of occupation by these different humans. As you'll recall, the modern site of Skhūl is very near the Neandertal site at Tabun; they're both on Mt. Carmel, mere steps from one another. Clearly, the dynamics of *Homo sapiens* evolution in the Near East are highly complex (Shea, 1998), and no simple model may adequately explain later hominid evolution.

FIGURE 14-5

Mt. Carmel, studded with caves, was home to *H. sapiens sapiens* at Skhūl (and to Neandertals at Tabun and Kebara).

Courtesy, David Frayer

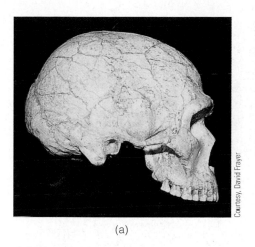

(a)

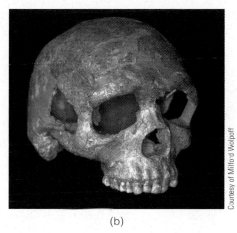

(b)

FIGURE **14-6**

(a) Skhūl 5. (b) Qafzeh 6. These specimens from Israel are thought to be representatives of early modern *Homo sapiens*. The vault height, forehead, and lack of prognathism are modern traits.

ASIA

There are six early anatomically modern human localities in China, the most significant of which are Liujiang, Upper Cave at Zhoukoudian, and Ordos in Mongolia (Fig. 14-8). The fossils from these Chinese sites are all fully modern, and all are considered to be from the Late Pleistocene with dates likely less than 40,000 ya. Upper Cave at Zhoukoudian has been dated to 27,000 ya and consists of three skulls found with cultural remains in a cave site that humans clearly regularly inhabited. The nearly complete human skull and partial skeleton from Liujiang Cave (in Guangxi Province) is also considered to be from the Late Pleistocene (although an older date has also been suggested). However, local farmers digging up some of the cave's limestone deposits for fertilizer originally found the remains, so it's no longer possible to determine their original context. It's thus unlikely that firm dates will ever be

FIGURE **14-7**

Time line of modern *Homo sapiens* discoveries. Note that most dates are approximations. Question marks indicate those estimates that are most tentative.

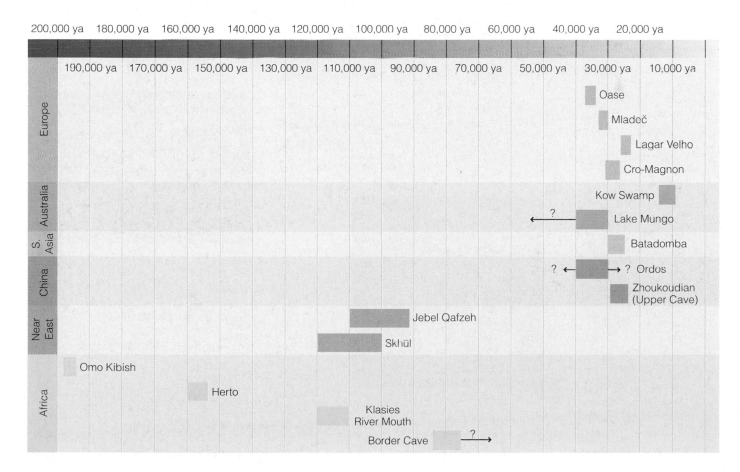

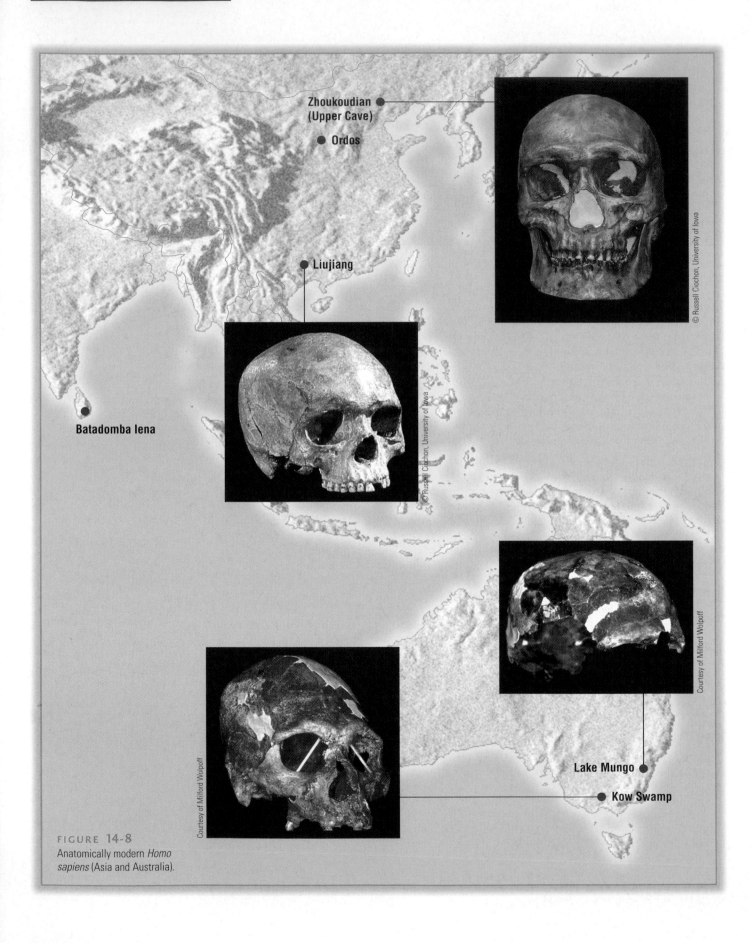

FIGURE 14-8
Anatomically modern *Homo sapiens* (Asia and Australia).

established, and Liujiang can't be regarded as the oldest anatomically modern material from China. Great antiquity has also been proposed for the Mongolian Ordos skull (Etler, personal communication), but this dating is not very secure and has therefore been questioned (Trinkaus, 2005).

In addition, some researchers (Tiemel et al., 1994) have suggested that the Jinniushan skeleton discussed in Chapter 13 (see p. 330) hints at modern features in China as early as 200,000 ya. If this date—as early as that proposed for direct antecedents of modern *H. sapiens* in Africa—should prove accurate, it would cast doubt on the complete replacement model. This position, however, is a minority view and is not supported by more recent and more detailed analyses. What's more, many Chinese paleoanthropologists take a position quite contrary to the complete replacement model and more in support of regional continuity. They thus see a continuous evolution first from Chinese *H. erectus* to premodern forms and finally to anatomically modern humans. This view is supported by Wolpoff, who mentions that materials from Upper Cave at Zhoukoudian "have a number of features that are characteristically regional" and that these features "are definitely not African" (1989, p. 83).*

In addition to the well-known finds from China, anatomically modern remains have been discovered in southern Asia. At Batadomba-lena, in southern Sri Lanka, modern *Homo sapiens* finds have been dated to 28,500 ya (Deraniyagala, 1992).

AUSTRALIA

During glacial times, the Indonesian islands were joined to the Asian mainland, but Australia was not. It's likely that by 50,000 ya, modern humans inhabited Sahul—the area including New Guinea and Australia. Bamboo rafts may have been the means of crossing the sea between islands, and doing so would've been dangerous and difficult. It's not known just where the future Australians came from, but Borneo, Java, and New Guinea have all been suggested.

Human occupation of Australia appears to have occurred quite early, with some archaeological sites dating to 55,000 ya. There's some controversy about dating of the earliest Australian human remains, which are all modern *H. sapiens*. The earliest finds so far discovered have come from Lake Mungo in southeastern Australia (see Fig. 14-8). In agreement with archaeological context and radiocarbon dates, the hominids from this site have been dated at approximately 30,000–25,000 ya. Newly determined age estimates, using electron spin resonance (ESR) and uranium-series dating (see p. 244), have dramatically extended the suggested time depth to about 60,000 ya (Thorne et al., 1999). The lack of correlation of these more ancient age estimates with other data, however, has some researchers seriously concerned (Gillespie and Roberts, 2000).

The recovery and sequencing of mitochondrial DNA from these prehistoric Australians is as intriguing—and controversial—as the early dating estimates (Adcock et al., 2001). The primary researchers are confident that these samples are authentically ancient, but the nagging possibility of contamination can't be entirely ruled out. Indeed, other researchers remain unconvinced that the mtDNA from Lake Mungo is ancient at all (Cooper et al., 2001). Obviously, because of the uncertainties, we'll need further corroboration for both the dating and DNA findings before passing judgment.

Unlike the more gracile early Australian forms from Lake Mungo are the Kow Swamp people, who are thought to have lived between about 14,000 and 9,000 ya (see Fig. 14-8). These fossils display certain archaic traits—such as receding foreheads, heavy supraorbital tori, and thick bones—that are difficult to explain since these features contrast with the postcranial anatomy, which matches that of recent native Australians.

CENTRAL EUROPE

Central Europe has been a source of many fossil finds, including the earliest anatomically modern *H. sapiens* yet discovered anywhere in Europe. Dated to 35,000 ya, the best dated

---

*Wolpoff's statement supports his multiregional hypothesis. His reference to Africa is a criticism of the complete replacement hypothesis.

of these early *H. sapiens* fossils come from recent discoveries at the Oase Cave in Romania (Fig 14-9). Here, cranial remains of three individuals were recovered, including a complete mandible and a partial skull (Fig. 14-10). While quite robust, these individuals are quite similar to later modern specimens, as seen in the clear presence of both a chin and a canine fossa (see Fig. 14-3, p. 358; Trinkaus et al., 2003).

Another early modern human site in Central Europe is Mladeč in the Czech Republic. Several individuals have been excavated here and are dated to approximately 31,000 ya. While there's some variation among the crania, including some with big browridges, Fred Smith (1984) is confident they're all best classified as modern *Homo sapiens* (see Fig 14-11a). After 28,000 ya modern humans are widely dispersed in Central and into western Europe

FIGURE **14-9**

Anatomically modern humans in Europe.

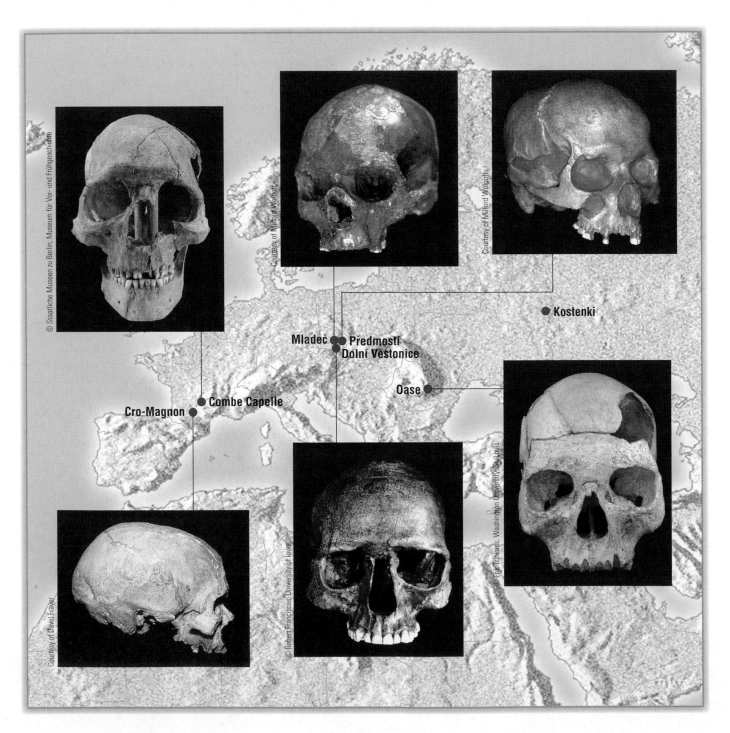

FIGURE **14-10**
Excavators at work within the spectacular cave at Oase in Romania. The floor is littered with the remains of fossil animals, including the earliest dated cranial remains of *Homo sapiens* in Europe.

(Trinkaus, 2005). A good example of one of these, also from the Czech Republic and dated at about 26,000 ya, comes from Dolní Věstonice—a site also famous for some of its archaeological remains (see Fig. 14-11b).

WESTERN EUROPE

For several reasons, one of them probably serendipity, western Europe and its fossils have received the most attention. Over the last 150 years, many of the scholars interested in this kind of research happened to live in western Europe, and the southern region of France happened to be a fossil treasure trove. Also, early on, discovering and learning about human ancestors caught the curiosity and pride of the local population.

As a result of this scholarly interest, beginning back in the nineteenth century, a great deal of data accumulated, and little reliable comparative information was available from elsewhere in the world. Consequently, theories of human evolution were based almost exclusively on

AT A GLANCE	Key Early Modern *Homo sapiens* Discoveries from Europe, Asia, and Australia	
Site	**Dates (ya)**	**Human Remains***
Abrigo do Lagar Velho (Portugal)	24,500	Four-year-old child's skeleton
Cro-Magnon (France)	30,000	8 individuals
Ordos (Mongolia, China)	40,000	1 individual
Kow Swamp (Australia)	14,000–9,000	Large sample (more than 40 individuals), including adults, juveniles, and infants
Lake Mungo (Australia)	?60,000–30,000	3 individuals, one a cremation

*Note: All fossils are classified as *H. sapiens sapiens*.

Courtesy of Milford Wolpoff

© Robert Franciscus, University of Iowa

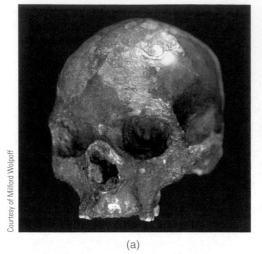

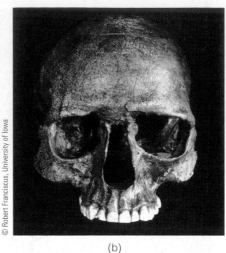

(a)   (b)

FIGURE 14-11

The Mladeč (a) and Dolní Věstonice (b) crania, both from the Czech Republic, represent good examples of early modern *Homo sapiens* in central Europe. Along with Oase in Romania, the evidence for early modern *Homo sapiens* appears first in central Europe before the later finds in western Europe.

Courtesy, David Frayer

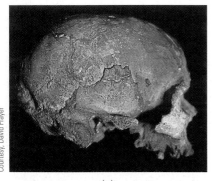

(a)

Courtesy of Milford Wolpoff

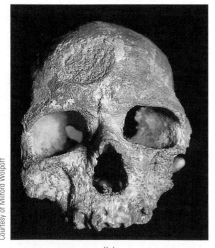

(b)

FIGURE 14-12

Cro-Magnon I (France). In this specimen, modern traits are quite clear. (a) Lateral view. (b) Frontal view.

Cro-Magnon (crow-man´-yon)

Aurignacian Pertaining to an Upper Paleolithic stone tool industry in Europe beginning at about 40,000 ya.

the western European material. It's only been in recent years, with growing evidence from other areas of the world and with the application of new dating techniques, that recent human evolutionary dynamics are being seriously considered from a worldwide perspective.

Western Europe has yielded many anatomically modern human fossils, but by far the best-known sample of western European *H. sapiens* is from the **Cro-Magnon** site. From a rock shelter in southern France, remains of eight individuals were discovered here in 1868.

The Cro-Magnon materials are associated with an **Aurignacian** tool assemblage, an Upper Paleolithic industry. Dated at about 28,000 ya, these individuals represent the earliest of France's anatomically modern humans. The so-called Old Man (CroMagnon I) became the original model for what was once termed the CroMagnon, or Upper Paleolithic, "race" of Europe (Fig. 14-12). Actually, of course, there's no such valid biological category, and CroMagnon I is not typical of Upper Paleolithic western Europeans—and not even all that similar to the other two male skulls found at the site.

Most of the genetic evidence, as well as the newest fossil evidence, from Africa argues against continuous local evolution producing modern groups directly from any Eurasian premodern population (in Europe, these would be Neandertals). Still, for some researchers, the issue isn't completely settled. With all the latest evidence, there's no longer much debate that a *large* genetic contribution from migrating early modern Africans influenced other groups throughout the Old World. What's being debated is just how much admixture might have occurred between these migrating Africans and the resident premodern groups. One group of researchers who have evaluated genetic evidence from living populations (Eswaran et al., 2005) suggests that significant admixture occurred in much of the Old World. What's more, for those paleoanthropologists who also think significant admixture ("assimilation") occurred in western Europe as well as elsewhere (e.g., Trinkaus, 2005), a recently discovered child's skeleton from Portugal provides some of the best evidence of ostensible interbreeding between Neandertals and anatomically modern *H. sapiens*. This important new discovery from the Abrigo do Lagar Velho site (see "A Closer Look," p. 367) was excavated in late 1998 and is dated to 24,500 ya—that's at least 5,000 years *later* than the last clearly Neandertal find. Associated with an Upper Paleolithic industry, and buried with red ocher and pierced shell, is a fairly complete skeleton of a 4-year-old child (Duarte et al., 1999). In studying the remains, Cidália Duarte, Erik Trinkaus, and colleagues found a highly mixed set of anatomical features. Many characteristics, especially of the teeth, lower jaw, and pelvis, were like those seen in anatomically modern humans. Yet, several other features—including lack of chin, limb proportions, and muscle insertions—were more similar to Neandertal traits. The authors thus conclude that "The presence of such admixture suggests the hypothesis of variable admixture between early modern humans dispersing into Europe and local Neandertal populations" (Duarte et al., 1999, p. 7608). They suggest that this new evidence strongly supports the partial replacement model while seriously weakening the complete replacement model. Of course, the evidence from one child's skeleton—while intriguing—certainly isn't going to convince everyone.

Hybridization in the Fossil Record: What *Exactly* Were Those Hominids Doing at Lagar Velho?

In 1999 researchers from Portugal announced an exciting discovery from the Lapedo Valley in central Portugal (Duarte et al., 1999). At the site of Lagar Velho, researchers excavated a Gravettian burial containing the largely complete skeleton of a 4-year-old child dated to around 24,500 ya (Fig. 1). What made this discovery particularly interesting was that the researchers claimed that the Lagar Velho child, as it's been called, represented a hybrid between Neandertals and modern humans: a Paleolithic lovechild of sorts. That is, the Lagar Velho child's anatomy was suggestive of generations of genetic admixture between indigenous Neandertal populations and modern humans who had migrated into Europe. Researchers looked to several morphological features as evidence of hybridization. For example, the mandible clearly exhibits a chin, which is a telltale sign of modernity. At the same time, though, this region recedes, as in Neandertals. In addition, aspects of the postcrania—such as limb proportions and robusticity of the skeleton—indicate the possible influence of Neandertal genes.

This interpretation of the Lagar Velho skeleton as a combination of both Neandertal and modern human morphology (which resulted from genetic admixture) is highly controversial. Adding to the controversy is the fact that the remains are those of a small child. Most anatomical characteristics used to define fossil species are normally based on adult skeletons, and there's no way to tell what this individual would have looked like once fully grown; we can only make predictions.

This isn't the first time that researchers have interpreted the morphology of hominid fossils as the result of hybridization. Later Neandertals such as those found at the sites of St. Césaire in France and from the upper levels at the site of Vindija in Croatia have also been regarded as the result of genetic admixture. While there's no consensus on whether or not these fossils are *actually* the product of hybridization, what makes the interpretation of the Lagar Velho remains so important is that they have stimulated significant discussion and research into the concept of genetic admixture in the fossil record. This discussion led paleoanthropologists to ask some important questions regarding the nature of population hybridization.

All of the proposed models of modern human origins must deal with, to some extent, the question of hybridization between Neandertals and modern humans. This is particularly true of the assimilation model since it's based on significant levels of genetic exchange between Neandertal and modern human populations. Thus, the ability for Neandertals and modern humans to hybridize speaks directly to one of the most frequently asked questions in paleoanthropology: "What happened to the Neandertals?" Did they go extinct due to competition with modern humans, or were they genetically assimilated by these new European inhabitants?

Looking for signs of hybridization in the fossil record is a challenging endeavor, for the obvious reason that we can't directly observe the breeding habits of fossil hominids. Researchers therefore must turn to other areas of inquiry to begin to understand the nature of genetic barriers that define a species. One type of study that's shedding new light on this issue is exemplified by the research of Trent Holliday of Tulane University. He and his colleagues have comprehensively investigated hybridization among extant species of primates as well as among other mammals. In particular, Holliday's study of genetic admixture in living animals has allowed researchers to understand not only the genetic markers associated with hybridization but also the morphological differences that result from the pairing of different species. By applying this type of research to the study of modern human origins, we can begin to address and test hypotheses regarding hybridization between Neandertals and modern humans.

© Portuguese Institute of Archaeology

FIGURE 1
The skeleton of the Lagar Velho child thought by some to be a Neandertal-modern human hybrid.

Something New and Different

As we've seen, by 25,000 years ago, modern humans had dispersed to all major areas of the Old World, and they would soon journey to the New World as well. But at about the same time, remnant populations of earlier hominids still survived in a few remote and isolated corners. We mentioned in Chapter 12 that populations of *Homo erectus* in Java managed to survive on this island long after their cousins had disappeared from other areas, for example, China and East Africa. What's more, even though they persisted well into the Late Pleistocene, physically these Javanese hominids were still very similar to other *H. erectus* (see p. 300).

Even more surprising, it seems that other populations branched off from some of these early inhabitants of Indonesia and either intentionally or accidentally found their way to other, smaller islands to the east. There, under even more extreme isolation pressures, they evolved in an astonishing direction. In late 2004, the world awoke to the startling announcement that an extremely small-bodied, small-brained hominid had been discovered in Liang Bua Cave on the island of Flores, east of Java (see Fig. 14-13). Dubbed the "Little Lady of Flores" or simply "Flo," the remains consist of an incomplete skeleton of an adult female (LB1) as well as additional pieces from nine other individuals, which the press have collectively nicknamed "hobbits." The female skeleton is remarkable in several ways (Fig. 14-14), though surprisingly similar to the Dmanisi hominids (from which they may be derived; see p. 302). First, she stood barely 3 feet tall—as short as the smallest australopithecine—and her brain, estimated at a mere 417 cm³ (Falk, 2005), was no larger than that of a chimpanzee (Brown et al., 2004). Possibly most startling of all, these extraordinary hominids were still living on Flores just 13,000 ya (Morwood et al., 2004, 2005)!

Where did they come from? As we said, their predecessors were probably *H. erectus* populations like those found on Java. How they got to Flores—some 400 miles away, partly over open ocean—is a mystery. There are several connecting islands, and to get between them, these hominids may have drifted across on rafts; but there's no way to be sure of this.

How did they get to be so physically different from all other known hominids? Here we're a little more certain of the answer. Isolated island populations can quite rapidly diverge from their relatives elsewhere—as we noted in "A Closer Look" in Chapter 5. Among such isolated animals, natural selection frequently favors reduced body size. For example, populations of dwarf elephants are found on islands in the Mediterranean as well as on some channel islands off the coast of southern California. And perhaps most interesting of all, dwarf elephants *also* evolved on Flores; they were found in the same geological beds with the little hominids. The evolutionary mechanism (called "insular dwarfing") thought to explain such extreme body size reduction in both the elephants and the hominids is an adaptation to a reduced amount of resources, leading through selection to smaller size.

Other than short stature, what did the Flores hominids look like? In their cranial shape, thickness of cranial bone, and dentition, they most resemble *Homo erectus*, and specifically

FIGURE **14-13**
Location of the Flores site in Indonesia.

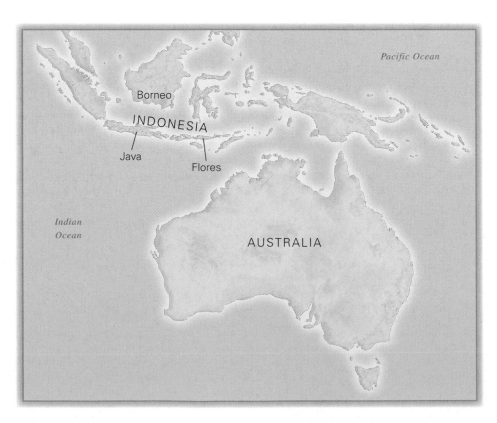

© Peter Brown

FIGURE **14-14**
Cranium of adult female *Homo floresiensis* from Flores, Indonesia, dated 18,000 ya.

those from Dmanisi. Still, they have some derived features that also set them apart from all other hominids. For that reason, many researchers have placed them in a separate species, *Homo floresiensis*.

In the two years following the first publication of the Flores remains, considerable controversy has arisen regarding their interpretation (Jacob et al., 2006; Martin et al., 2006). Some researchers have argued the small-brained find (LB1) is actually a pathological modern *H. sapiens* afflicted with a severe growth disorder called microcephaly.

The researchers who did most of the initial work reject this conclusion and provide some further details to support their original interpretation (for example, Dean Falk's further analysis of microcephalic endocasts—as reported in Bower, 2006).

The conclusion that among this already small-bodied island population the one individual found with a preserved cranium happened to be afflicted with a severe (and rare) growth defect is highly unlikely. Yet, it must also be recognized that long-term, extreme isolation of hominids on Flores leading to a new species showing dramatic body size dwarfing and even more dramatic brain size reduction, is also not very likely.

A third possibility has been suggested by U.C. Berkeley anthropologist Gary Richards. He argues that LB1 (and her fellow little Flores hominids) are normal *H. sapiens*, but ones that have had a microevolutionary change leading to unusually small body and brain size (Richards, 2006).

So where does this leave us? Because a particular interpretation is unlikely, it is not necessarily incorrect. We do know, for example, that such "insular dwarfing" has occured in other mammals (see p. 104). For the moment, the most comprehensive analyses suggest the possibility that a new hominid species (*H. floresiensis*) did, in fact, evolve on Flores. But this conclusion requires more detailed and more convincing evidence. There is a strong likelihood that DNA can be retrieved from the Flores bones and sequenced. Analysis of this DNA will go a long way to solving the mystery.

Technology and Art in the Upper Paleolithic

EUROPE

The cultural period known as the Upper Paleolithic began in western Europe approximately 40,000 years ago (Fig. 14-15). Upper Paleolithic cultures are usually divided into five different industries, based on stone tool technologies: (1) Chatelperronian, (2) Aurignacian, (3) Gravettian, (4) Solutrean, and (5) Magdalenian. Major environmental shifts were also apparent during this period. During the last glacial period, about 30,000 ya, a warming trend lasting several thousand years partially melted the glacial ice. The result was that much of Eurasia was covered by tundra and steppe, a vast area of treeless country dotted with lakes and marshes. In many areas in the north, permafrost prevented the growth of trees but permitted the growth, in the short summers, of flowering plants, mosses, and other kinds of vegetation. This vegetation served as an enormous pasture for herbivorous animals, large and small, and carnivorous animals fed off the herbivores. It was a hunter's paradise, with millions of animals dispersed across expanses of tundra and grassland, from Spain through Europe and into the Russian steppes.

Large herds of reindeer roamed the tundra and steppes, along with mammoths, bison, horses, and a host of smaller animals that served as a bountiful source of food. In addition, humans exploited fish and fowl systematically for the first time, especially along the southern tier of Europe. It was a time of relative abundance, and ultimately Upper Paleolithic people spread out over Europe, living in caves and open-air camps and building large shelters. Far more elaborate burials are also found, most spectacularly at the 24,000-year-old Sungir site near Moscow (Fig. 14-16), where grave goods included a bed of red

FIGURE **14-15**

Cultural periods of the European Upper Paleolithic and their approximate beginning dates.

GLACIAL	UPPER PALEOLITHIC (beginnings)	CULTURAL PERIODS
W Ü R M	17,000 – 21,000 – 27,000 – 40,000 –	Magdalenian Solutrean Gravettian Aurignacian Chatelperronian
Middle Paleolithic		Mousterian

369

FIGURE **14-16**
Skeleton of two teenagers, a male and a female, from Sungir, Russia. Dated 24,000 ya, this is the richest find of any Upper Paleolithic grave.

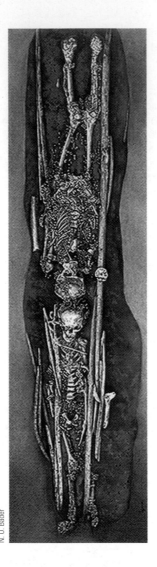

N. O. Bader

FIGURE **14-17**
(a) Burin. A very common Upper Paleolithic tool. (b) Solutrean blade. This is the best-known work of the Solutrean tradition. Solutrean stonework is considered the most highly developed of any Upper Paleolithic industry.

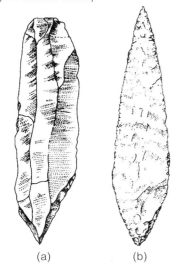

(a)   (b)

FIGURE **14-18**
Spear-thrower (atlatl). Note the carving.

Magdalenian   Pertaining to the final phase of the Upper Paleolithic stone tool industry in Europe.

burins   Small, chisel-like tools with a pointed end; thought to have been used to engrave bone, antler, ivory, or wood.

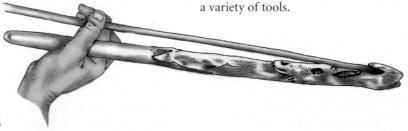

ocher, thousands of ivory beads, long spears made of straightened mammoth tusks, ivory engravings, and jewelry (Formicola and Buzhilova, 2004). During this period, either western Europe or perhaps portions of Africa achieved the highest population density in human history up to that time (see "A Closer Look," p. 371).

Humans and other animals in the midlatitudes of Eurasia had to cope with shifts in climatic conditions, some of them quite rapid. For example, at 20,000 ya another climatic "pulse" caused the weather to become noticeably colder in Europe and Asia as the continental glaciations reached their maximum extent for this entire glacial period, which is called the Würm in Eurasia.

As a variety of organisms attempted to adapt to these changing conditions, *Homo sapiens* had a major advantage: the elaboration of an increasingly sophisticated technology, and most likely other components of culture as well. In fact, probably one of the greatest challenges facing numerous Late Pleistocene mammals was the ever more dangerously equipped humans—a trend that has continued to modern times.

The Upper Paleolithic was an age of technological innovation that can be compared to the past few hundred years in our recent history of amazing technological change after centuries of relative inertia. Anatomically modern humans of the Upper Paleolithic not only invented new and specialized tools (Fig. 14-17) but, as we've seen, also greatly increased the use of—and probably experimented with—new materials, such as bone, ivory, and antler.

Solutrean tools are good examples of Upper Paleolithic skill and perhaps aesthetic appreciation as well (see Fig. 14-17b). In this lithic (stone) tradition, stoneknapping developed to the finest degree ever known. Using specialized flaking techniques, the artist/technicians made beautiful parallel-flaked lance heads, expertly flaked on both surfaces. The lance points are so delicate that they can be considered works of art that quite possibly never served, nor were they intended to serve, a utilitarian purpose.

The last stage of the Upper Paleolithic, known as the **Magdalenian**, saw even more advances in technology. The spear-thrower, or atlatl, was a wooden or bone hooked rod that acted to extend the hunter's arm, thus enhancing the force and distance of a spear throw (Fig. 14-18). For catching salmon and other fish, the barbed harpoon is a clever example of the craftsperson's skill. There's also evidence that the bow and arrow may have been used for the first time during this period. The introduction of much more efficient manufacturing methods, such as the punch blade technique (Fig. 14-19), provided an abundance of standardized stone blades. These could be fashioned into **burins** (see Fig. 14-17a) for working wood, bone, and antler; borers for drilling holes in skins, bones, and shells; and knives with serrated or notched edges for scraping wooden shafts into a variety of tools.

A CLOSER LOOK   Maybe, You Can Take It with You

The practice of deliberately burying the dead is an important and distinctive aspect of later human biocultural evolution. We saw in Chapter 13 that Neandertals buried their dead at a number of sites; but we also noted that the assortment of grave goods found in Neandertal burials was pretty sparse (see p. 343).

Something remarkable happened with the appearance and dispersal of modern humans. Suddenly—at least in archaeological terms—graves became much more elaborate. And, it wasn't just that many more items were placed with the deceased; it was also the kinds of objects. Neandertal graves sometimes contain a few stone tools and some unmodified animal bones, such as cave bear. But fully modern humans seem to have had more specialized and far more intensive cultural capacities. For example, from 40,000 years ago at Twilight Cave in Kenya, researchers have found 600 fragments of carefully drilled ostrich eggshell beads (Klein and Edgar, 2002). These beads aren't directly associated with a human burial, but they do show us an intensification of craft specialization and possibly a much greater interest in personal adornment.

A locale where such elaborate grave goods (including beads) have been found in association with Upper Paleolithic modern human burials is the famous Cro-Magnon site in southwestern France. Likewise, numerous elaborate grave goods were found with human burials at Grimaldi in Italy.

No doubt, the richest Upper Paleolithic burial sites are those at Sungir in Russia. Parts of several individuals have been recovered there, dating to about 24,000 ya. However, three individuals were found in direct association with thousands of ivory beads and other elaborate grave goods. Two of the individuals, a girl and boy aged about 9–10 and 12–13, were buried together head to head in a spectacular grave (see Fig. 14-16). The more than 10,000 beads excavated here likely once were woven into clothing, a task that would have been extraordinarily time-consuming. The two individuals were placed directly on a bed of red ocher, and with them were two magnificent spears made of straightened mammoth tusks—one of them more than 6½ feet (240 cm) long! Plus, there were hundreds of drilled fox canine teeth, pierced antlers, and ivory carvings of animals, as well as ivory pins and pendants (Formicola and Buzhilova, 2004).

Producing all of these items that were so carefully placed with these two young individuals took thousands of hours of labor. Indeed, one estimate suggests that it took 10,000 hours just to make the beads (Klein and Edgar, 2002). What were the Magdalenian people who went to all this trouble thinking? The double burial is certainly the most extravagant of any from the Upper Paleolithic, but another at Sungir is almost as remarkable. Here, the body of an adult male—perhaps about 40 years old when he died—was also found with thousands of beads, and he too was carefully laid out on a bed of red ocher.

Sungir is likely a somewhat extraordinary exception; still, far more elaborate graves are often found associated with early modern humans than was ever the case in earlier cultures. At Sungir, and to a lesser extent at other sites, it took hundreds or even thousands of hours to produce the varied and intricate objects.

The individuals who were buried with these valuable goods must have been seen as special. Did they have unique talents, were they leaders or children of leaders, or did they have some special religious or ritual standing? For sure, this evidence is the earliest we have from human history revealing highly defined social status. Thousands of years later, the graves of the Egyptian pharaohs express the same thing—as do the elaborate monuments seen in most contemporary cemeteries. The Magdalenians and other Upper Paleolithic cultures were indeed much like us. They too may have tried to defy death and take it with them!

By producing many more specialized tools, Upper Paleolithic peoples probably had more resources available to them; they may also have had an impact on the biology of these populations. Emphasizing a biocultural interpretation, C. Loring Brace of the University of Michigan has suggested that with more effective tools as well as the use of fire allowing for more efficient food processing, anatomically modern *H. sapiens* wouldn't have required the large teeth and facial skeletons seen in earlier populations.

In addition to their reputation as hunters, western Europeans of the Upper Paleolithic are even better known for their symbolic representation, or what has commonly been called art. Given uncertainties about what actually should be called "art," archaeologist Margaret Conkey of the University of California, Berkeley, refers to Upper Paleolithic cave paintings, sculptures, engravings, and so forth as "visual and material imagery" (Conkey, 1987, p. 423). We'll continue using the term *art* to describe many of these prehistoric representations, but you should recognize that we do so mainly as a cultural convention—and perhaps a limiting one.

It's also important to remember that there is an extremely wide geographical distribution of symbolic images, best known from many parts of Europe, but now also well documented from Siberia, North Africa, South Africa, and Australia. Given a 25,000-year time depth of what we call Paleolithic art, and its nearly worldwide distribution, we can indeed observe marked variability in expression.

(a) A large core is selected and the top portion is removed by use of a hammerstone.

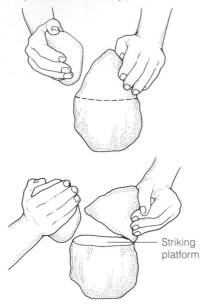

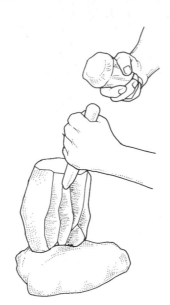

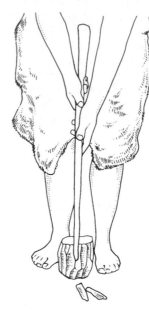

Striking platform

(b) The objective is to create a flat surface called a striking platform.

(c) Next, the core is struck by use of a hammer and punch (made of bone or antler) to remove the long narrow flakes (called blades).

(d) Or the blades can be removed by pressure flaking.

(e) The result is the production of highly consistent sharp blades, which can be used, as is, as knives; or they can be further modified (retouched) to make a variety of other tools (such as burins, scrapers, and awls).

FIGURE 14-19
The punch blade technique.

FIGURE 14-20
Magdalenian bone artifact. Note the realistic animal engraving on this object, the precise function of which is unknown.

Besides cave art, there are many examples of small sculptures excavated from sites in western, central, and eastern Europe. Perhaps the most famous of these are the female figurines, popularly known as "Venuses," found at such sites as Brassempouy, France, and Grimaldi, Italy. Some of these figures were realistically carved, and the faces appear to be modeled after actual women. Other figurines may seem grotesque, with sexual characteristics exaggerated, perhaps for fertility or other ritual purposes.

Beyond these quite well-known figurines, there are numerous other examples of what's frequently called portable art, including elaborate engravings on tools and tool handles (Fig. 14-20). Such symbolism can be found in many parts of Europe and was already well established early in the Aurignacian—by 33,000 ya. Innovations in symbolic representations also benefited from, and probably further stimulated, technological advances. New methods of mixing pigments and applying them were important in rendering painted or drawn images. Bone and ivory carving and engraving were made easier with the use of special stone tools (see Fig. 14-17). At two sites in the Czech Republic, Dolní Věstonice and Předmostí (both dated at approximately 26,000–27,000 ya), small animal figures were fashioned from fired clay. This is the first documented use of ceramic technology anywhere, and in fact it precedes later pottery invention by more than 15,000 years.

But it wasn't until the final phases of the Upper Paleolithic, particularly during the Magdalenian, that European prehistoric art reached its climax. Cave art is now known from more than 150 separate sites, the vast majority from southwestern France and northern Spain. Apparently, in other areas the rendering of such images did not take place in deep caves. Peoples in central Europe, China, Africa, and elsewhere certainly may have painted or carved representations on rock faces in the open, but these images long since would have eroded. So, we're fortunate that the people of at least one of the many sophisticated cultures of the Upper Paleolithic chose to journey belowground to create their artwork, preserving it not just for their immediate descendants, but for us as well. The most spectacular and most famous of the cave art sites are Lascaux and Grotte Chauvet in France and Altamira in Spain.

For example in Lascaux Cave, immense wild bulls dominate what's called the Great Hall of Bulls; and horses, deer, and other animals drawn with remarkable skill adorn the walls in black, red, and yellow. Equally impressive, at Altamira the walls and ceiling of an immense cave are filled with superb portrayals of bison in red and black. The "artist" even took advantage of bulges in the walls to create a sense of relief in the paintings. The cave is a treasure of beautiful art whose meaning has never been satisfactorily explained. It could have been religious or magical, a form of visual communication, or simply art for the sake of beauty.

Inside the cave called Grotte Chauvet, preserved unseen for perhaps 30,000 years, are a multitude of images, including dots, stenciled human handprints, and, most dramatically, hundreds of animal representations. Radiocarbon dating has placed the paintings during the Aurignacian, likely more than 35,000 ya, making Grotte Chauvet considerably earlier than the Magdalenian sites of Lascaux and Altamira (Balter, 2006).

AFRICA

Early accomplishments in rock art, possibly as early as in Europe, are seen in southern Africa (Namibia) at the Apollo 11 rock shelter site, where painted slabs have been identified dating to between 26 and 28 kya (Wendt, 1976; Freundlich et al., 1980; Vogelsang, 1998). In addition, incised ostrich eggshell fragments from the site may be much older (Kokis, 1988; Miller et al., 1999). Similarly, the Blombos Cave site is revealing amazing artifacts, including incised ochre fragments and various bone tools that are dated to 77 kya. In addition, more than forty tick shell beads have been found at Blombos Cave that are dated to this same early time range (Henshilwood and Sealey, 1997; Henshilwood et al., 2002; Henshilwood et al., 2004). In terms of stone tool technology, microliths (thumbnail-sized stone flakes hafted to make knives, saws, etc.) and blades characterize Late Stone Age* African industries. In central Africa there was also considerable use of bone and antler, some of it possibly quite early.

In terms of stone tool technology, microliths (thumbnail-sized stone flakes hafted to make knives, saws, etc.) and blades characterize Late Stone Age* African industries. In central Africa there was also considerable use of bone and antler, some of it possibly quite early. Excavations in the Katanda area of the eastern portion of the Democratic Republic of the Congo (Fig. 14-21) have shown remarkable development of bone craftwork. Dating of the site is quite early. Initial results using ESR and TL dating indicate an age as early as 80,000 ya (Feathers and Migliorini, 2001). From these intriguing data, preliminary reports by Alison Brooks of George Washington University and John Yellen of the National Science Foundation have demonstrated that these technological achievements rival those of the more renowned European Upper Paleolithic (Yellen et al., 1995).

Summary of Upper Paleolithic Culture

In looking back at the Upper Paleolithic, we can see it as the culmination of 2 million years of cultural development. Change proceeded incredibly slowly for most of the Pleistocene; but as cultural traditions and materials accumulated, and the brain—and, we assume, intelligence—expanded and reorganized, the rate of change quickened.

Cultural evolution continued with the appearance of early premodern humans and moved a bit faster with later premoderns. Neandertals in Eurasia and their contemporaries elsewhere added deliberate burials, technological innovations, and much more.

Building on existing cultures, late Pleistocene populations attained sophisticated cultural and material heights in a seemingly short—by previous standards—burst of exciting activity. In Europe and central Africa particularly, there seem to have been dramatic cultural innovations, among them big game hunting with powerful new weapons such as harpoons, spear-throwers, and possibly the bow and arrow. Other innovations included body ornaments, needles, "tailored" clothing, and burials with elaborate grave goods—a practice that may indicate some sort of status hierarchy.

This dynamic age was doomed, or so it seems, by the climatic changes of about 10,000 ya. As the temperature slowly rose and the glaciers retreated, animal and plant species were

---

*The Late Stone Age in Africa is equivalent to the Upper Paleolithic in Eurasia.

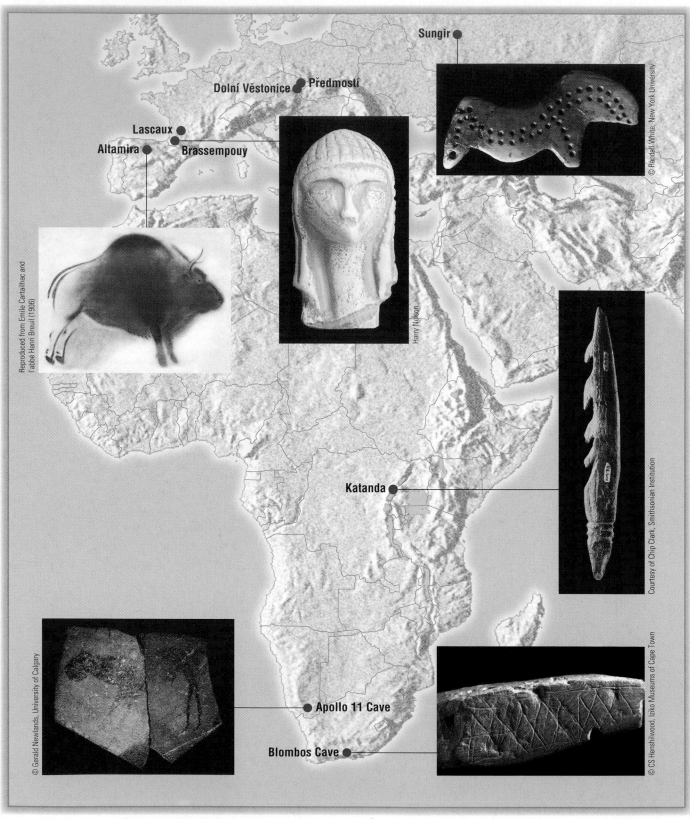

FIGURE 14-21

Symbolic artifacts from the Middle Stone Age of Africa and the Upper Paleolithic in Europe. It is notable that evidence of symbolism is found in Blombos Cave (77 kya) and Katanda (80 kya), both in Africa, a full 50 thousand years *before* any comparable evidence is known from Europe.

seriously affected, and in turn these changes affected humans. As traditional prey animals were depleted or disappeared altogether, humans had to seek other means of obtaining food.

Grinding hard seeds or roots became important, and as humans grew more familiar with propagating plants, they began to domesticate both plants and animals. Human dependence on domestication became critical, and with it came permanent settlements, new technology, and more complex social organization. This continuing story of human biocultural evolution will be the topic of the remainder of this text.

VISUAL SUMMARY

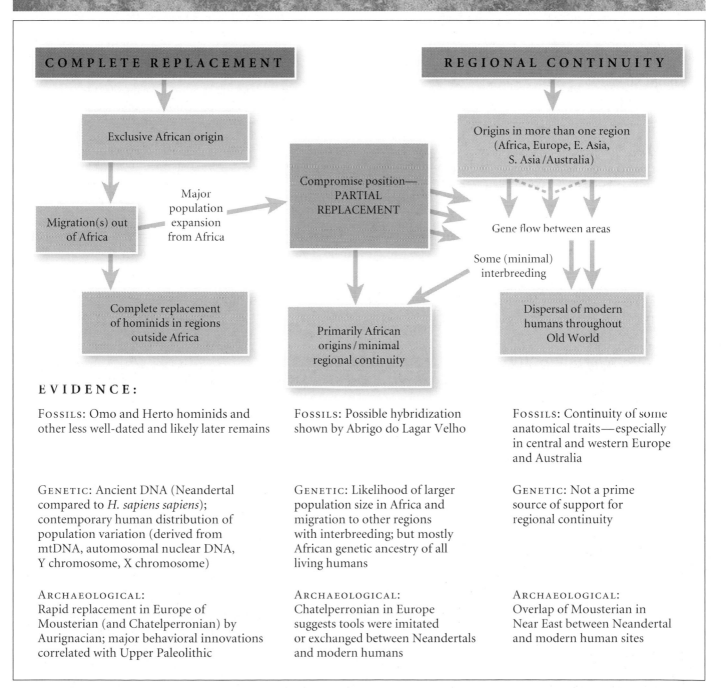

COMPLETE REPLACEMENT

Exclusive African origin

Migration(s) out of Africa

Major population expansion from Africa

Complete replacement of hominids in regions outside Africa

Compromise position—
PARTIAL REPLACEMENT

Primarily African origins / minimal regional continuity

REGIONAL CONTINUITY

Origins in more than one region (Africa, Europe, E. Asia, S. Asia / Australia)

Gene flow between areas

Some (minimal) interbreeding

Dispersal of modern humans throughout Old World

EVIDENCE:

FOSSILS: Omo and Herto hominids and other less well-dated and likely later remains

FOSSILS: Possible hybridization shown by Abrigo do Lagar Velho

FOSSILS: Continuity of some anatomical traits—especially in central and western Europe and Australia

GENETIC: Ancient DNA (Neandertal compared to *H. sapiens sapiens*); contemporary human distribution of population variation (derived from mtDNA, automosomal nuclear DNA, Y chromosome, X chromosome)

GENETIC: Likelihood of larger population size in Africa and migration to other regions with interbreeding; but mostly African genetic ancestry of all living humans

GENETIC: Not a prime source of support for regional continuity

ARCHAEOLOGICAL:
Rapid replacement in Europe of Mousterian (and Chatelperronian) by Aurignacian; major behavioral innovations correlated with Upper Paleolithic

ARCHAEOLOGICAL:
Chatelperronian in Europe suggests tools were imitated or exchanged between Neandertals and modern humans

ARCHAEOLOGICAL:
Overlap of Mousterian in Near East between Neandertal and modern human sites

Summary: Putting It All Together

For the past two decades, and there's no end in sight, researchers have fiercely debated the date and location of the origin of anatomically modern human beings. One hypothesis (complete replacement) claims that anatomically modern forms first evolved in Africa more than 100,000 ya and then, migrating out of Africa, completely replaced premodern *H. sapiens* in the rest of the world. Another school (regional continuity) takes a completely opposite view and maintains that in various geographical regions of the world, local groups of premodern *H. sapiens* evolved directly to anatomically modern humans. A third hypothesis (partial replacement) takes a somewhat middle position, suggesting an African origin but also accepting some later hybridization outside of Africa.

Recent research coming from several sources is beginning to clarify the origins of modern humans. Molecular evidence, as well as the dramatic new fossil finds from Herto in Ethiopia, suggests that a multiregional origin of modern humans is unlikely. Sometime, soon after 150,000 ya, complete replacement of all hominids outside Africa may have occurred when migrating Africans displaced the populations in other regions. However, such absolutely *complete* replacement will be very difficult to prove, and it's not really what we'd expect. More than likely, at least some interbreeding probably did take place. Still, it's looking more and more like there wasn't very much intermixing of migrating African populations with other Old World groups.

Archaeological evidence of early modern humans also paints a fascinating picture of our most immediate ancestors. The Upper Paleolithic was an age of extraordinary innovation and achievement in technology and art. Many new and complex tools were introduced, and their production indicates fine skill in working wood, bone, and antler. Cave art in France and Spain displays the masterful ability of Upper Paleolithic painters, and beautiful sculptures have been found at many European sites. Sophisticated symbolic representations have also been found in Africa and elsewhere. Upper Paleolithic *Homo sapiens* displayed amazing development in a relatively short period of time. The culture produced during this period led the way to still newer and more complex cultural techniques and methods.

In Table 14-1 you'll find a useful summary of the most significant fossil discoveries discussed in this chapter.

TABLE 14-1	Most Significant Modern *Homo sapiens* Discoveries Discussed in This Chapter		
Site	**Dates (ya)**	**Human Remains**	**Comments**
Abrigo do Lagar Velho (Portugal)	24,500	Four-year-old child's skeleton	Possible evidence of hybridization between Neandertals and modern *H. sapiens*
Cro-Magnon (France)	30,000	8 individuals	Famous site of early modern *H. sapiens,* but there are dozens of other sites in Europe and elsewhere
Oase Cave (Romania)	35,000	Portions of 3 crania	Earliest well-dated modern humans from Europe
Qafzeh (Israel)	110,000	Minimum of 20 individuals	Quite early site; shows considerable variation
Skhūl (Israel)	115,000	Minimum of 10 individuals	Earliest well-dated modern *H. sapiens* outside of Africa; also perhaps contemporaneous with neighboring Tabun Neandertal site
Herto (Ethiopia)	160,000–154,000	3 individuals and other fragments	Earliest well-dated modern humans; placed in separate subspecies (*H. sapiens idaltu*); location (in Africa) is notable

Critical Thinking Questions

1. What anatomical characteristics define *modern* as compared to *premodern* humans? Assume that you're analyzing an incomplete skeleton that may be early modern *H. sapiens*. Which portions of the skeleton would be most informative, and why?

2. Go through the chapter and list all the forms of evidence that you think support the complete replacement model. Now, do the same for the regional continuity model. What evidence do you find most convincing, and why?

3. Why are the fossils recently discovered from Herto so important? How does this evidence influence your conclusions in question 2?

4. What archaeological evidence shows that modern human behavior during the Upper Paleolithic was significantly different from that of earlier hominids? Do you think that early modern *H. sapiens* populations were behaviorally superior to the Neandertals? Be careful to define what you mean by *superior*.

5. Why do you think some Upper Paleolithic people painted in caves? Why don't we find such evidence of cave painting from a wider geographical area?

CHAPTER 15

Modern Human Biology: Patterns of Variation

KEY QUESTIONS

Is evolution still occurring in modern humans?

What is meant by race, and how useful is this concept in understanding the biology and evolution of our species?

Introduction

At some time or other, you've probably been asked to specify your "race" or "ethnic identity" on an application or census form. What did you think about that question? Did it make you uncomfortable? Usually, you can chose from a variety of racial/ethnic categories. Was it easy to pick an appropriate category? What about your parents and grandparents? Where would they fit in?

Notions about human diversity have played a large role in human relations for centuries, and they still influence political and social perceptions. While we'd like to believe that informed views have become almost universal, the gruesome tally of genocidal/ethnic cleansing atrocities in recent years tells us tragically that worldwide, we have a long way to go before tolerance becomes the norm.

Most people don't seem to understand the nature of human diversity, and worse yet, many seem quite unwilling to accept what science has to contribute on the subject. Many of the misconceptions, especially those regarding how *race* is defined and categorized, are no doubt rooted in cultural history over the last few centuries. Although many cultures have tried to come to grips with these issues, for better or worse, the most influential of these perspectives were developed in the Western world (that is, Europe and North America). The way many individuals still view themselves and their relationship to other peoples is a legacy of the last four centuries of racial interpretations.

In Chapters 3 and 4 we saw how physical characteristics are influenced by the DNA in our cells. We went on to discuss how individuals inherit genes from parents, and how variations in genes (alleles) can produce different expressions of traits. We also focused on how the basic principles of inheritance are related to evolutionary change.

In this chapter, we'll continue to discuss topics that directly relate to genetics, namely biological diversity in humans and how humans adapt physically to environmental challenges. After discussing historical attempts at explaining human phenotypic diversity and racial classification, we examine contemporary methods of interpreting diversity. In recent years, several new techniques have emerged that permit direct examination of the DNA molecule, revealing differences between individuals even at the level of single nucleotides. But, as discoveries of different levels of diversity emerge, geneticists have also shown that our species is remarkably uniform genetically, particularly when compared with other species.

 Click!

Go to the following media for interactives and exercises on topics covered in this chapter:

- Online Virtual Laboratories for Physical Anthropology, Fourth Edition
- Basic Genetics for Anthropology CD-ROM: Principles and Applications

Historical Views of Human Variation

The first step toward understanding diversity in nature is to organize it into categories that can then be named, discussed, and perhaps studied. Historically, when different groups of people came into contact with one another, they tried to account for the physical differences they saw. Because skin color was so noticeable, it was one of the more frequently explained traits, and most systems of racial classification were based on it.

As early as 1350 B.C., the ancient Egyptians had classified humans based on their skin color: red for Egyptian, yellow for people to the east, white for those to the north, and black for sub-Saharan Africans (Gossett, 1963). In the sixteenth century, after the discovery of the New World, several European countries embarked on a period of intense exploration and colonization in both the New and Old Worlds. One result of this contact was an increased awareness of human diversity.

Throughout the eighteenth and nineteenth centuries, European and American scientists concentrated primarily on describing and classifying the biological variation in humans as well as in nonhuman species. The first scientific attempt to describe the newly discovered variation between human populations was Linnaeus' taxonomic classification (see p. 22), which placed humans into four separate categories (Linnaeus, 1758). Linnaeus assigned behavioral and intellectual qualities to each group, with the least complimentary descriptions going to sub-Saharan, dark-skinned Africans. This ranking was typical of the period and reflected the almost universal European ethnocentric view that Europeans were superior to everyone else.

Johann Friedrich Blumenbach (1752–1840), a German anatomist, classified humans into five races. Although Blumenbach's categories came to be described simply as white, yellow, red, black, and brown, he also used criteria other than skin color. What's more, he emphasized that racial categories based on skin color were arbitrary and that many traits, including skin color, weren't discrete phenomena. Blumenbach pointed out that classifying all humans using such a system would completely omit everyone who didn't neatly fall into a specific category. Blumenbach and others also recognized that traits such as skin color showed overlapping expression between groups.

In 1842 Anders Retzius, a Swedish anatomist, developed the *cephalic index* as a method of describing the shape of the human head. The cephalic index, obtained by dividing maximum head breadth by maximum length and multiplying by 100, gives the ratio of head breadth to length. (The cephalic index does not measure actual head size.) The cephalic index is still used to assess head shape in individual skulls; but in the nineteenth century, it was viewed as a precise scientific technique that could be used to categorize groups of people. Also, because it quickly categorized people using a single number, the index provided a superficial but easy method for describing variation. Individuals with an index of less than 75 had long, narrow heads and were labeled "dolichocephalic." "Brachycephalic" individuals, with broad heads, had an index of over 80; and those whose indices were between 75 and 80 were "mesocephalic." Northern Europeans tended to be dolichocephalic, while southern Europeans were brachycephalic. Not surprisingly, these results led to heated and nationalistic debate over whether one group was superior to another.

By the mid-nineteenth century, populations were ranked essentially on a scale based on skin color (along with size and shape of the head), with sub-Saharan Africans at the bottom. The Europeans themselves were also ranked, so that northern, light-skinned populations were considered superior to their southern, somewhat darker-skinned neighbors.

To many Europeans, the fact that non-Europeans weren't Christian suggested that they were "uncivilized" and implied an even more basic inferiority of character and intellect. This view was rooted in a concept called **biological determinism**, which in part holds that there is an association between physical characteristics and such attributes as intelligence, morals, values, abilities, and even social and economic condition. In other words, cultural variations are *inherited* in the same way that biological variations are. It follows, then, that there are inherent behavioral and cognitive differences between groups and that some groups are *by nature* superior to others. Following this logic, it's a simple matter to justify the persecution and even enslavement of other peoples simply because their outward appearance differs from what is familiar.

After 1850, biological determinism was a constant theme underlying common thinking as well as scientific research in Europe and the United States. Most people, including such notable figures as Thomas Jefferson, Georges Cuvier, Benjamin Franklin, Charles Lyell, Abraham Lincoln, Charles Darwin, and Oliver Wendell Holmes, held deterministic (and what today we'd call racist) views. Commenting on this usually de-emphasized characteristic of more respected historical figures, the late evolutionary biologist Stephen J. Gould (1981, p. 32) remarked that "all American culture heroes embraced racial attitudes that would embarrass public-school mythmakers."

Francis Galton (1822–1911), Charles Darwin's cousin, shared an increasingly common fear among nineteenth-century Europeans that "civilized society" was being weakened by the failure of natural selection to completely eliminate unfit and inferior members (Greene, 1981, p. 107). Galton wrote and lectured on the necessity of "race improvement" and suggested government regulation of marriage and family size, an approach he called **eugenics**. Although eugenics had its share of critics, its popularity flourished throughout the 1930s.

biological determinism The concept that phenomena, including various aspects of behavior (e.g., intelligence, values, morals) are governed by biological (genetic) factors; the inaccurate association of various behavioral attributes with certain biological traits, such as skin color.

eugenics The philosophy of "race improvement" through the forced sterilization of members of some groups and increased reproduction among others; an overly simplified, often racist view that's now discredited.

Nowhere was it more attractive than in Germany, where the viewpoint took a horrifying turn. The false idea of pure races (see "Issue," p. 400) was increasingly extolled as a means of reestablishing a strong and prosperous state. Eugenics was seen as scientific justification for purging Germany of its "unfit," and many of Germany's scientists continued to support the policies of racial purity and eugenics during the Nazi period (Proctor, 1988, p. 143), when these policies served as justification for condemning millions of people to death.

But at the same time, many scientists were turning away from racial typologies and classification in favor of a more evolutionary approach. No doubt for some, this shift in direction was motivated by their growing concerns over the goals of the eugenics movement. Probably more important, however, was the synthesis of genetics and Darwin's theories of natural selection during the 1930s. As discussed in Chapter 4, this breakthrough influenced all the biological sciences, and some physical anthropologists soon began applying evolutionary principles to the study of human variation.

The Concept of Race

All contemporary humans are members of the same **polytypic** species, *Homo sapiens*. A polytypic species is composed of local populations that differ in the expression of one or more traits. Even *within* local populations, there's a great deal of genotypic and phenotypic variation between individuals.

In discussions of human variation, people have traditionally clumped together various characteristics, such as skin color, face shape, nose shape, hair color, hair form (curly or straight), and eye color. People who have particular combinations of these and other traits have been placed together in categories associated with specific geographical localities. Such categories are called *races*.

We all think we know what we mean by the word *race*, but in reality, the term has had various meanings since the 1500s, when English speakers first commonly used it. *Race* has been used synonymously with *species*, as in "the human race." Since the 1600s, *race* has also referred to various culturally defined groups, and this meaning is still common. For example, you'll hear people say, "the English race" or "the Japanese race," when they actually mean nationality. Another phrase you've probably heard is "the Jewish race," when the speaker is really talking about a particular ethnic and religious identity.

So, even though *race* is usually a term with biological connotations, it also has enormous social significance. And there's still a widespread perception that certain physical traits (skin color, in particular) are associated with numerous cultural attributes (such as language, occupational preferences, or even morality). As a result, in many cultural contexts a person's social identity is strongly influenced by the way he or she expresses those physical traits traditionally used to define "racial groups." Characteristics such as skin color are highly visible, and they make it easy to immediately and superficially place people into socially defined categories. However, so-called racial traits aren't the only phenotypic expressions that contribute to social identity. Sex and age are also critically important. But aside from these two variables, an individual's biological and/or ethnic background is still inevitably a factor that influences how he or she is initially perceived and judged by others.

References to national origin (for example, African, Asian) as substitutes for racial labels have become more common in recent years, both within and outside anthropology. Within anthropology, the term *ethnicity* was proposed in the early 1950s to avoid the more emotionally charged term, *race*. Strictly speaking, ethnicity refers to cultural factors, but the fact that the words *ethnicity* and *race* are used interchangeably reflects the social importance of phenotypic expression and demonstrates once again how phenotype is mistakenly associated with culturally defined variables.

In its most common biological usage, the term *race* refers to geographically patterned phenotypic variation within a species. By the seventeenth century, naturalists were beginning to describe races in plants and nonhuman animals. They had recognized that when populations of a species occupied different regions, they sometimes differed from one another in the expression of one or more traits. But even today, there are no established criteria for assessing races of plants and animals, including humans.

polytypic Referring to species composed of populations that differ in the expression of one or more traits.

Before World War II, most studies of human variation focused on visible phenotypic variation between large, geographically defined populations, and these studies were largely descriptive. Since World War II, the emphasis has shifted to examining the differences in allele frequencies within and between populations, as well as considering the adaptive significance of phenotypic and genotypic variation. This shift in focus occurred partly because of the Modern Synthesis in biology and partly because of further advances in genetics.

In the twenty-first century, the application of evolutionary principles to the study of modern human variation has replaced the superficial nineteenth-century view of race *based solely on observed phenotype*. Additionally, the genetic emphasis has dispelled previously held misconceptions that races are fixed biological entities that don't change over time and that are composed of individuals who all conform to a particular *type*.

Clearly, there are phenotypic differences between humans, and some of these differences roughly correspond to particular geographical locations. But certain questions must be asked. Is there any adaptive significance attached to observed phenotypic variation? Is genetic drift a factor? What is the degree of underlying genetic variation that influences phenotypic variation? These questions place considerations of human variation within a contemporary evolutionary framework.

Although, in part, physical anthropology is rooted in attempts to explain human diversity, no contemporary scholar subscribes to pre-Darwinian and pre–Modern Synthesis concepts of races (human or nonhuman) as fixed biological entities. Also, anthropologists recognize that race isn't a valid concept, especially from a genetic perspective, because the amount of genetic variation accounted for by differences *between* groups is vastly exceeded by the variation existing *within* groups. Many physical anthropologists also argue that race is an outdated creation of the human mind that attempts to simplify biological complexity by organizing it into categories. So, human races are a product of the human tendency to impose order on complex natural phenomena. In this view, simplistic classification may have been an acceptable approach some 150 years ago, but given the current state of genetic and evolutionary science, it's now meaningless.

Even so, some anthropologists continue to view variations in outwardly expressed phenotype as having the potential to yield information about population adaptation, genetic drift, mutation, and gene flow. Forensic anthropologists, in particular, find the phenotypic criteria associated with race to have practical applications. Law enforcement agencies frequently call on these scientists to assist in identifying human skeletal remains. Because unidentified human remains are often those of crime victims, identification must be as accurate as possible. The most important variables in such identification are the individual's sex, age, stature, and ancestry or "racial" and ethnic background. Using metric and nonmetric criteria, forensic anthropologists employ various techniques for establishing broad population affinity (that is, a likely relationship) for that individual. Generally, their findings are accurate about 80 percent of the time.

Some people object to racial taxonomies because traditional classification schemes are *typological*, meaning that categories are distinct and based on stereotypes or ideals that comprise a specific set of traits. So in general, typologies are inherently misleading because any grouping always includes many individuals who don't conform to all aspects of a particular type.

In any so-called racial group, there will be individuals who fall into the normal range of variation for another group based on one or several characteristics. For example, two people of different ancestry might vary in skin color, but they could share any number of other traits—height, shape of head, hair color, eye color, or ABO blood type. In fact, they could easily share more similarities with each other than they do with many members of their own populations (Fig. 15-1).

To further blur this picture, the characteristics that have traditionally been used to define races are *polygenic*; that is, they're influenced by several genes and therefore exhibit a continuous range of expression. So it's difficult, if not impossible, to draw distinct boundaries between populations with regard to many traits. This limitation becomes clear if you ask yourself, "At what point is hair color no longer dark brown but medium brown, or no longer light brown but dark blond?" It would also be instructive to look back at the illustration showing variability in eye-color phenotype (p. 77).

© Peter Johnson/CORBIS
© Charles & Josette Lenars/CORBIS
© Gallo Images/CORBIS
© Otto Lang/CORBIS
Lynn K Igore

FIGURE **15-1**
Some examples of phenotypic variation among Africans.
(a) San (South African)
(b) West African (Bantu)
(c) Ethiopian
(d) Ituri (Central African)
(e) North African (Tunisia)

The scientific controversy over race will fade as we increase our understanding of the genetic diversity (and uniformity) of our species. Given the rapid changes in genome studies, and because very few genes contribute to outward expressions of phenotype, dividing the human species into racial categories isn't a biologically meaningful way to look at human variation. But among the general public, variations on the theme of race will undoubtedly continue to be the most common view of human biological and cultural variation. Keeping all this in mind, it falls to anthropologists and biologists to continue exploring the issue so that, to the best of our abilities, accurate information about human variation is available to anyone who seeks informed explanations of complex phenomena.

Racism

Racism is based on the previously mentioned false belief that along with our physical characteristics, humans inherit such factors as intellect and various cultural attributes. Such beliefs also commonly rest on the assumption that one's own group is superior to other groups.

Since we've already alluded to certain aspects of racism, such as the eugenics movement and persecution of people based on racial or ethnic misconceptions, we won't belabor the point here. It's important, though, to point out that racism is hardly a thing of the past, and it's not restricted to Europeans and Americans of European descent. Racism is a cultural phenomenon, and it's found worldwide.

We end this brief discussion of racism with an excerpt from an article, "The Study of Race," by the late Sherwood Washburn, a well-known physical anthropologist who taught at the University of California, Berkeley. Although written many years ago, the statement is as fresh and applicable today as it was then:

Races are products of the past. They are relics of times and conditions which have long ceased to exist. Racism is equally a relic supported by no phase of modern science. We may not know how to interpret the form of the Mongoloid face, or why Rh is of high incidence in Africa, but we do know the benefits of education and of economic progress. We . . . know that the roots of happiness lie in the biology of the whole species and that the potential of the species can only be realized in a culture, in a social system. It is knowledge and the social system which give life or take it away, and in so doing change the gene frequencies and continue the million-year-old interaction of culture and biology. Human biology finds its realization in a culturally determined way of life, and the infinite variety of genetic combinations can only express themselves efficiently in a free and open society. (Washburn, 1963, p. 531)

Intelligence

As we've shown, belief in the relationship between physical characteristics and specific behavioral attributes is popular even today, but there's no scientific evidence to show that personality or any other behavioral trait differs genetically *between* human groups. Most scientists would agree with this last statement, but one question that produces controversy inside scientific circles and among laypeople is whether population affinity and intelligence are associated.

Genetic and environmental factors contribute to intelligence, although it's not possible to accurately measure the percentage each contributes. What can be said is that IQ scores and intelligence aren't the same thing. IQ scores can change during a person's lifetime, and average IQ scores of different populations overlap. Such differences in average IQ scores that do exist between groups are difficult to interpret, given the problems inherent in the design of the IQ tests. What's more, complex cognitive abilities, however they're measured, are influenced by multiple loci and are thus polygenic.

Innate factors set limits and define potentials for behavior and cognitive ability in any species. In humans, the limits are broad and the potentials aren't fully known. Individual abilities result from complex interactions between genetic and environmental factors. One product of this interaction is learning, and the ability to learn is influenced by genetic and other biological components. Undeniably, there are differences between individuals regarding these biological components. It's probably impossible, though, to determine what proportion of the variation in test scores is due to biological factors. Besides, innate differences in abilities reflect individual variation *within* populations, not inherent differences *between* groups. Comparing populations based on the results of IQ tests is a misuse of testing procedures. There's no convincing evidence *whatsoever* that populations vary in their cognitive abilities, regardless of what some popular books may suggest. Unfortunately, racist attitudes toward intelligence continue to flourish—despite the lack of evidence of mental inferiority of some populations and mental superiority of others, and despite the questionable validity of intelligence tests.

Contemporary Interpretations of Human Variation

Since the physical characteristics (such as skin color and hair form) used to define race are *polygenic*, precisely measuring the genetic influence on them hasn't been possible. So, physical anthropologists and other biologists who study modern human variation have largely abandoned the traditional perspective of describing superficial phenotypic characteristics in favor of examining differences in various allele frequencies.

Beginning in the 1950s, studies of modern human variation focused on the various components of blood as well as other aspects of body chemistry. Such traits as the ABO blood types are *phenotypes*, but they're also *direct* products of the genotype. (Recall that genes code for proteins, and the antigens on blood cells and many constituents of blood serum are partly composed of proteins; Fig.15-2). During the twentieth century, this perspective met with a great deal of success as eventually dozens of loci were identified and the frequencies of many specific alleles obtained from numerous human populations. Even so, in all these cases, it was the phenotype that was observed. Information about the underlying genotype remained largely unobtainable. Beginning in the 1990s, however, with the development of genomic studies, there's been a drastic shift in techniques. Using precise DNA sequencing, researchers can now directly identify genotypes. And in studying specific differences in DNA within and between human populations, we'll dramatically increase our knowledge of human variation.

HUMAN POLYMORPHISMS

Those traits that differ in expression among various populations and between individuals are most important in contemporary studies of human variation. Such characteristics with different phenotypic expressions are called **polymorphisms**. A genetic trait is *polymorphic* if the locus that governs it has two or more alleles. (Refer to p. 71 for a discussion of the ABO blood group system governed by three alleles at one locus.)

Understanding polymorphisms requires evolutionary explanations, and geneticists use polymorphisms as a principal tool to understand evolutionary processes in modern populations. By using these polymorphisms to compare allele frequencies between different populations, we can begin to reconstruct the evolutionary events that link human populations with one another.

By the 1960s, the study of *clinal distributions* of individual polymorphisms had become a popular alternative to the racial approach to human diversity. A **cline** is a gradual change in the frequency of a trait or allele in populations dispersed over geographical space. In humans, the various expressions of polymorphic characteristics exhibit a more or less continuous distribution from one region to another; most traits that show a clinal distribution are Mendelian. The distribution of the *B* allele in the Old World provides a good example of a clinal distribution (Fig. 15-3). Clinal distributions are generally thought to reflect

polymorphisms Loci with more than one allele. Polymorphisms can be expressed in the phenotype as the result of gene action (as in ABO), or they can exist solely at the DNA level within noncoding regions.

cline A gradual change in the frequency of genotypes and phenotypes from one geographical region to another.

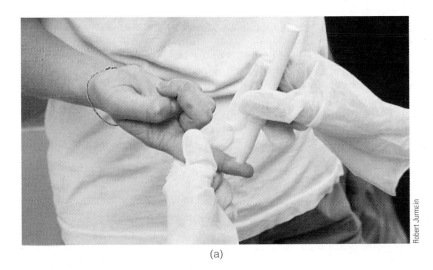
(a)

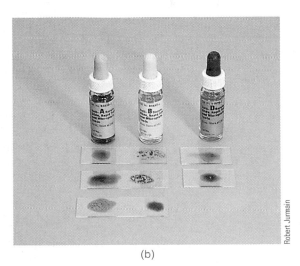
(b)

FIGURE **15-2**

(a) A blood sample is drawn. (b) To determine an individual's blood type, a few drops of blood are treated with specific chemicals. Presence of A and B blood type, as well as Rh, can be detected by using commercially available chemicals. The glass slides below the blue- and yellow-labeled bottles show reactions for the ABO system. The blood on the top slide (at left) is type AB; the middle is type B; and the bottom is type A. The two samples to the right depict Rh-negative blood (top) and Rh-positive blood (bottom).

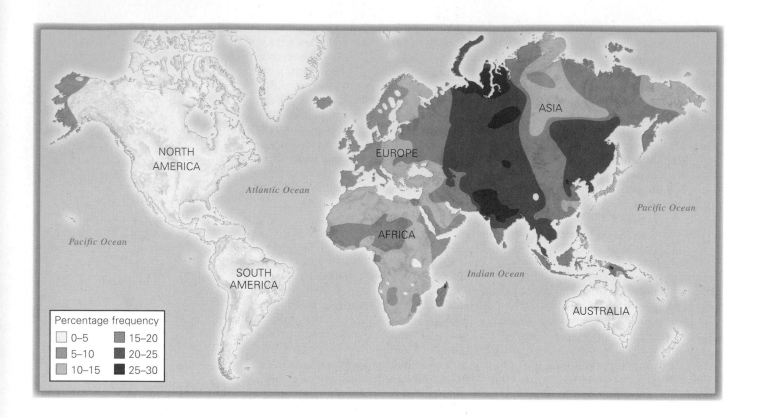

FIGURE 15-3

ABO blood group system. Distribution of the *B* allele in the indigenous populations of the world. (After Mourant et al., 1976.)

microevolutionary influences of natural selection and/or gene flow. Clinal distributions are thus explained in evolutionary terms.

The ABO system is interesting from an anthropological viewpoint because the frequencies of the *A*, *B*, and *O* alleles vary tremendously among humans. In most groups, *A* and *B* are only rarely found in frequencies greater than 50 percent; usually, frequencies for these two alleles are considerably lower. Most contemporary human populations are polymorphic for all three alleles.

On the other hand, in some native South American Indians, frequencies of the *O* allele reach 100 percent, and this allele is said to be "fixed" in these populations. (Actually, you could say that in these groups, the ABO blood system isn't a polymorphic trait.) Indeed, in most indigenous New World populations, the frequency of *O* is at least 80 percent. Uncommonly high frequencies of *O* are also found in northern Australia, and on some islands off the Australian coast, the frequency of *O* exceeds 90 percent. In these populations, the high frequencies of the *O* allele are probably due to genetic drift (founder effect), although the influence of natural selection can't be entirely ruled out.

Besides ABO, there are many other red blood cell phenotypes, each under the control of a different genetic locus. These include the well-known Rh blood group as well as the MN blood group (the MN group has been widely used in population studies; for example, see p. 393).

Some antigens on white blood cells are also polymorphic. Called human leukocyte antigen (HLA) in humans, these antigens are crucial to the immune response because they allow the body to recognize and resist potentially dangerous infections. What's interesting is that, unlike simple polymorphisms such as ABO (one locus, three alleles) or MN (one locus, just two alleles), HLA is governed by six loci together possessing *hundreds* of alleles. In fact, HLA is by far the most polymorphic genetic system known in humans (Knapp, 2002).

Because there are so many HLA alleles, they're useful in showing patterns of human population diversity. For example, Lapps, Sardinians, and Basques differ in allele frequencies from other European populations, and these data support allele frequency distributions for ABO, MN, and Rh (Fig. 15-4). Founder effect (that is, genetic drift) most likely explains the distinctive genetic patterning in these smaller, traditionally more isolated groups. Likewise, the unusual HLA allele frequencies found in many populations in Australia and New

Guinea probably result from founder effect. Natural selection also has influenced the evolution of HLA alleles in humans, especially as related to infectious disease. For example, certain HLA antigens appear to be associated with resistance to malaria and hepatitis B and perhaps to HIV as well.

A final physiological and evolutionary influence of HLA concerns male fertility. Recent data suggest that some HLA antigens are found in higher frequencies in infertile males, suggesting that there may be some influence of two or more HLA loci on sperm production and function (van der Ven et al., 2000).

Another well-studied polymorphism is the ability to taste an artificial substance called phenylthiocarbamide (PTC). While many people perceive PTC as extremely bitter, others don't taste it at all. The mode of inheritance follows a Mendelian pattern, with two alleles (T and t). The ability to taste PTC is a dominant trait, while the inability to taste it is recessive. So, "nontasters" are homozygous (tt) for the recessive allele. The frequency of PTC tasting varies considerably in human populations, and the evolutionary explanation for the patterns of variation isn't clear. It's possible, though, that the ability to perceive substances as unpleasantly bitter could, under certain circumstances, be selectively advantageous, especially in avoiding toxic plants (which are often bitter).

FIGURE 15-4
People in Sardinia, a large island off the west coast of Italy, differ in allele frequencies at some loci from other European populations.

PATTERNS OF POLYMORPHIC VARIATION

Examining single traits can give us information about potential influences of natural selection or gene flow. But this approach is limited when we try to sort out population relationships. Studying single traits, by themselves, can yield confusing interpretations regarding likely population relationships. A more meaningful approach is to study several traits simultaneously.

An excellent and early example of this approach to human diversity was undertaken by Harvard population geneticist R. D. Lewontin (1972). He calculated population differences in allele frequency for 17 polymorphic characteristics. In his analysis, he divided his sample into seven geographical areas, and he included several population samples within each region (Table 15-1). Next he calculated how much of the total genetic variability within our species could be accounted for by these population subdivisions, and the results were surprising. Only 6.3 percent of the total genetic variation was explained by differences between major population groups (Lewontin's seven geographical units). In other words, close to 94 percent of human genetic diversity occurs *within* these groups, not between them. The larger population subdivisions within the geographical clusters (for example, within Native Americans, the differences between subgroups such as Aleut and Yanomama) account for another 8.3 percent. Thus, geographical and local groups together account for just 15 percent of all human genetic variation, leaving the remaining 85 percent unaccounted for. This means that most of the genetic differences among human beings can be explained in terms

TABLE 15-1	Population Groupings Used by Lewontin in Population Genetics Study (1972)	
Geographic Group	**Examples of Populations Included**
Caucasians	Arabs, Armenians, Tristan da Cunhans
Black Africans	Bantu, San, U.S. blacks
Asians	Ainu, Chinese, Turks
South Asians	Andamanese, Tamils
Amerinds	Aleuts, Navaho, Yanomama
Oceanians	Easter Islanders, Micronesians
Australians	All treated as a single group

of differences from one village to another, one family to another, and—to a significant degree—one person to another, even within the same family.

As you can see, and as we mentioned earlier, the visible traits most often used to make racial distinctions (skin color, hair form, nose shape, and so on) don't provide an accurate picture of the actual pattern of *genetic variation*. Simple polymorphic traits provide a more objective basis for accurate biological comparisons of human groups. Indeed, Lewontin concluded his analysis with a ringing condemnation of traditional studies: "Human racial classification is of no social value and is positively destructive of social and human relations. Since such racial classification is now seen to be of virtually no genetic or taxonomic significance either, no justification can be offered for its continuance" (Lewontin, 1972, p. 397).

In addition, as we discussed earlier, there are even broader patterns of human diversity. At the species level, humans are an unusually homogeneous species compared to most other animals. For example, within-species variation of mtDNA is three to four times greater in both chimpanzees and gorillas than in humans. Even though our species is relatively uniform genetically, the variations that do exist reveal an interesting geographical pattern. Compared to all other areas, African populations show much more genetic variation. As emphasized in Chapter 14, this pattern of genetic diversity is thought to reflect a longer history of human occupation in Africa, with subsequent migrations to other parts of the world.

POLYMORPHISMS AT THE DNA LEVEL

The *Human Genome Project* has facilitated the direct study of both mitochondrial DNA and chromosomal (nuclear) DNA. So, we now have considerable insight into human variation *directly at the DNA level*. Using techniques described in Chapter 3, researchers can directly compare DNA sequences from different individuals and between populations.

What's more, new molecular technologies have uncovered a host of other regions of DNA variability. As explained in Chapter 3, much of the human genome consists of repeated DNA segments. In some cases there are only a few repeated segments, but in other cases there can be hundreds. One type of DNA repeat, called a *microsatellite*, is extraordinarily variable from person to person. In fact, as we discussed in Chapter 3, everyone is unique for his or her particular microsatellite arrangement, and using current analytical approaches, the individual pattern produces a distinctive "DNA fingerprint" (see p. 58).

Another kind of DNA segment, called an *Alu*, can also occasionally be copied, but not over and over (as in microsatellites). Instead, *Alu*s are DNA segments that typically are copied once and then insert randomly, perhaps elsewhere on the same chromosome; or, just as easily, they can "jump" and insert on some other chromosome. Several hundred of these *Alu*s have now been mapped in the human genome, and their patterns are quite informative concerning recent population history.

Finally, researchers are beginning to expand their approach and map patterns of variation at individual nucleotide sites. As you know, point mutations have been recognized for some time. But, what's only been recently appreciated is that such single-nucleotide alterations also frequently occur in *noncoding* portions of DNA. These sites, together with those in coding regions of DNA, are all referred to as *single-nucleotide polymorphisms* (SNPs). Already, more than a million such sites have been recognized; these SNPs are dispersed throughout the human genome (96 percent of them are in noncoding DNA), and they're extraordinarily variable (International SNP Map Working Group, 2001). So, at the beginning of the twenty-first century, geneticists have gained access to a vast biological "library" documenting the genetic history of our species.

Population geneticists are just beginning to take advantage of these new opportunities. While traditional polymorphic traits, such as ABO, are still being investigated, researchers are directing more and more attention to the remarkably variable DNA polymorphisms. These molecular applications are now being widely used to evaluate contemporary variation at a microevolutionary level, and this information provides far more accurate measures of within-group and between-group variation than was previously possible. Besides that, we can now use the vast amount of new data to more fully understand very recent events in human population history—including the varied roles of natural selection, genetic drift, gene flow, and mutation.

As an example of how far the study of human variation has moved toward a molecularly based approach, more than 95 percent of the papers presented at a recent anthropol-

population genetics   The study of the frequency of alleles, genotypes, and phenotypes in populations from a microevolutionary perspective.

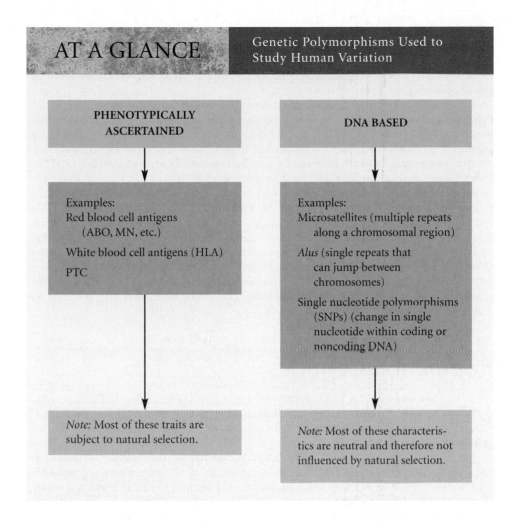

AT A GLANCE | Genetic Polymorphisms Used to Study Human Variation

PHENOTYPICALLY ASCERTAINED

Examples:
Red blood cell antigens
    (ABO, MN, etc.)

White blood cell antigens (HLA)

PTC

Note: Most of these traits are subject to natural selection.

DNA BASED

Examples:
Microsatellites (multiple repeats
    along a chromosomal region)

Alus (single repeats that
    can jump between
    chromosomes)

Single nucleotide polymorphisms
    (SNPs) (change in single
    nucleotide within coding or
    noncoding DNA)

Note: Most of these characteristics are neutral and therefore not influenced by natural selection.

ogy conference on population variation used DNA polymorphisms. Populations evaluated using direct DNA ascertainment come from every corner of the inhabited world. The information is increasing at an incredibly rapid rate, as indicated in a new online database called ALFRED (ALlele FREquency Database; see website at http://alfred.med.yale.edu/alfred). Recently, in just a 12-month period, the information in this database almost doubled (Kidd et al., 2003)!

These genetic data, including the more traditional polymorphisms such as blood groups and the vast new DNA-based evidence, all point in the same direction: Genetically, humans differ individually within populations far more than large geographical groups ("races") differ. Does this mean, as Richard Lewontin suggested more than 30 years ago (see p. 389), there's no biological value in further study and scientific understanding of geographical populations? Even with all our new information, the answer isn't entirely clear. Some of the newest genetic evidence from patterns of *Alus* (Bamshad et al., 2003) and microsatellites (Rosenberg et al., 2002) has found broad genetic correlations that quite consistently indicate an individual's geographical ancestry. We must consider some important points here, however. These geographically patterned genetic clusters aren't "races" as traditionally defined, and so they aren't closely linked to simple patterns of phenotypic variation (such as skin color). Besides that, the correlations are broad, so not all individuals can be easily classified. Many individuals, in fact, will likely be misclassified, even when using the best information for dozens of genetic loci.

This debate isn't entirely academic, and it really never has been. Just consider the destructive social impact caused over the last few centuries by misuse of the race concept. A contemporary continuation of the debate concerns the relationship of ancestry and disease. It's long been recognized that some disease-causing genes are more common in certain populations than in others (such as the allele causing sickle-cell anemia or that causing cystic fibrosis). The much more complete data on human DNA patterns have further expanded our knowledge, showing, for example, that some individuals are much more resistant than most people are to HIV infection (see Chapter 16 for further discussion). Does this mean that a person's ancestry provides valuable medical information in screening or even treating certain diseases?

Some experts argue that such information is medically helpful (e.g., Rosenberg et al., 2002; Bamshad and Olson, 2003; Burchard et al., 2003). What's more, official federal guidelines recently issued by the Food and Drug Administration recommend collection of ancestry data ("race/ethnic identity") in all clinical trials testing new drugs. Other researchers disagree, suggesting that such information is at best tenuous (King and Motulsky, 2002) or that it has no obvious medical use (e.g., Cooper et al., 2003).

Even the general public has weighed in on this issue, defeating an October 2003 California ballot measure that would have restricted the collection of "racial" or ethnic information on medical records. There are no easy answers to the questions we've raised, and this is an even stronger argument for an informed public. The subject of race has been contentious, and anthropology and other disciplines have struggled to come to grips with it. Our new genetic tools have allowed us to expand our knowledge at a rate far beyond anything seen previously. But increased information alone doesn't permit us to fully address all human concerns. How we address diversity, individually and collectively, must balance the potential scientific benefits against a history of social costs.

Population Genetics

As we defined it in Chapter 4, a *population* is a group of interbreeding individuals. More precisely, a population is the group within which an individual is most likely to find a mate. As such, a population is marked by a degree of genetic relatedness and shares a common **gene pool**.

In theory, this is a straightforward concept. In every generation, the genes (alleles) are mixed by recombination and rejoined through mating. What emerges in the next generation is a direct product of the genes going into the pool, which in turn is a product of who is mating with whom (see website at http://alfred.med.yale.edu/alfred).

In practice, however, defining and describing human populations is difficult. The largest population of *Homo sapiens* that could be described is the entire species. All members of a species are *potentially* capable of interbreeding but are incapable of fertile breeding with members of other species. Our species, like any other, is thus a *genetically closed system*. The problem arises not in describing who potentially can interbreed, but in determining the exact pattern of those individuals who are doing so.

Factors that determine mate choice are geographical, ecological, and social. If individuals are isolated on a remote island in the middle of the Pacific, there isn't much chance of their finding a mate outside the immediate vicinity. Such **breeding isolates** are fairly easily defined and are a favorite target of microevolutionary studies. Geography plays a dominant role in producing these isolates by severely limiting the range of available mates. But even within these limits, cultural rules can easily play a deciding role by prescribing who is most appropriate among those who are potentially available.

Human population segments are defined as groups with relative degrees of **endogamy** (marrying/mating within the group). But these aren't totally closed systems. Gene flow often occurs between groups, and individuals may choose mates from distant localities. With the modern advent of rapid transportation, greatly accelerated rates of **exogamy** (marrying/mating outside the group) have emerged.

Today most humans aren't clearly defined as members of particular populations, because they don't belong to a breeding isolate. Inhabitants of large cities may appear to be members of a single population; but within the city, there's a complex system of social, ethnic, and religious boundaries that are crosscut to form smaller population segments. Besides being members of these highly open local population groupings, we're simultaneously members of overlapping gradations of larger populations—the immediate geographical region (a metropolitan area or perhaps an entire state), a section of the country, the entire nation, and ultimately the whole species.

gene pool The total complement of genes shared by the reproductive members of a population.

breeding isolates Populations that are clearly isolated geographically and/or socially from other breeding groups.

endogamy Mating with individuals from the same group.

exogamy Mating pattern whereby individuals obtain mates from groups other than their own.

After identifying specific human populations, the next step is to find out what evolutionary forces, if any, are operating on this group. To determine whether evolution is taking place at a given genetic locus, we measure allele frequencies for specific traits. We then compare these observed frequencies with those predicted by a mathematical model called the **Hardy-Weinberg theory of genetic equilibrium**. This model gives us a baseline set of evolutionary expectations under *known* conditions.

The Hardy-Weinberg theory of genetic equilibrium establishes a set of conditions in a population where *no* evolution occurs. In other words, no evolutionary forces are acting, and all genes have an equal chance of recombining in each generation (that is, there's random mating of individuals). More precisely, the hypothetical conditions that such a population would be *assumed* to meet are as follows:

1. The population is infinitely large. This condition eliminates the possibility of random genetic drift or changes in allele frequencies due to chance.
2. There's no mutation. Thus, no new alleles are being added by molecular changes in gametes.
3. There's no gene flow. There is no exchange of genes with other populations that can alter allele frequencies.
4. Natural selection isn't operating. Specific alleles offer no advantage over others that might influence reproductive success.
5. Mating is random. There's nothing to influence who mates with whom. Thus, any female is assumed to have an equal chance of mating with any male.

If all these conditions are satisfied, allele frequencies won't change from one generation to the next (that is, no evolution will take place); as long as these conditions prevail, the population maintains a permanent equilibrium. Using this equilibrium model, population geneticists have a standard against which they can compare actual circumstances. Notice that the idealized conditions defining the Hardy-Weinberg equilibrium are just that: an idealized, *hypothetical* state. In the real world, no actual population would fully meet any of these conditions. But don't be confused by this distinction. By explicitly defining the genetic distribution that would be *expected* if *no* evolutionary change were occurring (that is, in equilibrium), we can compare the *observed* genetic distribution obtained in real human populations.

If the observed frequencies differ from those of the expected model, we can then say that evolution is taking place at the locus in question. The alternative, of course, is that the observed and expected frequencies don't differ enough that we can confidently say evolution is occurring at a locus in a population. In fact, this is often what happens; in such cases, population geneticists aren't able to delineate evolutionary changes at the particular locus under study.

The simplest way to do a microevolutionary study is to use a genetic trait that follows a simple Mendelian pattern and has only two alleles (*A*, *a*). As you recall from earlier discussions, there are then only three possible genotypes: *AA*, *Aa*, *aa*. Proportions of these genotypes (*AA:Aa:aa*) are a function of the *allele frequencies* themselves (percentage of *A* and percentage of *a*). To provide uniformity for all genetic loci, a standard notation is employed to refer to these frequencies:

Frequency of dominant allele *(A)* = *p*
Frequency of recessive allele *(a)* = *q*

Since in this case there are only two alleles, their combined total frequency must represent all possibilities. In other words, the sum of their separate frequencies must be 1:

$$p + q = 1 \text{ (100\% of alleles at the locus in question)}$$

(Frequency of *A* alleles) (Frequency of *a* alleles)

To determine the expected proportions of genotypes, we compute the chances of the alleles combining with one another into all possible combinations. Remember, they all have an equal chance of combining, and no new alleles are being added. These probabilities are a

Hardy-Weinberg theory of genetic equilibrium The mathematical relationship expressing—under ideal conditions—the predicted distribution of alleles in populations; the central theorem of population genetics.

direct function of the frequency of the two alleles. The chances of all possible combinations occurring randomly can be simply shown as

$$
\begin{array}{r}
p + q \\
\times \quad p + q \\
\hline
pq + q^2 \\
p^2 + pq \\
\hline
p^2 + 2pq + q^2
\end{array}
$$

Mathematically, this is known as a binomial expansion and can also be shown as:

$$(p + q)(p + q) = p^2 + 2pq + q^2$$

What we have just calculated is simply:

Allele Combination	Genotype Produced	Expected Proportion in Population
Chances of A combining with A	AA	$p \times p = p^2$
Chances of A combining with a;	Aa	$p \times q$
a combining with A	aA	$p \times q$ $= 2pq$
Chances of a combining with a	aa	$q \times q = q^2$

Thus, p^2 is the frequency of the *AA* genotype, *2pq* is the frequency of the *Aa* genotype, and q^2 is the frequency of the aa genotype, where p is the frequency of the dominant allele and q is the frequency of the recessive allele in a population.

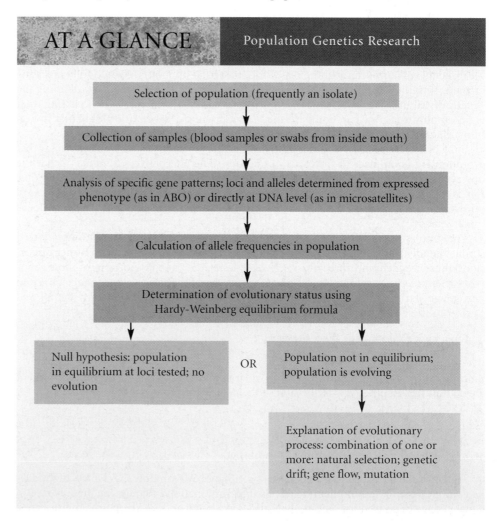

AT A GLANCE   Population Genetics Research

Selection of population (frequently an isolate)

↓

Collection of samples (blood samples or swabs from inside mouth)

↓

Analysis of specific gene patterns; loci and alleles determined from expressed phenotype (as in ABO) or directly at DNA level (as in microsatellites)

↓

Calculation of allele frequencies in population

↓

Determination of evolutionary status using Hardy-Weinberg equilibrium formula

Null hypothesis: population in equilibrium at loci tested; no evolution   OR   Population not in equilibrium; population is evolving

↓

Explanation of evolutionary process: combination of one or more: natural selection; genetic drift; gene flow, mutation

CALCULATING ALLELE FREQUENCIES

We can best demonstrate how geneticists use the Hardy-Weinberg formula by giving an example. Let's assume that a population contains 200 individuals, and we'll use the MN blood group locus as the gene to be measured. This gene produces two antigens (M and N) that are similar to the ABO antigens and are also located on red blood cells. Because the *M* and *N* alleles are codominant, we can ascertain everyone's phenotype by taking blood samples and testing them in a process very similar to that for ABO (see Fig. 15-2). From the phenotypes, we can then directly calculate the *observed* allele frequencies. So let's see what we can determine.

All 200 individuals are tested, and the observed data for the three phenotypes are as follows:

Genotype	Number of individuals*	Percent	Number of Alleles M	N
MM	80	40	160	0
MN	80	40	80	80
NN	40	20	0	80
Totals	200	100	240 + 160	= 400
		Proportion	.6 + .4	= 1

From these observed results, we can count the number of *M* and *N* alleles and thus calculate the observed allele frequencies:

p = frequency of M = .6

q = frequency of N = .4

The total frequency of the two alleles combined should always equal 1. As you can see, they do.

Next, we need to calculate the expected genotypic proportions. This calculation comes directly from the Hardy-Weinberg equilibrium formula: $p^2 + 2pq + q^2$.

p^2	=	(.6)(.6)	= .36
$2pq$	=	2(.6)(.4) × 2(.24)	= .48
q^2	=	(.4)(.4)	= .16
Total			1.00

There are only three possible genotypes: *MM, MN, NN*. The total of the relative proportions should equal 1. Again, as you can see, they do.

Finally, we need to compare the two sets of data, that is, the observed frequencies (what we actually found in the population) with the expected frequencies (those predicted by Hardy-Weinberg under conditions of genetic equilibrium). How do these two sets of data compare?

	Expected Frequency	Expected Number of Individuals	Observed Frequency	Actual Number of Individuals with Each Genotype
MM	.36	72	.40	80
MN	.48	96	.40	80
NN	.16	32	.20	40

We can see that although the match between observed and expected frequencies isn't perfect, it's close enough statistically to satisfy equilibrium conditions. Since our population isn't a large one, sampling may easily account for the small observed differences. Our population is therefore probably in equilibrium (that is, it's not evolving at this locus).

---

*Each individual has two alleles, so a person who's *MM* contributes two *M* alleles to the total gene pool. A person who's *MN* contributes one *M* and one *N*. For the *MN* locus, then, 200 individuals have 400 alleles.

| A CLOSER LOOK | Calculating Allele Frequencies: PTC Tasting in a Hypothetical Population |

For the PTC tasting trait, it's assumed there are two alleles, T and t. Also, while dominance is displayed, it's incomplete. So it's theoretically possible to ascertain the phenotypes of heterozygotes. To simplify calculations for this example, we assume that all heterozygotes can be ascertained.

In our population of 500 individuals, we find the following observed phenotypic frequencies:

Genotype	Number of Individuals	Percent	Number of Alleles T	t
TT	125	25	250	0
Tt	325	65	325	325
tt	50	10	0	100
Totals	500	100	575	425

Thus, the observed allele frequencies are

$$T(p) = .575$$
$$t(q) = .425$$

The expected genotypic proportions are

p^2	$=$	$(.575)(.575)$	$= .33$
$2pq$	$=$	$2(.575)(.425)$	$= .49$
q^2	$=$	$(.425)(.425)$	$= .18$

Now we compare the observed and expected genotypic frequencies:

	Expected Frequency	Expected Number of Individuals	Observed Frequency	Actual Number of Individuals with Each Genotype
TT	.33	165	.25	125
Tt	.49	245	.65	325
tt	.18	90	.10	50

These results show considerable departures of the observed genotypic proportions from those predicted under equilibrium conditions. Both types of homozygotes (TT and tt) are *less* commonly observed than expected, while the heterozygote (Tt) is *more* common than expected.

A statistical test (called a chi-square) can be performed to test the *statistical significance* of this difference. The results of this test are shown in Appendix C.

Of course, sometimes the observed allele frequencies do vary enough from equilibrium predictions to suggest that the population isn't in equilibrium or that it's evolving. For example, consider the locus influencing PTC tasting (see p. 387). What makes PTC tasting such a useful characteristic is how easy it is to identify. Unlike blood antigens such as ABO or MN, PTC tasting can be tested by simply having subjects place a thin paper strip on their tongues. This paper contains concentrated PTC, and people either taste it or they don't. So testing is quick, inexpensive, and it doesn't involve blood testing (a major concern, due to the risks of HIV or hepatitis infection).

With such an efficient means of screening subjects, we now consider a sample population of 500 individuals. The results from observing the phenotypes and calculations of expected genotypic proportions are shown in "A Closer Look." You'll find more examples of population genetics calculations in Appendix C.

Evolution in Action: Modern Human Populations

Once a population has been defined, it's possible to determine whether allele frequencies are stable (that is, in genetic equilibrium) or changing. As we've seen, the Hardy-Weinberg formula provides the tool to establish whether allele frequencies are indeed changing.

What factors initiate changes in allele frequencies? There are a number of factors, including those that

1. Produce new variation (that is, *mutation*)

2. Redistribute variation through *gene flow* or *genetic drift*

3. Select "advantageous" allele combinations that promote reproductive success (that is, *natural selection*)

Notice that factors 1 and 2 constitute the first stage of the evolutionary process, as first emphasized by the Modern Synthesis, while factor 3 is the second stage (see p. 79). There's also another factor, as implied by the condition of genetic equilibrium that under idealized conditions all matings are random. Thus, the evolutionary alteration (that is, deviation from equilibrium) is called **nonrandom mating**.

NONRANDOM MATING

Although sexual recombination doesn't itself alter *allele frequencies*, any consistent bias in mating patterns can alter the *genotypic proportions*. By affecting genotype frequencies, nonrandom mating causes deviations from Hardy-Weinberg expectations of the proportions p^2, $2pq$, and q^2. It therefore sets the stage for the action of other evolutionary factors, particularly natural selection.

A variety of nonrandom mating, called *assortative mating*, occurs when individuals of either similar phenotypes (positive assortative mating) or dissimilar phenotypes (negative assortative mating) mate more often than expected by Hardy-Weinberg predictions. However, in the vast majority of human populations, neither factor appears to have much influence.

Inbreeding is a second type of nonrandom mating, and it can have important medical and evolutionary consequences. Inbreeding occurs when relatives mate more often than expected. Such matings will increase the amount of homozygosity, since relatives who share close ancestors will more than likely also share more alleles than two unrelated people would. When relatives mate, their offspring have an increased probability of inheriting two copies of potentially harmful recessive alleles from a relative (perhaps a grandparent) they share in common. Many potentially deleterious genes, normally "masked" in heterozygous carriers, may be expressed in offspring of inbred matings and thereby "exposed" to the action of natural selection. Among offspring of first-cousin matings in the United States, the risk of congenital disorders is 2.3 times greater than it is for the overall population. Matings between especially close relatives—incest—often lead to multiple genetic defects.

All societies have some sort of incest taboo to ban matings between very close relatives, such as between parent and child or brother and sister. These matings thus usually occur less frequently than predicted under random mating conditions.

Whether incest is strictly prohibited by social proscriptions or whether biological factors also interact to condition against such behavior has long been a topic of debate among anthropologists. For many social, economic, and ecological reasons, exogamy is an advantageous strategy for hunting and gathering bands. Selective pressures may also play a part, since highly inbred offspring have a greater chance of expressing a genetic disorder and thereby lowering their reproductive fitness. What's more, inbreeding reduces genetic variability among offspring, potentially reducing reproductive success (Murray, 1980). In this regard, it's interesting to note that incest avoidance is widespread among vertebrates. Detailed studies of free-ranging chimpanzees indicate that they usually avoid incestuous matings within their family group, although exceptions do occur (Constable et al., 2001). In fact, adults of at least one sex in most primate species consistently establish themselves and then mate within groups other than the one in which they were reared. As we've seen, recognition of close kin apparently is an ability displayed by several (perhaps all) primates. Primatologists are currently investigating this fascinating aspect of our primate cousins (see p. 200). Apparently, both biological factors (in common with other primates) and uniquely human cultural factors have interacted during hominid evolution to produce this universal behavior pattern among contemporary societies.

nonrandom mating Patterns of mating in a population in which individuals choose mates preferentially.

inbreeding A type of nonrandom mating in which relatives mate more often than predicted under random mating conditions.

Human Biocultural Evolution

We've defined *culture* as the human strategy of adaptation. Human beings live in cultural environments that are continually modified by human activity; thus, evolutionary processes are understandable only within this *cultural* context. You'll recall that natural selection pressures operate within specific environmental settings. For humans and many of our hominid ancestors, this means an environment dominated by culture. For example, the sickle-cell allele hasn't always been an important genetic factor in human populations. Before the development of agriculture, humans rarely, if ever, lived close to mosquito-breeding areas. With the spread in Africa of **slash-and-burn agriculture**, perhaps in just the last 2,000 years, penetration and clearing of tropical rain forests occurred. This deforestation created open, stagnant pools that provided prime mosquito-breeding areas in close proximity to human settlements. DNA analyses have further confirmed such a recent origin and spread of the sickle-cell allele in West Africa. A recent study of a population from Senegal has estimated the origin of the Hb^S mutation in this group at between 1,250 and 2,100 years ago (Currat et al., 2002).

So quite recently, and for the first time, malaria struck human populations with its full impact; and it became a powerful selective force. No doubt, humans attempted to adjust culturally to these circumstances, and many biological adaptations also probably came into play. The sickle-cell trait is one of these biological adaptations. But there's a definite cost involved with such an adaptation. Carriers have increased resistance to malaria and presumably higher reproductive success, though some of their offspring may be lost through the genetic disease sickle-cell anemia. So there's a counterbalancing of selective forces with an advantage for carriers *only* in malarial environments. The genetic patterns of recessive traits such as sickle-cell anemia are discussed in Chapter 4.

Following World War II, extensive DDT spraying by the World Health Organization began systematic control of mosquito-breeding areas in the tropics. Forty years of DDT spraying killed many mosquitoes; but natural selection, acting on these insect populations, produced several DDT-resistant strains (Fig. 15-5). Accordingly, malaria is again on the rise, with several hundred thousand new cases reported annually in India, Africa, and Central America.

A genetic trait (such as sickle-cell trait) that provides a reproductive advantage to the heterozygote in certain environments is a clear example of natural selection in action among human populations. The precise evolutionary mechanism in the sickle-cell example is termed a **balanced polymorphism**. A polymorphism, as we've defined it, is a trait with more than one allele at a locus in a population. But when a harmful allele (such as sickle-cell) has a higher frequency than can be accounted for by mutation alone, a more detailed evolutionary explanation is required. In this case, the additional mechanism is natural selection.

This brings us to the other part of the term *balanced polymorphism*. By "balanced," we mean the interaction of selective pressures operating in a malarial environment. Some individuals (mainly homozygous normals) will be removed by the infectious disease malaria, and some (homozygous recessives) will die of the inherited disease sickle-cell anemia. Those with the highest reproductive success are the heterozygous carriers. But what alleles do they carry? Clearly, they're passing *both* the normal allele and the sickle-cell allele to offspring, thus maintaining both alleles at fairly high frequencies. Since one allele in this population won't significantly increase in frequency over the other allele, this situation will reach a balance and persist, at least as long as malaria continues to be a selective factor.

Another example of human biocultural evolution involves the ability to digest fresh milk. In all human populations, infants and young children have this ability, an obvious necessity for any young mammal. One ingredient of milk is the sugar *lactose*, which is broken

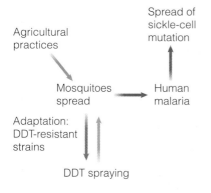

Agricultural practices → Mosquitoes spread → Human malaria → Spread of sickle-cell mutation

Adaptation: DDT-resistant strains ↕ DDT spraying

slash-and-burn agriculture   A traditional land-clearing practice involving the cutting and burning of trees and vegetation. In many areas, fields are abandoned after a few years and clearing occurs elsewhere.

balanced polymorphism   The maintenance of two or more alleles in a population due to the selective advantage of the heterozygote.

TABLE 15-2	Frequencies of Lactose Intolerance
Population Group	**Percent**
U.S. whites	2–19
Finnish	18
Swiss	12
Swedish	4
U.S. blacks	70–77
Ibos	99
Bantu	90
Fulani	22
Thais	99
Asian Americans	95–100
Native Australians	85

Source: Heredity, Evolution, and Society, by I. M. Lerner and W. J. Libby (San Francisco: W. H. Freem 1976).

down in humans and other mammals by the enzyme *lactase*. In most mammals, including humans, the gene coding for lactase production "switches off" in adolescence. Once this happens, if a person drinks too much fresh milk, the lactose ferments in the large intestine and causes diarrhea and severe gastrointestinal upset. Among many African and Asian populations, a majority of humankind today, most adults are intolerant of milk or any fresh dairy product (Table 15-2).

Evidence has suggested a simple dominant mode of inheritance for **lactose intolerance**. The environment also plays a role in expression of the trait—that is, whether a person will be lactose intolerant—since intestinal bacteria can somewhat buffer the adverse effects. Because these bacteria will increase with previous exposure, some tolerance can be acquired, even in individuals who genetically have become lactase deficient.

Why is there variation in lactose tolerance among human populations? Throughout most of hominid evolution, milk was unavailable after weaning. Perhaps, in such circumstances, continued action of an unnecessary enzyme might inhibit digestion of other foods. Thus, there *may* be a selective advantage for the gene coding for lactase production to switch off. So why can some adults (the majority in some populations) tolerate milk? The distribution of lactose-tolerant populations may provide an answer to this question, and it suggests a likely powerful cultural influence on this trait.

European groups, who are generally lactose tolerant, are partially descended from Middle Eastern populations. Often economically dependent on pastoralism, these people raised cows, sheep, and goats and no doubt drank considerable quantities of milk. In such a cultural environment, strong selection pressures would act to shift allele frequencies in the direction of more lactose tolerance. Modern European descendants of these populations apparently retain this ancient ability.

Even more informative is the distribution of lactose tolerance in Africa. For example, groups such as the Fulani and Tutsi, who have been pastoralists probably for thousands of years, have much higher rates of lactose tolerance than nonpastoralists do. Within Africa, the population pattern has become somewhat complicated, however, perhaps because of recent gene flow (Powell et al., 2003).

As we've seen, the geographical distribution of lactose tolerance is related to a history of cultural dependence on fresh milk products. There are, however, some populations that

lactose intolerance   The inability to digest fresh milk products, caused by the discontinued production of lactase—the enzyme that breaks down lactose, or milk sugar.

rely on dairying but aren't characterized by high rates of lactose tolerance. It's been suggested that such populations traditionally have consumed milk in the form of cheese and yogurt, in which the lactose has been broken down by bacterial action (Durham, 1981).

The interaction of human cultural environments and changes in lactose tolerance among human populations is another example of biocultural evolution. In the last few thousand years, cultural factors have initiated specific evolutionary changes in human groups. Such cultural factors have probably influenced the course of human evolution for at least 3 million years, and today they're of paramount importance.

VISUAL SUMMARY

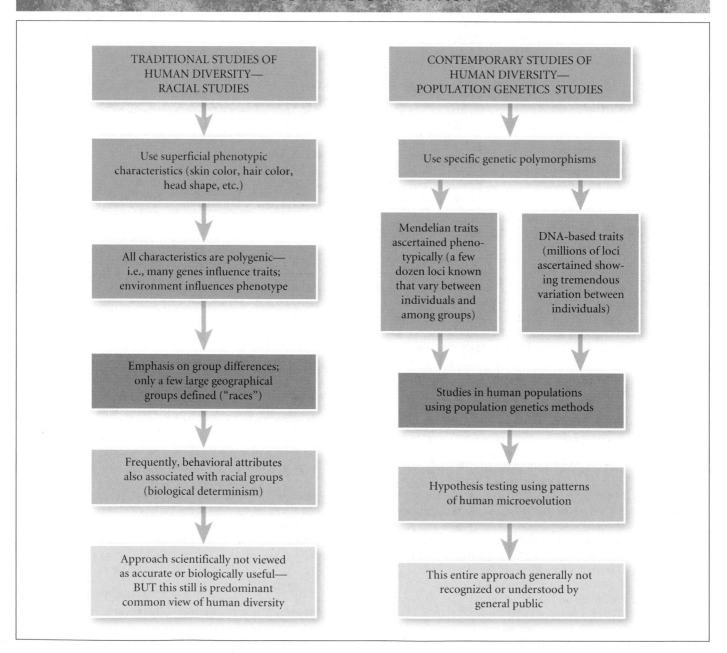

Summary: Putting It All Together

People obviously differ physically from each other, and some of this variation is superficially visible. Physically visible traits, long used in attempts to classify humans into clearly defined groups ("races"), have emphasized such features as skin color, hair color, hair form, head shape, and nose shape. However, all of these physical characteristics are not only influenced by numerous genetic loci but also modified by the environment. As a result, these traditional markers of race aren't reliable indicators of genetic relationships, and they're not biologically useful in depicting patterns of human diversity.

Since the middle of the twentieth century, more precise techniques have allowed far better understanding of actual patterns of *genetic* differences within our species. At first this genetic information was obtained from phenotypic expression of Mendelian traits such as blood groups. Analysis of several of these genetic polymorphisms proved useful in showing broad patterns, such as the high degree of within-population variation and the relatively minor amount of between-population variation.

Since the 1990s, the development and rapid application of comparative genomics has drastically expanded genetic data. Armed with these powerful new tools, population geneticists now use an array of precisely defined DNA sequences to investigate human population variation. Such population studies are aimed at reconstructing the microevolutionary population history of *Homo sapiens* and understanding the varied roles of natural selection, genetic drift, gene flow, and mutation.

For humans, of course, culture also plays a crucial evolutionary role. Interacting with biological influences, these factors define the distinctive *biocultural* nature of human evolution. Two excellent examples of recent human biocultural evolution involve the sickle-cell allele and lactose tolerance.

Critical Thinking Questions

1. Imagine you're with a group of three friends discussing human diversity and the number of races. One friend says there are three clearly defined races. A second claims there are five, while the third thinks there are nine. Would you agree with any of these views? Why or why not?

2. For the same group of friends mentioned in question 1 (none of whom have had a course in biological anthropology), how would you explain how scientific knowledge fits with their preconceived notions about human races?

3. Explain how the concept of race has developed in the Western world. What are the limitations of this approach?

4. In the twentieth century, how did the scientific study of human diversity change from the more traditional approach? Be sure to discuss *both* phenotypically ascertained polymorphisms and DNA-based polymorphisms.

5. Imagine you're a population geneticist about to begin a study of a human population. How will you select a population to study (one that can be defined fairly easily)? What kinds of characteristics will you measure in the group, and what kinds of methods and tools do you plan to use? Finally, what are you trying to learn about this population (in other words, what's your hypothesis)?

Racial Purity: A False and Dangerous Ideology

During the late nineteenth and early twentieth centuries, a growing sense of nationalism swept Europe and the United States. At the same time, an increased emphasis on racial purity had been coupled with the more dangerous aspects of what's known as *biological determinism* (see p. 380). The concept of pure races is based, in part, on the notion that in the past, races were composed of individuals who conformed to idealized types and who were similar in appearance and intellect. Over time, some variation had been introduced into these pure races through interbreeding with other groups, and increasingly, this type of "contamination" was viewed as a threat to be avoided.

In today's terminology, pure races would be said to be genetically homogenous, or to possess little genetic variation. Everyone would have the same alleles at most of their loci. Actually, we do see this situation in "pure breeds" of domesticated animals and plants, developed *deliberately* by humans through selective breeding. We also see many of the detrimental consequences of such genetic uniformity in various congenital abnormalities, such as hip dysplasia in some breeds of dogs.

With our current understanding of genetic principles, we're able to appreciate the potentially negative outcomes of matings between genetically similar individuals. For example, we know that inbreeding increases the likelihood of offspring who are homozygous for certain deleterious recessive alleles. We also know that decreased genetic variation in a species diminishes the potential for natural selection to act, thus compromising that species' ability to adapt to certain environmental fluctuations. What's more, in genetically uniform populations, individual fertility can be seriously reduced, potentially with disastrous consequences for the entire species. So, even if pure human races did exist at one time (and they didn't), theirs would not have been a desirable condition genetically, and they most certainly would have been at an evolutionary disadvantage.

During the latter half of the nineteenth century, many Americans and Europeans had come to believe that nations could be ranked according to technological achievement. It followed that the industrial societies of the United States and Europe were considered to be the most advanced and to have attained a "higher level of civilization" owing to the "biological superiority" of their northern European forebears. This concept arose in part from the writings of Herbert Spencer, a British philosopher who misapplied the principles of natural selection to societies in a doctrine termed *social Darwinism*. Spencer believed that societies evolved, and through competition, "less endowed" cultures and the "unfit" people in them would be weeded out. In fact, it was Spencer who coined the almost always misused phrase "survival of the fittest," and his philosophy became widely accepted on both sides of the Atlantic, where its principles accorded well with notions of racial purity.

In northern Europe, particularly Germany, and in the United States, racial superiority was increasingly embodied in the so-called Aryan race. *Aryan* is a term that's still widely used, albeit erroneously, with biological connotations. Actually, *Aryan* doesn't refer to a biological population, as most people who use the term intend it. Rather, it's a linguistic term that refers to an ancient language group that was ancestral to the Indo-European family of languages.

By the early twentieth century, the "Aryans" had been transformed into a mythical superrace of people whose noble traits were embodied in an extremely idealized "Nordic type." The true Aryan was held to be tall, blond, blue-eyed, strong, industrious, and "pure in spirit." Nordics were extolled as the developers of all ancient "high" civilizations and as the founders of modern industrialized nations. In Europe, there was growing emphasis on the superiority of northwestern Europeans as the modern representatives of "true Nordic stock," while southern and eastern Europeans were viewed as inferior.

In the United States, there prevailed the strongly held opinion that America was originally settled by Christian Nordics. Before about 1890, most newcomers to the United States had come from Germany, Scandinavia, Britain, and Ireland. But by the 1890s, the pattern of immigration had changed. The arrival of increasing numbers of Italians, Turks, Greeks, and Jews among the thousands of newcomers raised fears that society was being contaminated by immigration from southern and eastern Europe.

In the United States, there were additional concerns about the large population of former slaves and their descendants. As African Americans left the South to work in the factories of the North, many unskilled white workers felt economically threatened by competition. It was no coincidence that the Ku Klux Klan, which had been inactive for some years, was revived in 1915 and by the 1920s was preaching vehement opposition to African Americans, Jews, and Catholics in support of the supremacy of the white, Protestant "Nordic race." These sentiments were widespread in the general population, although they didn't always take the extreme form advocated by the Klan. One result of these views was the Immigration Restriction Act of 1924, which was aimed at curtailing the immigration of non-Nordics, including Italians, Jews, and eastern Europeans, in order to preserve America's "Nordic heritage."

To avoid the further "decline of the superior race," many states practiced policies of racial segregation until the mid-1950s. Particularly in the South, segregation laws resulted in an almost total separation of whites and blacks, except where blacks were employed as servants or laborers. There were also laws against marriage between whites and blacks in over half the states, and unions between whites and Asians were frequently illegal. In several states, marriage between whites and blacks was punishable as either a misdemeanor or a felony; astonishingly, some of these laws weren't repealed until the late 1950s or early 1960s. Likewise, in Germany by 1935, the newly instituted Nuremberg Laws forbade marriage or sexual intercourse between so-called Aryan Germans and Jews.

The fact that belief in racial purity and superiority led ultimately to the Nazi death camps in World War II is undisputed (except for continuing efforts by certain white supremacist and neo-Nazi organizations). It's one of the great tragedies of the twentieth century that some of history's most glaring examples of discrimination and viciousness were perpetrated by people who believed that their actions were based in scientific principles. In reality, there's absolutely no evidence to suggest that "pure" human races ever existed. Indeed, such an idea flies in the face of everything we know about natural selection, recombination, and gene flow. The degree of genetic uniformity throughout our species (compared to some other species), as evidenced by mounting data from mitochondrial and nuclear DNA analysis, argues strongly that there has always been gene flow between human populations and that genetically homogenous races are nothing more than fabrication.

The numerous abuses committed in the name of racial purity in the twentieth century were, in part, outgrowths of the rise of nationalism in Europe and the United States during the late nineteenth century. Unfortunately, however, prejudice based on a belief in racial purity and superiority is alive and well. The dogma preached by such white supremacist groups as White Aryan Resistance is no different from that espoused by the Nazi leadership in pre–World War II Germany. The dangers of such thinking have been manifested in incalculable human suffering. Now, early in the twenty-first century, we can only wonder if the generations who will see it to its conclusion will have learned from the mistakes of their predecessors.

CRITICAL THINKING QUESTIONS

1. Given what you know about evolutionary factors, discuss why the notion of "pure races" is inaccurate. Also discuss why you think the concept of racial purity has been (and remains) so prevalent.

2. What is the concept of an "Aryan race," and why is it incorrect? Is this concept dead today?

CHAPTER 16

Modern Human Biology: Patterns of Adaptation

Bill Hatcher / Getty Images

Frans Lemmen / Getty Images

OUTLINE

KEY QUESTIONS

Can patterns of evolution in contemporary human populations be linked to the role of natural selection?

Are there particular environmental (selective) factors to which human populations have adapted?

Introduction

We've all heard it said: "No two people are alike." It's an old expression, but it's true, and now that we're approaching the end of this book, you should know why. One exception to this old adage is identical twins, who are genetically the same, but even they don't look *exactly* alike, and they also have personality differences. You should also know why this is true.

In previous chapters, we explored the genetic bases for biological variation within and between human populations. We discussed how, as a species, humans are remarkably genetically uniform compared with our closest primate relatives. We've also placed these discussions within an evolutionary framework by emphasizing the roles of natural selection and genetic drift in human evolution.

With this foundation, we can turn our attention to some of the factors that have challenged us through our evolutionary journey and consider how we've met these challenges as a species, as populations, and as individuals. Except for the oceans, the highest mountain peaks, and Antarctica, we've managed to colonize the entire planet. But during this process, we've had to cope with ultraviolet (UV) radiation, altitude differences, temperature extremes, and infectious diseases. All of these factors, plus the fact that populations were separated from one another, have produced many kinds of variation in our species.

 Click!

Go to the following media for interactives and exercises on topics covered in this chapter:

- Online Virtual Laboratories for Physical Anthropology, Fourth Edition
- Basic Genetics for Anthropology CD-ROM: Principles and Applications

The Adaptive Significance of Human Variation

Today, biological anthropologists view human variation as the result of such evolutionary factors as genetic drift, founder effect, gene flow, and adaptations to environmental conditions, both past and present. Cultural adaptations have certainly played a critical role in the evolution of *Homo sapiens*, and although in this discussion we're primarily concerned with biological issues, we must still consider the influence of cultural practices on human adaptive responses.

To survive, all organisms need to maintain the normal functions of internal organs, tissues, and cells. What's more, they must accomplish this task in the context of an ever-changing environment. Even during the course of a single, seemingly uneventful day, there are numerous fluctuations in temperature, wind, solar radiation, humidity, and so on. Physical activity also places **stress** on physiological mechanisms. The body must accommodate all these changes by compensating in some way to maintain internal constancy, or **homeostasis**, and all life-forms have evolved physiological mechanisms that, within limits, achieve this goal.

Physiological response to environmental change is influenced by genetic factors. We've already defined adaptation as a response to environmental conditions in populations and individuals. In a narrower sense, adaptation refers to *long-term* evolutionary (that is, genetic) changes that characterize all individuals within a population or species.

Examples of long-term adaptations in *Homo sapiens* include some physiological responses to heat (sweating) or excessive levels of UV light (deeply pigmented skin near the equator). These characteristics are the results of evolutionary change in our species or in populations, and they don't vary because of short-term environmental change. For example, the ability to sweat isn't lost in people who spend their lives in predominantly cool areas. Likewise, individuals born with dark skin wouldn't become pale, even if they weren't ever exposed to sunlight.

stress In a physiological context, any factor that acts to disrupt homeostasis; more precisely, the body's response to any factor that threatens its ability to maintain homeostasis.

homeostasis A condition of balance, or stability, within a biological system, maintained by the interaction of physiological mechanisms that compensate for changes (both external and internal).

Acclimatization is another kind of physiological response to environmental conditions, and it can be short-term, long-term, or even permanent. The physiological responses to environmental stressors are at least partially influenced by genetic factors, but some can also be affected by duration and severity of the exposure, technological buffers (such as shelter, clothing), individual behavior, weight, and overall body size.

Hanna (1999) describes three main types of acclimatization. The simplest is a temporary and rapid adjustment to an environmental change (for example, tanning). Another example is one you may not know about, although you've probably experienced it: the rapid increase in hemoglobin production that occurs in people who live at lower elevations but travel to higher ones (see p. 412). (It's happened in your own body if you've spent a few days at a ski resort.) In both these examples, the physiological changes are temporary. Tans fade when exposure to sunlight is reduced, and hemoglobin production drops to original levels after returning to lower elevations.

A second type of acclimatization is permanent since, after exposure has ceased, the physical adjustments don't disappear. The third form, *developmental* acclimatization, results from exposure to an environmental challenge during growth and development. Because this kind of acclimatization is incorporated into an individual's physiology, it isn't reversible. An example of developmental acclimatization is the physiological responses we see in lifelong residents of high altitude (see p. 412).

In the next section, we present some of the many examples of how humans respond to environmental challenges. Some of these examples describe adaptations that characterize our entire species. Others are shared by most or all members of only certain populations. And a few illustrate acclimatization in individuals.

SOLAR RADIATION AND SKIN COLOR

Skin color is commonly cited as an example of adaptation through natural selection in humans. In general, pigmentation in indigenous populations prior to European contact (beginning around 1500) followed a particular geographical distribution, especially in the Old World. This pattern pretty much holds true today and Figure 16-1 shows that populations with the most pigmentation are found in the tropics, while lighter skin color is associated with more northern latitudes, especially the long-term inhabitants of northwestern Europe.

acclimatization Physiological responses to changes in the environment that occur during an individual's lifetime. Such responses may be temporary or permanent, depending on the duration of the environmental change and when in the individual's life it occurs. The *capacity* for acclimatization may typify an entire species or population, and because it's under genetic influence, it's subject to evolutionary factors such as natural selection or genetic drift.

FIGURE **16-1**
Geographical distribution of skin color in indigenous human populations. (After Biasutti, 1959.)

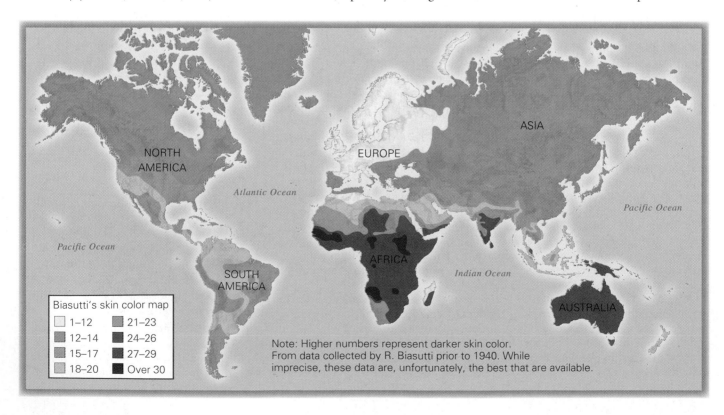

Biasutti's skin color map
1–12	21–23
12–14	24–26
15–17	27–29
18–20	Over 30

Note: Higher numbers represent darker skin color. From data collected by R. Biasutti prior to 1940. While imprecise, these data are, unfortunately, the best that are available.

Three substances influence skin color: hemoglobin, the protein carotene, and, most important, the pigment *melanin*. Melanin is a granular substance produced by specialized cells called melanocytes, located in the outer layer of the skin (see Fig. 16-2). All humans have approximately the same number of melanocytes, but they vary in the amount of melanin and the size of the melanin granules they produce.

Melanin is important because it acts as a built-in sunscreen by absorbing potentially dangerous UV rays that are present, but not visible, in sunlight. So melanin protects us from overexposure to UV radiation, which frequently causes genetic mutations in skin cells. These mutations can lead to skin cancer, which, if left untreated, can eventually spread to other organs and even result in death (see "A Closer Look" on pp. 408–409).

As we mentioned earlier, exposure to sunlight triggers a protective mechanism in the form of tanning, the result of temporarily increased melanin production (acclimatization). This response occurs in all humans except albinos, who carry a genetic mutation that prevents their melanocytes from producing melanin (refer to Fig. 4-10, p. 73). But even people who do produce melanin differ in their ability to tan. For instance, many people of northern European descent tend to have very fair skin, blue eyes, and light hair. Their cells obviously produce small amounts of melanin, but when exposed to sunlight, they have little ability to increase production. And in all populations, women tend not to tan as deeply as men.

Natural selection has favored dark skin in areas closest to the equator, where the sun's rays are most direct and where exposure to UV light is most intense and constant. In considering the cancer-causing effects of UV radiation from an *evolutionary* perspective, keep in mind these three points:

FIGURE **16-2**

Ultraviolet rays penetrate the skin and can eventually damage DNA within skin cells. The three major types of cells that can be affected are squamous cells, basal cells, and melanocytes. (See also "A Closer Look" on pp. 408–409.)

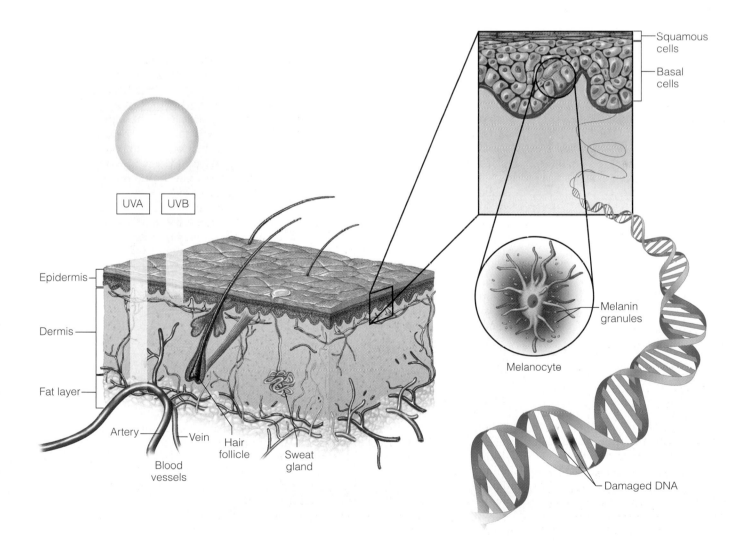

1. Early hominids lived in the tropics, where solar radiation is more intense than in temperate areas to the north and south.

2. Unlike modern city dwellers, early hominids spent their days outdoors.

3. Early hominids didn't wear clothing that would have protected them from the sun.

Under these conditions, UV radiation was probably a powerful agent selecting for optimum levels of melanin production in early humans, especially as they migrated out of the tropics.

There's an important objection to this hypothesis, however. As we mentioned in Chapter 4, natural selection can act only on traits that affect reproduction. Because cancers tend to occur later in life, after the reproductive years, it should theoretically be difficult for selection to act effectively against any factor that might predispose people to cancer. But in one African study, it was shown that all albino individuals in dark-skinned populations of Nigeria and Tanzania had either precancerous lesions or skin cancer by the age of 20 (Robins, 1991). This evidence suggests that even in early humans of reproductive age, less-pigmented skin could have reduced individual reproductive fitness in regions of intense sunlight.

Jablonski (1992) and Jablonski and Chaplin (2000) have provided substantial evidence for an additional explanation for the distribution of skin color, one that proposes an even greater role for natural selection than for skin cancer. This research concerns the degradation of folate by UV radiation. Folate is a B vitamin that isn't stored in the body and must be replenished through dietary sources. Adequate levels of folate are required for many developmental processes, including DNA synthesis; red blood cell formation; and, in males, sperm production. In pregnant women, insufficient levels of folate are associated with numerous fetal developmental disorders, including **neural tube** defects such as **spina bifida**. The consequences of severe neural tube defects can include pain, infection, paralysis, and failure of the brain to develop. Given the importance of folate to many processes related to reproduction, it's clear that maintaining adequate levels of this vitamin contributes to individual reproductive fitness.

Some studies have shown that UV radiation rapidly depletes folate serum levels both in laboratory experiments and in light-skinned individuals. These findings have implications for pregnant women, for children, and for the evolution of dark skin in early hominids. Jablonski (1992) proposed that the earliest hominids may have had light skin covered with dark hair, as is seen in chimpanzees and gorillas (who have darker skin on exposed body parts, for example, faces and hands). But as loss of body hair occurred in hominids, dark skin evolved as a protective response to the damaging effects of UV radiation on folate.

The folate hypothesis doesn't contradict the importance of the relationship between UV radiation and skin cancer. In fact, it reinforces the argument that UV radiation has been a major selective force in the geographical distribution of human skin color.

As hominids migrated out of Africa into Asia and Europe, they faced new selective pressures. In particular, those populations that eventually occupied northern Europe encountered cold temperatures and cloudy skies, sometimes during summer as well as in winter. Winter also meant fewer hours of daylight, and with the sun well to the south, solar radiation was indirect. What's more, to survive the cold, these populations used fire and wore animal skins and other types of clothing. Brace and Montagu (1977) proposed that because of reduced exposure to sunlight, the advantages of deeply pigmented skin in the tropics no longer applied, and selection for melanin production may have been relaxed.

However, relaxed selection for dark skin probably isn't adequate to explain the very depigmented skin seen in some northern Europeans. In fact, the need for a physiological UV filter conflicted with another biological necessity as people moved into areas with less direct solar radiation. That necessity was probably the production of vitamin D, and the theory concerning the role of vitamin D is called the *vitamin D hypothesis*.

Vitamin D is essential for the mineralization and normal growth of bones during infancy and childhood because it enables the body to absorb calcium (the major source of bone mineral) from dietary sources. (Vitamin D is also required for the continued mineralization of bones in adults.) Many foods, including fish oils, egg yolk, butter, cream, and liver, are good sources of vitamin D. But the body's primary source of vitamin D is its own ability to synthesize it through the interaction of UV light and a form of cholesterol found in skin cells. Therefore, adequate exposure to sunlight is essential to normal bone growth. Insufficient amounts of vitamin D during childhood result in *rickets*, a con-

neural tube   In early embryonic development, the anatomical structure that develops to form the brain and spinal cord.

spina bifida   A condition in which the arch of one or more vertebrae fails to fuse and form a protective barrier around the spinal cord.

dition that leads to bone deformities throughout the skeleton, especially the weight-bearing bones of the legs and pelvis. Thus, people with rickets frequently have bowed legs and pelvic deformities (Fig. 16-3). Pelvic deformities are of particular concern for women since they can lead to a narrowing of the birth canal. Without surgical intervention, this deformity frequently results in the death of both mother and infant during childbirth.

Jablonski and Chaplin (2000) have looked at the *potential* for vitamin D synthesis in people of different skin color based on the yearly average UV radiation at various latitudes (Fig. 16-4). Their conclusions support the vitamin D hypothesis to the point of stating that the requirement of vitamin D synthesis in northern latitudes was as important to natural selection as the need for protection from UV radiation in tropical regions.

There's substantial evidence, both historically and in contemporary populations, to support the vitamin D hypothesis. During the latter decades of the nineteenth century, African Americans in northern cities suffered a higher incidence of rickets than did African Americans who lived in the southern states, where exposure to sunlight is greater. (To alleviate this problem, the dairy industry began supplementing milk with vitamin D). Another example is seen in Britain, where darker-skinned East Indians and Pakistanis show a higher incidence of rickets than whites do (Molnar, 1983; Henderson et al., 1987).

Except for a person's sex, more social importance has been attached to skin color than to any other single human biological trait. Obviously, there's no reason this should be so. Aside from its probable adaptive significance relative to UV radiation, skin color is no more important physiologically than many other biological characteristics. But from an evolutionary perspective, skin color provides an outstanding example of how the forces of natural selection have produced geographically patterned variation as the result of two conflicting selective forces: the need for protection from overexposure to UV radiation, on the one hand, and the need for adequate UV exposure for vitamin D synthesis on the other.

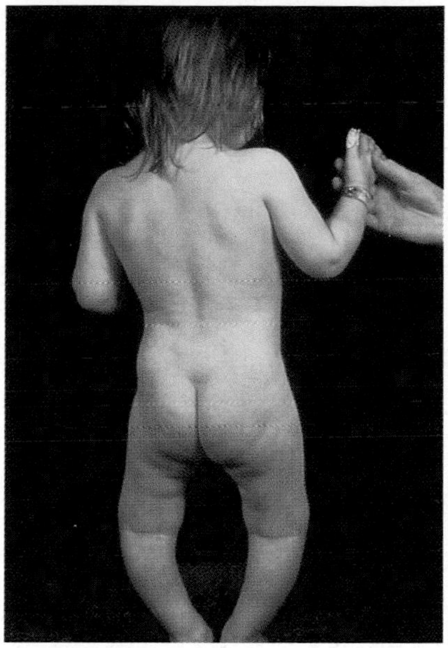

FIGURE 16-3
A child with rickets.

© Biophoto Associates / Photo Researchers, Inc.

FIGURE 16-4
Populations indigenous to the tropics (blue band) received enough UV radiation for vitamin D synthesis (year-round). The darker brown band shows areas where people with moderately melanized skin don't receive enough UV light for vitamin D synthesis for one month of the year. The lighter brown band shows areas where even light skin doesn't receive enough UV light for vitamin D synthesis during most of the year. (Adapted from Jablonski and Chaplin, 2000, 2002.)

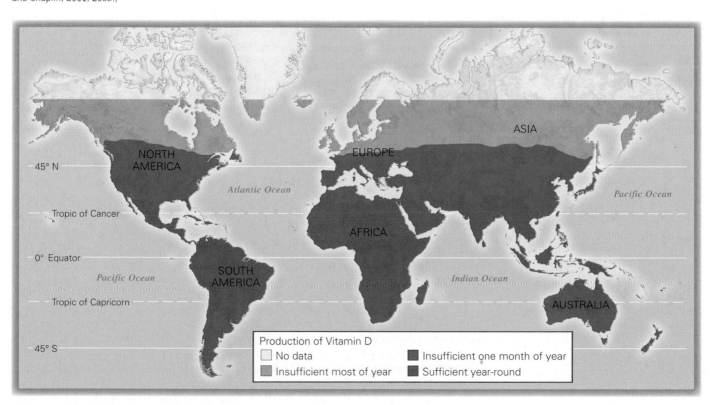

A CLOSER LOOK   Skin Cancer and UV Radiation

Even though we know we can't live without it, most people tend to take their skin for granted. The many functions of this complex organ (and skin *is* an organ) are vital to life. Yet most of us thoughtlessly expose our skin to any number of environmental assaults and especially abuse it with overexposure to the sun, practically to the point of charbroiling. For these reasons, we think it's appropriate here to examine a little more closely this watertight, evolutionary achievement that permits us to live on land, just as it allowed some vertebrates to leave the oceans several hundred million years ago.

Skin is composed of two layers, the epidermis and, just beneath it, the dermis (see Fig. 16-2). The upper portion of the epidermis is made up of flattened, somewhat overlapping *squamous* (scale-like) cells. Beneath these cells, near the base of the epidermis, are several layers of round *basal* cells. Interspersed within the basal cells are still two other cell types: *melanocytes*, which produce melanin, and *keratinocytes*, which are involved in vitamin D synthesis.

Skin cells are continuously produced at the base of the epidermis through mitosis. As they mature, they migrate to the surface, becoming flattened and avascular; that is, they have no direct blood supply. Approximately one month after forming, skin cells die in a process of genetically directed cellular suicide. The results of this suicidal act are the little white flakes people with dry skin are uncomfortably aware of. (Incidentally, in case you've been wondering, dead skin cells are a major component of common household dust.)

The dermis is composed of connective tissue and many structures, including blood vessels, lymphatic vessels, sweat glands, oil glands, and hair follicles. Together, the epidermis and dermis allow the body to retain fluid, help regulate body temperature, synthesize a number of essential substances, and provide protection from ultraviolet (UV) radiation.

There are three main types of UV radiation, but here we're concerned with only two: UVA and UVB. UVA has the longest wavelength and can penetrate through to the bottom of the dermis, while the medium-length UVB waves usually penetrate only to the basal layer of the epidermis (see Fig. 16-2).

The stimulation of vitamin D production by UVB waves is the only benefit we get from exposure to UV radiation. Following a sunburn, both UVB and UVA rays cause short-term suppression of the immune system. But because UVB is directly absorbed by the DNA within cells, it can potentially cause genetic damage, and this damage can lead to skin cancer.

You know that cancers are tumorous growths that invade organs, a process that often results in death, even after treatment. But you may not know that a cell becomes cancerous when a carcinogenic agent, such as UV radiation, damages its DNA and some DNA segments are more susceptible than others. The damage allows the affected cell to divide unchecked. Each subsequent generation of cells receives the mutant DNA, and with it, the potential to divide indefinitely. Eventually, cancer cells form a mass that invades other tissues. They can also break away from the original tumor and travel through the circulatory or lymphatic system to other parts of the body, where they establish themselves and continue to divide. For example, cells from lung tumors (frequently caused by carcinogenic agents in tobacco) can travel to the brain or parts of the skeleton and develop tumors in these new sites before the lung tumor is even detectable. (The former Beatle, George Harrison, died of brain cancer that had spread from the lungs. It's probably no coincidence that he was a heavy smoker when he was young.)

All three types of cells in the epidermis are susceptible to cancerous changes. The most common form of skin cancer is basal cell carcinoma (BCC), which affects about 800,000 people per year in the United States. Fortunately, BCCs are slow growing and, if detected early, can be successfully removed before they spread. They can appear as a raised lump and be uncolored, red-brown, or black (Fig.1a).

THE THERMAL ENVIRONMENT

Mammals and birds have evolved complex mechanisms to maintain a constant internal body temperature. While reptiles must rely on exposure to external heat sources to raise body temperature and energy levels, mammals and birds have physiological mechanisms that, within certain limits, increase or reduce the loss of body heat. The optimum body temperature for normal cellular functions is species-specific, and for humans it's approximately 98.6°F.

People are found in a wide variety of habitats, with thermal environments ranging from exceedingly hot (in excess of 120°F) to bitter cold (less than -60°F). In such extremes, particularly cold, human life wouldn't be possible without cultural innovations. But even accounting for the artificial environments in which we live, such external conditions place the human body under enormous stress.

Response to Heat   All available evidence suggests that the earliest hominids evolved in the warm-to-hot woodlands and savannas of East Africa. The fact that humans cope better with heat (especially dry heat) than they do with cold is testimony to the long-term adaptations to heat that evolved in our ancestors.

Squamous cell carcinomas (SCC) are the second most common skin cancer (Fig. 1b). They grow faster than BCCs, but they're also amenable to treatment if detected reasonably early. They usually appear as firm, pinkish lesions and may spread rapidly on skin exposed to sunlight.

The third form is malignant melanoma, a cancer of the melanocytes. Melanoma is thought to be caused by UVA radiation, and it accounts for only about 4 percent of all skin cancers. But while it's the least common of the three, melanoma is the fastest-growing and the deadliest, killing 30 to 40 percent of affected people. Melanoma looks like an irregularly shaped, very dark or black mole (Fig. 1c). In fact, it may be a mole that has changed because some of its cells have been damaged. It's extremely important to notice any changes in a mole or the appearance of a new dark, perhaps roughened spot on the skin and to have it examined as soon as possible. If a melanoma is less than a millimeter deep, it can be removed before it spreads. But if it has progressed into the dermis, it's likely that it's already spread to other tissues.

Brash et al. (1991) and Ziegler et al. (1994) determined that the underlying genetic factor in most non-melanoma skin cancers is a mutation of a gene called *p53* located on chromosome 17. This gene produces a protein, also called p53, which prevents any cell (not just skin cells) with damaged DNA from dividing until the damage is repaired. In addition, if the damage to a cell's DNA is too severe to repair, the p53 protein can cause the cell to die. Thus, *p53* is what's known as a tumor suppressor gene (Vogelstein et al., 2000).

Unfortunately, the *p53* gene is itself susceptible to mutation, and when certain mutations occur, it can no longer prevent cancer cells from dividing. Luckily, there are other tumor suppressor genes. In fact, damaged *p53* genes don't appear to be involved in melanoma. Instead, a UV-induced mutation in another tumor suppressor gene on chromosome 9 appears to be the culprit (NCBI, 2003).

BCCs and SCCs tend to appear in middle age, long after the underlying genetic damage occurred during childhood and adolescence. If you've had even one serious sunburn in your life, your odds of developing one of the nonmelanoma skin cancers have increased dramatically. Malignant melanomas can occur at any age, although the DNA damage can precede the development of cancer by several years. The best advice is don't take the threat of skin cancer lightly, and don't overexpose your skin to the sun. Wear a hat and a broad-based sunblock that will filter out both UVA and UVB rays. In other words, do your best to keep your tumor suppressor genes happy.

FIGURE 1

(a) Basal cell carcinoma. (b) Squamous cell carcinoma. (c) Malignant melanoma.

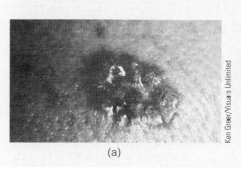

Ken Greer/Visuals Unlimited

(a)

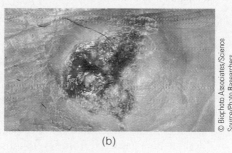

© Biophoto Associates/Science Source/Photo Researchers

(b)

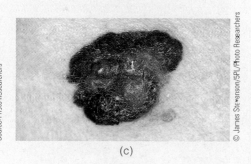

© James Stevenson/SPL/Photo Researchers

(c)

In humans, as well as some other species such as horses, sweat glands are distributed throughout the skin. This wide distribution of sweat glands makes it possible to lose heat at the body's surface through **evaporative cooling**, a mechanism that has evolved to the greatest degree in humans. In fact, perspiration is the most important factor in heat dissipation in humans.

The capacity to dissipate heat by sweating is seen in all human populations to an almost equal degree, with the average number of sweat glands per individual (approximately 1.6 million) being fairly constant. However, there's variation since people who aren't generally exposed to hot conditions do experience a period of acclimatization that initially involves significantly increased perspiration rates (Frisancho, 1993). An additional factor that enhances the cooling effects of sweating is increased exposure of the skin through reduced amounts of body hair. We don't know when in our evolutionary history the loss of body hair occurred, but it represents a species-wide adaptation.

Heat reduction through evaporation can be expensive, and indeed dangerous, in terms of water and sodium loss. For example, a person engaged in heavy work in high heat can lose up to 3 liters of water per hour. To appreciate the importance of this fact, consider that losing 1 liter of water is approximately equivalent to losing 1.5 percent of total body weight,

evaporative cooling A physiological mechanism that helps prevent the body from overheating. It occurs when perspiration is produced from sweat glands and then evaporates from the surface of the skin.

(a)

(b)

FIGURE 16-5

(a) This African woman has the linear proportions characteristic of many inhabitants of sub-Saharan Africa. (b) By comparison, the Inuit woman is short and stocky. These two individuals serve as good examples of Bergmann's and Allen's rules.

and losing 10 percent of body weight can be life threatening. So, water must be continuously replaced during exercise in heat.

There are two basic types of heat, arid and humid. Arid environments, such as those of the southwestern United States, the Middle East, and much of Africa, are characterized by high temperatures, wind, and low water vapor. Humid heat is associated with increased water vapor and is found in regions with a great deal of vegetation and precipitation, conditions found in the eastern and southern United States, parts of Europe, and much of the tropics. Because the increased water vapor in humid climates inhibits the evaporation of sweat on the skin's surface, humans adjust much more readily to dry heat. In fact, people exercising in dry heat may be unaware that they're sweating because the perspiration evaporates as soon as it reaches the skin's surface. While rapid evaporation increases comfort, it can lead to dehydration. Therefore, in dry heat it's important to keep drinking water, even if you aren't particularly thirsty.

Another mechanism for radiating body heat is **vasodilation**, which occurs when capillaries near the skin's surface widen to permit increased blood flow to the skin. The visible effect of vasodilation is flushing, or increased redness and warming of the skin, particularly of the face. But the physiological effect is to permit heat, carried by the blood from the interior of the body, to be emitted from the skin's surface to the surrounding air. (Some drugs, including alcohol, also produce vasodilation; this accounts for the increased redness and warmth of the face in some people after a couple of drinks.)

Body size and proportions are also important in regulating body temperature. In fact, there seems to be a general relationship between climate and body size and shape in birds and mammals. In general, within a species, body size (weight) increases as distance from the equator increases. In humans, this relationship holds up fairly well, but there are many exceptions.

Two rules that pertain to the relationship between body size, body proportions, and climate are *Bergmann's rule* and *Allen's rule*.

1. *Bergmann's rule (concerns the relationship of body mass or volume to surface area):* Among mammals, body size tends to be greater in populations that live in colder climates. This is because as mass increases, the relative amount of surface area decreases proportionately. Because heat is lost at the surface, it follows that increased mass allows for greater heat retention and reduced heat loss. (Remember our discussion of basal metabolic rate and body size in Chapter 7.)

2. *Allen's rule (concerns shape of body, especially appendages):* In colder climates, shorter appendages, with increased mass-to-surface ratios, are adaptive because they're more effective at preventing heat loss. Conversely, longer appendages, with increased surface area relative to mass, are more adaptive in warmer climates because they promote heat loss.

According to these rules, the most suitable body shape in hot climates is linear with long arms and legs. In a cold climate, a more suitable body type is stocky with shorter limbs. Considerable data gathered from several human populations generally conform to these principles. In colder climates, body mass tends, on average, to be greater and characterized by a larger trunk relative to arms and legs (Roberts, 1973). People living in the Arctic tend to be short and stocky while many sub-Saharan Africans, especially the East African pastoralists, are tall and linear (Fig. 16-5). But there's a lot of human variability regarding body proportions, and not all populations conform so obviously to Bergmann's and Allen's rules.

Response to Cold Human physiological responses to cold increase heat production and enhance heat retention. Of the two, heat retention is more efficient because less energy is required. This is an important point because energy is derived from dietary sources. Unless food resources are abundant, and in winter they frequently aren't, any factor that conserves energy can have adaptive value.

Short-term responses to cold include increased metabolic rate and shivering, both of which generate body heat, at least for a short time. **Vasoconstriction**, another short-term response, restricts heat loss and conserves energy. Humans also have a subcutaneous (beneath the skin) fat layer that provides insulation throughout the body. Behavioral modifications include increased activity, increased food consumption, and even curling up into a ball.

Increases in metabolic rate (the rate at which cells break up nutrients into their components) release energy in the form of heat. Shivering also generates muscle heat, as does voluntary exercise. But these methods of heat production are costly because they require an increased intake of nutrients to provide needed energy. (Perhaps this explains why we tend to have a heartier appetite during the winter and why we also tend to eat more fats and carbohydrates, the very sources of energy we require.)

In general, people exposed to chronic cold (meaning much or most of the year) maintain higher metabolic rates than do those living in warmer climates. The Inuit (Eskimo) people living in the Arctic maintain metabolic rates between 13 and 45 percent higher than observed in non-Inuit control subjects (Frisancho, 1993). What's more, the highest metabolic rates are seen in inland Inuit, who are exposed to even greater cold stress than coastal populations. Traditionally, the Inuit had the highest animal protein and fat diet of any population in the world. Their diet was dictated by the available resource base, and it served to maintain the high metabolic rates required by exposure to chronic cold.

Vasoconstriction restricts capillary blood flow to the surface of the skin, thus reducing heat loss at the body surface. Because retaining body heat is more economical than creating it, vasoconstriction is very efficient, provided temperatures don't drop below freezing. However, if temperatures do fall below freezing, continued vasoconstriction can allow the skin temperature to decrease to the point of frostbite or worse.

Long-term responses to cold vary among human groups. For example, in the past, desert-dwelling native Australian populations were subjected to wide temperature fluctuations from day to night. Since they wore no clothing and didn't build shelters, they built sleeping fires to protect themselves from nighttime temperatures that hovered only a few degrees above freezing. Also, they experienced continuous vasoconstriction throughout the night that permitted a degree of skin cooling most people would find extremely uncomfortable. But since there was no threat of frostbite, continued vasoconstriction helped prevent excessive internal heat loss.

By contrast, the Inuit experience intermittent periods of vasoconstriction and vasodilation. This compromise provides periodic warmth to the skin that helps prevent frostbite in below-freezing temperatures. At the same time, because vasodilation is intermittent, energy loss is restricted to retain more heat at the body's core.

These examples illustrate two of the ways adaptations to cold vary among human populations. Obviously, winter conditions exceed our ability to adapt physiologically in many parts of the world. So, if they hadn't developed cultural innovations, our ancestors would have remained in the tropics.

HIGH ALTITUDE

Studies of high-altitude residents have greatly contributed to our understanding of physiological adaptation. As you'd expect, altitude studies have focused on inhabited mountainous regions, particularly in the Himalayas, Andes, and Rocky Mountains. Of these three areas, permanent human habitation probably has the longest history in the Himalayas (Moore et al., 1998). Today, perhaps as many as 25 million people live at altitudes above 10,000 feet. In Tibet, permanent settlements exist above 15,000 feet; in the Andes, they can be found as high as 17,000 feet (Fig. 16-6).

Because the mechanisms that maintain homeostasis in humans evolved at lower altitudes, we're compromised by the conditions at higher elevations. At high altitudes, many factors produce stress on the human body. These include hypoxia (reduced available oxygen), more intense solar radiation, cold, low humidity, wind (which amplifies cold stress), a reduced nutritional base, and rough terrain. Of these, hypoxia exerts the greatest amount of stress on human physiological systems, especially the heart, lungs, and brain.

Hypoxia is caused by reduced barometric pressure. It's not that there is less oxygen in the atmosphere at high altitudes; rather, it's less concentrated. Therefore, to obtain the same amount of oxygen at 9,000 feet as at sea level, people must make certain physiological alterations that increase the body's ability to transport and efficiently use the oxygen that's available.

Reproduction, in particular, is affected through increased infant mortality rates, miscarriage, low birth weights, and premature birth. An early study (Moore and Regensteiner,

vasodilation Expansion of blood vessels, permitting increased blood flow to the skin. Vasodilation permits warming of the skin and facilitates radiation of warmth as a means of cooling. Vasodilation is an involuntary response to warm temperatures, various drugs, and even emotional states (blushing).

vasoconstriction Narrowing of blood vessels to reduce blood flow to the skin. Vasoconstriction is an involuntary response to cold and reduces heat loss at the skin's surface.

(a)

(b)

FIGURE 16-6

(a) A household in northern Tibet, situated at an elevation of over 15,000 feet above sea level. (b) La Paz, Bolivia, at just over 12,000 feet above sea level, is home to more than 1 million people.

1983) reported that in Colorado, infant deaths are almost twice as common above 8,200 feet (2,500 meters) as at lower elevations. One cause of fetal and maternal death is preeclampsia, a severe elevation of blood pressure in pregnant women after the twentieth gestational week. In another study of Colorado residents, Palmer et al. (1999) reported that among pregnant women living at elevations over 10,000 feet, the prevalence of preeclampsia was 16 percent, compared to 3 percent at around 4,000 feet. In general the problems related to childbearing are attributed to issues that compromise the vascular supply (and thus oxygen transport) to the fetus.

People born at lower altitudes and high-altitude natives differ somewhat in how they adapt to hypoxia. In people born at low elevations, acclimatization occurs upon exposure to high altitude. The responses may be short-term modifications, depending on duration of stay, but they begin within hours of the altitude change. These changes include an increase in respiration rate, heart rate, and production of red blood cells. (Red blood cells contain hemoglobin, the protein responsible for transporting oxygen to organs and tissues.)

Developmental acclimatization occurs in high-altitude natives during growth and development. This type of acclimatization is present only in people who grow up in high-altitude areas, not in those who moved there as adults. Compared to populations at lower elevations, lifelong residents of high altitude grow somewhat more slowly and mature later. Other differences include larger chest size, associated, in turn, with greater lung volume and larger heart. In addition to greater lung capacity, people born at high altitudes are more efficient at diffusing oxygen from blood to body tissues than migrants are. Developmental acclimatization to high-altitude hypoxia serves as a good example of physiological flexibility by illustrating how, within the limits set by genetic factors, development can be influenced by environmental factors.

There's evidence that entire *populations* have also genetically adapted to high altitudes. Indigenous peoples of Tibet who have inhabited regions higher than 12,000 feet for around 25,000 years may have made genetic (that is, evolutionary) accommodations to hypoxia. Altitude doesn't appear to affect reproduction in these people to the degree it does in other populations. Infants have birth weights as high as those of lowland Tibetan groups and higher than those of recent (20 to 30 years) Chinese immigrants. This fact may be the result of alterations in maternal blood flow to the uterus during pregnancy (Moore et al., 1991; Moore et al., 2006).

Another line of evidence concerns how the body processes glucose (blood sugar). Glucose is critical because it's the only source of energy used by the brain, and it's also used, although not exclusively, by the heart. Both highland Tibetans and the Quechua (inhabitants of high-altitude regions of the Peruvian Andes) burn glucose in a way that permits more efficient oxygen use. This implies the presence of genetic mutations in the mitochondrial DNA because mtDNA directs how cells process glucose. It also implies that natural selection has acted to increase the frequency of these advantageous mutations in these groups.

There's no certain evidence that Tibetans and Quechua have made evolutionary changes to accommodate high-altitude hypoxia. As yet, the genetic mechanisms underlying these populations' unique abilities haven't been identified. But the data strongly suggest that selection has operated to produce evolutionary change in these two groups. If further study supports these findings, we have an excellent example of evolution in action producing long-term adaptation at the population level.

Infectious Disease

Infection, as opposed to other disease categories such as degenerative or genetic disease, includes those pathological conditions caused by microorganisms (viruses, bacteria, and fungi). Throughout the course of human evolution, infectious disease has exerted enormous selective pressures on populations, so it's influenced the frequency of alleles that affect the immune response. Indeed, it's hard to overemphasize the importance of infectious disease as an agent of natural selection in human populations. But as important as infectious disease has been, its role in this regard isn't very well documented.

The effects of infectious disease on humans are mediated culturally as well as biologically. Innumerable cultural factors, such as architectural styles, subsistence techniques, exposure to domesticated animals, transportation, and even religious practices, affect how infectious disease develops and persists within and between populations.

Until about 10,000 to 12,000 years ago, all humans lived in small nomadic hunting and gathering groups. These groups rarely remained in one location more than a few days at a time, so they had little contact with refuse heaps that house disease **vectors**. But with the domestication of plants and animals, people became more sedentary and began living in small villages. Gradually, villages became towns; and towns, in turn, developed into densely crowded, unsanitary cities.

As long as humans lived in small bands, there wasn't much opportunity for infectious disease to affect large numbers of people. Even if an entire local group or band were wiped out, the effect on the overall population in a given area would have been negligible. Moreover, for a disease to become **endemic** in a population, sufficient numbers of people must be present. Therefore, small bands of hunter-gatherers weren't faced with continuous exposure to endemic disease.

But with the advent of settled living and association with domesticated animals, opportunities for disease increased. As sedentary life permitted larger group size, it became possible for several diseases to become permanently established in some populations. In addition, exposure to domestic animals, such as cattle and fowl, provided an opportune environment for the spread of several **zoonotic** diseases, such as tuberculosis. Close association with nonhuman animals has always been a source of disease for humans. But with the domestication of animals, humans greatly increased the spread of *zoonoses*, or infectious conditions that spread to humans through contact with nonhuman animals. The crowded, unsanitary conditions that characterized parts of all cities until the late nineteenth century, and that still persist in much of the world today, further added to the disease burden borne by human populations.

Malaria provides perhaps the best-documented example of how disease can act to change allele frequencies in human populations. In Chapter 4 you saw how, in some African and Mediterranean populations, malaria has altered allele frequencies at the locus governing hemoglobin formation. Despite extensive long-term eradication programs, malaria still poses a serious threat to human health. Indeed, the World Health Organization estimates the number of people currently infected with malaria to be between 300 and 500 million worldwide. And this number is increasing as drug-resistant strains of the disease-causing microorganism become more common (Olliaro et al., 1995).

Another example of the selective role of infectious disease is indirectly provided by AIDS (acquired immune deficiency syndrome). In the United States, the first cases of AIDS were reported in 1981. Since then, perhaps as many as 1.5 million Americans have been infected

vectors Agents that serve to transmit disease from one carrier to another. Mosquitoes are vectors for malaria, just as fleas are vectors for bubonic plague.

endemic Continuously present in a population.

zoonotic (zoh-oh-no´-tic) Pertaining to a zoonosis (*pl.,* zoonoses), a disease that's transmitted to humans through contact with nonhuman animals.

by HIV (human immunodeficiency virus), the agent that causes AIDS. However, most of the burden of AIDS is borne by developing countries, where 95 percent of all HIV-infected people live. According to World Health Organization estimates, between 33 and 46 million people were living with HIV/AIDS worldwide by the end of 2006. Sixty-five percent of these people were in sub-Saharan Africa. In addition, more than 25 million have died since 1981 (UNAIDS/WHO 2006 Report on the Global Aids Epidemic).

HIV is transmitted from person to person through the exchange of bodily fluids, usually blood or semen. It's not spread through casual contact with an infected person. Within six months of infection, most infected people test positive for anti-HIV **antibodies**, meaning that their immune system has recognized the presence of foreign antigens and is attempting to fight the infection. However, HIV is a "slow virus," and it may be present for years before the onset of severe illness. This asymptomatic state is called a "latency period," and the average latency period in the United States is more than 11 years.

Like all viruses, HIV must invade certain types of cells and alter the functions of those cells to produce more virus particles in a process that eventually leads to cell destruction. (The way HIV does this is different from that of many other viruses.) HIV can attack various types of cells, but it especially targets so-called T4 helper cells, which are major components of the immune system. As HIV infection spreads and T4 cells are destroyed, the patient's immune system begins to fail. Consequently, he or she begins to show symptoms caused by various **pathogens** that are commonly present but usually kept in check by a normal immune response. When an HIV-infected person's T cell count drops to a level indicating that immunity has been suppressed, and when symptoms of "opportunistic" infections appear, the patient is said to have AIDS.

By the early 1990s, scientists were aware of some patients who had been HIV positive for 10 to 15 years but continued to show few if any symptoms. This fact led researchers to suspect that some individuals are naturally resistant to HIV. This was shown to be true in late 1996 with the publication of two different studies (Dean et al., 1996; Samson et al., 1996) that demonstrated a mechanism for HIV resistance.

These two reports describe a genetic mutation that concerns a major protein "receptor site" on the surface of certain immune cells, including T4 cells. (Receptor sites are protein molecules that enable HIV and other viruses to invade cells.) In this particular situation, the mutant allele results in a malfunctioning receptor site to which HIV is unable to bind, and current evidence strongly suggests that people who are homozygous for this allele may be completely resistant to many types of HIV infection. In heterozygotes, infection may still occur; but the course of HIV disease is markedly slowed.

For unknown reasons, the mutant allele occurs mainly in people of European descent, among whom its frequency is about 10 percent. Samson and colleagues (1996) reported that in the Japanese and West African samples they studied, the mutation was absent; but Dean and colleagues (1996) reported an allele frequency of about 2 percent among African Americans. These researchers speculated that the presence of the allele in African Americans may be entirely due to genetic admixture (gene flow) with European Americans. They further suggest that this polymorphism exists in Europeans because of selective pressures favoring an allele that originally occurred as a rare mutation. But, it's important to understand that the original selective agent wasn't HIV. Instead, it was some other, as yet unidentified pathogen that requires the same receptor site as HIV. One possibility is bubonic plague, but it's largely been ruled out. Another, perhaps more likely suggestion is smallpox. In December 1999, Lalanie et al. (1999) reported that a poxvirus, related to the virus that causes smallpox, can use the same receptor site as HIV. While this conclusion hasn't yet been proved, or even really investigated, it offers an exciting avenue of research. It may reveal how a mutation that has been favored by selection because it provides protection against one type of infection can also increase resistance to another (AIDS).

Examples such as AIDS and the relationship between malaria and sickle-cell anemia are continuously revealing new insights into the complex interactions between disease organisms and their host populations. These insights in turn form a growing basis for understanding the many variations between individuals and populations that have arisen as adaptive responses to infectious disease.

Smallpox, once a deadly viral disease, may be a good example of how exposure to infectious agents can produce polymorphisms in host populations. During the eighteenth cen-

antibodies   Proteins that are produced by some types of immune cells and that serve as major components of the immune system. Antibodies recognize and attach to foreign antigens on bacteria, viruses, and other pathogens. Then other immune cells destroy the invading organism.

pathogens   Substances or microorganisms, such as bacteria, fungi, or viruses, that cause disease.

EXAMPLES

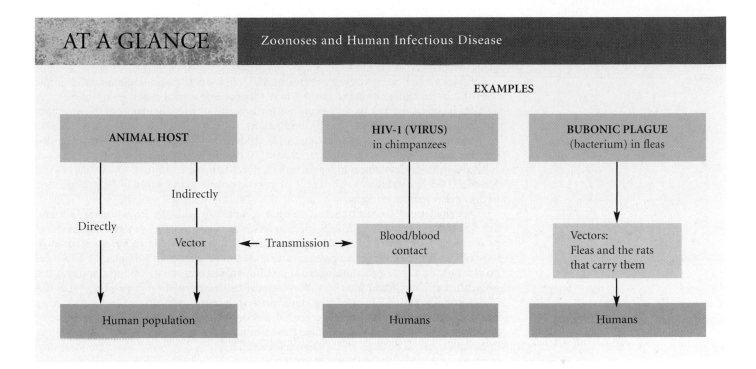

tury, smallpox is estimated to have accounted for 10 to 15 percent of all deaths in parts of Europe. But today, this once devastating killer is the only condition to have been successfully eliminated by modern medical technology. By 1977, through massive vaccination programs, the World Health Organization was able to declare the smallpox virus extinct, except for a few colonies in research labs in the United States and Russia.*

Smallpox had a higher incidence in persons with either blood type A or AB than in type O individuals, a fact that has been explained by the presence of an antigen on the smallpox virus that's similar to the A antigen. It follows that when some type A individuals were exposed to smallpox, their immune systems failed to recognize the virus as foreign and didn't mount an adequate immune response. So, in regions where smallpox was common in the past, it could have altered allele frequencies at the ABO locus by selecting against the A allele.

The Continuing Impact of Infectious Disease

It's important to understand that humans and pathogens exert selective pressures on each other, creating a dynamic relationship between disease organisms and their human (and nonhuman) hosts. Just as disease exerts selective pressures on host populations to adapt, microorganisms also evolve and adapt to various pressures exerted on them by their hosts.

Evolutionarily speaking, it's to the advantage of any pathogen not to be so virulent that it kills its host too quickly. If the host dies shortly after becoming infected, the viral or bacterial agent may not have time to reproduce and infect other hosts. Thus, selection sometimes acts to produce resistance in host populations and/or to reduce the virulence of disease organisms, to the benefit of both. However, members of populations exposed for the first

---

*Concern over the potential use of the smallpox virus by bioterrorists relates to these laboratory colonies. Although the virus is extinct outside these labs, some officials fear the possibility that samples of the virus could be stolen. Also, there are apparently some concerns that unknown colonies of the virus may exist in labs in countries other than Russia and the United States. Using disease organisms against enemies isn't new. In the Middle Ages, armies catapulted the corpses of smallpox and plague victims into towns under siege, and during the U.S. colonial period, British soldiers knowingly gave Native Americans blankets used by smallpox victims.

time to a new disease frequently die in huge numbers. This type of exposure was a major factor in the decimation of indigenous New World populations after Europeans introduced smallpox into Native American groups. And this has also been the case with the current worldwide spread of HIV.

Of the known disease-causing organisms, HIV provides the best-documented example of evolution and adaptation in a pathogen. It's also one of several examples of interspecies transfer of infection. For these reasons, we focus much of this discussion of evolutionary factors and infectious disease on HIV and AIDS.

The type of HIV responsible for the AIDS epidemic is HIV-1, which in turn is divided into three major subtypes comprising at least 10 different varieties (Hu et al., 1996; Gao, 1999). Another far less common type is HIV-2, which is present only in populations of West Africa. HIV-2 also exhibits a wide range of genetic diversity, and while some strains cause AIDS, others are less virulent.

Since the late 1980s, researchers have been comparing the DNA sequences of HIV and a closely related retrovirus called *simian immunodeficiency virus (SIV)*. SIV is found in chimpanzees and several African monkey species. Like HIV, SIV is genetically variable, and each strain appears to be specific to a given species and even subspecies of primate. SIV produces no symptoms in the African monkeys and chimpanzees that are its traditional hosts, but when injected into Asian monkeys, it eventually causes immune suppression, AIDS-like symptoms, and death. These findings indicate that the various forms of SIV have shared a long evolutionary history (perhaps several hundred thousand years) with a number of African primate species, and that these primates have developed ways of accommodating this virus, which is deadly to their Asian relatives. These results also substantiate long-held hypotheses that SIV and HIV evolved in Africa.

Comparisons of the DNA sequences of HIV-2 and the form of SIV found in one monkey species (the sooty mangabey) revealed that genetically, these two viruses are almost identical. These findings led to the generally accepted conclusion that HIV-2 evolved from sooty mangabey SIV. What's more, sooty mangabeys are hunted for food and kept as pets in west-central Africa, and the transmission of SIV to humans probably occurred through bites and the butchering of monkey carcasses.

But although the origin of HIV-2 was established, there was continuing debate over which primate species had been the source of HIV-1. So, a group of medical researchers (Gao et al., 1999) compared DNA sequences of HIV-1 and the form of SIV found in chimpanzees indigenous to west-central Africa. Their results showed that HIV-1 almost certainly evolved from the strain of chimpanzee SIV that infects the subspecies *Pan troglodytes troglodytes*, which is indigenous to central Africa.

Unfortunately for both species, chimpanzees are routinely hunted by humans for food in parts of West Africa (see pp. 118–120). So, the most probable explanation for the transmission of SIV from chimpanzees to humans is, as with sooty mangabeys, the hunting and butchering of chimpanzees (Gao et al., 1999; Weiss and Wrangham, 1999) (Fig. 16-7.)

So for all these reasons, HIV/AIDS is a zoonotic disease. The DNA evidence further suggests there were at least three separate human exposures to chimpanzee SIV, and at some point the virus was altered to the form we call HIV. When chimpanzee SIV was transmitted to humans is unknown. The oldest evidence of human infection is a frozen HIV-positive blood sample taken from a West African patient in 1959. There are also a few documented cases of AIDS infection by the late 1960s and early 1970s. Therefore, although human exposure to SIV/HIV probably occurred many times in the past, the virus didn't become firmly established in humans until the latter half of the twentieth century.

Severe acute respiratory syndrome (SARS) is another contemporary example of zoonotic transmission of disease. In early 2003 an outbreak of SARS in southern China surprised the world health community by quickly spreading through much of Asia, then to North America (especially Canada), South America, and Europe. It was due to travel that SARS spread so quickly around the world, even though it has a fairly low transmission rate. If modern technology didn't exist, this infection would have been confined to one or a few villages, and perhaps a small number of people would have died. But it would have been a fairly unremarkable event, and it certainly wouldn't have become widely known. In fact, this and many other similar scenarios have undoubtedly been repeated countless times during the course of human history.

When compared to HIV/AIDS, tuberculosis, influenza, and malaria, the threat from SARS is relatively minor. Still, it can be fatal especially in the elderly. Scientists don't know the exact mode of SARS transmission in humans, but most believe it's spread through close contact by means of infected droplets (that is, when people cough or sneeze). Many health officials believe it was initially transmitted to humans through contact either with domesticated animals or wild animals, such as civet cats, sold in Asian markets for food. Indeed, many of the influenza strains that frequently originate in China are believed to originate in pigs and fowl that live in very close contact with humans (Clarke, 2003).

From these SIV/HIV and SARS examples, you can appreciate how, by adopting various cultural practices, humans have radically altered patterns of infectious disease. The interaction of cultural and biological factors has influenced microevolutionary change in humans (as in the example of sickle-cell anemia) to accommodate altered relationships with disease organisms.

FIGURE **16-7**

These people, selling butchered chimpanzees, may not realize that by handling this meat they could be exposing themselves to HIV.

Until the twentieth century, infectious disease was the number one cause of death in all human populations. Even today, in many developing countries, as much as half of all mortality is due to infectious disease, compared to about 10 percent in the United States. For example, malaria is a disease of the poor in developing nations. Annually, there are an estimated 1 million deaths due to malaria. That figure computes to one malaria-related death every 30 seconds (Weiss, 2002)! Ninety percent of these deaths occur in sub-Saharan Africa, where 5 percent of children die of malaria before age 5 (Greenwood and Mutabingwa, 2002; Weiss, 2002). In the United States and other developed nations, with better living conditions and sanitation and especially with the widespread use of antibiotics and pesticides beginning in the late 1940s, infectious disease has given way to heart disease and cancer as the leading causes of death.

Optimistic predictions held that infectious disease would be a thing of the past in developed countries and, with the introduction of antibiotics and better living standards, in developing nations as well. But by the mid-1980s, such predictions were increasingly seen to be wrong. Between 1980 and 1992, the number of deaths in the United States in which infectious disease was the underlying cause rose from 41 to 65 per 100,000, an increase of 58 percent (Pinner et al., 1996). During that same period, there was a 25 percent increase in infectious disease mortality among people aged 65 and older, from 271 to 338 per 100,000. Additionally, AIDS contributed substantially to the increase in mortality due to infectious disease in the United States between 1980 and 1992.

Increase in the prevalence of infectious disease may partly be due to the overuse of antibiotics. It's estimated that half of all antibiotics prescribed in the United States are used to treat viral conditions such as colds and flu. Because antibiotics are completely ineffective against viruses, such therapy is not only useless but also may have dangerous long-term consequences. There's considerable concern in the biomedical community over the indiscriminate use of antibiotics since the 1950s. Antibiotics have exerted selective pressures on bacterial species that have, over time, developed antibiotic-resistant strains (an excellent example of natural selection). So, in the past few years we've seen the *reemergence* of many bacterial diseases, including influenza, pneumonia, tuberculosis, and cholera, in forms that are less responsive to treatment. In essence, we've altered the course of evolution in some microbial species, just as they've changed our own evolutionary course in the past and clearly continue to do so in the present.

Tuberculosis is now listed as the world's leading killer of adults by the World Health Organization (Colwell, 1996). In fact, the number of tuberculosis cases has risen 28 percent since the mid-1980s worldwide, with an estimated 10 million infected in the United States alone. Although not all infected persons develop active disease, an estimated 30 million are believed to have died from TB in the 1990s worldwide. One troubling aspect of the increase in tuberculosis infection is that newly developed strains of *Mycobacterium tuberculosis*, the bacterium that causes TB, are resistant to antibiotics and other treatments.

Cholera, a dangerous and often fatal gastrointestinal disease caused by a bacterium found in sewage-contaminated water, has periodically occurred in epidemic proportions throughout history, including outbreaks in the nineteenth century in New York, Philadelphia, and London. Currently, cholera claims about 100,000 lives annually in Asia alone, and an antibiotic-resistant strain has spread throughout Southeast Asia since the early 1990s. Besides threats posed by resistant strains of pathogens, other factors may contribute to the emergence (or reemergence) of infectious disease. Scientists are becoming increasingly concerned over the potential for global warming to expand the geographical range of numerous tropical disease vectors, such as mosquitoes. And the destruction of natural environments doesn't just contribute to global warming; it also has the potential of allowing disease vectors formerly restricted to local areas to spread to new habitats.

Fundamental to all these factors is human population size (see pp. 438–439); as it continues to soar, it causes more environmental disturbance and, through additional human activity, adds further to global warming. Moreover, in developing countries, where as much as 50 percent of mortality is due to infectious disease, overcrowding and unsanitary conditions increasingly contribute to increased rates of communicable illness. It's hard to conceive of a better set of circumstances for the appearance and spread of communicable disease, and it remains to be seen if scientific innovation and medical technology will be able to meet the challenge.

VISUAL SUMMARY

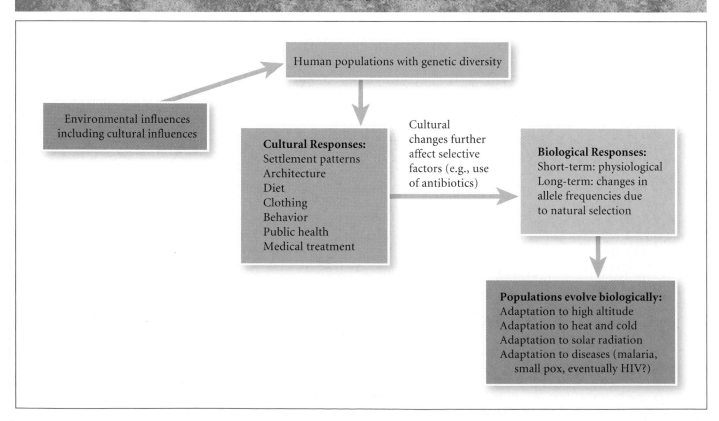

Summary: Putting It All Together

In this chapter, we've explored some of the many ways humans have adapted to environmental challenges as they evolved and migrated out of Africa to eventually inhabit most of the planet. We began with a brief discussion of acclimatization as a form of adaptation and the various ways it can occur.

We considered skin color and its adaptive value in response to conflicting selective pressures, all having to do with ultraviolet (UV) radiation. One reason we focused on skin color is that so much importance has been placed on it in the past, particularly in racial classification schemes. Also, skin color is an excellent example of how variations in a characteristic can develop rapidly in response to strong selective pressures. Heavily pigmented skin is adaptive in the tropics because it provides protection from UV radiation, which can cause skin cancer and degrade folate. But as people moved away from the tropics, dark skin became disadvantageous, because a decrease in sunlight meant insufficient exposure to UV radiation for the adequate production of vitamin D.

We also dealt with the various forms of acclimatization that have evolved in humans to deal with environmental stressors like heat, cold, and high altitude. And we emphasized the role of infectious disease in human evolution. We're still coping with infectious disease as we alter the environment and as global climate change facilitates the spread of disease vectors. Cultural innovations also have altered disease patterns and have increased the rate of spread of infectious conditions. Examples of this type of spread are HIV/AIDS and malaria.

Certainly, without cultural adaptations, our species never would have left the tropics. But, as in the case of sickle-cell anemia, HIV, and many bacterial diseases, some of our cultural innovations themselves have become selective agents. Many of our practices have had a nasty way of turning on us, and they continue doing so, often with devastating consequences. More than ever, we need to examine our biocultural interactions if we want to explain our history and perhaps predict our future.

Critical Thinking Questions

1. Why can we say that variations in human skin color are the result of natural selection in different environments? Why is less pigmented skin a result of conflicting selective factors?

2. Do you think that infectious disease has played an important role in human evolution? Do you think it plays a *current* role in human adaptation? How have human cultural practices influenced the patterns of infectious disease seen today? List as many examples as you can, including some not discussed in this chapter.

Molecular Applications in Modern Human Biology

As you've become aware, molecular data are revolutionizing anthropological studies of modern human biology. For example, numerous researchers using both mitochondrial and nuclear DNA are investigating population relationships spanning the last 100,000 years or so.

Anthropologists trying to untangle more recent population relationships also make good use of these same techniques. Dozens of studies have been completed, and hundreds more are in progress. The Y chromosome, especially, has been a focus of innovative research. It provides a particularly useful genetic tool, since (like mtDNA) most of the loci on the Y chromosome don't recombine during sexual reproduction. Therefore, except for mutations, Y chromosomes are passed intact over generations of related males.

Indeed, in the last decade, along with tremendously enhanced information coming from mtDNA, the X chromosome, and autosomes, Y chromosome molecular sequences have helped elucidate modern human origins (Underhill et al., 2001; Jobling and Tyler-Smith, 2003).

What's more, numerous microevolutionary insights have also been recently gained, such as those showing: (1) the gradual occupation of Europe by early farmers (in the last 5,000 years); (2) the imprint of genetic drift in small northern Asian populations; and (3) a quite recent occupation (dating to 20,000–10,000 ya) of the New World by North Asians; and (4) aspects of a Bantu expansion in Africa in the last 3,000 years. ("Bantu" is a linguistic term used to refer to many African ethnic groups who use the related languages of the Bantu language family. Today, all of southern Africa and sub-Saharan West Africa are occupied by Bantu-speaking people. But, these people are descendants of groups that began to expand out of what is now Nigeria between 3 and 4 thousand years ago. Eventually these groups displaced many indigenous populations.) It should be emphasized that in all these cases, genetic data are used in correlation with, and strongly corroborate, archaeological evidence.

Perhaps the most interesting discovery traces an expansion of populations from what is now Mongolia in central Asia, probably sometime in the last 1,000 years (ca. 1,300–700 ya). An unusual Y chromosome variant is found in about 8 percent of Asians today (i.e., a total of $1/200$ of all males in the world). Furthermore, the geographical patterns of genotypes trace back to Mongolia, and probably spread from there to its present distribution stretching from northeast China to Uzbekistan.

This genetic pattern can't be easily accounted for by natural selection. Alternatively, a team of international investigators has proposed a form of "social selection" in which only a few related males fathered a disproportionately large number of descendants (Zerjal et al., 2003). Presumably, this disproportionate contribution to the gene pool occurred not long before A.D. 1300.

Assembling these clues, Tatiana Zerjal, Chris Tyler-Smith (both from Oxford University), and colleagues raise a tantalizing suggestion. Was it Genghis Khan himself who happened to inherit the unusual Y chromosome and who then passed it to potentially dozens of sons (with many, in turn, also producing large broods)?

The timing and geography support this interesting hypothesis. Genghis Khan (ca.1160–1227), one of the most important military leaders in history, established what became the largest contiguous empire in history. At its greatest point, the Mongol Empire extended eastward, all the way from Iraq, across Asia to include much of modern China in the east. Presumably one of Khan's direct male ancestors first possessed the unique Y chromosome variant. Today, more than 15 million men have this same (or nearly identical) Y chromosome. How did it spread so quickly, and where did it originate? Allele frequency distribution strongly points to Mongolia as the area of origin. Moreover, the broader geographical pattern of contemporary high frequency of this genotype almost exactly coincides with the extent of the Mongol empire at the time of Genghis Khan's death (Fig. 1).

This same team of geneticists also discovered another intriguing Y chromosome variant found today among contemporary Mongolian and northern Chinese populations (Xue et al, 2005). In this group, it's hypothesized that up to 1.5 million men can trace their ancestry back to a very few male ancestors a few hundred years ago. The current data suggest that a mutation first arose in the Y chromosome of an early relative of members of the Qing Dynasty (who ruled in China, 1622–1912) and perhaps even can be originally traced to a single individual (Giocangge, who died in 1582). Again, these high status males seem to have been exceedingly successful in spreading their genes very quickly. Indeed, next to Genghis Khan, for the moment, Giocangge ranks as the second most prolific ancestor in history. These situations serve as examples of founder effect (see pp. 82–83). since a genetic variant, common in Asia, can be traced back to one very powerful individual, who, because of social factors was able to make a disproportionate contribution to the gene pool of generations that followed him.

So, was Genghis Khan responsible, and are all these 15 million living males his direct descendants? Perhaps. Certainly, some small group of Asian males who lived about 800 years ago was responsible, and most likely these males were part of the Mongol empire. Perhaps they were soldiers, who no doubt traveled widely and had numerous reproductive opportunities. It's not at all impossible that it was the greatest Mongol warrior of all (and his sons) who had the most mates and thus spread their genes very quickly indeed.

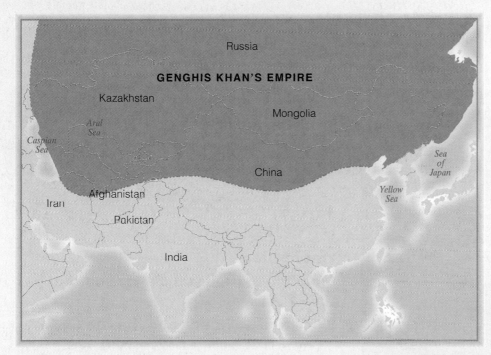

Source: Adapted from *Science News,* 163(6), February 8, 2003, p. 91.

One last tantalizing avenue of investigation might just help seal the case. Recently, archaeologists excavated a site in Mongolia that might be near the location of Genghis Khan's tomb (Travis, 2003). *If* the tomb is ever found, and *if* ancient DNA can be extracted and analyzed (including nuclear DNA), then just maybe there will be a solution to this intriguing inquiry!

SOURCES

Jobling, Mark A., and Chris Tyler-Smith. 2003. "The Human Y Chromosome: An Evolutionary Marker Comes of Age." *Nature Reviews Genetics* 4:598–612.

Travis, John. 2003. "Genghis Khan's Legacy?" *Science News* 163:91.

Underhill, P.A., G. Passarino, A.A. Lin, et al. 2001. "The Paleogeography of the Y Chromosome Binary Haplotypes and the Origins of Modern Human Populations." *Annals of Human Genetics* 65:43–62.

Xue, Yali, Tatiana Zerjal, Weidong Bao, et al. 2005. "Recent Spread of a Y Chromosomal Lineage in Northern China and Mongolia." *American Journal of Human Genetics* 77:1112-1116.

Zerjel, Tatiana, Yali Xue, Giorgio Bertorelle, et al. 2003. "The Genetic Legacy of the Mongols." *American Journal of Human Genetics* 72:717–721.

CHAPTER 17

Legacies of Human Evolutionary History

Courtesy Craig Mayhew and Robert Simmon, NASA

KEY QUESTIONS

How are humans part of a biological continuum that includes all living things?

Given that humans are part of a biological continuum, how does culture make us different from other species?

Introduction

By now, you've read 16 chapters that have emphasized human biological evolution and adaptation. You have followed along as we've talked about genetics, evolutionary factors, nonhuman primates, fossil hominids, and how humans vary from one another. But you have also learned that we're remarkably genetically uniform when compared to other primate species that have been studied.

You have accompanied us through geological time to the development of *Homo sapiens:* 225 million years of mammalian evolution, 65 million years of primate evolution, 6 million years of hominid evolution, and 2 million years of evolution of the genus *Homo.* So, what do you think now? Are we just another mammal—or just another primate? In most ways, of course, we *are* like other mammals and primates. But as we've emphasized throughout the text, modern human beings are the result of *biocultural evolution.* In other words, modern human biology and behavior have been shaped by the biological and cultural forces that operated on our ancestors. In fact, it would be fruitless to attempt an understanding of modern human biology and diversity without considering that humans have evolved in the context of culture. It would be like trying to understand the biology of fish without considering that they live in water.

In the two previous chapters, we've seen that modern human beings are a highly generalized species. This means that we can live in a great variety of climates, eat a wide variety of foods, and respond to most environmental challenges in myriad ways. For example, as human populations moved into cold northern climates, they were able to respond both physiologically and behaviorally to the environmental challenges they faced. As noted in Chapter 16, adaptations to cold include physiological responses to conserve or increase heat such as vasoconstriction of the capillaries, increased metabolic rate, and shivering. Considering these responses from an evolutionary perspective, we can assume that among the earliest human populations inhabiting cold regions of the world, those individuals who had genotypes and phenotypes enabling them to respond physiologically had more surviving offspring to pass along these characteristics. Behavioral and cultural adaptations to cold climates probably included fire, house structures, warm clothing, and hunting for foods that provided energy to withstand the cold. In these examples we see evidence of human adaptations to cold that are both biological and cultural and that are rooted in evolution.

In this chapter, we'll explore ways in which the legacies of human evolution continue to profoundly impact our behavior throughout our lives and the planet we inhabit. We begin with a view of the legacies of human evolution that affect each of us as individuals throughout our life course. Later we'll discuss how the legacies of our evolutionary history impact the Earth and other life-forms.

Evolution of Human Behavior and the Life Course

Examining human social behavior in an evolutionary framework is known as *behavioral ecology,* which we discussed in Chapter 7 in the context of primate behavior. Of course, humans are primates, and many biological anthropologists are interested in the extent to

 Click!

Go to the following media for interactives and exercises on topics covered in this chapter:

- Online Virtual Laboratories for Physical Anthropology, Fourth Edition

which evolution can explain contemporary human behaviors. Behavioral ecologists suggest that humans, like other animals, behave in ways that increase their fitness, or reproductive success. This includes behaviors affecting mating and parenting success. Finding mates and taking care of offspring require time and energy, and as we know all too well, both of these commodities exist in finite amounts. Thus, reproductive efforts require trade-offs in time, energy, and resources invested in mating and parenting. When we read about these concepts as they pertain to monkeys and apes, most of us probably find little to disagree with. But to suggest that evolutionary processes have an impact on human behavior today raises a lot of issues, some of which aren't so easily resolved.

For example, this view argues that natural selection isn't limited to physical and physiological responses, but has affected the way humans think—in other words, on human cognition, perception, and memory. An example of the argument goes something like this: The ability to remember a dangerous event that may have resulted in loss of life would be favorably selected if it prevented a person from being caught in a similar situation. The ability to distinguish a wildebeest (food) from a lion (danger) would be selectively favored. Likewise, economic behaviors involved in allocating resources to increase survival and reproductive success would be favored.

The study of how natural selection has influenced the way humans and other primates think is often called *evolutionary psychology*. Among the topics explored by evolutionary psychologists are mate attraction, sexuality, aggression, and violence. As you might guess, all of these are hot topics, and there's no end in sight for the controversy that surrounds them.

Because it implies that our behavior is constrained in ways that we may not be able to overcome, many people are uncomfortable with such an explicit evolutionary perspective on contemporary human behavior and thought. For example, it can be argued that individual males can increase their reproductive success by increasing the number of women they mate with. Women, meanwhile, are thought to best increase the health of their offspring (and thus their reproductive success) if they can find mates and other people who will supply resources to them and their children. At first glance, these two recipes for reproductive success seem to conflict. Further examination, however, reveals that the best route to reproductive success for males and females is a compromise between what's argued to be the best strategy for each sex. Males who "love 'em and leave 'em" usually end up with fewer surviving offspring in comparison with males who take on the role of providers.

Aggression and violence, particularly by males, is the subject of many books and papers in evolutionary psychology. A common approach is to contrast the behaviors of our two closest living relatives, the chimpanzees and bonobos. Most striking is that chimpanzee society seems to be based on male-male competition and aggression leading occasionally to violence both within and between troops, while bonobo society is described as a female-dominated community based on cooperation and peaceful interaction (Fig. 17-1). To Wrangham and Peterson (1996), these two behavior patterns represent the extremes of human societies and show potentials for both violence and peace that may be rooted in human evolutionary history. On the other hand, these and other authors acknowledge the role of culture and society in fostering aggression and violence in males. Mirroring some of the discussions of terrorism today, Wrangham and Peterson point out that chimpanzee communities with abundant resources have far fewer incidents of violence than do communities with limited resources; in general, bonobos live in areas of relative resource abundance. But whatever their roots, it appears to many observers that war, genocide, rape, rioting, and terrorism are unwelcome legacies of human evolutionary history. Unfortunately, because of recent events like the 2001 terrorist attacks and the wars in Afghanistan and Iraq, the arguments that violence and aggression are rooted in human evolutionary history resonate more profoundly and convincingly than they did when the first edition of this textbook was written. Perhaps by the next edition, the pendulum of thinking about world events will have swung toward the idea that peaceful cooperation is more fundamental to human behavior, a view held by primatologist Frans de Waal (1989; 1996; 1998) and many others.

In suggesting that some of our behaviors reflect our evolutionary history, we aren't saying there are "genes for" such behaviors (see p. 157). No matter how you cut it, human behavior is an extremely complex phenomenon, and its expression depends on a combination of myriad genes, environmental context, and individual experience. There's really

(a)   (b)

no way of predicting how an individual mother or father will allocate resources in the task of child rearing, but behavioral ecologists argue that patterns can be seen when populations (or even the entire species) are examined for allocation of parenting resources.

One aspect of behavioral ecology that may have less emotional baggage than reproductive and parenting strategies is how people make decisions about acquiring food. For example, when examining the hunting strategy on a given day for a band of foragers, behavioral ecologists predict that the hunters would pursue a strategy that maximizes return and minimizes time and energy invested (Fig. 17-2). In other words, they predict that the hunters would pursue an "optimal foraging strategy." But if the analysis considers only the calories in the food obtained, weighed against the calories expended in pursuit of the food item, the theory will always come up short because other important factors are left out of the model. What dangers were between the foragers and the foods that may have led them to take an alternate route or avoid a food patch or prey animal altogether? Does pursuit of a particular prey animal take them too far away from home when night falls? Does a smaller food or prey item provide additional resources, such as a pelt that's useful for clothing? And have the people been eating this food for several days, so that they'd like a bit of variety? All of

FIGURE **17-1**

(a) These chimpanzees exhibit an aggressive reaction when confronted by others. (b) The bonobos show more relaxed expressions.

FIGURE **17-2**

When these G/wi hunters plan their hunting strategy, they consider many factors in addition to calories expended and acquired.

these factors could explain why a band of hunters and gatherers might choose to pursue a food item of less caloric value and thus deviate from the prediction. To return to the idea of an optimal reproductive strategy, wouldn't similar complicating factors apply? Certainly, contemporary humans choose mates based on many more factors besides how many offspring they can produce or raise together.

Biocultural Evolution and the Life Cycle

Despite its limitations and challenges, examining human behavior as a product of evolution helps us explain and understand some aspects of our lives. It also allows us to make predictions that we can examine and test through field observations, demographic studies, and other methods. Examples from the human life cycle further illustrate how evolution has influenced human reproductive behavior and how reproduction is embedded in culture. In other words, we view the life cycle as a biocultural process. If we consider how a human develops from an embryo into an adult and examine the forces operating on that process, then we'll have a better perspective not only on how biology and culture influence our own lives but also on how our evolutionary history creates opportunities and sets limitations.

Of course, cultural factors interact with genetically based biological characteristics to widely varying degrees; these variable interactions influence how characteristics are expressed in individuals. Some genetically based characteristics will be exhibited no matter what the cultural context of a person's life happens to be. If a woman inherits two alleles for albinism, for example (see Chapter 4), she will be deficient in the production of the pigment melanin, resulting in lightly colored skin, hair, and eyes. This phenotype will emerge regardless of the woman's cultural environment. Likewise, the sex-linked trait for hemophilia (also described in Chapter 4) will be exhibited by all males who inherit it, no matter where they live.

Other characteristics, such as intelligence, body shape, and growth, reflect the interaction of environment and genes. We know, for example, that we're each born with a genetic makeup that influences the maximum height we can achieve in adulthood. But to reach that maximum height, we must be properly nourished during growth, and we must avoid many childhood diseases and other stresses that inhibit growth. What factors determine whether we are well fed and receive good medical care? In the United States, a person's socioeconomic status is probably the primary factor that determines their nutrition and health. Socioeconomic status is thus an example of a cultural factor that affects growth. But in another culture, diet and health status might be influenced by whether the person is male or female. In some cultures, males receive the best care in childhood and are thus often larger and healthier as adults than are females (Fig. 17-3). If there's a cultural value on slimness in women, young girls may try to restrict their food intake in ways that affect their growth; but if the culture values plumpness, the effect on diet in adolescence will likely be different. These are all examples of how cultural values affect growth and development.

As noted in earlier chapters, primatologists and other physical anthropologists view primate and human growth and development from an evolutionary perspective, with an interest in how natural

FIGURE 17-3

This is a mother with her twin children. The one on the left is a boy and is breast-fed. The girl, on the right, is bottle-fed. This illustrates both differential treatment of boys and girls in many societies and the potential negative effects of bottle-feeding.

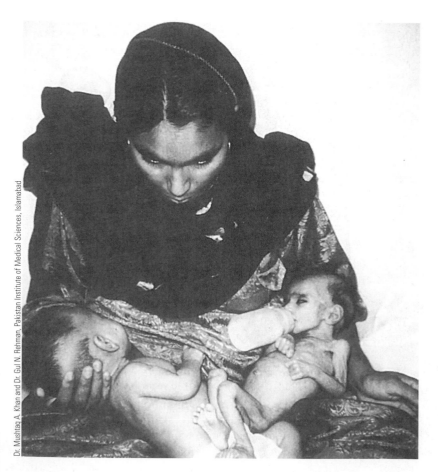

selection has operated on the life cycle from conception to death, a perspective known as *life history theory* (see p. 161). Why, for example, do humans have longer periods of infancy and childhood compared with other primates? What accounts for differences seen in the life cycles of such closely related species as humans and chimpanzees? Life history research seeks to answer such questions (e.g., Mace, 2000).

Life history theory begins with the premise that an organism has only a certain amount of energy available for growth, maintaining life, and reproducing. Energy that's invested in one of these processes is not available to another. So, the entire life course is a series of trade-offs among life history traits such as length of gestation, age at weaning, time spent in growth to adulthood, adult body size, and length of life span. For example, life history theory provides the basis for understanding how fast an organism will grow and to what size, how many offspring can be produced, how long gestation will last, and how long an individual will live. Crucial to understanding life history theory is its link to the evolutionary process: It is the action of natural selection that shapes life history traits, determining which ones will succeed or fail in a given environment. It's not clear whether life history theory works in contemporary human populations (Strassman and Gillespie, 2002), but it's a useful guide for examining the various life cycle phases from evolutionary and ecological perspectives.

Not all animals have distinct phases in their lives; among mammals, humans have more such phases than do other species (Fig. 17-4). Protozoa, among the simplest of animals, have only one phase; many invertebrates have two: larval and adult. Most primates have four phases—gestation, infancy, juvenile (usually called childhood in humans), and adult. Apes, humans, and perhaps monkeys have a phase between the juvenile phase and adulthood that's referred to as adolescence (the teenage years, in humans). Finally, for humans there's an additional sixth phase in women—the post-reproductive years following **menopause**. It could be argued that during the course of primate evolution, more recently evolved forms have longer life spans and more divisions of the life span into phases, or stages.

Most of these life cycle stages are well marked by biological transitions. The prenatal phase begins with conception and ends with birth; infancy is the period of nursing; childhood, or the juvenile phase, is the period from weaning to sexual maturity (puberty in humans); adolescence is the period from puberty to the end of growth; adulthood is marked by the birth of the first child and/or the completion of growth; and menopause is recognized as having occurred one full year after the last menstrual cycle. These biological markers are similar among higher primates. But for humans, there's an added complexity: The markers occur in cultural contexts that define and characterize them. Puberty, for example, has very different meanings in different cultures. A girl's first menstruation (**menarche**) is often marked with ritual and celebration, and a change in social status typically occurs with this biological transition. Likewise, menopause is often associated with a rise in status for women in non-Western societies, and it's commonly seen as a negative transition for women in many Western societies. As we'll see, collective and individual attitudes toward these life cycle transitions affect an individual's growth and development.

menopause The end of menstruation in women, usually occurring at around age 50.

menarche The first menstruation in girls, usually occurring in the early to mid-teens.

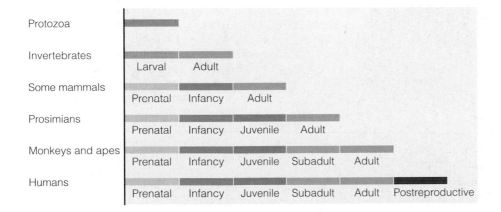

FIGURE **17-4**
Life cycle stages for various animal species.

GROWTH IN GESTATION, INFANCY, AND CHILDHOOD

A characteristic that humans share with most other primates is a relatively large brain compared with body size (see p. 183). In fact, the delivery of a large newborn head through a somewhat small pelvis is a challenge that modern humans share with many other primates, including most monkeys (Fig. 17-5). A further challenge for modern humans, though, is that human brains are somewhat undeveloped at birth, so the babies are more helpless and dependent on their caretakers than are most monkey infants. After a human infant is born, its brain continues growing much faster than any other part of the body except the eyeball. At birth, the human brain is about 25 percent of its adult size. By 6 months of age, the brain has doubled in size, reaching 50 percent of adult size. It reaches 75 percent of adult size at age 2½ years, 90 percent at age 5 years, and 95 percent by age 10 years. At adolescence there's only a small growth spurt, making the brain an exception to the growth curves for most other parts of the body. This pattern of brain growth, including the relatively small amount of growth before birth, is unusual among primates and other mammals. By contrast, most mammalian species have typically achieved at least 50 percent of adult brain size before birth. For humans, however, the narrow pelvis necessary for walking bipedally limits the size of the fetal head that can be delivered through it. That limitation, along with the value of having most brain growth occur in the more stimulating environment outside the womb, has resulted in human infants being born with far less of their total adult brain size than most other mammals are. (As we saw in Chapter 12, this pattern of delayed maturation was probably already established in hominid evolution by 1.5 million years ago [mya].)

Delayed brain growth may be particularly important for a species dependent on language. The human brain's language centers develop in the first three years of life, when the brain is rapidly expanding; these three years are considered a critical period for language

FIGURE 17-5
The relationship between the average diameter of the birth canal of adult females and average head length and breadth of newborns of the same species. (After Jolly, 1985.)

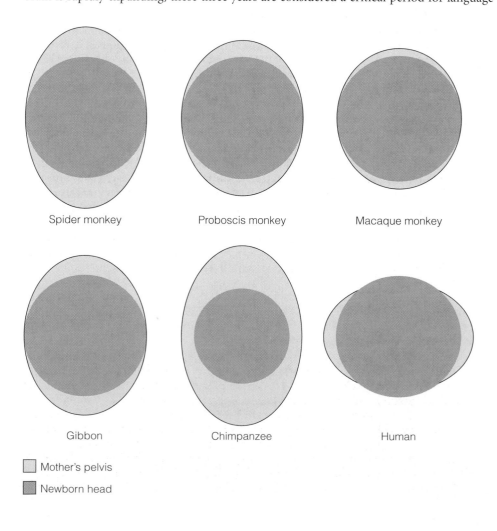

development in the human child. In fact, children who aren't exposed to speech during this period never develop fully normal language skills.

The narrow human pelvis adapted for bipedalism and the large newborn head offer another challenge in human development. Most primate infants are born head first, facing the front of the birth canal, making it easy for the mother to reach down and guide the infant out. Because of some modifications to the human pelvis, the infant is born facing the back of the birth canal. This means that the mother must reach behind her to pull the infant into the world. This added difficulty may explain why humans routinely seek assistance at birth, rather than delivering an infant alone as most mammals do. Although it's certainly possible for a woman to deliver an infant alone (Walrath, 2003), having someone else to guide the baby out, wipe its face so it can breathe, and prevent the umbilical cord from choking the infant can significantly reduce mortality associated with birth (Rosenberg and Trevathan, 2001). In fact, a survey of world cultures reveals that it's unusual to give birth alone, particularly to a first child. Assistance at birth may also enhance the relatively helpless infant's chances of survival. So for humans, birth is a life cycle event that typically takes place in the context of culture; it's a social rather than a solitary event, unlike that for most other mammals.

Infancy is defined for mammals as the period when nursing takes place, typically lasting about four years in humans. When we consider how unusual it is for a mother to breast-feed her child for even a year in the United States or Canada, this figure may surprise us. But considering that four or five years of breast feeding is the norm for chimpanzees, gorillas, orangutans, and for women in foraging societies, most anthropologists conclude that four years was the norm for most humans in the evolutionary past (Stuart-Macadam and Dettwyler, 1995).

Humans have unusually long childhoods and a slowed growth process, reflecting the importance of learning for our species. Childhood is the time between weaning and puberty when the child is growing taller, the brain is completing its growth, and technical and social skills are being acquired.

Before continuing to examine the life cycle from the vantage point of life history theory, let's take a look at factors that affect growth and development throughout the growing years.

NUTRITIONAL EFFECTS ON GROWTH AND DEVELOPMENT

Nutrition affects human growth at every stage of the life cycle. During pregnancy, for example, a woman's diet can profoundly affect the development of her fetus and the eventual health of the child. What's more, the effects are transgenerational, because a woman's own supply of eggs develops while she herself is *in utero*. So, if a woman is malnourished during pregnancy, the eggs that develop in her female fetus may be damaged in a way that affects her future grandchildren's health. And even if a baby girl whose mother was malnourished during pregnancy is well nourished from birth on (as often happens in adoptions), her growth, health, and future pregnancies appear to be compromised, perhaps even for several generations (Kuzawa, 2005). This information has clear implications for public health efforts that attempt to provide adequate nutritional support to pregnant women throughout the world.

Nutrients needed for growth, development, and body maintenance include proteins, carbohydrates, lipids (fats), vitamins, and minerals. The specific amount that we need of each of these nutrients coevolved with the types of foods that were available to human ancestors throughout our evolutionary history. For example, the specific pattern of amino acids required in human nutrition (the essential amino acids) reflects an ancestral diet high in animal protein. Unfortunately for modern humans, these coevolved nutritional requirements are often incompatible with the foods that are available and typically consumed today.

The ancestral diet, while perhaps high in animal protein, was probably low in fats, particularly saturated fats. The diet was also most likely high in complex carbohydrates (including fiber), low in salt, and high in calcium. We don't need to be reminded that the contemporary diet typically seen in many industrialized societies is just the opposite of the ancestral one. It's high in saturated fats and salt and low in complex carbohydrates, fiber, and calcium (Table 17-1). There's very good evidence that many of today's diseases in

TABLE 17-1	Preagricultural, Contemporary American, and Recently Recommended Dietary Composition		
	Preagricultural Diet	Contemporary Diet	Recent Recommendations
Total dietary energy (%)			
Protein	33	12	12
Carbohydrate	46	46	58
Fat	21	42	30
Alcohol	~0	(7–10)	—
P:S ratio*	1.41	0.44	1
Cholesterol (mg)	520	300–500	300
Fiber (g)	100–150	19.7	30–60
Sodium (mg)	690	2,300–6,900	1,000–3,300
Calcium (mg)	1,500–2,000	740	800–1,500
Ascorbic acid (mg)	440	90	60

*Polyunsaturated: saturated fat ratio.

Source: From *The Paleolithic Prescription*, by S. Boyd Eaton, Marjorie Shostak, and Melvin Konner (New York: Harper & Row, 1988).

industrialized countries are related to the lack of fit between our diet today and the one with which we evolved (Eaton, Shostak, and Konner, 1988; Eaton, Eaton, and Konner, 1999, Cordain, 2002).

Many of our biological and behavioral characteristics evolved because in the past they contributed to survival and reproductive success, but today these same characteristics may be maladaptive. An example is our ability to store fat. This capability was an advantage in the past, when food availability often alternated between abundance and scarcity. Those who could store fat during the times of abundance could draw on those stores during times of scarcity and remain healthy, resist disease, and, for women, maintain the ability to reproduce. Today, people with adequate economic resources spend much of their lives with a relative abundance of foods. Considering the number of disorders associated with obesity, the formerly positive ability to store extra fat has now turned into a liability. Our "feast or famine" biology is now incompatible with the constant feast many of us indulge in today.

Probably no disorder is as clearly linked with dietary and lifestyle behaviors as the form of diabetes mellitus that typically begins in later life. This form is referred to either as type 2 diabetes or NIDDM (non–insulin dependent diabetes mellitus). In 1900, diabetes ranked twenty-seventh among the leading causes of death in the United States; today it ranks seventh. And the threat to world health from this disease is growing, with projections of an increase in incidence between 2000 and 2010 of 57 percent in Asia, 50 percent in Africa, 44 percent in South America, and 23 percent in North America (Zimmet, Alberti, and Shaw, 2001). Part of this projected increase will be due to decreases in other causes of death (such as infectious diseases), but much of it has to do with lifestyle and dietary changes associated with modernization and globalization, especially the decrease in levels of daily activity and increase in dietary intake of fats and refined carbohydrates (Lieberman, 2003).

Rates for obesity and diabetes in the United States have grown over the last decade, and some fear that the increase is accelerating. In fact, medical and popular news reports refer to increases in obesity and diabetes as epidemics (Mokdad et al., 2001). Unlike many scourges that threaten our health, though, obesity and diabetes can usually be prevented by modifying diet and activity.

A CLOSER LOOK   Diabetes

What is diabetes? There are actually two different diseases that are referred to as diabetes. One, the less common, is type 1 diabetes (also called insulin dependent diabetes mellitus or IDDM and juvenile onset diabetes), which occurs when the immune system interferes with the body's ability to produce the insulin that converts sugars (glucose) into energy. This type is usually first recognized in childhood and requires lifelong insulin injections to avoid cell damage and death. It is unlikely that children with type 1 diabetes lived very long in the past. Type 2 diabetes, far more common today, is a problem with the way insulin is used in the body. Sometimes this is described as "insulin resistance" in that there may be sufficient insulin produced, but the cells are not able to utilize it, resulting in a buildup of glucose in the bloodstream that can result in a number of complications of the cardiovascular system, kidneys, and nervous system. If untreated, usually with diet modifications, weight control, and exercise, type 2 diabetes can also result in early death.

A few years ago, type 2 diabetes was something that happened to older people living primarily in the developed world. Sadly, this is no longer true. The World Diabetes Foundation estimates that 80% of the new cases of type 2 diabetes that appear between now and 2025 will be in developing nations and the World Health Organization (WHO) predicts that more than 70% of *all* diabetes cases in the world will be in developing nations in 2025. Furthermore, type 2 diabetes is occurring in children as young as 4 (Pavkov et al., 2006) and the mean age of diagnosis in the United States dropped from 52 to 46 between 1988 and 2000 (Koopman, et al., 2005). In fact, we predict that almost everyone reading this book has a friend or family member who has diabetes. What's happened to make this former "disease of old age" and "disease of civilization" reach what some have described as epidemic proportions?

Although there appears to be a genetic link (type 2 diabetes tends to run in families), most fingers point to lifestyle factors.

Two that have been implicated in the emergence of this epidemic are bad diets and no exercise. Noting that our current diets and low levels of activity are very different from those of our ancestors, proponents of evolutionary medicine suggest that diabetes is the price we pay for novel lifestyles that find people of all ages consuming diets high in sugars and other refined carbohydrates while they spend their days in front of TVs and computer monitors. The reason that diabetes incidence is increasing in developing nations is that these bad habits are also spreading to those nations.

Several decades ago, geneticist James Neel (1962) proposed that people who develop diabetes have "thrifty genotypes" that served their ancestors well when they lived under alternating feast and famine conditions and engaged in high levels of physical activity, but that today are nothing but trouble for people living under conditions of constant food availability and relative inactivity. Thus, what was formerly an asset (i.e., the ability to be thrifty and "save" calories for future use) is now a liability. Recent reviews, however, find the thrifty genotype hypothesis to be an oversimplification and a "thrifty phenotype hypothesis" has emerged to take its place. According to this view, poor fetal and early post-natal nutrition impose mechanisms of nutritional thrift upon the growing individual resulting in impaired glucose resistance throughout life (Hales and Barker, 2001). The long-term consequences of early malnutrition are thus impaired development of glucose metabolism and a far greater susceptibility to type 2 diabetes. Recognition of the role of early nutrition in predisposing to diabetes suggests that by improving maternal and prenatal health worldwide, we may be able to reduce the incidence of type 2 diabetes in a far more effective way than we can by urging people to change their diets and other aspects of their lifestyles.

It's clear that both deficiencies and excesses of nutrients can cause health problems and interfere with childhood growth (see pp. 406–407). Certainly, many people in all parts of the world, both industrialized and developing, suffer from inadequate supplies of food of any quality. We read daily of thousands dying from starvation due to drought, warfare, or political instability. The blame must be placed not only on the narrowed food base that resulted from the emergence of agriculture but also on the increase in human population that occurred when people began settling in permanent villages and having more children. Today, the crush of billions of humans almost completely dependent on cereal grains (Cordain, 1999) means that millions face undernutrition, malnutrition, and even starvation. Even with these huge populations, however, food scarcity may not be as big a problem as food inequality. In other words, there may be enough food produced for all people on earth, but economic and political forces keep it from reaching those who need it most.

So to summarize, our nutritional adaptations were shaped in environments that included times of scarcity alternating with times of abundance. The variety of foods consumed was so great that nutritional deficiency diseases were rare. Small amounts of animal foods were probably an important part of the diet in many areas of the world. In northern latitudes

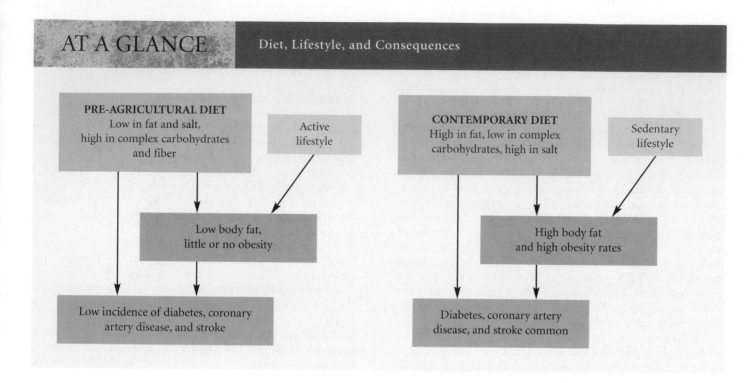

AT A GLANCE   Diet, Lifestyle, and Consequences

PRE-AGRICULTURAL DIET
Low in fat and salt, high in complex carbohydrates and fiber

Active lifestyle

Low body fat, little or no obesity

Low incidence of diabetes, coronary artery disease, and stroke

CONTEMPORARY DIET
High in fat, low in complex carbohydrates, high in salt

Sedentary lifestyle

High body fat and high obesity rates

Diabetes, coronary artery disease, and stroke common

after about 1 mya, meat was an important part of the diet. But because meat from wild animals is low in fats, the negative effects of high meat intake that we see today didn't occur. Our diet today is often incompatible with the adaptations that evolved in the millions of years preceding the development of agriculture. The consequences of that incompatibility include both starvation and obesity (Fig. 17-6).

ONSET OF REPRODUCTIVE FUNCTIONING IN HUMANS

Having reviewed nutritional factors that influence growth during childhood, let's return to the life cycle and follow it through until the end of life. Take another look at Figure 17-4 and you'll see that for most animals, the juvenile, or childhood, stage ends when adulthood begins. For humans and apes, and possibly some monkeys, there's an additional life cycle stage called adolescence. This is the time after reproductive functioning begins, when individuals may be mature in some ways but immature in others. For example, an adolescent girl of 14 may be capable of bearing children; but she's not yet fully grown herself, and she's often too immature socially and economically to successfully raise a child.

FIGURE **17-6**

Some people suffer from an overabundance of food (left), while others suffer from tragically insufficient amounts of food.

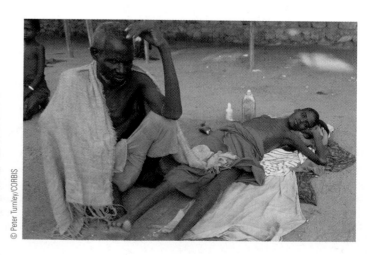

The onset of menarche in girls is affected by several factors, including genetic patterns (girls tend to become mature at about the same age as their mothers did), nutrition, stress, and disease. You'll remember from our discussion of life history theory that energy must be allocated among growth, body maintenance, and reproduction. During childhood most resources are directed toward growth; but at some point the body switches to allocating more energy to reproduction, and for girls this shift is somewhat abrupt. What "tells" the body that it's time to direct more energy to reproduction and less (or none) to growth? An early hypothesis was that the switch occurred when a girl had accumulated a certain amount of body fat (Frisch, 1988). This proposal made sense because of a trend toward lower age of menarche that's been noted in human populations in the past 100 years (see Figure 17-7) and the tendency for girls who are very active and thin to mature later than those who are heavier and less active. An alternative view that seems to fit the data better is Ellison's (2001) proposal that the critical growth parameter is not body fat but skeletal growth, specifically growth of the pelvis. We've already seen what a tight squeeze it is for the human infant to pass through the birth canal—imagine what it would be like for a fat 8-year-old girl to try to give birth! In this example, it can be seen that it's not only fat that is important for reproduction, but completion of skeletal growth as well.

Life history theory provides ways of predicting the timing of reproduction under favorable circumstances. For example, if early maturity results in higher numbers of surviving offspring, then it's predicted that natural selection would favor those members of a population who mature earlier. Until the advent of settled living, it's likely that females became pregnant as soon as they were biologically able to do so, that is, as soon as they finished growing. This would be an advantage because individual life expectancy would have been low. Paleodemographic studies indicate a mortality rate of at least 50 percent in subadults in preindustrial populations; and of the half that survived to adulthood, most didn't survive to age 50. Considering the reality of short life spans combined with the long period of infant dependency, producing offspring as early as possible may have contributed to the reproductive success of females, particularly early hominid females. By giving birth as soon as she reached sexual maturity, an early hominid female enhanced her chances of rearing even one offspring to the point it could survive without her.

The high rates of adolescent pregnancy that are seen in the United States and some other countries today reflect this ancient biological heritage. Today, however, there may be disadvantages to early maturity, including its effect on health in later life (Worthman, 1999). If delayed maturity is associated with higher-quality care of the offspring, then offspring survival may improve, resulting in a net increase in fitness for those who mature a few years

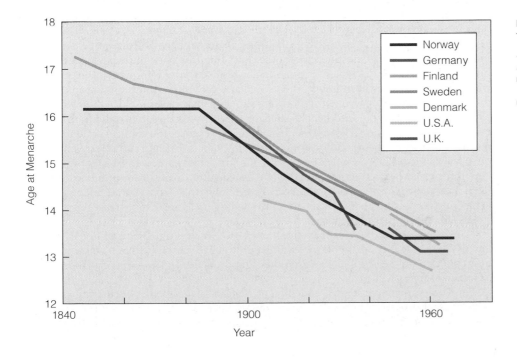

FIGURE **17-7**

The secular trend in age at menarche in Europe.

Source. Wood, James W., 1994 *Dynamics of Human Reproduction,* New York: Aldine de Gruyter; original redrawn from Eveleth, P.B. and J. M. Tanner, 1976, *Worldwide Variation in Human Growth,* Cambridge: Cambridge University Press.)

FIGURE 17-8

Human infants require extensive parental care, especially in the first few years of life.

later. Unfortunately, all too frequently today in many parts of the world, young girls become reproductively mature long before they're socially mature. And if they're also sexually active, they may become pregnant before finishing school or obtaining the skills necessary for economic self-sufficiency. This means that the quality of care they can provide their offspring may be compromised. We know that the infant mortality rate in humans rises rapidly as mothers' age at first birth decreases (Stearns, 1992). In most contemporary societies, it's likely that those who delay reproducing until they're emotionally, socially, and economically mature will have more surviving offspring than will those who begin their parenting careers before they themselves have matured. But if the young, maturing parents have enough help from their extended families, religious organizations, or government agencies, early childbearing may not compromise their reproductive fitness. Clearly, the road to reproductive success is more complicated than most early theories of behavioral ecology suggested, although they're useful models for predicting behavior.

What about the number of offspring produced at each birth? Primates such as monkeys, apes, and humans typically give birth to one infant at a time. Twins occur in apes and humans at about the same frequency, but the survival rate of twins (or triplets) is far lower than the survival rate of singletons. So, we can argue that humans are somewhat limited in the number of offspring resulting from each conception. Because we are mammals, we're also physiologically limited regarding the dependency of our offspring in the first few years of life, as discussed earlier in this chapter (Fig. 17-8). Apes (and, we assume, ancestral humans) breast feed their infants for three to four years, resulting in approximately a 4-year birth interval. That interval can be reduced with earlier weaning or, in the case of formula feeding, by not nursing at all. This means that contemporary humans can easily reduce the birth interval to less than 2 years, potentially doubling the number of offspring produced. But again, in most cases, the quality of parental care is compromised when there are too many dependent offspring. If the number of offspring reaching reproductive maturity is lower in individuals and families with 2-year birth intervals than in those with 4-year birth intervals, then natural selection will favor the latter.

While an evolutionary perspective can help us understand how natural selection has influenced the number of offspring, it can also help us understand parenting behaviors that may, at first glance, seem counter to the goal of increasing reproductive success. For example, in Chapter 7 we discussed infanticide in langurs and other species, noting that it seems counterproductive to the supposed goal of increasing reproductive success. The evolutionary perspective argues that when a male commits infanticide against another male's offspring, the first male can be interpreted as increasing his own reproductive success at the other male's expense. But what about situations when a mother kills her own offspring? Can this contribute to her reproductive success in any way? Sara Hrdy tackles such challenging questions in her book *Mother Nature: A History of Mothers, Infants, and Natural Selection* (1999). She points out that in many situations, maternal behavior defies the claim that mammals have a natural "instinct" for mother love. But if we place the behaviors in an evolutionary context, the discrepancies can often be resolved. For example, consider a mother who abandons her newborn infant when social and economic conditions are so dire that the child's chances of surviving very long are slim. She may have an older child whose life would be in jeopardy if the mother allocated her meager resources to two children. It might be better (in an evolutionary sense, *not* in a moral sense) to let the younger child die so the mother can bear another as soon as conditions and chances for child survival are improved, or so she can focus her resources on the older infant. This example illustrates the concept that for most measures of reproductive success, quality of offspring produced is more important than quantity. This is not to say that all maternal behaviors are adaptive. But a behavior that at first glance seems maladaptive may actually serve to increase reproductive success for the mother in the long run.

Can behavioral ecology explain the long period of reproductive sterility in human females following menopause? If increasing reproductive success is what it's all about, then how could natural selection favor cessation of reproductive functioning relatively early in a woman's lifetime?

For women, menopause—the end of menstruation—is a sign they're entering a new life cycle phase. Estrogen and progesterone production begin to decline toward the end of the reproductive years until ovulation (and thus menstruation) ceases altogether. This occurs at

senescence Decline in physiological function usually associated with aging.

about age 50 for women in all parts of the world. Throughout human evolution, most females (and males) didn't survive to age 50; so, few women lived much past menopause. But today this event occurs when women have as much as one-third of their active and healthy lives ahead of them. No other primates have such a long post-reproductive period. Female chimpanzees and monkeys experience decreased fertility in their later years, but most continue having reproductive cycles until their deaths. Occasional reports of menopause in apes and monkeys have been noted, but it's far from a routine and expected event.

Why do human females cease reproducing and then live such a long time when they can no longer reproduce? There are two questions here, one about cessation and one about living for so long after cessation. A theory about cessation of ovulation (menopause) suggests that it wasn't itself favored by natural selection; rather, it's an artifact of the extension of the human life span. It's been suggested that the maximum life span of the mammalian egg is 50 years (you'll recall that all the ova are already present before birth; see p. 57). Thus, although the human life span has increased over the past several hundred years, the reproductive life span has not. To put it another way, the long post-reproductive years and associated menopause in women have been "uncovered" by extension of life expectancy because many causes of death are now reduced (Sievert, 2006). Another proposal to explain menopause is that so much energy is needed "up front," for reproduction in the early years, that there's nothing left over by the time a woman reaches 50.

One theory for a long post-reproductive life relates to parenting. Because it takes about 12 to 15 years for a child to become independent, it's argued that females are biologically "programmed" to live 12 to 15 years beyond the birth of their last child (Mayer, 1982). This idea suggests that the maximum human life span for preagricultural humans was about 65 years, a figure that corresponds to what's known for contemporary hunter-gatherers and for prehistoric populations. One final explanation for the long post-reproductive period in human females has been proposed by behavioral ecologists and is known as the "grandmother hypothesis." This proposal argues that natural selection may have favored this long period in women's lives because by ceasing to bear and raise their own children, postmenopausal women would be freed to provide high-quality care for their grandchildren. (Fig. 17-9). In other words, an older woman would be more likely to increase her lifetime fitness by enhancing the survival of her older grandchildren (who share one-quarter of her genes) by providing food, shelter, and direct child care than she would by having her own, possibly low-quality infants (Hawkes, O'Connell, and Blurton Jones, 1997; but see Peccei, 2001). This is an example of the trade-offs considered by life history theory.

HUMAN LONGEVITY

Compared to most other animals, humans have a long life span (Table 17-2). Our maximum life span potential, estimated to be about 120 years, probably hasn't changed in the past several thousand years. But life expectancy at birth (the average length of life) has increased significantly in the past 100 years due to advances in medical care. The most important advance is likely treatment and prevention of infectious diseases, which typically take their toll on the young (Crews and Harper, 1998).

To some extent, aging is something we do throughout our lives. But we usually think of aging as **senescence**, the process of physiological decline in all systems of the body that occurs toward the end of the life course. Actually, throughout adulthood, there's a gradual decline in our cells' ability to synthesize proteins, in immune system function, in muscle mass (with a corresponding increase in fat mass) and strength, and in bone mineral density (Lamberts et al., 1997). This decline is associated with an increased risk for the chronic degenerative diseases that are usually listed as the causes of death in industrialized nations.

As you know, most causes of death that have their effects after the reproductive years won't be subjected to the forces of natural selection. What's more, in evolutionary terms,

James F. O'Connell

FIGURE **17-9**
Senior Hadza woman and grandchild.

TABLE **17-2**	Maximal Life Spans for Selected Species
Organism	**Approximate Maximum Life Span (in Years)**
Bristlecone pine	5,000
Tortoise	170
Rockfish	140
Human	120
Blue whale	80
Indian elephant	70
Gorilla	39
Domestic dog	34
Rabbit	13
Rat	5

Source: From "The Biology of Human Aging," by William A. Stini; in C. G. N. Mascie-Taylor and G. W. Lasker (eds.), *Applications of Biological Anthropology to Human Affairs* (Cambridge, UK: Cambridge University Press, 1991, p. 215).

FIGURE **17-10**

Telomeres are repeated sequences of DNA at the ends of chromosomes, and the sequences appear to be the same in all animals. They stabilize and protect the ends of chromosomes and, as they shorten with each cell division, the chromosomes eventually become unstable.

reproductive success isn't measured by how long we live. Instead, as we've emphasized throughout this textbook, it's measured by how many offspring we produce. So organisms need to survive only long enough to produce offspring and rear them to maturity. Most wild animals die young of infection, starvation, predation, injury, and cold. Obviously there are exceptions to this statement, especially in larger-bodied animals. Elephants, for example, may live over 50 years; and we know of several chimpanzees at Gombe that have survived into their forties.

Here's one explanation for why humans age and are affected by chronic degenerative diseases like atherosclerosis, cancers, and hypertension: Genes that enhance reproductive success in earlier years (and thus were favored by natural selection) may have detrimental effects in later years. These are referred to as **pleiotropic genes**, meaning that they have multiple effects at different times in the life span or under different conditions (Williams, 1957). For example, genes that enhance immune system functions in the early years may also damage tissue, so that cancer susceptibility increases in later life (Nesse and Williams, 1994). Alternatively, in later life, cancer-protecting genes may override genes for organ and tissue renewal.

Pleiotropy may help us understand evolutionary reasons for aging, but what are the causes of senescence (decline in physiological functions) in the individual? Much attention has been focused recently on free radicals, the highly reactive molecules that can damage cells. These by-products of normal metabolism can be protected against by antioxidants such as vitamins A, C, and E and by various enzymes (Kirkwood, 1997). Ultimately, damage to DNA can occur, in turn contributing to the aging of cells, the immune system, and other functional systems of the body. Additionally, there's evidence that programmed cell death is also a part of the normal processes of development that can obviously contribute to senescence.

Another hypothesis for senescence is known as the "telomere hypothesis." In this view, the DNA sequence at the end of each chromosome, known as the telomere, is shortened each time a cell divides (Fig. 17-10). Cells that have divided many times throughout the life course have short telomeres, eventually reaching the point where they can no longer divide and are unable to maintain healthy tissues and organs. Changes in telomere length have also been implicated in cancers. In the laboratory, the enzyme telomerase can lengthen telomeres, allowing the cell to continue to divide. For this reason, the gene for telomerase has been called the "immortalizing gene." But this may not be a good thing, since the only cells that can divide indefinitely are cancer cells. Although this research isn't likely to lead to a lengthening of the life span, it may contribute to a better understanding of cellular functions and of cancer.

Far more important than genes in the aging process, however, are lifestyle factors such as smoking, physical activity, diet, and medical care. Life expectancy at birth varies considerably from country to country and among socioeconomic classes within a country. Throughout the world, women have higher life expectancies than men do. A Japanese girl born in 2004, for example, can expect to live to age 86, a boy to age 79. Girls and boys born in that same year in the United States have life expectancies of 80 and 75. In contrast to these children in industrialized nations, girls and boys in Mali have life expectancies of only 47 and 44 (data from World Health Organization). Many African nations have seen life expectancy drop below 40 due to deaths from AIDS. For example, before the AIDS epidemic, Zimbabweans had a life expectancy of 65 years; today, life expectancy in Zimbabwe is less than 37 (Fig. 17-11).

EVOLUTIONARY MEDICINE

A few years ago, scholars in evolutionary theory, biological anthropology, and medicine joined forces to develop what many saw as a new field, referred to as either evolutionary or Darwinian medicine (Williams and Nesse, 1991; Nesse and Williams, 1994; Trevathan, Smith, and McKenna, 1999). There are several ways in which an evolutionary view can contribute to understanding contemporary health challenges. One is the recognition that the inevitable outcome of more and more aggressive interventions to fight pathogens that cause disease in humans will be stronger pathogens that eventually evolve resistance to therapies such as antibiotics. Because most of the viruses and bacteria that cause disease have very short generation times, it doesn't take long for strains that are resistant to antibiotics to emerge victorious. We've seen this occur with staphylococcal infections, some strains of tuberculosis, and *E. coli*. The pathogens that cause HIV and malaria mutate so fast that all attempts to develop a vaccine against them have failed so far. For the most part, the antibi-

pleiotropic genes Genes that have more than one effect; genes that have different effects at different times in the life cycle.

otic-pathogen arms race has led to the development of more and more lethal strains of disease, but the evolutionary process doesn't have to lead in that direction. In fact, one suggestion for beating disease-causing organisms like HIV and malaria is to turn the evolutionary process around by directing the process toward less and less virulence (Ewald, 1999; 1994). Ewald has called this procedure "domesticating" pathogens and cites as an example diphtheria, which has apparently evolved toward milder strains with vaccination. The primary argument is that medical interventions that are capable of responding to the *processes* of disease emergence and evolution are much more likely to be successful in the long run than those that target specific disease variants and their manifestations. Consider, for example, the influenza virus that appears every fall—medical researchers work hard to predict which strain will be the problem and target a vaccine against the one they select. If their prediction is wrong, an influenza epidemic could emerge.

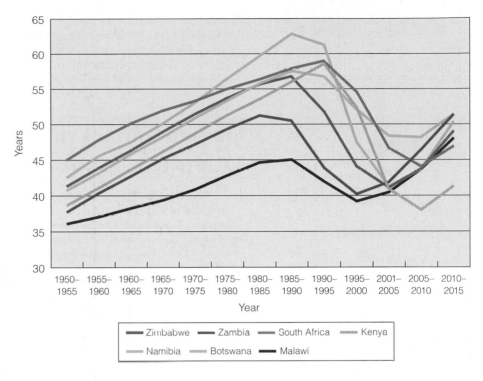

FIGURE 17-11

Changes in life expectancy due to AIDS in seven African nations. (From United Nations, 1998.)

The latest developments in assessing the complete genetic sequences of chimpanzees and humans have confirmed how few differences there are. But they've also pointed to tiny differences that may explain why humans are susceptible to diseases like cholera, malaria, and influenza while chimpanzees apparently aren't affected. For example, a molecule known as sialic acid differs in humans and chimpanzees by a single oxygen atom (Varki, 2001). The chimpanzee version of the sialic acid gene is the one found in other mammals, so it's been suggested that the human form is derived and most likely evolved after the chimpanzee and human lines split (see Chapter 9). Sialic acid serves as a binding site for organisms that cause diseases such as cholera, malaria, and some forms of influenza (Muchmore, Diaz, and Varki, 1998), and the discovery may lead to treatments for these diseases. It's also an important reminder that even one genetic difference between humans and chimpanzees can have extensive and as yet unforeseen impact.

Evolutionary medicine proponents also argue that knowing about the conditions under which humans evolved can contribute to understanding health problems and may point to potential solutions or interventions. As we noted when discussing nutrition, the human diet, activity levels, and other aspects of our lives evolved under very different conditions from the way we live our lives today. This "mismatch" of evolved bodies (sometimes referred to as "paleolithic bodies") and twenty-first-century lifestyles may account for diseases and disorders such as type 2 diabetes, atherosclerosis, hypertension, some cancers, diverticular diseases, and osteoporosis. Many popular books argue that by adopting some aspects of ancestral diets (lower fat, more complex carbohydrates, lower sodium, frequent small meals) and lifestyles (more exercise, less alcohol, no smoking, lower stress), we'll feel better, live longer, and lose weight (e.g., Cordain, 2002).

Evolutionary medicine also helps to distinguish traits that may have evolved because they enhanced survival and reproductive success in the past or are beneficial in one form (defenses) while negative in another (defects). For example, as discussed in Chapters 3 and 4, the sickle-cell allele is harmful in homozygotes; but if a person is heterozygous, he or she is protected against malaria. As another example, Tay-Sachs, found most commonly among Ashkenazi Jews, is a progressively deteriorating neurological disorder that usually results in death by age 4. One hypothesis is that the allele is maintained in somewhat high frequencies in this population because in the past it conferred survival advantages for the heterozygotes in the face of tuberculosis or influenza, which were common diseases in the ghettos of Europe where Jews were forced to live (Motulsky, 1995). Another example of a genetic polymorphism that's usually lethal in the homozygous form is cystic fibrosis, which may be protective against cholera for heterozygotes (Hill and Motulsky, 1999). With the addition of evolutionary theory to epidemiology and human genetics, populations that may be vulnerable to disease outbreaks may be identified in advance and appropriate preventive measures taken.

Human Impact on the Planet and Other Life-Forms

The figures cited earlier for life expectancy in various nations of the world remind us of the importance of diet, health care, and social environment for lifelong health and survival. Clearly, the data indicate that living conditions in Japan are more supportive of good health for the general population than are those in Kenya. At some level, we can measure a nation's success by indicators like infant mortality rates and life expectancy. But how do we measure the success of a species?

By most standards, *Homo sapiens* is a successful species. There are currently more than 6 billion human beings living on this planet. Each one of these individuals comprises upward of 20 trillion cells. Even so, we and all other multicellular organisms contribute but a small fraction of all the cells on the planet—most of which are bacteria. So if we see life ultimately as a competition among reproducing organisms, bacteria are the winners, hands down.

Evolutionary success can also be gauged by species longevity. As we've seen, fossil evidence indicates that *Homo sapiens* has been on the scene for at least 200,000 years and possibly as long as 400,000 years. Such time spans, seen through the perspective of a human lifetime, may seem enormous. But consider this: Our immediate predecessor, *Homo erectus*, had a species longevity of about 1.5 million years. In other words, we as a species would need to exist another million years simply to match *Homo erectus*! If considerations like these aren't humbling enough, remember that some sharks and turtles have thrived basically unchanged structurally for 400 million years (although many of these species are now seriously threatened).

No matter what criterion for success we use, there's no question that *Homo sapiens* has had an excessive impact on the earth and all other forms of life. In the past, humans had to respond primarily to challenges in the natural world; today, the greatest challenges for our species (and many others) are environments of our own making. Increasing population size is the main reason human impact has been so great. As human population pressure increases, more and more land is converted to crops, pasture, and construction sites, providing more opportunities for still more humans and leaving fewer (or no) habitats for most other species.

Scientists estimate that around 10,000 years ago, only about 5 million people inhabited the earth (not even half as many as live in Los Angeles County or New York City today). By the year 1650 there were perhaps 500 million, and by 1800, around 1 billion (Fig. 17-12). In other words, between 10,000 years ago and 1650 (a period of 9,650 years), population size doubled seven and a half times. On average, then, the doubling time between 10,000 years ago and 1650 was about 1,287 years. But from 1650 to 1800 it doubled again, which means that doubling time had been reduced to 150 years. And in the 37 years between 1950 and 1987, world population doubled from 2 billion to 4 billion. To state this problem in terms we can appreciate, we add 1 billion people to the world's population approximately every 11 years. That comes out to 90 to 95 million every year and roughly a quarter of a million every day—or more than 10,000 an hour.

The rate of growth is not equally distributed among all nations. The most recent United Nations report on world population notes that 95 percent of population growth is occurring in the developing world. Likewise, resources aren't distributed equally among all nations. Only a small percentage of the world's population, located in a few industrialized nations, controls and consumes most of the world's resources.

Efforts to slow the rate of world population growth have focused on improving women's education, health, and rights throughout the world, based on the idea that if women are educated, they choose to have fewer children and are able to achieve better health for the ones they do have. Despite resistance to this strategy in parts of the world, there's evidence of success; fertility rates have declined from 4.5 children per woman in 1970–1975 to 2.65 today (UN population 2004 revised). As with resources, however, most of the decline in fertility rates has been in the developed world. Realistic projections from the United Nations are that total fertility in all countries will reach 1.85 children per woman in 2050, with a total world population of slightly more than 9 billion people. These projections are based on continuing success at educating women and improving maternal and child health worldwide.

IMPACT ON BIODIVERSITY

In addition to huge numbers of people on the planet, another legacy of the human evolutionary process is expressed in the proposal recently put forth by biologist Stephen Palumbi (2001) that humans are the "world's greatest evolutionary force." What Palumbi means is that we humans, like no other species before us, have profound effects on the evolutionary histories of almost all forms of life, including the ability to alter global ecology and the potential to destroy ourselves and virtually all life on earth. Clearly, such wide and sudden impacts have no precedents in the fossil record. Even massive evolutionary catastrophes and mass extinctions didn't wreak the havoc that may result from modern human technology.

As we mentioned earlier (see p. 118), two major extinction events have occurred in the past 250 million years. A third major extinction event, possibly of the same magnitude, is occurring now; and according to some scientists, it may have begun in the late Pleistocene or early **Holocene** (Ward, 1994). Unlike all other mass extinctions, the current one hasn't been caused by continental drift, climate change (so far), or collisions with asteroids. Rather, these recent and ongoing extinctions are due to the activities of a single species—*Homo sapiens.*

Many scientists, in fact, believe that several large mammalian species were pushed toward extinction due to overhunting by earlier human populations, particularly near the end of the Pleistocene, some 10,000 years ago. In North America, at least 57 mammalian species became extinct, including the mammoth, mastodon, giant ground sloth, saber-toothed cat, several large rodents, and numerous grazing animals. Although climate change was undoubtedly a factor in these Pleistocene extinctions, hunting and other human

Holocene The most recent epoch of the Cenozoic. Following the Pleistocene, it's estimated to have begun 10,000 years ago.

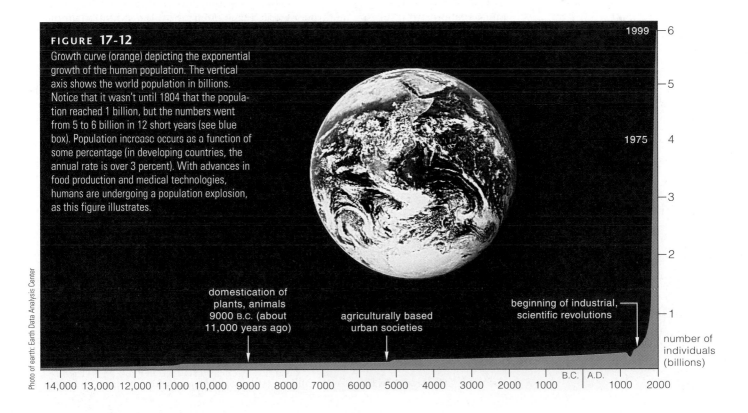

FIGURE 17-12

Growth curve (orange) depicting the exponential growth of the human population. The vertical axis shows the world population in billions. Notice that it wasn't until 1804 that the population reached 1 billion, but the numbers went from 5 to 6 billion in 12 short years (see blue box). Population increase occurs as a function of some percentage (in developing countries, the annual rate is over 3 percent). With advances in food production and medical technologies, humans are undergoing a population explosion, as this figure illustrates.

Photo of earth: Earth Data Analysis Center

domestication of plants, animals 9000 B.C. (about 11,000 years ago)

agriculturally based urban societies

beginning of industrial, scientific revolutions

number of individuals (billions)

14,000 13,000 12,000 11,000 10,000 9000 8000 7000 6000 5000 4000 3000 2000 1000 B.C. | A.D. 1000 2000

activities may also have been important (Guthrie, 2006; Worthy and Holdaway, 2002). Although there's some dispute over when humans first entered North America from Asia, it's certain that they were firmly established by at least 12,000 years ago (and probably earlier).

We have no direct evidence that early American big game hunters contributed to extinctions; but we do have evidence of what can happen to indigenous species when new areas are colonized by humans for the first time. Within just a few decades of human occupation of New Zealand, the moa, a large flightless bird, was exterminated. Madagascar serves as a similar example (Perez et al., 2005). In the past 1,000 years, after the arrival of permanent human settlement, 14 species of lemurs, in addition to other mammalian and bird species, have become extinct (Napier and Napier, 1985). One such species was *Megaladapis*, a lemur that weighed an estimated 300 pounds (Fleagle, 1999)! Lastly, scientists have debated for years whether the extinction of all large-bodied animals (some 60 species) in Australia during the late Pleistocene was due to human hunting and other activities or to climate change.

Since the end of the Pleistocene, human activities have continued taking their toll on nonhuman species. Today, however, species are disappearing at an unprecedented rate. Hunting, which occurs for reasons other than acquiring food, continues to be a major factor (see Issue, p. 118). Competition with introduced nonnative species, such as pigs, goats, and rats, has also contributed to the problem. But in many cases, the most important single cause of extinction is habitat reduction. We're all aware of the risk to such visible species as the elephant, panda, rhinoceros, tiger, and mountain gorilla, to name a few. These risks are real, and within your lifetime some of these species will certainly become extinct, at least in the wild. But the greatest threat to biodiversity is to the countless unknown species living in the world's rain forests (Fig. 17-13). By the year 2022, half the world's remaining rain forests will be gone if destruction continues at its current rate. This will result in a loss of between 10 and 22 percent of all rain forest species, or 5 to 10 percent of all plant and animal species on earth (Wilson, 1992).

Should we care about the loss of biodiversity? If so, why? In truth, many people don't seem very concerned. What's more, in explaining why we should care, we usually point out the benefits (known and unknown) that humans may derive from wild species of plants and animals. An example of such a benefit is the chemical taxol (derived from the Pacific yew tree), which may be an effective treatment for ovarian and breast cancer.

Undeniably, humans stand to benefit from continued research into potentially useful rain-forest products. Still, such anthropocentric reasons aren't the sole justification for preserving the earth's biodiversity. Each species the earth loses is the product of millions of years of evolution, and each one fills a specific econiche. Quite simply, the destruction of so many of the planet's life forms is within our power. But, we must ask ourselves, is it our right?

ACCELERATION OF EVOLUTIONARY PROCESSES

Another major impact of human activities is to accelerate the evolutionary process for hundreds of life-forms. Many of these changes have occurred over one human generation, rather than the millions of years that have been familiar in our discussions of evolution in this text. As noted earlier in this chapter and in Chapter 16, our use of antibiotics has directed the course of evolution of several infectious diseases to the point that many have become resistant to our antibiotics. Human-invented antibiotics have become the agents of natural selection directing the course of evolution of many bacteria to a more virulent state. It's even likely that human technology and lifestyles are responsible for the deadly nature of some of the so-called new diseases that have arisen in recent decades, such as HIV-AIDS (see pp. 415–418), dengue hemorrhagic fever, Legionnaire's disease,

FIGURE 17-13
Stumps of recently felled forest trees are still visible in this newly cleared field in Rwanda. The haze is wood smoke from household fires.

Lyme disease, and resistant strains of tuberculosis, *Staphylococcus*, and *E coli*. A few years ago, the fear of anthrax drove thousands of people to use antibiotics such as ciprofloxacin in the extremely unlikely event that they would be exposed to the deadly bacterium. Certainly, we understand the desire for preventive action by those at heightened risk. But if more harmful bacteria become resistant as a by-product of this practice, the risk to society from the overuse and improper use of this powerful class of antibiotics is potentially far greater. We could reach a point where we have no antibiotics strong enough to overpower dangerous bacteria that live and mutate in our midst.

A similar phenomenon has occurred with the overuse and misuse of insecticides and pesticides on agricultural crops (Palumbi, 2001). Insects evolve resistance to each new generation of toxic agents, eventually reaching a point where they're no longer affected by most of the insecticides used on the fields. Bt toxin *(Bacillus thuringiensis)* has been highly touted as an "organic" and environmentally friendly agent because it's naturally produced (often by the crops it protects), targets specific insect larvae, and isn't toxic to humans. Genes for producing Bt toxin have been engineered into millions of acres of plants but, unfortunately, recent evidence suggests that some insects are evolving resistance to it.

As we mentioned in Chapter 15, possibly the best-known insecticide to have altered the course of evolution of a species is DDT. When this insecticide was first developed, it was hailed as the best way to reduce malaria, eliminating the mosquitoes that transmit the disease. DDT was highly effective when it was first applied to mosquito-ridden areas; but soon, mosquitoes had evolved resistance to the powerful agent, rendering it almost useless in the fight against malaria. The use of DDT also proved disastrous to many bird species, including the bald eagle. The failure of other efforts to treat malaria has led to a recent call to begin using DDT again.

From these examples, it's clear that the process of evolution is something that can result in great harm for our species and planet. Certainly, none of the scientists working to develop antibiotics, insecticides, pesticides, and other biological tools intend to cause harm. But they may lack the understanding of the evolutionary process necessary to foresee long-term consequences of their work. As the great geneticist Theodosius Dobzhansky said, "Nothing in biology makes sense except in the light of evolution." Indeed, we can't afford even a single generation of scientists who lack knowledge about the process of evolution, which is responsible for the life-forms around us, both helpful and harmful. If human actions can cause an organism to evolve from a relatively benign state to a dangerously virulent state, then there's no reason we can't turn that process around. In other words, as noted earlier, it's theoretically possible to direct the course of evolution of a dangerous organism like HIV to a more benign, less harmful state (Ewald, 1999). But using evolution to solve health problems requires that medical researchers have a very sophisticated understanding of the evolutionary process, and evolutionary theory isn't usually offered as part of medical training (Nesse and Williams, 1994; Nesse, Stearns, and Omenn, 2006).

Is There Any Good News?

Now that you're thoroughly depressed about the potentially gloomy future of the earth and our species, is there any good news? In 2000, heads of state from almost 150 countries agreed to support a set of Millennium Development Goals that would help to reduce human misery throughout the world. Here are the eight goals:

1. Eradicate extreme poverty and hunger.
2. Achieve universal primary education.
3. Promote gender equity and empower women.
4. Reduce child mortality.
5. Improve maternal health.
6. Combat HIV/AIDS, malaria, and other diseases.
7. Ensure environmental sustainability.
8. Build a global partnership for development.

These goals set measurable targets that can be examined year after year to see how close we come to meeting them. There will be immense and expensive challenges, but this international agreement seems a good start toward concerted cooperative efforts to solve the major problems of the world today, and it goes a long way toward encouraging partnerships between rich and poor nations.

Although world population growth continues, it appears that the rate of growth has slowed somewhat. It's common knowledge among economists that as income and education increase, family size decreases; and as infant and child mortality rates decrease, families are having fewer children. In fact, it has frequently been argued that one of the best strategies for reducing family size and thus world population is to educate girls and women. Educated woman are more likely to be in the labor force and are better able to provide food for their families, seek health care for themselves and their children, delay marriage, and use family planning. In 1990, the international community adopted the World Declaration on Education for All. Since then, there have been steady increases in efforts to educate all segments of society. In fact, in some parts of the world, there have been so many efforts to improve education for girls that they're now favored by the gender gap in education.

With decreases in family size and improvements in education and employment opportunities for both men and women throughout the world, we're also likely to see improvements in environmental conservation and habitat preservation. A generally recognized phenomenon is that habitat destruction and poverty often go hand in hand. Although successes in Costa Rica can't be replicated everywhere, this small nation has been a model for making environmental concerns integral to social and economic development. Ecotourism, built on preserving the nation's abundant and beautiful natural resources, has now become its primary industry. Today, Costa Rica's poverty levels are the lowest in Central America.

Recently, several international agreements designed to preserve endangered species and habitats have been signed. These often mean the development of national parks and preserves. Figure 17-14 shows the increase in protected sites during the past 30 years.

There are also some international efforts to preserve primates, most notably the United Nations Great Ape Survival Project (GRASP). This project brings together great ape research and conservation organizations that have struggled to save the animals they care about with varying degrees of success and failure. Three UN Special Envoys have been appointed: Russell Mittermeier (Director of Conservation International), Jane Goodall (see p. 156), and Toshisada Nishida (see p. 195). By combining efforts and targeting resources, they hope to have the political and financial clout to halt the decline of great ape species (see also pp. 118–120).

Finally, in July, 2005, leaders from both developing and developed countries came together in Gleneagles, Scotland, to discuss new ways of reducing global poverty, especially

(see p. 156), (see p. 195), (see also pp. 118–120)

FIGURE 17-14

There has been a steady increase in the number and total area of the protected sites in the world in the past few decades.

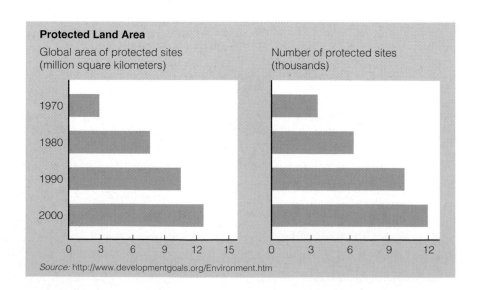

Source: http://www.developmentgoals.org/Environment.htm

in sub-Saharan Africa. The developed countries, including the European Union, the United States, Canada, and Australia, renewed commitments to double aid for Africa by 2010. Countries in Latin America and the Caribbean have made significant progress in meeting some of the goals, but countries in sub-Saharan Africa have fallen further behind than when earlier agreements were made. Aid from some countries hasn't come as quickly as originally hoped. Fortunately, some of the wealthiest individuals in the world (Bill and Melinda Gates, George Soros, Warren Buffet, Richard Branson, Ted Turner) have begun to invest their personal fortunes (or, in the cases of former U.S. Presidents Carter and Clinton, their diplomatic talents and charisma) in reducing poverty and poor health and in trying to achieve global peace and prosperity.

What should be obvious from these examples is that only by working together can nations and individuals of the world hope to bring about solutions to the world's problems. As we argued earlier in this chapter and in Chapter 8, despite occasional evidence to the contrary, cooperation may have been more important in human evolution than conflict. These international efforts illustrate how strongly we believe that to be the case. The question now is whether we have the collective will to see that our admirable goals are met. Many people believe that it's our only hope.

Are We Still Evolving?

In many ways, it seems that culture has enabled us to transcend most of the limitations our biology imposes on us. But that biology was shaped during millions of years of evolution, in environments very different from those in which most of us live today. There is, to a great extent, a lack of fit between our biology and our twenty-first-century cultural environment. Our expectations that scientists can easily and quickly discover a "magic bullet" to enable us to resist any disease that arises have been painfully dashed with death tolls from AIDS reaching catastrophic levels in many parts of the world.

Socioeconomic and political concerns also have powerful effects on our species today. Whether you die of starvation or succumb to disorders associated with overconsumption depends a great deal on where you live, what your socioeconomic status is, and how much power and control you have over your life. These are all factors not likely to be related to biology. They also affect whether you'll be killed in a war or spend most of your life in a safe, comfortable community. Your chances of being exposed to one of the "new" pathogens such as HIV, SARS, or tuberculosis have a lot to do with your lifestyle and other cultural factors. But your chances of dying from the disease, or failing to reproduce because of it, still have a lot to do with your biology. The 4.3 million children dying annually from respiratory infections are primarily those in the developing world, with limited access to adequate medical care—clearly a cultural factor. But in those same areas, lacking that same medical care, are millions of other children who aren't getting the infections or aren't dying from them. Presumably, among the factors affecting this difference is resistance afforded by genes. By considering this simple example, we can see that human gene frequencies are still changing from one generation to the next in response to selective agents such as disease; thus, our species is still evolving.

We can't predict whether we'll become a different species or become extinct as a species (remember, that's the fate of almost everything that has ever lived on earth). Will our brains get larger, or will our hands evolve solely to push buttons? Or will we change genetically, so that we no longer have to eat food? This is the stuff of science fiction, not anthropology. But as long as new pathogens appear or new environments are introduced by technology, there's little doubt that just like every other species on earth, the human species will either continue to evolve or become extinct.

Culture has enabled us to transcend many limits imposed by our biology. Today, people who never would have been able to do so in the past are surviving and having children. This in itself means we are evolving. How many of you would be reading this text if you had been born under the health and economic conditions prevalent 500 years ago?

VISUAL SUMMARY

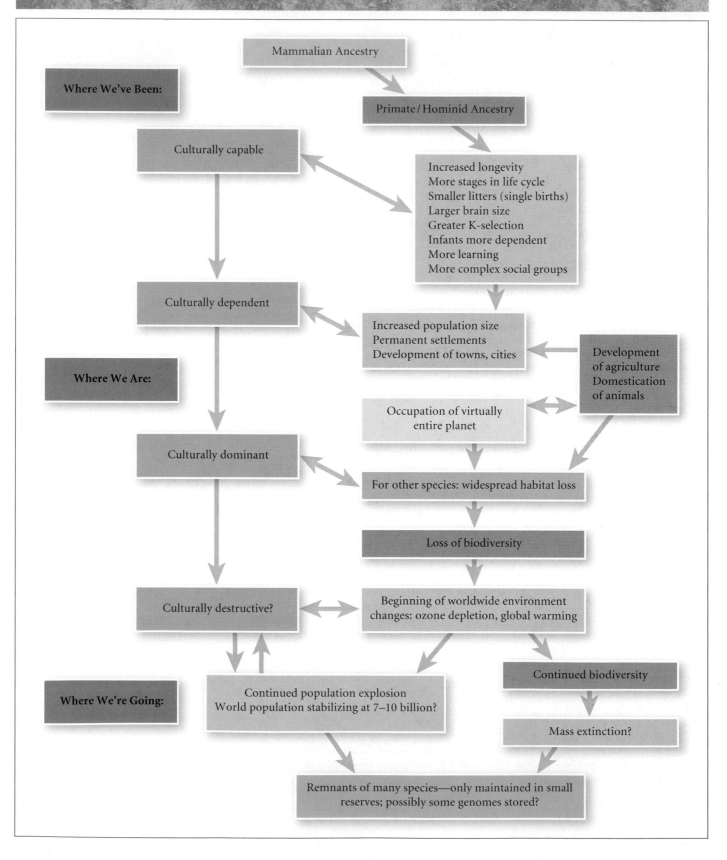

Mammalian Ancestry

Where We've Been:

Primate / Hominid Ancestry

Culturally capable

Increased longevity
More stages in life cycle
Smaller litters (single births)
Larger brain size
Greater K-selection
Infants more dependent
More learning
More complex social groups

Culturally dependent

Increased population size
Permanent settlements
Development of towns, cities

Development of agriculture
Domestication of animals

Where We Are:

Occupation of virtually entire planet

Culturally dominant

For other species: widespread habitat loss

Loss of biodiversity

Culturally destructive?

Beginning of worldwide environment changes: ozone depletion, global warming

Continued biodiversity

Where We're Going:

Continued population explosion
World population stabilizing at 7–10 billion?

Mass extinction?

Remnants of many species—only maintained in small reserves; possibly some genomes stored?

Summary: Putting It All Together

In this chapter, we've discussed legacies of human evolutionary history that leave their marks on us today. For the individual, these legacies include patterns of growth and nutritional requirements resulting from millions of years of biological evolution and thousands of years of cultural evolution. Our evolutionary history also means that human infants are relatively undeveloped at birth, especially in brain size, and require intense parental investment to reach adulthood and independence. For humans in society, legacies from evolutionary history include thought processes and behaviors that reflect natural selection operating on individuals to increase reproductive success, or fitness. A review of behavioral ecology summarizes the ways in which genes, environment, and culture have interacted to produce complex adaptations to equally complex challenges. Critical review of hypotheses for such human behaviors as aggression, violence, nurturance, and reproduction reveals the complexity of this interrelationship. Infusion of evolutionary theory into medicine may lead to improvements in human health. The final set of legacies reviewed in this chapter concerns the impact of the human species on the planet and other life-forms. Thanks to our amazing reproductive "success," the human population has reached more than 6 billion from an estimated base of about 5 million people 10,000 years ago. These numbers, coupled with technological developments, have turned humans into what Stephen Palumbi has called "the world's greatest evolutionary force." *Homo sapiens* has become a powerful agent of natural selection, influencing virtually every life-form on earth, causing the extinction of many species, and accelerating evolutionary change in others.

Studies of human evolution have much to contribute to our understanding of how we, as a single species, came to exert such control over our planet's destiny. It's a truly phenomenal story of how a small, apelike creature walking on two feet across the African savanna challenged nature by learning to make stone tools. From these humble beginnings came large-brained humans who, instead of stone tools, have telecommunications satellites, computers, and nuclear arsenals at their fingertips. The human story is indeed unique and wonderful. Our two feet have carried us not only across the plains of Africa, but onto the polar caps, the ocean floor, and even across the surface of the moon! Surely, if we can accomplish so much in so short a time, we can act responsibly to preserve our home and the wondrous creatures who share it with us.

Critical Thinking Questions

1. "Water is to fish as culture is to humans." What do you think this comparison means?

2. Give two examples of how culture and biology interact in meeting human nutritional requirements.

3. Compare and contrast the human preagricultural diet with that seen today (in places like the United States). Discuss at least one major health consequence of what has been called the "lack of fit" between the diet by which humans have evolved and the one many people now consume.

4. Is aging inevitable? Why do humans age?

5. How natural selection might act on such behaviors as mate selection, parenting, and aggression is controversial. Choose one of these, and first argue how natural selection *could* have shaped the way the behavior is expressed in humans. Then, critique your first argument and suggest some alternatives.

6. Describe circumstances under which adolescent pregnancy might be advantageous, in an evolutionary sense. What are some disadvantages of adolescent pregnancy for reproductive success?

7. Under what circumstances might natural selection favor infanticide in humans?

8. What are some proposed explanations for menopause in human females? Do other primates experience menopause?

9. Why do the authors of this text claim that human overpopulation is a major challenge facing our planet today? Do you agree or disagree? Why?

10. What is evolutionary medicine? Briefly discuss two ways in which understanding evolutionary theory or human evolutionary history may lead to improvements in human health.

11. How have humans contributed to the decrease of biodiversity on our planet?

12. Provide two examples of how human activities have affected the evolutionary pace of other life-forms.

13. Are we still evolving? What evidence is there that we're still subject to the forces of evolution?

ATLAS OF PRIMATE SKELETAL ANATOMY

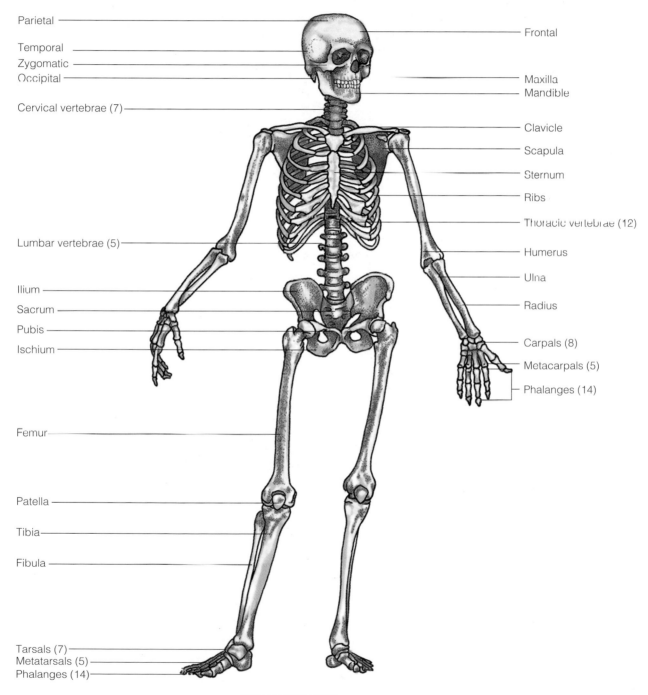

Parietal

Temporal

Zygomatic

Occipital

Cervical vertebrae (7)

Lumbar vertebrae (5)

Ilium

Sacrum

Pubis

Ischium

Femur

Patella

Tibia

Fibula

Tarsals (7)

Metatarsals (5)

Phalanges (14)

Frontal

Maxilla

Mandible

Clavicle

Scapula

Sternum

Ribs

Thoracic vertebrae (12)

Humerus

Ulna

Radius

Carpals (8)

Metacarpals (5)

Phalanges (14)

HUMAN SKELETON

FIGURE A-1

Human skeleton (*Homo sapiens*)—
bipedal hominid.

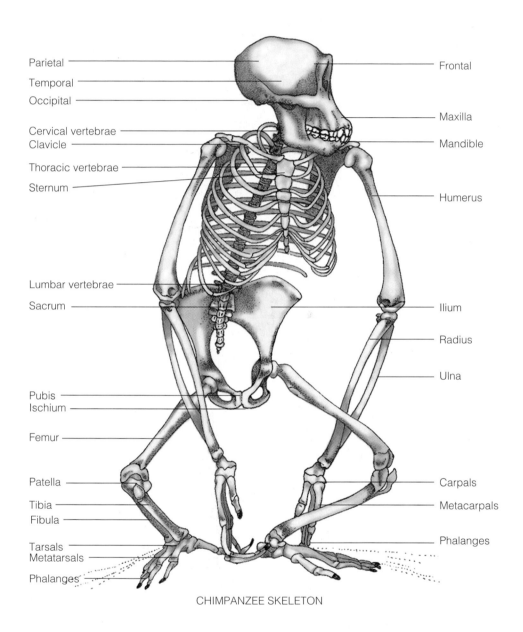

Parietal — Frontal

Temporal —

Occipital — Maxilla

Cervical vertebrae — Mandible
Clavicle —

Thoracic vertebrae — Humerus
Sternum —

Lumbar vertebrae —

Sacrum — Ilium

Radius

Ulna

Pubis —
Ischium —

Femur —

Patella — Carpals

Tibia — Metacarpals
Fibula —

Tarsals — Phalanges
Metatarsals —

Phalanges —

CHIMPANZEE SKELETON

FIGURE A-2
Chimpanzee skelton (*Pan troglodytes*)—
knuckle-walking pongid.

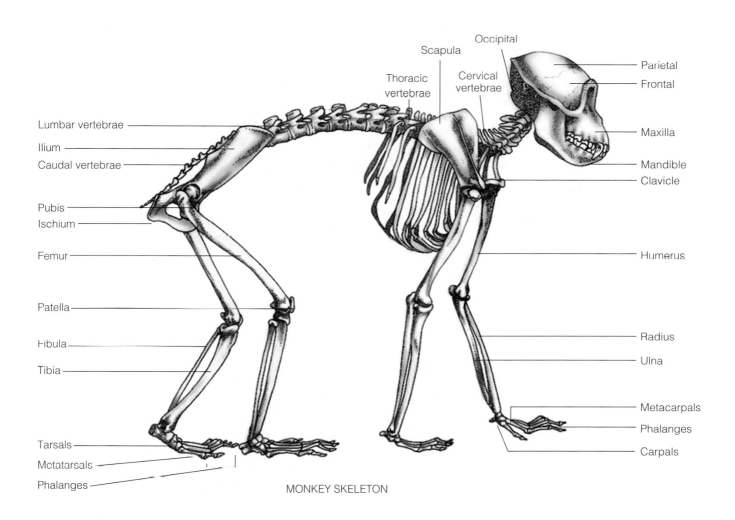

MONKEY SKELETON

FIGURE A-3
Monkey skeleton (rhesus macaque; *Macaca mulatta*)—a typical quadrupedal primate.

FIGURE A-4
Human cranium.
(continued on next page)

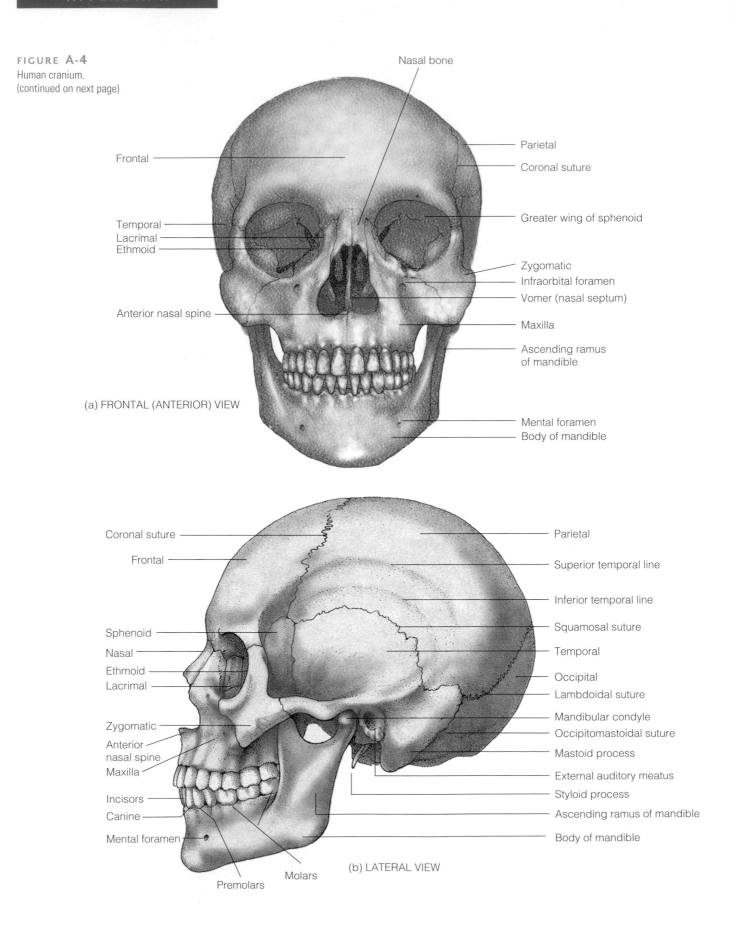

Nasal bone

Frontal

Parietal

Coronal suture

Greater wing of sphenoid

Temporal
Lacrimal
Ethmoid

Zygomatic

Infraorbital foramen

Vomer (nasal septum)

Anterior nasal spine

Maxilla

Ascending ramus
of mandible

(a) FRONTAL (ANTERIOR) VIEW

Mental foramen
Body of mandible

Coronal suture

Parietal

Frontal

Superior temporal line

Inferior temporal line

Squamosal suture

Sphenoid

Temporal

Nasal

Ethmoid

Occipital

Lacrimal

Lambdoidal suture

Mandibular condyle

Zygomatic

Occipitomastoidal suture

Anterior
nasal spine

Mastoid process

Maxilla

External auditory meatus

Incisors

Styloid process

Canine

Ascending ramus of mandible

Mental foramen

Body of mandible

(b) LATERAL VIEW

Premolars

Molars

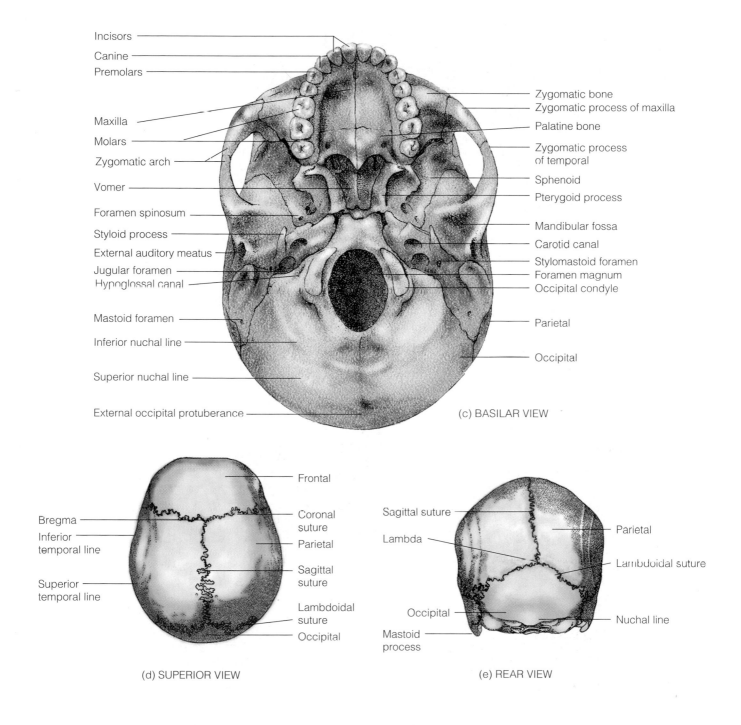

Incisors
Canine
Premolars
Maxilla
Molars
Zygomatic arch
Vomer
Foramen spinosum
Styloid process
External auditory meatus
Jugular foramen
Hypoglossal canal
Mastoid foramen
Inferior nuchal line
Superior nuchal line
External occipital protuberance

Zygomatic bone
Zygomatic process of maxilla
Palatine bone
Zygomatic process of temporal
Sphenoid
Pterygoid process
Mandibular fossa
Carotid canal
Stylomastoid foramen
Foramen magnum
Occipital condyle
Parietal
Occipital

(c) BASILAR VIEW

Bregma
Inferior temporal line
Superior temporal line

Frontal
Coronal suture
Parietal
Sagittal suture
Lambdoidal suture
Occipital

(d) SUPERIOR VIEW

Sagittal suture
Lambda
Occipital
Mastoid process

Parietal
Lambdoidal suture
Nuchal line

(e) REAR VIEW

FIGURE A-4
Human cranium.
(continued)

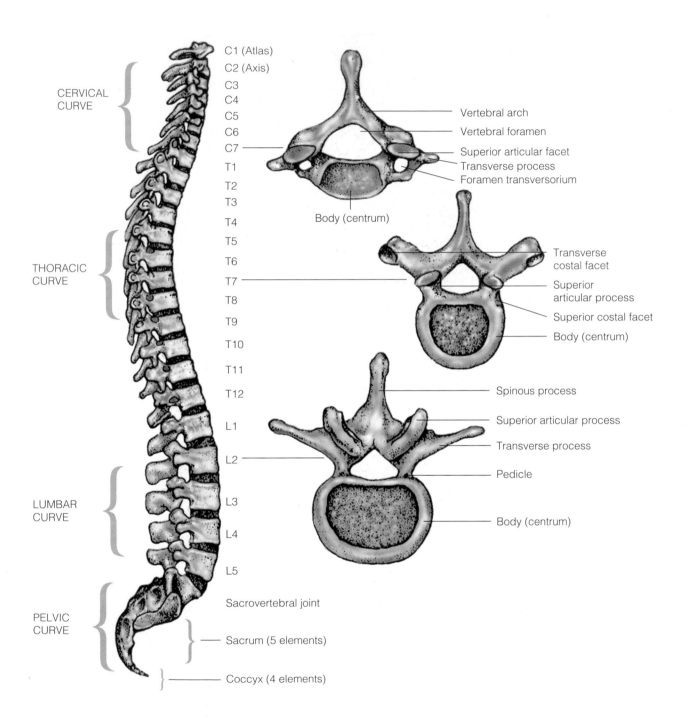

C1 (Atlas)
C2 (Axis)
C3
C4
C5
C6
C7

CERVICAL
CURVE

T1
T2
T3
T4

THORACIC
CURVE

T5
T6
T7
T8
T9
T10
T11
T12

L1

LUMBAR
CURVE

L2
L3
L4
L5

PELVIC
CURVE

Sacrovertebral joint

Sacrum (5 elements)

Coccyx (4 elements)

Vertebral arch
Vertebral foramen
Superior articular facet
Transverse process
Foramen transversorium

Body (centrum)

Transverse
costal facet

Superior
articular process

Superior costal facet

Body (centrum)

Spinous process

Superior articular process

Transverse process

Pedicle

Body (centrum)

FIGURE A-5
Human vertebral column (lateral view) and
representative cervical, thoracic, and lumbar
vertebrae (superior views).

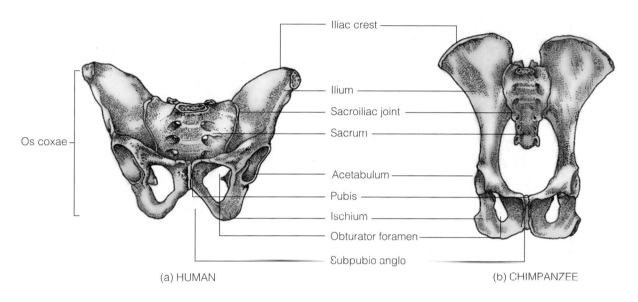

Iliac crest

Ilium

Sacroiliac joint

Sacrum

Acetabulum

Pubis

Ischium

Obturator foramen

Subpubic angle

Os coxae

(a) HUMAN

(b) CHIMPANZEE

FIGURE A-6
Pelvic girdles.

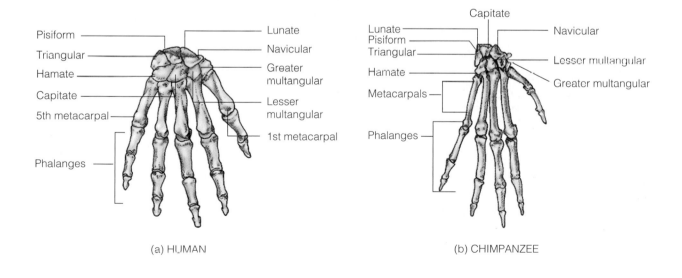

Pisiform

Triangular

Hamate

Capitate

5th metacarpal

Phalanges

Lunate

Navicular

Greater multangular

Lesser multangular

1st metacarpal

(a) HUMAN

Capitate

Lunate
Pisiform
Triangular

Hamate

Metacarpals

Phalanges

Navicular

Lesser multangular

Greater multangular

(b) CHIMPANZEE

FIGURE A-7
Hand anatomy.

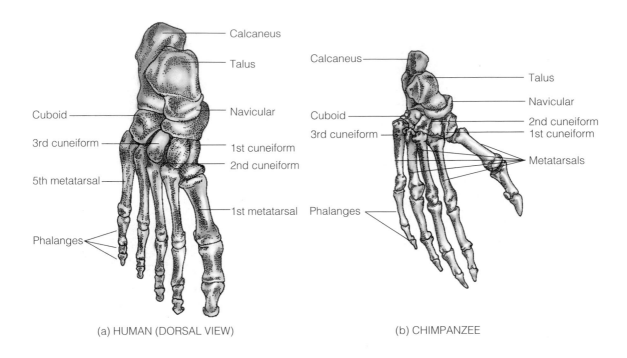

Calcaneus

Talus

Cuboid

Navicular

3rd cuneiform

1st cuneiform

2nd cuneiform

5th metatarsal

1st metatarsal

Phalanges

(a) HUMAN (DORSAL VIEW)

Calcaneus

Talus

Navicular

Cuboid

2nd cuneiform

3rd cuneiform

1st cuneiform

Metatarsals

Phalanges

(b) CHIMPANZEE

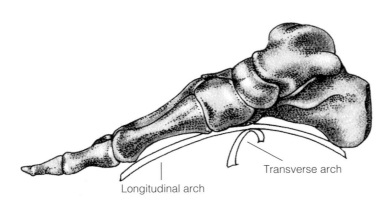

Transverse arch

Longitudinal arch

(c) HUMAN (MEDIAL VIEW)

FIGURE A-8
Foot (pedal) anatomy.

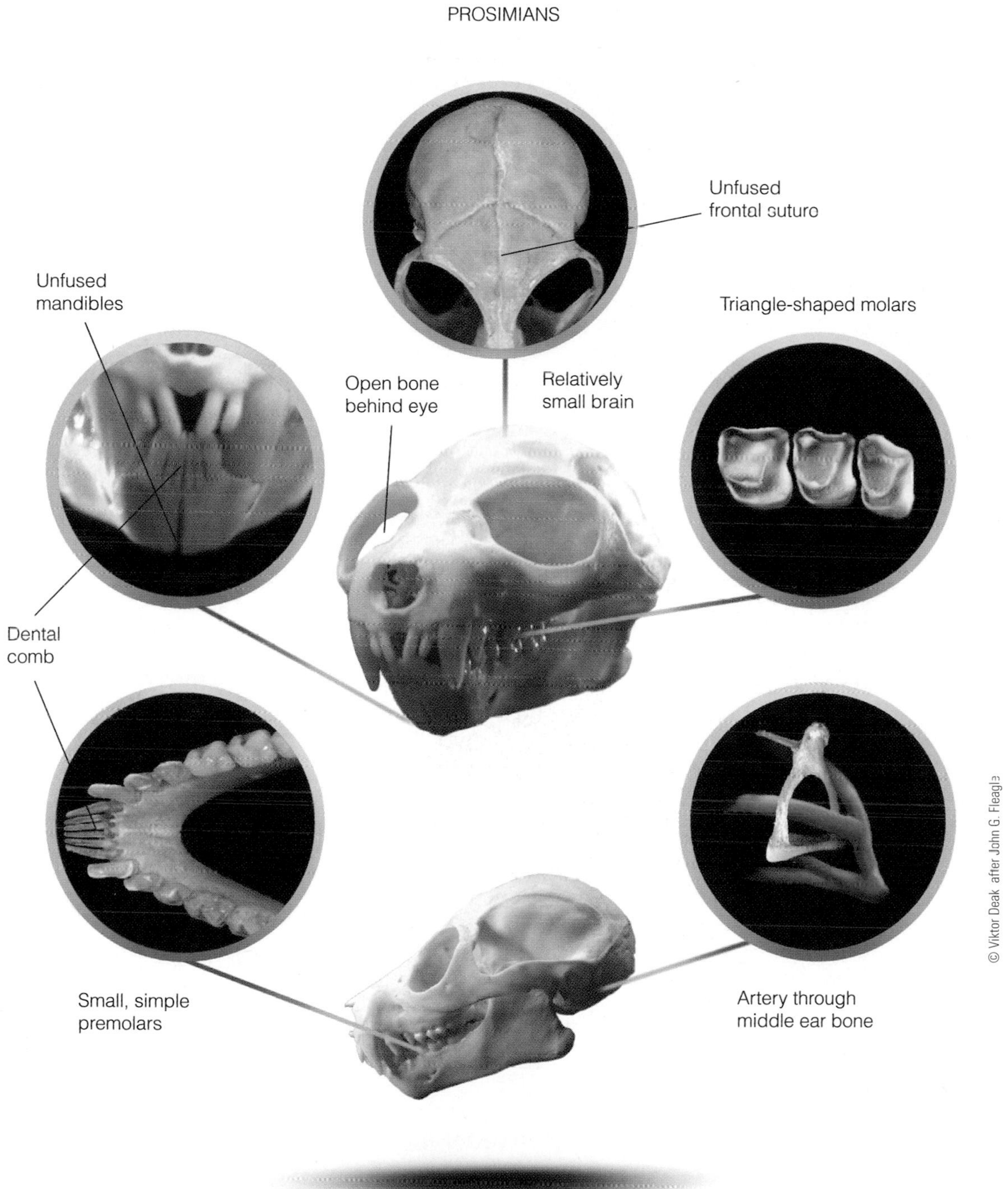

PROSIMIANS

Unfused
frontal suture

Triangle-shaped molars

Unfused
mandibles

Open bone
behind eye

Relatively
small brain

Dental
comb

Small, simple
premolars

Artery through
middle ear bone

© Viktor Deak after John G. Fleagle

FIGURE **A-9A**
Prosimian anatomy. Refer to At a Glance:
Prosimians vs. Anthropoids, Chapter 9, p. 215.

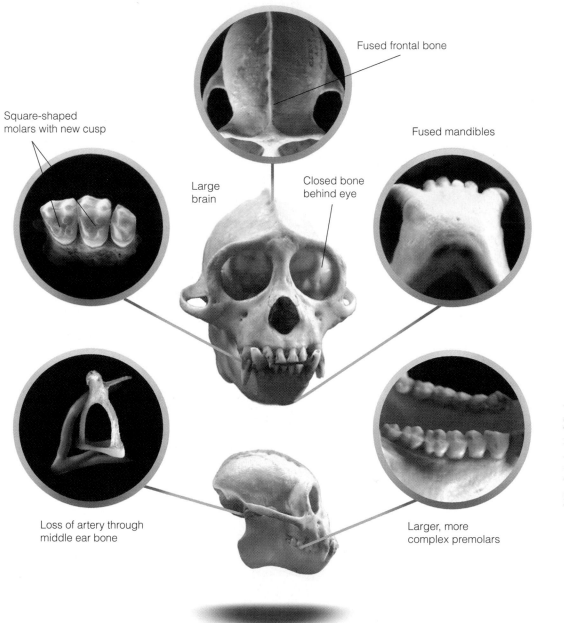

ANTHROPOIDS

Fused frontal bone

Square-shaped
molars with new cusp

Fused mandibles

Large
brain

Closed bone
behind eye

Loss of artery through
middle ear bone

Larger, more
complex premolars

© Viktor Deak, after John G. Fleagle

FIGURE A-9B
Anthropoid anatomy. Refer to At a Glance:
Prosimians vs. Anthropoids, Chapter 9, p. 215.

New World Monkeys

Old World Monkeys

Sideways-facing nostrils

Downward-facing nostrils

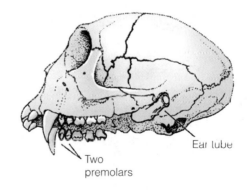

No ear tube

Three premolars

Ear tube

Two premolars

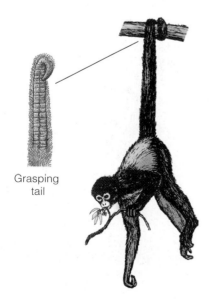

Grasping tail

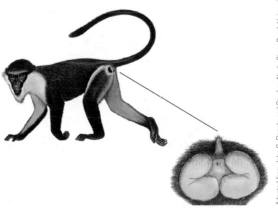

Ischial callosities

Adapted from John G. Fleagle and Stephen Nash, Stony Brook University, New York

FIGURE A-10

Comparison of New World Monkey and Old World Monkey anatomy. Refer to At a Glance: New World Monkeys vs. Old World Monkeys, Chapter 9, p. 219.

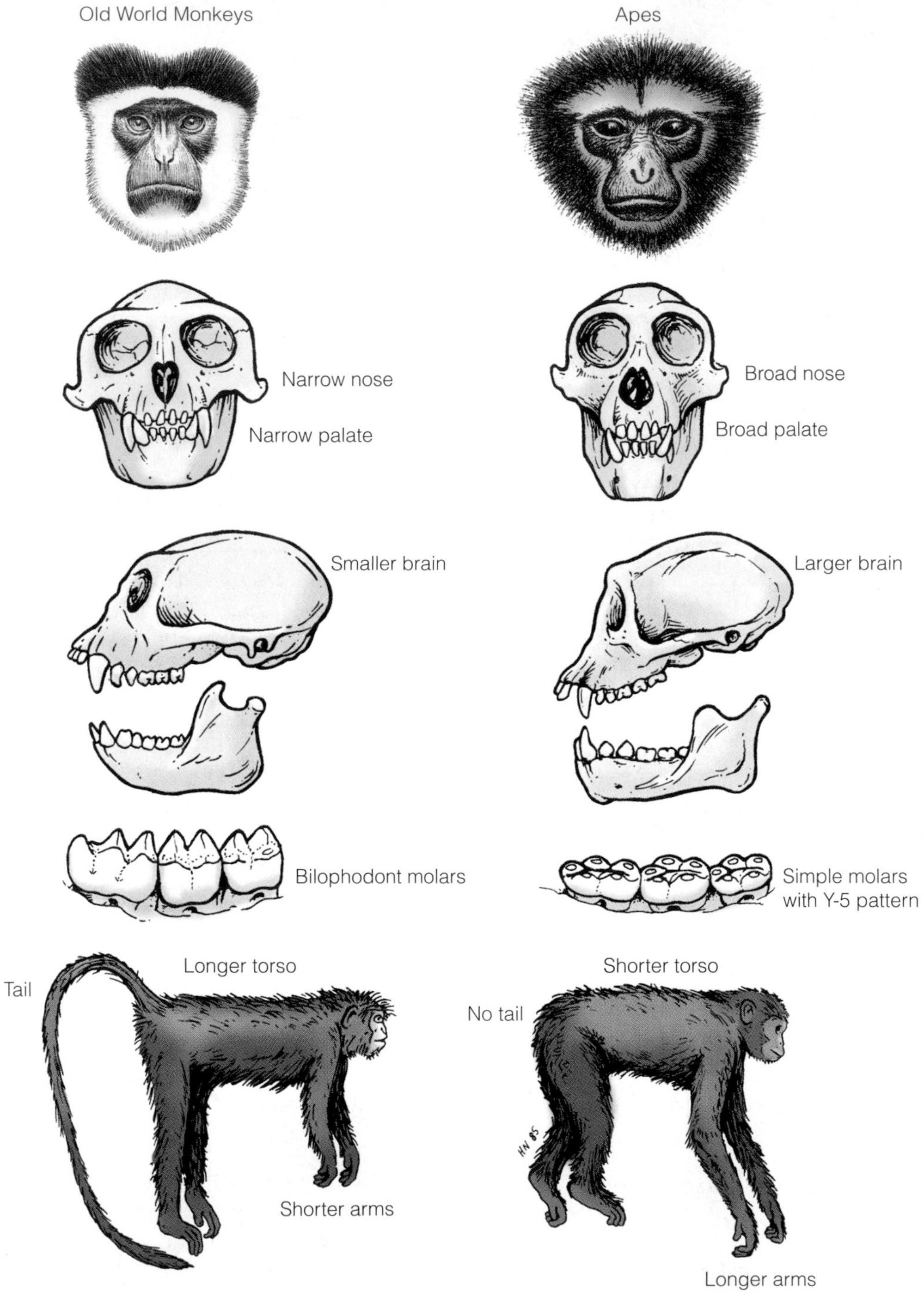

Old World Monkeys

Apes

Narrow nose

Broad nose

Narrow palate

Broad palate

Smaller brain

Larger brain

Bilophodont molars

Simple molars
with Y-5 pattern

Tail

Longer torso

Shorter torso

No tail

Shorter arms

Longer arms

Adapted from John G. Fleagle and Stephen Nash, Stony Brook University, New York

FIGURE A-11

Comparison of Old World Monkey and ape
anatomy. Refer to At a Glance: Old World
Monkeys vs. Apes, Chapter 9, p. 224.

SUMMARY OF EARLY HOMINID FOSSIL FINDS FROM AFRICA

Sahelanthropus

Taxonomic designation:
Sahelanthropus tchadensis

Year of first discovery: 2001

Dating: ~7 mya

Fossil material: Nearly complete cranium, 2 jaw fragments, 3 isolated teeth

Location of finds: Toros-Menalla, Chad, central Africa

Ardipithecus

Taxonomic designation:
Ardipithecus ramidus

Year of first discovery: 1992

Dating: Earlier sites, 5.8–5.6 mya; Aramis, 4.4 mya

Fossil material: Earlier materials: 1 jaw fragment, 4 isolated teeth, postcranial remains (foot phalanx, 2 hand phalanges, 2 humerus fragments, ulna). Later sample (Aramis) represented by many fossils, including up to 50 individuals (many postcranial elements, including at least 1 partial skeleton). Considerable fossil material retrieved from Aramis but not yet published; no reasonably complete cranial remains yet published.

Location of finds: Middle Awash region, including Aramis (as well as earlier localities), Ethiopia, East Africa

Orrorin

Taxonomic designation: *Orrorin tugenensis*

Year of first discovery: 2000

Dating: ~6 mya

Fossil material: 2 jaw fragments, 6 isolated teeth, postcranial remains (femoral pieces, partial humerus, hand phalanx). No reasonably complete cranial remains yet discovered.

Location of finds: Lukeino Formation, Tugen Hills, Baringo District, Kenya, East Africa

Australopithecus anamensis

Taxonomic designation: *Australopithecus anamensis*

Year of first discovery: 1965 (but not recognized as separate species at that time); more remains found in 1994 and 1995

Dating: 4.2–3.9 mya

Fossil material: Total of 22 specimens, including cranial fragments, jaw fragments, and postcranial pieces (humerus, tibia, radius). No reasonably complete cranial remains yet discovered.

Location of finds: Kanapoi, Allia Bay, Kenya, East Africa

Australopithecus afarensis

Taxonomic designation: *Australopithecus afarensis*

Year of first discovery: 1973

Dating: 3.6–3.0 mya

Fossil material: Large sample, with up to 65 individuals represented: 1 partial cranium, numerous cranial pieces and jaws, many teeth, numerous postcranial remains, including partial skeletons. Fossil finds from Laetoli also include dozens of fossilized footprints.

Location of finds: Laetoli (Tanzania), Hadar/Dikika (Ethiopia), also likely found at East Turkana (Kenya) and Omo (Ethiopia), East Africa

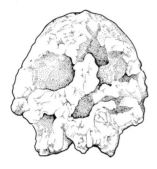

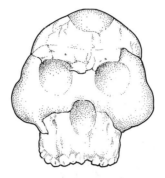

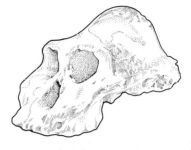

Kenyanthropus

Taxonomic designation:
Kenyanthropus platyops

Year of first discovery: 1999

Dating: 3.5 mya

Fossil material: Partial cranium, temporal fragment, partial maxilla, 2 partial mandibles

Australopithecus garhi

Taxonomic designation:
Australopithecus garhi

Year of first discovery: 1997

Dating: 2.5 mya

Fossil material: Partial cranium, numerous limb bones

Paranthropus aethiopicus

Taxonomic designation:
Paranthropus aethiopicus
(also called *Australopithecus aethiopicus*)

Year of first discovery: 1985

Dating: 2.4 mya

Fossil material: Nearly complete cranium

Location of finds: Lomekwi, West Lake Turkana, Kenya, East Africa

Location of finds: Bouri, Middle Awash, Ethiopia, East Africa

Location of finds: West Lake Turkana, Kenya

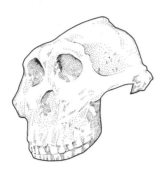

Paranthropus boisei

Taxonomic designation:
Paranthropus boisei (also called *Australopithecus boisei*)

Year of first discovery: 1959

Dating: 2.2–1.0 mya

Fossil material: 2 nearly complete crania, several partial crania, many jaw fragments, dozens of teeth. Postcrania less represented, but parts of several long bones recovered.

Location of finds: Olduvai Gorge and Peninj (Tanzania), East Lake Turkana (Koobi Fora), Chesowanja (Kenya), Omo (Ethiopia)

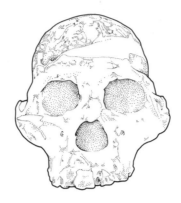

Australopithecus africanus

Taxonomic designation:
Australopithecus africanus

Year of first discovery: 1924

Dating: ~3.0?–2.0 mya

Fossil material: 1 mostly complete cranium, several partial crania, dozens of jaws/partial jaws, hundreds of teeth, 4 partial skeletons representing significant parts of the postcranium

Location of finds: Taung, Sterkfontein, Makapansgat, Gladysvale (all from South Africa)

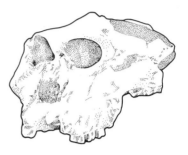

Paranthropus robustus

Taxonomic designation:
Paranthropus robustus (also called *Australopithecus robustusi*)

Year of first discovery: 1938

Dating: ~2–1 mya

Fossil material: 1 complete cranium, several partial crania, many jaw fragments, hundreds of teeth, numerous postcranial elements

Location of finds: Kromdraai, Swartkrans, Drimolen, Cooper's Cave, possibly Gondolin (all from South Africa)

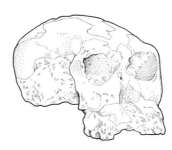

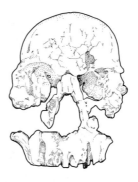

Early *Homo*

Taxonomic designation: *Homo habilis*

Year of first discovery: 1959/1960

Dating: 2.4–1.8 mya

Fossil material: 2 partial crania, other cranial pieces, jaw fragments, several limb bones, partial hand, partial foot, partial skeleton

Early *Homo*

Taxonomic designation: *Homo rudolfensis*

Year of first discovery: 1972

Dating: ~1.8 mya

Fossil material: 4 partial crania, 1 mostly complete mandible, other jaw pieces, numerous teeth, a few postcranial elements (none directly associated with crania)

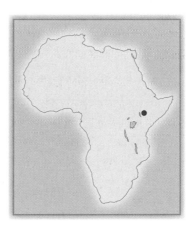

Location of finds: Olduvai Gorge (Tanzania), Lake Baringo (Kenya), Omo (Ethiopia), Sterkfontein (?) (South Africa)

Location of finds: East Lake Turkana (Koobi Fora), Kenya, East Africa

APPENDIX C
POPULATION GENETICS: THE MATH OF MICROEVOLUTION

Part A. Further Examples Using the Hardy-Weinberg Equilibrium Formula

EXAMPLE 1. HEMOGLOBIN BETA LOCUS IN WEST AFRICA

As discussed in Chapter 15, there is a high frequency of the Hb^S allele in parts of West Africa. One study (see p. 398) in a Senegalese group found a frequency of the Hb^S allele at 12 percent.

What follows is a hypothetical example for a Senegalese population of 4,000 individuals. Ascertainment is done on all individuals at 6 months of age. Because of incomplete dominance, all three phenotypes (and therefore all three genotypes) can be determined.

Observed frequencies:

	Number of Individuals	Hb^A Alleles	Hb^S Alleles
$Hb^A Hb^A$	3,070	6,140	——
$Hb^A Hb^S$	905	905	905
$Hb^S Hb^S$	25	——	50
Totals	4,000	7,045	955

Allele frequencies:

$Hb^A = p = 7,045/8,000 = .881$

$Hb^S = q = 955/8,000 = .119$

Expected genotypic frequencies:

$Hb^A Hb^A = p^2 = (.881)(.881) = .776$

$Hb^A Hb^S = 2pq = 2(.881)(.119) = .210$

$Hb^S Hb^S = q^2 = (.119)(.119) = .014$

Comparison of expected and observed frequencies:

	Expected Frequency	Expected No. Individuals	Observed Frequency	Observed No. Individuals
$Hb^A Hb^A$	.776	3,105	.767	3,070
$Hb^A Hb^S$	.210	839	.227	905
$Hb^S Hb^S$	.014	57	.006	25

As you can see, there is a noticeable difference between the expected and observed frequencies. There are fewer actual (observed) individuals of both homozygotes than expected and more heterozygotes than expected. Indeed, when performing a statistical test (see Part 2 of this appendix), the difference is statistically significant.

We can extend the example further. Let us assume that we again ascertain allele frequencies in this same population 30 years later, at which point there are 3,000 survivors.

Observed phenotypic frequencies:

	Number of Individuals	Hb^A Alleles	Hb^S Alleles
Hb^AHb^A	2,123	4,246	——
Hb^AHb^S	875	875	875
Hb^SHb^S	2	——	4
Totals	3,000	5,121	879

Allele frequencies:

$Hb^A = p = 5,121/6,000 = .854$

$Hb^S = q = 879/6,000 = .146$

Expected genotypic frequencies:

$Hb^AHb^A = p^2 = (.854)(.854) = .729$

$Hb^AHb^S = 2pq = 2(.854)(.146) = .249$

$Hb^SHb^S = q^2 = (.146)(.146) = .021$

Comparison of expected and observed frequencies:

	Expected Frequency	Expected No. Individuals	Observed Frequency	Observed No. Individuals
Hb^AHb^A	.729	2,188	.708	2,123
Hb^AHb^S	.249	748	.292	875
Hb^SHb^S	.021	64	.001	2

In this adult sample, the differences between the expected and observed frequencies are even greater than they were for the infant sample (and are even more highly statistically significant; see Part 2). Moreover, these differences are in the same direction as before: There are fewer homozygotes and more heterozygotes than expected under equilibrium conditions. A likely explanation for this pattern of allele frequencies would focus on natural selection. At age 6 months, there are slightly fewer Hb^AHb^A homozygotes than expected and considerably fewer Hb^SHb^S homozygotes than expected. Correspondingly, there are many more heterozygotes (Hb^AHb^S) than expected. These differences could arise from differential mortality of Hb^AHb^A individuals due to malaria (likely in early infancy) and Hb^SHb^S individuals due to sickle-cell anemia occurring both *in utero* and during early infancy.

These same factors would continue throughout childhood and early adulthood, so that by age 30, the effects of differential mortality due to both malaria and sickle-cell anemia are even more dramatic. While hypothetical, these figures represent a good example of how natural selection could operate on this population.

EXAMPLE 2. ADENOSINE DEAMINASE (ADA) IN A SRI LANKAN POPULATION

ADA is an enzyme present in many types of cells. The locus producing this enzyme has two common codominant alleles, A^1 and A^2. There are also very rare mutant alleles that can cause a fatal form of inherited immune deficiency.

From actual data derived from a polymorphic population in Sri Lanka,* the following observed frequencies were found. (*Note:* Because the alleles are codominant, the three phenotypes correspond directly to the three genotypes.)

	Number of Individuals	A^1 Alleles	A^2 Alleles
A^1A^1	113	226	——
A^1A^2	38	38	38
A^2A^2	3	——	6
Totals	154	264	44

Allele frequencies:

$A^1 = p = 264/308 = .857$

$A^2 = q = 44/308 = .143$

Expected genotypic frequencies:

$A^1A^1 = p^2 = (.857)(.857) = .734$

$A^1A^2 = 2pq = 2(.857)(.143) = .249$

$A^2A^2 = q^2 = (.143)(.143) = .020$

Comparison of expected and observed frequencies:

	Expected Frequency	Expected No. Individuals	Observed Frequency	Observed No. Individuals
A^1A^1	.734	113	.734	113
A^1A^2	.245	38	.247	38
A^2A^2	.020	3	.019	3

As you can clearly see, the expected and observed frequencies are nearly identical (in fact, the raw frequencies are identical). There is thus a probability of 1.0 that the null hypothesis is correct and a 0 percent confidence limit in rejecting the null hypothesis. This population at this locus thus appears to be in equilibrium. Such is often the case in actual population genetics studies, especially when the sample size is small.

EXAMPLE 3. DETERMINING THE NUMBER OF HETEROZYGOUS CARRIERS FOR PKU IN A HYPOTHETICAL POPULATION

Another way to apply the Hardy-Weinberg formula is to first *assume* equilibrium and then work the formula in reverse. For example, for many recessive traits where there is complete dominance (or nearly complete dominance), traditionally it has been impossible to ascertain the heterozygotes directly. However, if we make certain assumptions, we can use the formula to estimate the number of heterozygotes (i.e., carriers) in a population.

Let us assume that we are studying PKU in a group of 20,000 students at a university. PKU is an autosomal recessive disorder with an overall frequency in the United States of approximately 1/10,000 (see p. 70). In some subgroups (e.g., individuals of European descent), the frequency of PKU is higher.

In our hypothetical student population, we find two individuals with PKU (which was treated when the individuals were children). Because PKU is an autosomal recessive, the number of PKU homozygotes (2/20,000, or .0001) is equal to q^2.

If $q^2 = .0001$, then
$q = .01$ and $p = .99$

The frequency of the heterozygote is $2pq$:

$2(.99)(.01) = .0198$

The estimated number of carriers for PKU in the university student sample is

$(.0198)(20,000) = 198$

An interesting pattern is evident here. In the entire population, there is a total of 200 individuals who possess at least one PKU allele. Of these, the vast majority (99 percent) are carriers.

EXAMPLE 4. APPLYING THE HARDY-WEINBERG FORMULA TO ABO, A MORE COMPLEX GENETIC SYSTEM

In Chapter 15 and in the three examples given so far in this appendix, we have used examples of loci with only two alleles (and therefore just three possible genotypes). However, many loci are more complex, having three or more alleles. For example, ABO has three alleles and six genotypes (see Table 4–2, p. 71)

How do we utilize the Hardy-Weinberg equilibrium formula for a locus like ABO? First, there are three alleles, so the allele frequencies are designated as:

Frequency of $A = p$
Frequency of $B = q$
Frequency of $O = r$

Under equilibrium conditions, the genotypic frequencies would be calculated as follows:

$(p + q + r)^2 = 1$

This is an expansion of a trinomial (rather than the binomial used in a two-allele system). With a three-allele system like ABO, the genotypic frequency formula is

$p^2 + 2pq + 2pr + 2qr + q^2 = r^2 = 1$

There are six terms in this formula, each one representing a different genotype:

Term	Genotype Represented
p^2	AA
$2pq$	AB
$2pr$	AO
$2qr$	BO
q^2	BB
r^2	OO

We will not include actual numbers here. We simply wish to illustrate that population genetics calculations can be considerably more complex than implied by our earlier examples.

Part B. Statistical Evaluation: Testing Hardy-Weinberg Results

Following are the results using statistical tests comparing the expected and observed frequencies for the relevant examples shown in Chapter 15 as well as those discussed in this appendix. The test used is the chi-square (χ^2), which assumes that two variables are independent. In our examples, this independence is tested against a null hypothesis stating that there is equilibrium (in other words, the expected and observed frequencies do not differ any more than would be the case strictly as a result of chance). Further details concerning statistical approaches can be found in any introductory statistics text.

In the data tables that follow, all figures are shown as *raw* frequencies.

MN Data (from Chapter 15, p. 393) Contingency Table:

Observed frequencies	80	80	40
Expected frequencies	72	96	32

$\chi^2 = 2.76, p = .251$

The generally accepted confidence limit for rejection of the null hypothesis is less than or equal to .05. Thus, in this case, we cannot confidently reject the null hypothesis.

PTC Tasting Data (from Chapter 15, p. 393) Contingency Table:

Observed frequencies	125	325	50
Expected frequencies	165	245	90

$\chi^2 = 28.17, p < .0000$

This result is highly significant and allows us to reject the null hypothesis with a great deal of confidence. We are able to say there is less than one chance in 10,000 that the null hypothesis applies to these data.

Hemoglobin Beta Locus (Example 1, this appendix) Contingency Tables:

At 6 months:

Observed frequencies	3,070	905	25
Expected frequencies	3,105	839	57

$\chi^2 = 15.18, p = .0005$

This is a highly significant result that allows us to reject the null hypothesis with high confidence.

At Age 30:

Observed frequencies	2,123	875	2
Expected frequencies	2,188	748	64

$\chi^2 = 69.16, p < .0000$

This result is even more highly significant than at age 6 months, as there has been further disruption of equilibrium expectations (i.e., greater evidence of evolutionary shifts in allele frequencies).

GLOSSARY

Acclimatization Physiological responses to changes in the environment that occur during an individual's lifetime. Such responses may be temporary or permanent, depending on the duration of the environmental change and when in the individual's life it occurs. The *capacity* for acclimatization may typify an entire species or population, and because it's under genetic influence, it's subject to evolutionary factors such as natural selection or genetic drift.

Acheulian Pertaining to a stone tool industry from the Lower and Middle Pleistocene; characterized by a large proportion of bifacial tools (flaked on both sides). Acheulian tool kits are common in Africa, Southwest Asia, and western Europe, but they're thought to be less common elsewhere. Also spelled *Acheulean*.

Adaptation An anatomical, physiological, or behavioral response of organisms or populations to the environment. Adaptations result from evolutionary change (specifically, as a result of natural selection).

Adaptive niche An organism's entire way of life: where it lives, what it eats, how it gets food, how it avoids predators, and so on.

Adaptive radiation The relatively rapid expansion and diversification of life-forms into new ecological niches.

Affiliative Pertaining to amicable associations between individuals. Affiliative behaviors, such as grooming, reinforce social bonds and promote group cohesion.

Allele frequency In a population, the percentage of all the alleles at a locus accounted for by one specific allele.

Alleles Alternate forms of a gene. Alleles occur at the same locus on paired chromosomes and thus govern the same trait. But because they're different, their action may result in different expressions of that trait. The term is sometimes used synonymously with *gene*.

Allometry Also called *scaling;* the differential proportion among various anatomical structures (for example, the size of the brain in proportion to overall body size changes during the development of an individual). Scaling effects must also be considered when comparing species.

Alloparenting A common behavior in many primate species whereby individuals other than the parent(s) hold, carry, and in general interact with infants.

Allopatric Living in different areas; this pattern is important in the divergence of closely related species from each other and from their shared ancestral species because it leads to reproductive isolation.

Altruism Behavior that benefits another individual but at some potential risk or cost to oneself.

Amino acids Small molecules that are the components of proteins.

Analogies Similarities between organisms based strictly on common function, with no assumed common evolutionary descent.

Ancestral (primitive) Referring to characters inherited by a group of organisms from a remote ancestor and thus not diagnostic of groups (lineages) that diverged after the character first appeared.

Anthropocentric Viewing nonhuman organisms in terms of human experience and capabilities; emphasizing the importance of humans over everything else.

Anthropoids Members of a suborder of Primates, the *Anthropoidea* Traditionally, the suborder includes monkeys, apes, and humans.

Anthropology The field of inquiry that studies human culture and evolutionary aspects of human biology; includes cultural anthropology, archaeology, linguistics, and physical, or biological, anthropology.

Anthropometry Measurement of human body parts. When osteologists measure skeletal elements, the term *osteometry* is often used.

Antibodies Proteins that are produced by some types of immune cells and that serve as major components of the immune system. Antibodies recognize and attach to foreign antigens on bacteria, viruses, and other pathogens. Then other immune cells destroy the invading organism.

Antigens Large molecules found on the surface of cells. Several different loci govern various antigens on red and white blood cells. (Foreign antigens provoke an immune response.)

Arboreal Tree-living; adapted to life in the trees.

Archonta The superorder designated for the sister orders of tree shrews, flying lemurs, plesiadapiforms, and primates.

Artifacts Objects or materials made or modified for use by hominids. The earliest artifacts are usually made of stone or, occasionally, bone.

Association Relationships between components of an archaeological site. All the things artifacts are found with.

Assort To sort out or separate.

Aurignacian Pertaining to an Upper Paleolithic stone tool industry in Europe beginning at about 40,000 ya.

Australopithecine The colloquial name for members of the genus *Australopithecus* and *Paranthropus*. The term was first used as a subfamily designation, but it's now most often used informally.

Australopithecus An early hominid genus, known from the Plio-Pleistocene of Africa, characterized by bipedal locomotion, a relatively small brain, and large back teeth.

Autonomic Pertaining to physiological responses not under voluntary control. An example in chimpanzees would be the erection of body hair during excitement. An example in humans is blushing. Both convey information regarding emotional states; but neither behavior is deliberate, and communication is not intended.

Autosomes All chromosomes except the sex chromosomes.

Balanced polymorphism The maintenance of two or more alleles in a population due to the selective advantage of the heterozygote.

Behavior Anything organisms do that involves action in response to internal or external stimuli. The response of an individual, group, or species to its environment. Such responses may or may not be deliberate and they aren't necessarily the results of conscious decision making, as in one-celled organisms, insects, and many other species.

Behavioral ecology The study of the evolution of behavior, emphasizing the role of ecological factors as agents of natural selection. Behaviors and behavioral patterns have been selected for because they increase the reproductive fitness of individuals (i.e., they're adaptive) in specific environmental contexts.

Bilophodonty Molars that have 4 cusps, oriented in 2 parallel rows, that resemble ridges or "lophs." This is characteristic of Old World Monkeys.

Binocular vision Vision characterized by overlapping visual fields provided by forward-facing eyes. Binocular vision is essential to depth perception.

Binomial nomenclature In taxonomy, the convention established by Carolus Linnaeus whereby genus and species names are used to refer to species. For example, *Homo sapiens* refers to human beings.

Biocultural evolution The mutual, interactive evolution of human biology and culture; the concept that biology makes culture possible and that developing culture further influences the direction of biological evolution; a basic concept in understanding the unique components of human evolution.

Biological continuity Refers to a biological continuum. When expressions of a phenomenon continuously grade into one another so that there are no discrete categories, they exist on a continuum. Color is one such phenomenon, and life-forms are another.

Biological determinism The concept that phenomena, including various aspects of behavior (e.g., intelligence, values, morals) are governed by biological (genetic) factors; the inaccurate association of various behavioral attributes with certain biological traits, such as skin color.

Biological species concept A depiction of species as groups of individuals capable of fertile interbreeding but reproductively isolated from other such groups.

Biostratigraphy A relative dating technique based on regular changes seen in evolving groups of animals as well as presence or absence of particular species.

Bipedally On two feet. Walking habitually on two legs.

Blank In archaeology, a stone suitably sized and shaped to be further worked into a tool.

Brachiation A form of locomotion used by some primates; the animal suspends itself from a branch or other handhold and moves by alternately swinging from one forelimb to the other; also called arm swinging.

Breeding isolates Populations that are clearly isolated geographically and/or socially from other breeding groups.

Burins Small, chisel-like tools with a pointed end; thought to have been used to engrave bone, antler, ivory, or wood.

Catastrophism The view that the earth's geological landscape is the result of violent cataclysmic events. Cuvier promoted this view, especially in opposition to Lamarck.

Centromere The constricted portion of a chromosome. After replication, the two strands of a double-stranded chromosome are joined at the centromere.

Cercopithecines The subfamily of Old World monkeys that includes baboons, macaques, and guenons.

Chatelperronian Pertaining to an Upper Paleolithic industry found in France and Spain, containing blade tools and associated with Neandertals.

Chordata The phylum of the animal kingdom that includes vertebrates.

Christian fundamentalists Adherents to a movement in American Protestantism that began in the early twentieth century; this group holds that the teachings of the Bible are infallible and are to be taken literally.

Chromatin The loose, diffuse form of DNA seen when a cell isn't dividing. When it condenses, chromatin forms into chromosomes.

Chromosomes Discrete structures composed of DNA and protein found only in the nuclei of cells. Chromosomes are visible under magnification only during certain phases of cell division.

Chronometric dating (*chrono*, meaning "time," and *metric*, meaning "measure") A dating technique that gives an estimate in actual numbers of years.

Clade A group of organisms sharing a common ancestor. The group includes the common ancestor and all descendants.

Cladistics An approach to classification that attempts to make rigorous evolutionary interpretations based solely on analysis of certain types of homologous characters (those considered to be derived characters).

Cladogram A chart showing evolutionary relationships as determined by cladistic analysis. It's based solely on interpretation of shared derived characters. It contains no time component and does *not* imply ancestor-descendant relationships.

Classification In biology, the ordering of organisms into categories, such as orders, families, and genera, to show evolutionary relationships.

Cline A gradual change in the frequency of genotypes and phenotypes from one geographical region to another.

Clones Organisms that are genetically identical to another organism. The term may also be used in referring to genetically identical DNA segments, molecules, and cells.

Codominance The expression of two alleles in heterozygotes. In this situation, neither allele is dominant or recessive so they both influence the phenotype.

Colobines Common name for members of the subfamily of Old World monkeys that includes the African colobus monkeys and Asian langurs.

Communication Any act that conveys information, in the form of a message, to another individual. Frequently, the result of communication is a change in the recipient's behavior. Communication may not be deliberate, but may instead be the result of involuntary processes or a secondary consequence of an intentional action.

Complementary In genetics, referring to the fact that DNA bases form base pairs in a precise manner. For example, adenine can bond only to thymine. These two bases are said to be *complementary* because one requires the other to form a complete DNA base pair.

Conspecifics Members of the same species.

Context The environmental setting where an archaeological trace is found. *Primary* context is the setting in which the archaeological trace was originally deposited. A *secondary* context is one to which it has been moved (such as by the action of a stream).

Continental drift The movement of continents on sliding plates of the earth's surface. As a result, the positions of large landmasses have shifted drastically during the earth's history.

Continuum A set of relationships in which all components fall along a single integrated spectrum. All life reflects a single biological continuum.

Core area The portion of a home range containing the highest concentration and most reliable supplies of food and water. The core area is frequently the area that will be defended.

Core Stone reduced by flake removal; a core may or may not be used as a tool itself

Cortex Layer. In the brain, the cortex is the layer that covers the cerebral hemispheres, which in turn cover more primitive or older structures related to bodily functions and the sense of smell. It's composed of nerve cells called neurons, which communicate with each other and send and receive messages to and from all parts of the body.

Culture Behavioral aspects of human adaptation, including technology, traditions, language, religion, marriage patterns, and social roles. Culture is a set of *learned* behaviors transmitted from one generation to the next by nonbiological (i.e., nongenetic) means.

Cytoplasm The portion of the cell contained within the cell membrane, excluding the nucleus. The cytoplasm consists of a semifluid material and contains numerous structures involved with cell function.

Data Facts from which conclusions can be drawn; scientific information.

Dental ape An early ape that postcranially resembles a monkey, but dentally is hominoid (i.e., has a Y-5 molar configuration).

Dental formula Numerical device that indicates the number of each type of tooth in each side of the upper and lower jaws.

Deoxyribonucleic acid (DNA) The double-stranded molecule that contains the genetic code. DNA is a main component of chromosomes.

Derived (modified) Referring to characters that are modified from the ancestral condition and thus *are* diagnostic of particular evolutionary lineages.

Direct percussion Striking a core or flake with a hammerstone.

Displays Sequences of repetitious behaviors that serve to communicate emotional states. Nonhuman primate displays are most frequently associated with reproductive or agonistic behavior.

Diurnal Active during the day.

DNA (deoxyribonucleic acid) The double-stranded molecule that contains the genetic code. DNA is a main component of chromosomes.

Dominance hierarchies Systems of social organization wherein individuals within a group are ranked relative to one another. Higher-ranking individuals have greater access to preferred food items and mating partners than do lower-ranking individuals. Dominance hierarchies are sometimes referred to as pecking orders.

Dominant Describes a trait governed by an allele that's expressed in the presence of another allele (i.e., in heterozygotes). Dominant alleles prevent the expression of recessive alleles in heterozygotes. (This is the definition of *complete* dominance.)

Ecological niches The positions of species within their physical and biological environments, together making up the *ecosystem*. A species' ecological niche is defined by such components as diet, terrain, vegetation, type of predators, relationships with other species, and activity patterns, and each niche is unique to a given species.

Ecological species concept The concept that a species is a group of organisms exploiting a single niche. This view emphasizes the role of natural selection in separating species from one another.

Empirical Relying on experiment or observation; from the Latin *empiricus*, meaning "experienced."

Encephalization The proportional size of the brain relative to some other measure, usually some estimate of overall body size, such as weight. More precisely, the term refers to increases in brain size beyond what would be expected given the body size of a particular species.

Endemic Continuously present in a population.

Endocast A solid impression of the inside of the skull, often preserving details relating to the brain's size and surface features.

Endogamy Mating with individuals from the same group.

Endothermic (*endo*, meaning "within" or "internal") Able to maintain internal body temperature by producing energy through metabolic processes within cells; characteristic of mammals, birds, and perhaps some dinosaurs.

Environmental determinism An interpretation that links simple environmental changes directly to a major evolutionary shift in an organism. Such explanations tend to extremely oversimplify the evolutionary process.

Enzymes Specialized proteins that initiate and direct chemical reactions in the body.

Epochs Categories of the geological time scale; subdivisions of periods. In the Cenozoic, epochs include the Paleocene, Eocene, Oligocene, Miocene, and Pliocene (from the Tertiary) and the Pleistocene and Holocene (from the Quaternary).

Ethnocentric Viewing other cultures from the inherently biased perspective of one's own culture. Ethnocentrism often results in other cultures being seen as inferior to one's own.

Ethnographies Detailed descriptive studies of human societies. In cultural anthropology, an ethnography is traditionally the study of a non-Western society.

Eugenics The philosophy of "race improvement" through the forced sterilization of members of some groups and increased reproduction among others; an overly simplified, often racist view that's now discredited.

Euprimate The term *euprimate* means "true primate" and was coined by Elwyn Simons in 1972 (Conroy, 1990).

Evaporative cooling A physiological mechanism that helps prevent the body from over-heating. It occurs when perspiration is produced from sweat glands and then evaporates from the surface of the skin.

Evolution A change in the genetic structure of a population. The term is also frequently used to refer to the appearance of a new species.

Evolutionary systematics A traditional approach to classification (and evolutionary interpretation) in which presumed ancestors and descendants are traced in time by analysis of homologous characters.

Exogamy Mating pattern whereby individuals obtain mates from groups other than their own.

Exons Segments of genes that are transcribed and are involved in protein synthesis. (The prefix *ex–* denotes that these segments are expressed.)

Feature In archaeology, an immovable residue of human occupation, such as an ash pit.

Fertility The ability to conceive and produce healthy offspring.

Fitness Pertaining to natural selection, a measure of *relative* reproductive success of individuals. Fitness can be measured by an individual's genetic contribution to the next generation compared to that of other individuals. The terms *genetic fitness, reproductive fitness*, and *differential reproductive success* are also used.

Fixity of species The notion that species, once created, can never change; an idea dia-metrically opposed to theories of biological evolution.

Flake Thin-edged fragment removed from a core.

Flexed The position of the body in a bent orientation, with arms and legs drawn up to the chest.

Forensic anthropology An applied anthropological approach dealing with legal matters. Forensic anthropologists work with coroners and others in identifying and analyzing human remains.

Founder effect A type of genetic drift in which allele frequencies are altered in small populations that are taken from, or are remnants of, larger populations.

Free-ranging Pertaining to non-captive animals living in their natural habitat. Ideally, the behavior of wild study groups would be free of human influence.

Frugivorous Having a diet composed primarily of fruit.

Gametes Reproductive cells (eggs and sperm in animals) developed from precursor cells in ovaries and testes

Gene A sequence of DNA bases that specifies the order of amino acids in an entire protein, a portion of a protein, or any functional product. A gene may be made up of hundreds or thousands of DNA bases organized into coding and noncoding segments.

Gene flow Exchange of genes between populations.

Gene pool The total complement of genes shared by the reproductive members of a population.

Genetic drift Evolutionary changes—that is, changes in allele frequencies—produced by random factors. Genetic drift is a result of small population size.

Genetics The study of gene structure and action and the patterns of inheritance of traits from parent to offspring. Genetic mechanisms are the foundation for evolutionary change.

Genome The entire genetic makeup of an individual or species. In humans, it's estimated that each individual possesses approximately 3 billion DNA nucleotides.

Genotype The genetic makeup of an individual. Genotype can refer to an organism's entire genetic makeup or to the alleles at a particular locus.

Genus A group of closely related species.

Geological time scale The organization of earth history into eras, periods, and epochs; commonly used by geologists and paleoanthropologists.

Glaciations Climatic intervals when continental ice sheets cover much of the northern continents. Glaciations are associated with colder temperatures in northern latitudes and more arid conditions in southern latitudes, most notably in Africa.

Gracile Referring to smaller, more lightly built body/anatomical structure.

Grade A grouping of organisms sharing a similar adaptive pattern. Grade isn't necessarily based on closeness of evolutionary relationship, but it does contrast organisms in a useful way (e.g., *Homo erectus* with *Homo sapiens*).

Grooming Picking through fur to remove dirt, parasites, and other materials that may be present. Social grooming is common among primates and reinforces social relationships.

Half-life The time period in which one-half the amount of a radioactive isotope is converted chemically (into a daughter product). For example, after 1.25 billion years, half the 40K remains; after 2.5 billion years, one-fourth remains.

Hardy-Weinberg theory of genetic equilibrium The mathematical relationship expressing—under ideal conditions—the predicted distribution of alleles in populations; the central theorem of population genetics.

Hemispheres Two halves of the cerebrum that are connected by a dense mass of fibers. (The cerebrum is the large, rounded, outer portion of the brain.)

Hemoglobin A protein molecule that occurs in red blood cells and binds to oxygen molecules.

Heterodont Having different kinds of teeth; characteristic of mammals, whose teeth consist of incisors, canines, premolars, and molars.

Heterozygous Having different alleles at the same locus on members of a pair of chromosomes.

Holocene The most recent epoch of the Cenozoic. Following the Pleistocene, it's estimated to have begun 10,000 years ago.

Home range The total area exploited by an animal or social group; usually given for 1 year—or for the entire lifetime—of an animal.

Homeobox genes An evolutionarily ancient family of regulatory genes that directs the development of the overall body plan and the segmentation of body tissues.

Homeostasis A condition of balance, or stability, within a biological system, maintained by the interaction of physiological mechanisms that compensate for changes (both external and internal).

Hominidae The taxonomic family to which humans belong; also includes other, now extinct, bipedal relatives.

Hominids Colloquial term for members of the family Hominidae, which includes all bipedal hominoids back to the divergence from African great apes.

Hominoidea The formal designation for the superfamily of anthropoids that includes apes and humans.

Homo habilis A species of early *Homo*, well known from East Africa but perhaps also found in other regions.

Homologies Similarities between organisms based on descent from a common ancestor.

Homoplasy (*homo*, meaning "same," and *plasy*, meaning "growth") The separate evolutionary development of similar characteristics in different groups of organisms.

Homozygous Having the same allele at the same locus on both members of a pair of chromosomes.

Hormones Substances (usually proteins) that are produced by specialized cells; hormones travel to other parts of the body, where they influence chemical reactions and regulate various cellular functions.

Human Genome Project An international effort aimed at sequencing and mapping the entire human genome, completed in 2003.

Hybrids Offspring of individuals that differ with regard to certain traits or certain aspects of genetic makeup; heterozygotes.

Hypotheses A provisional explanation of a phenomenon. Hypotheses require verification or falsification through testing.

Inbreeding A type of nonrandom mating in which relatives mate more often than predicted under random mating conditions.

Intelligence Mental capacity; ability to learn, reason, or comprehend and interpret information, facts, relationships, and meanings; the capacity to solve problems, whether through the application of previously acquired knowledge or through insight.

Interglacials Climatic intervals when continental ice sheets are retreating, eventually becoming much reduced in size. Interglacials in northern latitudes are associated with warmer temperatures, while in southern latitudes the climate becomes wetter.

Interspecific Between species; refers to variation beyond that seen within the same species to include additional aspects seen between two different species.

Intraspecific Within species; refers to variation seen within the same species.

Introns Segments of genes that are initially transcribed and then deleted; therefore, they aren't expressed, that is, they aren't involved in protein synthesis.

Ischial callosities Patches of tough, hard skin on the buttocks of Old World monkeys and chimpanzees.

Island hop To travel from one island to the next.

Karyotype The chromosomal complement of an individual, or what is typical for a species. Usually displayed in a photomicrograph, the chromosomes are arranged in pairs and according to centromere size and position.

Knappers People (frequently archaeologists) who make stone tools.

K-selected Pertaining to an adaptive strategy (K-selection) whereby individuals produce relatively few offspring, in whom they invest increased parental care. Although only a few infants are born, chances of survival are increased for each individual because of parental investments in time and energy. Examples of nonprimate K-selected species are birds and canids (e.g., wolves, coyotes, and dogs).

Lactose intolerance The inability to digest fresh milk products, caused by the discontinued production of lactase—the enzyme that breaks down lactose, or milk sugar.

Last common ancestor (LCA) The final evolutionary link between two related groups.

Late Pleistocene The portion of the Pleistocene epoch beginning 125,000 ya and ending approximately 10,000 ya.

Lateralized Pertaining to lateralization, the functional specialization of the hemispheres of the brain for specific activities.

Life history traits Characteristics and developmental stages that influence rates of reproduction. Examples include longevity; age at sexual maturity; length of time between births, etc.

Line of weight transmission The line over which a significant weight load is carried; in a bone structure, the portion of the bone carrying the load will usually be reinforced (i.e., thicker/buttressed).

Lithic (*lith,* meaning "stone") Referring to stone tools.

Locus The position on a chromosome where a given gene occurs. The term is sometimes used interchangeably with *gene.*

Lumbar Pertaining to the lower back. Monkeys have a longer lumbar area than that seen in apes and humans.

Macroevolution Changes produced only after many generations, such as the appearance of a new species.

Magdalenian Pertaining to the final phase of the Upper Paleolithic stone tool industry in Europe.

Matrilines Groupings of females who are all descendants of one female (e.g., a female, her daughters, granddaughters, and their offpsring). Matrilines also include dependent male offspring. Among macaques, some matrilines are dominant to others, so that members of dominant matrilines have greater access to resources than do members of subordinate ones.

Megadont Big toothed.

Meiosis Cell division in specialized cells in ovaries and testes. Meiosis involves two divisions and results in four daughter cells, each containing only half the original number of chromosomes. These cells can develop into gametes.

Menarche The first menstruation in girls, usually occurring in the early to midteens.

Mendelian traits Characteristics that are influenced by alleles at only one genetic locus. Examples include many blood types, such as ABO. Many genetic disorders such as sickle-cell anemia and Tay-Sachs disease are also Mendelian traits.

Menopause The end of menstruation in women, usually occurring at around age 50.

messenger RNA (mRNA) A form of RNA that's assembled on a sequence of DNA bases. It carries the DNA code to the ribosome during protein synthesis.

Metabolism The chemical processes within cells that break down nutrients and release energy for the body to use. (When nutrients are broken down into their component parts, such as amino acids, energy is released and made available for the cell to use.)

Microevolution Small changes occurring within species, such as a change in allele frequencies.

Microliths (*micro*, meaning "small," and *lith*, meaning "stone") Small stone tools usually produced from narrow blades punched from a core; found especially in Africa during the latter part of the Pleistocene.

Microwear Polishes, striations, and other diagnostic microscopic changes on the edges of stone tools.

Middle Pleistocene The portion of the Pleistocene epoch beginning 780,000 ya and ending 125,000 ya.

Mitochondria Structures contained within the cytoplasm of eukaryotic cells that convert energy, derived from nutrients, into a form that's used by the cell.

Mitochondrial DNA (mtDNA) DNA found in the mitochondria; mtDNA is inherited only from the mother.

Mitosis Simple cell division; the process by which somatic cells divide to produce two identical daughter cells.

Molecules Structures made up of two or more atoms. Molecules can combine with other molecules to form more complex structures.

Morphological Pertaining to the form and structure of organisms.

Morphology The form (shape, size) of anatomical structures; can also refer to the entire organism.

Mosaic evolution A pattern of evolution in which the rates of evolution in one functional system vary from those in other systems. For example, in hominid evolution, the dental system, locomotor system, and neurological system (especially the brain) all evolved at markedly different rates.

Motor cortex That portion of the cortex involved in sending outgoing signals involved in muscle use. The motor cortex is located at the rear of the frontal lobe.

Mousterian Pertaining to the stone tool industry associated with Neandertals and some modern *H. sapiens* groups. Also called Middle Paleolithic. This industry is characterized by a larger proportion of flake tools than found in Acheulian tool kits.

Multidisciplinary Refers to research involving mutual contributions and cooperation of experts from various scientific fields (i.e., disciplines).

Mutation A change in DNA. *Mutation* refers to changes in DNA bases (specifically called point mutations) as well as to changes in chromosome number and/or structure.

Natal group The group in which animals are born and raised. (*Natal* pertains to birth.)

Natural selection The most critical mechanism of evolutionary change, first articulated by Charles Darwin; refers to genetic change or changes in the frequencies of certain traits in populations due to differential reproductive success between individuals.

Neocortex The more recently evolved portions of the cortex of the brain that are involved with higher mental functions and composed of areas that integrate incoming information from different sensory organs.

Neural tube In early embryonic development, the anatomical structure that develops to form the brain and spinal cord.

Nocturnal Active during the night.

Nondisjunction The failure of partner chromosomes or chromosome strands to separate during cell division.

Nonrandom mating Patterns of mating in a population in which individuals choose mates preferentially.

Nuchal torus (pertaining to the neck) A projection of bone in the back of the cranium where neck muscles attach; used to hold up the head.

Nucleotides Basic units of the DNA molecule, composed of a sugar, a phosphate, and one of four DNA bases.

Nucleus A structure (organelle) found in all eukaryotic cells. The nucleus contains chromosomes (nuclear DNA).

Olfaction The sense of smell.

Omnivorous Having a diet consisting of many food types (i.e., plant materials, meat, and insects).

Organelles Structures contained within cells. There are many organelle types, each performing specific functions.

Orthograde An upright body position; this term relates to the position of the head and torso during sitting, climbing, etc., and doesn't necessarily mean an animal is bipedal.

Osteology The study of skeletal material. Human osteology focuses on the interpretation of the skeletal remains from archaeological sites, skeletal anatomy, bone physiology, and growth and development. Some of the same techniques are used in paleoanthropology to study early hominids.

Paleanthropology The interdisciplinary approach to the study of earlier hominids—their chronology, physical structure, archaeological remains, habitats, and so on.

Paleomagnetism Dating method based on the earth's shifting magnetic pole.

Paleopathology The branch of osteology that studies the evidence of disease and injury in human skeletal (or, occasionally, mummified) remains from archaeological sites.

Paleoprimatologist A person who specializes in the study of the nonhuman primate fossil record.

Paleospecies Species defined from fossil evidence, often covering a long time span.

Pathogens Substances or microorganisms, such as bacteria, fungi, or viruses, that cause disease.

Pedigree chart A diagram showing family relationships; it's used to trace the hereditary pattern of particular genetic (usually Mendelian) traits.

Phenotype The observable or detectable physical characteristics of an organism; the detectable expressions of genotypes, frequently influenced by environmental factors.

Phenotypic ratio The proportion of one phenotype to other phenotypes in a group of organisms. For example, Mendel observed that there were approximately three tall plants for every short plant in the F^2 generation. This is expressed as a phenotypic ratio of 3:1.

Philopatric Remaining in one's natal group or home range as an adult. In most species, members of one sex disperse from their natal group as young adults, and members of the philopatric sex remain. In most of the nonhuman primate species, the philopatric sex is female.

Phylogenetic species concept Splitting many populations into separate species based on an identifiable parental pattern of ancestry.

Phylogenetic tree A chart showing evolutionary relationships as determined by evolutionary systematics. It contains a time component and implies ancestor-descendant relationships.

Phytoliths (*phyto*, meaning "hidden," and *lith*, meaning "stone") Microscopic silica structures formed in the cells of many plants, particularly grasses.

Placental A type (subclass) of mammal. During the Cenozoic, placentals became the most widespread and numerous mammals and today are represented by upwards of 20 orders, including the primates.

Pleiotropic genes Genes that have more than one effect; genes that have different effects at different times in the life cycle.

Pleiotropy A situation that occurs when the action of a single gene influences several seemingly unrelated phenotypic effects.

Pleistocene The epoch of the Cenozoic from 1.8 mya until 10,000 ya. Frequently referred to as the Ice Age, this epoch is associated with continental glaciations in northern latitudes.

Plio-Pleistocene Pertaining to the Pliocene and first half of the Pleistocene, a time range of 5–1 mya. For this time period, numerous fossil hominids have been found in Africa.

Point mutation A chemical change in a single base of a DNA sequence.

Polyandry A mating system wherein a female continuously associates with more than one male (usually 2 or 3), with whom she mates. Among nonhuman primates, this pattern is seen only in marmosets and tamarins.

Polygenic Referring to traits that are influenced by genes at two or more loci. Stature, skin color, eye color, and hair color are examples of polygenic traits. Many, but not all (eye color, for example), polygenic traits are influenced by environmental factors such as nutrition.

Polymerase chain reaction (PCR) A method of producing thousands of copies of a DNA segment using the enzyme DNA polymerase.

Polymorphisms Loci with more than one allele. Polymorphisms can be expressed in the phenotype as the result of gene action (as in ABO), or they can exist solely at the DNA level within noncoding regions.

Polypeptide chain A sequence of amino acids that may act alone or in combination with others as a functional protein.

Polytypic Referring to species composed of populations that differ in the expression of one or more traits.

Population Within a species, a community of individuals where mates are usually found.

Population genetics The study of the frequency of alleles, genotypes, and phenotypes in populations from a microevolutionary perspective.

Postcranial (*post,* meaning "after") In a quadruped, referring to that portion of the body behind the head; in a biped, referring to all parts of the body beneath the head (i.e., the neck down).

Prehensility Grasping, as by the hands and feet of primates.

Pressure flaking A method of removing flakes from a core by pressing a pointed implement (e.g., bone or antler) against the stone.

Primate paleontology The study of fossil primates, especially those that lived before the appearance of hominids.

Primates Members of the order of mammals *Primates* (pronounced "pry-may´-tees"), which includes prosimians, monkeys, apes, and humans.

Primatologists Scientists who study the evolution, anatomy, and behavior of nonhuman primates. Those who study behavior in noncaptive animals are usually trained as physical anthropologists.

Primatology The study of the biology and behavior of nonhuman primates (prosimians, monkeys, and apes).

Principle of independent assortment The distribution of one pair of alleles into gametes does not influence the distribution of another pair. The genes controlling different traits are inherited independently of one another.

Principle of segregation Genes (alleles) occur in pairs because chromosomes occur in pairs. During gamete formation, the members of each pair of alleles separate so that each gamete contains one member of each pair. During fertilization, the full number of chromosomes is restored, and members of gene or allele pairs are reunited.

Principle of superposition In a stratigraphic sequence, the lower layers were deposited before the upper layers. Or, simply put, the stuff on top of a heap was put there last.

Prosimians Members of a suborder of Primates, the Prosimii (pronounced "pro-sim´-ee-eye"). Traditionally, the suborder includes lemurs, lorises, and tarsiers.

Protein synthesis The assembly of chains of amino acids into functional protein molecules. The process is directed by DNA.

Proteins Three-dimensional molecules that serve a wide variety of functions through their ability to bind to other molecules.

Punctuated equilibrium The concept that evolutionary change proceeds through long periods of stasis punctuated by rapid periods of change.

Quadrupedal Using all four limbs to support the body during locomotion; the basic mammalian (and primate) form of locomotion.

Quantitatively Pertaining to measurements of quantity and including such properties as size, number, and capacity. When data are quantified, they're expressed numerically and can be tested statistically.

Random assortment The chance distribution of chromosomes to daughter cells during meiosis; along with recombination, the source of variation resulting from meiosis.

Recessive Describes a trait that isn't expressed in heterozygotes; also refers to the allele that governs the trait. For a recessive allele to be expressed, an individual must have two copies of it (i.e., the person must be homozygous).

Recognition species concept A depiction of species in which the key aspect is the ability of individuals to identify members of their own species for purposes of mating (and to avoid mating with members of other species). In theory, this type of selective mating is a component of a species concept emphasizing mating and is therefore compatible with the biological species concept.

Recombination (also sometimes called crossing over) The exchange of genetic material between homologous chromosomes during meiosis.

Recombinant DNA technology A process in which genes from the cell of one species are transferred to somatic cells or gametes of another species.

Regulatory proteins Proteins that can bind to DNA and modify the action of genes. Many are active only during certain stages of development.

Replicate To duplicate. The DNA molecule is able to make copies of itself.

Reproductive strategies The complex of behavioral patterns that contributes to individual reproductive success. The behaviors need not be deliberate, and they often vary considerably between males and females.

Reproductive success The number of offspring an individual produces and rears to reproductive age; an individual's genetic contribution to the next generation.

Reproductively isolated Pertaining to groups of organisms that, mainly because of genetic differences, are prevented from mating and producing offspring with members of other groups.

Rhinarium The moist, hairless pad at the end of the nose seen in most mammalian species. The rhinarium enhances an animal's ability to smell.

Ribonucleic acid (RNA) A single-stranded molecule, similar in structure to DNA. Three forms of RNA are essential to protein synthesis. They are messenger RNA (mRNA), transfer RNA (tRNA), and ribosomal RNA (rRNA).

Ribosomes Structures composed of a form of RNA called ribosomal RNA (rRNA) and protein. Ribosomes are found in the cell's cytoplasm and are essential to the manufacture of proteins.

Ritualized behaviors Behaviors removed from their original context and sometimes exaggerated to convey information.

Robust Referring to large, heavily built body/anatomical structure.

r-selected Pertaining to an adaptive strategy (r-selection) that emphasizes relatively large numbers of offspring and reduced parental care (compared to K-selected species). *K-selection* and *r-selection* are relative terms (e.g., mice are r-selected compared to primates but K-selected compared to many fish species).

Sagittal crest A ridge of bone that runs down the middle of the cranium like a short Mohawk. This serves as the attachment for the large temporal muscles, indicating strong chewing.

Science A body of knowledge gained through observation and experimentation; from the Latin *scientia*, meaning "knowledge."

Scientific method An approach to research whereby a problem is identified, a hypothesis (or provisional explanation) is stated, and that hypothesis is tested by collecting and analyzing data.

Scientific testing The precise repetition of an experiment or expansion of observed data to provide verification; the procedure by which hypotheses and theories are verified, modified, or discarded.

Sectorial Adapted for cutting or shearing; among primates, refers to the compressed (side-to-side) first lower premolar, which functions as a shearing surface with the upper canine.

Selective breeding A practice whereby animal and plant breeders choose which animals will be allowed to mate based on traits (such as coat color, body size, shape of face) they hope to produce in offspring. Animals that don't have the desirable traits aren't allowed to breed.

Selective pressures Forces in the environment that influence reproductive success in individuals.

Senescence Decline in physiological function usually associated with aging.

Sensory modalities Different forms of sensation (e.g., touch, pain, pressure, heat, cold, vision, taste, hearing, and smell).

Sex chromosomes In mammals, the X and Y chromosomes.

Sexual dimorphism Differences in physical characteristics between males and females of the same species. For example, humans are slightly sexually dimorphic for body size, with males being taller, on average, than females of the same population.

Sexual selection A type of natural selection that operates on only one sex within a species. It's the result of competition for mates, and it can lead to sexual dimorphism regarding one or more traits.

Shared derived Relating to specific character traits shared in common between two life-forms and considered the most useful for making evolutionary interpretations.

Sickle-cell anemia A severe inherited hemoglobin disorder in which red blood cells collapse when deprived of oxygen. It results from inheriting two copies of a mutant allele. This allele is caused by a single base substitution in the DNA.

Sister group Two lineages that diverged from a particular common ancestor. Since sister groups share a common ancestor, they are each other's closest relatives.

Slash-and-burn agriculture A traditional land-clearing practice involving the cutting and burning of trees and vegetation. In many areas, fields are abandoned after a few years and clearing occurs elsewhere.

Social structure The composition, size, and sex ratio of a group of animals. Social structures are the results of natural selection in specific habitats, and they influence individual interactions and social relationships. In many species, social structure varies, depending on different environmental factors. Thus, in most primate species, social structure should be viewed as flexible, not fixed.

Somatic cells Basically, all the cells in the body except those involved with reproduction.

Speciation The process by which a new species evolves from an earlier species. Speciation is the most basic process in macroevolution.

Species A group of organisms that can interbreed to produce fertile offspring. Members of one species are reproductively isolated from members of all other species (i.e., they cannot mate with them to produce fertile offspring).

Spina bifida A condition in which the arch of one or more vertebrae fails to fuse and form a protective barrier around the spinal cord.

Stable carbon isotopes Isotopes of carbon that are produced in plants in differing proportions, depending on environmental conditions. By analyzing the proportions of the isotopes contained in fossil remains of animals (who ate the plants), it's possible to reconstruct aspects of ancient environments (particularly temperature and aridity).

Stereoscopic vision The condition whereby visual images are, to varying degrees, superimposed. This provides for depth perception, or viewing the external environment in three dimensions. Stereoscopic vision is partly a function of structures in the brain.

Strategies Behaviors or behavioral complexes that have been favored by natural selection to increase individual reproductive fitness.

Stratigraphy Study of the sequential layering of deposits.

Stress In a physiological context, any factor that acts to disrupt homeostasis; more precisely, the body's response to any factor that threatens its ability to maintain homeostasis.

Subfossil Bone not old enough to have become completely mineralized as a fossil.

Sympatric Living in the same area; pertaining to two or more species whose habitats partly or largely overlap.

Taphonomy (*taphos*, meaning "dead") The study of how bones and other materials came to be buried in the earth and preserved as fossils. Taphonomists study the processes of sedimentation, the action of streams, preservation properties of bone, and carnivore disturbance factors.

Taxonomy The branch of science concerned with the rules of classifying organisms on the basis of evolutionary relationships.

Territorial Pertaining to the protection of all or a part of the area occupied by an animal or group of animals. Territorial behaviors range from scent marking to outright attacks on intruders.

Territory The portions of an individual's or group's home range actively defended against intrusion, particularly by conspecifics.

Theory A broad statement of scientific relationships or underlying principles that has been substantially verified through the testing of hypotheses.

Thermoluminiscence (TL) Technique for dating certain archaeological materials, such as stone tools, heated in the past, that release stored energy of radioactive decay as light upon reheating.

Theropods Small- to medium-sized ground-living dinosaurs, dated to approximately 150 mya and thought to be related to birds.

Transfer RNA (tRNA) The type of RNA that binds to specific amino acids and transports them to the ribosome during protein synthesis.

Transmutation The change of one species to another. The term *evolution* did not assume its current meaning until the late nineteenth century.

Uniformitarianism The theory that the earth's features are the result of long-term processes that continue to operate in the present as they did in the past. Elaborated on by Lyell, this theory opposed catastrophism and contributed strongly to the concept of immense geological time.

Upper Paleolithic A cultural period usually associated with modern humans, but also found with some Neandertals, and distinguished by technological innovation in various stone tool industries. Best known from western Europe, similar industries are also known from central and eastern Europe and Africa.

Variation (genetic) Inherited differences among individuals; the basis of all evolutionary change.

Vasoconstriction Narrowing of blood vessels to reduce blood flow to the skin. Vasoconstriction is an involuntary response to cold and reduces heat loss at the skin's surface.

Vasodilation Expansion of blood vessels, permitting increased blood flow to the skin. Vasodilation permits warming of the skin and facilitates radiation of warmth as a means of cooling. Vasodilation is an involuntary response to warm temperatures, various drugs, and even emotional states (blushing).

Vectors Agents that serve to transmit disease from one carrier to another. Mosquitoes are vectors for malaria, just as fleas are vectors for bubonic plague.

Vertebrates Animals with segmented, bony spinal columns; includes fishes, amphibians, reptiles, birds, and mammals.

Worldview General cultural orientation or perspective shared by members of a society.

Y-5 molar Molars that have 5 cusps with grooves running between them, forming a Y shape. This is characteristic of hominoids.

Zoonotic Pertaining to a zoonosis, a disease that's transmitted to humans through contact with nonhuman animals.

Zygomatic Cheekbone.

Zygote A cell formed by the union of an egg cell and a sperm cell. It contains the full complement of chromosomes (in humans, 46) and has the potential of developing into an entire organism.

BIBLIOGRAPHY

Adcock, Gregory J., Elizabeth S. Snow, Dennis Simon, et al.
  2001 "Mitochondrial DNA Sequences in Ancient
         Australians: Implications for Modern Human
         Origins." *Proceedings of the National Academy of
         Sciences, USA*, 98:537–542.

Aiello, L. C.
  1992 "Body Size and Energy Requirements." *In: The
         Cambridge Encyclopedia of Human Evolution*, J. Jones,
         R. Martin, and D. Pilbeam (eds.), Cambridge,
         England, UK: Cambridge University Press, pp. 41–45.

Aiello, L. C. and J. C. K. Wells
  2002 "Energetics and the Evolution of the Genus *Homo*.
         Annual Review of Anthropology, 31:323–338.

Alemseged, Z., F. Spoor, W. H. Kimbel et al.
  2006 "A Juvenile Early Hominin Skeleton from Dikika,
         Ethiopia." *Nature*, 443:296–301.

Altmann, J., G. Hausfater, and S.A. Altmann
  1988 "Determinants of Reproductive Success in Savannah
         Baboons, *Papio cynocephalus*." *In: Reproductive
         Success*, T. H. Clutton-Brock, (ed.), Chicago, IL:
         University of Chicago Press, pp. 403–418.

Anderson, R. P. and C. O. Handley
  2002 "Dwarfism in Insular Sloths: Biogeography, Selection,
         and Evolutionary Rate." *Evolution*, 56:1045–1058.

Ankel, Friderun
  1965 "Der Canalis Sacralis als Indikator für die Lange der
         Caudelregion der Primaten." *Folia Primatologica*,
         3:263–276.

Arsuaga, Juan-Luis, Carlos Lorenzo, Ana Gracia, et al.
  1999 "The Human Cranial Remains from Gran Dolina
         Lower Pleistocene Site (Sierra de Atapuerca, Spain)."
         Journal of Human Evolution, 37:431–457.

Arsuaga, J. L., I. Martinez, A. Gracia, et al.
  1997 "Sima de los Huesos (Sierra de Atapuerca, Spain): The
         Site." *Journal of Human Evolution*, 33:109–127.

Ascenzi, A., I. Bidditu, P. F. Cassoli, et al.
  1996 "A Calvarium of Late *Homo erectus* from Ceprano,
         Italy." *Journal of Human Evolution*, 31:409–423.

Asfaw, B., W. H. Gilbert, Y. Beyene, et al.
  2002 "Remains of *Homo erectus* from Bouri, Middle Awash,
         Ethiopia." *Nature*, 416:317–320.

Attenborough, David
  1987 *The First Eden: The Mediterranean World and Man*,
         Boston, MA: Little Brown.

Aureli, F., C. M. Schaffner, J. Verpooten, K. Slater, and G.
  Ramos-Fernandez
  2006 "Raiding Parties of Male Spider Monkeys: Insights
         into Human Warfare." *American Journal of Physical
         Anthropology*, 131:486–497.

Badrian, A. and N. Badrian
  1984 "Social Organization of *Pan paniscus* in the Lomako
         Forest, Zaire." *In: The Pygmy Chimpanzee*, Randall L.
         Susman (ed.), New York, NY: Plenum Press, pp.
         325–346.

Badrian, N., and R. K. Malenky
  1984 "Feeding Ecology of *Pan paniscus* in the Lomako Forest,
         Zaire." *In: The Pygmy Chimpanzee*, Randall L. Susman
         (ed.), New York, NY: Plenum Press, pp. 275–299.

Balter, Michael
  2006 "Radiocarbon Dating's Final Frontier." News Focus,
         Science, 313:1560–1563.

Baltimore, D,
  2001 "Our Genome Unveiled." *Nature*, 409:814–816.

Bamshad, Michael J.
  2003 "Human Population Genetic Structure and Inference
         of Group Membership." *American Journal of Human
         Genetics*, 72:578–589.

Bamshad, Michael J. and Steve E. Olson
  2003 "Does Race Exist?" *Scientific American*, 289:78–85.

Bartlett, Thad Q., Robert W. Sussman, and James M. Cheverud
  1993 "Infant Killing in Primates: A Review of Observed
         Cases with Specific References to the Sexual Selection
         Hypothesis." *American Anthropologist*, 95:958–990.

Barton, R. A. and R. L. M. Dunbar
  1997 "Evolution of the Social Brain." *In: Machiavellian
         Intelligence*, Vol. II., A. Whiten and R. Byrne (eds),
         Cambridge, UK: Cambridge University Press.

Beard, C.
2004   *The Hunt for the Dawn Monkey: Unearthing the Origins of Monkeys, Apes, and Humans.* Berkeley, CA: University of California Press.

Bearder, Simon K.
1987   "Lorises, Bushbabies & Tarsiers: Diverse Societies in Solitary Foragers." *In: Primate Societies,* Smuts, B. B., D. L. Cheney, and R. M. Seyfath (eds.), pp. 11–24.

Begun, David R.
1994   "Relations Among the Great Apes and Humans: New Interpretations Based on the Fossil Great Ape *Dryopithecus.*" *Yearbook of Physical Anthropology,* 37:11–63.

_____
2003   "Planet of the Apes." *Scientific American,* 289:74–83.

Begun, D. and A.Walker
1993   "The Endocast." *In: The Nariokotome* Homo erectus *Skeleton.* A. Walker and R. E. Leakey (eds.), Cambridge, MA: Harvard University Press, pp. 326-358.

Behrensmeyer, A. K., D. Western, and D. E. Dechant Boaz
1979   "New Perspectives in Vertebrate Paleoecology from a Recent Bone Assemblage." *Paleobiology,* 5:12–21.

Ben Shaul, D. M.
1962   "The Composition of the Milk of Wild Animals." *International Zoo Yearbook,* 4:333–342.

Berger, Thomas and Erik Trinkaus
1995   "Patterns of Trauma Among the Neandertals." *Journal of Archaeological Science,* 22:841–852.

Bergman, T. L., J. C. Beehner, D. L. Cheney, and R. M. Seyfarth
2003   "Hierarchical Classification by Rank and Kinship in Baboons." *Science,* 302:1234–1236.

Bermudez de Castro, J. M., J. Arsuaga, E. Carbonell, et al.
1997   "A Hominid from the Lower Pleistocene of Atapuerca, Spain. Possible Ancestor to Neandertals and Modern Humans." *Science,* 276:1392–1395.

Bermudez de Castro, J. M., M. Martinon-Torres, E. Carbonell, et al.
2004   "The Atapuerca Sites and their Contribution to the Knowledge of Human Evolution in Europe." *Evolutionary Anthropology,* 13:25–41.

Binford, L. R.
1981   *Bones: Ancient Men and Modern Myths.* New York, NY: Academic Press.

_____
1983   *In Pursuit of the Past.* New York, NY: Thames and Hudson.

Binford, Lewis R. and Chuan Kun Ho
1985   "Taphonomy at a Distance: Zhoukoudian, 'The Cave Home of Beijing Man'?" *Current Anthropology,* 26:413–442.

Binford, Lewis R. and Nancy M. Stone
1986a "The Chinese Paleolithic: An Outsider's View." *AnthroQuest,* 1986:14–20.

_____ 1986b "Zhoukoudian: A Closer Look." *Current Anthropology,* 27(5):453–475.

Bischoff, J. L., R. W. Williams, R. J. Rosebauer, et al.
2007   "High-Resolution U-series Dates from the Sima de los Huesos Hominids Yields 600+Ω/-66 kyrs: Implications for the Evolution of the Early Neanderthal Lineage." *Journal of Archaeological Science,* 34:763–770.

Bloch, Jonathan I. and Mary T. Silcox
2001   "New Basicrania of Paleocene-Eocene *Ignacius*: Re-evaluation of the Plesiadapiform-Dermopteran Link." *American Journal of Physical Anthropology,* 116:184–198.

Bloch, Jonathan I. and D. M. Boyer
2002   "Grasping Primate Origins." *Science,* 298:1606–1610.

Blumenschine, Robert J.
1986   *Early Hominid Scavenging Opportunities.* Oxford, UK: Bar International Series 283.

_____
1995   "Percussion Marks, Tooth Marks, and Experimental Determinants of the Timing of Hominid and Carnivore Access to Long Bones at FLK *Zinjanthropus,* Olduvai Gorge, Tanzania." *Journal of Human Evolution,* 29: 21–51.

Blumenschine, Robert J., and John A. Cavallo
1992   "Scavenging and Human Evolution." *Scientific American* (Oct.): 90–96.

Blumenschine, Robert J., and Charles R. Peters
1998   "Archaeological Predictions for Hominid Land Use in the Paleo-Olduvai Basin, Tanzania, During Lowermost Bed II Times." *Journal of Human Evolution* 34: 565–607.

Boaz, N. T. and A. K. Behrensmeyer
1976   "Hominid Taphonomy: Transport of Human Skeletal Parts in an Artificial Fluviatile Environment." *American Journal of Physical Anthropology,* 45:56–60.

Boaz, N. T. and R. L. Ciochon
2001   "The Scavenging of *Homo erectus pekinensis.*" *Natural History,* 110:46–51.

Boesch, C.
1996   "Social Grouping Tai Chimpanzees." *In: Great Ape Societies.* W. C. McGrew, L. Marchant, and T. Nishida (eds), Cambridge, UK: Cambridge University Press. pp. 101–113.

Boesch, C. and H. Boesch-Achermann
2000   *The Chimpanzees of the Tai Forest.* Oxford, UK: Oxford University Press.

Boesch, C. and H. Boesch
1989   "Hunting Behavior of Wild Chimpanzees in the Tai National Park." *American Journal of Physical Anthropology,* 78:547 573.

Boesch, C. P. Marchesi, N. Marchesi, et al.
1994   "Is Nut Cracking in Wild Chimpanzees a Cultural Behaviour?" *Journal of Human Evolution,* 26:325–338.

Borries, C., K. Launhardt, C. Epplen, et al.
1999   "DNA Analyses Support the Hypothesis that Infanticide is Adaptive in Langur Monkeys." *Proceedings of the Royal Society of London,* 266:901–904.

Bower, Bruce
2003   "The Ultimate Colonists." *Science News,* 164:10–12.

2006   "Evolution's Mystery Woman." *Science News,* 170:330–332.

Brace, C. L. and Ashley Montagu
1977   *Human Evolution* (2nd Ed.). New York, NY: Macmillan.

Brace, C. Loring, H. Nelson, and N. Korn
1979   *Atlas of Human Evolution* (2nd Ed.). New York, NY: Holt, Rinehart & Winston.

Brain, C. K.
1981   *The Hunters or the Hunted? An Introduction to African Cave Taphonomy.* Chicago, IL: University of Chicago Press.

Brash, D. E, J. A. Rudolph, J. A. Simon, et al.
1991   "A Role for Sunlight in Skin Cancer: UV-Induced p53 Mutations in Squamous Cell Carcinoma." *Proceedings of National Academy of Sciences, USA,* 88:10124–10128.

Bromage, Timothy G. and Christopher Dean
1985   "Re-evaluation of the Age at Death of Immature Fossil Hominids." *Nature,* 317:525–527.

Brown, P., T. Sutiikna, M. K. Morwood, et al.
2004   "A New Small-Bodied Hominin from the Late Pleistocene of Flores, Indonesia." *Nature,* 431:1055–1061.

Brown, T. M. and K. D. Rose
1987   "Patterns of Dental Evolution in Early Eocene Anaptomorphine Primates Comomyidael from the Bighorn Basin, Wyoming." *Journal of Paleontology,* 61:1–62.

Brunet, M., F. Guy, D. Pilbeam, et al.
2002   "A New Hominid from the Upper Miocene of Chad, Central Africa." *Nature,* 418:145–151.

Bshary, R. and R. Noe
1997   "Red Colobus and Diana Monkeys Provide Mutual Protection Against Predators." *Animal Behavior,* 54:1461–1474.

Buchan, J. C., S. C. Alberts, J. B. Silk, and J. Altmann
2003   "True Paternal Care in a Multi-male Primate Society." *Nature,* 425:179–180.

Bunn, Henry T.
1981   "Archaeological Evidence for Meat-eating by Plio-Pleistocene Hominids from Koobi Fora and Olduvai Gorge." *Nature,* 291:574–577.

Burchard, E. G., E. Ziv, N. Coyle, et al.
2003   "The Importance of Race and Ethnic Background in Biomedical Research and Clinical Practice." *New England Journal of Medicine,* 348:1170–1175.

Butzer, Karl W.
1974   "Paleoecology of South African Australopithecines: Taung Revisited." *Current Anthropology,* 15:367–382.

Cantalupo, Claudio and William D. Hopkins
2001   "Asymmetric Broca's Area in Great Apes." *Nature,* 414:505.

Caramelli, D., C. Lalueza-Fox, S. Condemi, et al.
2006   "A Highly Divergent mtDNA Sequence in a Neandertal Individual from Italy." *Current Biology,* 16:R630–R632.

Caramelli, David, Carlos Lalueza-Fox, Cristiano Vernesi, et al.
2003   "Evidence for Genetic Discontinuity Between Neandertals and 24,000-year-old Anatomically Modern Humans." *Proceedings of the National Academy of Sciences, USA,* 100:6593–6597.

Carroll, Sean B.
2003   "Genetics and the Making of *Homo sapiens.*" *Nature,* 422:849–857.

Cartailhac, Emile and Henri Breuil
1906   *La Caverne D'Altamira.* Monaco: Imprimerie de Monaco.

Cartmill, Matt
1972   "Arboreal Adaptations and the Origin of the Order Primates." *In: The Functional and Evolutionary Biology of Primates*, R. H. Tuttle (ed.), Chicago, IL: Aldine-Atherton, pp. 97–122.

———
1990   "Human Uniqueness and Theoretical Content in Paleoanthropology." *International Journal of Primatology*, 11:173–192.

———
1992   "New Views on Primate Origins." *Evolutionary Anthropology*, 1:105–111.

Cela-Conde, Camillo J. and Francisco J. Ayala
2003   "Genera of the Human Lineage." *Proceedings of the National Academy of Sciences, USA,* 100:7684–7689.

Charteris, J., J. C. Wali, and J. W. Nottrodt
1981   "Functional Reconstruction of Gait from Pliocene Hominid Footprints at Laetoli, Northern Tanzania." *Nature*, 290:496–498.

Chatterjee, Helen J.
2006   "Phylogeny and Biogeography of Gibbons: A Dispersal-Vicariance Analysis." *International Journal of Primatology*, 27:699–712.

Chen, F-C., and Li, W-H.
2001   "Genomic Divergences Between Humans and Other Hominoids and the Effective Population Size of the Common Ancestor of Humans and Chimpanzees." *American Journal of Human Genetics,* 68:444–456.

Cheney, Dorothy L.
1987   "Interaction and Relationships between Groups." *In: Primate Societies,* B. Smuts, D. L. Cheney, R. M. Seyfarth, et al. (eds.), Chicago, IL: University of Chicago Press, pp. 267–281.

Cheney, D. L., R. M. Seyfarth, S. J. Andelman, and P. C. Lee
1988   "Reproductive Success in Vervet Monkeys." *In: Reproductive Success.* T. H. Clutton-Brock, (ed.), Chicago, IL: University of Chicago Press. pp.384–402.

The Chimpanzee Sequencing and Analysis Consortium.
2005   "Initial Sequence of the Chimpanzee Genome and Comparison with the Human Genome." *Nature,* 437:69–87.

Ciochon, R. L. and A. B Chiarelli (eds.)
1980a   *Evolutionary Biology of the New World Monkeys and Continental Drift.* New York, NY: Plenum Press.

———
1980b   "Paleobiogeographic Perspectives on the Origin of Platyrrhini." *In: Evolutionary Biology of the New World Monkeys and Continental Drift,* New York, NY: Plenum Press, pp. 459–493.

Ciochon, Russell L. and Gregg G. Gunnell
2002   "Eocene Primates from Myanmar: Historical Perspectives on the Origin of Anthropoidea." *Evolutionary Anthropology*, 11:156–168.

Ciochon, Russell L., John J. Olsen, and Jamie James
1990a   *Other Origins: the Search for the Giant Ape in Human Prehistory.* New York, NY: Bantam.

Ciochon, Russell L., Dolores R. Piperno, and Robert G. Thompson
1990b   "Opal Phytoliths Found on the Teeth of the Extinct Ape *Gigantopithecus blacki*: Implications for Paleodietary Studies." *Proceedings of the National Academy of Sciences, USA,* 87:8120–8124.

Clark, A. G., S. Glanowski, R. Nielsen, et al.
2003.   "Inferring Nonneutral Evolution from Human-Chimp-Mouse Orthologous Gene Trios." *Science,* 302:1960–1963.

Clark, J. Desmond, Yonas Beyene, Gidoy Wold Gabriel, et al.
2003   "Stratigraphic, Chronological, and Behavioral Contexts of Pleistocene *Homo sapiens* from Middle Awash, Ethiopia." *Nature,* 423:747–752.

Clarke, R. J.
1985   "*Australopithecus* and Early *Homo* in Southern Africa." *In: Ancestors: The Hard Evidence,* E. Delson (ed.), New York, NY: Alan R. Liss, pp. 171–177.

Clarke, Ronald J. and Phillip V. Tobias
1995   "Sterkfontein Member 2 Foot Bones of the Oldest South African Hominid." *Science,* 269:521–524.

Cleveland, J. and C. T. Snowdon
1982   "The Complex Vocal Repertoire of the Adult Cotton-top Tamarin (*Saguinus oedipus oedipus*)." *Zeitschrift Tierpsychologie,* 58:231–270.

Colwell, Rita R.
1996   "Global Climate and Infectious Disease: The Cholera Paradigm." *Science,* 274:2025–2031.

Conkey, M.
1987　"New Approaches in the Search for Meaning? A Review of the Research in 'Paleolithic Art.'" *Journal of Field Archaeology,* 14:413–430.

Conroy, Glenn C.
1990　Primate Evolution. New York, NY: W. W. Norton.

————
1997　*Reconstructing Human Origins: A Modern Synthesis.* New York, NY: Norton.

Conroy, G. C., M. Pickford, B. Senut, J. van Couvering, and P. Mein
1992　"*Otavipithecus namibiensis,* First Miocene Hominoid from Southern Africa." *Nature,* 356:144–148.

Constable J. L., M. V. Ashley, J. Goodall, and A. E. Pusey
2001　"Noninvasive Paternity Assignment in Gombe Chimpanzees." *Molecular Ecology,* 10:1279–1300.

Cooper, Alan, Andrew Rambaut, Vincent Macaulay, et al.
2001　"Human Origins and Ancient DNA." Letter to *Science,* 282:1655–1656.

Cooper, Richard S., S. Kaufman, and Ryk Ward
2003　"Race and Genomics." *New England Journal of Medicine.* 348:1166–1170.

Cordain, L.
1999　"Cereal Grains: Humanity's Double-Edged Sword." *World Review of Nutrition and Diet,* 84:19–73.

————
2002　*The Paleo Diet: Lose Weight and Get Healthy by Eating the Food You Were Designed to Eat.* New York, NY: John Wiley and Sons, Inc.

Crews, D. E. and G. J. Harper
1998　"Ageing as Part of the Developmental Process." *In: The Cambridge Encyclopedia of Human Growth and Development,* S. J. Ulijaszek et al. (eds.) Cambridge, UK: Cambridge University Press, pp. 425–427.

Crook, J. H. and J. S. Gartlan
1966　"Evolution of Primate Societies." *Nature,* 210:1200–1203.

Cummings, Michael
2000　*Human Heredity. Principles and Issues* (5th Ed.). St. Paul, MN: Wadsworth/West Publishing Co.

Currat, M., G. Trabuchet, D. Rees, et al.
2002　"Molecular Analysis of the Beta-Globin Gene Cluster in the Niokholo Mandenka Population Reveals a Recent Origin of the Beta S Senegal Mutation." *American Journal of Human Genetics,* 70:207–223.

Curtin, R. and P. Dolhinow
1978　"Primate Social Behavior in a Changing World." *American Scientist,* 66:468–475.

De Bonis, Louis and George D. Koufos
1994　"Our Ancestors' Ancestor: *Ouranopithecus* Is a Greek Link in Human Ancestry." *Evolutionary Anthropology,* 3:75–83.

Daeschler, Edward B., Neil H. Shubin, and Farish A. Jenkins, Jr.
2006　"A Darwinian Tetrapod-Like Fish and the Evolution of the Tetrapod Body Plan." *Nature,* 440:757–763.

Dart, Raymond
1959　*Adventures with the Missing Link.* New York, NY: Harper & Brothers.

Darwin, Charles
1859　*On the Origin of Species.* A Facsimile of the First Edition, Cambridge, MA: Harvard University Press (1964).

————
1871　*The Descent of Man and Selection in Relation to Sex.* Princeton, NJ: Princeton University Press (1981).

Darwin, Francis (ed.)
1950　*The Life and Letters of Charles Darwin.* New York, NY: Henry Schuman.

Day, M. H. and E. H. Wickens
1980　"Laetoli Pliocene Hominid Footprints and Bipedalism." *Nature,* 286:385–387.

Deacon, T. W.
1992　"The Human Brain." *In: The Cambridge Encyclopedia of Human Evolution,* S. Jones, R. Martin, and D. Pilbeam (eds.), Cambridge, UK: Cambridge University Press, pp. 115–123.

Dean, Christopher, Meave G. Leakey, Donald Reid, et al.
2001　"Growth Processes in Teeth Distinguishing Modern Humans from *Homo erectus* and Earlier Hominins." *Nature,* 414:628–631.

Dean, M., M. Carring, C. Winkler, et al.
1996　"Genetic Restriction of HIV-1 Infection and Progression to AIDS by a Deletion Allele of the CKR5 Structural Gene." *Science,* 273:1856–1862.

Defleur, A, T. D. White, P. Valensi, et al.
1999　"Neanderthal Cannibalism at Moula-Guercy, Ardèche, France." *Science,* 286:128–131.

de Heinzelin, Jean, J. Desmond Clark, Tim D. White, et al.
1999　"Environment and Behavior of 2.5-Million-Year-Old Bouri Hominids." *Science,* 284:625–629.

de Lumley, Henry and M. de Lumley
1973   "Pre-Neanderthal Human Remains from Arago Cave in Southeastern France." *Yearbook of Physical Anthropology*, 16:162–168.

Dennell, Rubin and Wil Roebroeks
2005   "An Asian Perspective on Early Human Dispersal from Africa." *Nature*, 438:1099–1104.

Deragon, J. M. and P. Capy
2000   "Impact of Transposable Elements on the Human Genome." *Annals of Medicine* 32:264–273.

deReuter, J. R.
1986   "The Influence of Group Size on Predator Scanning and Foraging Behavior of Wedge-Capped Capuchin Monkeys *(Cebus olivaceus)*." *Behaviour*, 98:240–258.

Desmond, Adrian and James Moore
1991   *Darwin*. New York, NY: Warner Books.

DeVore, I. and S. L. Washburn
1963   "Baboon Ecology and Human Evolution." *In: African Ecology and Human Evolution*, F. C. Howell and F. Bourlière (eds.), New York, NY: Viking Fund Publication, No. 36, pp. 335–367.

de Waal, Frans
1982   *Chimpanzee Politics*. London, UK: Jonathan Cape.

———
1998   "No Imitation Without Identification." *Behavioral and Brain Sciences*, 21:689.

de Waal, F. and F. Lanting.
1997   *Bonobo: The Forgotten Ape*. Berkeley, CA: University of California Press.

———
1987   "Tension Regulation and Nonreproductive Functions of Sex in Captive Bonobos *(Pan paniscus)*." *National Geographic Research*, 3:318–335.

———
1989   *Peacemaking among Primates*. Cambridge, MA: Harvard University Press.

———
1996   *Good Natured: The Origins of Right and Wrong in Humans and Other Animals*. Cambridge, MA.: Harvard University Press.

———
1999   "Cultural Primatology Comes of Age." *Nature*, 399:635–636.

2005   *Our Inner Ape*. New York, NY: Penguin Group.

Dominy, N. J. and P. W. Lucas
2001   "Ecological Importance of Trichromatic Vision to Primates." *Nature*, 410:363–366.

Doran, D. M. and A. McNeilage
1998   "Gorilla Ecology and Behavior." *Evolutionary Anthropology*, 6:120–131.

Duarte, C., J. Mauricio, P. B. Pettitt, et al.
1999   "The Early Upper Paleolithic Human Skeleton from the Abrigo do Lagar Velho (Portugal) and Modern Human Emergence in Iberia." *Proceedings of the National Academy of Sciences, USA*, 96:7604–7609.

Dunbar, Robin
1998   "The Social Brain Hypothesis." *Evolutionary Anthropology*, 6(5):178–190.

———
2001   "Brains on Two Legs: Group Size and the Evolution of Intelligence." *In: Tree of Origin: What Primate Behavior Can Tell Us about Human Social Evolution*, Frans de Waal et al. (eds) Cambridge, MA: Harvard University Press, pp. 173–191.

Durham, William
1981   Paper presented to the Annual Meeting of the American Anthropological Association, Washington, D.C., Dec. 1980. Reported in *Science*, 211:40.

Eaton, S. Boyd, M. Shostak, and M. Konner
1988   *The Paleolithic Prescription*. New York, NY: Harper and Row.

Eaton, S. B., S. B. Eaton III and M. J. Konner
1999   "Paleolithic Nutrition Revisited." *In: Evolutionary Medicine*, W. R. Trevathan, J. J. McKenna, and E. O. Smith (eds.), New York: Oxford University Press, pp. 313–332.

Ehret, G.
1987   "Left Hemisphere Advantage in the Mouse Brain for Recognizing Ultrasonic Communication Calls." *Nature*, 325: 249–251.

Ehrlich, Paul R. and Anne H. Ehrlich
1990   *The Population Explosion*. New York, NY: Simon & Schuster.

Ellison, P. T
2001   *On Fertile Ground: A Natural History of Human Reproduction*. Cambridge, MA: Harvard University Press

Enard, W., M. Przeworski, S. E. Fisher, et al.,
2002 "Molecular Evolution of FOXP2, a Gene Involved in Speech and Language." *Nature*, 418:869–872.

Eswaran, V., H. Harpending, and A. R. Rogers
2005 "Genomics Refutes an Exclusively African Origin of Humans." *Journal of Human Evolution*, 49:1–18.

Ewald, P. W.
1994 *Evolution of Infectious Disease.* New York, NY: Oxford University Press.

———
1999 "Evolutionary Control of HIV and Other Sexually Transmitted Viruses." *In: Evolutionary Medicine*, W. R. Trevathan, E. O. Smith, and J. J. McKenna, (eds.), New York, NY: Oxford University Press.

Falguères, Christophe, Jean-Jacques Bahain, Yugi Yokoyama, et al.
1999 "Earliest Humans in Europe: The Age of TD6 Gran Dolina, Atapuerca, Spain." *Journal of Human Evolution*, 37:345–352.

Falk, Dean
1990 "Brain Evolution in *Homo*: The 'Radiator' Theory." *Behavioral and Brain Sciences*, 13:333–344.

Falk, D., C. Hildebolt, K. Smith, et al.
2005 "The Brain of LB1, *Homo floresiensis*." *Science*, 308:242–245.

Feathers, James K. and Elena Migliorini
2001 Luminescence Dating at Katanda – A Reassessment. *Quaternary Science Reviews* 20:961–966.

Fedigan, L. M.
1983 "Dominance and Reproductive Success in Primates." *Yearbook of Physical Anthropology*, 26:91–129.

Fischman, Josh
2005 "Family Ties." *National Geographic*, 207(April):16–27.

Fleagle, John
1988/1999 *Primate Adaptation and Evolution.* New York, NY: Academic Press. (2nd Ed.), 1999.

———
1994 "Anthropoid Origins." *In: Integrative Paths to the Past: Paleoanthropological Advances in Honor of F. Clark Howell*, R. Corruccini and R. Ciochon (eds.), Englewood Cliffs, NJ: Prentice Hall, pp. 17–35.

Foley, R. A.
1991 "How Many Species of Hominid Should There Be?" *Journal of Human Evolution*, 30: 413–427.

———
2002 "Adaptive Radiations and Dispersals in Hominin Evolutionary Ecology." *Evolutionary Anthropology*, 11(Supplement 1):32–37.

Formicola, Vincenzo and Alexandra P. Buzhilova
2004 "Double Child Burial from Sunghir (Russia): Pathology and Inferences for Upper Paleolithic Funerary Practices." *American Journal of Physical Anthropology*, 124:189–198.

Fossey, Dian
1983 *Gorillas in the Mist.* Boston, MA: Houghton Mifflin.

Foster, J. B.
1964 "Evolution of Mammals on Islands." *Nature*, 202:234–235.

Fouts, Roger S., D. H. Fouts, and T. T. van Cantfort
1989 "The Infant Loulis Learns Signs from Cross-Fostered Chimpanzees." *In: Teaching Sign Language to Chimpanzees*, R. A. Gardner, B. T. Gardner, and T. T. van Cantfort (eds.), Albany, NY: State University of New York Press, pp. 280–292.

Freundlich, J. C., H. Schwabedissen and E. Wendt
1980 "Köln Radiocarbon Measurements II." *Radiocarbon*, 22:68–81.

Frisancho, A. Roberto
1993 *Human Adaptation and Accommodation.* Ann Arbor, MI: University of Michigan Press.

Frisch, Rose E.
1988 "Fatness and Fertility." *Scientific American*, 258:88–95.

Froelich, J. W.
1970 "Migration and Plasticity Physique in the Japanese-Americans of Hawaii." *American Journal of Physical Anthropology*, 32:429.

Gabunia, Leo, Abesalom Vekua, David Lordkipanidze, et al.
2000 "Earliest Pleistocene Hominid Cranial Remains from Dmanisi, Republic of Georgia: Taxonomy, Geological Setting, and Age." *Science*, 288:1019–1025.

Galik, K., B. Senut, M. Pickford, et al.
2004 "External and Internal Morphology of the Bar, 1002'00 *Orrorin tugenensis* Femur." *Science*, 305:1450–1453.

Gao, Feng, Elizabeth Bailes, David L. Robertson, et al.
1999 "Origin of HIV-1 in the Chimpanzee *Pan troglodytes troglodytes*." *Nature*, 397:436–441.

Gardner, R. Allen, B. T. Gardner, and T. T. van Cantfort (eds.)
1989   *Teaching Sign Language to Chimpanzees.* Albany, NY: State University of New York Press.

Garner, K. J., Ryder, O. A.
1996   "Mitochondrial DNA Diversity in Gorillas." *Molecular Phylogenetics and Evolution,* 6:39–48.

Gebo, Daniel L., L.aura MacLatchy, R. Kityo, et al.
1997   "A Hominoid Genus from the Early Miocene of Uganda." *Science,* 276:401–404.

George, I., H. Cousillas, H. Richard, et al.
2002   "Song Perception in the European Starling: Hemispheric Specialization and Individual Variations." *C. R. Biol.,* 325:197–204.

Ghiglieri, Michael P.
1984   *The Chimpanzees of Kibale Forest.* New York, NY: Columbia University Press.

Giles, J. and J. Knight
2003   "Dolly's Death Leaves Researchers Woolly on Clone Ageing Issue." *Nature,* 421:776.

Gillespie, B. and R. G. Roberts
2000   "On the Reliability of Age Estimate for Human Remains at Lake Mungo." *Journal of Human Evolution,* 38:727–732.

Gingerich, Phillip D.
1985   "Species in the Fossil Record: Concepts, Trends, and Transitions." *Paleobiology,* 11:27–41.

Glantz, M. M. and T. B. Ritzman
2004   "A Re-Analysis of the Neandertal Status of the Teshik-Tash Child." *American Journal of Physical Anthropology,* 38:100–101.

Glazko, G. V. and M. Nei
2003   "Estimation of Divergence Times for Major Lineages of Primate Species." *Molecular Biology and Evolution,* (Supplement) 20:424–434.

Goodall, Jane
1986   *The Chimpanzees of Gombe.* Cambridge, NY: Harvard University Press.

Goodman, M., C. A. Porter, J. Czelusniak, et al.
1998   "Toward a Phylogenetic Classification of Primates Based on DNA Evidence Complemented by Fossil Evidence." *Molecular Phylogenetics and Evolution,* 9:585–598.

Goodman, S. and H. Schütz
2000   "The Lemurs of the Northeastern Slopes of the Réserve Spéciale de Manongarivo." *Lemur News,* 5:32.

Gossett, T. F.
1963   *Race, the History of an Idea in America.* Dallas, TX: Southern Methodist University Press.

Gould, Stephen
1981   *The Mismeasures of Man.* New York, NY: W. W. Norton.

———
1985   "Darwin at Sea—and the Virtues of Port." *In: The Flamingo's Smile. Reflections in Natural History,* Stephen Jay Gould, NY: W. W. Norton, pp. 347–359.

———
1987   *Time's Arrow, Time's Cycle.* Cambridge, NY: Harvard University Press.

Gould, Stephen Jay and Niles Eldredge
1977   "Punctuated Equilibria: The Tempo and Mode of Evolution Reconsidered." *Paleobiology,* 3:115–151.

Grant, P. R.
1982   "Variation in the Size and Shape of Darwin's Finch Eggs." *Auk,* 99:5–23.

———
1986   *Ecology and Evolution of Darwin's Finches.* Princeton, NJ: Princeton University Press.

Green, R. E., J. Krause, E. Ptak. et al.
2006   "Analysis of One Million Base Pairs of Neanderthal DNA." *Nature,* 444:330–336.

Greene, John C.
1981   *Science, Ideology, and World View.* Berkeley, CA: University of California Press.

Greenwood, B. and T. Mutabingwa
2002   "Malaria in 2000." *Nature,* 415:670–672.

Grine, F. E. and R. F. Kay
1988   "Early Hominid Diets From Quantitative Image-Analysis of Dental Microwear." *Nature,* 333:765–768.

Gross, Liza
2006   "Scientific Illiteracy and the Partisan Takeover of Biology." *PLoS Biol.,* 4:e167.

Groves, C. P.
2001a   *Primate Taxonomy.* Washington, DC: Smithsonian Institution Press.

———
2001b   "Why Taxonomic Stability Is a Bad Idea, or Why Are There So Few Species of Primates (or Are There?)." *Evolutionary Anthropology,* 10:191–197.

Grün, R. and C. B. Stringer
1991   "ESR Dating and the Evolution of Modern Humans." *Archaeometry,* 33:153–199.

Grün, R., C. B. Stringer, F. McDermott, et al.
2005   "U-series and ESR Analysis of Bones and Teeth Relating to the Human Burials from Skhūl." *Journal of Human Evolution,* 49:316–334.

Guthrie, R. D.
2006   "New Carbon Dates Link Climatic Change with Human Colonization and Pleistocene Extinction." *Nature,* 441:207–209.

Haile-Selassie, Y.
2001   "Late Miocene Hominids from the Middle Awash, Ethiopia." *Nature,* 412:178–181.

Haile-Selassie, Y., G. Suwa, and T. D. White
2004   "Late Miocene Teeth from Middle Awash, Ethiopia, and Early Hominid Dental Evolution." *Science,* 303:1503–1505.

Hales, C. N. and D. J. P. Barker
2001   "The Thrifty Phenotype Hypothesis." *British Medical Bulletin,* 60: 5–20.

Hanna, J. M.
1999   "Climate, Altitude, and Blood Pressure." *Human Biology,* 71:553–582.

Harlow, H. F.
195   "Love in Infant Monkeys." *Scientific American,* 200:68–74.

Harlow, H. F. and M. K. Harlow
1961   "A Study of Animal Affection." *Natural History,* 70:48–55.

Harrison, Terry, Xueping Ji, and Denise Su
2002   "On the Systematic Status of the Late Neogene Hominoids from Yunnan Province, China." *Journal of Human Evolution,* 43:207–227.

Hawkes, K., J. F. O'Connell, and N. G. Blurton Jones
1997   "Hadza Women's Time Allocation, Offspring Provisioning, and the Evolution of Long Postmenopausal Life Spans." *Current Anthropology,* 38:551–577.

Heaney, L. R.
1978   "Island Area and Body Size of Insular Mammals: Evidence from the Tri-colored Squirrel (*Callosciurus prevosti*) of Southeast Asia." *Evolution,* 32:29–44.

Heizmann, E. and D. R. Begun
2001   "The Oldest European Hominoid." *Journal of Human Evolution,* 41:465–481.

Henderson, J. B., M. G. Dunnigan, W. B. McIntosh, et al.
1987   "The Importance of Limited Exposure to Ultraviolet-Radiation and Dietary Factors in the Etiology of Asian Rickets: A Risk-Factor Model. *Quarterly Journal of Medicine,* 63:413–425.

Henshilwood, C. S. and J. C. Sealey
1997   "Bone Artefacts from the Middle Stone Age at Blombos Cave, Southern Cape, South Africa." *Current Anthropology,* 38:890–895.

Henshilwood, C. S., F. d'Errico, R. Yates, et al.
2002   "Emergence of Modern Human Behavior: Middle Stone Age Engravings from South Africa." *Science,* 295:1278–1280.

Henshilwood, C. S., F. d'Errico, M. Vanhaeren, et al.
2004   "Middle Stone Age Shell Beads from South Africa." *Science,* 304:404.

Henzi, P. and L. Barrett
2003   "Evolutionary Ecology, Sexual Conflict, and Behavioral Differentiation Among Baboon Populations." *Evolutionary Anthropology,* 12:217–230.

Hershkovitz, P.
1977   *Living New World Monkeys (Platyrrhini): With an Introduction to Primates.* Vol. 1. Chicago and London: University of Chicago Press.

Higham, Tom, Christopher Bronk Ramsey, Ivor Karavanic, et al.
2006   "Revised Direct Radiocarbon Dating of the Vindija G_1 Upper Paleolithic Neandertals." *Proceedings of the National Academy of Sciences,*103:553–557.

Hill, A., S. Ward, A. Deino, G. Curtis, and R. Drake
1992   "Earliest *Homo.*" *Nature,* 355:719–722.

Hill, A. V. S., and A. G. Motulsky
1999   "Genetic Variation and Human Disease: The Role of Natural Selection. *In: Evolution in Health and Disease,* S. Stearns (ed.), New York, NY: Oxford University Press, pp. 50–61.

Holloway, Ralph L.
1983   "Cerebral Brain Endocast Pattern of *Australopithecus afarensis* Hominid." *Nature,* 303:420–422.

————
1985   "The Poor Brain of *Homo sapiens neanderthalensis.*" *In: Ancestors, The Hard Evidence,* E. Delson (ed.). New York, NY: Alan R. Liss, pp. 319–324.

Hoffstetter, R.
1972   "Relationships, Origins, and History of the Ceboid Monkeys and the Caviomorph Rodents: A Modern Reinterpretation." *In: Evolutionary Biology* (Vol. 6), T. Dobzhansky, T. M. K. Hecht, and W. C. Steere (eds.), New York, NY: Appleton-Century-Crofts, pp. 323–347.

Houle, Alain
1998   "Floating Islands: A Mode of Long-Distance Dispersal for Small and Medium-Sized Terrestrial Vertebrates." *Diversity and Distribution*, 4:201–219.

_____
1999   "The Origin of Platyrrhines: An Evaluation of the Antarctic Scenario and the Floating Island Model." *American Journal of Physical Anthropology*, 109:541–559.

Howell, F. C.
1999   "Paleo-demes, Species, Clades, and Extinctions in the Pleistocene Hominin Record." *Journal of Anthropological Research*, 55:191–243.

Hrdy, Sarah Blaffer
1977   *The Langurs of Abu.* Cambridge, MA: Harvard University Press.

_____
1999   *Mother Nature: A History of Mothers, Infants, and Natural Selection.* New York, NY: Pantheon Books.

Hrdy, Sarah Blaffer, Charles Janson, and Carel van Schaik
1995   "Infanticide: Let's Not Throw Out the Baby with the Bath Water." *Evolutionary Anthropology,* 3:151–154.

Hu, Dale J., Timothy J. Dondero, Mark A. Rayfield, et al.
1996   "The Emerging Genetic Diversity of HIV. The Importance of Global Surveillance for Diagnostics, Research, and Prevention." *Journal of the American Medical Association*, 275:210–216.

The International SNP Map Working Group
2001   "A Map of Human Genome Sequence Variation Containing 1.42 Million Single Nucleotide Polymorphisms." *Nature*, 409:928–933.

Isaac, G.
1976   "Early Hominids in Action: A Commentary on the Contribution of Archeology to Understanding the Fossil Record in East Africa." *Yearbook of Physical Anthropology*, 1975, 19:19–35.

Isbell, L. A.
1994   "Predation on Primates: Ecological Patterns and Evolutionary Consequences." *Evolutionary Anthropology*, 3:61–71.

Isbell, L. A. and T. P. Young
1993   "Social and Ecological Influences on Activity Budgets of Vervet Monkeys and Their Implications for Group Living." *Behavioral Ecology and Sociobiology,* 32:377–385.

Izawa, K. and A. Mizuno
1977   "Palm-Fruit Cracking Behaviour of Wild Black-Capped Capuchin (*Cebus apella*)." *Primates*, 18:773–793.

IUCN (International Union for Conservation of Nature and Natural Resources)
1996/2004 Red List of Threatened Species. www.iucnredlist.org

Jablonski, N. G.
1992   "Sun, Skin Colour, and Spina Bifida: An Exploration of the Relationship between Ultraviolet Light and Neural Tube Defects." *Proceedings of the Australian Society of Human Biology*, 5:455–462.

Jablonski, N. G. (ed.)
1993   Theropithecus: *The Rise and Fall of a Primate Genus.* Cambridge: University of Cambridge Press.

Jablonski, N. G. and G. Chaplin
2000   "The Evolution of Skin Coloration." *Journal of Human Evolution*, 39:57–106.

_____
2002   "Skin Deep". *Scientific American*, 287:74–81.

Jacob, T., E. Indriati, R. P. Soejono, et al.
2006   "Pygmoid Australmelonesian *Homo sapiens* Skeletal Remains from Liang Bua, Flores: Population Affinities and Pathological Anomalies." *Proceedings of the National Academy of Sciences*, 103:13421–13426.

Janson, C. H.
1990   "Ecological Consequences of Individual Spatial Choice in Foraging Groups of Brown Capuchin Monkeys *Cebus apella*." *Animal Behavior*, 40:922–934.

_____
2000   "Primate Socio-ecology: The End of a Golden Age." *Evol. Anthropol.*, 9:73–86.

Jerison, H. J.
1973   *Evolution of the Brain and Behavior.* New York, NY: Academic Press.

Jia, L.
1975   *The Cave Home of Peking Man.* Peking: Foreign Language Press.

Jia, L. and W. Huang
1990   *The Story of Peking Man.* New York, NY: Oxford University Press.

Johanson, D. and M. Edey
1981   *Lucy: The Beginnings of Humankind.* New York: Simon & Schuster.

Jolly, Alison
1985   *The Evolution of Primate Behavior* (2nd Ed.). New York, NY: Macmillan.

Jolly, Clifford J.
1970   "The Seed-Eaters: A New Model of Hominid Differentiation Based on a Baboon Analogy." *Man,* New Series, 5:5–26.

———
1993   "Species, Subspecies, and Baboon Systematics." *In: Species, Species Concepts, and Primate Evolution,* W. H. Kimbel and L. B. Martin (eds.), New York, NY: Plenum Press, pp. 67–107.

Jungers, W. L.
1988   "New Estimates of Body Size in Australopithecines." *In: Evolutionary History of the "Robust" Australopithecines (Foundations of Human Behavior),* F. E. Grine (ed.), Somerset, NJ: Aldine Transaction, pp. 115–125.

Kano, T.
1992   *The Last Ape. Pygmy Chimpanzee Behavior and Ecology.* Stanford, CA: Stanford University Press.

Keeley, L. H. and N. Toth
1981   "Microwear Polishes on Early Stone Tools from Koobi Fora, Kenya." *Nature,* 293:464–465.

Kelley, R. I., D. Robinson, E. G. Puffenberger, et. al.
2002   "Amish Lethal Microcephaly: A New Metabolic Disorder with Severe Congenital Microcephaly and 2 Ketoglutaric Aciduria." *American Journal of Medical Genetics,* 112:318–326.

Kettlewell, H. B. D.
1956   "Further Selection Experiments on Industrial Melanism in the Lepidoptera." *Heredity,* 10:287–301.

Keynes, Randal
2002   *Darwin, His Daughter and Human Evolution.* New York, NY: Riverhead Books.

Keyser, André W.
2000   "New Finds in South Africa." *National Geographic,* (May):76–83.

Kidd, K. H. Rajeevan, M. V. Osier, et al.
2003   "ALFRED—the Allele FREquency Database—an Update." *American Journal of Physical Anthropology, Supplement,* 36:128 (Abstract).

Kimbel, W. H., R. C. Walter, D. C. Johanson, et al.
1996   "Late Pliocene *Homo* and Oldowan Tools From the Hadar Formation (Kada Hadar Member), Ethiopia. *Journal of Human Evolution,* 31:549–561.

Kimbel, W. H., T. D. White, and D. C. Johanson
1988   "Implications of KNM-WT-17000 for the Evolution of 'Robust' *Australopithecus.*" *In: Evolutionary History of the "Robust" Australopithecines (Foundations of Human Behavior),* F. E. Grine (ed.), Somerset, NJ: Aldine Transaction, pp. 259–268.

King, B. J.
2004   *Dynamic Dance: Nonvocal Communication in the African Great Apes.* Cambridge, MA: Harvard University Press.

King, B. J.
1994   *The Information Continuum.* Santa Fe, NM: School of American Research.

King, Marie-Claire and Arno G. Motulsky
2002   "Mapping Human History." *Science,* 298:2342–2343.

Kirk, E. Christopher and Elwyn L. Simons
2000   "Diet of Fossil Primates from the Fayum Depression of Egypt: a Quantitative Analysis of Molar Shearing." *Journal of Human Evolution,* 40:203–229.

Kirkwood, T. B. L.
2002   "Evolution of Ageing." *Mechanisms of Ageing and Development,* 123:737–745.

Klein, Richard G.
1989/1999 *The Human Career. Human Biological and Cultural Origins* (2nd Ed.). Chicago, IL: University of Chicago Press.

Klein, Richard G. and Blake Edgar
2002   *The Dawn of Human Culture.* New York, NY: John Wiley & Sons.

Knapp, Leslie A.
2002   "Evolution and Immunology." *Evolutionary Anthropology,* 11 (Supplement 1):140–144.

Kokis, J. E.
1988   "Protein Diagenesis Dating of Ostrich (*Struthio camelus*) Eggshell: an Upper Pleistocene Dating Technique." Unpublished M. A. Thesis, George Washington University.

Koopman, R. J., A. G. Mainous, V. A. Diaz, et al.
2005   "Changes in Age at Diagnosis of Type 2 Diabetes Mellitus in the United States, 1988 to 2000." *Annals of Family Medicine,* 3:60–69.

Kramer, Andrew
1993 "Human Taxonomic Diversity in the Pleistocene: Does *Homo erectus* Represent Multiple Hominid Species?" *American Journal of Physical Anthropology*, 91:161–171.

Krane S., Y. Itagaki, K. Nakanishi, et al.
2003 "'Venom' of the Slow Loris: Sequence Similarity of Prosimian Skin Gland Protein and Fel d 1 Cat Allergen." *Naturwissenschaften*, 90:60–62.

Krings, Matthias, Cristen Capelli, Frank Tscentscher, et al.
2000 "A View of Neandertal Genetic Diversity." *Nature Genetics*, 26:144–146.

Krings, Matthias, Anne Stone, Ralf W. Schmitz, et al.
1997 "Neandertal DNA Sequences and the Origin of Modern Humans." *Cell*, 90:19–30.

Kroeber, A. L.
1928 "Sub-human Cultural Beginning." *Quarterly Review of Biology*, 3:325–342.

Kulikov, Eugene E., Audrey B. Poltaraus, and Irina A. Lebedeva
2004 "DNA Analysis of Sunghir Remains: Problems and Perspectives." Poster Presentation, European Paleopathology Association Meetings, Durham, U.K, August 2004.

Kummer, H.
1968 *Social Organization of Hamadryas Baboons.* Chicago, IL: University of Chicago Press.

Kuzawa, C. W.
2005 "Fetal Origins of Developmental Plasticity: Are Fetal Cues Reliable Predictors of Future Nutritional Environments?" *American Journal of Human Biology*, 17, 5–21.

Lack, David
1966 *Population Studies of Birds.* Oxford: Clarendon.

Lahr, Marta Mirazon and Robert Foley
1998 "Towards a Theory of Human Origins: Geography, Demography, and Diversity in Recent Human Evolution." *Yearbook of Physical Anthropology*, 41:137–176.

Lai, C., S. Fisher, J. Hurst, et al.
2001 "A Forkhead-domain Gene is Mutated in a Severe Speech and Language Disorder." *Nature*, 413:519–523.

Lalani, A. S., J. Masters, W. Zeng, et al.
1999 "Use of Chemokine Receptors by Poxviruses." *Science*, 286:1968–71.

Lamberts, S. W. J., A. W. van den Beld, and A. J. van der Lely
1997 "The Endocrinology of Aging." *Science*, 278:419–424.

Leakey, M. D.
1971 "Remains of *Homo erectus* and Associated Artifacts in Bed IV at Olduvai Gorge, Tanzania." *Nature*, 232:380–383.

Leakey, M. D. and R. L. Hay
1979 "Pliocene Footprints in Laetolil Beds at Laetoli, Northern Tanzania." *Nature*, 278:317–323.

Leakey, M. G., C. S. Feibel, I. McDougall, and A. Walker
1995 "New Four-Million-Year-Old Hominid Species from Kanapoi and Allia Bay, Kenya." *Nature*, 376:565–571.

Leakey, M. G., F. Spoor, F. H. Brown, et al.
2001 "New Hominin Genus from Eastern Africa Shows Diverse Middle Pliocene Lineages." *Nature*, 410:433–440.

Lerner, I. M. and W. J. Libby
1976 *Heredity, Evolution, and Society.* San Francisco, CA: W. H. Freeman and Company.

Leroy, E. M., B. Kumulungui, X. Pourrut, et al.
2005 "Fruit Bats as Reservoirs of Ebola Virus." *Nature*, 438:575–576.

Leroy, E. M., P. Rouquet, P. Formenty, et al.
2004 "Multiple Ebola Virus Transmission Events and Rapid Decline of Central African Wildlife." *Science*, 303:387–390.

Lewontin, R. C.
1972 "The Apportionment of Human Diversity." *In: Evolutionary Biology* (Vol. 6), T. Dobzhansky, et al. (eds.), New York, NY: Plenum, pp. 381–398.

Li, T. and D. A. Etler
1992 "New Middle Pleistocene Hominid Crania from Yunxian in China." *Nature*, 357:404–407.

Lieberman, L. S.
2003 "Dietary, Evolutionary and Modernizing Influences on the Prevalence of Type 2 Diabetes." *Annual Review of Nutrition*, 23:345–377

Linnaeus, C.
1758 *Systema Naturae.*

Lister, A. M.
1989 "Rapid Dwarfing of Red Deer on Jersey in the Last Interglacial." *Nature*, 342:539–542.

Lomolino, M. V.
2005 "Body Size in Insular Vertebrates: Generality of the Island Rule." *Journal of Biogeography,* 32:1683–1699.

Lordkipanidze, David, Abesalom Vekua, Reid Ferring, et al.
2005 "The Earliest Toothless Hominin Skull." *Nature,* 434:717–718.

Lordkipandize D., A. Vekua, R. Ferring, P. Rightmire, et al.
2006 "A Fourth Hominid Skull from Dmanisi, Georgia." *The Anatomical Record: Part A,* 288:1146–1157.

Lovejoy, C. Owen
1981 "The Origin of Man." *Science,* 211:341 – 350

Mace, R.
2000 "Evolutionary Ecology of Human Life History: A Review." *Animal Behaviour* 59:1–10.

MacKinnon, J. and K. MacKinnon
1980 "The Behavior of Wild Spectral Tarsiers." *International Journal of Primatology,* 1:361 379.

Manson, J. H. and R. Wrangham
1991 "Intergroup Aggression in Chimpanzees and Humans." *Current Anthropology,* 32:369–390.

Martin, Richard D.
1990 *Primate Origins and Evolution: A Phylogenetic Reconstruction.* Princeton, NJ: Princeton University Press.

Martin, Robert D., Ann M. Maclaranon, James C. Phillips, and William B. Dobyns
2006 "Flores Hominid: New Species or Microcephalic Dwarf?" *The Anatomical Record*: Part A, 288:1123–1145.

Masataka, N.
1983 "Categorical Responses to Natural and Synthesized Alarm calls in Goeldi's Monkeys (*Callimico goeldi*)." *Primates.* 24:40–51.

Mayer, Peter
1982 "Evolutionary Advantages of Menopause." *Human Ecology,* 10:477–494.

Mayr, Ernst
1970 *Population, Species, and Evolution.* Cambridge, MA: Harvard University Press.

McBrearty, Sally and Nina G. Jablonski
2005 "First Fossil Chimpanzee." *Nature,* 437:105–108.

McCrossin, M. L., B. R. Benefit, and S. N. Gitau, et al.
1998 "Fossil Evidence for the Origins of Terrestriality among Old World Monkeys and Apes." *In: Primate Locomotion: Recent Advances,* E. Strasser, J. G. Fleagle, H. M. McHenry, and A. L. Rosenberger (eds.), New York, NY: Plenum, pp. 353–396.

McDougall, I.; F. H. Brown, J. G. Fleagle
2005 "Stratigraphic Placement and Age of Modern Humans from Kibish, Ethiopia." *Nature,* 433: 733–736.

McGrew, W. C.
1992 *Chimpanzee Material Culture. Implications for Human Evolution.* Cambridge: Cambridge University Press.

———
1998 "Culture in Nonhuman Primates?" *Annual Review of Anthropology,* 27:301–328.

McGrew, W. C. and E. G. Tutin
1978 "Evidence for a Social Custom in Wild Chimpanzees?" *Man,* 13:234–251.

McHenry, Henry
1988 "New Estimates of Body Weight in Early Hominids and Their Significance to Encephalization and Megadontia in 'Robust' Australopithecines." *In: Evolutionary History of the "Robust" Australopithecines (Foundations of Human Behavior),* F. E. Grine (ed.), Somerset, NJ: Aldine Transaction, pp. 133–148.

———
1992 "Body Size and Proportions in Early Hominids." *American Journal of Physical Anthropology,* 87:407–431.

McKusick, V. A. (with S. E. Antonarakis, et al.)
1998 *Mendelian Inheritance in Man.* (12th Ed.). Baltimore, MD: Johns Hopkins University Press.

Mervis, J.
2006 "Judge Jones Defines Science—And Why Intelligent Design Isn't." *Science,* 311:34.

Miles, H. Lyn Whire
1990 "The Cognitive Foundations for Reference in a Signing Orangutan." *In: Language and Intelligence in Monkeys and Apes: Comparative Developmental Perspectives,* S. T. Parker and K. R. Gibson (eds.), New York, NY: Cambridge University Press, pp. 511–539.

Miller, Ellen R., Gregg F. Gunnell, and Richard D. Martin
2005 "Deep Time and the Search for Anthropoid Origins." *Yearbook of Physical Anthropology,* 48:60–95.

Miller, G. H., P. B. Beaumont, A. S. Brooks, et al.
1999a "Earliest Modern Humans in South Africa Dated by Isoleucine Epimerization in Ostrich Eggshell." *Quaternary Science Reviews*, 18:1537–1548.

Miller, G. H., J. W. Magee, B. J. Johnson, et al.
1999b "Pleistocene extinction of *Genyornis newtoni*: Human Impact on Australian Megafauna." *Science*, 283:205–208.

Miller, Steven F., Jessica L. White, and Russell L. Ciochon
2007 "Assessing Mandibular Shape Variation in *Gigantopithecus* and '*Indopithecus*' Using a Geometric Morphometrics Approach." *American Journal of Physical Anthropology*, in press.

Mokdad, A. H., B. A. Bowman, and E. S. Ford
2001 "The Continuing Epidemics of Obesity and Diabetes in the United States." *Journal of the American Medical Association* 286: 1195–1200.

Molnar, Stephen
1983 *Human Variation. Races, Types, and Ethnic Groups* (2nd Ed.). Englewood Cliffs, NJ: Prentice-Hall.

Moore, L. G. and J. G. Regensteiner
1983 "Adaptation to High Altitude." *Annual Reviews of Anthropology*, 12:285–304.

Moore, L. G., S. Niermeyer, and S. Zamudio
1998 "Human Adaptation to High Altitude: Regional and Life-Cycle Perspectives." *American Journal of Physical Anthropology*, Suppl. 27:25–64.

Moore, L.G., M. Shriver, L. Bemis, and E. Vargas
2006 "An Evolutionary Model for Identifying Genetic Adaptation to High Altitude." *Advance in Experimental Medicine and Biology* , 588:101–118.

Moore, L. G., S. Zamudio, J. Zhuang, et al.
1999 "Oxygen Transport in Tibetan Women During Pregnancy at 3,658 M." *American Journal of Physical Anthropology*, 114:42–53.

Morwood, M. J., P. Brown, T. Jatmiko, et al.
2005 "Further Evidence for Small-Bodied Hominins from the Late Pleistocene of Flores, Indonesia." *Nature*, 437:1012–1017.

Morwood, M. J., R. P. Suejono, R. G. Roberts, et al.
2004 "Archaeology and Age of a New Hominin from Flores in Eastern Indonesia." *Nature*, 431:1087–1091.

Motulsky, A. G.
1995 "Jewish Diseases and Origins." *Nature Genetics*, 9:99–101.

Muchmore, E. A., S. Diaz , and A. Varki
1998 "A Structural Difference Between the Cell Surfaces of Humans and the Great Apes. *American Journal of Physical Anthropology*, 107:187–98.

Murphy, W. J., E. Elzirik, W. E. Johnson, et al.
2001 "Molecular Phylogenetics and the Origins of Placental Mammals." *Nature*, 409:614–618.

Murray, R. D.
1980 "The Evolution and Functional Significance of Incest Avoidance." *Journal of Human Evolution*, 9:173–178.

Napier, John
1967 "The Antiquity of Human Walking." *Scientific American*, 216:56–66.

Napier, J. R. and P. H. Napier
1967 *A Handbook of Living Primates*. New York, NY: Academic Press.

——————
1985 *The Natural History of the Primates*. London: British Museum of Natural History.

Nakatsukasa, Masato, Carol V. Ward, and Alan Walker, et al.
2004 "Tail Loss in *Proconsul heselonsi*." *Journal of Human Evolution*, 46:777–784.

NCBI (National Center for Biological Information).
2003 Bookshelf: Genes and Disease. www.ncbi.nlm.nih.gov/books/bv.fcgi?rid=gnd.section.104

Neal, J. V.
1962 "Diabetes Mellitus: A Thrifty Genotype Rendered Detrimental By 'Progress'?" *Am. J. Human Genet.*, 14:353–362.

Nesse, R. M., S. C. Stearns, and G. S. Omenn
2006 "Medicine Needs Evolution." *Science*, 311:1071.

Nesse, R. M. and G. C. Williams
1994 *Why We Get Sick. The New Science of Darwinian Medicine.* New York, NY: Vintage Books.

Ni, Xijun, Yuanqing Wang, Yaoming Hu, and Chuankui Li
2004 "A Euprimate Skull from the Early Eocene of China." *Nature*, 427:65–68.

Nishida, T.
1991 "Comments.: *In:* "Intergroup Aggression in Chimpanzees and Humans," J. H. Manson and R. Wrangham, *Current Anthropology*, 32:369–390, pp. 381–382.

Nishida, T., M. Hiraiwa-Hasegawa, T. Hasegawa, and Y. Takahata
1985 "Group Extinction and Female Transfer in Wild Chimpanzees in the Mahale National Park, Tanzania." *Zeitschrift Tierpsychologie,* 67:284–301.

Nishida, T., H. Takasaki, and Y. Takahata
1990 "Demography and Reproductive Profiles." *In: The Chimpanzees of the Mahale Mountains,* T. Nishida (ed.), Tokyo: University of Tokyo Press, pp. 63–97.

Nishida, T., R. W. Wrangham, J. Goodall, and S. Uehara
1983 "Local Differences in Plant-feeding Habits of Chimpanzees between the Mahale Mountains and Gombe National Park, Tanzania." *Journal of Human Evolution,* 12:467–480.

Noe, R. and R. Bshary
1997 "The Formation of Red Colobus-Diana Monkey Associations Under Predation Pressure from Chimpanzees. *Proceedings of the Royal Society of London, (B) Biological Science,* 264:253 259.

Noonan, James P., Graham Coop, Sridhar Kudaravalli, et al.
2006 "Sequencing and Analysis of Neanderthal Genomic DNA." *Science,* 314:1113–1118.

Nowak, Ronald M.
1999 *Walker's Primates of the World.* Baltimore, MD: Johns Hopkins University Press.

Oakley, Kenneth
1963 "Analytical Methods of Dating Bones." *In: Science in Archaeology,* D. Brothwell and E. Higgs (eds.), New York, NY: Basic Books, Inc.

Oates, J. F.
1999 *Myth and Reality in the Rain Forest: How Conservation Strategies are Failing in West Africa.* Berkeley, CA: University of California Press.

Oates, John F., Michael Abedi-Lartey, W. Scott McGraw, et al.
2000 "Extinction of a West African Red Colobus Monkey." *Conservation Biology,* 14:1526–1532.

Olliaro, P.
1996 "Malaria, the Submerged Disease." *Journal of the American Medical Association,* 275:230–233.

Ovchinnikov, Igor V., Anders Gotherstrom, Galina P. Romanova, et al.
2000 "Molecular Analysis of Neanderthal DNA from the Northern Caucasus." *Nature,* 404:490–493.

Padian, Kevin and Luis M. Chiappe
1998 "The Origin of Birds and Their Flight." *Scientific American,* 278:38–47.

Pagel, M., C. Venditti, and A. Meade
2006 "Large Punctuational Contribution of Speciation to Evolutionary Divergence at the Molecular Level." *Science,* 314:119–121.

Paine, M.
2001 "Source of the Australasian Tektites?" *Meteorite,* http//www.meteor.co.nz/

Palmer, S. K., L. G. Moore, D. Young, et al.
1999 "Altered Blood Pressure Course During Normal Pregnancy and Increased Preeclampsia at High Altitude (3100 meters) in Colorado." *Am. J. Obstet. Gynecol.,* 189:1161–1168.

Palumbi, Stephen R.
2001 *The Evolution Explosion: How Humans Cause Rapid Evolutionary Change.* New York, NY: W. W. Norton.

Parés, Josef M. and Alfredo Pérez-González
1995 "Paleomagnetic Age for Hominid Fossils at Atapuerca Archaeological Site, Spain." *Science,* 269:830–832.

Park, Edwards
1978 "The Ginsberg Caper: Hacking it as in Stone Age." *Smithsonian,* 9:85–96.

Pavkov, M. E., R. L. Hanson, W. C. Knowler, et al.
2006 "Secular Trends in the Prevalence and Incidence Rate of Type 2 Diabetes." *Diabetes,* 55:A224–A224 Suppl.

Pearson, Helen
2006 "What is a Gene?" *Nature,* 441:399–401.

Peccei, Jocelyn Scott
2001 "Menopause: Adaptation or Epiphenomenon?" *Evolutionary Anthropology,* 10:43–57.

Penny, D.
2004 "Our Relative Genetics." *Nature,* 427:208–209.

Pennisi, Elizabeth
2001 "The Human Genome." *Science,* 291:1177–1180.

Peres, C. A.
1990 "Effects of Hunting on Western Amazonian Primate Communities." *Biological Conservation* 54:47–59.

Perez, V. R., L. R. Godfrey, M. Nowak-Kemp, et al.
2005 Evidence of Early Butchery of Giant Lemurs in Madagascar." *Journal of Human Evolution,* 49:722–742.

Perkins, Sid
2003 "Learning from the Present." *Science News*, 164:42–44.

Phillips, K. A.
1998 "Tool Use in Wild Capuchin Monkeys." *American Journal of Primatology*, 46:259–261.

Phillips-Conroy, J. E., C. J. Jolly, P. Nystrom, and H. A. Hemmalin
1992 "Migration of Male Hamadryas Baboons into Annubis Groups in the Awash National Park, Ethiopia." *International Journal of Primatology*, 13:455–476.

Pickford, Martin and Hidemi Ishida
1998 "Interpretation of *Samburupithecus*, an Upper Miocene Hominoid from Kenya." *Comptes Rendus de l'Académie des Sciences*, Ser. 11A, *Earth and Planetary Science*, 326:299–306.

Pickford, Martin and Brigitte Senut
2001 "The Geological and Faunal Context of Late Miocene Hominid Remains from Lukeino, Kenya." *Comptes Rendus de l'Académie des Sciences*, Ser. 11A, *Earth and Planetary Science*, 332:145–152.

Pilbeam, D.
1982 "New Hominoid Skull Material from the Miocene of Pakistan." *Nature*, 295:232–234.

———
1996 "Genetic and Morphological Records of the Hominoidea and Hominid Origins: A Synthesis." *Molecular Phylogenetics and Evolution*, 5:155–168.

Pilbeam, David, Michael D. Rose, and John C. Barry, et al.
1990 "New *Sivapithecus* Humeri from Pakistan and the Relationship of *Sivapithecus* and *Pongo*." *Nature*, 348:237–239.

Pinner, R. W., S. M. Teutsch, L. Simonson, et al.
1996 "Trends in Infectious Diseases Mortality in the United States." *Journal of the American Medical Association*, 275:189–193.

Poremba, A., M. Malloy, R. C. Saunders, et al.
2004 "Species-specific Calls Evoke Asymmetric Activity in the Monkey's Temporal Poles." *Nature*, 427:448–451.

Potts, Richard
1984 "Home Bases and Early Hominids." *American Scientist*, 72:338–347.

———
1991 "Why the Oldowan? Plio-Pleistocene Toolmaking and the Transport of Resources." *Journal of Anthropological Research*, 47:153–176.

———
1993 "Archeological Interpretations of Early Hominid Behavior and Ecology." *In: The Origin and Evolution of Humans and Humanness*, D. T. Rasmussen (ed.), Boston, MA: Jones and Bartlett, pp. 49–74.

———
2003 Paper presented at the Paleoanthropology Association Annual Meetings, Tempe, AZ, April.

Potts, Richard and Pat Shipman
1981 "Cutmarks Made by Stone Tools from Olduvai Gorge, Tanzania." *Nature*, 291:577–580.

Powell, K. B.
2003 "The Evolution of Lactase Persistence in African Populations." *American Journal of Physical Anthropology*, Supplement 36:170 (Abstract).

Proctor, Robert
1988 "From Anthropologie to Rassenkunde." *In: Bones, Bodies, Behavior. History of Anthropology* (Vol. 5), W. Stocking, Jr. (ed.), Madison, WI: University of Wisconsin Press, pp. 138–179.

Pusey, A., J. Williams, and J. Goodall
1997 "The Influence of Dominance Rank on the Reproductive Success of Female Chimpanzees." *Science*, 277:828–831.

Raaum, Ryan L., Kirstin N. Sterner, and Colleen M. Noviello, et al.
2005 "Catarrhine Primate Divergence Dates Estimated from Complete Mitochondrial Genomes: Concordance with Fossil and Nuclear DNA Evidence." *Journal of Human Evolution*, 48:237–257.

Rak, Y.
1983 *The Australopithecine Face*. New York, NY: Academic Press.

Rasmussen, D. T. (ed.)
1993 *The Origin and Evolution of Humans and Humanness*. Boston, MA: Jones and Bartlett.

Reithman, H. C., Z. Xiang, S. Paul, et al.
2001 "Integration of Telomere Sequences with the Draft Human Genome Sequence." *Nature*, 409:948–951.

Relethford, John H.
2001 *Genetics and the Search for Modern Human Origins*. New York, NY: Wiley-Liss.

Renne, P. R., W. D. Sharp, A. L. Deino, et al.
1997 "^{40}Ar/^{39}Ar Dating into the Historic Realm: Calibration Against Pliny the Younger." *Science*, 277:1279–1280

Reno, P. L., R. S. Meindl, M. A. McCollum, and C. O. Lovejoy
2003   "Sexual Dimorphism in *Australopithecus afarensis* Was Similar to that of Modern Humans." *Proceedings of the National Academy of Sciences*, 100:9404–9409.

Reno, P. L., R. S. Meindl, M. A. McCollum, et al.
2005   "The Case is Unchanged and Remains Robust: *Australopithecus afarensis* Exhibits Only Moderate Skeletal Dimorphism: A Reply to Plavcan et al., 2005." *Journal of Human Evolution*, 49:279–288.

Richards, Gary D.
2006   "Genetic, Physiologic, and Ecogeographic Factors Contributing to Variation in *Homo sapiens*: *Homo floresiensis* Reconsidered." *Journal of Evolutionary Biology*, 19:1744–1767.

Riddle, Robert D. and Clifford J. Tabin
1999   "How Limbs Develop." *Scientific American*, 280:74–79.

Ridley, Mark
1993   *Evolution*. Boston, MA: Blackwell Scientific Publications.

Rightmire, G. P.
1998   "Human Evolution in the Middle Pleistocene: The Role of *Homo heidel-bergensis*." *Evolutionary Anthropology*, 6:218–227.

————
2004   "Affinities of the Middle Pleistocene Cranium from Dali and Jinniushan." *American Journal of Physical Anthropology*, Supplement 38:167 (Abstract).

Roberts, D. F.
1973   *Climate and Human Variability*. An Addison-Wesley Module in Anthropology, No. 34. Reading, MA: Addison-Wesley.

Robins, A. H.
1991   *Biological Perspectives on Human Pigmentation*. Cambridge: Cambridge University Press.

Robinson, J. T.
1972   *Early Hominid Posture and Locomotion*. Chicago, IL: University of Chicago Press.

Rose, M. D.
1991   "Species Recognition in Eocene Primates." *American Journal of Physical Anthropology, Supplement*, 12:153 (Abstract).

Rosenberg, K. and W. Trevathan
2001   "The Evolution of Human Birth." *Scientific American*, 285:72–77.

Rosenberg, Noah A., Jonathan K. Prichard, James L. Weber, et al.
2002   "Genetic Structure of Human Populations." *Science*, 298:2381–2385.

Ross, C. F.
2000   "Into the Light: The Origin of Anthropoidea." *Annual Review of Anthropology*, 29:147–194.

Rossie, J. B. and L. MacLatchy
2006   "A New Pliopithecoid Genus from the Early Miocene of Uganda." *Journal of Human Evolution*, 50:568–586.

Rovner, I.
1983   "Plant Opal Phytolith Analysis: Major Advances in Archaeobotanical Research." *In: Advances in Archaeological Method and Theory*, M. B. Schiffer (ed.), New York, NY: Academic Press, pp. 225–266.

Ruff, C. B. and Alan Walker
1993   "The Body Size and Shape of KNM-WT 15000." *In: The Nariokotome* Homo erectus *Skeleton*, A. Walker and R. E. Leakey (eds.), Cambridge, MA: Harvard University Press, pp. 234–265.

Rumbaugh, D. M.
1977   *Language Learning by a Chimpanzee: The Lana Project*. New York, NY: Academic Press.

Ruvolo, M., D. Pan, S. Zehr, T. Goldberg, et al.
1994   "Gene Trees and Hominoid Phylogeny." *Proceedings of the National Academy of Sciences*, 91:8900–8904.

Sagan, C.
1977   *The Dragons of Eden: Speculations on the Evolution of Human Intelligence*. Random House.

Samson, M., F. Libert, B. J. Doranz, et al.
1996   "Resistance to HIV-1 Infection in Caucasian Individuals Bearing Mutant Alleles of the CCR-5 Chemokine Receptor Gene." *Nature* 382:722–725.

Savage-Rumbaugh, S.
1986   *Ape Language: From Conditioned Responses to Symbols*. New York, NY: Columbia University Press.

Savage-Rumbaugh, S. and R. Lewin
1994   *Kanzi: The Ape at the Brink of the Human Mind*. New York, NY: John Wiley and Sons.

Savage-Rumbaugh, S., K. McDonald, R. A. Sevic, W. D. Hopkins, and E. Rupert
1986   "Spontaneous Symbol Acquisition and Communicative Use by Pygmy Chimpanzees (*Pan paniscus*)." *Journal of Experimental Psychology: General*, 115:211–235.

Sawada, Y., M. Pickford, T. Itaya, et al.
1998 "K-Ar Ages of Miocene Hominoidea (*Kenyapithecus* and *Samburupithecus*) from Samburu Hills, Northern Kenya." *Comptes Rendus de l'Académie des Sciences, Ser. 11A, Earth and Planetary Science*, 326:445–451.

Schmid, P.
1983 "Front Dentition of the Omomyiformes (Primates)." *Folia Primatologica*, 40:1–10.

Schmitz, Ralf W., David Serre, Georges Bonani, et al.
2002 "The Neandertal Type Site Revisited: Interdisciplinary Investigations of Skeletal Remains from the Neander Valley, Germany." *Proceedings of the National Academy of Sciences*, 99:13342–13347.

Schrago, C. G. and C. A. M. Russo
2003 "Timing the Origin of New World Monkeys." *Molecular Biology and Evolution*, 20:1620–1625.

Schwartz, Jeffrey H.
1984 "What Is a Tarsier?" *In: Living Fossils*, Niles Eldridge and Steven M. Stanley (eds.), New York, NY: Springer Verlag, pp. 38–49.

Scott, Eugenie C.
2004 *Evolution vs. Creationism*. Westport, CT: Greenwood Press.

Scriver, C. R.
2001 *The Metabolic and Molecular Bases of Inherited Disease*. New York, NY: McGraw Hill.

Seehausen, O.
2002 "Patterns of Fish Radiation Are Compatible with Pleistocene Dessication of Lake Victoria and 14,600 Year History for Its Cichlid Species Flock." *Proceedings of the Royal Society of London (Biological Science)*, 269:491–497.

Seiffert, E. R., Elwyn Simons, and Timothy M. Ryan et al.
2005a "Additional Remains of *Wadilemur elegans*, a Primitive Stem Galagid from the Late Eocene of Egypt." *Proceedings of the National Academy of Sciences, USA*, 102:11396–11401.

Seiffert, Erik, Elwyn Simons, William C. Clyde, et al.
2005b "Basil Anthropoids from Egypt and the Antiquity of Africa's Higher Primate Radiation." *Science*, 310:300–304.

Semaw, S., P. Renne, W. K. Harris, et al.
1997 "2.5-million-Year-Old Stone Tools from Gona, Ethiopia." *Nature*, 385:333–336.

Senut, Brigitte, Martin Pickford, Dominique Grommercy, et al.
2001 "First Hominid from the Miocene (Lukeino Formation, Kenya)." *Comptes Rendus de l'Académie des Sciences*, Ser. 11A, *Earth and Planetary Science*, 332:137–144.

Serre, David, André Langaney, Marie Chech, et al.
2004 "No Evidence of Neandertal mtDNA Contribution to Early Modern Humans." *PloS Biology*, 2:313–317.

Seyfarth, Robert M.
1987 "Vocal Communication and Its Relation to Language." *In: Primate Societies*, B. Smuts, D. L. Cheney, R. M. Seyfarth, et al. (eds.), Chicago, IL: University of Chicago Press, pp. 440–451.

Seyfarth, Robert M., Dorothy L. Cheney, and Peter Marler
1980a "Monkey Responses to Three Different Alarm Calls." *Science*, 210:801–803.

———
1980b "Vervet Monkey Alarm Calls." *Animal Behavior*, 28:1070–1094.

Shea, John J.
1998 "Neandertal and Early Modern Human Behavioral Variability." *Current Anthropology*, 39 (Supplement):45–78.

Shindler, K.
2006 *Discovering Dorothea: The Life of the Pioneering Fossil-Hunter Dorothea Bate*. London: Harper Collins Ltd.

Shipman, Pat
1983 "Early Hominid Lifestyle. Hunting and Gathering or Foraging and Scavenging?" Paper presented at 52nd Annual Meeting, American Association of Physical Anthropologists, Indianapolis, IN.

Shubin, Neil H., Edward B. Daeschler, and Farish A. Jenkins Jr.
2006 "The Pectoral Fin of *Tiktaalik roseae* and the Origin of the Tetrapod Limb." *Nature*, 440:764–771.

Shublin, Neil, Cliff Tabin, and Sean Carroll
1997 "Fossil Genes, and the Evolution of Animal Limbs." *Nature*, 388:639–648.

Sibley, C. and J. E. Ahlquist
1984 "The Phylogeny of the Hominoid Primates as Indicated by DNA-DNA Hybridization." *Journal of Molecular Evolution*, 20:2–15.

Sievert, Lynette Leidy
2006 *Menopause: A Biocultural Perspective*. New Brunswick, NJ: Rutgers University Press.

Silcox, Mary T.
2001   *A Phylogenetic Analysis of Plesiadapiformes and Their Relationship to Euprimates and Other Archontans.* Unpublished PhD dissertation, Johns Hopkins University School of Medicine, Baltimore, MD.

Silk, J. B., S. C. Alberts, and J. Altmann
2003   "Social Bonds of Female Baboons Enhance Infant Survival." *Science,* 302:1231–1234.

Simerly, C., T. Dominko, C. Navara, et al.
2003   "Molecular Correlates of Primate Nuclear Transfer." *Science,* 300:297.

Simons, E. L.
1976   "The Fossil Record of Primate Phylogeny." *In: Molecular Anthropology: Genes and Proteins in the Evolutionary Ascent of the Primates,* Morris Goodman (ed.), New York, NY: Plenum Press, pp. 35–62.

Skaletsky, H., T. Kuroda-Kawaguchi, P. J. Minx, et al.
2003   "The Male-Specific Region of the Human Y Chromosome is a Mosaic of Discrete Sequence Classes." *Nature,* 423:825–837.

Smith, F. H.
1984   "Fossil Hominids from the Upper Pleistocene of Central Europe and the Origin of Modern Europeans." *In: The Origins of Modern Humans.* F. H. Smith and F. Spencer (eds.), New York, NY: Alan R. Liss, pp. 187–209.

———
2002   "Migrations, Radiations and Continuity: Patterns in the Evolution of Late Pleistocene Humans. *In: The Primate Fossil Record.* W. Hartwig (ed.), Cambridge: Cambridge University Press, pp.437–456.

Smith, F. H., A. B. Falsetti, and S. M. Donnelly
1989   "Modern Human Origins." *Yearbook of Physical Anthropology,* 32:35–68.

Smith, F. H., I. Jankovic, and I. Karavanic
2005   "The Assimilation Model, Modern Human Origins in Europe, and the Extinction of Neandertals." *Quaternary International,* 137:7–19.

Smith, F. H., E. Trinkaus, P. B. Pettitt, et al.
1999   "Direct Radiocarbon Dates for Vindija G1 and Velika Pécina Late Pleistocene Hominid Remains." *Proceedings of the National Academy of Sciences,* 96:12281–12286.

Smith, T., K. D. Rose, and P. Gingerich
2006   "Rapids Asia-Europe-North America Geographic Dispersal of Earliest Eocene Primate *Teilhardina* During the Paleocene-Eocene Thermal Maximum." *Proceedings of the National Academy of Sciences, USA,* 103:11223–11227.

Smuts, Barbara
1985   *Sex and Friendship in Baboons.* Hawthorne, NY: Aldine de Gruyter.

Smuts, B., D. L. Cheney, R. M. Seyfarth, et al. (eds.)
1987   *Primate Societies.* Chicago, IL: University of Chicago Press.

Snyder, M. and M. Gerstein
2003   "Genomics. Defining Genes in the Genomics Era." *Science,* 300:258–260.

Sponheimer, Matt and Julia A. Lee-Thorp
1999   "Isotopic Evidence for the Diet of an Early Hominid, *Australopithecus africanus.*" *Science,* 283:368–370.

Sponheimer, M., B. H. Passey, D. J. de Ruiter, et al.
2006   "Isotopic Evidence for Dietary Variability in the Early Hominin *Paranthropus robustus.*" *Science,* 314:980–982.

Stanford, Craig
1999   *The Hunting Apes: Meat Eating and the Origins of Human Behavior.* Princeton, NJ: Princeton University Press.

———
2001   "The Ape's Gift: Meat-Eating, Meat-sharing, and Human Evolution." *In: Tree of Origin,* F. de Waal (ed.), Cambridge, MA: Harvard University Press, pp. 95–117.

Stearns, S. C.
1992   *The Evolution of Life Histories.* Oxford: Oxford University Press.

Steklis, H. D.
1985   "Primate Communication, Comparative Neurology, and the Origin of Language Reexamined." *Journal of Human Evolution,* 14:157–173.

Stelzner, J. and K. Strier
1981   "Hyena Predation on an Adult Male Baboon." *Mammalia,* 45:106–107.

Sterner, K. N., R. L. Raaum, Y. P. Stewart, and T. R. Disotell
2006   "Mitochondrial Data Support an Odd-Nosed Colobine Clade." *Molecular Phylogenetics and Evolution,* 40:1–7.

Strassman, B. I. and B. Gillespie
2002   "Life-history Theory, Fertility, and Reproductive Success in Humans." *Proceedings of the Royal Society of London B*, 269:553–562.

Strier, Karen B.
2003   *Primate Behavioral Ecology* (2nd Ed.). Boston, MA: Allyn and Bacon.

Stringer, C. B. and P. Andrews
1988   "Genetic and Fossil Evidence for the Origin of Modern Humans." *Science*, 239:1263–1268.

Struhsaker, T. T.
1967   "Auditory Communication among Vervet Monkeys (*Cercopithecus aethiops*)." *In: Social Communication Among Primates*, S. A. Altmann (ed.), Chicago, IL: University of Chicago Press.

———
1975   *The Red Colobus Monkey*. Chicago, IL: University of Chicago Press.

Struhsaker, T. T. and L. Leland
1979   "Socioecology of Five Sympatric Monkey Species in the Kibale Forest, Uganda." *In: Advances in the Study of Behavior*, Vol. 9. J.S. Rosenblatt, R.A. Hinde, C. Beer, and M.C. Busnel (eds.), New York, NY: Academic Press, pp. 159–229.

———
1987   "Colobines: Infanticide by Adult Males." *In: Primate Societies*, B. Smuts, D. L. Cheney, R. M. Seyfarth, et al. (eds.), Chicago, IL: University of Chicago Press, pp. 83–97.

Stuart-Macadam, P. and K. A. Dettwyler
1995   *Breastfeeding: Biocultural Perspectives*. Hawthorne, NY: Aldine de Gruyter.

Sugiyama, Y.
1965   "Short History of the Ecological and Sociological Studies on Non-Human Primates in Japan." *Primates*, 6:457–460.

Suomi, Stephen J., Susan Mineka, and Roberta D. DeLizio
1983   "Short- and Long-Term Effects of Repetitive Mother-Infant Separation on Social Development in Rhesus Monkeys." *Developmental Psychology*, 19:710–786.

Sumner, D. R., M. E. Morbeck, and J. Lobick
1989   "Age-Related Bone Loss in Female Gombe Chimpanzees." *American Journal of Physical Anthropology*, 72:259.

Susman, Randall L. (ed.)
1984   *The Pygmy Chimpanzee: Evolutionary Biology and Behavior*. New York, NY: Plenum.

Susman, Randall L., Jack T. Stern, and William L. Jungers
1985   "Locomotor Adaptations in the Hadar Hominids." *In: Ancestors: The Hard Evidence*, E. Delson (ed.), New York, NY: Alan R. Liss, pp.184–192.

Sussman, Robert W.
1991   "Primate Origins and the Evolution of Angiosperms." *American Journal of Primatology*, 23:209–223.

Sussman, R. W., J. M. Cheverud, and T.Q. Bartlett
1995   "Infant Killing as an Evolutionary Strategy: Reality or Myth?" *Evolutionary Anthropology*, 3:149–151.

Swisher, C. C., W. J. Rink, S. C. Anton, et al.
1996   "Latest *Homo erectus* of Java: Potential Contemporaneity with *Homo sapiens* in Southwest Java." *Science*, 274:1870–1874.

Szalay, F. S. and E. Delson
1979   *Evolutionary History of the Primates*. New York, NY: Academic Press.

Tattersall, I., E. Delson, and J. Van Couvering
1988   *Encyclopedia of Human Evolution and Prehistory*. New York, NY: Garland Publishing.

Tavaré, S., C. R. Marshall, O. Will, et al.
2002   "Using the Fossil Record to Estimate the Age of the Last Common Ancestor of Extant Primates." *Nature*, 416:726–729.

Tenaza, R. and R. Tilson
1977   "Evolution of Long-Distance Alarm Calls in Kloss' Gibbon." *Nature*, 268:233–235.

Teresi, Dick
2002   *Lost Discoveries. The Ancient Roots of Modern Science – from the Babylonians to the Maya*. New York, NY: Simon and Schuster.

Thieme, H.
1997   "Lower Palaeolithic Hunting Spears from Germany." *Nature*, 385:807–810.

Thorne, A., R. Grün, G. Mortimer, et al.
1999   "Australia's Oldest Human Remains: Age of the Lake Mungo 3 Skeleton." *Journal of Human Evolution*, 36:591–612.

Tiemel, C., Y. Quan, and W. En
1994   "Antiquity of *Homo sapiens* in China." *Nature*, 368:55–56.

Tobias, Phillip
1971 *The Brain in Hominid Evolution.* New York, NY: Columbia University Press

——— 1983 "Recent Advances in the Evolution of the Hominids with Especial Reference to Brain and Speech." Pontifical Academy of Sciences, *Scripta Varia*, 50:85–140.

Trevathan, W. R., E. O. Smith, and J. J. McKenna
1999 *Evolutionary Medicine.* New York, NY: Oxford University Press.

Trinkaus, E.
2005 "*Early Modern Humans.*" *Annual Reviews of Anthropology*, 34:207–230.

Trinkaus, E., S. Milota, R. Rodrigo, et al.
2003 "Early Modern Human Cranial Remains from Pestera cu Oase, Romania." *Journal of Human Evolution*, 45:245–253.

Trinkaus, E. and P. Shipman
1992 *The Neandertals.* New York, NY: Alfred A. Knopf.

UNAIDS/WHO
2006 Report on the Global AIDS Epidemic. http://data.unaids.org/pub/GlobalReport/2006/2006_GR_enpdf

United Nations World Population Prospects
2004 Revision. http://esa.un.org/unpp/

Ungar, Peter S., and Richard F. Kay
1995 "The Dietary Adaptations of European Miocene Catarrhines." *Proceedings of the National Academy of Sciences, USA*, 92:5479–5481.

van der Ven, K., R. Fimmers, G. Engels, et al.
2000 "Evidence for Major Histocompatability Complex-Mediated Effects on Spermatogenesis in Humans." *Human Reproduction*, 15:189–196.

van Schaik, C. P., M. Ancrenaz, G. Bogen, et al.
2003 "Orangutan Cultures and the Evolution of Material Culture." *Science*, 299:102–105.

Van Valen, L.
1973 "Pattern and the Balance of Nature." *Evolutionary Theory*, 1:31–49.

Varki, A.
2000 "A chimpanzee genome project is a biomedical imperative." *Genome Research*, 8:1065–1070.

Vialet, A., L. Tianyuan, D. Grimaud-Herve, et al.
2005 "Proposition de Reconstitution du Deuxième Crâne d'*Homo erectus* de Yunxian (Chine)." *Comptes rendus. Palévol*, 4:265–274.

Vigilant, L., M. Hofreiter, H. Siedel, and C. Boesch
2001 Paternity and Relatedness in Wild Chimpanzee Communities. *Proceedings of the National Academy of Sciences*, 98:12890–12895.

Vignaud, P., P. Duringer, H. MacKaye, et al.
2002 "Geology and Palaeontology of the Upper Miocene Toros-Menalla Hominid Locality, Chad." *Nature*, 418:152–155.

Villa, Paola
1983 *Terra Amata and the Middle Pleistocene Archaeological Record of Southern France.* University of California Publications in Anthropology, Vol. 13. Berkeley, CA: University of California Press.

Visalberghi, E.
1990 "Tool Use in *Cebus.*" *Folia Primatologica*, 54:146–154.

Vogel, Gretchen
2001 "Objection #2: Why Sequence the Junk?" *Science*, 291:1184.

Vogelsang, R.
1998 *The Middle Stone Age Fundstellen in Süd-west Namibia.* Köln: Heinrich Barth Institut.

Vogelstein, B., D. Lane, and A. J. Levine
2000 "Surfing the p53 Network." *Nature,* 408:307–310.

Vrba, Elisabeth S.
1992 "Mammals as a Key to Evolutionary Theory". *Journal of Mammalogy*, 73:1–28.

Wagner, Gunter A.
1996 "Fission-Track Dating in Paleoanthropology." *Evolutionary Anthropology*, 5:165–171.

Walker, A.
1976 "Remains Attributable to *Australopithecus* from East Rudolf." *In: Earliest Man and Environments in the Lake Rudolf Basin*, Y. Coppens (ed.), Chicago, IL: University of Chicago Press, pp. 484–489.

——— 1991 "The Origin of the Genus *Homo*." *In: Evolution of Life*, S. Osawa and T. Honjo (eds.), Tokyo: Springer-Verlag, pp. 379–389.

1993   "The Origin of the Genus *Homo*." In: *The Origin and Evolution of Humans and Humanness*, D. T. Rasmussen (ed.), Boston, MA: Jones and Bartlett, pp. 29–47.

2002   "New Perspectives on the Hominids of the Turkana Basin, Kenya." *Evolutionary Anthropology*, 11 (Supplement):38–41.

Walker, Alan and R. E. Leakey
1993   *The Nariokotome* Homo erectus *Skeleton.* Cambridge, MA: Harvard University Press.

Walrath, D.
2003   "Rethinking Pelvic Typologies and the Human Birth Mechanism." *Current Anthropology*, 44:5–31.

Walsh, P. D., K. A. Abernathy, M. Bermejo, et al.
2003   "Catastrophic Ape Decline in Western Equatorial Africa." *Nature,* 422:611–614.

Ward, Carol V.
2005   "Torso Morphology and Locomotion in *Proconsul nyanzae*." *American Journal of Physical Anthropology*, 92:321–328.

Ward, Peter
1994   *The End of Evolution.* New York, NY: Bantam.

Washburn, S. L.
1963   "The Study of Race." *American Anthropologist*, 65:521–531.

Washburn, S. L. and I. DeVore
1961   "The Social Life of Baboons." *Scientific American*, 204:62–71.

Washburn, S. L. and C. S. Lancaster
1968   "The Evolution of Hunting." *In: Man the Hunter*, R. B. Lee and I. DeVore (eds.), Chicago, IL: Aldine de Gruyter, pp. 293–303.

Waterston, R. H., K. Lindblad-Toh, E. Birney, et al. (Mouse Genome Sequencing Consortium)
2002   "Initial Sequencing and Comparative Analysis of the Mouse Genome." *Nature,* 421:520–562.

Watson, J. B. and F. H. C. Crick
1953a   "Genetical Implications of the Structure of the Deoxyribonucleic Acid." *Nature,* 171:964–967.

1953b   "A Structure for Deoxyribonucleic Acid." *Nature,* 171:737–738.

Weiner, J. S.
1955   *The Piltdown Forgery.* London: Oxford University Press.

Weiner, Steve, Qinqi Xu, Paul Goldberg, et al.
1998   "Evidence for the Use of Fire at Zhoukoudian, China." *Science,* 281:251–253.

Weiss, Kenneth
2003   "Come to Me My Melancholic Baby!" *Evolutionary Anthropology*, 12:3–6.

Weiss, Robin A. and Richard W. Wrangham
1999   "From *Pan* to Pandemic." *Nature,* 397:385–386.

Weiss, U.
2002   "Nature Insight: Malaria." *Nature,* 415:669.

Wendt, W. E.
1976   "'Art Mobilier' from the Apollo 11 Cave, South West Africa: Africa's Oldest Dated Works of art." *South African Archaeological Bulletin,* 31:5–11.

Westgate, John W.
1994   "Eocene Forest-Swamp." *National Geographic Research and Exploration*, 10:80–91.

Westgate, John and C. T. Gee
1990   "Paleoecology of a Middle Eocene Mangrove Biota (Vertebrates, Plants, and Invertebrates) from Southwest Texas." *Palaeogeography, Palaeoclimatology, Palaeoecology,* 78:163–177.

White, T.D.
1986   "Cut Marks on the Bodo Cranium: A Case of Prehistoric Defleshing." *American Journal of Physical Anthropology*, 69:503–509.

2003   "Early Hominids—Diversity or Distortion?" *Science,* 299:1994–7.

White, T. D., B. Asfaw, D. DeGusta, et al.
2003   "Pleistocene *Homo sapiens* from Middle Awash Ethiopia." *Nature,* 423:742–747.

1995   "Corrigendum (White, et al., 1994)". *Nature,* 375:88.

White, T. D. and N. Toth
1988   "Engis: Preparation Damage, Not Ancient Cutmarks." *American Journal of Physical Anthropology,* 78:361–367.

White, T.D., Giday WoldeGabriel, B. Asfaw, et al.
2006   "Asa Issie, Aramis and the Origin of *Australopithecus*." *Nature,* 440:883–889.

Whiten, A., J. Goodall, W. C. McGrew, et al.
1999   "Cultures in Chimpanzees." *Nature*, 399:682–685.

Wildman, Derek E., Monica Uddin, Guozhen Liu, et al.
2003   "Implications of Natural Selection in Shaping 99.4% Nonsynonymous DNA Identity Between Humans and Chimpanzees: Enlarging Genus *Homo*." *Proceedings of the National Academy of Sciences*, 100:7181–7188.

Williams, J. M.
1999   *Female Strategies and the Reasons for Territoriality in Chimpanzees. Lessons from Three Decades of Research at Gombe.* Unpublished Ph.D. Thesis. University of Minnesota.

Wilmut, I., A. E. Schnieke, J. McWhir, et al.
1997   "Viable Offspring Derived from Fetal and Adult Mammalian Cells." *Nature*, 385:810–813.

Wilson, E. O.
1992   *The Diversity of Life*. Cambridge, MA: The Belknap Press of Harvard University Press.

———
2002   *The Future of Life*. New York, NY: Alfred A. Knopf.

Wilson, John A.
1966   "A New Primate from the Earliest Oligocene, West Texas, Preliminary Report." *Folia Primatologica*, 4:227–248.

Wilson, John A. and Fred Szalay
1976   "New Adapid Primate of European Affinities from Texas." *Folia Primatologica*, 25:294–312.

Wolpoff, Milford H.
1983   "*Ramapithecus* and Human Origins. An Anthropologist's Perspective of Changing Interpretations." *In: New Interpretations of Ape and Human Ancestry*, Russell L. Ciochon and Robert S. Corruccini (eds.), New York, NY: Plenum Press, pp. 651–676.

———
1989   "Multiregional Evolution: The Fossil Alternative to Eden." *In: The Human Revolution*, P. Mellars and C. B. Stringer (eds.), Princeton, NJ: Princeton University Press, pp. 62–108.

———
1999   *Paleoanthropology*. 2nd ed. New York, NY: McGraw-Hill.

Wolpoff, M., A.G. Thorne, F.H. Smith, et al.
1994   "Multiregional Evolutions: A World-Wide Source for Modern Human Populations." *In: Origins of Anatomically Modern Humans*, M. H. Nitecki and D. V. Nitecki (eds.), New York, NY: Plenum Press, pp. 175–199.

Wolpoff, M. H., J. Hawks, D. Frayer, and K. Hunley
2001   "Modern Human Ancestry at the Peripheries: A Test of the Replacement Theory." *Science*, 291:293–297.

Wolpoff, Milford H., Brigitte Senut, Martin Pickford, and John Hawks
2002   "Paleoanthropology (Communication Arising): *Sahelanthropus* or '*Sahelpithecus*'"? *Nature*, 419:581–582.

Woo, J.
1966   "The Skull of Lantian Man." *Current Anthropololgy*, 5: 83–86.

Wood, Bernard
1991   *Koobi Fora Research Project IV: Hominid Cranial Remains from Koobi Fora*. Oxford: Clarendon Press.

———
1992   "Origin and Evolution of the Genus *Homo*." *Nature*, 355:783–790.

———
2002   "Hominid Revelations from Chad." News and Views, *Nature*, 418:133–135.

Wood, Bernard and Mark Collard
1999a   "The Human Genus." *Science*, 284:65–71.

———
1999b   "The Changing Face of Genus *Homo*." *Evolutionary Anthropology*, 8:195–207.

Wood, B. and B. G. Richmond
2000   "Human Evolution: Taxonomy and Paleobiology." *Journal of Anatomy*, 197:19–60.

Worthman, C. M.
1999   "Evolutionary Perspectives on the Onset of Puberty." *In: Evolutionary Medicine.* W. R. Trevathan, E. O. Smith, and J. J. McKenna (eds.), New York, NY: Oxford University Press.

Worthy, T. W. and R. N. Holdaway.
2002   *The Lost World of the Moa: Prehistoric Life of New Zealand*. Bloomington, IN: Indiana University Press.

Wrangham, R. W.
1990   "An Ecological Model of Female-Bonded Primate Groups." *Behaviour,* 75:262–300.

Wrangham, R. W. and B. B. Smuts
1980   "Sex Differences in the Behavioural Ecology of Chimpanzees in Gombe National Park, Tanzania." *J. Reprod. Fert., Supplement,* 28:13–31.

Wrangham, R., A. Clark, and G. Isabiryre-Basita
1992   "Female Social Relationships and Social Organization of Kibale Forest Chimps." *In: Topics in Primatology,* vol. 1, *Human Origins,* T. Nishida, W. McGrew, P. Marler, et al. (eds), Tokyo: Tokyo University Press, pp. 81–98.

Wrangham, R. and D. Peterson
1996   *Demonic Males: Apes and the Origins of Human Violence.* New York, NY: Houghton Mifflin.

Wu, Rukang and Xingren Dong
1985   "*Homo erectus* in China." *In: Palaeoanthropology and Palaeolithic Archaeology in the People's Republic of China,* R. Wu and J. W. Olsen (eds.), New York, NY: Academic Press, pp. 79–89.

Wu, X. and F. E. Poirier
1995   *Human Evolution in China.* Oxford: Oxford University Press.

Wu, X., L. A. Schepartz, D. Falk, and L. Wu
2006   "Endocranial Cast of Hexian *Homo erectus* from South China." *American Journal of Physical Anthropology,* 130:445–454.

Wuehrich, B.
1998   "Geological Analysis Damps Ancient Chinese Fires." *Science,* 28:165–166.

Yamei, H., R. Potts, Y. Baoyin, et al.
2000   "Mid-Pleistocene Acheulean-like Stone Technology of the Bose Basin, South China." *Science,* 287:1622–1626.

Yellen, J. E., A. S. Brooks, E. Cornelissen, et al.
1995   "A Middle Stone Age Worked Bone Industry from Katanda, Upper Semliki Valley, Zaire." *Science,* 268:553–556.

Young, David.
1992   *The Discovery of Evolution.* Cambridge: Natural History Museum Publications, Cambridge University Press.

Zhang, J., Y. Zhang, and H. E. Rosenberg
2002   "Adaptive Evolution of a Duplicated Pancreatic Ribonuclease Gene in a Leaf-eating Monkey." *Nature Genetics,* 30:411–415.

Zhu, R. X., Z. S. An, R. Potts, et al.
2003   "Magnetostratigraphic Dating of Early Humans in China." *Earth Science Reviews,* 61:341–359.

Zhu, R. X., R. Potts, K. A. Xie, et al.
2004   "New Evidence on the Earliest Human Presence at High Latitudes in Northeast Asia." *Nature,* 431:559–562.

Zhu, R. X., R. X. Zhu, K. A. Hoffman, et al.
2001   "Earliest Presence of Humans in Northeast Asia." *Nature,* 413:413–417.

Ziegler, A., A. S. Jonason, D. J. Leffellt, et al.
1994   "Sunburn and p53 in the Onset of Skin Cancer." *Nature,* 372:773–776.

Zimmet, P., K. G. M. M. Alberti, and J. Shaw
2001   "Global and Societal Implications of the Diabetes Epidemic." *Nature,* 414:782–787.

CREDITS

vi, Biophoto Associates/Photo Researchers, Inc.; **vii,** bottom left, Kevin Schafer/CORBIS; top right, Noel Rowe; **viii,** top left, Manoj Shah/The Image Bank; bottom right, © Russell Ciochon, University of Iowa; **ix,** National Museums of Kenya; **x,** top left, © Russell Ciochon, University of Iowa; bottom right © Randall White, New York University; **xi,** David L. Brill/Atlanta; **xii,** Craig King, Armed Forces DNA Identification Laboratory; **xiii,** top left © Russell Ciochon, University of Iowa; bottom right © Russell Ciochon, University of Iowa; **xiv,** AP/Wide World Photos; **1,** top, Robert Jurmain; bottom left, Courtesy Bonnie Pedersen/Arlene Kruse; center right, Lynn Kilgore; bottom right, Lynn Kilgore; **2,** Courtesy, Peter Jones; **3,** © Bettmann/CORBIS, **4,** left, Lynn Kilgore; top right, Lynn Kilgore; **7,** top, © Kenneth Garrett/NGS Image Collection; right, Lynn Kilgore; **8,** top, Courtesy, Judith Regensteiner; bottom, Courtesy, Judith Regensteiner; **9,** top left, Robert Jurmain; right, Courtesy, Bonnie Pedersen/Arlene Kruse; bottom, Lynn Kilgore; **10,** top, Courtesy, Lorna Pierce/Judy Suchey; center, Provided by D. France; **11,** Courtesy, Linda Levitch; **18,** © Russell L. Ciochon, University of Iowa; **21,** Loon, J. van (Johannes); **23,** American Museum of Natural History; **24,** top left, Mathieu-Ignace van Brée; center, With permission from the Master of Haileybury; bottom, © National Portrait Gallery, London; **25,** top, The Natural History Museum, London; bottom, © Bettmann/CORBIS; **27,** Dogs surrounding wolf: Lynn Kilgore and Lin Marshall; wolf: John Giustina/Getty Images; **28,** © National Portrait Gallery, London; **29,** top, Michael Tweedie/Photo Researchers; bottom, Breck P. Kent/Animals Animals; **36,** Biophoto Associates/Photo Researchers, Inc.; **37,** Courtesy, Dr. Michael S. Donnenberg; **39,** top, A. Barrington Brown/Photo Researchers, Inc.; bottom, The Novartis Foundation; **46,** Lynn Kilgore; **48,** © Dr. Stanley Flegler/Visuals Unlimited; **50,** © Biophoto Associates/Science Source/Photo Researchers; **52,** Ifti Ahmed; **58,** Cellmark Diagnostics, Abingdon, UK; **59,** Courtesy of Advanced Cell Technology, Inc., Worcester, Massachusetts; **64,** Francis Leroy/Photo Researchers, Inc.; **65,** Raychel Ciemma and Precision Graphics; **73,** Norman Lightfoot/Photo Researchers; **76,** Ray Carson, University of Florida News and Public Affairs; **77,** Lynn Kilgore; **80,** Reprinted, with permission, from the Annual Review of Genetics, Volume 10 ©1976 by Annual Reviews www.annualreviews.org; **83,** Lynn Kilgore; **91,** Courtesy, Margaret Maples; inset: ©Bettmann/CORBIS; **93,** Craig King, Armed Forces DNA Identification Laboratory; **94,** © Shawn Gould; **104,** Drawing by Robert Greisen; **114,** J. C. Stevenson/Animals Animals; **118,** Courtesy, John Oates; **119,** Karl Ammann; **121,** David Haring/Duke Lemur Center; **123,** Lynn Kilgore; **126,** Lynn Kilgore; **127,** Lynn Kilgore; **128,** Howler species: Raymond Mendez/Animals Animals; Spider monkey: Robert L. Lubeck/Animals Animals; Prince Bernhard's titi: Marc van Roosmalen; Tamarin: © Zoological Society of San Diego, photo by Ron Garrison; Muriqui: Andrew Young; White-faced capuchins: © Jay Dickman/CORBIS; Squirrel monkey: © Kevin Schafer/CORBIS; Uakari: R. A. Mittermeier/Conservation International; **129,** Baboon: Arlene Kruse/Bonnie Pedersen; Macaque: Jean De Rousseau; Gibbon: Lynn Kilgore; Tarsier: David Haring, Duke University Primate Zoo; Orangutan: © Tom McHugh/Photo Researchers, Inc.; Langur: Joe MacDonald/Animals Animals; Lemur: Fred Jacobs; Loris: San Francisco Zoo; Cercopithecus: Robert Jurmain; Colobus: Robert Jurmain; Galagos: Bonnie Pedersen/Arlene Kruse; Chimpanzee: Bonnie Pedersen/Arlene Kruse;

Mountain gorilla: Lynn Kilgore; **131,** © Russell L. Ciochon, University of Iowa; **136,** Lynn Kilgore; **137,** top, Courtesy, Fred Jacobs; center, Courtesy, Fred Jacobs; bottom left, Courtesy, San Francisco Zoo; bottom right, Courtesy, Bonnie Pedersen/Arlene Kruse; **138,** David Haring, Duke University Primate Zoo; **139,** top left, Marc van Roosmalen; top center, © Andrew Young; top right, R. A. Mittermeier/Conservation International; bottom left, Kevin Schafer/CORBIS; bottom right, © Jay Dickman/CORBIS; **140,** top left, © Zoological Society of San Diego, photo by Ron Garrison; top right, Raymond Mendez/Animals Animals; bottom left, Robert L. Lubeck/Animals Animals; **141,** top, Robert Jurmain; bottom left, right, Courtesy, Bonnie Pedersen/Arlene Kruse; **142,** Lynn Kilgore; **143,** Lynn Kilgore; **144,** left, Noel Rowe; right, Lynn Kilgore; **145,** Lynn Kilgore; **146,** left, Lynn Kilgore; right, Robert Jurmain, photo by Jill Matsumoto/Jim Anderson; **147,** Courtesy, Ellen Ingmanson; **154,** Lynn Kilgore; **156,** bottom left, Courtesy, Jean De Rousseau; bottom right, Courtesy, John Oates; **158,** Russ Mittermeier; **159,** Lynn Kilgore; **162,** Courtesy, John Oates; **164,** Time Life Pictures/Getty Images; **165,** left, © Chris Hellier/CORBIS; right, © Theo Allofs/CORBIS; **166,** Lynn Kilgore; **167,** Lynn Kilgore; **169,** top, Lynn Kilgore; center left, Robert Jurmain; center right, Courtesy, Meredith Small; bottom left, Courtesy, Arlene Kruse/Bonnie Pedersen; bottom right, Courtesy, Arlene Kruse/Bonnie Pedersen; **170,** Lynn Kilgore; **172,** top, Joe MacDonald/Animals Animals; bottom, © Peter Henzi; **173,** top left, Robert Jurmain; top right, Robert Jurmain; bottom left, Courtesy, David Haring, Duke University Primate Center; bottom center, © Tom McHugh/Photo Researchers, Inc.; bottom right, Courtesy, Arlene Kruse/Bonnie Pedersen; **174,** Harlow Primate Laboratory, University of Wisconsin; **175,** Lynn Kilgore; **180,** Tetsuro Matsuzawa; **184,** Courtesy, Wally Welker, University of Wisconsin—Madison; **185,** David Bygott, Anthro Photo; **186,** Lynn Kilgore; **188,** Rose A. Sevcik, Language Research Center, Georgia State University; photo by Elizabeth Pugh; **189,** © Royalty-Free/CORBIS; **192,** top, Lynn Kilgore; bottom, Manoj Shah/The Image Bank; **193,** Tetsuro Matsuzawa; **195,** Curt Busse; **200,** Jim Moore/Anthro Photo; **202,** Courtesy of John Kappelman, University of Texas; **204,** *Carpolestes*: Courtesy of Jonathan Bloch; *Plesiadapis:* © John Fleagle and Stephen Nash; *Mahgarita*: © Stephen Nash; *Rooneyia*: © Stephen Nash; *Branisella*: Courtesy of M. Takai; *Homunculus*: © Richard Kay; **205,** *Adapis*: © John Fleagle and Stephen Nash; *Dryopithecus*: Courtesy of David Begun; *Pliopithecus*: © Russell Ciochon; *Ouranopithecus*: Courtesy of Louis de Bonis; *Parapithecus*: Courtesy of Elwyn Simons; *Sivapithecus*: Courtesy of David Pilbeam; *Lufengpithecus*: © Russell Ciochon; *Teihardina*: Courtesy of Xijum Ni; *Aegyptopithecus*: Courtesy of Elwyn Simons; *Theropithecus brumpti*: © Russell Ciochon; *Amphipithecids*: © Russell Ciochon; *Gigantopithecus*: © Russell Ciochon; *Catopithecus*: Courtesy of Elwyn Simons; *Micropithecus*: © John Fleagle and Stephen Nash; *Proconsul*: © The Natural History Museum, London; *Kenyapithecus*: Courtesy of Monte McCrossin; *Archaeolemur*: © Russell Ciochon; *Megaladapis*: © Russell Ciochon; *Victoriapithecus*: Courtesy of Brenda Benefit; **206,** Drawings by Robert Greisen; **208,** © Russell Ciochon, University of Iowa; **209,** Courtesy of Jonathan Bloch, Florida Museum of Natural History; **210,** top, Courtesy of Xijum Ni, IVPP, Chinese Academy of Sciences; bottom, Courtesy of Thierry Smith, Royal Belgium Institute of Natural Science; **211,** © Russell Ciochon, University of Iowa; **212,** top, © Russell Ciochon, University of Iowa; bottom, Courtesy of James Westgate, Lamar University; **213,** © Stephen Nash, Stony Brook University, New York; **215,** Courtesy of Elwyn Simons, Duke University Primate Center; **216,** © Russell Ciochon, University of Iowa; **217,** top, © John Fleagle, Stony Brook University; center, bottom, Courtesy of Elwyn Simons, Duke University Primate Center; **218,** top, Courtesy of Richard Kay, Duke University; bottom, © John Fleagle, Stony Brook University, New York;

INDEX

World Political Map

80°N

GREENLAND
(KALAALLIT NUNAAT)
(Den.)

ARCTIC CIRCLE

ALASKA
(U.S.)

ICELAND

60°N

CANADA

UNITED
KINGDOM

IRELAND
(EIRE)

40°N

*Atlantic
Ocean*

AZORE IS.
(Port.)

PORTUGAL

SPAIN

UNITED STATES

CANARY IS.
(Sp.)

MOROCCO

TROPIC OF CANCER

BAHAMAS

MEXICO

CUBA

DOMINICAN REP.

HAITI

CAPE VERDE IS.

MAURITANIA

20°N

HAWAII
(U.S.)

BELIZE
HONDURAS

JAMAICA

PUERTO
RICO (U.S.)

ANTIGUA & BARBUDA
GUADELOUPE (Fr.)
DOMINICA
MARTINIQUE (Fr.)
BARBADOS
GRENADA
TRINIDAD & TOBAGO

SENEGAL
GAMBIA

GUINEA BISSAU

GUINEA

SIERRA LEONE

IVORY
COAST

LIBERIA

EQUATORIAL

GUATEMALA
EL SALVADOR

NICARAGUA

NETHERLANDS
ANTILLES (Neth.)

*Pacific
Ocean*

COSTA RICA

PANAMA

VENEZUELA

GUYANA

SURINAME
FRENCH GUIANA
(Fr.)

COLOMBIA

GALAPAGOS IS.
(Ecuador)

ECUADOR

EQUATOR

0°

BRAZIL

WESTERN
SAMOA

AMERICAN
SAMOA (U.S.)

SOCIETY IS.
(Fr.)

FRENCH
POLYNESIA
(Fr.)

PERU

TONGA

TAHITI (Fr.)

BOLIVIA

PARAGUAY

20°S

TROPIC OF CAPRICORN

PITCAIRN IS.
(U.K.)

EASTER ISLAND
(Chile)

CHILE

*Atlantic
Ocean*

URUGUAY

40°S

ARGENTINA

0   500   1000   1500 miles
0   1000   2000 kms
Equatorial Scale

FALKLAND IS.
(U.K.)

60°S

ANTARCTIC CIRCLE

80°S

180° 160°W 140°W 120°W 100°W 80°W 60°W 40°W 20°W